CORPORATE TAXATION

Examples and Explanations

CORPORATE TAXATION

Examples and Explanations

Second Edition

Cheryl D. Block

Professor of Law
The George Washington University

ASPEN LAW & BUSINESS
A Division of Aspen Publishers, Inc.
Gaithersburg   New York

Permissions
Aspen Law & Business
1185 Avenue of the Americas
New York, NY 10036

2 3 4 5 6 7 8 9 0

Printed in the United States of America

Library of Congress Cataloging-in-Publication Data

Block, Cheryl D., 1955-
    Corporate taxation : examples and explanations / Cheryl D. Block.—2nd ed.
        p.   cm.
    Includes index.
    ISBN 0-7355-2027-5 (alk. paper)
    1. Corporation — Taxation — Law and legislation — United States. I. Title.

    KF6465 .B557 2001
    343.7305'267 — dc21
                                            00-053603

About Aspen Law & Business
Legal Education Division

With a dedication to preserving and strengthening the long-standing tradition of publishing excellence in legal education, Aspen Law & Business continues to provide the highest quality teaching and learning resources for today's law school community. Careful development, meticulous editing, and an unmatched responsiveness to the evolving needs of today's discerning educators combine in the creation of our outstanding casebooks, coursebooks, textbooks, and study aids.

ASPEN LAW & BUSINESS
A Division of Aspen Publishers, Inc.
A Wolters Kluwer Company
www.aspenpublishers.com

To Hannah Ruth, whose arrival brought unimaginable joy to my life and gave me the happiest possible reason to delay this project.

And to Chad, whose love and support helped me to finish it.

NOTICE

As this Second Edition went to print, Congress retroactively repealed §536(a) of the Ticket to Work and Work Incentives Improvement Act of 1999, Pub. L. No. 106-170, 113 Stat. 1860 (1999). Section 536(a) of that Act added a new §453(a)(2), which disallowed installment reporting for most accrual basis taxpayers. As one of its last acts, the 106th Congress repealed this recent amendment and instructs that the Internal Revenue Code "shall be applied and administered as if that subsection (and the amendments made by that subsection) had not been enacted." Installment Tax Correction Act of 2000, Pub. L. No. 106-573, 114 Stat. 3061, §2(b) (2000). Consequently, accrual basis taxpayers are entitled to use installment reporting as provided in §453. Any references in this Second Edition should be read as if §453(a)(2) had not been enacted.

Visit *www.corptax-ee.com* for further semiannual updates, corrections, and addenda.

Summary of Contents

Contents

Preface

Corporate taxation has a reputation, among law students at least, as one of the most difficult courses in the law school curriculum. This perception magnifies as Congress continues its seemingly endless amendment process, regularly revising the Internal Revenue Code in general, and Subchapter C, in particular. Some of these revisions appear eminently sensible and others do not. Few of them can be said to simplify, however. The Taxpayer Relief Act of 1997 and the Miscellaneous Trade and Technical Corrections Act of 1999 are the last in this long series of legislative revisions, and their provisions are included, as appropriate, throughout this book. The Treasury Department has also entered the fray, recently rethinking and revising several of its longstanding positions, particularly in the area of tax-free reorganizations. With this book, I hope to assist in unraveling the mysteries of Subchapter C, dealing with corporate taxpayers and their shareholders.

Two unique features of this book distinguish it from other books on corporate taxation. First, and most important, are the series of questions and answers (referred to as "examples" and "explanations") at the end of each chapter, with the exception of introductory Chapters 1 through 3 on "Preliminary Matters" and Chapter 11, an introductory chapter to the tax-free reorganization materials. For years, my students have been asking me whether a corporate tax book existed that offered hypothetical questions along with *answers*. Now it does. These problems should help to test your understanding and give you an opportunity to apply the textual material from each chapter. While I have attempted to make the problems as realistic as possible, they are unlike transactions in the real world in that the problems at the end of each chapter focus on the particular issues addressed in that chapter. Real world corporate transactions may not be quite so "compartmentalized," but instead involve multiple issues in the same transaction. Once you have mastered the problems in these chapters, you should be in a position to advance to problems that combine multiple corporate tax issues. Although different professors look for different things in student responses to examination questions, the answers provided in the examples and explanations sections reflect the kind of answers I hope to see from my students.

The second unique feature of this book is that it includes numerous diagrams. I have joked with my students over the years that many corporate transactions were planned out by creative tax planners on cocktail napkins. In many cases, the most difficult aspects of corporate taxation involve understanding the underlying transaction itself. Once you can "see" the transaction, the tax consequences often fall right into place. I encourage you to get into a regular habit of diagraming corporate transactions. Practice diagramming the transactions described in the examples and explanations sections.

One last problem in studying corporate tax is simply deciding where to start. One possibility is to start with incorporation, or birth, of the corporation and end with liquidation, or death, of the corporation. This is sometimes referred to as the "cradle to grave" approach. Another possibility is to begin with distributions. Since corporations are first taxed on their profits and shareholders are taxed *again* on those profits when they are distributed as dividends, double taxation really is the heart of the corporate tax regime. Why not start at the heart with distributions? A strong case can be made for either technique. Texts and courses on corporate taxation take different approaches. This book adopts the "cradle to grave" approach, modified by considering corporate liquidations prior to the more complex materials on tax-free reorganizations. Nevertheless, each of the chapters that follows is designed to operate independently so that the book can be used as a study guide regardless of the approach used in your particular course of study.

Perhaps the best advice that I can offer students is to work always to see the big picture, and not to get lost in the minutia that can sometimes be so overwhelming. In particular, I hope to assist students in developing skills that will enable them to identify the details that really matter in getting at the big picture. With the proper focus, corporate tax turns out not to be nearly as difficult as one first imagined. Better yet, corporate tax can be — dare I say it? — *fun*.

February 2001   *Cheryl D. Block*

Acknowledgments

I would like to thank my students and colleagues over the years, who have helped me think through the issues reflected here. Also, special thanks go to my colleagues, Professors Karen Brown and Robert Peroni, who were always willing to listen, guide and commiserate, especially when complex legislative changes made our lives difficult. I am very grateful for the help of my research assistants, particularly Pamela Burke, Tejpal Chawla, Daniel Fisher, Bernard Gallagher, Karen Howat, and Jim Keller, and to the George Washington University Law School, which provided funding for my research assistants, as well as summer research grants. I am also grateful for proofreading assistance from Christina Verleger and for the assistance of the secretaries at the George Washington University Law School, particularly David Foss. Finally I would like to thank my extended family, and the Osborn family of Miami, Oklahoma.

CORPORATE
TAXATION

Examples and Explanations

PART ONE

Some Preliminary Matters

1

Introduction

The Corporate Income Tax—A Double Tax Regime

Beginning immediately after passage of the Sixteenth Amendment in 1913,[1] and continuing to the present, Congress has routinely imposed a direct tax on both personal and corporate incomes.[2] Corporate profits are subject to a corporate level tax under §11 of the Internal Revenue Code[3] and a second tax on the same profits will be imposed when the profits are distributed to the shareholders in the form of dividends.[4] Even if the shareholders sell their stock before receiving distributions, the price received for the stock presumably will include the stock's pro rata share of profits. As a result, the gain reported from sale of the stock should reflect the stockholder's share of

---

1. The Sixteenth Amendment permits Congress to "lay and collect taxes on incomes, from whatever source derived, without apportionment among the several states." U.S. CONST. amend. XVI.

2. An earlier statute imposing an income tax upon both personal and corporate income was held unconstitutional. In 1909, Congress successfully levied a tax on corporations that was held to be constitutional as an indirect or *excise* tax not subject to the apportionment clause. Flint v. Stone Tracy Co., 220 U.S. 107, 171 (1911).

3. A small business corporation that makes a proper election under Subchapter S generally will not be subject to the corporate level tax imposed by §11. See I.R.C. §1363. There also are three exceptions to the corporate tax listed in §11 for mutual savings banks conducting a life insurance business, insurance companies, and regulated investment companies and real estate investment trusts (REIT). I.R.C. §11(c). Each of these types of business entities is covered under different Subchapters of the Internal Revenue Code and is beyond the scope of this book.

4. I.R.C. §301. For further discussion of ongoing corporate distributions, see Chapter 5.

undistributed profits. One way or the other, the shareholders will pay a tax.[5] Since the corporation pays taxes on profits and is not entitled to any deduction for dividends paid to shareholders, the effect of the corporate and shareholder taxes often is double taxation of corporate income.

The double tax imposed on corporations should be distinguished from the single tax imposed on other forms of business organization. A partnership, for example, is not subject to income tax at the partnership level.[6] Instead, income, loss, deductions, and credits are "passed-through" and reported on each participant's individual tax return. If a partnership has income for the year, the partnership itself will have no tax liability, but each partner will report a share of the income on his or her individual tax return. In addition, certain corporations with a limited number of shareholders may achieve similar pass-through status by making an election to be an S Corporation under Subchapter S of the Internal Revenue Code.[7] Like a partnership, an S Corporation is not itself a taxpaying entity, but instead generally passes items of income, loss, deduction, and credit through to its shareholders for reporting on their individual returns.[8] In addition, changes to state business law in virtually all 50 states have created authority for an increasing number of new types of business entities, such as limited liability companies (LLCs) and limited liability partnerships (LLPs). Under new "check-the-box" regulations, such entities with two or more members will automatically be treated as partnerships for tax purposes unless they elect to be treated as corporations.[9]

The focus of this book will be on corporations that have *not* made an election under Subchapter S and, thus, are subject to the rules of Subchapter C of the Internal Revenue Code.[10] In contrast to pass-through entities such a partnership, S Corporation, or LLC, when a *C Corporation* earns a profit, the shareholder pays no immediate tax. Although the value of the stock may increase, the shareholder pays no tax until the corporation makes a distribu-

---

5. There is one important distinction between dividends and gains from the sale of stock, however. Dividends received by shareholders are considered "ordinary income" and taxed at the individual income tax rates provided in I.R.C. §1. Gains from the sale of stock generally are considered capital gains and taxed under preferential capital gains rates. I.R.C. §1(h).

6. I.R.C. §701. Partnerships generally are governed by Subchapter K, entitled "Partners and Partnerships." I.R.C. §§701-761.

7. I.R.C. §1362 (election); §1361 (S Corporation defined); §1363 (effect of election). Subchapter S Corporations are considered briefly in Chapter 2.

8. I.R.C. §§1363, 1366.

9. For further discussion of these new types of business entities, see Chapter 2.

10. The modern statutory provisions on the corporate income tax can be found primarily in Subchapter C ("Corporate Distributions and Adjustments"), located within Subtitle A ("Income Taxes"), Chapter 1 ("Normal Taxes and Surtaxes") of Title 26 of the United States Code ("The Internal Revenue Code"). Corporations governed by the provisions of Subchapter C often are simply referred to as "C Corporations."

tion or the shareholder sells the shares. Similarly, the shareholder is not entitled to immediately deduct a share of the corporation's losses. The decreased value of the shares will be reflected in a lower gain, or perhaps a loss, on the ultimate sale of the shares.

At this point you may be wondering why two otherwise similar businesses, one operated as a partnership, S Corporation, or LLC, and the other operated as a C Corporation, should have different tax burdens. You would not be alone. Over the years, policy makers and commentators have debated the wisdom of the separate corporate income tax. Several proposals have recommended eliminating the corporate level tax altogether or otherwise fully "integrating" the corporate and individual income taxes. Alternative proposals for partial integration have also been considered. Such proposals for partial integration would provide corporate deductions for dividends paid or shareholder credits on dividends received.

Despite its critics, the double corporate tax regime reflected in Subchapter C of the Internal Revenue Code has proved quite tenacious. This tenacity may be more surprising given that the percentage of revenue generated by the corporate income tax is rather low. In 1999, for example, the federal government raised only 10% of its revenue from the corporate income tax, as opposed to 48% from the individual income tax.[11] While the percentages are small, the volume of revenue raised by the corporate income tax is substantial, and elimination of the corporate income tax would be politically quite difficult.[12] Corporate income taxation continues to be a subject of great interest and importance to taxpayers, policy makers, and academics alike. This book assumes Subchapter C's continued vitality.

Computation and Rate Structure for the Tax on Corporate Income

General Computation and Rates

Under corporate law and for federal income tax purposes, the corporation is regarded as a person and computes income in much the same way that individual taxpayers do.[13] The corporation will first determine its gross

---

11. Exec. Office of the Pres., Office of Management & Budget, Budget of the United States Government: Fiscal Year 2001, Analytical Perspectives 47, 91 (2000). The remainder of federal receipts is derived from social insurance taxes, contributions, and other excise taxes. The percentage of federal revenue raised through the corporate income tax has hovered in the 10-12% range for the last 10 years and is expected to continue in that range through at least 2005, under existing law. *Id.*

12. In 1999, for example, the corporate income tax raised approximately $184.7 billion. *Id.*

13. The Internal Revenue Code itself provides that "where not otherwise distinctly expressed or manifestly incompatible with the intent [of Title 26, t]he term 'person'

income[14] and then subtract available deductions to determine taxable income. Of course, there are some differences in the types of income that corporations, as opposed to individuals, are likely to receive and also some differences in allowable deductions.

Like the personal income tax, the corporate income tax uses a graduated set of rates that generally increase as corporate income rises. The stated marginal rates of taxation for corporate income are 15%, 25%, 34%, and 35%.[15] In addition, however, corporations with incomes over $100,000 are subject to a 5% surtax with a cap of $11,750 and corporations with incomes over $15,000,000 are subject to an additional 3% surtax with a cap of $100,000.[16] The stated top marginal rate of taxation of 35% for corporations is slightly lower than the stated top marginal rate for individuals of 39.6%.[17] Unlike individual taxpayers, corporations are not eligible for preferential rates on capital gains.

The Corporate Alternative Minimum Tax

Over the years, Congress has provided many exclusions, deductions, and credits through special provisions of the Internal Revenue Code. Many individual and corporate taxpayers have taken advantage of these special provisions to dramatically reduce their overall tax liability. In extreme cases, taxpayers that were *financially* profitable, showed little or no income for *tax* purposes. In response, Congress enacted the alternative minimum tax (AMT) designed "to ensure that no taxpayer with substantial economic income can avoid significant tax liability by using exclusions, deductions, and credits because, however worthy their goals, they become counterproductive when taxpayers are allowed to use them to avoid virtually all tax liability."[18] Pro-

---

shall be construed to mean and include . . . an association, company or corporation." I.R.C. §7701(a)(1).

14. I.R.C. §61(a) makes no distinction between individuals and corporations in its definition of gross income.

15. I.R.C. §11(b).

16. The 5% surtax and the additional 3% surtax have the effect of creating a top marginal corporate tax rate of 43%. However, since the surtaxes are capped, the corporate rate goes back down to 35% once the caps have been met. The resulting corporate rate structure is: 15%, 25%, 34%, 35%, 40%, 43%, 35%.

17. The individual income tax uses a five-tier rate structure. The marginal rates for the personal income tax are 15%, 28%, 31%, 36%, and 39.6%. I.R.C. §1. Although there is no formal surtax included in the personal income tax rate structure, Congress achieves results similar to the corporate surtaxes through a phase-out of the personal exemption for individuals with incomes above specified threshold amounts, I.R.C. §151(d)(3), and an overall limitation on itemized deductions for taxpayers with incomes over specified amounts. I.R.C. §68.

18. S. Fin. Comm. Rep. No. 313, 99th Cong., 2d Sess. 518-519 (1986).

19. Recent legislative efforts to substantially revise the corporate alternative mini-

visions in §§55 through 58 impose an alternative minimum tax for both corporations and individuals.[19]

In addition to simply computing regular taxable income, corporate taxpayers also must compute alternative minimum taxable income (AMTI).[20] This is done by making various adjustments to taxable income as required in special provisions in §§56 through 58. The details and mechanics of these adjustments are beyond the scope of most introductory corporate taxation courses. For introductory purposes, it should be sufficient to note that the basic idea of the adjustments is to provide a picture of the taxpayer's income that more accurately measures *economic* income. So, for example, the corporation may be required to recompute its taxable income by using a less accelerated method of depreciation than that used to compute the regular tax.[21] In computing its AMTI, the corporation also is required to add various "items of tax preference" to its taxable income pursuant to §57. These tax preference items effectively add back into the taxpayer's taxable income amounts reflecting excess depletion allowances, intangible drilling cost deductions, tax-exempt interest, and other listed items. Finally, certain losses that were permissible for purposes of computing taxable income may be denied for purposes of computing the AMTI.[22]

The corporation's "tentative minimum tax" is 20% of the AMTI that exceeds an exemption amount of $40,000.[23] In addition to the regular tax computed under §11, the corporation will be liable for an additional tax to the extent that its tentative minimum tax exceeds its regular tax for the taxable year.[24] Thus, a corporation that otherwise finds itself in a tax bracket of less than 20% under the regular tax rates provided in §11, may discover that it owes additional tax under the alternative minimum tax.

Penalty Taxes on Undistributed Corporate Income

Recall that the distinctive feature of corporate taxation generally is a *double* tax on corporate profits through imposition of both a *corporate* level tax on

---

mum tax failed with veto of the Taxpayer Refund and Relief Act of 1999, H.R. 2488, 106th Cong., 2d Sess. The final bill would have reduced the corporate AMT through revisions in computation. The House version of the bill would have repealed the corporate AMT altogether.

20. S Corporations generally are not subject to the corporate AMT. In addition, under a provision effective for tax years beginning in 1998, certain small corporations with average gross receipts of $5 million or less will be effectively exempt from the corporate alternative minimum tax. Taxpayer Relief Act of 1997, Pub. L. No. 105-34, 111 Stat. 788, §401 (codified at I.R.C. §55(e)).

21. See I.R.C. §56(a).

22. See I.R.C. §58.

23. I.R.C. §55(b)(1)(B), (d)(2). This provision also permits a reduction for an alternative minimum tax foreign tax credit.

24. I.R.C. §55(a)(1).

income and a *shareholder* level tax on distributions. Some corporations developed techniques to avoid the shareholder level tax by simply failing to make corporate distributions. Congress responded with penalty taxes on accumulated earnings and personal holding companies. Each of these provisions is designed to prod corporations into making distributions that will be subject to the shareholder level tax.

a) The Accumulated Earnings Tax

The accumulated earnings penalty tax is imposed upon corporations "availed of for the purpose of avoiding the income tax with respect to its shareholders . . . by permitting earnings and profits to accumulate instead of being divided or distributed."[25] Such an inquiry obviously depends upon facts peculiar to the particular corporation. According to §533, a corporation that permits earnings and profits to "accumulate beyond the reasonable needs of the business" has acted with the prohibited tax avoidance motive. Not surprisingly, disputes between the taxpayer and the government in accumulated earnings penalty tax cases center upon identifying the "reasonable needs of the business." Special provisions in §537 and corresponding §537 regulations address these issues.[26] Once it is factually determined that the corporation is subject to the accumulated earnings penalty tax, a tax is imposed upon "accumulated taxable income" at the 39.6% top marginal tax rate imposed on individuals.[27] For this purpose, "accumulated taxable income" is computed based upon taxable income, with adjustments as provided in §535. Perhaps most important among these adjustments is a credit for amounts that *were* retained for reasonable needs of the business.[28]

b) The Personal Holding Company Tax

When the personal holding company rules were first adopted in 1934, individual income tax rates were much higher than corporate tax rates. Individual taxpayers found that they could reduce their tax liability on personal service income or income from personal assets by incorporating. The problem was especially acute in the case of small, closely held businesses, whose shareholders could easily manipulate corporate affairs for nonbusiness purposes. In response, Congress adopted the personal holding company

---

25. I.R.C. §532(a). Since personal holding companies are subject to a separate set of penalty provisions, such corporations are exempted from the accumulated earnings tax. I.R.C. §532(b)(1).

26. The details of these provisions are beyond the scope of these introductory materials.

27. I.R.C. §§532, 535.

28. I.R.C. §535(c).

(PHC) rules to prevent this abuse by taxing certain shareholders on undistributed corporate earnings at the top marginal individual tax rate.

Today's individual and corporate tax rates no longer present individual taxpayers an incentive to shelter their personal income at lower corporate rates. Nevertheless, an incentive remains to retain corporate earnings so as to avoid, or defer, the shareholder level of the corporate double tax. The accumulated earnings tax provisions discussed above arguably should be sufficient to address the problem of retained earnings. On the other hand, as a practical matter, the accumulated earnings penalty is often more difficult to impose since it requires a subjective finding of tax avoidance. Thus, Congress has retained the more objective personal holding company rules.

Under the PHC provisions, a penalty tax is imposed upon undistributed personal holding company income at the top individual marginal tax rate of 39.6%.[29] Since the PHC penalty tax is directed at small businesses whose shareholders can easily manipulate corporate affairs, the penalty only applies to corporations if "at any time during the last half of the taxable year more than 50 percent in value of its outstanding stock is owned, directly or indirectly, by or for not more than 5 individuals."[30] In addition, the penalty only applies if at least 60% of the corporation's adjusted ordinary gross income constitutes "personal holding company income."[31] "Personal holding company income" is defined as the portion of adjusted ordinary gross income consisting of listed types of personal service or personal asset income, such as amounts under personal service contracts,[32] dividends,[33] rents,[34] and the like. The details and mechanics of the personal holding company penalty tax are beyond the scope of most introductory corporate taxation courses. For introductory purposes, it should be sufficient to note that certain small, closely held corporations may be subject to this penalty tax in addition to the regular corporate tax provided in §11.

Affiliated Corporations

Each corporation subject to tax under Subtitle A of the Internal Revenue Code is required to file a corporate tax return.[35] Certain "affiliated groups of corporations," however, are extended the privilege of filing a "consolidated return" in lieu of separate returns.[36] Affiliated groups are chains of

---

29. I.R.C. §541.
30. I.R.C. §542(a)(2).
31. I.R.C. §542(a)(1).
32. I.R.C. §543(a)(7).
33. I.R.C. §543(a)(1).
34. I.R.C. §543(a)(2).
35. I.R.C. §6012(a)(2).
36. I.R.C. §1501; see also §6012(e).

corporate entities connected through stock ownership with a common parent corporation.[37] A parent corporation is "affiliated" to its subsidiary if it possesses at least 80% of the total voting power *and* 80% of the total value of the stock of the subsidiary.[38] Congress granted affiliated corporations the privilege of filing consolidated returns, but left most of the details regarding consolidated filing to the Treasury Department.[39] Complex and extensive regulations now govern the computation of federal income tax for corporations filing consolidated returns. In fact, many modern corporate transactions are structured by tax lawyers and accountants to take advantage of special consolidated return provisions. While this book does not attempt a comprehensive analysis of the consolidated return regulations, several of the more significant issues related to consolidated return reporting are considered throughout the chapters that follow.

Capital Gains vs. Ordinary Income Rates: The Influence on Subchapter C

Difference in Tax Treatment for Capital Gains and Losses

For federal income tax purposes, gain and loss from the sale of a "capital asset" is treated differently from ordinary income and loss. Corporations are allowed losses from the sale or exchange of capital assets only to the extent of gain from such sales or exchanges.[40] Thus, for any given taxable year, capital losses may be used only to offset capital gains. Individual taxpayers are subject to similar capital loss restrictions, but will be entitled to deduct a maximum of $3000 in capital losses even if capital losses exceed capital gains for the taxable year.[41]

With regard to gains, individual taxpayers generally are eligible for lower tax rates on net capital gains than the top marginal rate applicable to ordinary income under §1. Before the Taxpayer Relief Act of 1997, §1(h) effectively imposed a maximum rate of 28% on net capital gains for individuals. The 1997 Act's amendments to §1(h) include a complex set of capital gains rate

---

37. I.R.C. §1504(a)(1).

38. I.R.C. §1504(a)(2).

39. I.R.C. §1502 grants broad authority to the Secretary of the Treasury to prescribe regulations governing consolidated returns for affiliated corporations.

40. I.R.C. §1211(a). Unused corporate capital losses are subject to carryback and carryforward rules under §1212(a).

41. I.R.C. §1211(b). Unused individual capital losses may be carried forward under rules provided in §1212(b).

reductions. Briefly summarized, the amendments effectively reduce the maximum capital gain rate for most capital assets from 28% to 20%. The rate drops still further to 18% in 2001 for certain capital assets held for more than five years.[42] Capital gains and losses are further broken into short- or long-term gains or losses. A long-term capital gain or loss is a gain or loss from the sale or exchange of an asset held for more than one year.[43] Until recently, preferential capital gains rates were applicable only to net long-term capital gains.[44] The 1997 revisions to the capital gains provisions in §1(h) technically do not change the one-year holding period incorporated into the long-term capital asset definition. At the same time, since the various capital gains rate reductions in amended §1(h) require different holding periods, the distinction between long- and short term capital gain has become somewhat less meaningful.

For purposes of an introductory course in corporate taxation, one need not master all of the complexities of the capital gain and loss rules. It should be sufficient to recognize that capital loss restrictions and the rate differential for taxation of ordinary income versus capital gains raise especially significant issues for corporate taxpayers and their shareholders. Corporate taxpayers may attempt to classify losses as ordinary, rather than capital, in order to avoid the loss limitation rules. On the gain side, many corporate transactions are driven by shareholders' desire to convert profit that might otherwise have been taxed at high ordinary income rates into gains taxable at lower capital gains rates. Several Subchapter C provisions and case-law doctrines were designed by Congress and the courts precisely to thwart such efforts. Commentators have argued that much of Subchapter C's complexity could be eliminated simply by providing for taxation of ordinary income and capital gains at the same rates. Many reformers had high hopes for the Tax Reform

---

42. Taxpayer Relief Act of 1997, Pub. L. No. 105-34, 111 Stat. 788, §311 (codified at I.R.C. §1(h)). Under the new rules, the reduced 20% rate will not apply to certain gain from collectibles. I.R.C. §1(h)(4)-(6). Also, a 25% rate generally will apply to recapture gain from certain depreciable assets. *Id.* at §1(h)(1)(D), (4). In addition, individual taxpayers investing in certain "qualified small business stock" may defer tax on gain from the sale of such stock by purchasing other "qualified small business stock" within 60 days of the sale. Taxpayer Relief Act of 1997 at §313 (codified at I.R.C. §1045). Ultimately, even the sale of this replacement stock may be eligible for a 50% exclusion under special provisions for the sale of "qualified small business stock" in I.R.C. §1202.

43. I.R.C. §1222(3), (4). The period of time during which the taxpayer has held a capital asset typically is referred to as the "holding period." One recurring issue in corporate taxation is whether the sale or exchange of stock or other assets begins a *new* holding period or whether, instead, an earlier holding period should be "tacked on." I.R.C. §1223 resolves many of these questions. Discussion of §1223 and specific holding period issues will be included in subsequent chapters as the issues arise.

44. "Net long-term capital gain" is defined as "the excess of long-term capital gains for the taxable year over the long-term capital losses for such year." I.R.C. §1222(7).

Act of 1986, which briefly eliminated the difference in rates. Even in 1986, however, it was clear that the equalization of rates would not last very long. Anticipating a possible future increase in ordinary income rates, Congress provided in 1986 that the rate on net capital gains would not exceed 28%.[45] Not surprisingly, Congress increased ordinary income rates in 1990 and again in 1993. The capital gains rate was protected from these increases as a result of the congressional preemptive strike included in the 1986 Act. For many capital assets, the Taxpayer Relief Act of 1997 reduced the capital gains rate from 28% to 20%, with still further reductions scheduled to take effect in the future. A significant differential between ordinary income and capital gains rates is now back in place. This increased differential undoubtedly will result in renewed emphasis on statutory provisions and case-law doctrines addressing corporate transactions designed by taxpayers to convert profits that should otherwise have been taxed as ordinary income into capital gains eligible for lower tax rates.

One common theme underlying much of the discussion that follows is the influence of the capital gains/ordinary income distinction on corporate transactions and on the development of Subchapter C. An in-depth discussion of the capital asset definition and the substantial volume of case law surrounding it is beyond the scope of this book on corporate tax. What follows in this introduction is a very brief discussion of the capital asset definition as applied in the corporate setting.[46] Specific transactions that raise capital gain versus ordinary income issues appear throughout the text and, particularly, in the examples at the end of chapters.

Overview of Capital Asset Definition

The term "capital asset" is rather expansively defined in I.R.C. §1221(a) as "property held by the taxpayer" *except* eight specifically listed items that are *not* considered capital assets.[47] Four of these exceptions are especially relevant for corporate businesses.[48] First, the §1221 definition excludes "stock in trade," inventory, or "property held by the taxpayer primarily for sale to

---

45. Pub. L. No. 99-514, §101(a), 100 Stat. 2085.

46. For a useful detailed analysis of the capital asset definition, see Edward Yorio, Federal Income Tax Rulemaking: An Economic Approach, 51 Fordham L. Rev. 1 (1982).

47. Continuing the tradition of definitions in the negative, "ordinary income" is defined as "any gain from the sale or exchange of property which is neither a capital asset nor property described in section 1231(b)." I.R.C. §64.

48. In addition to the four exceptions discussed in the text, §1221 includes exceptions in §1221(a)(3) for copyrights, literary, musical, or artistic compositions; in §1221(a)(5) for publications of the United States government; in §1221(a)(6)-(7) for certain financial instruments; and in §1221(a)(8) for supplies used or consumed in the ordinary course of business. These new subparagraphs were added by the Tax

customers in the ordinary course, of . . . [the taxpayer's] trade or business."[49] Thus, when a corporation sells goods or services to customers in the ordinary course of its business, the profit or loss will be treated as ordinary income or loss. In addition, when a corporation sells its inventory, any profit or loss will be treated as ordinary. Congress recently added a second, and related, exception for "supplies of a type regularly used or consumed by the taxpayer in the ordinary course of a trade or business of the taxpayer."[50] This new exception should reduce technical arguments as to whether or not a particular asset fits the definition of "stock in trade" or property "primarily for sale to customers" under §1221(a)(1) and clarifies that regular business assets, as opposed to investment assets, generally will not be classified as capital assets. Third, the capital asset definition excludes "accounts or notes receivable acquired in the ordinary course of trade or business for services rendered or from the sale of property described in paragraph (1)."[51] Fourth, the capital asset definition explicitly excludes depreciable trade or business property or real property used in a trade or business.[52] Thus, according to the terms of the capital asset definition itself, a corporate sale of depreciable equipment or real estate used for business purposes should result in ordinary income or loss. With regard to such sales of depreciable equipment or real estate, however, Congress has provided a special set of rules in §1231 under which gains or losses are treated as capital when gains from the sale of §1231 assets exceed losses from §1231 assets for the taxable year.[53] Thus, sales of depreciable property or real property used in a trade or business may be treated as capital gain or loss pursuant to §1231 even though these assets have otherwise been excluded from the definition of a "capital asset" under §1221(2).

From the shareholder's perspective, stock generally is considered a capital asset.[54] Thus, when a shareholder sells his or her stock, the gain will be considered capital gain. The shareholder is entitled to this favorable treatment even though the stock reflects an indirect interest in the underlying assets of the corporation, which may or may not be capital assets. This capital

---

Relief Extension Act of 1999, Pub. L. No. 106-170, 113 Stat. 1860, 1928-1929, tit. V, §532 (codified at I.R.C. §1221(a)(6)-(8)).

49. I.R.C. §1221(a)(1).
50. I.R.C. §1221(a)(8).
51. I.R.C. §1221(a)(4).
52. I.R.C. §1221(a)(2).
53. I.R.C. §1231(a).
54. However, if the shareholder is a dealer in securities, her gains from the sale of securities generally will not be considered gain from the sale of a capital asset. I.R.C. §1236. In addition, the Code contains some special rules under which gains from the sale of stock will be treated as ordinary income. See, e.g., the discussion of §306 stock in Chapter 7.

gain should be distinguished from dividend income, which is taxed to individual shareholders at ordinary income rates.[55]

Nonrecognition in the Subchapter C World

Under general federal income tax principles, realized gains and losses must be recognized for tax purposes unless the Code provides an explicit nonrecognition rule.[56] Familiar examples of such explicit nonrecognition rules in the noncorporate setting include the provisions allowing for like-kind exchanges and involuntary conversions.[57] The basic rationale for these rules is that a transaction that merely changes the form of a taxpayer's investment should not yet be considered a taxable event. The usual corollary to such nonrecognition rules is a substituted basis provision designed to assure that the gain or loss left unrecognized will be preserved for the future. Subchapter C contains numerous nonrecognition provisions as well. For example, if structured properly, the formation of a corporation will be a nonrecognition event.[58] In addition, certain corporate reorganizations are covered by nonrecognition rules.[59] Given the possibility of a tax-free reorganization, parties to a corporate acquisition are confronted with the choice between a tax-free acquisition with substituted basis rules or a taxable acquisition with cost or fair market value basis rules. Of course, these issues will be considered in depth in subsequent chapters. For the moment, it is worth noting that nonrecognition and substituted basis rules play an important part in Subchapter C and corporate tax planning. These principles serve as a thread that runs through much of the study of corporate taxation.

Incidence of the Corporate Tax

Although the corporation itself pays the corporate level tax, controversy continues in identifying the taxpayers who bear the ultimate burden of the corporate income tax. Economists describe the problem as determining the *incidence* of the corporate income tax. Since the corporation itself is a fictional entity, it cannot bear the ultimate burden of taxation. To say that the incidence of the corporate tax falls upon the corporation, then, really is to

---

55. I.R.C. §61(a)(7).

56. I.R.C. §§61(a)(3), 1001(c).

57. I.R.C. §§1031 (like-kind exchanges), 1033 (involuntary conversions).

58. I.R.C. §351. For a detailed discussion of this provision, see Chapter 4.

59. I.R.C. §§354, 361. For a detailed discussion of tax-free reorganizations, see Chapters 11-14.

say that the shareholder "owners" of the corporation bear the tax. Taxes paid by the corporation arguably reduce profits otherwise available for distribution to the shareholder owners. Focusing upon the short run, it may well be that the corporation's shareholders bear the corporate tax burden. Over time, however, corporations may discover that they can shift the burden of the tax forward to consumers of the corporation's goods or services. By increasing the price of goods or services to cover tax costs, corporations can preserve profits for the shareholders and shift the corporate tax burden to consumers. Alternatively, corporations in the long run may shift the burden of taxation backwards to suppliers or to employees by reducing the amount paid for goods or services purchased in order to cover tax costs. Savvy investors will move their investments to those corporations that successfully shift the tax burden. The extent to which such shifting occurs and the direction of such shifting is the subject of much debate and the incidence question remains unresolved. Resolution of this debate fortunately is not essential for a reasonably thorough investigation of Subchapter C.[60]

---

60. For a good discussion of both sides of the debate, see J. Gregory Ballentine, Equity, Efficiency, and the U.S. Corporation Income Tax (1980); Joseph A. Pechman, Federal Tax Policy 141-146 (5th ed. 1987).

2

Choice of Form and Entity Classification

Introduction

Before jumping full speed into Subchapter C, students of corporate taxation should consider a few preliminary matters. Advisors of new businesses often assist the client in choosing an appropriate business form. Once the business form is chosen, the advisor next must assure that the business entity achieves the desired classification for tax purposes. Over the past 20 years, changes in state law have created a substantial number of new types of unincorporated business entities. In addition to the Subchapters C and S incorporated forms, business taxpayers now face a sometimes dizzying array of options for unincorporated entities.[1] New "check-the-box" rules effectively make tax classification elective for most business taxpayers, thus making it reasonably simple to achieve the taxpayer's desired tax status.[2] This loosening of tax classification rules has altered the balance for business taxpayers such that the choice of business form now should be far less tax-driven than in the past.

This chapter first briefly addresses the nontax and tax issues surrounding the choice of a particular type of entity or organization for engaging in

---

1. The variety of different forms of business entities has swollen to the point that several commentators advocate that state governments move to a unified business entity code. See, e.g., Thomas F. Blackwell, The Revolution Is Here: The Promise of a Unified Business Entity Code, 24 Iowa J. Corp. L. 333 (1999); Robert R. Keatinge, Universal Business Organization Legislation: Will It Happen? Why and When, 23 Del. J. Corp. L. 29 (1998); John H. Matheson and Brent O. Olson, A Call for a Unified Business Organization Law, 65 Geo. Wash. L. Rev. 1 (1996).

2. A discussion of the Treasury Department's "check-the-box" regulations follows later in this chapter.

business activity. The second part of this chapter considers the entities to which Subchapter C applies and the proper classification of business entities for federal income tax purposes.

Choice of Business Form

The Options

At the outset, any business entity must consider the various options for structuring the business. A single individual who owns and operates a business may choose either to incorporate or to operate as a sole proprietor, simply reporting income and loss on a separate business schedule on an individual tax return.[3] Assuming more than one participant in the enterprise, the traditional options are general or limited partnership, Subchapter S corporation, and Subchapter C corporation. Additional options now include newer types of business entities known as limited liability companies (LLCs), limited liability partnerships (LLPs) and limited liability limited partnerships (LLLPs).[4]

Ideally, the choice of business form should be animated largely by nontax considerations. Horizontal equity demands that similarly situated taxpayers be taxed alike. If one accepts that a business operated as a partnership is similarly situated to the same business operated as a corporation, the two entities should be taxed in similar fashion. This is a significant "if." Some would argue that there are significant differences. Proposals for integrating the corporate and individual income taxes so as to reduce or eliminate the separate tax on corporate income would go some of the way towards creating more horizontal equity between different forms of business organization. Tax factors play a significant, if not determinative, role in choosing the form of doing business. A complete discussion of these issues is beyond the scope of this book. What follows is a brief overview of the nontax and tax issues that businesses will consider in choosing the appropriate form of doing business.

---

3. Virtually all states also now recognize single-member limited liability companies (LLCs). Certain single-owner organizations, including LLCs, "can choose to be recognized or disregarded as entities separate from their owners." Treas. Reg. §301.7701-1(a)(4). One commentator recently referred to the latter option as "the tax nothing" — "a single- member entity that is disregarded for federal income tax purposes and treated as a mere extension of its owner . . ." David S. Miller, The Tax Nothing, 74 Tax Notes 619 (1997). A limited liability company with only one member is considered a "disregarded entity."

4. Most states impose more filing and registration requirements on these new types of entities than on the more traditional partnerships.

Nontax Factors

The key nontax factor that most businesses consider is limited liability. For high-risk businesses, limited liability often is essential in order to attract sufficient capital from investors. Sole proprietors and partners in a general partnership generally are personally liable for the torts, debts, and other obligations of the business and are entitled to actively participate in business management. Whether under Subchapter C or Subchapter S, the corporate form offers the advantage of limited liability. On the other hand, shareholder investors cannot participate directly in management, but simply are entitled to elect a Board of Directors to manage the corporate business affairs. The traditional option for investors seeking limited liability without incorporating has been the limited partnership. Several restrictions make the limited partnership unattractive to some businesses, however. First, a limited partnership offers limited liability only to the limited partners; the partnership must have at least one general partner who will be personally liable. Second, limited partners may not actively engage in the management of business affairs.

In recent years, many states have adopted statutes authorizing new and different business entities with some measure of limited liability, but without the restrictions imposed on limited partnerships. The limited liability company (LLC) generally is an unincorporated business organization all of whose members have limited liability, but whose members still are entitled to participate in the management of the business.[5] The limited liability partnership (LLP) is a general partnership that provides its partners with limited liability for some or all partnership obligations. The early LLP statutes provided protection only from vicarious liability for the malpractice or negligence of another partner sounding in tort. Later generation LLP statutes extended this protection to cover negligence and malpractice actions, whether sounding in tort, contract, or otherwise. Third generation LLP statutes finally provide full vicarious liability protection.[6] The most recent addition to the business organization options available in some states is the

---

5. The first LLC statute was adopted by Wyoming in 1977. Wyo. Stat. §§17-15-101 to 136 (1977 & Supp. 1995). Since that time, all 50 states and the District of Columbia have adopted LLC statutes. For a history of the development of LLC statutes, see generally Susan Pace Hamill, The Origins Behind the Limited Liability Company, 59 Ohio St. L.J. 1459 (1998); Larry E. Ribstein, The Emergence of the Limited Liability Company, 51 Bus. Law. 1 (1995).

6. LLPs generally do not provide protection against liability for activities in which the partner was personally involved or directly responsible for the supervision of the individual personally involved. For a useful discussion of the evolution of these different generations of LLP statutes, see Robert R. Keatinge, Allan G. Donn, George W. Coleman, and Elizabeth G. Hester, Limited Liability Partnerships: The Next Step in the Evolution of the Unincorporated Business Organization, 51 Bus. Law. 147 (1995).

limited liability limited partnership (LLLP). This new entity is a limited partnership providing traditional limited liability to the limited partners, but also providing limited liability to the *general* partners to the same extent permitted a partner in an LLP.[7]

A second nontax factor in choosing a business form is management. A corporation offers the centralized management of an elected Board of Directors. While it is possible to achieve comparable centralization of management in other business forms, the formal and simple structure of a corporate Board of Directors is appealing to many desiring centralized management for the business. On the other hand, the LLC generally offers greater flexibility with regard to management, effectively permitting management by either members or managers. In addition, even an otherwise manager-managed LLC can provide authority to nonmanagers to bind the LLC on particular matters through a specialized operating agreement. In choosing between a member-managed LLC and an LLP, one must keep in mind that partners generally have equal management rights. Thus, decisions on issues such as salary generally must be unanimous. In contrast, the LLC offers the flexibility of majority rule through a specialized operating agreement. Along with this flexibility, however, comes the risk of a "squeeze out" for minority LLC members.

As a third nontax factor, businesses must consider access to capital markets. Corporate stock may be easier to market to investors and may provide greater ease of transferability. Fourth, the corporate form may offer advantages with respect to benefits available to employees such as qualified deferred compensation plans, profit-sharing and stock-option plans.

A fifth consideration in the choice of business form is the "ease of exit" or dissolution. Corporations generally have an indefinite life, while partnerships can be dissolved easily through the withdrawal of any partner. LLCs generally fit somewhere in the middle. Many state LLC statutes provide no statutory right to disassociate or withdraw.

As a sixth consideration, business participants choosing among different types of unincorporated business entities should carefully examine the state statute with regard to restrictions on distributions, rules with regard to profit-sharing ratios, and other financial matters.

A final factor is the cost of formation. A corporation, whether Subchapter C or S, requires Articles of Incorporation and By-Laws and must register with the state of incorporation and often with other states in which it does business. LLCs and LLPs also generally must register with the state. The legal costs of generating the necessary documents along with filing and registration fees makes the expense of incorporating a significant factor, particularly for many small businesses. Although a business would be well

---

7. See, e.g., Colo. Rev. Stat. Ann., §§7-60-144, 7-62-109 (1995); Del. Code Ann., tit. 6, §1553 (Supp. 1994).

advised to have a partnership agreement, such an agreement is not required. Similarly, an LLC operating agreement is advisable for LLCs, but is not required in all states. Additionally, in most cases, partnerships need not register with the state or pay fees associated with such registration.

Tax Factors

a) Double Taxation

From a tax point of view, the double taxation provided for in Subchapter C is a distinct disadvantage.[8] This disadvantage to Subchapter C may not appear as serious if the corporation plans to reinvest profits as working capital and not pay out regular dividends. Several problems must be considered, however. First, the Code imposes penalty taxes on certain undistributed corporate earnings.[9] Second, it may be difficult for such a corporation to raise capital to the extent that investors expect dividends to be paid. Finally, even though the double tax impact can be delayed through certain accumulations of capital, it cannot be avoided entirely. Upon liquidation or upon sale of the stock, the shareholders must report gain or loss.

Pass-through entities, such as general or limited partnerships, Subchapter S corporations, as well as LLCs, LLPs, and LLLPs that are classified as partnerships for tax purposes, offer the advantage of a single federal income tax.[10] Where there are profits, the advantage of a single layer of tax may be obvious. In addition, if the partnership or other pass-through entity suffers an operating loss, each partner or member will report his or her share of the loss on an individual tax return. Individual taxpayers often seek out such losses in order to reduce gains from other activities. A member's ability to use such losses from a pass-through entity is severely restricted through various provisions in the Code.[11] On the other hand, a shareholder in a

---

8. For a contrary view, see John W. Lee, A Populist Political Perspective of the Business Tax Entities Universe: Hey the Stars Might Lie But the Numbers Never Do, 78 Tex. L. Rev. 885 (2000).

9. See brief discussion of the accumulated earnings and personal holding company penalty taxes in Chapter 1.

10. Although the single tax advantage is available to pass-through entities for *federal* tax purposes, some states *do* impose an entity level income and/or franchise tax.

11. For example, a partner's losses are limited to the extent of the partner's basis in the partnership interest. I.R.C. §704(d). In addition, partners can only deduct losses to the extent that their partnership interest basis reflects amounts for which the partner is personally "at risk." I.R.C. §465. Finally, passive investors, such as limited partners, can only deduct losses from investments in passive activities to the extent that they have gain from passive activities. I.R.C. §469. A comprehensive discussion of these provisions is beyond the scope of this book. In choosing between the partnership and Subchapter S pass-through business forms, members should be aware that the loss limitations applicable to partners under Subchapter K can differ from those under Subchapter S. For example, although both Subchapters provide that a

corporation will never have the opportunity to report a corporate loss on her individual tax return.

Subchapter S corporations seem to offer the best of both worlds. On the one hand, the shareholder has limited liability. At the same time, the business profits are subject to only one layer of tax. Until recently, however, availability of the Subchapter S election was quite limited. First, it was available only to corporations with 35 or fewer individual shareholders.[12] Second, the S corporation can issue only one class of stock and, until recently, was not entitled to hold stock in a subsidiary corporation. Congress recently increased the permissible number of shareholders to 75 and extended permissible shareholders to include certain tax-exempt corporations and "electing small business trusts."[13] In addition, an S corporation now may hold stock in a C corporation or a qualified subchapter S subsidiary.[14] Although the recent changes make Subchapter S tax treatment more widely available, many large business entities still cannot qualify for Subchapter S status or may find it still too restrictive. The LLC and LLP provisions in many states seem to solve many of these problems. A properly structured LLC or LLP provides the double advantages of limited liability and a single layer of taxation on business income, assuming that the LLC or LLP chooses partnership classification for federal income tax purposes.[15] In addition, LLCs, in particular, allow members more flexibility to "custom fit" an operating agreement to their business needs. At the same time, state provisions for such businesses do not restrict the number of members that can participate.

b) Tax Rate Issues

There was a time when taxpayers used corporations as tax shelters. Shortly after World War II, the individual income tax rate was significantly higher than the corporate tax rate. Individuals would place their assets in a corporation so that profits would be taxed at the significantly lower corporate rate. Even though there was a second shareholder level tax on distributed earnings, this shareholder tax could be deferred for significant periods of time by accumulating earnings, or it could be eliminated entirely by leaving the stock upon death to beneficiaries who acquired the stock with a stepped-up basis under I.R.C. §1014.

---

member's loss deduction cannot exceed the member's basis, Subchapters K and S have different rules for the computation of basis.

12. I.R.C. §1361(b)(1) (prior to amendment by the Small Business Job Protection Act of 1996).

13. Small Business Job Protection Act of 1996, §§1301 and 1302(b), Pub. L. No. 104-188, 110 Stat. 1755 (codified at I.R.C. §1361(b), (c)(2), (e)).

14. *Id.* at §1308(b), adding I.R.C. §1361(b)(3).

15. The entity classification issues under new "check-the-box" regulations are discussed later in this chapter.

Over the years, the differential between the top corporate and the top individual income tax rates has been dwindling. For the first time in 1986, the top corporate rate was set just slightly higher than the top individual rate. Since tax rate changes in 1993, the top individual rate has been slightly higher than the top corporate rate. In any event, there is now only a modest difference between the top individual and the top corporate rates. Surely, few think of a Subchapter C corporation as a tax shelter opportunity any longer.[16] One must look carefully at the anticipated earnings of the business and the anticipated tax bracket of primary shareholders before making any decisions regarding business form based upon rate structure.[17] Another factor that should be considered is the extent to which any gains might be capital gains. Since individual taxpayers are eligible for significantly lower tax rates on their capital gains income under §1(h), capital gains earned by the corporation will be taxed at a higher rate than those earned by individual high-bracket taxpayers.

Given the differences in tax rates and double taxation on corporate earnings, one may well wonder why businesses choose the corporate form at all. Some larger entities simply have no option. They need the corporate advantages of limited liability and centralized management and are ineligible for Subchapter S status. The centralized management permitted to an LLC under various "opt out" provisions under state law may prove too unwieldy. A small business may plan to make distributions only rarely. If the shareholders of such a corporation hold onto the stock until death, the stock basis is stepped up to fair market value under §1014, with the result that little or no shareholder level tax is paid. Finally, many larger business entities wish to provide certain profit-sharing and stock-option plans that can be offered only through the corporate form.

Classification of the Business Entity

Initial Classification Issues

Federal tax law includes three primary categories of organizations recognized as entities separate from their owners: corporations (or other entities taxable as corporations), partnerships, and trusts.[18] Since each of these entities is governed by a distinct tax regime with its own special rules, proper classifica-

---

16. But see Lee, *supra* note 8.

17. In order to discourage individuals subject to higher rates from setting up corporations to receive income from their personal services, taxable at the lower corporate rate, Congress provides in I.R.C. §11(b)(2) that the graduated corporate rates are not available to a "qualified personal service corporation" as defined in §448(d)(2). Such personal service corporations will be subject to a flat tax of 35%.

18. Treas. Reg. §301.7701-1(b).

tion of the organization is essential in determining the proper tax conse-quences of the organization's activities and transactions.[19] Although the Treasury Department recently revised and simplified its §7701 regulations under which organizations are classified for federal income tax purposes, many of the basic classification rules remain unchanged.[20] As before, the label attached to a particular enterprise for state law purposes will not be deter-minative for federal income tax purposes.[21]

Also as before, the first step under the entity classification regulations is to be sure that a separate tax entity has actually been created. The mere co-ownership of property or sharing of expenses does not necessarily create a separate tax entity. A joint venture or other contractual arrangement creates a separate entity for tax purposes if the participants "carry on a trade, business, financial operation, or venture and divide the profits therefrom."[22] Once it is established that the organization is a separate entity for tax pur-poses, the entity must further be classified as a corporation, partnership, or trust under rules provided in Treasury regulations §§301.7701-2, 3, and 4.

According to the regulations, a separate tax entity not properly classified as a trust, or otherwise subject to special treatment, is a "business entity." Such a business entity with two or more members will be classified as a corporation or a partnership for tax purposes.[23] Before turning to the dis-tinction between corporations and partnerships, then, it is necessary first to establish that the organization is not an ordinary trust.[24] Generally speaking, an ordinary trust does not involve "associates in a joint enterprise for the conduct of business for profit."[25] Instead, the usual trustee simply is respon-sible for protecting and conserving property for trust beneficiaries. The §7701 regulations distinguish such an ordinary trust from a business or commercial trust, providing that "[t]he fact that any organization is techni-cally cast in the trust form, by conveying title to property to trustees for the benefit of persons designated as beneficiaries, will not change the real char-acter of the organization if the organization is more properly classified as a business entity."[26] Once it is established that the organization in question is

---

19. Corporations generally are subject to Subchapter C (§§301-384), partnerships to Subchapter K (§§701-761) and trusts to Subchapter J (§§641-692).

20. Revisions to the §7701 entity classification regulations were effective as of January 1, 1997. T.D. 8697, 61 Fed. Reg. 66,584 (Dec. 18, 1996).

21. Treas. Reg. §301.7701-1(a).

22. Treas. Reg. §301.7701-1(a)(2).

23. Treas. Reg. §301.7701-2(a).

24. The rules for purposes of this distinction have not significantly changed even under the revised regulations. See Treas. Reg. §301.7701-4.

25. Treas. Reg. §301.7701-4(a).

26. Treas. Reg. §301.7701-4(b).

a *business* entity with two or more members, the entity must be further classified as either a corporation or a partnership.

Incorporated Entities

An entity properly incorporated under state law or properly organized under a state joint-stock company or joint-stock association statute generally will be treated as a corporation for federal income tax purposes.[27] In rare cases, however, a corporation otherwise properly incorporated under state law will be disregarded for federal income tax purposes. For example, the Supreme Court case of Commissioner v. Bollinger[28] involved a group of real-estate partnerships that created a corporation for the sole purpose of holding nominal title to property and borrowing necessary funds for the partnership real-estate business. The lender had suggested that the partnerships establish a corporation to hold nominal title to the collateral and borrow the necessary funds since the interest rate the lender could charge corporate borrowers under the state usury law was higher than the rate for noncorporate borrowers. The corporation had no other assets, liabilities, employees, or bank accounts. In *Bollinger,* the Court disregarded the corporation, finding that the corporate entity was acting as agent for the partnerships, which were the true owners of the property. Thus, the Court upheld the partnerships' reporting of income and loss on their partnership tax returns and the pass-through of such income and loss to the individual partners. This is not to suggest, however, that the *Bollinger* result will be common. As a general rule, once investors choose to incorporate, the corporation is viewed as a separate entity for tax purposes and the shareholders generally will be bound for tax purposes by their decision to incorporate, for better or for worse, until they liquidate the corporation. The *Bollinger* decision does leave open the possibility, however, that in certain limited circumstances, a properly incorporated entity will be disregarded for tax purposes.

Certain Unincorporated Entities: Per Se Corporations

In addition to formally incorporated businesses and joint-stock companies or associations, the Internal Revenue Code and regulations also automatically classify certain *unincorporated* entities as corporations for federal tax purposes. For example, §7704 automatically classifies certain publicly traded partnerships as corporations. For purposes of this provision, a publicly traded

---

27. Treas. Reg. §301.7701-2(b)(1), (3).
28. 485 U.S. 340 (1988).

partnership is "any partnership if (1) interests in such partnership are traded on an established securities market, or (2) interests in such partnership are readily tradeable on a secondary market (or the substantial equivalent thereof)."[29] This Code provision was a response to the growth of "master limited partnerships" in the 1980s. Such investments were often available on established securities markets and gave investors, otherwise ineligible for pass-through tax treatment under Subchapter S, the advantages of limited liability and the opportunity to participate in huge business conglomerates without the disadvantage of the corporate double tax. Since these publicly traded partnerships so resemble corporations, §7704 *deems* them to be corporations for federal tax purposes. The §7701 regulations also automatically classify as corporations certain other business entities such as insurance companies,[30] certain state-chartered banks,[31] government-owned businesses,[32] and certain foreign entities.[33]

Associations Taxable as Corporations: Movement from the "Corporate Resemblance" Test to the New Elective Regime

The Internal Revenue Code itself defines the term "corporation" to include "associations, joint-stock companies, and insurance companies."[34] Before the recently promulgated "check-the-box" regulations, the distinction between an "association" taxable as a corporation and an unincorporated business entity *not* taxed as a corporation was determined under a six part "corporate resemblance" test taken from the Supreme Court's 1935 decision in Morrissey v. Commissioner.[35] The old §7701 regulations identified six charac-

---

29. I.R.C. §7704(b). The publicly traded partnership is deemed to have transferred all of its assets to a newly formed corporation in exchange for stock and to have distributed the stock to its partners in liquidation of their partnership interests. I.R.C.§7704(f). An exception to the §7704 rules is provided for certain publicly traded partnerships more than 90% of whose income consists of "passive-type" income. I.R.C. §7704(c).

30. Treas. Reg. §301.7701-2(b)(4).

31. Treas. Reg. §301.7701-2(b)(5).

32. Treas. Reg. §301.7701-2(b)(1), (6).

33. Treas. Reg. §301.7701-2(b)(8). This provision contains a list of particular business entities formed in specifically named foreign countries that will be treated as per se (or automatic) corporations. Other foreign business entities will be eligible to elect partnership or corporate status for U.S. tax purposes. Issues related to foreign corporations and the general international implications of the new entity classification regulations are beyond the scope of this book.

34. I.R.C. §7701(a)(3).

35. 296 U.S. 344 (1935). The government in *Morrissey* sought to treat an entity organized as a trust under state law as an "association" taxable as a corporation for

teristics ordinarily found in a pure corporation, which, taken together, distinguished it from other organizations. The six factors were:

1. associates,
2. objective to carry on business for joint profit,
3. continuity of life,
4. centralization of management,
5. limited liability, and
6. free transferability of interests.[36]

Based upon this old facts and circumstances analysis, if an organization more nearly resembled a corporation than a partnership or trust, the organization was classified as an association taxable as a corporation. The §7701 entity classification regulations first promulgated in 1960 had a distinct bias in favor of partnership rather than corporate classification for unincorporated business entities. At that time, groups of professionals, otherwise unable to organize as corporations due to state laws prohibiting professional incorporation, sought corporate status for tax purposes in order to take advantage of employee benefits then available only to corporate employees. Dr. Kintner and his medical partners successfully established themselves as an association treated as a corporation for tax purposes in order to be eligible to participate in a qualified pension plan.[37] The old detailed §7701 entity classification regulations, often referred to as the "Kintner regulations," were specifically designed to prevent groups such as Dr. Kintner and associates from achieving corporate status for tax purposes. Given this history, it is not surprising that the old regulations were distinctly biased in favor of partnership classification.

Over time, the government's interest in classification cases changed considerably. For one thing, most states adopted professional incorporation laws permitting professionals to achieve corporate status directly. In addition, fringe benefits such as pension plans, that were available only to corporate employees, are now more widely available. It is no longer necessary for professionals to achieve corporate status in order to take advantage of such fringe benefits. Most important, the tax shelter industry that flourished after adoption of the old "Kintner regulations" depended upon successful classification of the entity as a limited partnership. Until the Tax Reform Act of 1986, a limited partnership offered the combined advantages of limited liability to limited partners and a pass-through of losses to individual limited partners who could use such losses to offset other income. The partnership entity permitted investors to "pass-through" their share of losses and other

---

federal income tax purposes. After applying its six-part "corporate resemblance" test, the Court concluded that the entity more nearly resembled a corporation than a trust. *Id.* at 360.

36. *Id.*

37. United States v. Kintner, 216 F.2d 418 (9th Cir. 1954).

deductions from the business onto their individual tax returns, thus offsetting other income. Ironically, the partnership bias of the old §7701 regulations worked to the government's disadvantage in its early battle against tax shelters.

Instead of fighting the battle against tax shelters through changes in the classification rules, the government fought the battle through changes enacted by the Tax Reform Act of 1986, which disallowed the deduction of many losses that had been so attractive to the tax-shelter industry.[38] The Treasury Department became more relaxed in blessing partnership classification for different types of business entities, thus making it easy for many business entities to avoid the double corporate tax.[39] The Treasury Department recognized that the growth of different types of business entities under state law had blurred the traditional distinctions between corporations and partnerships. Through their statutory LLC, LLP, and LLLP provisions, many states, as a practical matter, have already given taxpayers opportunities to create business entities providing the corporate advantage of limited liability while avoiding the corporate disadvantage of double taxation.

In proposing its new entity classification regulations, the Treasury Department noted that "[o]ne consequence of the increased flexibility under local law in forming a partnership or other unincorporated business organization is that taxpayers generally can achieve partnership tax classification for a nonpublicly traded organization that, in all meaningful respects, is virtually indistinguishable from a corporation."[40] The new "check-the-box" regulations eliminate the corporate resemblance test, replacing the formalistic rules of the old regulations "with a much simpler approach that generally is elective,"[41] now making explicit the previously de facto elective nature of the entity classification rules.

The New Elective Classification Regulations: Check-the-Box

Under new "check-the-box" regulations, a business entity that is not *automatically* classified as a corporation under §301.7701-2 is considered an "eligible entity."[42] An eligible entity with two or more members can elect

---

38. For example, the passive loss rules in I.R.C. §469 now prohibit passive investors, such as limited partners, from deducting losses from their limited partnership investments, except to the extent that they have gain from passive investment activity.

39. For example, in numerous recent rulings, the Service has agreed to classify companies organized under new state limited liability company statutes as partnerships for tax purposes. See discussion earlier in this chapter.

40. Notice of Proposed Rulemaking, PS-43-95, Fed. Reg. (May 10, 1996).

41. T.D. 8697, 61 Fed. Reg. 66,584 (Dec. 18, 1996) (explanation of provisions).

42. Treas. Reg. §301.7701-3(a). Entities automatically classified as corporations were discussed earlier in this chapter.

classification as either an association taxable as a corporation or a partnership. An eligible entity with a single member can elect classification as an association taxable as a corporation or to be disregarded as an entity separate from its owner.[43] Presumably, most business entities will prefer the pass-through tax treatment offered by partnership classification to the double taxation regime of Subchapter C. Consequently, the regulations provide a default partnership classification rule — if no election is filed for a domestic entity with two or more members, the entity will be treated as a partnership. Similarly, since it is presumed that most individual owners will prefer to avoid Subchapter C double taxation, a default rule provides that if no election is filed for a domestic single-owner entity, the entity "will be disregarded as an entity separate from its owners."[44]

Since the default rules are explicit, the regulations clarify that "elections are necessary *only when* an eligible entity chooses to be classified initially as other than the default classification or when an eligible entity chooses to change its classification." In other words, an entity that wishes *corporate* tax status must make a formal election; other entities need do nothing. The regulations now define a partnership for tax purposes as "a business entity that is not a corporation . . . and that has at least two members."[45]

Given that "check-the-box" rules permit an election to change entity classification, a business entity need not be stuck with its initial tax classification choice.[46] However, the regulations include special rules aimed at taxpayer attempts to use repeated changes in tax status for manipulative or abusive purposes. Thus, if an eligible entity elects to change its classification, it generally will not be permitted *again* to change its classification for a period of 60 months.[47]

Recently finalized regulatory amendments add details regarding the tax consequences that flow from an elective change in classification.[48] For example, if a partnership elects to become an association, the regulations provide that the partnership is thereby deemed to contribute its assets and liabilities to the association in exchange for stock, followed by an immediate liquidation of the partnership in which stock is distributed to the partners.[49] If an

---

43. *Id*. See also Treas. Reg. §301.7701-2(a).

44. Treas. Reg. §301.7701-3(b)(1).

45. Treas. Reg. §301.7701-2(c)(1).

46. Treas. Reg. §7701-3(c)(1)(i).

47. Treas. Reg. §7701-3(c)(1)(iv). The Commissioner has authority, however, to waive this rule upon a greater than 50% change in ownership. *Id*.

48. Treas. Reg. §7701-3(g) (added by T.D. 8844, 64 Fed. Reg. 66,591. (Nov. 29, 1999)).

49. *Id*. at §7701-3(g)(1)(i). Tax consequences of the "deemed formation transaction" would be governed by §351, which is discussed in Chapter 4. Tax consequences of the "deemed partnership liquidation" would be governed by Subchapter K partnership rules.

eligible entity that previously elected to be classified as an association later elects to change its classification to partnership, the association will be deemed to have distributed all of its assets and liabilities to the shareholders in liquidation, followed by an immediate contribution of the assets and liabilities to the partnership.[50]

From the moment the "check-the-box" regulations were enacted, taxpayers have been busy designing clever transactions, perceived as abusive by the Treasury Department, that use these rules to reduce tax liability.[51] Taxpayers have particularly focused on transactions involving the one member "disregarded entity," popularly referred to as the "tax nothing."[52] In the meantime, the Treasury Department has proposed additional amendments to the "check-the-box" regulations designed to address perceived abuses involving foreign eligible entity changes in tax classification.[53] Stay tuned. Clearly, the "check-the-box" saga will continue.

Summary and Implications

New elective regulations simplify and liberalize entity classification rules. Given the availability of LLC and other new business forms, these "check-the-box" regulations effectively offer business owners the opportunity to easily achieve limited liability without incurring the double taxation of Subchapter C. Under the old "corporate resemblance" test, a limited partnership, LLC, LLP, or LLLP bore the risk that the Treasury Department might reclassify it as a corporation for tax purposes if the organization had more corporate than noncorporate characteristics. Under the new regulations, such eligible business entities simply can choose a tax classification by election.

The "check-the-box" rules were intended to simplify tax classification issues and reduce the extraordinary number of hours government and private accountants and lawyers were spending on them. Yet major simplification continues to appear elusive. Already, a familiar cycle is emerging. Taxpayers design complex transactions to use new statutes or regulations to their tax

---

50. Treas. Reg. §7701-3(g)(1)(ii). Tax consequences of the "deemed liquidation transaction" would be governed by §§331 and 336 or §§332 and 337, which are discussed in Chapters 8 and 9. The "deemed partnership contribution" would be governed by Subchapter K partnership rules.

51. Accounting firms have even published detailed descriptions of such transactions. See, e.g., a description of the "Bond & Option Sales Strategy" (BOSS) by PriceWaterhouse Coopers, 1999 Tax Notes Today 233-258.

52. For a description of these developments, see David S. Miller, The Strange Materialization of the Tax Nothing, 87 Tax Notes 685 (2000).

53. Notice of Proposed Rulemaking, 64 Fed. Reg. 66,591 (Nov. 29, 1999) ("Changes in Entity Classification: Special Rule for Certain Foreign Eligible Entities"). A detailed discussion of these foreign eligible entity issues is beyond the scope of this book.

advantage in ways that were unanticipated or were not desired by Congress or the Treasury Department. The government then responds to such "loopholes" with an amendment to the statute or regulations designed to attack the transaction. The government response often is complex and narrowly focused on the tax shelter of the moment, thus adding to the complexity of the Code and regulations.

The Internal Revenue Code includes specific definitions of the terms "corporation" and "partnership" in §7701. Given these definitions, some have questioned even the Treasury Department's authority to promulgate elective classification rules.[54] Since the rules are so favorable to most taxpayers, however, a legal challenge to the regulations may not be imminent. In the meantime, some have suggested that Congress explicitly codify or, at least, provide clear legislative authority for elective classification rules.[55]

As the Joint Committee on Taxation recently observed, the enhanced ability to choose partnership treatment, "places increased pressure on the rules governing the taxation of partnership income, making it more important to identify and, if possible, correct provisions in the partnership tax rules that give anomalous results, create problems in application, or are anachronistic."[56] More significantly, the new "check-the-box" regime undoubtedly will stimulate policymakers to rethink the need for the different tax regimes in Subchapter C (corporations), Subchapter K (partnerships), and Subchapter S (small-business corporations) and place increasing emphasis on proposals for integrating the federal individual and corporate income taxes.

---

54. Staff of Joint Comm. on Tax'n, Review of Selected Entity Classification and Partnership Tax Issues, 105th Cong., 2d Sess. (Comm. Print 1997).

55. *Id.*

56. *Id.* at 1.

3

The Corporate Capital Structure

Introduction[1]

Once a business chooses to operate in the corporate form, it must decide how to raise capital and otherwise structure the corporate organization. Corporations typically raise capital through issuing stock or through borrowing. The investor who purchases stock holds an equity interest while the lender holds a debt or creditor interest in the corporate enterprise. In either case, the investor or lender expects a return on funds placed or "invested" with the corporation. Shareholders may receive that return from dividends paid on the stock and from profit upon later sale of the stock. Lenders receive their return from interest payments.[2] The corporation is obligated to pay its lenders before it pays its shareholders. Thus, an equity interest is regarded as *subordinate* or *junior* to a debt interest in the corporation. Put another way, the debt interest is regarded as *preferred* or *senior* to the equity interest. An equity interest generally carries greater risk than a debt interest *in the same corporation.*[3]

---

1. This chapter will provide only a brief overview of the corporate capital structure as necessary to understand the related tax issues. For a more detailed analysis, see Bayless Manning and James J. Hanks, Jr., Legal Capital (3d ed. 1990); Lewis D. Solomon and Alan R. Palmiter, Corporations: Examples and Explanations, ch. 4 (3d ed. 1999).

2. A lender might also receive value by selling or exchanging the note at a gain. Such a gain generally would result from changes in interest rates and should not be regarded as gain from the investment in the corporation itself.

3. Generalizations are more difficult when comparing different corporations. A debt interest in a new, highly speculative corporation may be more risky than an equity interest in a well-established, economically healthy corporation.

Creditors generally are entitled only to a repayment of the principal and a fixed rate of interest. As a result, although creditors are preferred in the sense that they are entitled to payment before the common shareholders, they are limited in that their rate of return generally is fixed. Unlike the creditor, the common shareholder's rate of return is unlimited, giving the shareholder the opportunity to participate in the economic growth of the corporation. A holder of stock or equity decides "to embark upon the corporate adventure, taking the risks of loss . . . so that he may enjoy the chances of profit."[4]

Many smaller corporations have only one class of equity outstanding. This simple voting common stock typically allows the shareholders to vote for members of the board of directors. It also gives the shareholders an unlimited interest in the earnings of the corporation after all creditors have been paid and an unlimited right to share in assets upon liquidation.[5] Other corporations may have more complex capital structures, including additional classes of common stock either with greater or lesser voting rights, or sometimes, no voting rights at all. Corporations may also issue preferred stock, which also may be either voting or nonvoting. Preferred stock generally provides for a fixed rate of return before the common shareholders are entitled to be paid. Thus, for example, 6% preferred stock may offer investors a fixed 6% rate of return on the stock's stated value before the common shareholders are paid. Unlike a creditor, the preferred shareholder is not *entitled* to a 6% return regardless of corporate performance.[6] Preferred shareholders are paid only after creditors have been paid, but before the common shareholders. Thus, in the corporate pecking order, preferred shareholders are senior or preferred to common shareholders, but subordinate or junior to creditors or note holders.

Distinguishing Debt from Equity

Why Does It Matter?

Many corporate tax provisions cannot be properly applied until one first identifies the instrument at issue as debt or equity. The descriptions that

---

4. United States v. Title Guarantee & Trust Co., 133 F.2d 990, 993 (6th Cir. 1993).

5. This is not to suggest that the shareholders are entitled to dividends. Dividends will be paid by the corporation only when they are declared by the board of directors. If the corporation should liquidate, however, the holders of common stock are entitled to all residual assets left after the creditors and other more senior equity holders have been paid.

6. Preferred stock that is *cumulative* is entitled to accrued, but unpaid, dividends from prior years before common shareholders may receive a dividend. If the preferred

follow provide a brief sampling of the kinds of issues that require a distinction between debt and equity instruments.

One issue of great concern to corporations is whether payments with respect to a particular instrument will qualify as deductible interest expense. Interest payments are deductible to the corporation,[7] whereas distributions to shareholders with respect to stock are not deductible. The recipient of a corporate payment must also distinguish interest receipts from dividend receipts. A corporation holding stock in another corporate enterprise is entitled to a dividends-received deduction on payments with respect to an equity interest,[8] but is not entitled to any deduction on interest receipts with respect to a debt instrument. In addition, holders of debt issued with "original issue discount"[9] (OID) will be required to include the interest reflected in this discount for each day during the taxable year that he or she held the debt instrument.[10] These OID rules generally will not apply to equity instruments.[11]

The debt-equity distinction also is critical in determining the tax consequences of incorporation. Upon formation of a corporation, contributors will be entitled to nonrecognition of gain upon receipt of *stock* in return for the property contributed.[12] If the investor receives a debenture or some other form of debt instead of stock in return for a contribution to a corporation, the transfer of property will not qualify for nonrecognition treatment. In somewhat parallel fashion, the corporate reorganization rules provide nonrecognition where the shareholders receive stock in a reorganization.[13] When shareholders receive notes or other evidence of indebtedness they are con-

---

stock is *noncumulative,* the corporation has no continuing obligation to later pay undeclared dividends from prior years. Preferred stock also may be either *participating* or *nonparticipating.* Participating preferred shareholders are entitled not only to the preferred rate of return, but also share with the common shareholders when dividends beyond the dividend preference are declared.

7. I.R.C. §163. There are, however, a limited number of circumstances in which corporate interest will not be deductible. See, e.g., I.R.C. §§279, 247.

8. I.R.C. §243.

9. "Original issue discount" is defined as the excess of the stated redemption price at maturity over the issue price. I.R.C. §1273(a)(1).

10. I.R.C. §1272(a)(1).

11. Rules similar to the OID rules may apply, however, to certain preferred stock redeemable at a price higher than the issue price. Here, the difference between the redemption and issue price resembles the discount element in an OID debt instrument. Under its authority under §305(c), the Treasury Department requires ratable inclusion of income of the redemption premium over the period of time during which the stock cannot be called for redemption. Treas. Reg. §1.305-5(b). For further discussion of §305(c), see Chapter 7.

12. I.R.C. §351. The nonrecognition rules for contributions in return for stock are discussed in more detail in Chapter 4.

13. For discussion of corporate reorganizations, see Chapters 11-14.

sidered to have received taxable boot. Thus, distinguishing debt from equity will be important to shareholders participating in an otherwise tax-free reorganization.

Redemption provides another example of the significance of the distinction between equity and debt. Payments to a shareholder in redemption of stock will be treated under §302 as either sale or exchange or dividend income.[14] In contrast, retirement of debt instruments will be governed by special rules in §1271. Another example involves the loss of corporate value. When corporate stock loses its value, the shareholders may be entitled to a deduction for the loss of worthless stock under §165. On the other hand, when a debt becomes worthless, the lender may be entitled to a bad debt deduction under §166. The distinction also is important in determining eligibility for an election to be treated as a Subchapter S corporation. To be eligible for such an election, the corporation generally may have only one class of stock.[15] The corporation must be careful that any other financial instruments issued not be classified as equity or stock for purposes of these rules.

Why Should It Matter?

Corporate issues of stock and debt are simply alternative methods of raising corporate capital. From a finance theory perspective, an argument can be made that changes in a firm's capital structure will not change the firm's overall value.[16] In other words, from an *economic,* as opposed to a tax, point of view, it should make little difference whether the corporation raises funds through debt or equity. Why, then, should there be any difference in the tax treatment of debt and equity? This question goes to the very heart of the corporate tax itself. One could eliminate much of the discrepancy between debt and equity by treating all corporate financial instruments as debt. Thus, corporations would be entitled to deduct all payments to investors and all holders of financial instruments would be required to report "interest" income as it accrued under rules similar to the original issue discount rules. The double tax on corporate earnings effectively would be eliminated. On the other hand, one could treat all financial instruments as equity, thus disallowing any interest deductions on corporate financial instruments. Unless the interest deduction was eliminated for all business taxpayers, this

---

14. For a more thorough discussion of redemptions, see Chapter 6.

15. I.R.C. §1361(b)(1)(D).

16. See discussion of this theory in Richard A. Brealey & Stewart C. Myers, Principles of Corporate Finance, chs. 17 and 18 (6th ed. 2000). This theoretical conclusion only holds, however, before taking into account the costs of the corporate tax, bankruptcy and certain other expenses.

would discriminate in favor of noncorporate businesses still eligible for the interest deduction.

The Tax Advantages of Debt vs. Equity

Common wisdom suggests that debt financing is encouraged by tax provisions favoring debt over equity. Although this is generally true, the case often is overstated. Perhaps the most frequently cited tax advantage to debt over equity is the deductibility of corporate interest payments on debt in contrast to the nondeductibility of corporate dividend payments on stock. In contrast to interest, however, the payment and timing of *dividends* is at the discretion of the board of directors. Corporations may choose to accrue earnings rather than distribute them as dividends. These accrued earnings should be reflected in an increased value for the shares. If the shareholders sell their stock, gain is reported as capital gain as opposed to ordinary income. Moreover, the gain on the shares may never be taxed to the shareholders at all if they hold the shares until they die, leaving the stock to their heirs with a stepped-up basis under §1014. In other words, an investor in a corporation that accrues earnings can convert what would have been ordinary dividend income into capital gain upon the later sale of the stock or can even avoid tax on the accrued earnings altogether through a stepped-up basis in the shares upon death.[17] Such investors will have a preference for equity over debt.

Another tax advantage to debt financing is that amounts received upon retirement of corporate debt are considered "as amounts received in exchange," and thus generally are treated as capital gains,[18] whereas amounts received upon the redemption of stock must meet one of the safe-harbors of §302 in order to achieve the same result.[19] Thus, it will be easier to achieve capital gain treatment upon retirement of debt.

Despite the advantage of interest deductions to the paying corporation on debt instruments, a corporate shareholder generally will prefer equity, since dividends paid to corporations are entitled to a dividends-received deduction under §243.[20] In the end, the tax advantages to debt financing from the paying corporation's perspective must be balanced against the slight

---

17. The accumulated earnings tax, personal holding company rules, and related provisions in the Code were designed to prevent some of the perceived abuses from such accumulations. See Chapter 1.

18. I.R.C. §1271(a)(1). Note, however, that debt retirement will result in ordinary income in certain cases where there was an intention to call the debt instrument before maturity. I.R.C. §1271(a)(2)(A). In addition, ordinary income will result to the extent of unamortized original issue discount, I.R.C. §1272, and to the extent of any accrued market discount. I.R.C. §1276.

19. The tax treatment of redemptions is covered in Chapter 6.

20. See Chapter 5 for detailed discussion of the §243 dividends-received deduction.

preference that the individual shareholders may have and the strong preference that corporate shareholders may have for equity financing.

Congress has responded to the perceived bias toward debt financing by disallowing corporate interest deductions in certain cases thought to be abusive or where interest deductions seemed particularly inappropriate. For example, in an effort to curb the growing numbers of tax-induced leveraged buy-outs, §279 disallows interest deductions on corporate indebtedness incurred to acquire certain stock of another corporation. In addition, special net operating loss provisions restrict the carryback of certain losses attributable to interest expense incurred in connection with a major stock acquisition or excess distribution.[21]

Having considered some of the reasons why the debt-equity distinction is important and briefly explored the generally perceived bias towards equity financing built into the corporate tax regime, the next step is to study the factors that assist in making the debt-equity distinction.

Absence of a Precise Standard

Although distinguishing debt from equity is important in determining the proper tax consequences of many corporate transactions, actually making the distinction often is no easy task. Variations in the types and terms of financial instruments are as boundless as the creativity of financial planners, tax lawyers, and accountants. Making the debt-equity distinction can be a frustrating exercise. There are no precise rules, but rather a number of factors to be applied in a facts and circumstances balancing act. As the court pointed out in one major case:

> neither any single criterion nor any series of criteria can provide a conclusive answer in the kaleidoscopic circumstances which individual cases present. . . . The various factors . . . are only aids in answering the ultimate question whether the investment, analyzed in terms of its economic reality, constitutes risk capital entirely subject to the fortunes of the corporate venture or represents a strict debtor-creditor relationship. Since there is often an element of risk in a loan, just as there is an element of risk in an equity interest, the conflicting elements do not end at a clear line in all cases.[22]

Reclassification of a debt instrument as equity for tax purposes will result in disallowance of interest deductions to the corporation and taxation of dividends to the shareholders. Reclassification of an equity interest as a debt interest will result in disallowance of the §243 dividends-received deduction

---

21. I.R.C. §172(b)(1)(E), (h).

22. Fin Hay Realty Co. v. United States, 398 F.2d 694, 696-697 (3d Cir. 1968) (citations omitted).

to any corporate shareholder and the allowance of interest deductions to the paying corporation.

Despite many years of effort, there are no precise rules distinguishing debt from equity. In 1969, Congress authorized the Treasury Department to "prescribe such regulations as may be necessary or appropriate to determine whether an interest in a corporation is to be treated . . . as stock or indebtedness (or as in part stock and in part indebtedness)."[23] An unusual Code provision, §385, offers merely suggestions to the Treasury Department as to factors it may include in regulations distinguishing debtor-creditor relationships from corporation-shareholder relationships.[24] These suggested factors are:

1. whether there is a written unconditional promise to pay on demand or on a specified date a sum certain in money in return for an adequate consideration in money or money's worth and to pay a fixed rate of interest;
2. whether there is subordination to or preference over any indebtedness of the corporation;
3. the ratio of debt to equity of the corporation;
4. whether there is convertibility into the stock of the corporation; and
5. the relationship between holdings of stock in the corporation and holdings of the interest in question.[25]

It took 11 years before the Treasury Department ever issued proposed regulations. Although these regulations were finalized, the effective date was delayed several times and the regulations never became effective. Later proposed regulations were ultimately withdrawn. Despite the passage of decades, still no §385 regulations exist. Where does that leave things? No worse, and perhaps just a tiny bit better than before §385 was enacted. Before §385, courts were using a facts and circumstances analysis in deciding the difference between debt and equity and continue to do so. In the meantime, §385 provides at least a sense of the Congress regarding the types of factors that courts should examine in deciding cases.

Rather than thinking of debt and equity as two distinct categories, one should imagine a continuum with debt at one extreme and equity at the other. Financial instruments appear in many different forms, some with both debt and equity characteristics. These instruments are often referred to as

---

23. I.R.C. §385(a). The parenthetical language at the end of the sentence was actually added later. Pub. L. No. 101-239, §7208(a)(1) (1989).

24. Under §385(c), characterization of the instrument by the issuer is binding on the issuer and on all holders, but not binding on the Internal Revenue Service. Provision was made, however, for holders to treat an instrument inconsistently with the issuer's classification upon proper disclosure. I.R.C. §385(c)(2).

25. I.R.C. §385(b).

hybrid securities. Taxpayers, tax advisors, the Treasury Department, and courts struggle with these hybrid securities to determine whether they are closer on the continuum to debt and therefore should be classified as debt or whether, instead, they are closer to equity and therefore should be classified as equity for tax purposes.[26]

Overview of Factors Used to Distinguish Debt from Equity

This overview of factors is designed to give you a flavor of the inquiry used to distinguish debt from equity. Keep in mind that the analysis adopts an overall facts and circumstances test and that no one of the following factors will determine the outcome.

a) Observing the Formalities of a Debt Instrument

The first factor listed in §385 may be useful in identifying those instruments that come closest to classic or straight debt. Where there is a "written unconditional promise to pay on demand or on a specified date a sum certain in money in return for an adequate consideration in money or money's worth, and to pay a fixed rate of interest," the instrument is likely to be regarded as debt. Such a written obligation has the earmarks of a debt instrument. A key element here is the payment of reasonable interest. An instrument that fails to provide for the payment of interest will virtually never be classified as debt. In addition, to be sure that an instrument will be classified as debt, it is best to have a reasonably close fixed maturity date rather than a demand note or a maturity date long after the issuance of the note.

To be respected as genuine debt, it is also important that certain formalities be observed. The note holder should act like a reasonable creditor, taking reasonable steps to enforce payment. In addition, it should be relatively clear that the corporation will have sufficient cash flow to meet its debt obligation. If the holder of the corporate note agrees to extensions of the maturity date or does not otherwise insist on payments in accordance with the terms of the note, the note may be suspect. Even if the formalities normally associated with debt instruments are strictly observed, the debt may nevertheless be classified as equity if, after consideration of other relevant

---

26. More recently, Congress, the Treasury Department, and the courts have considered bifurcation of financial instruments so that they may be treated as part debt and part equity. For further discussion of these bifurcation possibilities, see *infra*.

factors, the instrument more resembles equity than debt. A discussion of some of those factors follows.

b) The Debt-Equity Ratio or Thin Capitalization

When a corporation issues excessive liabilities relative to the capital contributions that it has received, the holders of corporate notes bear significant risk. Such a corporation is regarded as "thinly capitalized." Even though the instrument may bear all of the formalities normally associated with a debt instrument, the holders of this debt are depending largely on the profitability of the enterprise rather than underlying assets to assure payment. This type of risk is more typically associated with an equity investment. At some point, the debt-equity ratio is so large that the instrument should be regarded as an equity investment. For many years, the courts have considered the debt-equity ratio as one of the many factors to be considered in distinguishing debt from equity. Congress also listed the debt-equity ratio as one of the five factors that the Treasury was to consider in promulgating regulations.[27] Although there is general agreement that the debt-equity ratio is significant, it is hard to quantify just how excessive the ratio needs to be before serious red flags should be waved. One commentator reports that a 3 to 1 ratio will generally withstand attack.[28] Another set of issues involves the proper method for computing a debt-equity ratio. These include debates over whether to use aggregate debt figures as opposed to separate figures for debt to inside shareholder lenders and outside lenders, or separate figures for recourse and nonrecourse debt.

c) Subordination to Other Claims

Another important factor in distinguishing debt from equity is subordination to other claims. Creditor's claims generally take priority over equity holder's claims. Thus, if an instrument specifies the holder's claims are subordinate to general creditor claims, the instrument is more likely to be classified as equity. A corporation may issue several different classes of debt, some of which are subordinated to other classes of debt. By itself, the subordination to some other creditor claims will not cause the subordinated debt to be reclassified as equity if the subordinated debt continues to be senior to preferred and common shares.

---

27. I.R.C. §385(b)(3).
28. Boris I. Bittker and James S. Eustice, Federal Income Taxation of Corporations and Shareholders ¶4.04[3] (7th ed. 2000).

d) Contingency of Payment

In the case of straight or classic debt, the obligation to pay interest is unconditional. On the other hand, a corporation's obligation to pay interest to the holder of a financial instrument may be contingent upon a certain level of corporate profits or may be left to the discretion of the board of directors in some way. The risk associated with a debt instrument subject to such a contingency is more like the risk associated with an equity interest in the corporation. Such contingency is an important factor suggesting that the financial interest is an equity interest.

e) Right to Participate in Profits

One key element that distinguishes an equity holder from a debt holder is the right of the equity holder to participate in the corporation's economic growth. When the holder of an obligation is entitled to share in profits of the corporate enterprise above and beyond the interest specified in the note, this factor will weigh heavily in favor of an equity classification.[29]

In addition, when a note or debenture is convertible into stock, the note holder has the potential to ultimately share in the corporation's economic growth by exercising the conversion privilege. Thus, the conversion privilege is another factor weighing in favor of an equity classification.

f) Voting and Other Rights of Control

Voting rights and managerial rights are equity characteristics. Lenders typically are not entitled to vote or otherwise participate in the management of the corporation. The presence of such rights can be a factor that causes a financial instrument to be classified as equity. Some debt instruments carry limited voting or other managerial rights designed to protect the lender. For example, the lender may be entitled to vote only on specific major corporate changes such as a merger or acquisition or only if quarterly earnings fall below a specified amount. Such limited voting rights should not cause the debt to be reclassified as equity.

g) Identity Between Shareholders and Creditors

When the shareholders of a corporation also lend money to the corporation, the notes taken in return should be regarded with special scrutiny. The notes are particularly prone to being reclassified as equity if the shareholders hold these notes in the same proportions that they own stock. Put another way,

---

29. It also may be possible to bifurcate the instrument so that the fixed interest received is treated as interest and the additional profit treated as dividend.

the debt classification is safer where the identity of debt and equity holders is different and where those who own both debt and equity hold different proportions of each.

h) Acquisition of Essential Assets

Some courts have considered the fact that a note was issued to shareholders in return for essential assets necessary for the corporation's business as an equity factor. The idea here is that corporations do not typically acquire their core assets through debt issued to shareholders. A shareholder who purports to sell such essential assets to a corporation in return for a note will be subject to special scrutiny. This is perhaps the most questionable of the many debt-equity factors discussed. The premise behind this factor appears to be flawed. There is no reason to believe that a corporation would not acquire its essential assets with debt. Many corporations borrow from outside lenders in order to acquire the core assets needed to start a business; a loan from a shareholder to acquire such assets should not be viewed differently.

i) Intent of the Parties

Some courts have explored the intent to establish a debtor-creditor relationship in deciding whether to reclassify a note as equity. Intent tests are difficult to apply. Best applied, an intent test should look to the reasonable expectation of the lender that the debt will be repaid, focusing on objective criteria.[30] Many of the criteria that a lender will look to in developing an expectation regarding repayment are the same factors discussed above. The factors begin to circle upon themselves and overlap.

Bifurcation of Hybrid Securities

Many financial instruments include both features of ordinary debt and ordinary equity. Until recently, it was necessary to classify such hybrid securities entirely as either debt or equity. Under this "unitary" approach, one must examine all of the instrument's characteristics to determine whether the instrument is more "debt-like" or "equity-like." Recent amendments to §385 now authorize the Secretary to prescribe regulations to determine "whether an interest in a corporation is to be treated . . . as stock or indebtedness (*or as in part stock and in part indebtedness*)."[31] This bifurcation approach will take off some of the pressure by eliminating the need to pick

---

30. One case that took this approach to intent was Gilbert v. Commissioner, 248 F.2d 399 (2d Cir. 1957), *appeal after remand*, 262 F.2d 512 (2d Cir.), *cert. denied*, 359 U.S. 1002 (1959).

31. I.R.C. §385(a) (emphasis added). The parenthetical language was added in 1989. Pub. L. No. 101-239, §7208(a)(1), 103 Stat. 2337.

one camp or the other in the case of complex hybrid securities. On the other hand, the bifurcation process itself may be complex and controversial as well.[32]

One example of a bifurcation rule already in place is a special rule applicable to certain high-yield discount obligations. Under §163(e)(5), such obligations are bifurcated for tax purposes into a "debt portion," for which an interest deduction will be permitted to the corporation and a "dividend portion" on which no deductions will be permitted to the corporation. If the recipient shareholder is a corporation, it will be entitled to a dividends-received deduction on the dividend portion.[33]

Losses from Investments in the Corporate Enterprise

General Losses

Losses suffered by shareholders or creditors generally will be deductible. The key question for investors, however, is whether the loss will be treated as capital or ordinary loss. For most taxpayers, ordinary loss is preferable for several reasons. First, it can be deducted against ordinary income. Second, the taxpayer is permitted more generous carryback of the loss to earlier tax years under §172. A capital loss, on the other hand, is more limited. Individual taxpayers' capital losses first can be used to offset capital gains. Excess losses are deductible, but subject to a $3000 cap for any single taxable year.[34] Losses beyond the $3000 limit may be carried forward, but not backward.[35]

Losses from worthless securities are considered capital losses under §165(g). For purposes of this provision, a security includes not only shares of stock, but also options to acquire stock, and bonds, debentures, notes, certificates or other evidence of indebtedness issued by the corporation with

---

32. An earlier Treasury Department proposal called for bifurcation with respect to certain debt obligations with both fixed and contingent obligations. The Treasury Department later withdrew its proposal to treat the noncontingent portion as debt and the contingent portion "in accordance with economic substance." In other words, the contingent portion would likely have been treated as equity. 59 Fed. Reg. 64,884 (Dec. 16, 1994). The Treasury Department's notice accompanying the withdrawal cited commentators who "argued that there is rarely a unique set of components into which a contingent payment debt instrument can be bifurcated. In addition, commentators questioned whether it is appropriate to bifurcate a contingent debt instrument because it is often unclear how the contingent components should be taxed." *Id.* at 64,885.

33. I.R.C. §163(e)(5)(B).

34. I.R.C. §1211(b).

35. I.R.C. §1212(b).

interest coupons or in registered form.[36] Thus, for purposes of §165, if an instrument is classified as stock or equity, the loss when the stock becomes worthless will be a capital loss. Moreover, even if the instrument is classified as debt, if the debt carries interest coupons or is in registered form, the loss will also be capital loss.

On the other hand, if the taxpayer owns a debt instrument that is not registered and that has no interest coupons, a loss upon worthlessness of the debt will be considered a bad debt subject to the rules of §166. A nonbusiness bad debt held by an individual taxpayer is deductible only as a capital loss. Business bad debts, on the other hand, can be deducted as ordinary losses. To constitute a business bad debt, the loss must be proximately related to the taxpayer's business.[37] This has proven to be a very difficult test for most taxpayers to meet.[38]

Section 1244 Stock Losses

Before the enactment of §1244, investors who suffered a loss from sale or exchange of the stock in a small business were limited to a capital loss. This result seemed particularly inequitable to such investors given the alternative of Subchapter S or partnership provisions under which the investors would have been entitled to pass-throughs of ordinary losses from the business investment. Responding to this concern, Congress created a special class of stock in §1244. When an individual or a partnership suffers certain losses on §1244 stock, the loss can be treated as an ordinary loss.[39] This ordinary loss treatment is only available to the individual or partnership to which the stock was issued. In addition, there is a $50,000 cap for individuals and a $100,000 cap for joint filers on the ordinary loss than can be taken. Any excess loss will be treated as a capital loss. Since the ordinary loss provisions are available only to the person who was issued the shares initially, a transferor who receives §1244 stock from the individual or partnership to which it was originally issued will not be entitled to the special loss treatment provided by §1244. Early versions of §1244 contained many technical requirements creating many traps for the unwary. Over the years, the restrictions and technical requirements have eased substantially, making the present version

---

36. I.R.C. §165(g)(2).

37. Treas. Reg. §1.166-5(b).

38. See, e.g., Whipple v. Comm'r, 373 U.S. 193 (1963); United States v. Generes, 405 U.S. 93 (1972).

39. Congress imposes certain limitations on the amount of ordinary loss in cases where the shareholder contributed loss property in the first instance to the corporation in return for the stock. In effect, losses that were built-in through the contribution of loss property are not permitted as §1244 ordinary losses. For more details regarding the implementation of this policy, see I.R.C. §1244(d)(1).

of §1244 much less complex. Although §1244 ordinary loss treatment originally was available only with respect to common stock, it is now available for losses on preferred stock as well.

To qualify as §1244 stock, the corporation must be a domestic United States corporation. In addition, the corporation must be a small business corporation at the time the stock is issued. A corporation will qualify as a small business corporation if, at the time the stock is issued, the aggregate money and property received for stock, contributions to capital, or paid in surplus does not exceed $1 million.[40] In addition, the stock must have been issued in return for money or other property. Finally, during the five-year period prior to sustaining loss, the corporation must have received more than 50% of its receipts from sources other than royalties, rents, dividends, interest, annuities, and sale or exchanges of stock or securities. Put more simply, more than 50% of the income during that five-year period should not be from passive sources. This requirement was designed to limit the ordinary loss provisions to those corporations that are substantially engaged in an active trade or business.

Gains from Investment in the Corporate Enterprise

Investors' gains received from the sale or exchange of stock or debt generally are treated as capital gain.[41] The lower capital gains rate is designed, in part, to encourage more corporate investment. Some policymakers have been interested in stimulating investment in smaller, new, higher-risk enterprises. Responding to this concern, Congress has recently added several new provisions applicable to "qualified small business stock," as defined in §1202.[42] "Qualified small business corporations" are distinguished from other C corporations based largely upon aggregate gross assets.[43] Also, the corporation must be engaged in an active trade or business during substantially all of the taxpayer's holding period for the stock.[44] The Taxpayer Relief Act of 1997 added a new provision that permits individual investors to defer, or "roll

---

40. For purposes of this provision, the amount taken into account for property is the adjusted basis of the property to the corporation less any liability relating to the property. I.R.C. §1244(c)(3).

41. Among others, there are exceptions for certain recapture items and in the case of collapsible corporations.

42. Omnibus Budget Reconciliation Act of 1993, Pub. L. No. 103-66, 107 Stat. 312, §13113(a), adding I.R.C. §1202.

43. The cut-off point to be eligible is aggregate gross assets not exceeding $50 million. See I.R.C. §1202(d)(1)(A).

44. I.R.C. §1202(c)(2), (e).

over," gain from the sale of "qualified small business stock" by acquiring other qualified small business stock within 60 days.[45] Ultimately, individual shareholders are entitled to deduct 50% of any gain from a sale or exchange of such stock held for more than five years.[46] Through this special category of stock, Congress, in effect, provides reduced capital gains rates for investors in §1202 "small business stock" corporations.

Conclusion

The corporation makes two basic decisions regarding its capital structure. First, the corporation must decide on the types and classes of stock that will make up the equity structure of the enterprise. Second, the corporation must decide on the appropriate mix of debt and equity. Such decisions ideally should be made independent of tax considerations. The first category of decisions on the equity structure itself come closer to meeting this ideal. Most corporations decide on the equity structure of the enterprise based largely on nontax considerations. Different classes and kinds of stock are issued to reflect the different types of contributions made and the different levels of risk that investors are willing to undertake. On the other hand, decisions regarding the appropriate mix of debt and equity often are heavily influenced by tax considerations.

An in-depth discussion of all of the financial and other nontax considerations that go into determining corporate capital structure is beyond the scope of this book. The above materials on capital structure are meant only to provide a brief introduction to the alternative capital structures and categories of financial instruments available and some of the tax issues involved.

---

45. Taxpayer Relief Act of 1997, Pub. L. No. 105-34, 111 Stat. 788, §313 (codified at I.R.C. §1045).

46. I.R.C. §1202(a). The gain eligible for such preferential treatment is subject to limitations provided in §1202(b).

PART TWO

Corporate Formation

4

Incorporation and Other Contributions to Capital

Introduction

The corporate enterprise typically receives funds in one of three ways. First, the corporation raises capital through equity contributions.[1] Second, the corporation may borrow funds. Third, the corporation receives operating funds through the sale of its goods or services and through returns on its investments. This chapter will consider primarily the first of these forms of fundraising—equity contributions from shareholders. At the time of formation, the initial shareholders of the corporation make equity contributions in return for stock. Keep in mind, however, that the principles considered in this chapter are not limited to the initial incorporation transaction. The provisions considered in this chapter cover subsequent capital contributions as well.[2]

In the typical incorporation transaction, the incorporating shareholders transfer cash, other property, or services to the corporation in return for

---

1. Although equity contributions usually come from shareholders, nonshareholders may occasionally make capital contributions as well.

2. Some of the peculiar issues raised by capital contributions made *after* the initial formation of the corporation are considered later in this chapter. In addition, §351 often will have a role to play in connection with various corporate reorganizations. The relationship between §351 and the reorganization provisions will be discussed in detail in Chapter 12.

stock.[3] Cash contributions in return for stock do not raise tax consequences of great significance to the contributing shareholders. There is no unrealized gain or loss to be recognized by the shareholders in the case of a cash purchase at fair market value.[4] A shareholder who purchases stock for cash simply holds the stock with a cost basis. More significant tax issues arise when shareholders contribute appreciated or depreciated property in return for stock. When a shareholder contributes property in exchange for stock, two assets are created out of one—the original asset and the corporate stock now reflecting an indirect ownership of the same asset. The value of the contributed property, now held by the corporation, is also reflected in the newly issued stock held by the shareholder. Subchapter C addresses not only the questions of gain or loss to the respective parties, but also the appropriate basis of the contributed property in the corporation's hands and of the stock in the shareholder's hands. Absent special nonrecognition rules, gain or loss realized from the exchange would be recognized to the shareholder and to the corporation.[5] As we shall see, however, a properly structured shareholder contribution to capital will be treated as a nonrecognition event to the contributing shareholders under §351 and to the corporation under §1032. The shareholder nonrecognition provided by §351 will not necessarily be permanent, however. Corollary basis rules defer shareholder gains or losses not recognized at the time of the §351 exchange for potential taxation upon later sale or exchange of stock received in the exchange.

Shareholder Nonrecognition: §351 Eligibility Requirements and Underlying Policy

Overview

Shareholders in an incorporation transaction will not recognize any gain or loss on the exchange if they satisfy the three major requirements of §351(a).

---

3. The transferring shareholders may be individuals or corporations. The newly formed corporation may be a new business or a continuation of an existing business previously operated in sole proprietorship, partnership, or other noncorporate form.

4. Different issues emerge if the shareholder purchases stock from the corporation at less than fair market value. If a shareholder is permitted to purchase stock at a discount, it will be important to know the underlying circumstances. For example, if the discount was offered in exchange for services rendered and was not offered as part of a qualified stock purchase or stock option plan, the discount will be taxable as compensation under the provisions of §§61 and 83.

5. I.R.C. §§61(a)(3), 1001(c). Treas. Reg. §1.1002-1(c) (listing §351 as an exception to the recognition requirement of §1001(c)). Some might argue that the

First, there must be a contribution of property. Second, the contribution must be solely in exchange for stock and, third, the contributors must control the corporation immediately after the exchange. This overview will summarize each of these three elements and the tax policy considerations behind the requirements. A more detailed discussion of each requirement follows in subsequent sections.

The first requirement for nonrecognition treatment is that the shareholders transfer *property*. Congress does not provide a comprehensive definition for purposes of applying these provisions, but merely identifies items that will *not* be considered property.[6] The Internal Revenue Service and the courts construe the term "property" broadly to include cash and real or intangible property.[7] Most important among the exceptions to the broad scope of the property definition is the contribution of services.[8] Individuals establishing a corporation often contribute past or future services in return for stock. Such service contributions are not considered contributions of property and will *not* qualify for nonrecognition treatment. The rationale for excluding service contributions is that payment for services, regardless of the form of payment, is compensation and should be taxed to the recipient shareholder as ordinary income. Horizontal equity would be violated if those receiving cash compensation for services to the corporation were taxed, but those receiving stock compensation were not.

The second requirement to qualify for shareholder nonrecognition treatment is that property be contributed *solely in exchange for stock*.[9] By taking only stock in return for property, the shareholders continue their relationship with the assets contributed. This "continuity of interest" requirement is really the heart of §351.[10] The clearest example of this continuity of interest is the sole proprietor who incorporates an ongoing business by contributing all of the business assets to a newly formed corporation in return for 100% of the corporation's stock. Immediately before incorporating, the sole proprietor

---

corporation does not even realize a gain upon receipt of a contribution to capital. This argument is considered later in the section of this chapter on tax consequences to the corporation.

6. I.R.C. §351(d).

7. The shareholder who contributes only cash does not have any realized gain or loss, but nevertheless has contributed property. Shares received for cash will count toward meeting the §351 control tests discussed below. See, e.g., Holstein v. Comm'r, 23 T.C. 923, 924 (1955).

8. I.R.C. §351(d)(1); Treas. Reg. §1.351-1(a)(1)(i).

9. I.R.C. §351(a). After the Taxpayer Relief Act of 1997, certain types of preferred stock will not qualify for purposes of §351. The significance of this change will be considered later in this chapter.

10. Continuity of interest also is the heart of similar nonrecognition rules applicable to reorganization transactions. See Treas. Reg. §1.368-1(b). For complete coverage of reorganizations, see Chapters 11-14.

held a direct interest in the assets used in the business enterprise. Immediately after incorporation, the shareholder holds 100% of the stock of a new corporation and, thus, holds a continued, albeit now indirect, interest in the business assets. The assets contributed presumably are no different than they were before and business customers probably will not even notice a difference in operations.

At first blush, the "solely in exchange for stock" language suggests that shareholders will not be eligible for nonrecognition treatment unless they receive *only* stock in return for contributed property. As is often the case with the Internal Revenue Code, the bark of the "solely in exchange for stock" language is louder than its bite. Shareholders *may* receive something in addition to stock from the corporation in the incorporation exchange. Such additional property often is referred to as "boot."[11] Receipt of boot from the corporation will not completely disqualify the shareholder from nonrecognition treatment, *but* the shareholder receiving boot in an incorporation transaction *will* be taxed on realized gain to the extent of the boot.[12]

The third requirement for nonrecognition treatment is that the person or persons contributing property be in *control* of the corporation immediately after the exchange.[13] The control test provided in §368(c) includes two parts. To satisfy the control test, the contributing shareholder group must own 1) "stock possessing at least 80% of the *total combined voting power* of all classes of stock entitled to vote," and 2) "at least 80% of the *total number of shares* of all other classes of stock."[14] As a shorthand, this book will sometimes refer to both parts of the test together as the "80% control test" or simply the "control test."

Exceptions to Nonrecognition Rules

Even if an exchange meets the above three requirements under §351, nonrecognition treatment is not available in the case of a transfer of property to an investment company.[15] According to Treasury regulations, a transfer is made to an investment company when the transfer results in the diversification of the transferor's assets *and* the transferee company is "a regulated investment company, a real estate investment trust, or a corporation more than 80% of value of whose assets . . . are held for investment and are readily marketable stocks or securities, or interests in regulated investment compa-

---

11. To help with this concept, think of the shareholder as receiving stock and other property *to boot*.

12. I.R.C. §351(b)(1).

13. I.R.C. §§351(a), 368(c).

14. I.R.C. §368(c) (emphasis added). For purposes of meeting the total number of shares part of the control test, the Service takes the position that 80% of the total number of shares of *each class* is required. Rev. Rul. 59-259, 1959-2 C.B. 115.

15. I.R.C. §351(e)(1).

nies or real estate investment trusts."[16] In such cases, Congress was concerned that, absent a special §351 exception, it would be too easy for a shareholder to diversify investments without recognition of taxable gain by contributing appreciated property in exchange for stock in a highly diversified investment corporation. Congress recently expanded this definition of investment corporation, adding to the types of assets considered in applying the regulatory 80% test. A corporation now will be considered an investment corporation if more than 80% of the value of its assets includes stock, securities, other equity interests in a corporation, debt, options, futures contracts, foreign currencies, and other specifically listed items.[17]

Another transaction not covered by §351 is a transfer of property by a debtor in a Title 11 bankruptcy case where the stock received in the exchange is used to satisfy indebtedness of the debtor.[18] Nevertheless, such a bankruptcy transaction can be structured to obtain nonrecognition under the reorganization provisions in §368(a)(1)(G).[19]

Why Permit Nonrecognition for Incorporation Transactions?

Now that we have briefly considered the three major requirements that must be met to qualify for nonrecognition treatment, let's take a step back to consider the policy behind §351. Why does Congress permit shareholders to defer recognition of gain or loss from transfers of property to a controlled corporation? For one thing, corporations need capital to function. To tax either the shareholder or the corporation on transactions through which corporations raise capital might serve as an impediment to incorporation or capital formation. Thus, the simplest explanation for the §351 nonrecognition rule is that Congress wished to encourage, or at least not to discourage, corporate formations. More generally, the legislative history reflects an interest in "facilitating business adjustments."[20]

A second justification often given for §351 is that the transaction reflects a mere change in form.[21] A contributing shareholder group that satisfies the "continuity of interest" requirement established through the "solely in ex-

---

16. Treas. Reg. §1.351-1(c)(1).

17. Taxpayer Relief Act of 1997, Pub. L. No. 105-34, 111 Stat. 788, §1002(a) (codified, as amended, at I.R.C. §351(e)(1)).

18. I.R.C. §351(e)(2).

19. See Chapter 11.

20. The legislative history of one of the early predecessors to §351 suggests that nonrecognition was provided, in part, to "permit business to go forward with readjustments required by existing conditions." S. Rep. No. 275, 67th Cong., 1st Sess. 11-12 (1921); S. Rep. No. 398, 68th Cong., 1st Sess. 17-18 (1924).

21. "The underlying assumption [of §351] is that the new property is substantially a continuation of the old investment still unliquidated." Treas. Reg. §1.1002-1(c).

change for stock" element, and also meets the 80% control test, arguably is merely changing the form of the business investment. The shareholders have a continued interest in their old assets now reflected in stock and they continue to exercise control over those assets through their controlling interest in the corporation.

Despite its mere change-in-form rationale, the scope of §351 is quite broad, extending nonrecognition to several transactions that arguably reflect more than a simple change in form. For example, §351 does not limit the number of transferors. Hundreds, thousands, or even millions of transferors may exchange property in return for stock. This often is the case in underwriting transactions where the public is considered to be part of the transferring control group. As another example, imagine a sole proprietor who, along with hundreds of similar investors, exchanges an interest in a small convenience store for stock in a large corporation operating a nationwide chain of convenience stores. A sole proprietor who transfers property in return for a minority interest in a large corporation effectively loses direct control over assets contributed. Nevertheless, this minority shareholder will receive nonrecognition treatment as part of the control group in a §351 transaction.

Even if one accepts the above explanations for §351 nonrecognition, an additional challenge is to explain the policy behind limiting nonrecognition to transferors who receive an 80% controlling interest in the corporation.[22] And, even if the control requirement can be justified, why does Congress use 80% control rather than 50% or some other measure of control?[23] There is little legislative history explaining the rationale for requiring control. One limited explanation for the control test is that it prevents "corporations with readily marketable stock from using their stock to buy goods and supplies on a tax-free basis to their vendors."[24] Without the 80% control requirement, a vendor could accept a small percentage of a another corporation's stock as payment for goods and services. The vendor could effectively sell property without recognizing any gain or loss. Perhaps the best explanation one can offer for the control requirement is that it does appear to strengthen the continuity of interest element and the chance that the exchange represents a mere change in form.

---

22. It should be noted, for example, that parallel nonrecognition is provided in Subchapter K for transfers to a partnership in return for a partnership interest. These provisions do not require receipt of a controlling partnership interest. I.R.C. §721.

23. Since many significant corporate events such as acquisition or liquidation require a supermajority vote of the shareholders, 80% control is sometimes referred to as organic control whereas 50% control is referred to as managerial control.

24. Ronald Jensen, Of Form and Substance: Tax-Free Incorporations and Other Transactions Under Section 351, 11 Va. Tax Rev. 349, 398 (1991).

A Closer Look at the §351 Requirements

a) The Transfer Requirement

As its first requirement, §351 permits nonrecognition of gain or loss only "if property is transferred to a corporation." Two terms are important here. Notice that §351 refers to *transfers* of property. The transfer requirement generally will not be problematic. Most §351 contributions represent complete conveyances of property. Questions may arise, however, in the case of transfers falling short of complete conveyance. The courts have tended to interpret the transfer of property requirement broadly, holding, for example, that a contribution of a lease qualifies for nonrecognition treatment.[25] For purposes of §351, the term transfer does not carry the same meaning as "sale or exchange." For example, the Court of Claims held that contribution of a nonexclusive license to use certain patents qualified as a "§351 transfer" even though the license transfer would not have been considered a "sale or exchange" under §1001.[26]

b) The Property Requirement

To qualify for §351 nonrecognition, the transferors must contribute *property*. As noted earlier, the term property is rather broadly construed for purposes of §351. Thus, property includes cash and other assets, including a transferor corporation's own stock[27] or a corporate or individual transferor's note. In addition, in the case of an existing corporation, the holder of a corporation's debt may exchange the debt obligation in return for stock. The debt will be considered property as long as it is evidenced by a security. Thus, a bond or debenture holder who exchanges the debt interest for equity (stock) will not recognize any gain or loss on the exchange attributable to the *principal* amount of the debt. Gain or loss will be recognized with regard to *interest* accrued while the transferor held the debt.[28] Debts of the transferee corpo-

---

25. R&J Furniture Co. v. Comm'r, 20 T.C. 857 (1953), *acq* 1954-1 C.B. 6, *rev'd on other grounds,* 221 F.2d 795 (6th Cir. 1955); see also Rev. Rul. 55-540, 1955-2 C.B. 39, 43.

26. E.I. DuPont de Nemours & Co. v. United States, 471 F.2d 1211 (Ct. Cl. 1973).

27. Rev. Rul. 74-503, 1974-2 C.B. 117. Note that the definition of property in §317(a), which excludes stock in the corporation making the distribution, applies only to Part I of Subchapter C (Distributions by Corporations) and, thus, is not applicable to §351.

28. I.R.C. §351(d)(3) explicitly excludes from the definition of property, "interest on indebtedness of the transferee corporation which accrued on or after the beginning of the transferor's holding period." Similarly, if the bond was a market discount bond, the accrued market discount must be recognized upon an exchange of the bond for stock. I.R.C. §1276(a), (c), (d)(1)(C).

ration that are *not* evidenced by a security are explicitly excluded from the definition of property under §351.[29] Since open-account indebtedness is not considered "property" for purposes of §351, a transferor of such indebtedness for stock will recognize gain or loss — generally loss in the form of a bad-debt deduction.

The most significant exception to the breadth of the §351 transfer of property requirement is the exception for services. A transfer of either past or future *services* is not considered a transfer of property.[30] A transferor who contributes *only* services will not qualify for nonrecognition treatment and the entire value of stock received for such services will be taxable as ordinary compensation income. If the shareholder contributes both property *and* services, nonrecognition will apply only to the extent that stock was received in return for property. The amount eligible for nonrecognition and the amount subject to tax will be determined based upon the relative fair market value of the property and the services contributed. To illustrate, suppose that a shareholder contributed property worth $90,000 and services worth $10,000 in return for $100,000 worth of stock. In this case, $90,000 worth of stock has been received in return for property. Gain or loss on the property exchange will not be taxed. The remaining $10,000 worth of stock has been received for services, resulting in $10,000 of ordinary compensation income to the contributing shareholder.[31]

A combination of the service contribution restriction and the control test may generate further problems. Because services are not considered property for purposes of §351, a transferor who has contributed *only* services cannot be counted as part of the control group. Consequently, if one shareholder contributes services in return for 21% of the stock and another contributes property in return for 79% of the stock, nonrecognition treatment is unavailable to *both* the service *and* the property contributor. The service contributing shareholder has taxable compensation income. Moreover, the property contributing shareholder fails the control test and is ineligible for nonrecognition treatment.[32] The lesson here is that in order to assure nonrecognition treatment for the property contributing shareholders, the "service only" shareholder should never receive more than 20% of the stock.

---

29. I.R.C. §351(d)(2).

30. I.R.C. §351(d). The regulations clarify that stock "issued for services rendered or to be rendered to or for the benefit of the issuing corporation will not be treated as having been issued in return for property." Treas. Reg. §1.351-1(a)(1)(i).

31. For a similar example with similar results, see Treas. Reg. §1.351-1(a)(2), ex. (3).

32. If the service shareholder also contributed some property, then *all* of his shares could be counted toward meeting the control test unless the property contribution was of nominal value and made primarily for the purposes of qualifying the property contributor for nonrecognition treatment. See Treas. Reg. §1.351-1(a)(1)(ii). See also Treas. Reg. §1.351-1(a)(2), ex. (3).

Another concern under §351(d) is determining whether certain "service-flavored" property is "property" or "service" for purposes of the §351 rules. The case of United States v. Frazell[33] provides a good illustration. The taxpayer in *Frazell* performed geological services for an oil and gas partnership in return for a contingent interest in the assets of the partnership. The court held that the taxpayer's contribution of this contingent partnership interest to a corporation in return for stock was not a contribution of "property" for purposes of §351.[34] Despite the taxpayer's loss in *Frazell*, the courts have been reasonably liberal in holding that various contributions of "service-flavored" property were eligible for nonrecognition treatment.[35]

Contributions of intellectual property would appear to be particularly vulnerable to attack under the §351(d) service restriction. As one court observed, "[t]he difficulty in determining whether payments to a creator of an invention or valuable commercial process are compensation for services or payments for the sale of a patent or other capital assets stems from the fact that an invention is merely the fruit of the inventor's labor, and that payment for the invention itself necessarily compensates the inventor for his services in creating the invention."[36] Despite this difficulty, the courts generally have held that stock issued in return for patents, copyrights, trademarks, and trade secrets is stock issued for property rather than for services. Moreover, even the Service agrees that where a "transferor agrees to perform services in connection with a transfer of property, tax-free treatment will be accorded if the services are *merely ancillary and subsidiary to* the property transfer."[37] Thus, receipt of stock in return for property and ancillary know-how will receive nonrecognition treatment under §351.[38]

---

33. 335 F.2d 487 (5th Cir. 1964), *cert. denied*, 380 U.S. 961 (1965).

34. There was some dispute in *Frazell* as to whether the taxpayer's partnership interest had vested prior to his making the corporate contribution. The court found that either the taxpayer had already received a vested partnership interest in return for services ineligible for nonrecognition under I.R.C. §721 or received stock in return for services ineligible for nonrecognition under I.R.C. §351. The §721 rules for contributions to a partnership parallel the §351 rules for contributions to a corporation. In either case, the court held that the taxpayer made a *service* contribution in return for compensation, as opposed to a *property* contribution in return for a partnership interest or for stock. 335 F.2d at 490.

35. See, e.g., United States v. Stafford, 727 F.2d 1043 (11th Cir. 1984) (letter of credit held to be "property" for purposes of §721); E.I. DuPont de Nemours & Co. v. United States, 471 F.2d 1211 (Ct. Cl. 1973) (nonexclusive license on patent held to be "property" for purposes of §351).

36. Ofria v. Comm'r, 77 T.C. 524, 535 (1981), *nonacq.* 1983-2 C.B. 1.

37. Rev. Rul. 64-56, 1964-1 C.B. 133, 134 (emphasis added).

38. For an excellent overall discussion of §351 "transfer of property" concerns in intellectual property cases, see J. Clifton Fleming, Jr., Domestic Section 351 Transfers of Intellectual Property: The Law as It Is vs. the Law as the Commissioner Would Prefer It to Be, 16 J. Corp. Tax 99 (1989).

c) The Solely in Exchange for Stock Requirement

To qualify for §351(a) nonrecognition, shareholders contributing property must receive *stock* in return. Anything other than stock will be considered "boot" and will be covered by special rules in §351(b). After the Taxpayer Relief Act of 1997, certain limited kinds of preferred stock may now be treated as boot as well.[39] Although determining whether or not the shareholders have received "stock" is not usually difficult, a few issues have emerged under the §351 exchange for stock requirement. Treasury Department regulations take the position that "for purposes of §351, stock rights or stock warrants are not included in the term 'stock.'"[40] On the other hand, the Tax Court has held that a contract right to receive additional shares of stock upon the corporation's achieving a specified net earnings goal was "stock" under §351.[41]

Although §351 once permitted nonrecognition where property was exchanged for "stock" *or* "securities," securities are now considered boot. In some limited circumstances, however, a long-term corporate security or debt may have so many equity characteristics that it will be reclassified as an equity interest for tax purposes.[42] Receipt of a debt instrument that has been reclassified as stock should be considered receipt of stock under §351 and

---

39. The Act amended §351 which now provides that "nonqualified preferred stock" will be treated as boot for purposes of §351(b). Taxpayer Relief Act of 1997, Pub. L. No. 105-34, 111 Stat. 788, §1014(a) (codified, as amended, at I.R.C. §351(g)). This change is considered more fully below in the section entitled "Effect of Boot."

40. Treas. Reg. §1.351-1(a)(1)(ii). The Treasury Department recently issued final regulations defining the circumstances under which stock rights or warrants will be considered securities for purposes of the *reorganization* nonrecognition provisions. Treas. Reg. §1.354-1(e). This new treatment of warrants is discussed in Chapters 11-13.

41. Hamrick v. Comm'r, 43 T.C. 21 (1964) *acq.* 1966-2 C.B. 5, *vacated and remanded* per parties' agreement, 17 A.F.T.R. 2d 357 (4th Cir. 1965). See also Carlberg v. United States, 281 F.2d 507 (8th Cir. 1960), where the court held that "stock" included "certificates of contingent interest" for purposes of §354. These certificates entitled the holders to reserved shares of stock to be released pending the settlement of substantial corporate liabilities. The Service takes the position that ordinary stock rights and warrants are distinguishable from the unusual contractual rights in *Hamrick* and *Carlberg*. Rev. Rul. 66-112, 1966-1 C.B. 68. For a critical view of the Service's position, see Boris I. Bittker & James S. Eustice, Federal Income Taxation of Corporations and Shareholders, ¶3.03[2] (7th ed. 2000).

42. See, e.g., Burr Oaks Corp. v. Comm'r, 43 T.C. 635 (1965), *aff'd*, 365 F.2d 24 (7th Cir. 1966), *cert. denied*, 385 U.S. 1007 (1967), where the court held that a promissory note issued by the corporation should be treated as preferred stock. As a result, the exchange was recast as a §351 contribution rather than a sale. A discussion of the distinction between §351 contributions and sales to the corporation follows later in this chapter. For a general discussion of the debt-equity distinction, see Chapter 2.

the transferors receiving such an instrument should be eligible for nonrecognition.

d) Control Immediately After the Exchange Test

(i)   Who Can Be Considered a Member of the Control Group?

Under §351(a), the "person or persons" transferring property in return for stock must control the corporation immediately after the exchange. Members of the control group may include individuals, trusts, estates, partnerships, associations, companies, or corporations.[43] Several transferors may be involved, and because it is often impractical or impossible for all of them to simultaneously transfer property in return for stock, the regulations permit some flexibility. According to the regulations, a simultaneous exchange by all parties is not required, but the rights of the parties must have been previously defined and "the execution of the agreement [must] proceed with an expedition consistent with orderly procedure."[44] In other words, if the transactions can be viewed as part of an integrated plan of incorporation, contributing shareholders under the plan will be considered part of the "control group" even if all of the exchanges did not take place simultaneously.

Public offering transactions provide a good illustration of some of these control test issues. Many corporations raise capital by offering stock for sale to the public and may engage the services of an underwriter. Such transactions raise a number of questions. Is the underwriter counted as a member of the control group? Does the public count as a part of the control group? Does the control group have control immediately after the exchange if the purchases are not simultaneous, but are taking place over a period of time?

Two basic types of underwriting arrangements should be considered here. First, the corporation may enter into a *best efforts* underwriting contract. With this contract, the underwriter agrees to exercise his or her best efforts to sell a specified amount of stock to the public, receiving stock and perhaps additional compensation or commissions in return. The underwriter does not purchase stock directly and incurs no risk, other than loss of rights to stock and other commissions, upon failure to sell the specified number of shares. Since the underwriter serves merely as agent selling stock on behalf of the corporation, the underwriter in a best efforts contract is not part of the §351 transferor group and stock received by the underwriter is not be counted toward meeting the 80% control test.

An alternate form of underwriting is the *firm commitment* contract in which the underwriter actually purchases stock from the corporation and

---

43. Treas. Reg. §1.351-1(a)(1).
44. *Id.*

undertakes to sell the shares to the general public. In contrast to the best efforts contract, the underwriter in a firm commitment contract must retain the shares if efforts to sell them are unsuccessful. Since the firm commitment underwriter actually transfers its own property and assumes the risk of reselling the stock, the Treasury Department originally took the position that the underwriter should be counted as a member of the control group.[45] In recently finalized regulations, however, the Treasury Department recognized the reality that the successful firm commitment underwriter's stock ownership is merely transitory. Thus, the new regulations take the position that the same control measuring principles should apply whether the underwriting agreement is a best efforts contract or firm commitment contract in which the underwriter's stock ownership is transitory. In both cases, "if a person acquires stock of a corporation from an underwriter in exchange for cash . . . , the person who acquires stock from the underwriter is treated as transferring cash directly to the corporation in exchange for stock of the corporation and the underwriter is disregarded."[46] In other words, the purchasing public is considered part of the control group, but the underwriter is not.

(ii)   Control "Immediately After the Exchange": Is Momentary Control Sufficient?

Another significant issue in interpreting the "immediately after the exchange" requirement is the length of time that the control group must retain control. What if the transferor group has momentary control of the corporation, but then falls below the required 80% control as a result of stock transfers to others who were not part of the control group? Early case law suggests that where the transferor group has a binding agreement at the time of incorporation to transfer stock to members not in the control group, those shares should not be counted toward meeting the control test.[47]

The major case on point is American Bantam Car Co. v. Commissioner,[48] in which the incorporators entered into a best efforts contract with an underwriter. Immediately after transferring property to the corporation in return for common stock, the incorporators met the 80% control test. Some of the incorporators' stock was placed in an escrow account from which the underwriter was to receive common shares upon successfully marketing preferred shares to the general public. More than a year later, the underwriter had satisfied the best efforts contract requirements and received stock from the escrow account. Transfer of the stock from this account caused the incorporators' control to fall below the required 80%. The Court held that

---

45. Rev. Rul. 78-294, 1978-2 C.B. 141 (Situation 2).

46. Treas. Reg. §1.351-1(a)(3).

47. See, e.g., Intermountain Lumber Co. v. Comm'r, 65 T.C. 1025 (1976).

48. 11 T.C. 397 (1948), *aff'd per curiam*, 177 F.2d 513 (3d Cir. 1949), *cert. denied*, 339 U.S. 920 (1950).

the incorporators had obtained the necessary 80% control immediately after the exchange and that the transaction was covered by the nonrecognition rules of §351.[49]

Despite its off-hand remark that the "statutory words 'immediately after the exchange' require control for no longer period; in fact, momentary control is sufficient,"[50] the Court recognized that in some cases apparent momentary control will not be sufficient. If the series of steps involved in the incorporation are part of an integrated plan, the "exchange" will not be viewed as complete until the necessary steps in the plan have been completed and the control test should be applied after completion of steps in the integrated plan. Applying a "mutual interdependence" test to the facts in *American Bantam*, the Court concluded that the underwriting arrangement was not a "sine qua non in the general plan, without which no other step would have been taken."[51] The underwriter's right to the escrowed shares was contingent and ownership of the shares remained with the incorporators until the underwriter satisfied the best efforts contract conditions.

Based upon cases such as *Intermountain Lumber* and *American Bantam*, it would seem that a post-incorporation sale of stock by the transferor group pursuant to a binding contract could cause an incorporation exchange to fail §351 control requirements. New continuity-of-interest regulations applicable to tax-free reorganizations, however, may call this assumption into question. With these new regulations, the Treasury Department has announced a significant change of position regarding post-reorganization stock transfers. Such transfers, even if pursuant to a binding contract, will not cause a reorganization to violate continuity-of-interest principles as long as the transfers are made to unrelated parties.[52] The Treasury Department has not yet indicated what impact this change of position may have in the context of §351 exchanges.

Disproportionate Contributions and Other Variations

Ordinarily, stock received by contributing shareholders is proportionate to the value of property contributed. Thus, if shareholders A and B each contribute 50% of the total value to Corporation X, one would expect each to get 50% of the value of X stock in return. Nevertheless, stock received

---

49. Interestingly enough, the taxpayer in *American Bantam* was the *corporation;* not the incorporators. In a §351 transaction, the corporation takes a substituted basis from the incorporating shareholders. To avoid this result and instead receive a cost basis, American Bantam took the position that the incorporators did *not* meet the 80% control test and that the transaction was not covered by §351.

50. 11 T.C. at 404.

51. *Id.* at 406.

52. The new continuity-of-interest regulations are discussed in detail in Chapter 11.

need not necessarily "be substantially in proportion to . . . [the] interest in the property immediately prior to the transfer."[53] In the case of a disproportionate contribution, however, "the entire transaction will be given tax effect in accordance with its true nature."[54]

To illustrate, suppose that mother and daughter decide to incorporate a family business. They agree that each will receive 50% of the stock. The combined capital contributions will be $100,000. In a proportionate contribution, each would contribute $50,000 of the total $100,000 in return for 50% of the stock. Instead, mother contributes property worth $90,000 and daughter contributes property worth only $10,000. According to Treasury regulation §1.351-1(b)(1), the disproportionate nature of the contributions will not disqualify mother and daughter from §351 nonrecognition treatment. However, the transaction will be "given tax effect in accordance with its true nature." In deciding the "true nature" of the transaction, it will be necessary to examine the facts and circumstances to determine the reason that the "losing" party in the disproportionate exchange agreed to take less than her fair share. In the mother/daughter case, the most likely explanation is that mother was making a gift to daughter.[55] Mother will be viewed as first contributing 90% of the total contributions ($90,000) in return for 90% of the stock and then as making a gift of 40% of the shares ($40,000 worth of stock) to daughter. The daughter is viewed as first contributing 10% of the total contributions ($10,000) in return for 10% of the stock and then as receiving an additional 40% ($40,000 worth of stock) as a gift from mom. The daughter is deemed to receive a tax-free gift[56] and her basis for the gift shares will be governed by the gift-basis rules.[57] Mother may be required to pay a gift tax on this transfer.[58]

Operation of Shareholder Nonrecognition Rules

Overview of Basis Rules: Deferral of Gain or Loss

If a contribution to the corporation meets the requirements of §351(a), gain or loss will not be recognized to the contributing shareholder. The nonrec-

---

53. Treas. Reg. §1.351-1(b)(1).

54. *Id.*

55. See particularly examples (1) and (2) in Treas. Reg. §1.351-1(b)(2). Other explanations for disproportionate contributions may be that one contributor is paying another for services rendered or to satisfy other obligations.

56. I.R.C. §102.

57. I.R.C. §1015.

58. I.R.C. §2501.

ognition will not necessarily be permanent, however. Congress preserves unrecognized gain or loss through the basis rules in §358.[59] Section 358(a) provides that the shareholder's basis in property permitted to be received without recognition of gain or loss (the stock) shall be the same as that of the property exchanged (the property transferred to the corporation), subject to certain adjustments that will be considered below. This is a type of substituted basis labeled by Congress as "exchanged basis."[60] A simple example is perhaps the best way to illustrate the deferral provided by the combination of §§351 and 358. Suppose that shareholder A has been operating a business as sole proprietor and decides to incorporate, transferring real estate with a basis of $20,000 and a fair market value of $200,000 to a newly formed corporation in return for 100% of the corporation's common stock. The value of the stock received presumably is equal to the value of the corporation's only asset — $200,000. Under §351, the shareholder's $180,000 *realized* gain will not be recognized. A's basis in the common shares received will be an "exchanged basis" of $20,000 from the contributed real estate. If A later sells the stock for $200,000, A will then recognize the $180,000 gain previously deferred.[61] Thus, recognition of gain from the incorporation is deferred until ultimate disposition of the shares.[62]

---

59. The shareholder may permanently escape recognition only if he or she dies before disposing of the shares. In such event, the shareholder's heirs will inherit the stock with a fair market value basis at the time of death. I.R.C. §1014.

60. See I.R.C. §7701(a)(44), which defines "exchanged basis" as basis "determined in whole or in part by reference to other property held at any time by the person for whom the basis is to be determined."

61. In addition to determining the *amount* of gain, the shareholder will need to know the *character* of the gain. I.R.C. §1223(1) allows the shareholder to compute the stock's holding period by including the period of ownership of the transferred asset if: 1) the stock received has the same basis in whole or in part as the property exchanged; and 2) if the property exchanged was a capital asset. In the example in text, the shareholder received an exchanged basis under §358, thus satisfying the first condition. Assuming that the real estate transferred was a capital asset and assuming that A had held the real estate for one year, A's gain from sale of the stock will be long-term capital gain. These holding period rules will be considered further in the Examples and Explanations section below.

62. Use of the term "deferred" does not mean that the gain or loss later recognized upon sale of the stock will be precisely the amount of gain or loss realized at the time of contribution. The value of the property contributed may increase or decrease. If so, the value of the stock presumably will also increase or decrease. Gain later recognized may be more or less than the $180,000 realized gain at the time of contribution. Note, though, that the same would be true if the shareholder had retained the property. Later sale of the property at a price lower than $200,000 would reduce the gain below $180,000. The important point here is that the "exchanged basis" preserves the gain or loss at the level it would have been if the shareholder had retained the contributed property and later sold it directly.

Effect of Boot

a) Taxation of "Boot Gain": §351(b)(1)

Under §351(a), the transfer to the corporation must be *solely in exchange for stock*. Any property other than qualified stock of the transferee corporation received by the shareholders in the §351 exchange is referred to as boot.[63] After setting out the "solely in exchange for stock" requirement in §351(a), Congress then loosens the requirement with the "boot exception" in §351(b). If §351(a) would apply *but for* the fact that some boot was received in the exchange, §351(b) provides that gain (if any) will be recognized, but not in excess of the boot received.[64] Returning to shareholder A in the example above, assume that instead of receiving $200,000 worth of stock in exchange for her real estate (basis $20,000), A received $170,000 worth of stock and $30,000 in cash boot. A's *realized gain* is still $180,000.[65] A's receipt of $30,000 boot will not jeopardize the nonrecognition transaction altogether, but she will be required to report gain to the extent of the money (boot) received. Of the $180,000 realized gain, A will recognize only a $30,000 "boot gain." The remaining $150,000 of realized gain remains unrecognized; it is not affected by the boot.[66]

After computing A's gain from the transaction, the next step is to determine A's basis in the $170,000 worth of stock. A begins with a §358(a) exchanged basis of $20,000 from the contributed real estate. Shareholder A must then make adjustments, first decreasing basis by the amount of money received ($30,000)[67] and next increasing basis by the amount of gain recognized upon the exchange (also $30,000).[68] To better understand these adjustments, think of basis as a running account of the taxpayer's investment. To the extent of the $30,000 cash received, shareholder A has "cashed out"

---

63. Boot may take the form of cash, other property, or "nonqualified preferred stock" as provided in I.R.C. §351(g). Under §357(a), however, the corporation's assumption of a transferring shareholder's liability is not considered boot. Incorporations involving assumption of liabilities are considered later in this chapter.

64. I.R.C. §351(b).

65. Her amount realized includes the stock and the cash totaling $200,000. From this, she must subtract her basis of $20,000.

66. As a practical matter, the payment of cash boot upon formation of a new corporation is rare. Keep in mind that while §351 is most often associated with the initial formation of a corporation, it is not so limited. In fact, §351 applies to *any* transfer to a corporation controlled by the transferror that meets the §351 requirements. Cash boot may be more common in connection with such subsequent contributions. The more common form of boot in an initial incorporation is a corporate security.

67. I.R.C. §358(a)(1)(A)(ii).

68. I.R.C. §358(a)(1)(B)(ii).

of her investment in the corporate enterprise. Since she took this cash out, shareholder A has already recovered this part of her investment and her basis must be reduced accordingly. On the other hand, this "cashing out" caused shareholder A to have $30,000 in taxable gain. This gain is an increased cost ("tax cost") in her corporate investment and should increase her basis. Even after these adjustments, shareholder A's basis remains at $20,000.

If shareholder A later sells her stock for $170,000, her gain from the sale will be $150,000.[69] Adding together the $30,000 boot gain from the initial transaction and the $150,000 gain collected upon later sale, we discover that her total gain from the two transactions is $180,000. This is precisely the unrealized appreciation lurking in the property when she transferred it to the corporation in the first place. The §351 exchange rules required her to report $30,000 of gain at the outset, but permitted her to defer the remaining $150,000 until ultimate sale of the stock.

You probably noticed that when the dust settled after shareholder A's §358 adjustments, basis had been reduced by $30,000 and then increased by $30,000, leaving her where she started with an exchanged basis in her common shares of $20,000. Why bother with these adjustments if they simply wash each other out? Although this particular example results in a wash, this will not be the outcome in all cases. A variation on the above hypothetical will help to illustrate. Suppose that shareholder A's basis in the contributed property had been $185,000 as opposed to $20,000. Again assume that the property is valued at $200,000 when she contributes it to the corporation in return for $170,000 worth of stock and $30,000 cash boot. Remember that §351(b) requires recognition of gain, *if any,* but not in excess of the boot. In this variation, A's *realized* gain from her contribution is only $15,000.[70] Thus, shareholder A will recognize "boot gain" of only $15,000 under §351(b). The receipt of $30,000 boot results in *full* recognition of her realized gain. Surely, shareholder A should not be taxed on more than her realized gain. As for basis, shareholder A must first decrease her exchanged basis of $185,000 by the $30,000 money received and then must increase by the $15,000 gain recognized, leaving a $170,000 basis in the stock. If she should later sell her shares for $170,000, she will have no further taxable gain. This is sensible, since she has already been fully taxed on her realized gain from the contributed property. The downward and upward adjustments required by §358 do not precisely wash each other out in this variation of the hypothetical.

If shareholder A received other property instead of cash boot, the analysis would be similar to that considered above. Assume, for example, that

---

69. From her $170,000 amount realized, subtract her §358 exchanged basis of $20,000.

70. A's amount realized is $200,000 ($170,000 worth of stock plus the $30,000 cash she received). From this, she subtracts her $185,000 basis.

shareholder A transferred her real estate (basis $20,000) to the corporation in return for stock worth $170,000 and a piece of artwork worth $30,000. The gain from this transaction is precisely the same as it was above. Of the $180,000 realized gain, a "boot gain" of $30,000 (the fair market value of the property received) will be recognized. Two basis questions now must be addressed, however. As for A's basis in the stock received, the answer remains the same — the exchanged basis of $20,000 is first decreased by the fair market value of the property ($30,000) and then increased by the gain recognized on the exchange (also $30,000).[71] The basis in the artwork is simply its fair market value of $30,000.[72] Shareholder A's fair market value basis in the boot makes sense. After all, she was taxed on the full value of the artwork. It is as if she received cash boot and then used the cash to purchase the asset. In effect, she has a "tax cost" basis in the boot property.

b) Securities, Notes, or Other Evidence of Indebtedness as Boot

Prior to the Omnibus Budget Reconciliation Act of 1989, securities of the transferee corporation issued in a §351 exchange were not considered boot. Today, however, any securities transferred to a contributing shareholder in return for property in a §351 exchange will be considered boot. Ordinarily, when a shareholder receives boot, the gain, if any, is taxed to the extent of the fair market value of the boot. The gain must be reported entirely in the taxable year of the §351 exchange. When a shareholder receives boot in the form of notes or securities, however, timing issues arise. Given that payments on the boot notes or securities will occur over time, the shareholder may be entitled to take advantage of installment reporting under §453. Under the installment method, the shareholder would recognize boot gain as payments were received, thus deferring tax on the gain and spreading the recognition over the period of the installment obligation. There is no explicit statutory authority for treating notes or securities received in a §351 transaction under the installment method. However, Congress *did* provide special rules for installment reporting with respect to notes or securities received as boot in other similar nonrecognition transactions such as like-kind exchanges and reorganizations.[73] In proposed regulations, the Service explicitly takes the position that transferors who receive corporate notes, securities, or other evidence of indebtedness as boot in a §351 transaction are entitled to installment reporting of boot gain.[74]

---

71. I.R.C. §358(a)(1)(A)(i), (a)(1)(B)(ii).

72. I.R.C. §358(a)(2).

73. I.R.C. §453(f)(6).

74. Prop. Treas. Reg. §1.453-1(f)(3). The proposed regulations also provide details regarding the mechanics of applying the installment method.

c) "Nonqualified Preferred Stock" Treated as Boot

Prior to the Taxpayer Relief Act of 1997, §351(a) nonrecognition extended to qualifying exchanges of property for *any* type of stock of the transferee corporation. Anything *other* than stock received by the transferors is considered boot. As noted in the preceding paragraphs, such boot includes corporate securities and other evidences of indebtedness. Over the years, the number of different types of stock, debt, and other financial instruments has exploded. In particular, tax and financial planners have created categories of preferred stock that closely resemble debt. By offering transferors "debt-like" preferred stock or preferred stock with built-in redemption features, planners were able to structure incorporation transactions without any §351(b) boot gain in which the transferors received a preferred stock instrument much like a security or one which was reasonably certain to be quickly redeemed.

Included among the provisions of the Taxpayer Relief Act of 1997 is a new §351(g), which declares that §351(a) nonrecognition shall *not* apply to the transfer of property to a corporation in exchange for "nonqualified preferred stock."[75] Instead, "nonqualified preferred stock" will be treated as boot under §351(b). For purposes of this provision, preferred stock is "stock which is limited and preferred as to dividends and does not participate in corporate growth to any significant extent."[76] Preferred stock is classified as *nonqualified* under any of four stated circumstances, the first three of which relate to redemption rights. Preferred stock is nonqualified: 1) if the stockholder has a right to require that the issuing corporation or a related person redeem or purchase the shares within 20 years of issue;[77] 2) if redemption of the shares is mandatory within 20 years of issue;[78] or 3) if the issuing corporation or a related person has the right to redeem or purchase the shares within 20 years and "it is more likely than not that such right will be exercised."[79] The focus in these three cases is on shares that are reasonably likely to be redeemed and, thus, converted to cash in the hands of the holders. Congress is no longer willing to offer nonrecognition to those who transfer property to a corporation in exchange for such redeemable stock.[80]

---

75. The 1997 Tax Act redesignated the *old* §351(g) as §351(h) and inserted a *new* §351(g). Taxpayer Relief Act of 1997, Pub. L. No. 105-34, 111 Stat. 788, §1014(a).

76. I.R.C. §351(g)(3).

77. I.R.C. §351(g)(2)(A)(i). Such shares often are referred to as "puttable."

78. I.R.C. §351(g)(2)(A)(ii).

79. I.R.C. §351(g)(2)(A)(iii). Such shares often are referred to as "callable."

80. Despite incorporating one of the three redemption features, preferred stock will not be classified as nonqualified if the redemption right or obligation to purchase is subject to a contingency which makes the likelihood of redemption or purchase remote. I.R.C. §351(g)(2)(B). Other specific exceptions to the classification rules appear in I.R.C. §351(g)(2)(C).

The last listed circumstance that will result in a nonqualified preferred stock classification is when the dividend rate for the preferred stock "varies, in whole or in part . . . , with reference to interest rates, commodity prices, or other similar indices."[81] Where dividends on stock are tied to such market factors, rather than to the earnings of the corporation itself, the preferred stock resembles debt. Since securities are now treated as boot under §351(b), Congress has decided to treat such debt-like preferred stock as boot as well.

To illustrate §351(g), imagine that shareholder A again transfers real estate with a basis of $20,000 and a fair market value of $200,000 to a newly formed corporation in exchange for 100% of the corporation's common stock, valued at $170,000, and 100% of the corporation's preferred stock, valued at $30,000. Shareholder A has a right to "put" the preferred shares within five years from the date of issue; in other words, shareholder A can *require* the corporation to redeem these preferred shares. Prior to the 1997 Tax Act changes, shareholder A was entitled to nonrecognition treatment on all of the $180,000 realized gain from this exchange. Under new §351(g), however, the redemption feature makes the preferred stock *nonqualified*. As a result, the preferred shares will be treated as boot. Shareholder A now will recognize $30,000 "boot gain" just as if she had received cash or other boot.

Although nonqualified preferred stock is treated as boot for purposes of §351(b), the Conference Report clarifies that, until Treasury regulations require a different result, the nonqualified stock will still be treated as stock for purposes of the control test under §§351(a) and 368(c).[82] Imagine, for example, that two individual shareholders transfer appreciated property to a newly formed corporation in exchange for stock. Shareholder A receives all of the corporation's common stock and Shareholder B receives all the corporation's nonqualified preferred stock. Shareholder B surely will have "boot gain" under §351(b). Nevertheless, the preferred shares will be considered stock for purposes of determining control under §368(c). Since Shareholders A and B have "control" of the corporation immediately after the exchange, Shareholder A will be entitled to §351(a) nonrecognition treatment.

If shareholders transfer *multiple* properties in exchange for stock and boot, §351(b) gain must be computed on an asset-by-asset basis. A portion of the boot received must be allocated to each asset based upon the fair market value of the asset.[83] Boot gain will be recognized with respect to each gain asset transferred. Boot gain from each asset will be reflected as ordinary income, short-term capital gain, long-term capital gain, or recapture income, as appropriate. Thus, the asset-by-asset approach effectively preserves the character of gain for each individual asset.

---

81. I.R.C. §351(g)(2)(A)(iv).
82. H.R. Rep. No. 105-220, 105th Cong., 2d Sess. 561 (1997).
83. Rev. Rul. 68-55, 1968-1 C.B. 140.

d) No Recognition of Loss: §351(b)(2)

Although the payment of boot triggers recognition of gain, losses are not recognized. Section 351(b)(2) specifically disallows loss recognition when property other than stock (boot) is received in connection with a §351 exchange. The rationale here probably is that it otherwise would be too easy for shareholders to have it both ways, avoiding gain on §351(a) exchanges, but recognizing loss under §351(b) merely by including boot along with the transfer of stock from the corporation.

When shareholders receive boot in exchange for multiple assets in a §351 exchange, they may be tempted to argue that the "gain (if any)" language in §351(b) refers to *aggregate* gain from the assets contributed. If successful, the shareholders could use losses from the loss assets to offset gains from the gain assets contributed, resulting in a lower boot gain on the exchange. The asset-by-asset approach described above prevents this end-run around §351(b)(2). Under this approach, no gain is recognized and no loss is permitted with respect to the boot allocated to the loss assets.[84]

Tax Consequences to the Corporation

Nonrecognition Rule: §1032

With regard to the corporation, Congress provides a nonrecognition rule that somewhat parallels the §351 shareholder nonrecognition rules. Under §1032(a), "no gain or loss shall be recognized to a corporation on the receipt of money or other property in exchange for stock." This nonrecognition rule also applies to previously issued treasury stock later redeemed by the corporation.[85]

One explanation for the nonrecognition provided in §1032 is potential hardship. Corporations need capital to begin operations. Taxing capital contributions would impose additional financial burdens on a corporation just as it was trying to get off the ground.[86] Put differently, §1032 nonrecognition may be simply an encouragement to incorporate. Another explanation for §1032 may be that most contributions arguably do not involve genuine gain to the corporation. At least upon initial incorporation, the

---

84. See Examples and Explanations, Example 6, *infra*.

85. See Treas. Reg. §1.1032-1(a), which provides that the "disposition by a corporation of shares of its own stock (including treasury stock) for money or other property does not give rise to taxable gain or deductible loss to the corporation regardless of the nature of the transaction or the facts and circumstances involved."

86. Note that §1032 is not by its terms limited to contributions at the time of incorporation. In this respect, §1032 is similar to §351.

corporation's stock has not appreciated in the corporation's hands. The stock has no value until it is issued.

Although it is useful to think of §1032 as a parallel to §351, several differences between the two provisions should be pointed out. First, under §1032 *any* issuance of the corporation's own stock in return for money or other property is a nonrecognition event to the issuing corporation. Unlike §351, there is no requirement that a group receiving the shares meet an 80% control test. In addition, distributions of stock for services are covered by §1032. Treasury Regulation §1.1032-1(a) provides that a "transfer by a corporation of shares of its own stock . . . as compensation for services is considered, for purposes of section 1032(a), as a disposition by the corporation of such shares for money or other property." Finally, the basis rules that apply on the corporate side are similar, but not quite the same as the shareholder basis rules provided in §358.

The Corporate Basis Rules: §362

Operating together, the §351 shareholder nonrecognition rule and the §358 shareholder basis rule establish a deferral rather than permanent nonrecognition of the shareholder's gain or loss with respect to assets contributed to the corporation. The effect of the §1032 *corporate* nonrecognition rule in conjunction with the §362 basis rule is slightly different. First of all, arguably there is no corporate level gain from the shareholder contribution that should be deferred. Unlike the shareholder, the corporation has not disposed of appreciated or depreciated assets. Thus, §362 does not adopt an "exchanged" basis rule parallel to §358. Instead, the corporation's basis in property acquired in a §351 exchange is "the same as it would be in the hands of the transferor, increased in the amount of gain recognized to the transferor on such transfer."[87] In other words, the corporation takes the *contributing shareholder's* basis or "steps into the shoes of" the contributing shareholder. The Code refers to this type of basis as "transferred basis."[88] Suppose again that shareholder A contributes real estate with a basis of $20,000 and a fair market value of $200,000 to Corporation X in return for 100% of X's common stock. Corporation X will have no taxable gain from receipt of the property under §1032. Corporation X's basis in the property under §362 will be a "transferred basis" from the shareholder of $20,000. This transferred basis assures that the *shareholder* level gain or loss from the §351 contribution is preserved in the *corporation's* hands. If Corporation X sold

---

87. I.R.C. §362(a).

88. I.R.C. §7701(a)(43) defines "transferred basis property" as property having a basis "determined in whole or in part by reference to the basis in the hands of the donor, grantor, or other transferror." Note that both "exchanged basis" and "transferred basis" are forms of "substituted basis." I.R.C. §7701(a)(42).

the real estate contributed by A for $200,000, the corporation would be required to report a taxable gain of $180,000. This is precisely the amount of gain that the shareholder would have had if she sold the property herself.[89]

The only required adjustment to the corporation's basis in contributed property under §362(a) is an *increase* in the amount of the shareholder's gain recognized on the §351 exchange.[90] Since the corporation's §362 basis is designed to preserve the *shareholder* level gain or loss from the contributed property, this upward adjustment is necessary to reflect the portion of shareholder realized gain that has already been recognized. If shareholder A received $170,000 worth of stock and $30,000 boot from Corporation X in exchange for real estate with a basis of $20,000 and a fair market value of $200,000, shareholder A would report $30,000 in gain pursuant to §351(b)(1).[91] Corporation X's basis in the real estate now would be a transferred basis from shareholder A of $20,000, increased by the $30,000 gain recognized to shareholder A. Thus, the real estate will have a basis of $50,000 in the corporation's hands. If the corporation were to sell the real estate for $200,000, it would recognize a $150,000 gain — precisely the portion of $180,000 realized shareholder gain that was left unrecognized at the time of the §351 exchange.

Notice that both §§358 and 362 use a form of "substituted basis" and both provisions preserve the gain or loss left unrecognized to the shareholder under §351. Congress thus has preserved the shareholder level gain in two places. The shareholder will recognize the gain deferred upon later sale of the stock and the corporation will recognize the same gain deferred upon later sale of the contributed property. Is this overkill? Will it result in double taxation of the same gain? The answer to the latter question is yes. Surely, there lurks the possibility that shareholder A's unrecognized gain from appreciation in the contributed real estate will be taxed once at the shareholder level and again at the corporate level. The answer to the first question is more difficult and controversial. By its very nature, Subchapter C creates a double tax. Certainly, corporate income is taxed first to the corporation and again to the shareholders when it is distributed. The combination of

---

89. If the asset in question was a capital asset, the gain would be capital gain. With regard to holding periods, the corporation will be entitled to include or "tack" the shareholder's holding period because the property in the corporation's hands has the same basis as it would have in the hands of the shareholder from whom the property was acquired. I.R.C. §1223(2).

90. Recent amendments to §362 added a *new* §362(d), which limits the amount of this increase in certain cases involving the assumption of liabilities by the corporation. A discussion of this new provision is included in the discussion of the effect of liabilities later in this chapter.

91. Shareholder A's tax treatment in this example was considered in detail in the section on boot earlier in this chapter.

§§358 and 362 extends this double tax to *pre-contribution appreciation* as well.[92]

Contribution vs. Sale

The rules considered up to this point deal with contributions of property to a controlled corporation in return for stock. Sometimes, however, shareholders wish to "sell" rather than contribute property to the corporation. In such transactions, the corporation often issues a promissory note to the shareholder in return for the property. Whether the shareholder "sells" property in exchange for a promissory note or contributes property to the corporation in exchange for stock, the shareholder's "return" will be taxable. In the case of a "sale," the seller's return takes the form of interest taxable as ordinary income.[93] In the case of a "contribution," the shareholder's return takes the form of dividends also taxable as ordinary income.[94]

Given the valuable nonrecognition provided by §351, why might a shareholder prefer to sell an asset to the corporation? Remember that §351 is a two-way street, providing nonrecognition for both gains *and losses*. A shareholder may wish to sell property to the corporation in order to recognize a loss. Unfortunately for certain shareholders attempting to avoid §351 nonrecognition of loss by "selling" the property to the corporation, the related party rules of §267 may prohibit the shareholder from deducting any loss in such a transaction.[95] Thus, a *controlling* shareholder cannot recognize a loss upon sale of property to the controlled corporation.

Another reason that a shareholder might arrange a "sale" rather than a "contribution" is to limit risk. A creditor's relationship with the corporation is less risky than an equity holder's relationship with the corporation. The

---

92. In a case where a shareholder challenged the double taxation of pre-contribution appreciation, the court upheld the constitutionality of the provisions. In Perthur Holding Co. v. Comm'r, Judge Learned Hand commented that the double tax "may be unfair, but it is not unconstitutional. This was something the shareholder should have considered when he 'put on a corporate dress.'" 61 F.2d 785, 786 (2d Cir. 1932), *cert. denied*, 288 U.S. 616 (1933).

93. Payments of *principal* will be taxable to the extent of the gain upon the asset sold. This gain will be capital or ordinary depending upon the character of the asset sold. Assuming that the shareholder takes a promissory note in return for the sale, the sale will be treated as an installment sale unless the shareholder elects not to use the installment method. I.R.C. §453(d)(1).

94. For a complete discussion of corporate distributions, including dividends, see Chapter 5.

95. An individual owning, directly or indirectly, more than 50% of the value of the corporation's outstanding stock is considered "related" to the corporation for purposes of §267. See I.R.C. §267(b)(2).

corporate planner considering shareholder "sales" to the corporation to reduce risk should proceed with caution, however. Other creditors may turn to corporate law in order to achieve priority over creditors who are also major or controlling shareholders.

A shareholder also may attempt to "sell" property to the corporation to provide the corporation with a cost basis in the property under §1012 rather than a transferred basis under §362. A corporation may find it particularly attractive to "buy" depreciable property from the shareholder when the cost basis would result in significantly higher depreciation allowances than a transferred basis. A final reason the shareholder may arrange a "sale" to the corporation is to provide the corporation with a deduction for interest payments. A corporation can deduct interest payments on a promissory note,[96] but cannot deduct dividend payments to shareholders.

Until recently, the "sale" versus "contribution" issue was more complex than it is today. As amended in 1989, §351 only provides nonrecognition for transfers of property to the corporation in return for stock. Before 1989, §351 provided nonrecognition for transfers in return for "stock *or* securities." While it was clear that short-term notes were not securities for purposes of *old* §351, long-term notes fell into a gray area in which it was difficult to predict whether or not a particular note would be designated a security eligible for §351 nonrecognition.[97] Given that §351 now applies only to transfers in exchange for stock, transfers of property in exchange for long-term *securities* no longer fall into any gray area. Gain upon such exchanges is now taxable to the extent of the securities received as boot. There remains a risk, however, that a sale for a long-term note will be reconstrued as a contribution for *stock*. In some cases, the promissory note received had so many equity characteristics that the purported sale was deemed to be an exchange of property for *stock* and, thus, treated as a §351 nonrecognition exchange rather than a sale.[98] Even under §351 as revised, a formal sale in exchange for a debenture or note may be disregarded and viewed, in substance, as a disguised equity contribution in return for stock. Among the factors that courts have considered in distinguishing a sale from an equity contribution are: 1) the capital and credit structure of the corporation; 2) the extent of risk borne by the noteholders; 3) the extent of control of the noteholders over business operations; 4) whether the "price" of the property

---

96. I.R.C. §163(a).

97. See, e.g., Nye v. Comm'r, 50 T.C. 203 (1968), *acq.* 1969-2 C.B. xxiv (purported sales to the corporation in return for promissory notes held to be §351 exchanges of property for securities).

98. See, e.g., Burr Oaks Corp. v. Comm'r, 43 T.C. 635 (1965), *aff'd*, 365 F.2d 24 (7th Cir. 1966), *cert. denied*, 385 U.S. 1007 (1967) (promissory notes received by the taxpayers in return for property treated as preferred stock for §351 purposes).

was proportionate to its fair market value; and 5) whether payments on notes were subordinated to other creditors and dividends.

Additional Contributions to Capital

Shareholder Level Issues

a) Nonrecognition

So far, this chapter has focused upon the initial formation of a corporation. Neither §351 or §1032, by its terms, is limited to contributions upon the initial formation of the corporation. Subsequent transfers to a corporation also will qualify for shareholder nonrecognition treatment if they meet all of the §351 requirements. Most importantly, the person or persons transferring property to the corporation in return for stock must be in control of the corporation immediately after the exchange. This requirement is easily met if all members of the original transferor group again transfer property to the corporation. On the other hand, if one or more members of the initial transferor group subsequently contribute additional appreciated property for additional shares of stock and, immediately after the transfer, the subsequent contributors hold less than 80% control, the exchange will not qualify for §351 nonrecognition unless the subsequent contributions are part of an "integrated plan" under which a group of persons meeting the control test contribute additional property to the corporation.[99] Suppose that, aware of this lurking problem, the subsequent contributors convinced enough other shareholders to make nominal contributions so that the group of contributing shareholders now had control immediately after the exchanges? Although the combined contributions might literally satisfy all of the requirements of §351, the Treasury Regulations provide that stock "issued for property which is of relatively small value in comparison to the value of the stock . . . already owned . . . by the person who transferred such property, shall not be treated as having been issued in return for property *if the primary purpose of the transfer is to qualify under this section the exchanges of property by other persons transferring property*."[100] In other words, if the primary purpose of the nominal contributions of the other shareholders was to qualify the sub-

---

99. Given that the contribution does not qualify for §351 nonrecognition, the §358 basis rules also will not apply. Therefore, the contributing shareholder's basis in the stock received will be a cost basis. In this case, the cost would include both the actual cost of the property contributed (the shareholder's basis) plus "tax cost" incurred from the taxable contribution. In other words, the shareholder's basis in the new shares should be equal to the fair market value of the property contributed.

100. Treas. Reg. §1.351-1(a)(1)(ii) (emphasis added).

sequent contributors for §351 nonrecognition treatment, the stock held by the nominal contributors will not be counted toward meeting the control test.[101] One question that comes to mind here is what constitutes property that is "of relatively small value in comparison to the value of stock already owned"? At what point are the contributions of the other shareholders substantial enough to be counted? The answer to this question is not entirely clear, but the Treasury Department has suggested in a Revenue Procedure that the transaction should be safe if the purchase represents 10% of the value already owned.[102]

Another question that may arise involves subsequent shareholder contributions for which the shareholder receives *no* additional shares of stock. Suppose, for example, that one of the original shareholders voluntarily contributes additional appreciated property to the corporation and gets nothing in return? The shareholder simply is making an additional contribution to capital. At least as to voluntary pro rata payments by shareholders, Treasury Regulations confirm this treatment, providing that such payments "are in the nature of assessments upon, and represent an additional price paid for, the shares of stock held by the individual shareholders."[103] In other words, if *all* shareholders contribute additional money or property in proportion to their stock interests, the contributions simply will be treated as additional price paid for the original shares. No taxable gain to the shareholders will result from contributions of appreciated property under such circumstances. The regulations do not speak as clearly to additional voluntary contributions that are not pro rata. It has generally been assumed that even voluntary non pro rata contributions will not trigger taxable gain or loss to the contributing shareholders.[104] Further support for this view is provided by the Supreme Court's opinion in Commissioner v. Fink.[105] In order to increase the attractiveness of the corporation to outside investors, the controlling shareholders in *Fink* voluntarily surrendered a non pro rata portion of their shares, receiving no consideration in return. The Supreme Court disallowed the shareholders' ordinary loss deduction, holding that the stock surrender effectively was a contribution to capital or additional cost of stock.[106]

---

101. The validity of this regulation was tested and upheld in Kamborian v. Comm'r, 56 T.C. 847 (1971), *aff'd*, 469 F.2d 219 (1st Cir. 1972).

102. Rev. Proc. 77-37, 1977-2 C.B. 568 (stating requirements for purpose of receiving an advance letter ruling).

103. Treas. Reg. §1.118-1.

104. Boris I. Bittker and James S. Eustice, Federal Income Taxation of Corporations and Shareholders ¶3.13[1] (7th ed. 2000).

105. 483 U.S. 89 (1987).

106. *Id.* at 99-100. The basis in the surrendered shares was reallocated among the shares retained.

b) Basis

When a shareholder makes a subsequent contribution to the corporation that qualifies for §351 nonrecognition, basis in the new shares is determined under the "exchanged" basis rules of §358. If the contribution does not qualify for nonrecognition, the shareholder will receive a cost basis in the new shares. If *no* new shares are received for the subsequent contribution, the contribution to capital regulations discussed above simply view the contribution as an additional price paid for the stock.[107] Thus, in the simple case where a shareholder makes a cash contribution to capital, the shareholder's basis in his existing shares of stock is increased by the amount of money contributed. Upon a subsequent contribution of appreciated property, however, the question is whether the existing stock's basis should be increased by the basis of the property contributed or by the fair market value. If the difference between basis and fair market value does not result in taxable gain or loss, as assumed above, the original stock basis should be increased by the basis of the property contributed.[108] This approach applies an "exchanged basis" principle consistent with §358. An increase to the original stock basis, reflecting the fair market value of contributed property, should be permitted only in cases where the gain or loss was recognized to the shareholder upon the subsequent contribution.

Corporate Level Issues

Under §1032, a corporation issuing its *own* stock in return for money or other property has no taxable gain. Money or other property received by the corporation *without* issuing stock also will not be taxed according to §118(a), which simply provides that "[i]n the case of a corporation, gross income does not include any contribution to the capital of the taxpayer." This general provision covers even nonshareholder contributions to capital. The §118 capital contribution exclusion does not apply, however, to "any contribution in aid of construction or any other contribution as a customer or potential customer."[109] Apparently, the focus of this "contribution in aid" exception is contributions to public utilities by transferors who stand to directly benefit from the contribution.[110] Contributions from such "direct beneficiaries" generally are not considered contributions to capital.[111]

---

107. Treas. Reg. §1.118-1.

108. This approach is confirmed by dicta in Comm'r v. Fink, 483 U.S. 89, 94 (1987).

109. I.R.C. §118(b).

110. H.R. Rep. No. 426, 99th Cong., 1st Sess. 644 (1985).

111. Congress recently reinstituted an exclusion for certain qualifying contributions to water and sewerage disposal utilities. I.R.C. §118(c), added by the Small Business Job Protection Act, Pub. L. No. 104-108, 110 Stat. 1755, §1613(a)(1).

The §362 "transferred basis" rules explicitly apply not only to §351 contributions, but also to property acquired "as paid-in surplus or as a contribution to capital."[112] Thus, the corporation's basis in property received as a contribution to capital generally is the same basis as in the hands of the transferor.[113] If the contribution to capital comes from a nonshareholder, however, the basis in property other than money will be zero.[114]

Effect of Liabilities: §357 and Related Matters

The General Rule: §357(a)

a) Contributions with Liabilities

Sole proprietors, partners, and other noncorporate business entities may choose to incorporate after operating for a time in the noncorporate setting. As part of the incorporation transaction, it is quite common for the newly formed corporation to assume liabilities of the old business. In addition, contributions of property to the corporation may be subject to an outstanding mortgage or the corporation may assume the mortgage on the property.

For example, suppose that shareholder A purchased real estate for $20,000, paying $10,000 down and incurring a $10,000 mortgage for the remainder of the purchase price. After the property has appreciated to a fair market value of $200,000, but before making any payments on the mortgage, shareholder A transfers the property to the corporation in return for 100% of the common stock plus the corporation's assumption of the $10,000 mortgage. In this example, the net value of shareholder A's contribution to the corporation is $190,000. In return for her contribution shareholder A receives $190,000 worth of stock and is relieved of a $10,000 liability. Her *realized* gain is $180,000.[115] Under the basic §351 rules, shareholder A should be eligible for nonrecognition except that gain, if any, *will* be recognized to the extent of the boot. The tax issue here is whether or not relief from liability is considered boot, requiring shareholder A to report a $10,000 "boot gain."

---

112. I.R.C. §362(a)(2).

113. But see Treas. Reg. §1.1032-3, discussed at the end of this chapter.

114. I.R.C. §362(c).

115. Amount realized ($200,000) less adjusted basis ($20,000). The amount realized from a disposition must include the fair market value of property received plus any liabilities assumed. Crane v. Comm'r, 331 U.S. 1 (1947); Comm'r v. Tufts, 461 U.S. 300 (1983). The taxpayer's cost basis in this situation is $20,000, including the $10,000 down payment plus the $10,000 borrowed cost.

Early in corporate tax history, the Supreme Court held in United States v. Hendler that the corporation's assumption of liabilities in a nonrecognition transaction was the equivalent of the receipt of boot by the shareholder.[116] As a result, many incorporators were required to report "boot gain" where liabilities were transferred to the corporation in an incorporation exchange. Shortly thereafter, Congress legislatively overruled *Hendler*. Today, the general rule of §357(a) provides that if another party assumes a liability of the transferor as part of the consideration in a §351 exchange, the assumption shall not be treated as boot and shall not prevent the exchange from being within §351.[117] Thus, the corporation's assumption of shareholder A's $10,000 mortgage in the above hypothetical is not considered boot.

The next question in a §351 exchange involving liabilities is the shareholder's basis in shares received upon the exchange. Recall that under §358(a), the shareholder's basis in stock received in the §351 transfer is an "exchanged basis" from the property contributed, reduced by the amount of money received and increased by the amount of gain recognized. Even though the assumption of liability is *not* considered money received under the general rule of §357(a), §358 provides that the assumption "shall, *for purposes of this section,* be treated as money received by the taxpayer on the exchange."[118] In other words, the corporation's assumption of the transferror's liability is *not* considered boot in applying the basic §351 nonrecognition rule, but *is* considered boot for purposes of computing the shareholder's stock basis. This dichotomy can best be understood by focusing on the value received by the shareholder upon a contribution of liabilities in an incorporation transaction. The contributing shareholder gains from the corporate transaction to the extent that he or she is relieved of a liability. This gain is analogous to "discharge of indebtedness" income. In §357(a), Congress simply provides temporary relief from taxation on this gain. At the same time, the §358 basis rules attempt to preserve this discharge of indebtedness type gain for later taxation by treating the liability as money received for purposes of computing *basis,* reducing the shareholder's stock basis by the amount of the liability.

Shareholder A in our example received $190,000 worth of stock and $10,000 worth of relief from liability, totaling $200,000. Her total *realized* gain was $180,000. Since §358 now requires a decrease in basis for the liability assumed, shareholder A will reduce her exchanged basis of $20,000

---

116. 303 U.S. 564 (1938).

117. I.R.C. §357(a). Until recently, §357 was not limited to the *assumption* of liability, but also included a reference to another party acquiring property from the transferor *subject to* a liability. Congress amended §357 in 1999, eliminating references to transfers subject to liabilities. These changes will be discussed in detail later in this chapter.

118. I.R.C. §358(d)(1) (emphasis added).

from the real estate by the $10,000 liability, resulting in a stock basis of $10,000.[119] If she later sells her stock for $190,000, her taxable gain will be $180,000 — precisely the amount of gain deferred in the §351 transaction. Failure to reduce her basis by the $10,000 liability would result in a taxable gain of only $170,000 on the later sale, thus permitting her to permanently escape taxation on her earlier discharge of indebtedness income.

b) What Constitutes Assumption of Liability?

Two different terms often are used to refer to liability transfers: 1) transfers *subject to* a liability, and 2) transfers in which the transferee *assumes* the liability. When property is merely *subject to* a liability, this generally means that the property transferred is still subject to forfeiture for nonpayment of the debt. The transferee is not otherwise personally liable for payment of the debt. On the other hand, when the transferee *assumes* a liability, the property itself is still subject to forfeiture *and* the transferee is also personally liable for nonpayment. In other words, the transferee's other assets may be required to satisfy the debt obligation.

Until recently, the statutory language regarding liabilities in §357 and related provisions generally referred to circumstances in which "another party assumes a liability of the transferor or acquires property from the transferor subject to a liability." Thus, the same tax treatment applied regardless of whether the property transferred was merely *subject to* the liability or the liability was *assumed* by the transferee corporation. Recent amendments to §357 deleted the references to property that was acquired subject to a liability.[120] Today, §357(a)(2) reads more simply, covering only the case where, "as part of the consideration, another party to the exchange assumes a liability of the taxpayer. . . ." At the same time, however, the §357 amendments added a *new* §357(d), which defines the extent to which liabilities shall be treated as having been assumed. Rest assured that any apparent simplification in §357(a) is outweighed by the potential complexities added by new §357(d).[121]

Under new §357(d), *recourse* liabilities are considered assumed "if, as determined on the basis of all facts and circumstances, the transferee has agreed to, and is expected to, satisfy such liability . . . , whether or not the transferor has been relieved of such liability."[122] *Nonrecourse* liabilities gen-

---

119. I.R.C. §§358(a), (d)(1).

120. Miscellaneous Trade and Technical Corrections Act of 1999, Pub. L. No. 106–36, 113 Stat. 127, §3001 (codified, as amended, at I.R.C. §357).

121. For a discussion of some of these complexities, see John Bogdanski, Section 357(d)—Old Can, New Worms, 27 J. Corp. Tax'n 17, 23 (2000).

122. I.R.C. §357(d)(1)(A).

erally are considered assumed "by the transferee of any asset subject to such liability."[123]

c) Multiple Assets Securing the Same Liability

Under a special exception in new §357(d)(2), the amount of nonrecourse liabilities assumed will be reduced in certain cases where the transferor owned *multiple* assets subject to the liability transferred. In fact, the §357 amendments themselves were designed to eliminate a particular transaction in which taxpayers were interpreting the "subject to a liability" language to achieve what the government thought to be abusive tax results.

Perhaps the best way to make sense of new §357(d) is to understand the transaction it was designed to attack. Imagine that X Corporation has three separate assets, each with a basis of zero and a fair market value of $50. All three assets are subject to aggregate nonrecourse liabilities of $100. In other words, the properties are cross-collateralized for the aggregate debt. X decides to incorporate subsidiaries A, B, and C, transferring one of the three assets to each subsidiary. Each of the assets remains subject to the entire $100 liability. If §357(c) imposes a tax on the excess of liabilities over basis, X Corporation will be required to report a $100 §357(c) gain for each transfer, totaling $300. Under §357(d)(2), the nonrecourse liability treated as assumed will be reduced by the lesser of "the amount of such liability which an owner of other assets not transferred to the transferee and also subject to the liability has agreed with the transferee to, and is expected to, satisfy" or the fair market value of the other property. In effect, the amount of liability viewed as assumed by each subsidiary in the above example must be reduced by the portion of nonrecourse liability attributable to assets *not* transferred. Thus, the liabilities considered assumed by each A, B, and C will be $33.33, resulting in an overall §357(c) gain of only $100. If anything, the *old* result appeared harsh and the new result seems preferable from the taxpayer's point of view. Where was the abuse? Recall that the transferee corporation's basis in the assets under §362 is a transferred basis, *increased in the amount of the gain recognized by the transferor.* Under the old rules, if subsidiaries A, B, and C were each entitled to increase basis in the assets received by the §357(c) gain, each of them would have a $100 basis in the asset received from X. In fact, the real concern driving the recent amendments was the use of §357(c) to create artificial basis under §362. The abuse becomes more clear if A, B, and C are domestic corporations entitled to the step-up in basis under §362, while X is a foreign corporation not subject to U.S. tax on the §357(c) gain. Not surprisingly, the recent amendments also added a new §362(d), which parallels §357(d), denying the full step-up in basis.[124]

---

123. I.R.C. §357(d)(1)(B).

124. I.R.C. §362(d), added by Pub. L. No. 106–36, §3001(e) (codified, as amended, at I.R.C. §362). This new provision includes two limitations on the

Exceptions to the §357(a) General Rule

a) Tax Avoidance Purpose: §357(b)

An assumption of liability *will* be considered boot if the principal purpose of the taxpayer was to avoid federal income tax on the exchange or was not a bona fide business purpose.[125] When might this be the case? Suppose that shareholder A from the earlier example had purchased the real estate for $20,000 cash many years ago. After the property had appreciated to $200,000, but before incorporating, A pledged the real estate as collateral for a $10,000 bank loan, using the borrowed funds to take a personal vacation. If A later transfers the property along with the liability to the corporation in return for $190,000 worth of stock, the assumption of liability arguably is for a tax avoidance purpose or, at least, is not for a bona fide business purpose. Shareholder A has effectively "cashed out" $10,000 from corporate solution, using the funds for personal reasons. In such a case, shareholder A would be required under §357(b) to treat the $10,000 as money (boot) received in the exchange and would be required to report a $10,000 "boot gain." Under §358, the exchanged basis of $20,000 from the real estate would be first reduced by the $10,000 liability and then increased by the $10,000 gain recognized, leaving shareholder A's stock basis at $20,000. If she were later to sell her shares for $190,000, the taxable gain would be only $170,000. Since she already would have been taxed on $10,000 of the $180,000 realized gain at the time of the initial incorporation, this application of the §358 basis adjustments provides a sensible result.

b) Liabilities in Excess of Basis: §357(c)

The second exception to the general rule of §357(a) is invoked simply when liabilities exceed the shareholder's basis in the property transferred. Going

---

corporation's increase in basis to reflect gains recognized by the shareholders on the exchange. First, §362(d)(1) provides that "in no event shall the basis of any property be increased . . . above the fair market value of such property . . . by reason of any recognition to the transferor as a result of the assumption of a liability." Second, §362(d)(2) directly addresses the concern with multiple assets securing the same liability. If a transferor with multiple assets securing a liability does not transfer all of those assets to the corporation, and if nobody was subject to tax on the §357(c) gain with respect to the transferred assets, the corporation's increase in basis under §362 "shall be determined as if the liability assumed by the transferee equaled such transferee's ratable portion of such liability determined on the basis of the relative fair market value . . . of all the assets subject to such liability." I.R.C. §362(d)(2)(B).

125. I.R.C. §357(b). The statute refers to the *taxpayer's* principal purpose, taking into account the nature of the liability and the circumstances. Nevertheless, the regulations require the shareholder to file a statement indicating the "*corporate* business reason for assumption by the controlled corporation." Treas. Reg. §1.351-3(a)(6) (emphasis added).

back to the example above, suppose that shareholder A's contribution to the corporation was a building that she purchased for $20,000 and was worth $200,000 at the time of contribution. As above, the purchase price was paid with $10,000 in cash and $10,000 was mortgaged. Now imagine that the shareholder took $15,000 in depreciation deductions with respect to the building before contributing the building to the corporation, thus reducing her basis in the building to $5000.[126] Upon contribution, the corporation assumes the $10,000 liability. Although the assumption of liability *ordinarily* will not be considered boot under the general rule of §357(a), §357(c) requires treating the excess of liabilities assumed over the total adjusted basis of the property transferred as "gain from the sale or exchange of a capital asset or of property which is not a capital asset, as the case may be." Under this provision, shareholder A would report a taxable gain of $5000 — the excess of the $10,000 liability assumed by the corporation over the $5000 basis of the building at the time of contribution.[127] Under §358, shareholder A's basis in the stock would be an exchanged basis from the building ($5000) decreased by the $10,000 liability assumed,[128] and increased by the amount of the gain recognized.[129] After these adjustments, shareholder A's stock basis will be zero.[130]

To better understand the logic of §357(c), recall that the general rule in §357(a) gives shareholders the benefit of nonrecognition even though gain was technically realized from the corporation's assumption of liabilities. In most cases, the §358 basis rules will be sufficient to defer this "discharge of indebtedness type" income for taxation upon the later sale or disposition of the shares. If the shareholder's basis is reduced by the full amount of the liability, subsequent gain from sale or disposition of the stock will include an additional amount reflecting the previously realized, but unrecognized, gain. Problems arise, however, when the liability is *greater* than the shareholder's basis in the property. Returning to our hypothetical, recall that shareholder A had a *realized* gain of $195,000 on the §351 exchange.[131] Absent the

---

126. I.R.C. §1016(a)(2) requires a downward adjustment to basis for depreciation on the theory that the depreciation is an advance recovery of the taxpayer's capital or investment.

127. Note that the property in this example is §1250 "recapture" property (depreciable real property). I.R.C. §1250(c). Under §1250(a), gain from the exchange would be ordinary income. Although §1250 generally applies notwithstanding other provisions, §1250(h), Congress provided an exception for certain tax-free exchanges, including §351. Under this exception, the §1250(a) gain shall not exceed the gain that would have been taken into account absent §1250. I.R.C. §1250(d)(3). In other words, shareholder A will report $5000 taxable gain under §357(c). This gain will be treated as ordinary income under §1250(a).

128. I.R.C. §358(d)(1).

129. I.R.C. §358(a)(1)(B)(ii).

130. Exchanged basis ($5000) less liability ($10,000) plus gain recognized ($5000).

131. Her $200,000 amount realized includes the fair market value of the stock

§357(c) exception, shareholder A in our example would be subject to the general rule in §357(a) and would report no gain upon transferring the building to the corporation along with the corresponding mortgage. Under §358, the stock basis would be the exchanged basis of $5000 from the building reduced by the liability of $10,000, resulting in a basis of –$5000 — a *negative* basis. At least in theory, shareholder A could be left with a negative basis in the shares.[132] Upon later sale of the stock for $190,000, the shareholder simply would report a $195,000 taxable gain.[133]

Despite this theoretical possibility, Congress, the Treasury Department, and most courts remain unwilling to embrace the notion of a negative basis.[134] Recognizing this "hang-up" over negative basis helps to explain the need for §357(c). Without negative basis, the §358 basis rules cannot preserve all of A's discharge of indebtedness type gain for later taxation. Since her basis in the building is only $5000, but her relief from liability is $10,000, the best that can be achieved is a reduction in basis to zero, thus preserving only part of the realized, but unrecognized, gain from the corporation's assumption of liabilities. The legislative solution to this dilemma adopted by §357(c) is to force shareholder A to recognize $5000 of the realized gain (the excess of liabilities over basis) at the time of her transfer to the corporation. Now we need not be concerned that her basis in the stock will be zero and that her gain on subsequent sale of the shares for $190,000 will be limited to $190,000. The other $5000 in gain was already taxed at the time of the incorporation transfer, for a total taxable gain of the proper $195,000.

c) Avoiding the §357(c) "Trap"

A contributing shareholder faced with the possibility of a §357(c) gain may wish to avoid tax upon the excess of liabilities over basis in one of two basic ways: 1) decrease the liabilities assumed by the corporation, or 2) increase the basis of assets transferred. The most direct and obvious way to achieve

---

($190,000) plus the relief from liability ($10,000). Subtracting her basis of $5000 leaves a gain of $195,000. Note that her realized gain in this example is $15,000 higher than in previous examples. In effect, this additional gain is a recapture of the $15,000 taken in prior depreciation deductions.

132. For a discussion of the theoretical possibilities, see George Cooper, Negative Basis, 75 Harv. L. Rev. 1352 (1962); J. Clifton Fleming, Jr., The Highly Unavoidable Section 357(c): A Case Study in Traps for the Unwary and Some Positive Thoughts About Negative Basis, 16 J. Corp. Tax 1 (1990). See also Judge Kozinski's colorful discussion of negative basis in Peracchi v. Comm'r, 143 F.3d 487, 491 (9th Cir. 1998) ("But skeptics say that negative basis, like Bigfoot, doesn't exist.").

133. Amount realized ($190,000) less adjusted basis (–$5000).

134. But see Easson v. Comm'r, 294 F.2d 653 (9th Cir. 1961); Parker v. Delaney, 186 F.2d 455 (1st Cir. 1950) (concurring opinion of Judge Magruder), *cert. denied,* 341 U.S. 926 (1951).

either of these results, however, requires the commitment of additional resources. Surely, the contributing shareholder may pay off some or all of the liabilities prior to transferring assets to the corporation. In the alternative, the contributing shareholder may invest additional resources in the corporation, thus increasing the basis of property transferred. For example, the shareholder might simply increase the basis of the assets transferred to the corporation by contributing additional cash to cover the difference between the liabilities assumed and the basis in the property contributed.[135] Shareholders unwilling or unable to invest additional resources of their own might first borrow the necessary cash from a third-party lender and then transfer the cash to the corporation along with the other property subject to liabilities.[136] This option not only avoids §357(c) by increasing the basis in the assets transferred, but also may produce interest deductions on the borrowing.

Another approach recently attempted by several taxpayers is for the contributing shareholder to issue a promissory note to the corporation covering the difference between liabilities assumed and basis of the transferred assets. This option is not very different from borrowing cash and then contributing the cash to the corporation. The shareholder simply is borrowing from the corporation itself rather than a third-party lender. As long as the shareholder's promissory note is a bona fide debt to the corporation, the source of the borrowing arguably should not alter the outcome. In each case, the shareholder is making a contribution with borrowed funds. The economic effect of the transactions is the same. The arguable problem with this approach is that the statute itself does not support it. Based upon the traditional tax wisdom that the maker does not have a basis in his own note, the Internal Revenue Service takes the position that contribution of the shareholder's own note does not increase the basis of the assets transferred and, thus, is ineffective in avoiding §357(c) gain.[137]

Until recently, most courts addressing the issue had agreed with the Service.[138] Two recent controversial opinions have reached a different result. In a case before the Second Circuit, Lessinger v. Commissioner, the taxpayer incorporated a business previously operated as a sole proprietorship. The liabilities transferred exceeded the basis of the property transferred by approximately $250,000, resulting in a potential §357(c) gain. In fact, the liabilities transferred exceeded even the fair market value of the assets transferred. In other words, the business had a negative net worth at the time of incorporation.[139]

---

135. For purposes of §357(c), cash contributed is treated as having a basis equal to the cash amount.

136. See, e.g., Edwards v. Comm'r, 19 T.C. 275 (1952), acq. 1953-1 C.B. 4.

137. See, e.g., Rev. Rul. 68-629, 1968-2 C.B. 154.

138. See, e.g., Alderman v. Comm'r, 55 T.C. 662 (1971).

139 Lessinger v. Comm'r, 872 F.2d 519 (2d Cir. 1989).

In addition to the other assets and liabilities transferred, Mr. Lessinger undertook an obligation to the corporation for the $250,000 difference between liabilities and basis.[140] Mr. Lessinger argued that his obligation was additional "property" transferred to the corporation in return for stock and that this additional property had a basis equal to the $250,000 face value of the note. The effect of including this additional basis in the overall basis of the assets transferred was to eliminate the §357(c) gain, since the liabilities assumed no longer exceeded the basis of the assets transferred.

The obvious problem with this logic is that a taxpayer ordinarily has no basis in his *own* obligation to pay. Even if the obligation is considered "property" for purposes of §351, transfer of the obligation does not alter the §357(c) computation if the obligation has a zero basis. The Second Circuit in *Lessinger* conceded that the note had a zero basis in Mr. Lessinger's hands. On the other hand, the court found that the note in the *corporation's* hands had a basis equal to its face amount.[141] Moreover, the Second Circuit concluded that, at least in the situation presented, §357(c)'s reference to liability in excess of basis is a reference to the *transferee corporation's* basis in the obligation.[142] The combined effect of these two unusual holdings was that Mr. Lessinger's obligation was found to be effective in increasing the basis of the assets transferred for purposes of §357(c), thus eliminating any gain from the excess of liabilities over the basis of the transferred property.

It is easy to understand the court's sympathy for Mr. Lessinger. In an *economic* sense, he did not realize any gain from incorporating a sole proprietorship with a negative net worth. Moreover, Mr. Lessinger could have avoided §357(c) gain by borrowing cash from a third party and then contributing the cash. The only difference between the cash and the note transactions is that in the latter case, the taxpayer is borrowing from the corporation rather than a third party.[143] Finally, the court did not see this as a case of deliberate tax evasion. In fact, Mr. Lessinger incorporated his business only when his lender refused to provide additional working capital to him as a sole proprietor because state usury laws allowed the lender to

---

140. The original obligation was not in the form of a promissory note and both the shareholder's and the corporation's record keeping were somewhat sloppy. The shareholder later executed a promissory note for the debt. Despite the initial informalities and the failure to pay interest on the note, the court concluded that the obligation was a real debt. *Id.* at 524.

141. The court finds that "the corporation should have a basis in its obligation from Lessinger, because it incurred a cost in the transaction involving the transfer of the obligation by taking on the liabilities of the proprietorship that exceeded its assets, and because it would have to recognize income upon Lessinger's payment of the debt if it had no basis in the obligation." *Id.* at 525.

142. *Id.* at 526.

143. The court explicitly noted the similarity of the two transactions and expressed its fear that a contrary ruling would create a "trap for the unwary." *Id.* at 528.

charge higher interest rates to corporations. The court noted that if the government had prevailed in the case, it would be "the factor's demand for higher interest [that] led Lessinger into a §351 'trap.'"[144]

While most commentators seem to agree that the *result* in *Lessinger* is sensible from a policy point of view, they have been critical of the opinion.[145] Providing the corporation with a face value basis in the transferring shareholder's note is inconsistent with §362's requirement that the corporation's basis in a §351 transaction be the same as that of the transferring shareholder.[146] Moreover, §357(c)'s reference to the excess of liabilities over the "adjusted basis of the property transferred" is virtually always interpreted to mean the adjusted basis in the transferring shareholder's (not in the corporation's) hands.[147]

Despite its loss in the Second Circuit, the government continued to litigate vigorously, presumably hoping to create a split among the circuits and take the issue to the Supreme Court. Much to everyone's surprise, these efforts backfired when the Ninth Circuit issued its decision in Peracchi v. Commissioner.[148]

In response to a demand for additional capital to meet state minimum premium-to-asset ratios for his closely held corporation, Mr. Peracchi contributed real estate encumbered by liabilities in excess of his basis in the property. In an attempt to avoid the §357(c) trap, Peracchi also contributed his own unsecured personal promissory note to the corporation, arguing, as Mr. Lessinger had, that the note had a basis equal to its face amount.

The Ninth Circuit shared the *Lessinger* court's concern that the §357(c) trap could have been avoided through transactions that were economically equivalent to the contribution of a promissory note. For example, the court noted that "Peracchi could have borrowed $1 million from a bank and

---

144. 143 F.3d 487 (9th Cir. 1998).

145. Fleming, *supra* note 132; Michael Megaard and Susan Megaard, Can Shareholder's Note Avoid Gain on Transfer of Excess Liabilities?, 71 J. Tax'n. 244 (1989); Louis S. Nunes, Comment, Taking Section 357(c) Out of the Scheme of Things: Has the Second Circuit Stranded This Section of the Internal Revenue Code?, 65 Tul. L. Rev. 663 (1991). *Contra* Kenneth Brewer, The Zero Basis Hoax, 63 Tax Notes 457 (1994).

146. To get around §362, the court simply says in a footnote that §362 "cannot be applied to the corporation's valuation of its receivable from the taxpayer" because the purpose of §362 was to prevent the corporation from getting a new, stepped-up basis for depreciation purposes. 872 F.2d at 525, n.4.

147. Treas. Reg. §1.357-2(a). The court responds by noting that in most cases, the corporation takes its basis from the shareholder under §362. Here, however, the court concludes that §362 does not apply to the note. "Consideration of 'adjusted basis' in section 357(c) . . . normally does not require determining whether the section refers to the 'adjusted basis' in the hands of the transferor-shareholder or the transferee-corporation, because the basis does not change." 872 F.2d at 526.

148. 143 F.3d 487 (9th Cir. 1998).

contributed cash to [the corporation] along with the properties. Because cash has a basis equal to face value, Peracchi would not have faced any section 357(c) gain."[149] On the other hand, the Ninth Circuit was unwilling to adopt the Second Circuit's twisted and unconventional interpretation of the statutory language in §§357(c) and 362. Instead, the court rejected the traditional tax wisdom regarding a taxpayer's basis in his or her own note, finding that Mr. Peracchi *did* have a basis in his personal promissory note contributed to the corporation. To reach this conclusion, the court reasoned that the corporation's creditors could enforce Peracchi's note in the event of the corporation's bankruptcy. Since the corporation was "an operating business which is subject to a non-trivial risk of bankruptcy or receivership,"[150] the court found that Peracchi had increased his exposure to risk and was entitled to "a step-up in basis to the extent he will be subjected to economic loss if the underlying investment turns unprofitable."[151] The court was careful, however, to limit its holding to cases where the note was worth approximately its face amount.[152]

Although the *Peracchi* opinion's reasoning is superficially more appealing than that of *Lessinger,* criticism of the opinion has been similarly severe.[153] Most significant, its finding that the taxpayer had a basis in his own note is contrary to well-established precedent. While the court was careful to limit its holding to the facts of the case before it, this holding could have serious implications far beyond the §357 context.

Most agree that some solution is necessary, however. If shareholders can borrow cash from third parties to get around §357(c), they should be able to borrow from the corporation as well. Although recent changes to §357(c) were aimed at transactions involving cross-collateralized assets,[154] the amendments may have some impact on the issues raised in the *Lessinger* and *Peracchi*

---

149. *Id.* at 493.

150. *Id.* at 493, n.14.

151. *Id.* at 493.

152. Since the taxpayer's net worth far exceeded the face value of the note, the court was prepared to conclude, in this case, that Peracchi's note was worth its face value. *Id.* at 493–494, n.15.

153. The opinion itself includes an unusually vigorous dissent. *Id.* at 497 ("Peracchi says a lot about economic realities. I see nothing real about that maneuver. I see, rather, a bit of sortilege that would have made Merlin envious. The taxpayer has created something—basis—out of nothing.") See also Richard M. Lipton and Joseph E. Bender, *Peracchi* and Making Something Out of Nothing, or Does Debt Have a Zero Basis to Its Maker and Further Ruminations on the Substance and Form of Transactions, 77 Taxes 13, 20 (1999) ("One of the interesting aspects of the Ninth Circuit's decision in *Peracchi* is its total disregard for authorities . . . "); Michael M. Megaard and Susan L. Megaard, Risky Business: Can Shareholder's Own Note Truly Avoid Section 357(c) Gain?, 89 J. Tax'n 89, 72–74 (1998).

154. See earlier discussion in this chapter on multiple assets securing the same liability.

cases. The new rules provide a facts-and-circumstances test, under which recourse liabilities are considered assumed "if the transferee has agreed to, and is expected to, satisfy . . . [the] liability."[155] Thus, another way to avoid §357(c) gain when recourse liabilities exceed the transferor's basis in contributed property would be to establish that the transferee corporation is not expected to satisfy the liability. Given that this argument may not be available in many cases, an amendment designed to address the issue more directly may be necessary. Short of such an amendment to the statute, one proposed narrow solution would be to treat the shareholder in the Lessinger-type situation as having purchase-money debt owed to the corporation. Ordinarily, a buyer who borrows from the seller is deemed to first borrow cash from the seller and then to transfer the cash in exchange for the property. In this way, the buyer with purchase money debt has the same basis in the property that a buyer with a third-party mortgage would have. If the shareholder who transfers a personal note to the corporation is deemed first to have borrowed the cash and then to transfer the cash as part of the §351 exchange, the §357(c) trap is avoided without distorting the language of the statute.[156] A broader solution would be to repeal §357(c) altogether and simply have taxpayers reduce their basis in the stock by the full amount of liabilities *even if* this results in a negative basis.[157] For the moment, §357(c) continues to present messy problems for taxpayers. Congress and the courts have yet to agree on a solution.

d) Comparison of §357(b) and (c)

When the liability assumed exceeds the basis of property transferred, §357(c) provides for recognition only of the excess at the time of the transfer. In contrast, if §357(b) applies, the entire assumption of liability is treated as boot. Thus, if shareholder A contributed property with a basis of $5000 subject to a mortgage of $10,000, the §357(b) exception would result in a $10,000 gain whereas the §357(c) exception would result in only a $5000 gain at the time of incorporation. In cases involving tax avoidance or lack of bona fide business purpose, Congress imposes the harsher provision, requiring that the *entire* assumption of liability be considered boot. In other cases, Congress imposes tax only to the extent necessary to avoid the sticky negative basis problem and, at the same time, to assure that the entire realized gain at the time of the transfer is deferred through use of the substituted basis

---

155. I.R.C. §357(d)(1)(A).

156. J. Clifton Fleming, Jr., A Second Look at the Zero Basis Hoax, 64 Tax Notes 811 (1994).

157. See Fleming, *supra* note 132.

provisions in §358. In situations where both exceptions apply to the transaction, the harsher rule of §357(b) will prevail.[158]

e) Special Rules Applicable to Accounts Payable: §357(c)(3)

When a business previously operated in sole proprietor, partnership, or other noncorporate form later incorporates, the newly formed corporation may assume the business accounts payable for goods and services purchased prior to incorporation. To treat such accounts payable as liabilities for purposes of §357(c) would create hardships for some taxpayers. To illustrate, suppose that shareholder B decides to incorporate his business, transferring assets with a basis of $50,000 and a fair market value of $150,000 to a new solely owned corporation. The new corporation also assumes business accounts payable totaling $200,000.[159] Assume further that B's business was using the cash basis method of accounting. If the accounts payable were considered liabilities for purposes of §357(c), shareholder B would have a $150,000 gain — the excess of the $200,000 in liabilities over the $50,000 basis in the property contributed. If shareholder B had paid the accounts before incorporating, he could have taken a business expense deduction. As a cash basis taxpayer, however, he cannot take business deductions for payables that have not yet been paid, nor will transfer of the accounts payable to the corporation trigger a business deduction for shareholder B. Absent some statutory relief, the taxpayer in this case would have §357(c) gain resulting from the corporation's assumption of the accounts payable, but no offsetting deduction for the business expense.

Responding to this hardship, Congress added §357(c)(3)(A), which provides that liabilities that would give rise to a deduction will not be considered liabilities for purposes of §357(c)(1). Thus, in the above example, shareholder B would not take any business deductions for the $200,000 in accounts payable not yet paid, the payables would not be counted as liabilities, and shareholder B would have no gain or loss from the incorporation transaction.[160] The *corporation* now should be entitled to deduct its payments on the accounts payable.[161]

Notice that the hardship to which Congress responded with §357(c)(3) generally is not a concern with accrual basis taxpayers. If shareholder B's

---

158. Treas. Reg. §1.357-2(a).

159. Assume that these payables included salaries due employees and other payables for which a business expense deduction would be available.

160. The assumption of such accounts payable will not cause a reduction in the contributing shareholder's basis under §358 either. I.R.C. §358(d)(2).

161. See Rev. Rul. 80-198, 1980-2 C.B. 113.

business had used the accrual method of accounting, a business deduction would have been taken at the time the accounts payable were accrued, presumably prior to incorporation. As an accrual basis taxpayer, shareholder B would have a $200,000 basis in the accounts payable. Adding this to the $50,000 basis from the other assets, his overall basis of $250,000 in the assets transferred would exceed the assumed liabilities of $200,000. He would no longer have to worry about §357(c) gain.

Section §357(c)(3)(B) deals with the case of a liability, such as the accrual basis taxpayer's accounts payable in the above example, that results "in the creation of, or an increase in, the basis of any property." So, for example, payables incurred in connection with the purchase of, and reflected in the basis of, depreciable property will not be protected by the §357(c)(3) exception. If incurrence of a liability has created or increased basis, the hardship addressed in §357(c)(3) is not present. Hence, the exception to the exception in §357(c)(3)(B). Despite §357(c)(3)(A), "basis producing liabilities" still are considered liabilities for purposes of §357(c).

One potential hardship circumstance seems to have slipped through the cracks between §357(c)(3)(A) and (B), however. Even an accrual basis taxpayer may have *contingent* liabilities that do not necessarily "give rise to a deduction" under §357(c)(3)(A), nor have they yet created a basis under §357(c)(3)(B). The Treasury Department recently addressed just such a case involving a transfer of contingent environmental liabilities for potential soil and ground water remediation as part of a §351 exchange.[162] The Service concluded that "[w]hile §357(c)(3) explicitly addresses liabilities that give rise to deductible items, the same principle applies to liabilities that give rise to capital expenditures as well."[163] The corporate transferor had not taken any deduction with respect to the contingent liabilities, nor had the liabilities resulted in the creation of basis. The Service determined that such liabilities should not be counted in determining whether liabilities exceed basis pursuant to §357(c).

The Corporation's Transfer of Its Own Stock— Special Issues Under §351

A corporate transferor may transfer its *own* stock to a newly formed or existing subsidiary in return for subsidiary stock under §351.[164] As noted earlier, the transferor corporation's stock is considered property for purposes

---

162. Rev. Rul. 95-74, 1995-2 C.B. 36.

163. *Id.* at 37.

164. If a corporate parent contributes 80% or more of its own stock to its subsidiary in a §351 exchange, the subsidiary effectively becomes the parent and the parent becomes the subsidiary. This role reversal, referred to in the trade as a "corporate inversion," raises a number of complex tax issues, which will be considered in subsequent chapters.

of §351. Nonrecognition treatment is available under §351 as long as the transferor corporation has control immediately after the exchange. In measuring such control immediately after the exchange, the Code specifically provides that "the fact that any corporate transferor distributes part or all of the stock which it receives in the exchange to its shareholders shall not be taken into account."[165] Thus, the transferor corporation may distribute the subsidiary stock to its shareholders, maintaining only brief direct control. This subsequent distribution of subsidiary stock to the parent corporation's shareholders may be eligible for nonrecognition as a tax-free corporate division.[166]

A related issue upon a parent corporation's creation of a subsidiary is the subsidiary corporation's basis in the parent stock. Under §362, the subsidiary's basis will be the same as it would be in the hands of the transferor corporation, increased in the amount of any gain recognized by the transferor. Since a corporation has a zero basis in its newly issued stock or reissued treasury stock,[167] the subsidiary takes the parent's stock with a zero basis.

One might expect the parent corporation's basis in its subsidiary's stock to be governed by the §358 basis rules for stock received by a contributing shareholder in a §351 exchange. When the transferor is a corporation exchanging its *own* stock or securities, however, the §358 rules do not apply.[168] Instead, regulations under §1032 require the corporate transferor to use §362 to determine its basis.[169] Thus, the parent corporation also will have a zero basis in its subsidiary's stock.

Commentators have criticized the "zero basis" rule suggesting that "[t]he concern with the zero basis result is that the parent that contributes its stock to a subsidiary appears improperly to have been denied its statutory right to issue its stock without recognition, because the subsidiary may recognize gain when it later disposes of the zero basis parent stock."[170]

New regulations offer limited relief to subsidiaries confronted with this "zero basis" problem upon acquiring money or property in exchange for parent corporation stock. For example, imagine that a parent corporation (P) issues additional shares of its stock to its subsidiary (S) in order to enable the subsidiary to acquire a truck from a third party. In accordance with the plan, S immediately exchanges the recently issued P stock for the truck. Without special relief, S would recognize gain to the extent that the fair market value of the truck received exceeded S's zero basis in the P stock.

---

165. I.R.C. §351(c).

166. For a detailed discussion of §351(c), divisive reorganizations, and other tax-free corporate divisions, see Chapter 14.

167. Rev. Rul. 74-503, 1974-2 C.B. 117.

168. I.R.C. §358(e).

169. Treas. Reg. §1.1032-1(d).

170. Jasper L. Cummings, Jr., The Silent Policies of Conservation and Cloning of Tax Basis and the Corporate Applications, 48 Tax L. Rev. 113, 133 (1992).

Under limited conditions, the new regulations treat the transaction as if, immediately before the exchange of P stock for the truck, S *purchased* P's stock from P for fair market value with cash contributed to S by P.[171] The effect of this deemed purchase is to provide S with a fair market value basis, as opposed to a zero basis, in the P shares. Assuming an immediate arm's-length exchange of the P stock for the truck, there should be no taxable gain to S upon the exchange. In addition to a plan to acquire money or other property, eligibility for such special treatment requires that 1) S *immediately* transfer the P stock in exchange for money or property from someone other than P; 2) S acquire the P stock in a transaction in which, but for the special rule, S would have a §362 basis in the P stock; 3) the party receiving the P stock not get a substituted basis (i.e., the transaction must be taxable to the third party); and 4) the P stock not be exchanged for other P stock.[172]

EXAMPLES

The following questions apply the materials just discussed and add some nuances and details not specifically considered.

An Easy Question

1.   Viola and Sebastian agree to form Sail Away, Inc., a small family boat rental business. Viola contributes 20 sailboats purchased for $70,000 but worth $170,000 at the time of incorporation. Sebastian contributes a small piece of waterfront property and a dock purchased many years ago for $30,000, with a fair market value of $150,000, plus cash of $20,000. In return for the contributions, each receives 50% of the 200 authorized common shares of Sail Away stock. Tax consequences to Viola? To Sebastian? To Sail Away, Inc.?

Variations on a Theme From Question 1

2a. What result if Viola's sailboats were originally purchased for $180,000?

2b. What result if Viola received 75% of the stock and Sebastian 25%?

2c. What result if Sebastian's contribution consisted of services worth $70,000 and property worth $100,000 (basis still $30,000)? What if he contributed only services valued at $170,000?

2d. What result if Viola made her contribution in exchange for $160,000 worth of stock plus a Sail Away security valued at $10,000? How would your answer change if Viola's basis in the property contributed had been $180,000?

---

171. Treas. Reg. §1.1032–3(b), (e)(1), ex. 1.
172. Treas. Reg. §1.1032–3(c).

2e. What if Sebastian later makes an additional contribution of $20,000 cash and receives no additional shares? Would your answer be different if he contributes property worth $20,000 (basis $5000)? What if he receives some additional shares for the subsequent contribution?

Transfer of Control

3. Antonio incorporated his shipping business by contributing all of his ships and their cargo to a newly formed corporation in return for 100% of the stock. At the time of incorporation, Antonio committed himself to transferring 25% of the stock to his good friend Bassanio in order to help him with some financial problems. What tax consequence to Antonio and the newly formed corporation? Would your answer be different if Antonio had not come up with the idea to help his friend by this transfer of stock until after he had already incorporated the business?

The Publicly Held Setting

4. Sir Falstaff has decided to incorporate a publishing business and needs to raise capital through sales of stock to the public. He arranges for Falstaff's, Inc. to have two classes of stock: Class A common and Class B 6% nonvoting preferred. The articles of incorporation authorized 1000 shares of Class A common and 5000 shares of Class B preferred. The preferred shares are to be sold to the public for cash. Falstaff incorporates by transferring a printing press and other assets to the corporation in return for 75% of the common stock. His friend Nym contributes additional capital in return for 25% of the Class A common shares. Together, they approach an underwriter who agrees to sell 4500 Class B preferred shares to the public. If successful, the underwriter is to receive the remaining 500 Class B preferred shares. What tax consequences to Falstaff, Nym, the corporation, the underwriter, and the public if the underwriter is successful?

Return of Boot

5. Oberon and Puck agree to establish Oberon Spirits, Inc. (OSI), to manufacture and sell fine wines and spirits. At the time of incorporation, two classes of stock are authorized: 1) voting common stock; and 2) 6% nonvoting preferred stock with a redemption feature mandating redemption of the shares at a specified premium 10 years from the date of issue. Oberon contributes land for a winery with a basis of $75,000 and a fair market value of $500,000. Puck contributes a wine cellar already filled with fine wines he has collected over the years. Puck's basis for the wines and the cellar was $20,000, and its fair market value at the time of contribution was $500,000. In return for his contribution, Oberon receives 100 shares of common stock.

Puck, on the other hand, receives only 50 shares of common stock valued at $250,000 and OSI securities bearing 8% interest and payable over 10 years, also valued at $250,000.

5a. What tax consequence to Oberon, Puck and the corporation?

5b. What if, instead of the OSI securities, Puck received OSI 6% nonvoting preferred stock valued at $250,000?

5c. What if Puck received *only* OSI 6% nonvoting preferred stock valued at $500,000 in exchange for his contribution?

5d. What if Puck's basis for the wine cellar and wines had been $450,000?

Problems with Boot, Liabilities, and Other Twists

6a. Prospero and his daughter Miranda decide to establish a corporation to sell island real estate. Prospero has been collecting real estate over the years. He has one parcel with a basis of $30,000 and a fair market of $100,000, and another parcel has a basis of $170,000 and a fair market value of $100,000. Prospero has held parcel one for six months and parcel two for five years. Prospero contributes the two parcels in return for 80% of the stock (worth $190,000) plus $10,000 cash boot. Miranda contributes only one parcel with a basis of $70,000, a fair market value of $90,000, to the corporation in return for 20% of the stock. The corporation takes Miranda's property subject to a mortgage of $40,000. What tax consequence to Prospero, Miranda, and the corporation?

6b. What result if Miranda's parcel was subject to a mortgage in the amount of $80,000?

6c. How might your answer to 6b. change if Miranda had taken out the $80,000 mortgage against her property just one week prior to contributing the property as part of the incorporation exchange, using the $80,000 to pay off her personal debts?

7. Assume that Prospero had been operating a real-estate business as a sole proprietor prior to incorporation. At the time of incorporation, he had already contracted for the sale of the land parcel with a basis of $30,000 and a fair market value of $100,000, but had not yet received payment. He contributes the sale contract to a new corporation in exchange for all of the corporation's stock. In addition, the corporation assumes $150,000 in accounts payable previously incurred by the proprietorship for salaries and other business expenses. What tax consequence to Prospero and the corporation?

EXPLANATIONS

1. Viola has contributed property to the corporation, solely in exchange for stock, and immediately after the exchange, she and Sebastian together control 100% of the stock of the corporation. Thus, Viola will qualify for

nonrecognition under §351. Presumably, the value of her 50% stock interest is equal to 50% of the value of the corporation's assets — $170,000. Her $100,000 realized gain ($170,000 amount realized less $70,000 basis in the sailboats) will not be recognized. Viola's basis in her 100 shares of Sail Away stock will be an exchanged basis of $70,000 under §358. Should she later sell the stock for $170,000, she will recognize a $100,000 gain at that time. Note that her stock is a capital asset, the sale of which will result in capital gain or loss. The sailboats Viola contributed were presumably *not* capital assets, however. Thus, she will not be able to tack the period during which she owned the boats onto the stock holding period under §1223(1). If Viola sells the stock within the first year, her gain will be short-term capital gain. If she waits more than one year before selling the shares, her gain will be long-term capital gain from the sale of stock.

Sebastian also has met the requirements of §351. Sebastian's 50% stock interest presumably is also worth $170,000. He effectively purchased $20,000 worth of stock for cash and received the remaining $150,000 worth of stock in exchange for property. His $120,000 realized gain from transfer of the waterfront property ($150,000 amount realized less $30,000 basis in the property) will not be recognized. Sebastian's basis in the stock will include his exchanged basis of $30,000 from the property plus the $20,000 cash contributed for a total of $50,000. Should he later sell the stock for $170,000, he will recognize a capital gain of $120,000. Assuming Sebastian's property was a capital asset, he will be entitled to tack on the period for which he held the property under §1223(1). Thus, even if Sebastian sells his shares the day after incorporation, his gain will be long-term capital gain.

Sail Away, Inc. will have no gain from the receipt of the sailboats, the waterfront property, or the cash under §1032. Its basis in the boats under §362 will be a transferred basis from Viola of $70,000. Since these are not capital assets, any gain from the sale of these boats would result in ordinary income. As for the waterfront property, it will have a transferred basis from Sebastian of $30,000. If the property is considered a capital asset in Sail Away's hands, any gain from sale of the property will be capital gain. Moreover, Sail Away will be entitled to tack on the period during which Sebastian owned the land so that the gain will be long-term capital gain even if the property is sold within the first year. I.R.C. §1223(2).

2a. If Viola's sailboats originally had been purchased for $180,000, but were worth only $170,000 at the time of contribution, she would have realized a *loss* of $10,000 upon the exchange. Notice that §351 nonrecognition is not elective and applies to both gains and losses. Thus, Viola will *not* be able to recognize the loss. Her basis in the stock will be an exchanged basis of $180,000 from the sailboats contributed. Should she later sell her shares for $170,000, she will recognize the $10,000 loss at that time. If Viola wanted to recognize her loss immediately, she should have sold the boats to a third party and contributed cash to the corporation. Sail Away's basis in the boats under §362 would now be $180,000.

2b. If Viola received 75% of the stock and Sebastian only 25% in return for equal contributions from each of $170,000, it would be important to know *why* Viola received a disproportionately greater share of stock than she would otherwise be entitled to. If Sebastian agreed to allow her the extra shares simply out of "detached and disinterested generosity," the transaction will be viewed in two steps. It will be assumed that the stock first was received in proportion to the relative contributions from each and then that Sebastian made a gift to Viola. Thus, Sebastian will be viewed as first receiving 50% of the stock with a basis of $50,000 ($30,000 exchanged basis from the property plus $20,000 cash). He next will be viewed as transferring half of his stock (25% of the total shares) to Viola as a gift. The receipt of the gift will be tax-free to Viola under §102. Her basis in the gift shares will be $25,000 under §1015.[173] Thus, Viola's basis for her full 75% will now be $95,000 (her $70,000 exchanged basis from the property contributed plus $25,000 §1015 basis in the gift shares). Sebastian may be required to pay a gift tax on the transfer of the shares to Viola under §2501. After the gift, Sebastian's basis in his remaining stock will be $25,000.

If Sebastian agreed to allow Viola to take the extra 25% because Viola had worked for several years in Sebastian's real-estate firm without any salary and was due $85,000 in back pay, the transaction still would first be viewed as if each received 50% of the stock worth $170,000. Sebastian would then be viewed as transferring half ($85,000 worth) to Viola as compensation. Viola will report the $85,000 as taxable compensation income. Her basis in the 75% will include her exchanged basis of $70,000 plus a tax cost basis of $85,000 for a total of $155,000. Sebastian, on the other hand, will be left with a basis of $25,000 in his remaining shares and will be entitled to a business expense deduction for salary paid to Viola, assuming that his business was on a cash basis and he had not previously deducted the expense.

2c. If Sebastian contributed services worth $70,000 and property worth $100,000 in exchange for $170,000 worth of stock, he effectively is receiving $70,000 worth of stock as compensation for services and $100,000 worth of stock in exchange for property. He should report $70,000 as ordinary compensation income. The $70,000 realized gain from the property contribution ($100,000 amount realized less $30,000 basis in the property) will not be recognized. Sebastian's basis in the stock will include an exchanged basis of $30,000 from the property *plus* a cost basis of $70,000 from the stock received for services totaling $100,000. Note that even though *part* of Sebastian's contribution was in the form of services, his full 50% can be counted for purposes of the control tests since he also contributed property.

---

173. Since she received half of Sebastian's shares, she will take half of his basis.

Thus, Viola and Sebastian together will still satisfy the §368(c) control tests. Sail Away would be entitled to a $70,000 ordinary and necessary business expense deduction under §162 for compensation paid.

If Sebastian made his entire contribution in the form of services worth $170,000, he would be required to report $170,000 in ordinary compensation income and would hold the stock with a $170,000 basis. Moreover, since he contributed no property, his 50% share would not be counted toward meeting the control test. By itself, Viola's 50% interest does not meet the control test, making her ineligible for §351 nonrecognition. Viola now must report her $100,000 gain ($170,000 amount realized less $70,000 basis in the sailboats) from the exchange of property for stock. Her basis in the stock now will be a $100,000 "cost" or fair market value basis. Sail Away would be entitled to a $170,000 ordinary and necessary business expense deduction under §162 for compensation paid.

2d. The additional $10,000 in Sail Away securities will be treated as boot to Viola. Of her $100,000 realized gain from the §351 exchange ($170,000 amount realized from stock and securities received less $70,000 basis in the sailboats), she will recognize gain only to the extent of the $10,000 boot. I.R.C. §351(b)(1). Assuming that the sailboats were not capital assets, her gain will be ordinary income. To compute her basis in the stock, Viola will start with a §358 exchanged basis of $70,000, decreased by the $10,000 fair market value of the boot securities and increased by the $10,000 gain. I.R.C. §358(a)(1)(A)(i), (B)(ii). Thus, her basis in the shares will remain at $70,000. Her basis in the Sail Away securities will be the $10,000 fair market value. I.R.C. §358(a)(2). Sail Away's basis in the sailboats under §362 would be $80,000 ($70,000 transferred basis increased by the $10,000 gain recognized by Viola).

If Viola's basis in the contributed property had been $180,000, she would have a realized loss of $10,000. Under §351(b)(2), however, she will not be entitled to recognize this loss. Under §358, her $180,000 exchanged basis in the stock would be decreased by the $10,000 fair market value of the boot securities received, leaving her with a basis of $170,000. If she later sells hers shares for $160,000, she will recognize the $10,000 loss at that time. Sail Away's basis in the sailboats under §362 would be a transferred basis of $180,000. Sail Away would not report any gain upon receipt of the cash pursuant to §118.

2e. If Sebastian later makes an additional cash contribution without receiving any additional shares of stock, he simply has made a cash contribution to capital and will be entitled to increase the basis in his stock to reflect the additional $20,000 payment. Treas. Reg. §1.118-1. Thus, his total basis for the shares now will be $70,000.

Sebastian's contribution of property worth $20,000 (basis $5000) for no additional shares should also be viewed as an additional contribution to capital. Section §351 is not invoked here since this was not an exchange of property for stock. One issue here is whether or not Sebastian must recognize a gain of $15,000 from disposition of this appreciated property. Unless the transfer of property is being used in payment of an assessment, at least one commentator assumes that the realized gain will not be taxed. Boris I. Bittker and James S. Eustice, Federal Income Taxation of Corporations and Shareholders ¶3.13 (7th ed. 2000). Assuming that Sebastian is not taxed on the transfer, he should increase his basis in the stock by the $5000 basis (rather than the fair market value) of the property contributed. Sail Away's basis in the property under §362(a)(2) would be $5000.

If Sebastian received additional shares in return for his subsequent contribution of property, the transaction would be tested under §351. Sebastian now has contributed property solely in exchange for stock. Unless Sebastian alone meets the 80% control tests immediately after this transfer, he will not be eligible for nonrecognition. He should try to convince Viola to make more than a nominal contribution at the same time.

3.   Given Antonio's binding commitment, the transaction may be viewed as an "integrated transaction," which is not complete until after Antonio transfers the 25% interest to Bassanio. Thus, Antonio would be viewed as controlling only 75% of the stock and so would not have the requisite 80% control immediately after the exchange. Since his friend Bassanio contributed no property to the corporation, his 25% would not be counted toward meeting the control test. Antonio would be required to recognize any gain or loss from his contribution. If Antonio had not come up with the idea to transfer the shares until after incorporation, the transaction presumably would not be treated as an integrated transaction. Since the initial §351 exchange and the subsequent transfer are separate tax events, Antonio would have the requisite 80% control "immediately after the exchange."[174]

4.   In order to qualify for nonrecognition treatment, the person or persons contributing property must have control immediately after the exchange. To meet this requirement, the group must have 80% of the total combined voting power. Falstaff and Nym together meet this requirement since only the common shares have voting rights. The question here involves the second part of the control test. Under §368(c) the transferor group must also have 80% of the total number of shares of all other classes of stock. Thus, to qualify for §351 nonrecognition, the transferor group must show that it controls more than 80% (4000) of the total 5000 nonvoting preferred shares immediately after the exchange. To meet the tests of control *immediately after the*

---

174. The Treasury Department's recent change of position regarding the effect of post-reorganization transfers on continuity of interest may signal that the government will rethink its position on post-incorporation transfers as well. For a detailed discussion of these new regulations, see Chapter 11.

exchange, Treasury regulations indicate that the contributions of property in exchange for stock test need not be simultaneous, but the rights of the parties must be previously defined and the execution of the agreement must proceed with an expedition consistent with orderly procedure. Treas. Reg. §1.351-1(a)(1). Since the underwriter in a best efforts underwriting is acting merely as agent on behalf of the corporation, the underwriter is not considered part of the control group. On the other hand, the shares sold to the public will be counted toward meeting the control tests as long as the underwriting plan has proceeded expeditiously. The public is viewed as transferring cash directly to the corporation in return for stock and, therefore, is included in the control group along with Falstaff and Nym. See Treas. Reg. §1.351-1(a)(3). The group now has 100% of the voting stock and 90% (4500 out of 5000) of the total number of all other classes of stock. Consequently, Falstaff and Nym are eligible for §351 nonrecognition upon their transfers of property in exchange for stock. The corporation is eligible for nonrecognition upon the receipt of property and cash under §1032. Its basis in contributed property is determined under §362. The underwriter must report ordinary compensation income upon receipt of the 500 Class B preferred shares. The public simply has contributed cash in exchange for stock. The public's basis in the shares will be equal to the cash contributed.

5a. Oberon's realized gain of $425,000 ($500,000 amount realized less $75,000 basis in winery) will not be recognized. His stock will take a §358 exchanged basis of $75,000 from the winery property contributed. Of Puck's $480,000 realized gain ($500,000 amount realized less $20,000 basis in wines and cellar), he will recognize gain under §351(b)(1) to the extent of the $250,000 boot received in the form of OSI securities.[175] Puck's common stock basis under §358 will be his $20,000 exchanged basis decreased by the $250,000 boot and then increased by the $250,000 gain recognized, leaving him still with a basis of $20,000 in the stock. His basis in the OSI securities will be fair maket value ($250,000) pursuant to §358(a)(2). OSI will report no gain or loss upon receipt of the land, wine cellar, and wines under §1032. Its basis in the land will be a transferred basis of $75,000 under §362. Its basis in the wine cellar and wines under §362 will be $270,000 (a transferred basis of $20,000 increased by the $250,000 gain recognized by Puck).

5b. Since the 6% OSI nonvoting preferred stock received by Puck is subject to a mandatory redemption clause within less than 20 years from the date of issue, the stock will be classified as "nonqualified preferred stock" under new §351(g)(2)(A)(ii). As a result, the preferred stock will be treated as boot pursuant to new §351(g)(1). Again, of his $480,000 realized gain, Puck will

---

175. Under regulations proposed by the Treasury Department, Puck would be entitled to report boot gain from the 10-year debt instrument under the installment method. Prop. Treas. Reg. §1.453-1(f)(3).

recognize "boot gain" to the extent of the $250,000 boot received in the form of OSI nonqualified preferred stock. Puck's common stock basis under §358 will be the same as it was in the answer to question 5a. His basis in the preferred stock will be fair market value ($250,000) pursuant to §358(a)(2). OSI's basis in the wine cellar and wines would still be $270,000, as above.

5c. If Puck received *only* OSI 6% nonvoting preferred stock in exchange for his contribution, Puck will not be eligible for §351(a) nonrecognition, since he will have received *only* boot in exchange for his contribution. In this case, Puck received $500,000 worth of boot. Under §351(b), Puck must report gain, if any, to the extent of the boot received. Thus, Puck will report his entire $480,000 realized gain. Since Puck's preferred shares are considered "other property," the basis of these shares will be fair market value ($500,000) under §358(a)(2). This fair market value basis makes sense since Puck has now been fully taxed with respect to the appreciated value of the wine cellar contributed to the corporation.

One remaining concern is whether Oberon remains eligible for §351(a) nonrecognition. Recall that §§351(a) and 368(c) require the transferors to have *both* 80% of the total combined voting power *and* 80% of the total number of shares of all other classes of stock immediately after the exchange. If Puck's nonvoting preferred shares cannot be counted for purposes of the control test, Oberon's eligibility for nonrecognition is threatened. For the moment, the Conference Report for the Taxpayer Relief Act of 1997 clarifies that the preferred stock *will* be considered stock for purposes of §§351(a) and 368(c). H.R. Rep. 105-220 at 561 (1997). Thus, the control test is met and Oberon should remain eligible for §351(a) nonrecognition on the winery contribution in exchange for common stock. OSI will have a $150,000 basis in the wine cellar and wines.

5d. If Puck's basis in the wines and cellar had been $450,000, his realized gain upon the contribution would have been only $50,000 ($500,000 amount realized less $450,000 basis in contributed property). Although he received $250,000 boot, he can be taxed only to the extent of his $50,000 gain. Puck's stock basis under §358 will be his $450,000 exchanged basis decreased by the $250,000 boot and increased in the amount of the $50,000 gain, leaving him with a basis of $250,000 in the OSI stock. Notice that his basis in the boot now is equal to its fair market value of $250,000. Since he has already been taxed upon the full realized gain, there should be no further taxable gain upon a sale of the boot for $250,000. OSI's basis in the wine cellar and wines under §362 will be $500,000 (a transferred basis of $450,000 increased by the $50,000 gain recognized by Puck).

6a. The tax consequences to Prospero are a bit tricky in this problem. Note that Prospero has made an overall contribution of property worth $200,000 and that the overall basis in the property contributed was $200,000. Taking these two contributions together, it would appear that there is no realized gain or loss. Although Prospero has received $10,000 in boot, he will argue that there is no taxable gain from the boot since no gain was realized. Remember, however, that §351(b)(2) specifies that no loss shall be allowed in §351 transactions even where boot is paid by the corporation. To accept Prospero's argument here would be to allow his $70,000 loss from the second parcel to offset the $70,000 gain from the first parcel, thus allowing him a loss. Rev. Rul. 68-55 addresses this problem by requiring an asset-by-asset approach in such cases. An allocation must be made based upon the fair market value of each asset. Since the two parcels were of equal value, each represents 50% of the total property contributed. Thus, 50% of the boot ($5000) will be deemed to have been received for the first parcel and 50% (the remaining $5000) for the second parcel. The realized gain on the first parcel was $70,000. Of this gain, $5000 will be recognized as boot gain. As for parcel two, no loss will be recognized despite the receipt of $5000 boot attributable to it pursuant to §351(b)(2).

The appropriate character of Prospero's boot gain raises some interesting questions. Notice that parcel one was a capital asset held for only six months, while parcel two was a capital asset held for five years. Example 1, included in Treas. Reg. §357–2(b), seems to suggest that since half of the assets contributed, by reference to fair market value, were short term and the other half were long term, half of the boot gain should be short-term capital gain and the other half should be long-term capital gain. This result would not make sense as applied to Prospero. Only parcel one had any realized gain at all. In Prospero's case, the most sensible result would be to attribute the boot gain entirely to parcel one, resulting in $5000 of short-term capital gain.

Prospero's stock basis will be an overall exchanged basis of $200,000 from the two properties contributed decreased by the $10,000 cash boot and increased by the $5000 taxable gain, leaving him with a $195,000 stock basis. Should he later sell the shares for $190,000, he will recognize a $5000 loss. This later loss will offset the $5000 gain recognized at the time of incorporation. In the end, his overall net gain or loss from both transfers is zero.

Miranda's contribution of property with a basis of $70,000, fair market value of $90,000, and subject to a mortgage of $40,000 results in a realized gain of $20,000 ($90,000 amount realized less $70,000 basis).[176] Under the general rule of §357(a), the corporation's taking property subject to a liability is not considered boot. Consequently, Miranda will not be required to recognize gain upon the transfer. This result assumes that there was no tax

---

176. Given the $40,000 mortgage, the net value of Miranda's contribution of property is only $50,000. Her amount realized on the exchange includes $50,000 worth of stock received and $40,000 from the liability, for a total of $90,000.

avoidance motive triggering the inclusion of liability as boot under §357(b). Notice also that Miranda has no §357(c) gain since the $40,000 liability transferred does not exceed the $70,000 basis in the contributed property. Even though the liability is not considered boot under §357, her §358 exchanged basis of $70,000 in the stock must be decreased by the $40,000 liability under §358(d), leaving her with a basis of $30,000 in the stock. If she later sells her stock for $50,000, she will report the $20,000 realized gain left unrecognized upon the §351 exchange. Under §1032, the corporation would not recognize any gain upon receipt of the properties from Prospero and Miranda. Under §362, the corporation would take a $70,000 transferred basis in the parcel contributed by Miranda. As for the properties contributed by Prospero, the corporation would begin with a transferred basis of $30,000 in parcel one and $100,000 in parcel two. Pursuant to §362, the corporation is entitled to increase its basis in assets contributed by the $5000 in boot gain recognized by Prospero. Since parcel one had a realized gain, while parcel two had a realized (but unrecognized) loss, the most sensible approach would be for the corporation to add $5000 to its basis in parcel one, leaving the corporation with a total basis of $35,000 for parcel one and $100,000 for parcel two.[177]

6b. If Miranda contributed the same property to the corporation subject to an $80,000 mortgage, the results would be different. Now the mortgage of $80,000 exceeds her $70,000 basis in the contributed property by $10,000. Under §357(c), this $10,000 excess of liabilities over basis must be recognized as gain from the sale of the contributed property. Her basis in the stock under §358 will be an exchanged basis of $70,000 reduced by the $80,000 liabilities assumed and increased by the $10,000 gain recognized. Thus, her basis in the shares will be zero. Under §362, the corporation's basis would be $80,000 (a transferred basis of $70,000 increased by the $10,000 gain recognized by Miranda).

6c. When Miranda took out a mortgage just before incorporating and then used the mortgage proceeds for personal reasons unrelated to the business, she distinctly raised the likelihood that the Service will assert, pursuant to §357(b), that her principal purpose with respect to the corporation's assumption of her liability was to avoid federal income tax or that her principal purpose was not a bona fide business purpose. Recall that in question 6b. Miranda recognized only $10,000 in boot gain (the excess of the $80,000 of liabilities over her $70,000 basis in the contributed property). In contrast, if the exchange is governed by §357(b), the *entire* $80,000 of liability

---

177. The regulations, however, suggest that the §362 basis increase should be apportioned based upon the relative fair market values of the contributed assets. See Treas. Reg. §1.357–2(b), ex. 1, 2. This result does not make sense, as applied to the situation in question 6, where one of the assets is a gain asset and the other asset is a loss asset.

assumed will be treated as money received by Miranda on the exchange. As a result, she would recognize her *entire* realized gain of $20,000. Under §358, Miranda would begin with a $70,000 exchanged basis, reduced by the $80,000 of liabilities assumed and increased by the $20,000 gain recognized, resulting in a $10,000 basis in her stock. This result makes sense. Since she contributed property with a $10,000 net value to the corporation ($90,000 fair market value less $80,000 mortgage liability), she presumably received stock worth $10,000 on the §351 exchange. Since she has already recognized her entire realized gain with respect to the contributed property, she has no further gain to be deferred through substituted basis rules. Under §362, the corporation would take a $70,000 transferred basis increased by the $20,000 gain recognized to Miranda, resulting in a total basis of $90,000.

7. If Prospero contributed parcels of land which he had already contracted to sell, the first question that arises is whether this might be an impermissible assignment of income to the corporation. In Hempt Brothers, Inc. v. United States, 490 F.2d 1172 (3d Cir. 1974), the court concluded that the assignment of income doctrine would not override §351 nonrecognition where the assignment was of accounts for goods and services sold in the regular course of business and the change of business form had a business purpose and was not for tax avoidance purposes. There does not appear to be a tax avoidance motive in this case. The corporation will report income upon the receipt of payments from the land sale contract and will take deductions upon payment of the accounts payable for salary and other business expenses.

Another problem is that if the accounts payable of $150,000 are considered liabilities for purposes of §357(c), the overall liabilities exceed the $30,000 basis of property contributed, resulting in a potential $120,000 taxable gain under §357(c)(1). Since the accounts payable would give rise to a deduction to Prospero if he had paid them, §357(c)(3) does not consider them liabilities for purposes of §357(c)(1).

PART THREE

Corporate Midlife Events

5

Nonliquidating Distributions

Introduction

A useful place to begin studying the tax consequences of corporate distributions is the relationship of shareholders to the corporations in which they hold shares. A shareholder is essentially an owner of the corporate enterprise whose ownership interest typically provides three significant rights: 1) the right to exercise control through voting,[1] 2) entitlement to a share of the corporation's earnings, and 3) entitlement to a share of the corporation's net assets upon liquidation.[2] One obvious way that shareholders receive payment for their share of earnings and assets is through sale of the stock itself. Short of terminating their stock ownership, however, shareholders often receive their share of earnings and/or assets through different types of corporate distributions.

This chapter considers nonliquidating corporate distributions made to shareholders during the corporation's lifetime. The most common example is a simple pro rata cash distribution in which the amount of each shareholder's distribution is determined according to his or her proportionate interest in the corporation. Immediately after the distribution, the shareholders continue to hold the same proportionate interests that they held immediately before the distribution. In other words, the distribution has not altered the basic relationship among shareholders or between the sharehold-

---

1. Not all shares carry the right to vote, however. Certain classes of stock may be designated nonvoting. Nonvoting preferred is a common example.

2. This three-part ownership analysis is nicely spelled out in Himmel v. Comm'r, 338 F.2d 815 (2d Cir. 1964).

ers and the corporation. One may be tempted to think of this distribution as a "dividend." For tax purposes, however, "dividend" is a term of art with a precise statutory meaning.

Before embarking upon a detailed discussion of typical nonliquidating or operating distributions, it will be useful to note other types of corporate distributions through which shareholders may receive their shares of earnings and/or assets. In a redemption, the corporation distributes cash or other property to its shareholders in return for its own stock, thus reducing the number of outstanding shares.[3] In a liquidating distribution, the corporation distributes its net assets after payment of liabilities to its shareholders at or about the time of its termination as a going concern.[4] Other distributions may be made in connection with a formal corporate restructuring such as a reorganization.[5] This chapter will cover only nonliquidating distributions other than redemptions.[6] Keep in mind that the distribution rules considered in this chapter generally preserve the double tax on corporate income. Income is taxed once when it is earned by the corporation and again when it is distributed to the shareholders.

Tax Consequences to the Shareholders

Overview of §301 Distributions with Respect to Stock

The starting point for determining tax consequences to shareholders receiving corporate distributions is §301, which addresses distributions of property by a corporation to a shareholder *with respect to* the corporation's stock.[7] For purposes of §301, property includes money, securities, and any other property *except* stock in the corporation making the distribution (or rights to acquire such stock).[8] The §301 rules apply only to distributions made "with

---

3. Redemption is a unique type of nonliquidating distribution that will be considered fully in Chapter 6. For the moment, however, note that a pro rata redemption does not alter the basic relationship among shareholders. As a result, such redemptions are treated for tax purposes according to the nonliquidating or operating distribution rules. See I.R.C. §302(d).

4. Liquidating distributions are governed by I.R.C. §§331, 332, 336, and 337. For complete coverage of liquidations, see Chapters 8 and 9.

5. The term "reorganization" is defined for tax purposes in I.R.C. §368. For complete coverage of reorganizations, see Chapters 11-14.

6. As a form of shorthand, the remainder of this chapter will refer to these distributions as "nonliquidating" or "operating distributions."

7. I.R.C. §301(a) (emphasis added).

8. I.R.C. §317(a). A corporation distributing its *own* stock is making a "stock dividend." Stock dividends are covered by §305 and will be considered in Chapter 7.

respect to" the distributing corporation's stock. Corporations may make distributions for other reasons, however. For example, a shareholder also may be an employee of or a lender to the corporation. In such cases, the distribution may not be made "with respect to" stock, but instead with respect to an employment or lender relationship. What appears to be a §301 distribution actually may be payment of salary or repayment of a debt.[9] When the shareholder wears more than one hat, a facts and circumstances analysis will be necessary to distinguish distributions made with respect to stock, and thus subject to §301, from payments covered by other provisions of the Code.

Section 301(c) breaks nonliquidating corporate distributions into three distinct parts. First, the portion of the distribution that is a dividend is includible in the shareholder's gross income under §301(c)(1). Dividend income is treated as ordinary income, in contrast to gain from the sale of the underlying stock, which often will be capital gain. Second, the portion of the distribution that is not a dividend shall be applied against and reduce the shareholder's adjusted basis in the stock pursuant to §301(c)(2). Finally, any remaining portion of the distribution shall be treated as gain from the sale or exchange of property under §301(c)(3).

A Closer Look at the §301 Trilogy

By including the dividend portion of the corporate distribution in gross income, §301(c)(1) repeats what we already know from the general definition of gross income in §61(a)(7), which specifically lists dividends as items to be included in gross income. Neither of these provisions provides a definition of "dividend," however. A "dividend" is defined in §316 as any distribution of property made by a corporation to its shareholders out of earnings and profits accumulated after 1913 (accumulated e&p) or out of earnings and profits of the taxable year (current e&p).[10] Without getting into details for the moment, it should at least be clear that an operating distribution may be entirely a dividend, partially a dividend (to the extent that it is paid to shareholders out of earnings and profits), or not a dividend at all (if the corporation has no earnings and profits).[11]

---

9. The reverse situation also presents concerns. A payment that appears to be salary, repayment of a debt, or other nondividend payment in fact may be a disguised or constructive dividend. Constructive dividends will be considered later in this chapter.

10. *Current* e&p is computed "as of the close of the taxable year without diminution by reason of any distributions made during the taxable year." I.R.C. §316(a)(2). Thus, the status of current e&p on the precise date of the distribution generally is not relevant. In contrast, *accumulated* e&p on the date of the distribution will be relevant. These details will be explored further in Example 3 of the Example and Explanations section below.

11. Several details concerning the §316 dividend rules are not addressed here in the text. The Examples and Explanation section below explores additional details, including a discussion of the differences in computing current as opposed to accumulated e&p.

The last two parts of the §301(c) trilogy deal with the excess portion of the distribution determined *not* to be a dividend after application of the §316 dividend test. The portion of the distribution that is *not* a dividend is applied against and reduces the shareholder's adjusted basis in the stock under §301(c)(2). This second part of the distribution rule trilogy is a tax-free recovery of the taxpayer's investment (basis) in the stock. Finally, since basis cannot be reduced below zero,[12] and since the shareholder should not receive *more* than his or her investment back tax free, §301(c)(3) requires the shareholder to treat any remaining portion of the distribution as gain from the sale or exchange of property. Since stock generally is held as a capital asset, the gain or loss from this deemed sale or exchange generally will be capital gain or loss.

Why Limit Dividends to Amounts Paid Out of Earnings and Profits?

A closer look at the "dividend" definition in §316 will help to understand the e&p limitation. Imagine that shareholder A contributes 100X dollars to form a new solely owned corporation.[13] Before the corporation has earned any profit, the corporation distributes 100X dollars.[14] Shareholder A arguably has no economic gain from this receipt and should report no taxable gain since the distribution was simply a return of the original investment. This is precisely the result achieved by §§301 and 316. Since the corporation has no earnings and profits, the distribution will not be treated as a dividend. Instead, under §301(c)(2), the portion of the distribution that is not a dividend (in this case, the full 100X) is a tax-free recovery of capital and will be applied against shareholder A's stock basis. Applying the 100X distribution against the 100X original stock basis now will reduce shareholder A's stock basis to zero. Additional distributions to the shareholder before the corporation has earned a profit will be treated under §301(c)(3) as gain from a fictional sale or exchange of the shareholder's stock.[15]

Imagine now that shareholder A's corporation earns a 100X profit in its

---

12. Negative basis certainly is a theoretical possibility. Nevertheless, Congress and the Treasury Department have never opted to use it. The concept of negative basis was addressed in connection with the discussion of §357(c) in Chapter 4.

13. Assume for purposes of discussion that the contribution was tax free under §351 and that the shareholder's basis under §358 was also 100X.

14. You may be wondering how the corporation could distribute the 100X and still survive. Assume that the corporation had excess cash on hand, either from borrowing or from gross receipts before paying expenses. In other words, the corporation had available cash, but no economic profit.

15. Since the stock basis has already been reduced to zero, no further basis remains to be recovered tax free under §301(c)(2).

first year of operations. The corporation's distribution of 100X to the shareholder at the end of the first year theoretically might be construed either as a distribution of the 100X profit *or* as a distribution of the underlying 100X capital contributed by the shareholder. The statutory provisions in §§301 and 316 effectively adopt a "profits first" ordering rule under which earnings and profits are deemed to be distributed before capital. Since the corporation has current e&p, the 100X distribution to shareholder A in this example is a taxable dividend under §301(c)(1) and the shareholder's 100X stock basis is not reduced.

The underlying rationale of §316 appears to be that when a corporation makes distributions that are *not* out of e&p or profit, the corporation is dipping into its capital. In a tax regime that taxes only *net* income, shareholders must be entitled, at some point, to receive a tax-free return of their original investment. When the corporation makes a distribution before it has a profit, the shareholders arguably are recovering the capital they have invested in the corporation and which is reflected in the shareholder's stock basis. Once the shareholder has recovered this investment from the corporation without tax, basis in the stock should be reduced by the amount of the distribution. Failure to reduce basis would permit a potential double tax-free recovery of capital.

Although the recovery of capital notion often is cited as the rationale for the dividend definition, it is not an entirely satisfactory explanation of §316. The use of both accumulated and current e&p sometimes produces results inconsistent with a logical application of recovery of capital principles. To illustrate, imagine that shareholder A contributes 100X to form a corporation. In the first year of operations, the corporation incurs a deficit. In year two, the corporation has some current earnings, but not enough to make up the prior year's deficit. The corporation thus has an accumulated deficit or a negative accumulated e&p account. From shareholder A's perspective, the corporation has not yet been profitable overall. Nevertheless, a distribution will result in dividend income to shareholder A to the extent of *current* e&p. A corporation with an accumulated deficit, but current earnings, might avoid this "nimble dividend" result for its shareholders simply by deferring distributions until a subsequent year in which there is no current e&p. Thus, not only can the §316 two-part dividend definition sometimes produce results inconsistent with recovery of capital principles, but the rules also can be easily manipulated by careful timing of distributions.

Application of the two-part e&p definition can yield results inconsistent with a recovery of capital rationale in other ways as well. Suppose that shareholder A above sold his stock to shareholder B at the end of year one (a deficit year) and before any distributions were made. Concerned about buying into a deficit corporation, shareholder B agreed to pay only 90X for the shares. Assume further that the corporation remains in a deficit position for year two. Shareholder B will have no dividend income upon a corporate distribution of 100X in year two, since the corporation has no e&p. Instead, the 100X distribution will be treated first as a tax-free recovery of shareholder B's 90X basis in the shares under §301(c)(2) and then as a 10X gain from the sale or exchange of stock under §301(c)(3). Notice that the corporate investment has been profitable as to shareholder B, who received a distribution in excess of the price paid for the shares. To the extent of the excess 10X received over the 90X paid for the stock, application of the dividend definition arguably results in a windfall sale or exchange treatment to shareholder B.

Given the weaknesses of recovery of capital theory as a satisfactory explanation for the §316 two-part dividend definition, one must look elsewhere for answers. The corporate tax history books may shed some light. Until 1936, the dividend definition referred only to accumulated e&p. At that time, corporations were subject to an undistributed profits tax. Corporations were entitled to deduct dividends paid in computing undistributed earnings subject to the old tax, but distributions out of *current* earnings made by a corporation with an *accumulated deficit* were not considered dividends. Hence, they were not deductible for purposes of the undistributed earnings tax. As relief for these corporations, Congress added what is now §316(a)(2) including distributions out of *current* e&p as dividends. The undistributed profits tax was repealed long ago, but the two-part dividend definition remains.

The Tax Stakes: Timing and Character of Shareholder Income

a) A Matter of Timing

What is really at stake for the shareholder applying the §301 distribution rules is the timing and character of income reporting. Sooner or later, the shareholder will be required to pay tax on his or her share of corporate profit.[16] Profits retained by the corporation presumably increase the value of the corporation's stock. This increased value should be reflected in a higher gain to the shareholder upon ultimate sale of the stock. If instead, the corporation passes profit on to its shareholders through distributions, the shareholders will report immediate income to the extent that the distributions are dividends under §316. In effect, the corporation's dividend payments accelerate the shareholder's liability for tax upon his or her share of corporate profit. This is consistent with realization principles. A shareholder who re-

---

16. One notable exception is the shareholder who holds onto stock until death and passes the stock on to heirs with a stepped-up basis under I.R.C. §1014.

ceives a distribution has realized a gain to the extent of the distribution. Distributed profits have left the corporation and are no longer reflected in an increased value in the shares themselves. If no shareholder tax on the dividend is collected at this point, there may never be an opportunity to collect a shareholder level tax upon this profit.

Timing also is at stake when the corporation makes a distribution that is *not* out of e&p. Typically, the owner of a non-wasting asset must wait for final disposition of the asset to recover his or her capital through a basis offset to the amount realized from the sale under §1001. Owners of stock arguably should be subject to the same rules. After all, if the corporation has truly dipped into capital so as to reduce its overall net worth, this will ultimately be reflected in a lower price paid for the shares. Just like any other owner of a non-wasting asset, the shareholder simply would report a lower gain, or perhaps even report a loss, upon sale of the asset. Nevertheless, the §301 rules offer shareholders a uniquely accelerated recovery of capital. Unlike owners of other non-wasting assets, shareholders may receive a tax-free recovery of capital under §301(c)(2) *without* disposing of the shares. In the meantime, they have in hand the value represented by the corporate distribution. Over the years, proposals have been made to repeal the §316 e&p limitation altogether so that shareholders would be taxed on distributions regardless of their corporate source.[17] Overall gain or loss from the stock ownership would be computed upon final disposition of the shares. Since no such proposals have been adopted, shareholders retain the privilege of an advanced recovery of stock basis upon receipt of certain corporate distributions without disposing of the underlying stock.

b) The Character Issue

The increased value from a corporation's retained profits presumably will be reflected in the gain reported by the shareholders upon sale or exchange of the stock. Gain from a shareholder's sale or exchange of stock held for investment typically is capital gain, historically eligible for lower preferential tax rates.[18] On the other hand, profits distributed to shareholders as dividends are taxed to the shareholders at higher ordinary income rates. Thus, in addition to accelerating the *timing* of a shareholder level tax, corporate

---

17. Among the first of these proposals was from Professor William Andrews in an article entitled Out of Its Earnings and Profits: Some Reflections on the Taxation of Dividends, 69 Harv. L. Rev. 1403 (1956). For more recent proposals, see Staff of the Senate Comm. on Finance, The Reform and Simplification of the Income Taxation of Corporations, 98th Cong., 1st sess. 77 (1983); S. Rep. No. 99-47, 99th Cong., 1st Sess. (1985).

18. For a brief discussion of capital gains preferences, see Chapter 1.

dividend distributions may change the *character* of the shareholder level tax from capital gain to ordinary income.[19]

In-Kind Distributions

Not all distributions to shareholders are made in the form of cash or its equivalent. On occasion, particularly in the case of small, closely held corporations, distributions are made in-kind. For example, a corporation might distribute an asset in its investment portfolio or an asset no longer needed for ongoing operations. From the shareholder's perspective, such distributions are governed by the same rules in §§301 and 316 discussed above.

There will be some practical differences in application of the rules, however. First, determining the amount of the distribution will be more difficult than it is in the case of cash distributions. Section 301(b)(1) simply provides that the amount of the distribution is the amount of money received plus the fair market value of other property received.[20] Thus, determining the amount of an in-kind distribution will require valuation of the property distributed. Once the amount of an in-kind distribution has been determined, the tax consequences will depend upon the outcome of the §301(c) trilogy. In other words, the shareholder will have dividend income to the extent of e&p, tax-free recovery of capital on excess amounts to the extent of stock basis, and sale or exchange gain on the remainder of the distribution.

The recipient shareholder of an in-kind distribution does have one additional concern that the cash recipient does not — determining basis in the property received. Section 301(d) simply provides that the basis of such property shall be its fair market value. This fair market value basis makes sense because the shareholder has taken the value of the distribution into account for tax purposes. Since the receipt is taxable, the shareholder receives a "tax cost" basis as if she had first received cash and then purchased the property.

Definitions of Earnings and Profits

General Concepts

Given the importance of earnings and profits in identifying dividends for purposes of §316, it is surprising that the Internal Revenue Code provides

---

19. The Code imposes some penalties on excessive retention of earnings in order to prevent corporations from deliberately using a retained earnings technique to reduce ordinary dividend income to their shareholders. These issues were considered briefly in Chapter 1.

20. When the shareholder assumes or takes property subject to liabilities, the amount of the distribution is reduced by the amount of the liability. I.R.C. §301(b)(2). This point is considered below in a separate section on distributions involving liabilities.

no definition.[21] Even the Treasury Department regulations are of limited assistance. Because the Code has not provided a definition, the rules regarding computation of e&p have been developed in an ad hoc fashion through scattered legislation, cases, regulations, rulings, and common sense accounting.

The concept of earnings and profits is distinct from that of taxable income.[22] Nevertheless, taxable income is a useful place to start in computing e&p. A corporation generally must use the same method of accounting for e&p purposes that it employs for computing taxable income.[23] In order to arrive at e&p from taxable income, corporate accountants must make various upward and downward adjustments to taxable income. The Internal Revenue Code fails to provide a comprehensive list of such adjustments, but Congress at least provides a hint as to the purpose of the adjustments in its title to §312(n): "Adjustments to Earnings and Profits to More Accurately Reflect Economic Gain and Loss." In computing *taxable* income, Congress permits certain exemptions and deductions purely for economic or social policy reasons and not because the exemptions or deductions are necessary to accurately represent the corporation's economic profits. The earnings and profits account theoretically provides a truer picture of the corporation's *economic* income or profit than taxable income can.

Upward Adjustments

Two basic categories of upward adjustments must be made to taxable income to compute e&p. The first category involves certain items that were excluded from taxable income, but must be added back for e&p purposes. One major upward adjustment in this first category is contained not in the Code itself, but in Treas. Reg. §1.312-6, which provides that e&p includes exempt income. Even though certain corporate income may be exempt from federal income tax, it must be added back to taxable income in computing e&p. A common example is interest on certain bonds and other obligations excluded from gross income under §103. In addition, a corporate shareholder must add back to taxable income the amount subtracted under the §243 dividends-received deduction. The rationale for these upward adjustments is that income exempt from tax at the corporate level nevertheless represents part of the corporation's profit or economic income. Distributions of such profits to the shareholders should be taxable to the same extent as other distribu-

---

21. Despite its lack of a statutory definition, the Code does list certain necessary adjustments to earnings and profits "to more accurately reflect economic gain and loss." I.R.C. §312(n). Some of these adjustments are considered later in this section.

22. Accountants and others familiar with financial accounting should be aware that e&p for purposes of §316 also is distinct from the concept of "retained earnings" for purposes of the corporate balance sheet.

23. Treas. Reg. §1.312-6(a).

tions of profit. Failure to include this income in e&p would provide a *double* benefit; income would be exempt at both the corporate and the shareholder level.[24]

The second category of upward adjustments involves differences in timing for e&p purposes. Although Treas. Reg. §1.312-6(a) generally requires the taxpayer to use the same method of accounting for taxable income and e&p purposes, certain timing-related e&p adjustments operate as exceptions. A good example of an upward adjustment in this category is found in §312(n)(5), which requires that e&p be computed as if the installment method had not been used even though the corporation uses the installment sale method in determining taxable income. Although §453 installment reporting permits deferral for taxable income purposes, the full gain from an installment sale is realized at the time of sale. To arrive at e&p from taxable income, the corporate taxpayer here must add back any gain from the sale that has been deferred through use of the installment method.[25]

Another example of a timing related upward adjustment to taxable income involves depreciation. Although the corporation may use an accelerated method of depreciation for income tax purposes, §312(k) requires the corporation to compute depreciation on a straight-line method for e&p purposes. Thus, to arrive at e&p from taxable income, the corporate taxpayer must add back the excess of accelerated over straight-line depreciation.

Downward Adjustments

In addition to upward adjustments, corporate taxpayers will also make some downward adjustments to taxable income to determine e&p. The corporation will be entitled to deduct certain items for e&p purposes that are not otherwise deductible for tax purposes. As with the upward adjustments, these downward adjustments to taxable income assure that e&p is a more accurate reflection of economic gain or loss. These adjustments reflect expenses that deplete economic resources but are otherwise nondeductible for tax purposes. The most common example is federal income tax.[26] Although not deductible for taxable income purposes, federal income tax is deductible in

---

24. Exemption of income at the corporate level does not mandate exemption at the shareholder level. To the contrary, Congress often is careful to retain at least one level of tax rather than permit income to escape tax at both levels.

25. Recent amendments to §453, however, disallow installment reporting for most accrual basis taxpayers. I.R.C. §453(a)(2) (added by the Ticket to Work and Work Incentives Improvement Act of 1999, Pub. L. No. 106-170, 113 Stat. 1860, §536 (1999)). Since most corporations use the accrual method, §312(n)(5) is no longer significant for them. They now must report the full amount of gain for both taxable income and earnings and profits purposes.

26. Certain tax penalties paid also will reduce e&p. See Rev. Rul. 57-332, 1957-2 C.B. 231.

computing e&p. The timing of the downward adjustment for federal income tax paid has been settled through rulings and case law. A cash basis taxpayer, for example, reduces earnings and profits for the year in which the tax is actually paid.[27] An accrual basis taxpayer, on the other hand, can deduct federal income tax liability from e&p in the year that the liability accrues.[28] Although the corporation cannot deduct dividends paid in computing its taxable income, dividends paid will reduce e&p as provided in §312.[29]

Additional Timing Issues

The Internal Revenue Code contains several provisions that allow temporary nonrecognition or deferral of income. The e&p related issues presented by such nonrecognition items are different from those raised by the exempt income adjustment discussed above. The exempt income items discussed above are permanently excluded from the tax base. If they are to be included in e&p, they must be included when they are received. Nonrecognition/deferral items, on the other hand, will be included in the taxpayer's taxable income for some later year. Such deferral items generally enter into e&p in the year they are recognized, not in the year they are realized.[30] We studied one example of nonrecognition/deferral rules earlier in §351. Additional examples can be found in the like-kind exchange rules of §1031, involuntary conversion rules of §1033 and the relief from discharge of indebtedness income in §108.

In the case of affiliated corporations, a member of a corporate consolidated group will compute its e&p in the same manner as if it had filed a separate return. The consolidated return regulations provide a few exceptions, however. For example, under the consolidated return regulations, if one member of a consolidated group sells property to another, the gain or loss from the intercompany transaction is deferred.[31] The intercompany gain or loss is not included in taxable income in the year of sale, but instead will be included later "to produce the same effect on consolidated taxable income

---

27. Helvering v. Alworth Trust, 136 F.2d 812 (8th Cir.), *cert. denied*, 320 U.S. 784 (1943); Rev. Rul. 70-609, 1970-2 C.B. 78.

28. James Armour, Inc. v. Comm'r, 43 T.C. 295, 310 (1964).

29. The §312 adjustments to earnings and profits following a corporate distribution will be considered later in this chapter.

30. See I.R.C. §312(f)(1); Bangor & Aroostook R.R. v. Comm'r, 193 F.2d 827 (1st Cir. 1951), *cert. denied*, 343 U.S. 934 (1952). One notable exception to this general timing rule is the installment sale adjustment in I.R.C. §312(n)(5) discussed above.

31. Treas. Reg. §1.1502-13(c)(1). See particularly Treas. Reg. §1.1502-13(c)(7), ex. 1. A realized gain or loss to the selling corporation that is deferred under the consolidated return regulations is called an "intercompany item."

(and consolidated tax liability) as if [the corporations] were divisions of a single corporation, and the intercompany transaction was a transaction between divisions."[32] So, for example, gain or loss from the property sale would be included in taxable income when the property is disposed of *outside* of the consolidated group. In computing e&p, the selling member of the group will not take the deferred gain or loss into account until it is included in the taxable income of the group.[33] This special rule for deferred intercompany transactions is consistent with the treatment of other deferral transactions, such as like-kind exchanges, in which the item is not included in e&p until the income is included in taxable income. Under consolidated return regulations, the e&p of the lower-tier members of a consolidated group is annually transferred or "tiered up" to the common parent so that the common parent reflects the e&p for the entire group.[34]

Special Rules for Corporate Shareholders

The Dividends-Received Deduction: §243

Corporations often wear two hats. In addition to paying a corporate level tax, a corporation may own shares in another corporation and thus be subject to a shareholder level tax as well. When a corporation wearing its shareholder hat receives a distribution from another corporation, it will be subject to the same §301 rules discussed above. Unlike an individual shareholder, however, a corporate shareholder receiving a distribution from a domestic (U.S.) corporation will be entitled to a special dividends-received deduction under I.R.C. §243.[35] The rationale for this special deduction is reasonably straightforward. Without the deduction, corporate profits would be taxed first to the corporation that earned them, again to the corporate shareholder receiving the distribution, and yet again to the individual shareholder upon receipt of a distribution from the second corporation. Although Congress provided for a double tax on corporations, it did not intend a triple, or potentially even more extensive, multi-tiered tax in the case of longer corporate ownership chains.

---

32. Treas. Reg. §1.1502-13(c)(1).
33. Treas. Reg. §1.1502-33(a).
34. Treas. Reg. §1.1502-33(b).
35. Corporations that are members of an affiliated group and receive "qualifying dividends" are eligible for a 100% deduction of dividends received. I.R.C. §243(a)(3), (b)(1). Small business investment companies are also entitled to a 100% deduction. I.R.C. §243(a)(2). Other corporations are entitled to only 70%. I.R.C. §243(a)(1).

Special Rules for Corporations Filing a Consolidated Return

Corporations that are affiliated, as defined in §1504, are entitled to file a consolidated return. Although the same basic §301 rules will apply to a distribution from one member to another member of a consolidated group, there are some differences. In most cases, an intercompany distribution is not included in the gross income of the member receiving the distribution.[36] This exclusion effectively achieves the same result as taking a 100% dividends-received deduction. Notice, however, that it also permits the distributee to exclude the excess distribution that would otherwise have been taxable as capital gain under §301(c)(3). In keeping with the "single entity" theory underlying the consolidated return regulations, both the dividend income under §301(c)(1) and the capital gain under §301(c)(3) are deferred through a corresponding negative adjustment to the distributee corporation's basis in stock in the distributing corporation.[37]

Congressional Response to Dividends-Received Deduction Abuses

Although the dividends-received deduction is designed to eliminate multiple layers of taxation beyond the existing double tax, it also has been subject to abuse by corporations seeking to classify otherwise taxable receipts as deductible dividends. Congress on several occasions has reconsidered the deduction, adding several anti-abuse provisions.[38] For example, Congress has imposed holding period requirements to prevent corporations from purchasing stock immediately before and selling immediately after a distribution simply to take advantage of the §243 deduction.[39]

Another restriction disallows the §243 deduction when the distributing corporation is a tax-exempt organization. Section 243 is designed to eliminate multiple layers of tax *beyond* the basic double tax of Subchapter C. It is not designed to eliminate the corporate level tax altogether. Assuming that the tax-exempt distributing corporation paid no tax on the income when it was received, a §243 deduction to the recipient corporate shareholder would

---

36. Treas. Reg. §1.1502-13(f)(2)(ii).

37. *Id.*; Treas. Reg. §1.1502-32. See particularly Treas. Reg. §1.1502-13(f)(7), ex. 1.

38. This book will not provide in-depth coverage of anti-avoidance provisions in this area. What follows in the text is a brief discussion of some of the anti-abuse rules.

39. See I.R.C. §246(c).

eliminate the corporate level tax altogether. Consequently, §246(a) denies the dividends-received deduction in the case of distributions from tax-exempt corporations.

Corporations also arguably abused the §243 deduction in certain leveraged stock investments. For example, corporations would purchase stock for their investment portfolios with borrowed funds. Absent statutory restrictions, dividends from such leveraged stock would be entitled to a dividends-received deduction, effectively excluding all, or a portion, of the dividend from taxable income. In addition, the corporation would be entitled to deduct interest expense incurred in connection with the debt-financed purchase. The combination of §243 and interest deductions provided a net tax loss from the transaction that could be used to shelter other corporate income. Congress responded with limitations on the §243 deduction in the case of debt-financed portfolio stock. Section 246A restricts the §243 deduction in the case of dividends on debt-financed portfolio stock through a formula that reduces the dividends-received deduction to the extent of the "average indebtedness percentage."[40]

Another transaction designed by corporations to take advantage of the §243 deduction is known as "dividend stripping." To illustrate, assume that Corporation X hears that Corporation Y is about to distribute a substantial dividend. It purchases Y shares for $200 and shortly thereafter receives a $50 dividend. As a corporate shareholder, X is entitled to a dividends-received deduction with respect to the $50 distribution. Given a 70% dividends-received deduction under §243(a)(1), only $15 of the $50 distribution is subject to tax and the remaining $35 effectively is excluded. After the dividend distribution, the value of the Y shares drops to $150. Corporation X now sells the shares for $150 and, absent statutory restrictions, would take a $50 capital loss. Congress responded to this type of transaction with the "extraordinary dividend" rules in §1059. In the case of an "extraordinary dividend"[41] issued on stock held for less than two years,[42] the corporate shareholder must reduce basis in the stock by the nontaxed portion of the dividend.[43] In the example above, Corporation X's $200 cost basis is reduced by $35 to $165. Thus, X's capital loss will be limited to $15.

---

40. Another investment-related abuse of the dividends-received deduction has been the use of hedging transactions. Congress responded to hedging designed to reduce the risk of loss by disallowing the §243 deduction in certain hedging transactions. I.R.C. §246(c)(1)(B). The precise mechanics of §§246A and 246(c) are not covered in this book.

41. Extraordinary dividends are those where the amount of the dividend equals or exceeds specified percentages of the taxpayer's adjusted basis in the stock. I.R.C. §1059(c).

42. Certain exceptions will apply. See, e.g., §1059(d)(6), (e)(3).

43. I.R.C. §1059(b). Under recent amendments to §1059 an extraordinary dividend may even trigger an immediate *gain* to the extent that the nontaxed portion of

Dividends-Received Deduction in a "Bootstrap Acquisition"

Another creative use of the §243 dividends-received deduction is to reduce a corporate shareholder's potential gain from the sale of stock. One of the landmark cases in this area is Waterman Steamship Corporation v. Commissioner.[44] The parent corporation, Waterman Steamship, received a $3.5 million cash offer for all of its stock in two subsidiary corporations. Since the parent's basis in the subsidiary shares was only $700,000, such a sale of stock would have resulted in a $2.8 million taxable capital gain. Waterman Steamship counterproposed a sale at the reduced price of $700,000 to be completed after its subsidiaries had declared and paid dividends amounting to $2.8 million. This might appear to be quite a deal to the buyer. How often does the counteroffer from the seller come in at a substantially *lower* price? The rub was that the dividend was paid in the form of a short-term (30 day) promissory note. This note was paid with funds borrowed by the purchasing corporation from its major stockholder shortly after the purchaser acquired control of Waterman Steamship's subsidiaries. The end result here is that the selling corporation has $3.5 million cash ($2.8 million in distributions from its subsidiaries and $700,000 from the buyer) in connection with the sale of its subsidiaries.[45] Waterman Steamship argued that the $2.8 million was a cash dividend received when it was both legal and equitable owner of the subsidiaries' stock. It argued that the cash dividend should not be taxed pursuant to the consolidated return regulations, which effectively exclude inter-corporate dividends in provisions paralleling §243. The government, on the other hand, argued that the so-called dividend in substance was part of the sales price paid for the stock. The Tax Court agreed with the taxpayer, but the Fifth Circuit reversed, holding that the subsidiaries acted as "a mere conduit for passing the payment through to the seller. We agree with the Commissioner. The so-called dividend and sale were one transfer. The note was but one transitory step in a total, pre-arranged plan to sell the stock."[46] The selling corporation in *Waterman Steamship* wound up with a busted bootstrap acquisition.

Other corporate sellers have avoided the pitfalls displayed in this case

the dividend exceeds the corporate shareholder's basis in the stock. Taxpayer Relief Act of 1997, Pub. L. No. 105-34, 111 Stat. 788, §1011(a) (codified at I.R.C. §1059(a)(2)).

44. 430 F.2d 1185 (5th Cir. 1970), *cert. denied*, 401 U.S. 939 (1971).

45. This type of transaction sometimes is called a "bootstrap acquisition" since a substantial portion of the funds for the acquisition appear to come from the seller itself rather than from the buyer. The seller thus uses its own funds to "bootstrap" the sale.

46. 430 F.2d at 1192.

and arranged successful sales of stock with pre-sale distributions of cash or other unwanted assets.[47] For example, in *TSN Liquidating Corporation v. United States*,[48] the selling corporation (TSN) arranged for an in-kind distribution of approximately $1.8 million of assets from its target subsidiary immediately prior to selling the subsidiary stock to the purchasing corporation for approximately $800,000. Immediately after the sale transaction, the purchaser contributed substantial capital to the target subsidiary, the effect of which was to reinfuse the target's assets previously distributed to TSN. TSN, of course, claimed the distribution as a dividend eligible for a §243 deduction. Relying on *Waterman Steamship,* the government countered that the alleged dividend should be treated as part of the purchase price upon sale of the subsidiary stock. The Fifth Circuit disagreed and held for the taxpayer. The court noted that the distribution in *Waterman Steamship* "was clearly a sham, designed solely to achieve a tax free distribution of assets ultimately funded by the purchaser."[49] In contrast to the *Waterman Steamship* "sham" distribution, TSN's subsidiary distributed assets that were unwanted by the buyer and ultimately were retained by TSN. The court also noted that there was no suggestion that TSN had a tax avoidance motive, adding that "[t]he fact that the dividend may have had incidental tax benefit to the taxpayer, without more, does not necessitate the disallowance of dividend treatment."[50]

The *TSN* and *Litton Industries* cases illustrate that it still is possible to successfully structure a bootstrap acquisition through a pre-sale dividend distribution of assets by a target subsidiary, deductible by the selling parent under §243. Taxpayers should tread carefully, however, in planning such transactions. First, it is important that there be some business reason for the distribution, usually that the distributed assets were unwanted by the buyer. The parent ideally should avoid an immediate sale or exchange of the assets received in the pre-sale distribution. Finally, the taxpayer must take into account the basis deduction in its subsidiary stock, and potential taxable gain, that can result if the distribution is treated as an "extraordinary dividend" under §1059.[51]

---

47. See, e.g., Litton Industries, Inc. v. Comm'r, 89 T.C. 1086 (1987), *acq. in result in part,* 1988-2 C.B. 1.

48. 624 F.2d 1328 (5th Cir. 1980).

49. *Id.* at 1335.

50. *Id.* at 1336.

51. Section 1059 distributions are considered further in the section entitled "Special Issues for Corporate Shareholders" in Chapter 6. The selling parent corporation must also take into account that in determining the extent of the dividend, special rules for computing e&p are imposed on distributions to 20% shareholders by I.R.C. §301(e).

Tax Consequences to the Distributing Corporation

In-Kind Distributions: §311

a) In General

A corporation does not realize or recognize any gain or loss upon a simple cash distribution to its shareholders. In contrast, in-kind distributions can have significant tax consequences. Do not be misled by §311(a), which provides a general nonrecognition rule for the distributing corporation upon distributions of property with respect to stock. This so-called general rule is virtually swallowed by the exception provided in §311(b). When a corporation distributes *appreciated* property, §311(b) requires that the distributing corporation recognize gain "as if such property were sold to the distributee at its fair market value." In other words, the distributing corporation must treat the appreciated property as if it had been sold to the shareholders, triggering taxable gain.[52] Given the gain recognition required by §311(b), what remains of the §311(a) "general rule" simply is a loss disallowance rule. In the end, Congress does *not* provide a two-way street for in-kind operating distributions. Corporations must recognize gain upon distribution of appreciated property, but cannot recognize loss upon distribution of depreciated property.[53]

The explanation for the statutory inversion of the "general rule" and its "exception" in §311 is historical. Not long ago in corporate tax history, corporate level nonrecognition of *both* gain and loss upon in-kind distributions was the general rule. This old nonrecognition rule often is attributed to the famous 1935 decision of the United States Supreme Court in General Utilities & Operating Company v. Helvering.[54] The General Utilities company owned stock in the Islands Edison Company originally purchased for $2000, but worth approximately $1 million. Rather than sell the stock directly, General Utilities distributed the stock to its shareholders, who then

---

52. If the in-kind distribution is from one member to another member of a consolidated group, a distribution of appreciated property still triggers a gain under §311(b). However, under the consolidated return regulations, the §311(b) gain will be deferred as if property had been transferred within divisions of a single corporation. In general, the deferred gain will be taxed when the distributed property leaves the consolidated group. Treas. Reg. §1.1502-13(f)(7), ex. 1.

53. This should be contrasted with liquidating distributions. Unlike §311, §336 provides that "gain *or loss* shall be recognized to a liquidating corporation on the distribution of property in complete liquidation." I.R.C. §336(a) (emphasis added). Liquidating distributions will be more fully considered in Chapter 8.

54. 296 U.S. 200 (1935).

sold the shares. The issue for the court was whether the distribution of this highly appreciated stock required General Utilities to report a taxable gain on the difference between the fair market value of the stock and its $2000 basis. The Supreme Court held that there was no taxable gain.[55] The government's concern with this transaction should not be hard to discern. The distributing corporation disposed of its highly appreciated Islands Edison stock, transferring $1 million in value to its shareholders. Although the $1 million value was reported as dividend income to the shareholders, the corporation has reported no gain or loss. The corporation has effectively escaped the corporate level portion of the double tax on corporate income. If the corporation had sold the Islands Edison stock directly to the buyer and distributed the cash proceeds from the sale to its shareholders, two levels of tax would have been collected.

Surprisingly, Congress first indicated its approval of the *General Utilities* decision by initially codifying the nonrecognition rule in §311(a).[56] In piecemeal fashion over the years, however, Congress has chipped away at, and finally repealed, the *General Utilities* nonrecognition rule as applied to distributions of appreciated property, and replaced it with the gain recognition rule now found in §311(b). Rather than repeal §311(a) entirely, Congress left it in place and added §311(b). The gain recognition rule now in §311(b) reflects the congressional judgment that corporations should not be able to escape corporate level taxation on appreciation in corporate assets distributed to shareholders.

Imagine that Corporations X and Y each hold an asset with a basis of 110X and a fair market value of 150X. Corporation X arranges to sell the asset for 150X and later distributes 150X cash to its sole shareholder. In contrast, Corporation Y distributes the asset directly to its sole shareholder, who later sells the asset for 150X. These two economically similar transactions now will result in similar tax consequences. Corporation X will recognize a 40X taxable gain on the sale under §§61(a)(3) and 1001 and the shareholder will report income from the cash distribution under the §301 rules. Similarly, Corporation Y will recognize a 40X gain upon the distribution under §311(b) and the shareholder will report gain from the in-kind distribution under the §301 rules. In each case, the character of the corporation's gain as capital or ordinary will depend upon the character of the asset.

Switching to loss property, suppose that Corporation X sold an asset with a basis of 110X and a fair market value of 100X and later distributed the 100X cash proceeds to its sole shareholder, while Corporation Y simply

---

55. In quite cursory fashion, the Court simply said that the corporation derived no taxable gain from the distribution of appreciated stock: "This was no sale; assets were not used to discharge indebtedness." *Id.* at 206.

56. Congress initially provided a parallel nonrecognition rule for liquidating distributions as well. These rules and the relevant *General Utilities* history in the liquidation context are considered in Chapter 8.

distributed the loss asset directly to the shareholder. Corporation X is entitled to recognize the 10X loss upon sale of the asset, but Corporation Y will *not* be entitled to deduct the 10X loss. Since this is not a distribution of appreciated property, the §311(a) nonrecognition rule will apply. In this case, the two similar economic transactions do *not* have similar tax results.

b) Why the Lack of Symmetry in §311?

Why does Congress require recognition of gain upon distributions of appreciated property but prohibit recognition of loss upon distributions of depreciated property? Congress has historically been concerned with the possibilities for manipulation of loss recognition.[57] This is particularly true where the parties to the transaction are related.[58] If both gains and losses were recognized upon corporate distributions, corporations might be motivated to leave gains unrealized by holding onto appreciated assets, but realize losses by distributing loss assets. One might respond with the observation that a corporation wishing to avoid gains but realize losses can achieve this result by holding onto appreciated property and selling depreciated property in the marketplace. Cash received from the sale could then be distributed to the shareholders. A sale of loss property in the marketplace can be distinguished from a distribution of loss property to the shareholders, however, since the marketplace sale actually causes the property to leave the corporate family. Recognition of the loss in this case comes at a price; the corporation *and* its shareholders must relinquish control over the property. If losses were recognized upon in-kind distributions, corporations would be able to receive the tax benefit of the loss while keeping the property in the corporate family's hands.[59]

Adjustments to E&P: §312

Remember that shareholders report taxable dividends only to the extent of the corporation's e&p. Once a distribution is made out of earnings and

---

57. In fact, even in connection with liquidating distributions, upon which loss recognition *is* generally allowed, §336(d) imposes limitations on loss recognition in certain cases. These limitations will be discussed further in Chapter 8.

58. See, e.g., I.R.C. §267(a), which disallows losses from sales or exchanges between related parties. Related parties, for purposes of §267, include an individual and a corporation in which the individual owns more than 50% in value of the outstanding stock. I.R.C. §267(b)(2).

59. The real concern for manipulation evolves from the relationship of corporation and shareholder. Congress fears that the corporation will take a loss, but still retain control of the property indirectly through its shareholders. This is more likely to be a problem with respect to controlling shareholders. Some would argue that the §267 restriction on losses between related parties is a sufficient response to the loss manipulation possibility and that the §311 restriction is overly broad.

profits, the e&p distributed is no longer available for future dividend distributions. Accordingly, §312(a) requires the distributing corporation to decrease its earnings and profits after making a distribution with respect to its stock. Although a corporation might find itself with a negative e&p account from operating business losses, §312(a) effectively prohibits the corporation from *creating* a deficit in e&p through distributions since e&p can only be reduced after a corporate distribution "to the extent thereof."

Following a cash distribution, the distributing corporation simply decreases e&p by the amount of money distributed.[60] Adjustments following in-kind distributions of property can be slightly more involved. To illustrate, suppose again that Corporation Y distributes an asset with a basis of 110X and a fair market value of 150X. As a result of this in-kind distribution of appreciated property, §312(b)(1) first requires the distributing corporation to *increase* e&p by the excess of fair market value over basis of the property distributed. In other words, e&p is increased to the extent of the 40X corporate gain just recognized under §311(b).[61] Corporation Y next must decrease e&p to reflect the distribution. Under the "general rule" for e&p adjustments following corporate distributions, the corporation would decrease e&p by the *adjusted basis* of the property distributed.[62] In the case of *appreciated* property, however, the Code instructs the corporation to substitute the words "fair market value" for "adjusted basis."[63] In other words, Corporation Y in the above example would now decrease e&p by the full 150X fair market value of the distributed asset. While the statutory language is cumbersome, the result is sensible. If Corporation Y had never been taxed upon the 40X gain from appreciation in the distributed asset and had never reflected that gain in e&p, it might make sense to limit the downward adjustment to e&p from the distribution to the 110X basis in the asset. In fact, the "general" e&p adjustment rule in §312(a)(3) actually is a relic left over from the days when the *General Utilities* nonrecognition rule prevailed, and even distributions of appreciated property did not result in taxable gain to the distributing corporation. Just as the §311(b) exception virtually swallows the §311(a) "general rule" regarding recognition of gain or loss upon in-kind distributions of property, the §312(b) exception similarly virtually swallows the §312(a)(3) "general rule" regarding corporate adjustments to e&p after in-kind distributions.

The §312(a)(3) "general rule" decreasing e&p by the adjusted basis of the property distributed *will* apply to distributions of loss property. Suppose

---

60. I.R.C. §312(a)(1).

61. In fact, since the §311 gain is included in the corporation's taxable income and since the e&p computation will begin with taxable income, the language of §312(b)(1) may be unnecessary. The gain certainly should not be counted in e&p twice.

62. I.R.C. §312(a)(3).

63. I.R.C. §312(b)(2).

again that Corporation Y distributes property with a basis of 110X and a fair market value of 100X. When loss property is distributed, §312(a)(3) simply requires that e&p be reduced by the adjusted basis of the property. Although §311(a) disallows the loss for tax purposes, the corporation is still entitled to reduce e&p by the 110X adjusted basis of the property distributed, thus reducing the e&p amounts available for future distributions. This is a sensible result since the corporation's "cost" or investment in the distributed property was 110X and this amount has left the corporation and is no longer available for future distribution.

No Deductions for Dividends Paid

As opposed to many other corporate payments, dividends are not deductible to the distributing corporation. For example, reasonable salary payments to employees (including shareholder employees) are deductible trade or business expenses under §162. In addition, interest costs incurred by a corporation will often be deductible under §163. The different tax treatment afforded to dividends and interest has motivated corporations to raise capital through debt rather than equity and has spawned a host of additional problems that are dealt with in other chapters of this book.[64]

Distributions Involving Liabilities

Shareholder Tax Consequences

If the shareholder either assumes a liability, or takes property subject to a liability, in connection with an in-kind distribution, §301(b)(2) provides that the amount of the distribution will be reduced (but not below zero) by the amount of such liability. After all, when a shareholder takes on a liability in connection with an in-kind distribution, the value of the property to the shareholder is reduced to the extent that she must incur debt in order to retain the property. Imagine, for example, that the corporation distributes property with a fair market value of 150X that is subject to a 100X mortgage to shareholder A. The *amount* of shareholder A's distribution under §301(b)(2) is 50X—the *net* value of the distribution after taking the liability into account.[65]

Even though the fair market value of the property distributed is reduced

---

64. See, e.g., the treatment of sales vs. contributions to a controlled corporation in Chapter 4.

65. Whether or not this 50X distribution is taxable as a dividend depends on the outcome of the same §§301 and 316 shareholder distribution analysis considered earlier in this chapter.

by liabilities to determine the *amount* of the distribution, the shareholder still is entitled to a fair market value *basis* in the property under §301(d). Thus, shareholder A's basis in the distributed property is 150X. This full fair market value basis simply extends to the shareholder the same right to include borrowing in basis that is provided to all taxpayers;[66] the shareholder is given the benefit of a presumption of repayment of the debt and is entitled to include borrowing in advance as a "cost."

Interesting issues arise when the shareholder takes on a debt with respect to the distributed property that *exceeds* the fair market value of the property. For example, imagine that shareholder A took the distributed property worth 150X subject to a 200X mortgage. The *amount* of the distribution now would be zero, since §301(b)(2) prohibits a reduction below zero. Under §301(d), shareholder A's basis in the distributed property would be limited to its 150X fair market value. As a result, the shareholder cannot include the full amount of the 200X liability in the distributed property's basis. What is *really* happening when a shareholder receives an in-kind property distribution where a recourse liability assumed exceeds the value of the property? In this example, shareholder A must pay 50X more for the property than its worth. At least in the case of operating distributions, such a situation might be construed as a shareholder contribution of 50X to the corporation's capital. The shareholder arguably should receive an increase in his or her stock basis reflecting the excess of the liability over fair market value.[67]

Distributing Corporation Tax Consequences

When a corporation makes an in-kind distribution in connection with which the shareholders either assume a liability or take property subject to a liability, additional corporate level considerations arise. According to general tax principles, the amount realized to the seller must include the amount of liabilities when a buyer either assumes or purchases property subject to liabilities.[68] Since §311(b) requires the corporation to treat the distribution

---

66. In its landmark opinion in Crane v. Comm'r, 331 U.S. 1, 11 (1947), the Supreme Court concluded that the taxpayer's basis in property included her mortgage. The Court reached this result in *Crane* even though the liability involved was a *nonrecourse* mortgage. The Court points out the longstanding practice of the Treasury Department allowing taxpayers to use the full value of property (undiminished by liabilities) for purposes of depreciation and continued acceptance of this practice by Congress. It is now well settled that basis includes borrowing.

67. Treas. Reg. §1.118-1. For an in-depth discussion of contributions to capital, see Chapter 3.

68. This rule serves as a corollary to the rule that borrowing is included in basis. If borrowing was included in the seller's basis in the property, the buyer's assumption of the liability must be included in amount realized upon resale. Comm'r v. Tufts, 461 U.S. 300 (1983); Crane v. Comm'r, 331 U.S. 1 (1947); Treas. Reg. §1.1001-2(a).

as a sale to the shareholder, the "amount realized" to the corporation upon the distribution includes liabilities taken on by the shareholders. Corporate level gain upon an in-kind distribution ordinarily is measured by the fair market value of the property distributed over its adjusted basis.[69] Suppose, for example, that Corporation X distributes property with a basis of 80X and a fair market value of 150X to shareholder A, subject to a 100X mortgage on the property. Corporation X will report a taxable gain of 70X under §311(b). In this case, the 150X amount realized includes both the 100X liability taken on by the shareholder and the additional 50X value in the appreciated property.

While the term "fair market value" *ordinarily* refers to the price that a willing seller and an unrelated buyer would agree to in the marketplace, the Code requires that the fair market value of the property "be treated as *not less than* the amount of [the] liability" when liabilities are involved in an in-kind distribution.[70] Thus, when the liabilities *exceed* fair market value, corporate level gain under §311 will be measured by the excess of *liabilities* over adjusted basis. To illustrate, imagine that the mortgage in the above example was 200X instead of 100X. Even though the fair market value of the property was only 150X, the amount realized to the corporation upon its distribution of the property to its shareholder now would be 200X, resulting in a 120X taxable gain.[71] This twist on the general rule is simply a codification in the corporate distribution context of the holding in Commissioner v. Tufts.[72] In *Tufts*, the Supreme Court held that when a buyer assumes or takes property subject to a liability, the amount realized from the sale must include the full amount of the liability *even if* the liability *exceeds* the fair market value of the property.[73]

---

69. I.R.C. §311(b). This gain formula is no different from the formula used upon sales of property generally. See I.R.C. §1001.

70. I.R.C. §336(b). Section 336 generally covers the tax consequences to corporations upon *liquidating* distributions. With respect to nonliquidating distributions, §311(b)(2) entitled "Treatment of Liabilities," provides that "[r]ules similar to the rules of section 336(b) shall apply for purposes of this subsection." Notice that §336(b) applies to both recourse and nonrecourse debt. *Cf.* Treas. Reg. §1.1001-2(c), ex. 8.

71. Notice that this gain reflects 70X appreciation in the property's value and an additional 50X from excess liability over the value of the property.

72. 461 U.S. 300 (1983).

73. Since the acceptance of excess recourse liabilities might be viewed as a shareholder contribution to capital, one might argue that the corporation should receive this excess as a tax-free contribution to capital under §§118 or 1032. For a detailed discussion of these sections, see Chapter 3. Under this view, the corporation's gain, contrary to *Tufts*, should be limited to fair market value over basis. This view would require repeal of §336(b). The argument against this view is that *Tufts* requires full inclusion of liabilities in amount realized because the liabilities were included in the corporation's basis when the funds were borrowed. This basis from borrowing may

For distributions involving liabilities, §312(c) requires that "proper adjustment" be made to e&p for liabilities to which distributed property is subject or which are assumed by shareholders. This language is not very helpful. What is the proper adjustment? Relief from a liability generates income or profit. In the old world under *General Utilities*, "proper adjustment" required an increase in e&p to the extent of the liability.[74] "Proper adjustment" for liabilities under §312(c) in the world after repeal of *General Utilities* is more confusing. A more detailed analysis of the necessary adjustment is provided in the Examples and Explanations section below.[75]

Constructive Dividends

In addition to actual dividends, corporations sometimes engage in activity which is *deemed* to result in dividend treatment. One common example is the closely held company in which the shareholders also are involved in day-to-day management activities for which they receive salary. If the corporation pays salaries in excess of what is reasonable, the excess may be viewed as a constructive dividend to the employee-shareholder to the extent that the corporation has sufficient e&p to cover the excess payment. Another common constructive dividend is free service or property provided by the corporation to a shareholder-employee or officer. From the shareholder's perspective, both dividends and salary are taxable as ordinary income. There is one important distinction, however. Salary payments are fully taxable without regard to the corporation's e&p account. On the other hand, a constructive dividend is taxable as a dividend under §301 only to the extent of the corporation's e&p. From the corporation's perspective, the distinction is even more significant. Salary payments are deductible business expenses whereas dividend distributions are not deductible.

EXAMPLES

Some Beginning Questions

1.   Curly is the sole shareholder of Beautiful Pups, Inc., (BPI) a dog-grooming business. BPI employs Mo to run the day-to-day operations. At

---

have resulted in depreciation or other deductions. *Crane* and *Tufts* require symmetry in the inclusion of borrowing in both basis and amount realized. Thus, full inclusion of the recourse liability as provided in §336(b) may be warranted. Resolution of this debate is beyond the scope of this book.

74. In convoluted fashion, the regulations talk about reducing the reduction. Treas. Reg. §1.312-3. The effect of reducing the reduction is an increase.

75. See Example 7.

the end of the year in question, BPI has current e&p of $100,000 and accumulated e&p of $300,000. BPI distributes cash of $100,000 to Curly. Curly's basis in the shares is $5000. Tax consequences to Curly? Tax consequences to BPI? What issues are raised if, instead of hiring incompetent Mo as the manager, Curly manages the business himself?

2a. What if BPI in the above problem had no current e&p?

2b. What if BPI had $100,000 in current e&p, but no accumulated e&p?

2c. What if BPI had $100,000 in current e&p, but an accumulated deficit?

2d. What if BPI had $25,000 in current e&p and $25,000 in accumulated e&p?

2e. What if BPI had no e&p at all?

3. Curly, Mo, and Larry each were the sole owners of Stooges Plumbing during one-third of the first taxable year of Stooges operations. Curly owned all the shares for the first period from January 1 through March 31, during which time the company had $100,000 in e&p. Mo owned the shares from April 1 through June 30, during which time the company had $200,000 in e&p. Larry owned the shares for the final period, during which time the corporation suffered a $150,000 loss. Each received a $100,000 distribution from the corporation during his term of ownership. How should Curly, Mo, and Larry treat these distributions for tax purposes? What if the above distributions took place in the second year of operations and, in addition to the current e&p, Stooges had $25,000 in its accumulated e&p account?

Computing Earnings and Profits

4. Stooges Plumbing is a cash basis corporation (although C corporations generally cannot use the cash method, assume that Stooges is excepted from this restriction by §448(b)(3)). Its income and expenses for the taxable year were as follows:

Gross receipts from plumbing services	$200,000
Ordinary and necessary expenses for salaries and supplies	50,000
Income from tax-exempt bonds	10,000
Accelerated depreciation on equipment: equipment has a useful life of 10 years and its original basis was $5000.	750
Realized but unrecognized gain from like-kind exchange under §1031	1,000
Federal income tax liability for the prior taxable year paid in the current taxable year	5,000

Compute Stooges' e&p for the taxable year.

Adding Complexities at the Corporate Level

5.   On December 31, Minstrel Singers, Inc. distributes to its shareholders an old Boesendorfer grand piano with a fair market value of $125,000 and a basis to the corporation immediately before the distribution of $75,000. Assume that the corporation had sufficient e&p to cover the distribution. What tax consequence to Minstrel Singers, Inc.? To the shareholders? What if Minstrel Singers had no e&p before the distribution?

6.   In Example 5, what if the basis of the property to the corporation immediately before the distribution had been $60,000 and the fair market value of the property had been $50,000?

7.   What if the property described in Example 5 was subject to a mortgage of $100,000 and the shareholders took the property subject to the mortgage?

The Corporate Shareholder

8a. MicroMac, Inc. is a large computer corporation that owns 80% of MiniMac, Inc. a subsidiary corporation. The remaining 20% of MicroMac's stock is owned by individual minority shareholders. The two corporations do not file a consolidated return. MiniMac has been extremely profitable and declares a pro rata distribution from e&p of $50,000. Of this total amount, $35,000 is distributed to MicroMac as the parent company and $15,000 is distributed to the minority shareholders. What are the tax consequences of the distribution to both MicroMac and to the minority shareholders? Would the results be different if the subsidiary corporation was tax exempt?

8b. How would your answer to Example 8a change if MicroMac and MiniMac *did* file a consolidated return as affiliated corporations under §1504?

9.   On January 1, MicroMac, Inc. purchased shares of IBM stock for $100,000. On January 15 of the same year, IBM paid a $2000 dividend on these shares. MicroMac sold its IBM shares on January 30 of the same year. What are the tax consequences to MicroMac upon receipt of the dividend?

A Sneaky Question

The precise issue raised by the following question was not discussed in the text above. Test your skills by intuiting an answer based on concepts that were discussed:

10. Corporation Y is a publishing company and Corporation Z manufactures paper. Both corporations are wholly owned by shareholder A. Last year, Corporation Y spent $500,000 for paper purchased from Corporation Z. If Y had paid the prices normally charged to Z's other customers, the bill would

have been $750,000. What are the tax consequences, if any, of these events to shareholder A and Corporations Y and Z?

EXPLANATIONS

Some Beginning Questions

1. Curly will have a fully taxable dividend of $100,000 under §§301(c)(1) and 61(a)(7) since the corporation has sufficient e&p to cover the distribution. His $5000 basis in the BPI stock will remain unchanged. After the distribution, BPI's e&p account must be reduced by the amount of money distributed pursuant to §312(a)(1). The question here is whether the distribution comes out of current or accumulated e&p since there is enough of either to cover the distribution. The flush language of §316(a) provides that "except as otherwise provided, every distribution is made out of earnings and profits to the extent thereof, *and from the most recently accumulated earnings and profits.*" See also Treas. Reg. §1.316-2(a). Under these rules, current e&p must be exhausted before dipping into accumulated earnings. BPI's current e&p will be reduced to zero or "wiped out." I.R.C. §312(a)(1). The accumulated e&p account remains at $300,000. There will be no deduction to BPI for the dividend paid.

The issue raised if Curly manages the business himself is whether the distribution was "made by a corporation *with respect to its stock.*" I.R.C. §301(a). Where the same person wears both an employee and shareholder hat, the §301 rules may not apply at all if the distribution is viewed as made to an employee. Whether the distribution is made to Curly as employee or shareholder will be determined under the facts and circumstances. If the payment to Curly is viewed as compensation for his services, Curly will have §61(a)(1) salary or compensation income. If viewed as a payment with respect to stock, Curly will have §61(a)(7) dividend income. In either case, the income will be taxed at ordinary income rates. What difference does it make? Virtually none, from Curly's perspective, since the corporation had sufficient e&p to cover a dividend distribution in any case. From BPI's perspective, on the other hand, the distinction is quite important. If viewed as a payment to an employee, the corporation can take a deduction for an ordinary and necessary salary expense under §162. In contrast, a dividend payment to a shareholder is nondeductible.

2a. Even if BPI had no current e&p, Curly would still be required to report $100,000 in §301 dividend income, since there is sufficient accumulated e&p to cover the distribution. I.R.C. §316 clearly refers to accumulated *or* current e&p. BPI's accumulated e&p account would be reduced to $200,000. I.R.C. §312(a)(1).

2b. If BPI had only current e&p of $100,000, but no accumulated e&p, Curly would still have a fully taxable dividend. Section 316 includes dividends paid out of current *or* accumulated e&p. This distribution would wipe out BPI's e&p.

2c. If BPI had an accumulated deficit, but nevertheless had $100,000 of current earnings, the dividend to Curly would still be taxable, again because §316 uses the word "or" rather than "and." This "nimble dividend" result arguably is inconsistent with recovery of capital principles. Since Curly is the original shareholder and the corporation has not yet been profitable, the distribution of funds arguably should be treated as a recovery of capital.

2d. If BPI had only $25,000 in current and $25,000 in accumulated e&p, Curly's taxable dividend would be limited to the extent of the $50,000 combined e&p. He would receive $5000 as a tax-free recovery of capital under §301(c)(2) and reduce the basis in his shares from $5000 to zero. The remaining $45,000 would be treated as gain from the sale or exchange of stock under §301(c)(3). If Curly has held the stock for the proper holding period under §1222, the gain will be treated as long-term capital gain. Regarding the corporation's e&p adjustment following the distribution, recall that the distribution can only reduce e&p *to the extent thereof.* I.R.C. §312(a). Consequently, both BPI's current and accumulated e&p accounts are reduced to zero, but not below.

2e. If the corporation had no e&p at all, Curly would receive $5000 as a tax-free recovery of capital under §301(c)(2) and reduce his basis in the shares to zero. The remaining $95,000 would be §301(c)(3) gain. If Curly held the stock for the proper holding period under §1222, the gain would be long-term capital gain.

3. Since this is the first year of Stooges operations, it has no accumulated e&p. The net current e&p at the end of year one was $150,000. I.R.C. §316(a) provides that *current* e&p is to be "computed as of the close of the taxable year without diminution by reason of any distributions made during the taxable year and without regard to the amount of the earnings and profits at the time the distribution was made." Thus, the particular status of the *current* e&p account at the time of each distribution is irrelevant. Current e&p of $150,000 was not sufficient to cover the $300,000 total distributions, however. Under these circumstances, the dividend portion of each distribution is determined by using a ratio, the numerator of which is total current e&p and the denominator of which is total distributions. See Treas. Reg. §1.316-2(b). In our case, this ratio would be $150,000/$300,000 or ½. Thus, Curly, Mo, and Larry will each be taxed upon a dividend of $50,000, one-half of the $100,000 each received. The remaining half of each distribution will be tax-free recovery of capital to the extent of their bases in the stock under §301(c)(2) with any excess treated as gain from the sale of stock under §301(c)(3).

   If, in addition to this year's e&p, Stooges also had $25,000 in accumulated e&p, you would first look to and "wipe out" the current e&p account as described above so that each still would have a $50,000 dividend from current e&p. In addition, according to Treas. Reg. §1.316-2(b), distributions not out of *current* e&p shall be considered taxable dividends to the extent of accumulated e&p "available on the date of the distribution." Under this rule, Curly, as the first shareholder receiving a distribution during the taxable year, would have an additional $25,000 in taxable dividend (for a total of $75,000), thus wiping out the accumulated e&p account. Mo and Larry would be left with only the $50,000 dividend computed above. This problem illustrates that, in contrast to current e&p, the status of accumulated e&p account at the time of the distribution is relevant. See also Treas. Reg. §1.316-2(c) (example).

Computing Earnings and Profits

4. The first step in computing e&p for Stooges Plumbing is to determine taxable income. To compute taxable income, deductible expenses must be subtracted from gross receipts received for plumbing services:

Gross receipts	$200,000
Less ordinary expenses	50,000
	150,000
Less accelerated depreciation	750
	$149,250 Taxable Income

To arrive at e&p from taxable income, Stooges must make two upward adjustments. First, the $10,000 in exempt income must be added back. Treas. Reg. §1.312-6. In addition, Stooges must add back the excess of accelerated over straight-line depreciation. I.R.C . §312(k). If Stooges used straight-line depreciation for its 10-year asset with a $5000 basis, yearly depreciation would be $500 per year. Thus the excess of accelerated ($750) over straight-line ($500) is $250. Stooges total upward adjustments amount to $10,250:

Exempt income	$10,000
Excess depreciation	250
	$10,250

Stooges must also adjust taxable income downward for its $5000 federal income tax liability. Since Stooges is a cash basis taxpayer, federal income tax paid in the taxable year reduces e&p for the taxable year even though the tax was due for the prior taxable year.

To summarize, Stooges' e&p for the taxable year is computed as follows:

Taxable income	$149,250
plus upward adjustments	10,250
	159,500
less downward adjustment	5,000
	$154,500

The realized, but unrecognized, gain from the like-kind exchange will not be taken into account for taxable income *or* e&p purposes. This gain will enter into taxable income and e&p when it is recognized. I.R.C. §312(f)(1).

Adding Complexities at the Corporate Level

5.   Upon distribution of the piano, Minstrel must report a taxable gain as if the piano had been sold to the shareholders at its fair market value. I.R.C. §311(b). Thus, Minstrel will report a gain of $50,000 ($125,000 fair market value less $75,000 basis). Minstrel's e&p first will be increased by the $50,000 gain and then decreased by the $125,000 fair market value. I.R.C. §312(a), (b).

The amount of the distribution to the shareholders in this case is $125,000, the fair market value of the property distributed. I.R.C. §301(b). There was sufficient e&p to cover the distribution. Thus, the entire $125,000 will be treated as an ordinary income dividend to the shareholders. The shareholders will have a basis of $125,000 (fair market value) in the piano. I.R.C. §301(d).

If there was no e&p immediately before the distribution on December 31, the issue is whether the distribution *itself* creates any e&p that will result in dividend treatment to shareholders. The answer is yes. Under §312(b) e&p is increased by the excess of fair market value over adjusted basis. Thus, the $50,000 gain recognized to Minstrel under §311(b) will also increase its e&p. As a result, the shareholders will report $50,000 of the distribution as taxable dividend. The remaining $75,000 will be recovery of capital to the extent of basis in the shares with any excess treated as gain from the sale of stock.

After an in-kind distribution, §312(a)(3) requires that e&p be decreased by the adjusted basis of property distributed. In the case of appreciated property, however, §312(b) provides that "(a)(3) shall be applied by substituting 'fair market value' for 'adjusted basis.' " Although the fair market value here is $125,000, the §312(a) adjustment cannot reduce e&p below zero. In our problem, e&p will be decreased from $50,000 to zero.

Unfortunately, the mechanics of §312 here can be rather confusing. One distribution causes three significant tax events. First, the distribution results in corporate gain. This gain increases e&p. Second, the distribution results in a taxable dividend to the shareholders to the extent of e&p. Finally, the distribution reduces e&p. Since all of these tax events are taking place simultaneously through one economic event, one may be confused as to the order in which to consider the tax consequences. Sections 312(a) and (b) provide an inelegantly drafted, but common sense, answer requiring the corporation to first increase e&p by the gain recognized and then decrease e&p by fair market value of the property distributed. Tax consequences to the shareholders must be determined after the increase to e&p, but before the decrease reflecting the distribution.

After working through the problem, you probably noticed that we first increased e&p from zero to $50,000 and then immediately decreased e&p back to zero again. If these two numbers simply wash each other out, you may be asking: why bother? The reason is that unless we went through this exercise, the shareholders would have wound up with no dividend. By temporarily increasing e&p, the corporation generated at least some e&p to cover the distribution, thus making the distribution at least partially taxable to the shareholders.

One final issue here is the basis of the piano now in the shareholders' hands. Section 301(d) simply provides that the basis is fair market value, here $125,000. Since the corporation paid tax on the corporate level gain and the shareholders paid tax on the distribution to the extent provided in §301(c), this result now seems appropriate. In the world before *General Utilities* repeal, this step-up in basis to the shareholders resulted in a permanent nonrecognition of the corporate level gain on the distributed property.

6. Although the corporation has realized a $10,000 loss, the loss will not be recognized. This question illustrates the limited function of the general rule of §311(a), which provides that no gain or loss shall be recognized on corporate distributions. The "general rule" in §311(a) now effectively operates as a disallowance of loss rule. After the distribution, the corporation's e&p will be reduced under §312(a)(3) by the $60,000 adjusted basis of the property distributed. E&p cannot be reduced below zero by the distribution. If the corporation had no e&p before the distribution was made, e&p will remain at zero.

The shareholders in this case received a distribution of $50,000 — the fair market value of the property. I.R.C. §301(b)(1). If the corporation has sufficient e&p, this will be a dividend to the shareholders. If the corporation had no e&p, the distribution will be treated as a tax-free recovery of capital to the extent of basis and thereafter as gain from the sale of stock. The shareholders' basis in the property is its fair market value of $50,000. I.R.C. §301(d).

7. Adding the assumption of a mortgage to Example 5 will not change the tax results to the corporation. The corporation must still report a gain of $50,000 ($125,000 amount realized less $75,000 basis) upon distribution

of the piano. The corporation is treated as if it sold the property to the shareholders at fair market value. Since the shareholders are assuming a liability, they are "paying" $100,000 of the price of this fictional purchase through assumption of the debt, and the remaining $25,000 with other "consideration." The amount realized of $125,000 thus includes the $100,000 mortgage.

From the shareholders' perspective, the distribution must be reduced by the amount of the liabilities under §301(b)(2). Thus, the shareholders have received a $25,000 distribution ($125,000 less $100,000). The distribution will be treated as a dividend to the extent of e&p. Despite receiving only a $25,000 distribution, the shareholders will take the piano with a full fair market value basis of $125,000 under §301(d). This too reflects the *Crane* notion that borrowed amounts are included in basis. Including the liability in basis presumes that the taxpayer will pay the liability.

One sticky issue remains — what adjustment to e&p should be made following the distribution? E&p will first be increased by the amount of the gain ($50,000) under §312(b)(1). Thereafter, e&p must be reduced by the fair market value of the property ($125,000) under §312(a) as modified by §312(b)(2). In addition, however, §312(c) requires "proper adjustment" for liabilities. The role of §312(c) after repeal of *General Utilities* is not entirely clear. On the one hand, given repeal of *General Utilities*, the corporation now must include the liability in amount realized on the distribution under §311. The resulting gain is included in taxable income and e&p. As a result, one might argue that no further adjustment is "proper." On the other hand, a closer look at what has been distributed out of corporate solution shows that the corporation has distributed property worth $125,000 subject to a mortgage of $100,000, or a *net* distribution of only $25,000. (Remember that this is the amount of the distribution to the shareholders figured above.) After taking the gain of $50,000 into account, then, perhaps the corporation should be limited to an e&p reduction of $25,000. Perhaps, then, "proper adjustment" for liabilities *does* require something further. Using the convoluted language of Treas. Reg. §1.312-3, we might reduce the $125,000 reduction by the $100,000 mortgage, leaving a decrease to e&p of $25,000. The latter approach seems to be the right answer here because it more accurately reflects the economic substance of the distribution.

The Corporate Shareholder

8a. Both MicroMac, Inc. and its minority shareholders have received a §301(c)(1) dividend. The minority shareholders will report their $15,000 share as ordinary dividend income. As a corporate shareholder, MicroMac can take a dividends-received deduction under §243. If the affiliated group has made the proper election and if the dividend is otherwise a "qualifying dividend" under §243(b), MicroMac will receive a 100% dividends-received deduction. I.R.C. §243(a)(3). The effect of this 100% deduction is to exclude the dividend from MicroMac's income.

If the subsidiary paying the dividend was a tax-exempt entity, the parent MicroMac would not be entitled to a dividends-received deduction. I.R.C. §246(a). The dividends-received deduction is designed to eliminate multiple layers of tax *beyond* the double tax. If the distributing corporation is exempt from tax and the corporate shareholder can take a dividends-received deduction, the government would collect a full tax only at the shareholder level.

8b. The only change would be that MicroMac, the distributee member of the consolidated group, would simply exclude the amount of the dividend, rather than first include the dividend and then take a §243 deduction. The effect of this treatment is the same as the §243 deduction—no tax upon the dividend distribution. In addition, under recently adopted consolidated return regulations, MicroMac would be required to reduce its basis in its MiniMac shares by the amount of the excluded dividend. Treas. Reg. §1.1502-13(f)(2).

9. MicroMac is not eligible for the §243 deduction since it did not own the IBM shares for the required holding period. I.R.C. §246(c). Thus, the dividend would be taxable to MicroMac to the extent of IBM's e&p. This holding period requirement prevents corporations from taking the §243 deduction on stock purchased recently in anticipation of a quick dividend payment otherwise eligible for a dividends-received deduction. Since §246(c) disallows the §243 deduction, no portion of the dividend is left untaxed for purposes of §1059(b). Thus, no further restrictions will apply.

A Sneaky Question

10. Corporation Z has made a bargain sale to Corporation Y. Ordinarily, such a bargain would have no immediate tax consequence. Given the relationship of the two corporations, however, some interesting tax consequences emerge. Here, Corporation Z has given up $250,000 in value that has been transferred to Corporation Y. The reason for the special arrangement here was the common ownership of the two corporations. The sale may be viewed as a *constructive dividend* of $250,000 to shareholder A followed by a contribution by A of the same $250,000 to Corporation Y. Under this approach, A will have dividend income to the extent that Corporation Z has e&p to cover the distribution and will receive an increase to basis in the Y shares reflecting the $250,000 contribution.[76]

---

76. Of course, not all payments between commonly controlled corporations will be treated as constructive dividends. This problem is designed simply to point out that possibility and to give some sense of the scope of constructive dividend principles.

6

Redemption Distributions

Introduction

A redemption distribution is a special type of nonliquidating distribution with one major distinguishing factor: the corporation in a redemption distributes cash or other property *in return for its own stock*.[1] At a minimum, a corporation's purchase of its own shares alters the capital structure by reducing the total shares outstanding. Moreover, unless the redemption is pro rata as to all shareholders, the redemption will alter the relative ownership interests of shareholders. In contrast, the nonliquidating distributions discussed in Chapter 5 generally did not alter the capital structure of the corporation or the relationships among shareholders or between shareholders and the corporation.

In some cases, a redemption simply reduces the number of outstanding shares and otherwise leaves the relative shareholder interests unchanged. For example, imagine a corporation with two unrelated shareholders, each of whom holds 1000 shares of stock representing 50% of the total 2000 outstanding shares. If the corporation pays cash to redeem 200 shares from each shareholder, the total number of shares outstanding is reduced from 2000 to 1600. Each shareholder now owns 800 shares. Despite this reduction in the *number* of shares, each shareholder still holds a 50% interest in the corporation. The corporation has less cash in its coffers and each of the shareholders has more cash in his or her pocket. How is this different from

---

1. I.R.C. §317(b) provides that "stock shall be treated as redeemed by a corporation if the corporation acquires its stock from a shareholder in exchange for property, whether or not the stock so acquired is cancelled, retired or held as treasury stock."

an operating distribution by which the corporation might distribute the same cash to the shareholders? The obvious answer is that in the redemption case, the corporation purchased back its own stock. From an economic perspective, however, the transactions are not very different. In either case, the shareholders have taken cash out of the corporation without changing their relative interests in the corporation. If the transaction had been structured as an operating distribution when the corporation had sufficient earnings and profits, the shareholders would have treated the distribution as a taxable dividend. When redemptions take on the quality of an operating distribution, they too will be handled under the §301 distribution rules considered in Chapter 5.

Varying the example above, imagine that the corporation decided to redeem completely the 1000 shares from one of its shareholders, reducing the total number of outstanding shares from 2000 to 1000. The redeemed shareholder no longer holds any shares and the remaining shareholder's interest has increased from 50% to 100%.[2] Unlike the pro rata redemption described above, this redemption rather dramatically alters the shareholders' relative interests. The redeemed shareholder effectively has sold her entire interest back to the corporation, thus reducing her interest in the corporation from 50% to zero. From the redeemed shareholder's perspective, this redemption takes on the quality of a sale.[3]

Taken together, these examples should begin to illustrate the challenge for drafters of the Internal Revenue Code with regard to redemptions. The key problem is distinguishing those redemptions that should be handled under the §301 distribution rules and those that should be treated simply as sales of stock by the shareholders to the corporation. Individual shareholders generally will prefer sale or exchange treatment. First of all, such treatment allows a basis offset that would not be available if the redemption was treated as a §301 distribution.[4] Second, if the stock has lost value, the shareholder will be entitled to use the loss for tax purposes at the time of the redemption.[5] Third, since stock generally is a capital asset, sale treatment at a gain

---

2. Tax consequences to the remaining shareholders upon this increase in their proportionate interest in the corporation are considered in a separate section later in this chapter.

3. The redemption distribution will be treated as a sale under the §302(b)(3) "complete termination of interest" provision, which is discussed in detail later in this chapter.

4. Assuming that there is sufficient e&p to cover the distribution, a §301 distribution will result in taxable ordinary income without any basis offset. If there is not sufficient e&p, the shareholder may receive a tax-free recovery of basis under the §301(c) rules. For complete discussion of the rules covering §301 distributions, see Chapter 5.

5. In assessing the value of this advantage, one must consider that the shareholder's ability to deduct the loss may be limited since the loss is likely to be capital loss.

will result in capital gains eligible for preferential capital gains rates. Corporate shareholders, on the other hand, may prefer dividend treatment to take advantage of the §243 dividends-received deduction.[6]

This chapter focuses primarily upon the rules designed to distinguish "sale redemptions" from "distribution redemptions." Note that these rules concern the proper tax treatment of the shareholders. From the corporation's perspective, a redemption distribution is not significantly different from other nonliquidating distributions. The final sections of this chapter consider tax consequences to the corporation.

Tax Consequences to Redeemed Shareholders

Overview

Prior to 1954, redemption distributions simply were treated as sales *unless* they were "essentially equivalent to the distribution of a taxable dividend."[7] This early statutory language was simple, but not especially helpful. After all, the very point of the redemption distribution rules was to distinguish those redemptions that should be treated as sales from those that should be treated as dividends. In this early period, decisions as to when distributions were essentially equivalent to a dividend and, therefore, taxable as a dividend, were left to the courts. Each such case required a facts and circumstances analysis and shareholders were left with tremendous uncertainty as to the outcome. In 1954, Congress enacted §302, under which individual shareholders could be certain of sale or exchange treatment upon receipt of redemption distributions meeting the precise tests provided within its §302(b) "safe harbor" provisions. For the most part, the provisions enacted in 1954 are those still found in §302(b) today.

A brief look at the structure of §302 is a good place to start. First, §302(a) provides that if one of the four paragraphs of subsection (b) applies, a corporate redemption of stock will be treated as "a distribution in part or full payment in exchange for the stock"—a sale. If the redemption does not fit within one of the paragraphs of subsection (b), the redemption will be treated as a distribution of property to which the distribution rules of §301 apply.[8] Thus, §302 is designed to distinguish sale or exchange redemptions

---

6. For discussion of the dividends-received deduction available to corporate shareholders, see Chapter 5. Special issues related to redemptions from corporate shareholders are considered later in this chapter.

7. Internal Revenue Code of 1939, §115(g).

8. I.R.C. §302(d).

from distribution redemptions to be treated under the nonliquidating distribution rules considered in Chapter 5. *Unless* the exchange fits within one of the descriptions in §302(b), the redemption will be treated under the §301 distribution rules.[9]

The §302(b) Tests for Sale or Exchange Treatment

a) Complete Termination of Interest: §302(b)(3)

The simplest of the §302(b) rules provides sale or exchange treatment for redemptions "in complete redemption of all of the stock owned by the shareholder." A classic illustration of §302(b)(3) is a redemption distribution to one of two 50% shareholders in exchange for all of the redeemed shareholder's stock. Treating the redemption as full payment in exchange for the stock in accordance with §302(a) makes sense if the shareholder's interest in the corporation is terminated by a complete redemption. Sale or exchange gain would result from the shareholder's sale of the stock to an independent third party. The tax consequences should be no different simply because the buyer happened to be the corporation itself.

A few twists should be noted here. First, in determining whether or not a particular shareholder's interest has been completely terminated, constructive ownership rules shall apply.[10] Under these constructive ownership or attribution rules, the redeemed shareholder is deemed to own shares owned by certain related parties for purposes of testing the redemption distribution under §302(b). For example, if the two shareholders in the above example were husband and wife, the redemption of all of the shares from one of them would not qualify under §302(b)(3), since the redeemed shareholder would be considered to own the spouse's shares even after the redemption and thus, the redeemed shareholder's interest will not have been completely terminated.[11]

Second, a complete redemption need not take place at one instant. A series of redemption distributions may be considered part of a complete termination of interest if the "individual redemptions constitute, in substance, the component parts of a single sale or exchange of the entire stock interest" and if the "redemptions are pursuant to a firm and fixed plan to

---

9. Note that §302(a) is entitled "General Rule." Given that only those redemptions that meet the requirements of subsection (b) are covered, this title can be a bit misleading.

10. The §318 constructive stock ownership rules will apply for purposes of all of the §302(b) tests. I.R.C. §302(c)(1). These rules are considered in detail later in this chapter.

11. I.R.C. §318(a)(1)(A)(i).

eliminate the stockholder from the corporation."[12] Deciding whether a series of redemptions is part of an integrated plan to completely terminate the shareholder requires a facts and circumstances analysis.[13]

b) Substantially Disproportionate Distribution: §302(b)(2)

Even if the shareholder's interest is not completely terminated, sale or exchange treatment may be available if his or her interest in the corporation is substantially reduced. In the §302(b)(2) "substantially disproportionate distribution" safe harbor, Congress provides precise mathematical tests to measure the extent of the shareholder's reduction in interest. This mathematical rule is designed to provide some certainty to shareholders concerning the percentage of stock that must be redeemed so as to qualify as a substantially disproportionate distribution. Congress determined by fiat that when there has been greater than a 20% reduction in the shareholder's voting interest *and* where the resulting interest is not a controlling interest, the shareholder has relinquished sufficient interest in the corporation to qualify for sale treatment. Thus, §302(b)(2) imposes the following two-part test:

i)   The 50% Threshold Test

As a threshold, §302(b)(2) shall not apply "unless immediately after the redemption the shareholder owns less than 50% of the total combined voting power of all classes of stock entitled to vote."[14] If the redeemed shareholder holds 50% or more of the combined voting power immediately after the redemption, the shareholder retains *control* of the corporation. A proportionate reduction that still leaves the shareholder with a controlling voting interest immediately after the redemption is not substantial enough to qualify for §302(b)(2) sale or exchange treatment.

ii)   The 80% Disproportionate Distribution Tests

The second part of the mathematical test involves a before and after analysis of stock ownership. The percentage of voting stock owned by the shareholder

---

12. Bleily & Collishaw, Inc. v. Comm'r, 72 T.C. 751, 756 (1979), *aff'd*, 647 F.2d 169 (9th Cir. 1981).

13. The Court in *Bleily & Collishaw* stated: "Generally, a gentleman's agreement lacking written embodiment, communication, and contractual obligations will not suffice to show a fixed and firm plan. . . . On the other hand, a plan need not be in writing, absolutely binding, or communicated to others to be fixed and firm although these factors all tend to indicate that such is the case." *Id.*

14. I.R.C. §302(b)(2)(B).

immediately *after* the redemption must be less than 80% of the percentage of voting stock owned by the shareholder immediately *before* the redemption.[15] In other words, there should be at least a 20% reduction in the shareholder's voting interest in the corporation. If less than 20% of the shareholder's voting interest is "sold" back to the corporation through the redemption, the shareholder's interest in the corporation relative to the other shareholders has not changed substantially. In such cases, Congress has determined that the transaction looks more like a distribution and should not qualify for sale treatment under §302(b)(2).

To illustrate, suppose that Corporation X has two unrelated shareholders, A and B, each of whom owns 50 of the 100 common voting shares outstanding and the corporation redeems 25 shares from A for cash. Immediately *before* the redemption, shareholder A owned 50% of the stock and immediately *after* the redemption, owns 25 of the remaining 75 shares or $33\frac{1}{3}$%. Shareholder A meets the 50% threshold test since her interest is less than 50% of the voting stock immediately after the redemption. Also, the $33\frac{1}{3}$% owned immediately after the redemption is less than 80% of the 50% owned immediately before the redemption, so the redemption will qualify under §302(b)(2).[16]

In addition to the 80% test applied to voting stock, §302(b)(2) requires that the 80% test also be applied to the common stock of the corporation, whether voting or nonvoting. Thus, if the corporation has outstanding any nonvoting common stock in addition to voting stock, the 80% test must be met for the total common shares as well as for the voting shares alone.

c) Redemptions Not Equivalent to Dividends: §302(b)(1)

i)   History

Section 302(b)(1) simply provides for sale treatment "if the redemption is not essentially equivalent to a dividend." Unlike the other provisions in §302(b), the "not essentially equivalent to a dividend" rule has a long history

---

15. I.R.C. §302(b)(2)(C). The language of the statute refers to the "ratio which the voting stock of the corporation owned by the shareholder immediately after the redemption bears to all of the voting stock of the corporation at such time," I.R.C. §302(b)(2)(C)(i), and the "ratio which the voting stock of the corporation owned by the shareholder immediately before the redemption bears to all of the voting stock of the corporation at such time," I.R.C. §302(b)(2)(C)(ii). For simplicity, these ratios will simply be referred to as the percentages of stock owned by the shareholder immediately after and immediately before the redemption respectively.

16. One way to figure the results under the 80% test is to create the ratio that the percentage ownership after the redemption bears to the percentage ownership before the redemption. In our example, this ratio would be $33\frac{1}{3}$/50 or $66\frac{2}{3}$%. Since this ratio

and interpretation of the statutory language in §302(b)(1) has been developed substantially through case law. This language carried over from the simple, but not especially helpful, provision in the 1939 Internal Revenue Code. The House version of the 1954 Code would have eliminated the "essentially equivalent to a dividend" language,[17] but the Senate insisted on retaining the old language, noting that the House version "appeared unnecessarily restrictive, particularly in the case of redemptions of preferred stock that might be called by the corporation without the shareholder having any control over when the redemption may take place."[18]

Given this history, modern §302(b)(1) has been quite narrowly construed and is the §302(b) sale or exchange provision of last resort for most shareholders. The landmark case interpreting §302(b)(1) is United States v. Davis,[19] which involved a closely held corporation owned by the taxpayer, his wife, and his children. Responding to the corporation's need for additional capital, the taxpayer contributed cash in return for some nonvoting preferred stock. The corporation was to "repay" the cash by later redeeming the shares. Since the taxpayer's basis in the nonvoting preferred shares was equal to the cash contributed, he expected little or no taxable gain from the later redemption. Unfortunately for Mr. Davis, the redemption did not qualify as a complete termination of his interest under §302(b)(3) since only his preferred shares were redeemed. Similarly, the redemption did not qualify for the §302(b)(2) substantially disproportionate distribution safe harbor. In the end, the taxpayer's argument for sale treatment hinged upon the §302(b)(1) "essentially equivalent to a dividend" test. Since his wife and children owned all of the other shares of the corporation, the taxpayer was deemed to be a 100% owner of the corporation both before and after the redemption through operation of the constructive ownership rules.[20] Developing what is commonly known as the "meaningful reduction" test, the Court ruled that to be eligible for sale or exchange treatment under §302(b)(1), "a redemption must result in a meaningful reduction of the shareholder's proportionate interest in the corporation."[21] Since Mr. Davis was deemed to be a 100% owner both before and after the redemption, he had experienced *no* reduction in interest at all. The redemption

---

is less than 80%, the redemption meets the 80% test. Another is first to compute 80% of the pre-redemption ratio. Since 80% of 50% is 40%, anything *less than* a 40% interest immediately after the redemption would be sufficient to qualify shareholder A for sale treatment under the §302(b)(2).

17. H.R. Rep. No. 1337, 83d Cong., 2d Sess. 35 (1954).

18. S. Rep. No. 1622, 83d Cong., 2d Sess. 44 (1954).

19. 397 U.S. 301 (1970). The Supreme Court in *Davis* provides a rather detailed description of the history behind §302(b)(1).

20. I.R.C. §318(a)(1).

21. United States v. Davis, 397 U.S. 301, 313 (1970).

distribution in exchange for his nonvoting preferred stock was treated as a dividend.

If a shareholder's reduction in interest is to be meaningful, there at least must be *some* reduction. The import of the *Davis* decision is that redemption of a sole shareholder (or a "constructive" sole shareholder such as Mr. Davis) is *always* equivalent to a dividend and can never get sale treatment. The hardship in *Davis* should be reasonably evident. If the taxpayer had *lent* the necessary capital to the corporation and later been repaid, he would have had no taxable gain from the corporation's repayment of principal. By providing the needed capital to the corporation in the form of a contribution in exchange for stock, the taxpayer in *Davis* found himself with a taxable dividend upon redemption of the stock.[22] The dissenters in *Davis* argued vigorously for a bona fide business purpose exception, particularly in the case of closely held corporations. Despite this call for a bona fide business exception, the *Davis* meaningful reduction test continues to rule the day. A redemption from a sole shareholder, actual or constructive, will *never* qualify for sale treatment under §302.

ii)   The Aftermath of *Davis*

Although the *Davis* case gave birth to the meaningful reduction test, the Court in that particular case found no reduction at all. Thus, the Court left open the question of how much reduction would qualify as "meaningful" in cases where a corporate redemption causes at least *some* reduction in the shareholder's interest. The *Davis* meaningful reduction test requires a facts and circumstances analysis and each case must be examined on its own merits. Nevertheless, cases and rulings interpreting the meaningful reduction test appear to fall into two categories.

The first includes redemptions from majority shareholders. When the shareholder held a majority interest immediately before the redemption and continues to hold a dominant voting interest immediately after the redemption, virtually *no* reduction in interest will be considered meaningful. Rev. Rul. 75-502 provides a good illustration of the Treasury Department's position. In that ruling the shareholder's interest in the corporation was reduced from 57% to 50%. The remaining 50% was owned by a single unrelated shareholder. Although the shareholder (an estate) continued to hold 50% after the redemption, its voting control was eliminated since the other 50% shareholder now held effective veto power, or at least the power to create a stalemate. The Treasury Department ruled that the redemption

---

22. Note, however, that the taxpayer in the *Davis* case was entitled to add the basis in the redeemed preferred stock to his basis in the common shares he continued to hold, thus reducing future gain from the sale of the common shares. *Id.* at 307, n.9.

qualified for sale or exchange treatment under §302(b)(1). The Ruling added that if the reduction had been less than 7% "the redemption would not qualify under section 302(b)(1) because the estate would continue to have dominant voting rights in X by virtue of its ownership of more than 50% of the X stock."[23] The logic here resembles the 50% threshold test under §302(b)(2). The reduction in interest is not thought to be substantial enough to justify sale or exchange treatment if the shareholder still exercises voting control even after the redemption. Despite this similarity, the Treasury Department's interpretation of §302(b)(1) allows more flexibility than the rigid 50% threshold test of §302(b)(2). The redemption involved in Rev. Rul. 75-502 would not have met the threshold test of §302(b)(2), which requires that the shareholder's interest immediately after the redemption be *less than* 50%. Under the facts and circumstances of that ruling, the reduction was considered meaningful since only two shareholders remained after the redemption. By implication, the Ruling suggests that had the remaining 50% of the stock been held by many shareholders, as opposed to one, the 50% interest owned by the taxpayer after the redemption would have left effective dominant voting rights with the redeemed shareholder. The reduction in that instance would not have been considered meaningful.

Although a shareholder who retains dominant voting rights after a redemption will have difficulty using §302(b)(1), there is one set of circumstances in which a case for meaningful reduction might succeed. For example, in Wright v. United States,[24] the court held that a reduction from 85% to 61.7% was meaningful since the shareholder lost the two-thirds voting control required by state law for various corporate actions. The shareholder in *Wright* retained *managerial* control, but nevertheless lost what might be referred to as *organic* control.[25] The Treasury Department, however, refused to consider the loss of organic control as a meaningful reduction in a case where no action requiring a two-thirds vote was contemplated at the time of the redemption.[26]

The second category of §301(b)(1) cases involves redemptions from minority shareholders, who will have a much easier time arguing that a meaningful reduction has taken place. In contrast to the uphill battle facing the majority shareholder in qualifying for §301(b)(1) sale treatment, it appears that almost *any* reduction in interest will qualify the minority shareholder. For example, in Rev. Rul. 76-385[27] a reduction from a .0001118%

23. Rev. Rul. 75-502, 1975-2 C.B. 111.

24. 482 F.2d 600 (8th Cir. 1973).

25. Since most states and articles of incorporation provide two-thirds voting rules only in the case of major organic changes such as merger or acquisition, I will refer to a loss of a dominant two-thirds interest as a loss of organic control.

26. Rev. Rul. 78-401, 1978-2 C.B. 127.

27. 1976-2 C.B. 92.

interest to a .0001081% interest in Z Corporation was considered meaning-ful. The ruling points out that the redemption "involves a minority share-holder whose relative stock interest in Z is minimal and who exercises no control over the affairs of Z."[28] This was precisely the kind of case the Senate was worried about when it added back the "not essentially equivalent to a dividend" provision. Recall that the Senate Finance Committee voted to leave this language in the statute to protect "redemptions of preferred stock which might be called by the corporation without the shareholder having any control over when the redemption may take place."[29] Even though a min-uscule reduction may be sufficient for minority shareholders, the Treasury Department continues to insist on at least *some* reduction. For example, in Rev. Rul. 81-289, the proportionate interest of the minority shareholders remained at exactly .02% before and after the redemption distribution. The minority shareholders in this ruling were not entitled to sale treatment under §302(b)(1) since they experienced no reduction.

d) Partial Liquidations: §302(b)(4)

The last sale or exchange redemption in §302(b)(4) has a rather different focus from the first three. The first three of the §302(b) tests focus on the extent of the *shareholder's* proportionate reduction in interest in the corpo-ration relative to other shareholders. In contrast, the (b)(4) partial liquidation provision views the redemption from the *corporation's* perspective, looking to the extent of corporate contraction. In fact, even a pro rata redemption distribution might qualify for sale or exchange treatment under §302(b)(4).[30] In addition, unlike the other §302(b) provisions, §302(b)(4) is limited to *noncorporate* shareholders. Section 302(b)(4) permits sale or exchange treat-ment to a noncorporate shareholder if the distribution is "in partial liquida-tion of the distributing corporation."

Unfortunately, the general definition of "partial liquidation" in §302(e)(1) is quite vague. This provision sets out two requirements for classification as a partial liquidation. First, the distribution must be "not essentially equivalent to a dividend (*determined at the corporate level rather than at the shareholder level.*)"[31] Second, the distribution must be "pursuant to a plan and occur within the taxable year in which the plan is adopted or within the succeeding taxable year."[32] Although some issues may arise re-

---

28. *Id.*
29. S. Rep. No. 1622, 83d Cong., 2d Sess. 44 (1954).
30. See I.R.C. §302(e)(4).
31. I.R.C. §302(e)(1)(A) (emphasis added).
32. I.R.C. §302(e)(1)(B).

garding what constitutes a "plan" and the date on which the plan was adopted, this second requirement is reasonably straightforward.

The first requirement is more problematic. One might immediately notice parallels with the language in §302(b)(1). Recall that, as interpreted by the Supreme Court in the *Davis* case, a (b)(1) "not essentially equivalent to a dividend" distribution required a "meaningful reduction" in the *shareholder's* interest. Although it uses the same initial language, §302(e) asks us to make the "not essentially equivalent to a dividend" determination at the *corporate* level. Taking this instruction to heart, it should be clear that the *Davis* shareholder level meaningful reduction test will not apply to partial liquidation distributions. The meaning of "not essentially equivalent to a dividend" determined at the corporate level lies in old case law and regulations promulgated under the predecessor to §302(b)(4).[33] Under these cases and regulations, a distribution was not essentially equivalent to a dividend from the corporate perspective when the distribution reflected a "genuine contraction of the corporate business."[34] Even in its earlier incarnations, the "corporate contraction" doctrine was highly fact specific and the outcome of any particular case was difficult to predict. Now that the partial liquidation provision has been moved to §302(b)(4), the extent to which the corporate contraction doctrine will be applied as before is uncertain.

Responding to this uncertainty, Congress provides a partial liquidation safe harbor in §302(e)(2). Taxpayers meeting the more specific requirements in §302(e)(2) will be assured that the distribution is a partial liquidation for purposes of §302(b)(4).[35] Here again, the definition has two requirements. First, the distribution must be "attributable to the distributing corporation's ceasing to conduct, or consists of the assets of, a qualified trade or business."[36] Second, the distributing corporation must be "actively engaged in the conduct of a qualified trade or business immediately after the distribution."[37] A qualified trade or business is one that was "(A) conducted throughout the 5-year period ending on the date of redemption, and (B) was

---

33. Much of the language in §302(b)(4) originated in old §346. Thus, the regulations under this now repealed provision may be instructive. See Treas. Reg. §1.346-1. Oddly enough, even though the old partial liquidation statute itself has been repealed, the regulations remain in place.

34. Treas. Reg. §1.346-1(a)(2). An example in the regulations taken from an earlier case is "the distribution of unused insurance proceeds recovered as a result of a fire which destroyed part of the business causing a cessation of a part of its activities." *Id.*

35. The "safe harbor" definition in §302(e)(2) is not exclusive. It states that "distributions which meet the requirement of paragraph (1)(A) [the general definition] shall include *(but shall not be limited to)* a distribution meeting the requirements of . . . this paragraph." I.R.C. §302(e)(2) (emphasis added).

36. I.R.C. §302(e)(2)(A).

37. I.R.C. §302(e)(2)(B).

not acquired by the corporation within such period in a transaction in which gain or loss was recognized in whole or in part."[38] In this safe-harbor definition, we see more clearly the concept of corporate contraction. The safe harbor here envisions a corporation that was engaged in two or more businesses and is distributing the assets of, or ceasing to conduct, one of its businesses.[39] The five-year requirements are designed to avoid "abusive" transactions in which the corporation might use an earnings surplus to invest in a new business and then distribute the recently acquired business shortly thereafter to its shareholders. A direct corporate distribution of earnings to shareholders who had an interest in the acquisition followed by a *shareholder* purchase of the new business would have resulted in dividend income to the shareholders. If the redemption distribution of the new business qualified for sale or exchange treatment under §302(b)(4), the shareholders would be able to bail out corporate earnings at capital gains rates and with a basis offset. The 5-year restriction in §302(e)(3) prevents this type of quick bailout.[40]

A Look at Attribution Rules: §318

Overview

In determining the percentage ownership of stock before and after a redemption for purposes of applying the §302(b) rules discussed above,[41] the shareholder must include not only shares *actually* owned but also shares *constructively* owned.[42] The rationale for these constructive ownership or attribution rules is that shareholders are presumed to exercise control over shares held by certain related parties. For example, suppose that taxpayer W's shares are completely redeemed by a closely held corporation in which she and her husband own all of the stock. Even though the wife no longer owns any shares *directly*, she is considered to own her husband's shares *indirectly*.

---

38. I.R.C. §302(e)(3).

39. One should note the similarities between a partial liquidation as defined in §302(e)(2) and a corporate split-off pursuant to §355. Split-offs and the similarities to partial liquidations will be considered further in Chapter 13.

40. Notice that the bailout can be achieved, however, if the shareholders and the corporation are prepared to wait out the five-year period.

41. Since §302(b)(4) focuses on the extent of corporate contraction rather than on the shareholder's proportionate interest, the attribution rules will have little or no bearing in the case of a partial liquidation.

42. I.R.C. §302(c)(1) states that "§318(a) shall apply in determining the ownership of stock."

The constructive ownership rules *presume* that she still exercises control over the corporate enterprise to the extent of her husband's interest.

The constructive stock ownership rules in §318 come into play only when another provision of the Code expressly makes them applicable.[43] The §302 stock redemption rules are among the Code provisions expressly referring to §318.[44] Pursuant to §302(c), the attribution rules apply only for purposes of testing the *redeemed* shareholder's proportionate interest in the corporation immediately before and immediately after the redemption distribution and then applying the various §302(b) tests for sale or exchange treatment.

One interesting issue to arise over the years is whether the presumption of control that underlies the family attribution rules in §318(a)(1) can be rebutted by evidence of family hostility. A series of colorful cases involving family discord has raised this issue with mixed results. Most courts have taken the view that evidence of discord cannot be used to avoid family attribution. These courts view the §318 rules as irrebuttable.[45] As most colorfully put by the court in *David Metzger Trust,* "[t]he pattern, intensity, and predicted duration of a family fight are difficult enough for the solomonic justice of our domestic relations courts. It is hardly the basis for a soundly administered tax policy. The fixity of the attribution rules then in this sense is not their weakness but their strength."[46] Evidence of family discord may nevertheless be relevant in one limited context. In connection with the "not essentially equivalent to a dividend" safe harbor in §302(b)(1) at least one court has indicated that family discord may be taken into account in determining whether or not a reduction in interest is meaningful under the *Davis* test.[47]

Categories of Attribution

The §318 attribution rules include four categories of relationships that will cause the shares of one shareholder to be constructively owned by another. First, §318(a)(1) provides for attribution among certain family members. Second, §318(a)(2) provides for attribution *from* entities such as partnerships

---

43. I.R.C. §318(a).

44. I.R.C. §302(c)(1).

45. David Metzger Trust v. Comm'r, 693 F.2d 459 (5th Cir. 1982), *cert. denied,* 463 U.S. 1207 (1983); Cerone v. Comm'r, 87 T.C. 1 (1986). *Contra* Robin Haft Trust v. Comm'r, 510 F.2d 43 (1st Cir. 1975).

46. David Metzger Trust v. Comm'r, 693 F.2d at 467.

47. Cerone v. Comm'r, 87 T.C. at 22. Note, however, that the attribution rules must first be applied in determining whether or not there has been any reduction in interest and to determine the extent of the reduction. Evidence of family discord then can be considered as a factor in assessing whether or not the reduction was meaningful.

or corporations to the individual partners or shareholders and, third, §318(a)(3) provides for attribution *to* entities such as partnerships or corporations from the individual partners or shareholders. Finally, §318(a)(4) provides that any person who has an option to purchase stock shall be considered as owning the stock.

a) Family Attribution: §318(a)(1)

An individual will be considered to own stock that is owned directly or indirectly by his or her spouse, children, grandchildren, or parents under §318(a)(1). Notice that the relationships specified here are, for the most part, lineal. This provision does *not* call for attribution between siblings, for example.[48]

b) Attribution *from* Entities: §318(a)(2)

Section 318(a)(2) provides attribution rules for stock owned by a partnership, estate, trust, or corporation. Stock owned directly or indirectly by a partnership or estate shall be considered as owned *proportionately* by its partners or beneficiaries.[49] For example, suppose that partners A and B each hold a one-half interest in Partnership X. Partnership X owns 100 shares in Corporation Y. Each partner will be considered to constructively own one-half of the partnership's stock for purposes of §302.

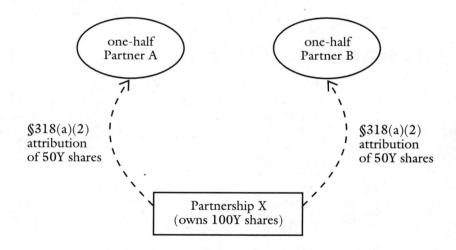

---

48. In contrast, different constructive ownership rules applicable for purposes of *other* provisions of the Code *do* provide attribution for siblings. I.R.C. §267(b)(1). Note too that §318(a) limits the lineal attribution to children, grandchildren, and parents, whereas §267 applies attribution to all lineal descendants. I.R.C. §267(c)(4).

49. I.R.C. §318(a)(2)(A). According to the regulations, beneficiary "includes any person entitled to receive property of a decedent pursuant to a will or pursuant to laws of descent and distribution. A person shall no longer be considered a beneficiary

Similarly, beneficiaries of a trust will be considered to own stock of the trust in proportion to their actuarial interests in the trust.[50] Finally, any person[51] who directly or indirectly owns 50% or more in value of the stock in a corporation will be considered to own stock owned by the corporation in proportion to the value of stock owned.[52] For example, imagine that shareholders A and B each own a 50% interest in Corporation X and Corporation X holds 100 Y shares. Each shareholder is deemed to own 50% of the stock owned by Corporation X.

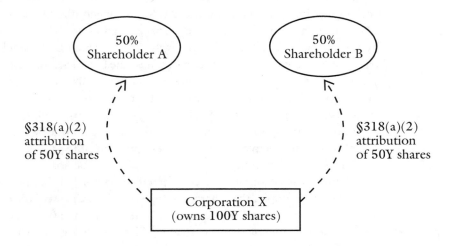

Notice the difference between the partnership/ estate attribution rule and the corporation attribution rule. The former applies regardless of the extent of the partner or beneficiary's interest in the entity. Thus, even a 10% partner would be considered to own 10% of the partnership's stock. A 10% shareholder in a corporation, on the other hand, would not be viewed as constructively owning any stock owned by the corporation. Perhaps the difference here simply reflects differences in the entities themselves. A share-

---

of an estate when all property to which he is entitled has been received by him, when he no longer has a claim against the estate arising out of having been a beneficiary, and when there is only a remote possibility that it will be necessary for the estate to seek the return of property or to seek payment from him by contribution or otherwise to satisfy claims against the estate or expenses of administration." Treas. Reg. §1.318-3(a).

50. I.R.C. §318(a)(2)(B)(i). In addition, stock owned by any portion of a trust of which a person is considered a "grantor" will be considered owned by the grantor. I.R.C. §318(a)(2)(B)(ii).

51. It should be noted that the statute uses the term "person" as opposed to "individual" for purposes of the entity attribution rules in §318(a)(2) and (a)(3). "Person" is a broad term that includes corporations and other entities.

52. I.R.C. §318(a)(2)(C).

holder has little control over affairs of the corporation unless he or she holds a controlling interest permitting election of his or her chosen representatives to the Board of Directors. On the other hand, partners generally have control proportionate to their interest in the partnership. Under §318(a)(2) *from* the entity attribution, only stock proportionate to the person's interest in the entity will be attributed from the entity to the individual.

c) Attribution *to* Entities: §318(a)(3)

Section 318(a)(3) provides attribution rules for stock owned by persons *to* entities in which they hold an interest. Stock owned directly or indirectly by a partner in a partnership or a beneficiary of an estate is considered owned by the partnership or estate respectively. Stock owned by a beneficiary of a trust is considered owned by the trust unless the beneficial interest is a remote contingent interest.[53] Finally, if any person owns 50% or more of the stock in a corporation, the corporation will be considered to own that person's stock. Note that unlike the §318(a)(2) *from* the entity rules, the rules for attribution *to* the entity are not proportional rules. In other words, when the §318(a)(3) constructive ownership rules apply, *all* of the stock owned by the related person is attributed to the entity. When a person is in control of a corporation, the corporation is considered to own *all* of that person's stock. Imagine, for example, that shareholders A and B each own 50% of the stock in Corporation X. Each of the shareholders also owns 50 shares of stock in Corporation Z. All of these Z shares will be attributed to Corporation X under §318(a)(3).

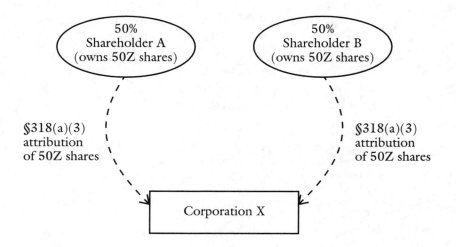

---

53. A beneficial interest is considered remote if "under the maximum exercise of discretion by the trustee in favor of such beneficiary, the value of such interest, computed actuarially, is 5% or less of the value of the trust property." I.R.C. §318(a)(3)(B)(i).

d) Options Treated as Stock: §318(a)(4)

Under §318(a)(4), a person with an option to acquire stock is considered to actually own the shares for purposes of testing a redemption distribution under §302(b). A warrant or convertible security will be considered an option under this rule if it provides the holder a right to obtain stock at his or her election and if there are no contingencies with respect to the election.[54]

Multiple Attribution

Each of the attribution rules discussed above provides that stock owned *directly or indirectly* by one person shall be considered owned by another. A person may own stock *indirectly* via attribution from another. Lest there be any doubt, the operating rules in §318(a)(5) provide, with two exceptions, that stock *constructively* owned shall be considered *actually* owned for purposes of applying the attribution rules. For example, suppose that A is a partner in Partnership X. A's mother owns 50 shares in Corporation Z. Under §318(a)(1), A is considered to own her mother's shares. In a second application of attribution rules under §318(a)(3)(A), the partnership is considered to own the stock just attributed to A. Thus, the partnership constructively owns shares actually owned by the mother of one of its partners.

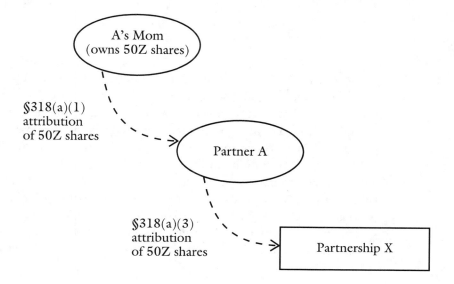

Although the general operating rule of §318(a)(5) allows unlimited multiple attribution, two exceptions to the general rule provide for a cut-off of attribution in certain cases. The first exception applies to family attribu-

---

54. Rev. Rul. 68-601, 1968-2 C.B. 124. See also Rev. Rul. 89-64, 1989-1 C.B. 91.

tion. Stock constructively owned by an individual under the family attribution rules shall not be considered as owned by her for purposes of *again* applying the family attribution rules in order to make another the constructive owner of such stock.[55] This family attribution cut-off prevents multiple applications of the attribution rules to pass constructive ownership to family members not included in the §318(a)(1) provision directly. For example, recall that §318(a)(1) does not provide for direct attribution between siblings. Without the family attribution cut-off, one sibling's stock might have been attributed to another in a two-step process. First, one child's stock is attributed to a parent under §318(a)(1). Next, absent the cut-off rule, the stock would be attributed to the other child in a second application of §318(a)(1). Since §318(a)(5)(B) prevents a double application of family attribution, one sibling will not be considered to own stock of another.[56]

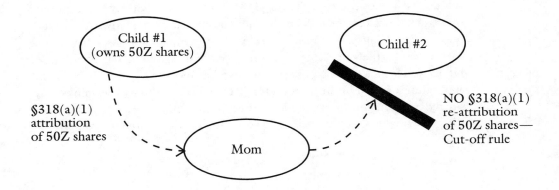

A second exception to the general multiple attribution operating rule applies to entities. Under §318(a)(5)(C), "stock constructively owned by a partnership, estate, trust, or corporation by reason of the application of paragraph (3) shall not be considered as owned by it for purposes of applying paragraph (2) in order to make another the constructive owner of such stock."[57] This attribution cut-off is similar to the family attribution cut-off above. As an example, suppose that Partnership X has two equal and unrelated partners, A and B. Partner A owns stock in Z corporation. The Z stock is constructively owned by the partnership under §318(a)(3). Absent the special cut-off, partner B now might be considered to own one-half of these shares under §318(a)(2).[58] The attribution of shares from one partner to

---

55. I.R.C. §318(a)(5)(B).

56. You might think of the §318(a)(5)(B) rule as the "(1)/(1) cut-off."

57. You might think of the §318(a)(5)(C) rule as the "(3)/(2) cut-off."

58. Keep in mind that §318(a)(2) provides for proportionate attribution and partner B holds a one-half partnership interest.

another partner is prevented through the attribution cut-off found in §318(a)(5)(C) much in the same way that the attribution between siblings is prevented by §318(a)(5)(B).

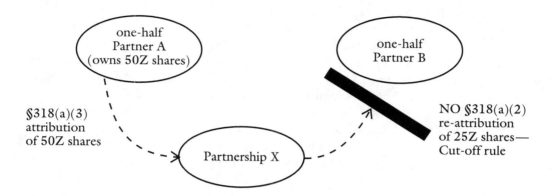

This seems a sensible result. There is no reason to assume that one partner has control over a corporation in which an unrelated partner happens to hold stock.

As you can imagine, multiple application of the attribution rules and operation of the attribution cut-offs can be quite complex. In each case above, we considered only one example of operation of the attribution cut-offs. Keep in mind that many other applications are possible. Moreover, where multiple attribution is not cut off by one of the operating rules, applications of the rules can be seemingly endless. Since application of the constructive ownership rules tends to be somewhat mechanical, more involved problems can best be considered in the Examples and Explanations section below.[59]

Waiver of Family Attribution Rules: §302(c)(2)

a) Waiver by Individual Shareholders

In the family business setting, application of constructive ownership rules made it virtually impossible for a redeemed shareholder to receive sale treatment on the redemption. Even if his or her shares were completely redeemed, constructive ownership from other family members prevented the redemption from qualifying as a complete termination of interest under §302(b)(3). Responding to these concerns, Congress allows the redeemed shareholder to waive only *family* attribution under §318(a)(1) and only in the case of §302(b)(3) complete terminations of interest.[60] Using the family

---

59. See Examples 5 and 6 at the end of this chapter.
60. I.R.C. §302(c)(2)(A).

attribution waiver, it is now possible for one family member to retire from the family business by having the corporation purchase all of his or her shares in a redemption that qualifies as a complete termination of interest under §302(b)(3). Shares held by the remaining family members will not be attributed to the redeemed shareholder.

To qualify for the waiver, three important conditions must be met. First, immediately after the redemption, the redeemed shareholder must have "no interest in the corporation (including an interest as officer, director, or employee), other than an interest as a creditor."[61] Remember that the attribution rules are based on the assumption that related parties retain control and influence over the corporation even though they may not own any shares directly. The redeemed shareholder's agreement to forgo any interest in the corporation undercuts this assumption of control. Second, the redeemed shareholder cannot acquire any such interest in the corporation within 10 years of the redemption distribution.[62] Third, the redeemed shareholder must file an agreement to notify the Secretary of any reacquisition within the 10-year period. Should such reacquisition occur, the statute of limitations will be extended for one year from the date of notification to the Secretary.[63] In such cases, the taxes for the year of redemption will be recomputed to treat the redemption as a dividend rather than as a sale.

The requirement that the redeemed shareholder forgo any interest in the corporation other than an interest as a creditor is really the heart of the waiver provision. Congress is willing to ignore the presumption of continued control through other family members' shares only if the retiring family member no longer has any interest in the corporate enterprise other than as a creditor and does not reacquire such an interest for a period of ten years. The precise boundaries of the "no interest" condition have been somewhat difficult to define, however.

The statutory language permitting the retiring shareholder to continue as a creditor gives corporations flexibility to completely redeem a family member with a promissory note providing for payment on an installment basis. This will be a convenient tool where corporate funds are limited or otherwise needed for operations or expansion. The Treasury Department was concerned, however, that corporations might create special creditor relation-

---

61. I.R.C. §302(c)(2)(A)(i).

62. I.R.C. §302(c)(2)(A)(ii). The statute provides an exception for stock acquired by bequest or inheritance.

63. I.R.C. §302(c)(2)(A)(iii). Another concern in applying the family attribution waiver provisions was that family businesses would engage in pre-redemption stock shuffling so as to permit a later redemption of one family member to receive sale treatment. Congress responded to this concern by creating an exception to the waiver rules in cases where the distributee received any of the redeemed stock within 10 years prior to redemption from a related party. This exception will apply only if one of the principal purposes of the acquisition was tax avoidance. I.R.C. §302(c)(2)(B).

ships with retiring family members that really disguised a greater continuing interest in the corporate enterprise than one would expect for the ordinary creditor. Responding to this concern, the regulations provide that:

> a person will be considered a creditor only if the rights of such person with respect to the corporation are not greater or broader in scope than necessary for the enforcement of his claim. Such claim must not in any sense be proprietary and must not be subordinate to the claims of general creditors. An obligation in the form of a debt may thus constitute a proprietary interest. For example, if under the terms of the instrument the corporation may discharge the principal amount of its obligation to a person by payments, the amount or certainty of which are dependent upon the earnings of the corporation, such a person is not a creditor of the corporation. Furthermore, if under the terms of the instrument the rate of purported interest is dependent upon earnings, the holder of such instrument may not, in some cases, be a creditor.[64]

Several courts have held arrangements to create only a creditor interest even under circumstances where the retiring shareholder's interest maintained arguably proprietary characteristics. For example, in Dunn v. Commissioner,[65] an installment agreement with the retiring shareholders provided for postponement of any installment payment that would cause the corporation to fall below the net working capital requirement or to violate the 50% net profit retention clause under the corporation's franchise agreement with General Motors. The government argued that the postponement provision in the redemption agreement subordinated the shareholder's claim and that the payments were dependent upon the corporation's earnings. Ruling for the shareholders, the Second Circuit noted that only the *timing* of the payments, as opposed to the amounts, were in any way dependent upon the corporation's earnings. While conceding that an ordinary trade creditor would have greater right to insist on payment than the retiring shareholders, the court observed that this "is just the difference between any trade creditor selling on current account and a long-term creditor, secured or unsecured."[66] The court found that general creditors would have no greater rights than the retiring shareholders if the corporation were to liquidate. The rulings in *Dunn* and several other cases suggest that the courts will be somewhat lenient and allow the corporation some leeway in structuring installment agreements with retiring shareholders to take unusual circumstances into account.[67] Even the Service has agreed that an arms-length leasehold interest retained by the redeemed shareholder is not prohibited under the waiver rules as long as the

---

64. Treas. Reg. §1.302-4(d).

65. 615 F.2d 578 (2d Cir. 1980).

66. *Id.* at 583.

67. See, e.g., Estate of Leonard v. Comm'r, 61 T.C. 554 (1974), *nonacq.* 1978-2 C.B. 3.

rental payments to the redeemed shareholder are not subordinated to general creditor claims or dependent upon the corporation's earnings.[68]

Another issue in interpreting the "no interest" condition is whether the retiring family member can continue in some advisory or independent consultant capacity as long as he has no formal interest as an officer, director, or employee. The Tax Court took the rather liberal position that the test for purposes of §302(c)(2)(A)(i) was whether the taxpayer had "a financial stake in the corporation or managerial control after the redemption."[69] Merely providing services to the corporation, even for compensation, was not considered by the Tax Court to be an interest in the corporation for purposes of applying the waiver rule. The Ninth Circuit, at least, disagrees. In Lynch v. Commissioner, the Ninth Circuit Court of Appeals rejected the Tax Court approach, stating that "[a]n individualized determination of whether a taxpayer has retained a financial stake or continued to control the corporation after the redemption is inconsistent with Congress' desire to bring a measure of certainty to the tax consequences of a corporate redemption. We hold that a taxpayer who provides post-redemption services, either as an employee or an independent contractor, holds a prohibited interest in the corporation because he is not a creditor."[70]

b) Waiver by an Entity

As originally drafted, the waiver rules permitted only the waiver of family attribution under §318(a)(1) by individual distributees. In 1982, Congress added a narrow provision permitting entities to waive family attribution under limited circumstances.[71] If a person with an interest in an entity owns stock indirectly by family attribution under §318(a)(1), the stock will again be attributed to the entity under §318(a)(3). As a result, an otherwise complete redemption of the entity's interest will fail the §302(b)(3) complete termination of interest test. Under §302(c)(2)(C), the *entity* may waive the *family* attribution to its beneficiary. Notice, however, that the waiver is limited to §318(a)(1) family attribution. If the person owned any shares *directly,* these would be attributed to the entity under §318(a)(3). No waiver is available to the entity under §318(a)(3).

To illustrate, suppose that A is the beneficiary of X's estate. X's estate owns 50 Corporation Z shares. The remaining 50 Z shares are owned by A's

---

68. Rev. Rul. 77-467, 1977-2 C.B. 92.

69. Lynch v. Comm'r, 83 T.C. 597, 606-607 (1984), *rev'd,* 801 F.2d 1176 (9th Cir. 1986). Similar language was used in Cerone v. Comm'r, 87 T.C. 1, 31 (1986); Seda v. Comm'r, 82 T.C. 484, 488 (1984); Lewis v. Comm'r, 47 T.C. 129, 135 (1966).

70. 801 F.2d 1176, 1179 (9th Cir. 1986).

71. I.R.C. §302(c)(2)(C).

mother.[72] Z Corporation redeems all of the shares owned directly by the X Estate. A multiple application of the attribution rules[73] will result in the Estate's constructively owning A's mother's shares.

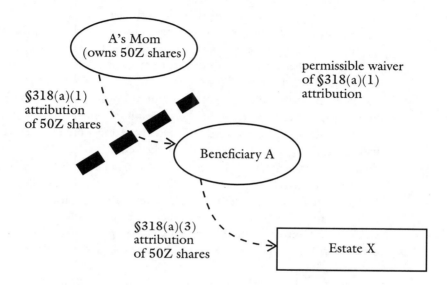

Under these circumstances, the estate may waive the attribution from A's mother to A if the conditions of §302(c)(2)(C) are met. These conditions require that the entity *and* each related person meet the (c)(2)(A) waiver requirements.[74] In our example, both the Estate *and* beneficiary A must have no interest other than as a creditor and agree not to acquire such an interest within 10 years. In addition, each related party must agree to be jointly and severally liable for any deficiency resulting from acquisition of an interest within the 10-year period.[75] If the estate and its beneficiary meet the conditions and file an appropriate waiver, the estate will qualify for sale or exchange treatment under §302(b)(3). If A owned 50% of the Z stock directly rather than by attribution from her mother, A's Z shares would be attributed to the estate and the estate would be ineligible for sale or exchange treatment under any of the safe harbors since the estate would be constructively a 100% owner both before and after the redemption.

---

72. Notice that A herself owns no Z shares.

73. An (a)(1)-(a)(3) combination. Notice that this multiple attribution is similar to the multiple attribution in the partnership example, *supra* p. 159. The partnership in that example also could use the entity waiver rule discussed here to avoid family attribution from Partner A's Mom.

74. I.R.C. §302(c)(2)(C)(i)(I).

75. I.R.C. §302(c)(2)(C)(i)(II).

The Mystery of Disappearing Basis

Application of the §318 attribution rules in connection with a §302 redemption distribution may result in dividend treatment to a shareholder whose stock is completely redeemed. Consider the simple closely held family corporation in which stock is owned entirely by the husband and wife. Even if the husband's shares are completely redeemed upon his retirement, the redemption distribution will not meet any of the §302(b) sale or exchange tests unless the husband files a proper waiver of family attribution. He is deemed to own 100% of the corporation both immediately before and immediately after the redemption. As a result, the husband will have ordinary dividend income to the extent of the corporation's earnings and profits and will receive no offset for his basis in the redeemed shares. In the ordinary dividend situation, the absence of a basis offset is not especially troubling. After all, the shareholder receiving a dividend distribution still owns the stock and will get the basis offset upon ultimate sale of the stock. In the complete redemption context, however, the redeemed shareholder no longer holds any stock. Sale treatment was prevented due to application of the constructive ownership rules. What happens to the redeemed shareholder's basis in the shares no longer owned? One bad solution to the mystery of disappearing basis would be to let the basis quietly disappear. This would be unfair to the taxpayer who should receive a recovery of his or her capital investment at some point.

The best clue to an answer to this "mystery of disappearing basis" can be found in the regulations. In Treasury Regulation §1.302-2(c), example (2), husband and wife (H and W) each owned one-half of Corporation X. H had originally purchased all of the stock for $100,000 and had later given one-half to W. All of H's stock is later redeemed in a transaction determined to be a dividend as opposed to a sale redemption. Without further elaboration, the example states that "immediately after the transaction, W holds the remaining stock of Corporation X with a basis of $100,000."

The regulatory example resolves the mystery by permitting the husband's basis in the shares redeemed to be transferred to the wife. When *she* later sells the remaining shares, *she* will get the basis offset. Keeping in mind that the mystery should arise only in cases where attribution rules prevent sale treatment, it appears that basis in the redeemed shares should be transferred to those remaining shareholders from whom the attribution occurred. These mysteries are explored further in the Examples and Explanations section below.

Special Issues for Corporate Shareholders

Individual shareholders tend to think of the §302(b) provisions as "safe harbors" since they prefer the preferential capital gains rates and basis offset available in a §302 sale or exchange redemption to §301 ordinary dividend income. Such individual shareholders often will insist that the corporation carefully structure a redemption transacton to fit within one of the §302(b) provisions. *Corporate* shareholders, on the other hand, have very different interests with respect to redemption transactions; they are unlikely to think of the §302(b) provisions as "safe harbors" at all. Instead, corporate shareholders tend to prefer §301 dividend treatment so that they can take advantage of the §243 dividends-received deduction available only to corporate shareholders. Thus, corporate shareholders may insist that a redemption transaction be structured deliberately to *flunk* the §302(b) tests. One of the more famous such transactions in recent memory involved a redemption of DuPont shares from Seagram's, one of DuPont's major corporate shareholders. Through a carefully structured redemption distribution designed to flunk §302(b), Seagram's tried to dispose of most of its interest in DuPont for cash, short-term notes and warrants without reporting *any* capital gains tax on an approximately $6 billion gain. Instead, Seagram's hoped to treat the cash and notes as an intercorporate dividend, eligible for a §243 corporate dividends-received deduction. This particular transaction inspired numerous reform proposals, culminating in amendments included in the Taxpayer Relief Act of 1997.[76]

Rather than adopt changes to the §302 redemption rules, Congress responded with narrowly targeted special provisions in the §1059 extraordinary dividend rules. Under §1059(e), as amended, certain redemption distributions are treated as §1059(a) "extraordinary dividends." If the redemption distribution is classified as an "extraordinary dividend" under §1059(e), the shareholder receiving the redemption distribution will be required to reduce its basis in its remaining shares by the nontaxed portion of the dividend. So, for example, under §1059, Seagram's would be required to reduce its basis in the DuPont shares by the nontaxed portion of the dividend; in other words, to the extent that it was able to escape tax on the distribution through the §243 dividends-received deduction. In addition, to the extent that the nontaxed portion of the distribution exceeds the shareholder's basis in the remaining shares, §1059(a)(2) now triggers an immediate recognition of capital gain.

Details of the amended §1059 rules are beyond the scope of most basic courses in corporate taxation. For the moment, the lesson to be highlighted

---

76. Pub. L. No. 105-34, 111 Stat. 788, §1011 (codified at I.R.C. §1059(a)(2), (e)).

from this episode is that individual shareholders and corporate shareholders have different interests with regard to classification of redemption distributions. Historically, the Treasury Department has been rather rigid in its application of the §302(b) tests, making them harder to satisfy. This government strategy was designed to prevent individual shareholders from too easily achieving sale or exchange treatment on redemption distributions, thus escaping §301 ordinary income. The government's rigid application of the §302(b) rules, however, has played into the hands of corporate shareholders, who actually *prefer* §301 treatment. Congress has responded with special rules in §1059 designed to reduce the tax advantages of certain dividend redemption transactions.

Redemptions of Stock to Pay Death Taxes: §303

After the death of one of its shareholders, a closely held corporation often redeems shares from the decedent's estate. Absent special rules, the estate might be required to report the distribution as a dividend under the §301 distribution rules after applying the §302 redemption analysis incorporating constructive ownership from other family members. Responding to the hardship faced by some family businesses forced to liquidate the business in order to pay estate and other death taxes, Congress enacted §303, which provides sale or exchange treatment upon the redemption of shares included in determining the gross estate of a decedent.[77]

Pursuant to §303(a), a redemption distribution will be treated as a sale or exchange to the extent that it does not exceed the sum of death taxes and the funeral and administrative expenses allowed as deductions. Special limitations in §303(b) require that the distribution be made within specified periods measured from the date of death of the decedent.[78] More important, as a threshold, §303(b)(2) limits the application of the special sale or exchange rule of §303(a) to cases where the value of the corporation's stock included in the gross estate exceeds 35% of the excess of the value of the gross estate over funeral, administrative, taxes, and other expenses.[79] The idea here is to limit this antihardship provision to those estates for which

---

77. I.R.C. §303(a).

78. I.R.C. §303(b)(1). This period will vary depending upon circumstances, but is generally tied to the period for assessment, redetermination of deficiency, or payment of estate tax by installment.

79. I.R.C. §303(b)(2)(A)(i), (ii) (referring to the value of the gross estate over the sum allowable as deduction under §§2053 and 2054). Section 303(b)(2)(B) provides special rules for purposes of computing stock ownership in meeting the 35% requirement.

stock in the corporation represents a substantial proportion of the estate's assets.[80]

Redemptions Related to Inter-Shareholder Transfers and Bootstrap Acquisitions

Inter-Shareholder Transfers

a) In General

Redemption distributions sometimes are used as part of a plan to transfer control of a corporation. Imagine, for example, that shareholder A wishes to retire from a corporation equally owned by unrelated shareholders A, B, and C. If shareholders B and C simply "bought out" shareholder A's interest using their own funds, shareholder A would report gain or loss upon the sale. As an alternative, the corporation might redeem shareholder A's stock using corporate funds. Such a redemption would eliminate shareholder A's one-third interest and simultaneously increase shareholder B and C's interests from one-third to one-half each. Since the shareholders are unrelated, no shares will be attributed under §318, and shareholder A will treat the redemption as a sale or exchange complete termination of interest under §302(b)(3). Notice that the tax consequences to shareholder A are no different than they were in the case of a direct sale — sale or exchange gain upon disposition of the shares.

What about the remaining shareholders whose interest in the corporation is increased by reason of a redemption of another? Is this increase in relative interest in the corporation taxable? To answer this question, a closer look at what has really happened is necessary. The corporation in the above example presumably redeemed shareholder A's stock at fair market value. Although shareholder B and C's *percentage* of shares has increased, the *net worth* of the shares they own remains unchanged. For example, assume that the corporation's overall net worth was $3 million, so that each of the three shareholders' interests immediately before the redemption was worth $1 million. After the $1 million redemption distribution to shareholder A, shareholders B and C each hold a 50% interest in the corporation with an overall net worth of $2 million. Thus, the value of shareholder B and C's interests remains $1 million apiece. As a general rule, the increase in the remaining shareholders' relative interests resulting from the redemption of

---

80. On the other hand, notice that §303 sale or exchange treatment is available even if the family does not use redemption proceeds to pay death taxes. To some, this provision might appear to be a windfall to the estate, which already benefits from the stepped-up basis in assets provided in §1014.

another shareholder is not taxable.[81] Interestingly enough, in Holsey v. Commissioner,[82] the court reached this result even though the redemption was at *less* than fair market value. Imagine that shareholder A in the above hypothetical received only $750,000 in redemption of his one-third interest in the corporation. In other words, the redemption price was 25% below the fair market value of his interest. In such a case, shareholders B and C receive not only an increase in their *percentage* interests from one-third to one-half, but also an increase in the *value* of their shares from $1 million to $1,125,000.[83] Under similar circumstances, the Third Circuit in *Holsey* conceded that "the taxpayer was benefited indirectly by the distribution. The value of his own stock was increased, since the redemption was for less than book value, and he became sole stockholder. But these benefits operated only to increase the value of the taxpayer's stock holdings; they could not give rise to taxable income within the meaning of the Sixteenth Amendment until the corporation makes a distribution to the taxpayer or his stock is sold."[84] In other words, the court found no *realized* gain to the continuing shareholder.

One key exception to the general rule that the continuing shareholder's interest increase resulting from redemption of another shareholder is not taxable is the "primary and unconditional obligation" exception. According to the Treasury Department and the courts, when the continuing shareholder is subject to an "unconditional obligation to purchase the retiring shareholder's stock, the satisfaction by the corporation of his obligation results in a constructive distribution to him."[85] Imagine, for example, that shareholders B and C had a binding "buy-sell" agreement obligating them to purchase shareholder A's shares upon request. If, instead, the corporation redeems shareholder A's stock, the corporation has relieved shareholder B and C's obligation.[86] Since the redemption distribution satisfied shareholder B and

---

81. See, e.g., Holsey v. Comm'r, 258 F.2d 865 (3d Cir. 1958).

82. *Id.*

83. Before the redemption, shareholders B and C each owned one-third of a corporation worth $3 million. After the redemption, they each own one-half of a corporation worth $2.25 million.

84. 258 F.2d at 868.

85. Rev. Rul. 69-608, 1969-2 C.B. 42. This ruling is especially useful since it provides numerous illustrations of corporate buy-sell agreements, indicating those that do, and those that do not, create an unconditional obligation to purchase. See also Wall v. United States, 164 F.2d 462 (4th Cir. 1947); Sullivan v. United States, 363 F.2d 724 (8th Cir. 1966), *cert. denied*, 387 U.S. 905 (1967).

86. Notice that the courts and the Service view the satisfaction of the obligation by the corporation as a constructive dividend to the continuing shareholder. This suggests that the earnings and profits of the corporation are relevant. If the corporation has no e&p, there will be no dividend, but rather recovery of capital and sale or exchange gain under §301(c). If the transaction was viewed as a pure relief from indebtedness, the extent of the corporation's earnings and profits would not be relevant.

C's "primary and unconditional obligation," they will be required to report their increase in proportionate interest as a constructive dividend.[87]

b) Redemptions Incident to Divorce

Unique tax issues arise in the divorce setting when a redemption of shares from one spouse effectively transfers control of the corporation to the other spouse. A common scenario is a corporation owned entirely by husband and wife. Upon divorce, the parties may choose to have the corporation completely redeem the shares of one spouse, leaving the other spouse as sole owner of the corporation. Under the general redemption principles just considered, the redeemed spouse would report sale or exchange gain under §302(b)(3).[88] The nonredeemed spouse would not have any taxable income from the resulting increased interest in the corporation unless the redemption distribution satisfied a "primary and unconditional obligation" to purchase the redeemed spouse's shares.

The unique twist in the divorce setting, however, is the §1041 nonrecognition rule for property transfers "incident" to divorce.[89] Ordinarily, §1041 permits nonrecognition to both the transferring and the transferee spouse or former spouse on direct transfers of property incident to divorce. In addition, the Treasury Department has concluded that certain property transfers to third parties *on behalf of* a spouse also should be eligible for §1041 nonrecognition.[90] Among the property transfers mentioned in temporary regulations is one "required by a divorce or separation instrument."[91] For example, pursuant to a divorce decree, one spouse may transfer property to a third-party lender in satisfaction of the other spouse's debt. Under the temporary regulation, the property transferred to the third party first is viewed as if it had been transferred directly from the transferring spouse to

---

87. Another risk for the remaining shareholders whose interests are increased as a result of another shareholder's redemption is that their proportionate interest increase will be treated as a "deemed" stock dividend taxable under §305(c). A detailed discussion of the §305(c) constructive stock dividend rules appears in Chapter 7. In the meantime, note simply that the risk to the remaining shareholders of a taxable "deemed" stock dividend is low as long as their increase in proportionate interest results from an "isolated redemption," as opposed to a series of periodic redemptions.

88. Since the spouses are no longer married, the ex-spouse's shares are not constructively owned under the §318 attribution rules. The redemption distribution should easily qualify for sale or exchange treatment as a §302(b)(3) complete termination of interest.

89. I.R.C. §1041(a)(2). The nonrecognition provided in §1041 applies more broadly to transfers of property between spouses generally and to transfers between former spouses that are incident to divorce. Since the redemption issue tends to arise in the divorce context, this discussion is limited to transfers incident to divorce.

90. Temp. Treas. Reg. §1.1041-1T(c).

91. Temp. Treas. Reg. §1.1041-1T(b).

the other spouse and immediately thereafter by the nontransferring spouse to the third party.[92]

In a controversial case involving a corporation wholly owned by husband and wife, the Ninth Circuit held that the wife's transfer of her shares to the corporation in complete redemption pursuant to a divorce decree was a transfer "on behalf of" the husband covered by the temporary regulation.[93] As a result, the wife was entitled to §1041 nonrecognition rather than §302 sale or exchange treatment upon receipt of cash from the corporation in exchange for her redeemed stock. Given this §1041 treatment to the wife, the transaction should have been viewed under the regulations as a direct transfer of the stock from the wife to her husband, followed by a transfer of the stock by the husband to the "third party" corporation in complete redemption. In other words, the wife's transfer of shares to the corporation "on behalf of" her husband should shift tax liability for the sale or exchange gain on redemption to the husband.

Odd results emerged, however, because the tax consequences to the husband were decided in a separate case in which the Tax Court decided that it was not bound by the Ninth Circuit's holding that the property transfer was covered by §1041. The Tax Court believed that the legal issue in the husband's case did not turn on §1041, but rather on whether there was a constructive dividend to the husband. The court held that there was no constructive dividend to the nonredeemed husband whose proportionate interest in the corporation increased as a result of the wife's redemption since he did not have a "primary and unconditional obligation" to purchase the wife's shares.[94] In the end, neither husband nor wife paid tax on the approximately $450,000 paid out by the corporation in the redemption distribution.

This end result arguably is inconsistent with the policies underlying both §1041 and §302. Nonrecognition is provided under §1041 for property transfers between spouses and between ex-spouses incident to divorce because married taxpayers are thought to represent a single economic unit. Although §1041 provides nonrecognition at the time of transfer, the transferee spouse takes the property with a substituted basis from the transferring spouse.[95] This substituted basis is designed to preserve gain or loss unrecognized at the time of transfer for recognition upon later disposition of the property. In other words, gain or loss will be recognized when the property leaves the marital unit.

In the case of the Arnes divorce, the wife's shares were not transferred

92. *Id.*

93. Arnes v. United States, 981 F.2d 456 (9th Cir. 1992). See also Craven v. United States, 215 F.3d 1201 (11th Cir. 2000).

94. Arnes v. Comm'r, 102 T.C. 522 (1994).

95. I.R.C. §1041(b).

to the husband, but were completely redeemed for cash. In contrast to the ordinary §1041 transaction, Mr. Arnes took no property with a substituted basis. Unless one of the spouses is subject to tax at the time of the redemption, gain or loss with respect to the redeemed shares will never be recognized for tax purposes.[96] This result is inconsistent with §302, which requires shareholder level recognition of taxable income when funds or property are withdrawn from the corporation in a redemption distribution.[97] As suggested by Judge Beghe in his concurring opinion in the husband's tax case, one solution to this "whipsaw" effect to the government would be to "interpret §1041 and the temporary regulation so that no redemption of one spouse will be considered to be 'on behalf of' the remaining spouse unless it discharges that spouse's primary and unconditional obligation to purchase the subject stock."[98] Under this approach, a redemption treated as a §1041 nonrecognition event to the redeemed spouse would always result in a constructive dividend to the nonredeemed spouse. In such cases, the government would collect a shareholder level tax on the redemption distribution, but the burden of this tax would be shifted to the nonredeemed spouse.

Other Bootstrap Acquisitions

The inter-shareholder "buy out" situations just discussed involved the departure of one shareholder from the corporation and the acquisition of his or her interest by the remaining shareholders. Instead of using their own funds, the remaining shareholders use *corporate* assets to fund the acquisition. Such an acquisition may be called a "bootstrap acquisition." Even outside purchasers can structure a corporate acquisition so that all or a part of the funds for the acquisition come from the target corporation's assets. The landmark case in this area is Zenz v. Quinlivan.[99]

In *Zenz*, the buyer intended to acquire complete control over the target corporation owned by a single shareholder. Instead of a direct purchase of all of the shares, the buyer first purchased a small amount of stock from the selling shareholder. Shortly thereafter, the corporation redeemed all the selling shareholder's remaining shares. The selling shareholder presumably

---

96. In a case appealable to the Sixth Circuit, the Tax Court declined to follow and announced its disagreement with the Ninth Circuit's decision in the *Arnes* case. Blatt v. Comm'r, 102 T.C. 77 (1994).

97. Recall that the focus of §302 simply is to distinguish redemption distributions treated as sales or exchanges from those treated under the §301 distribution rules. In other words, the focus generally is on the *character* of the taxable income resulting from the distribution.

98. 102 T.C 522, 538. See also the extensive discussion in the dissenting opinions in Read v. Comm'r, 114 T.C. 14, 46-55 (2000) (Ruwe, J., dissenting); *id.* at 55-66 (Halpern, J., dissenting).

99. 213 F.2d 914 (6th Cir. 1954).

was indifferent as to whether she sold *all* of her stock to the buyer directly or sold only part of the stock and had the rest redeemed. Assuming that the redemption qualified as a §302(b)(3) complete termination of her interest, she would treat all of her gain as capital gain from the sale of stock in either case.

"Zenz-Out" Transaction

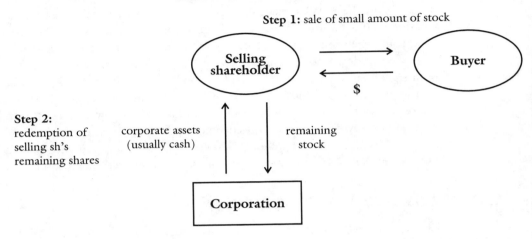

Step 1: sale of small amount of stock

Selling shareholder

Buyer

$

Step 2: redemption of selling sh's remaining shares

corporate assets (usually cash)

remaining stock

Corporation

From the buyer's viewpoint, the transaction was arranged in this fashion for at least two reasons. First, the buyer was concerned about the corporation's high earnings and profits accounts, which would later prove to be a source of taxable dividends should he receive distributions from the corporation. By buying only a small amount of stock and having the corporation use its earnings and profits to redeem the rest from the sole shareholder, the e&p account was reduced pursuant to §312.[100] Second, the buyer would have to come up with substantial funds to purchase *all* of the stock. By buying a small amount and having the corporation redeem the rest, the buyer got 100% control of the corporation without having to use substantial funds of his own. This type of acquisition is also known as a "bootstrap acquisition," since the buyer is bootstrapping on corporate funds to take over the corporation.

Concerned that this structure was a deliberate device to evade tax, the Service argued in *Zenz* that the shareholder should not be entitled to §302(b)(3) complete termination of interest treatment and should report the redemption distribution as a dividend. Conceding that the transaction was arranged to minimize taxes for both parties, the court nevertheless held that the redeemed shareholder was entitled to sale treatment. She literally satisfied the requirements of §302(b)(3) and she *intended* a complete liquidation of her holdings in the corporation.

---

100. I.R.C. §312(n)(7).

Notice that the redemption in the *Zenz* case took place *after* the sale of stock. This too was part of the overall plan. If the redemption had *preceded* the acquisition, it would have been a partial redemption from a sole shareholder and, thus, arguably taxable as a dividend to the shareholder. By having the acquisition precede the redemption, this problem was avoided and the redeemed shareholder qualified for §302(b)(3) sale or exchange treatment. Since *Zenz*, several courts have held, and the Service has conceded, that a "Zenz-like" bootstrap acquisition can still effectively provide §302(b)(3) sale or exchange redemption treatment to the selling/redeemed shareholder even if the redemption precedes the purchase of shares, as long as the two steps clearly are part of an overall integrated plan.[101]

The Service has also approved the *Zenz* bootstrap technique for acquisition transactions that do not completely terminate the selling shareholder's interest. In Rev. Rul. 75-447, for example, shareholders A and B, each with 50 shares, wanted to bring a new equal shareholder, C, into the business.[102] The corporation first issued 25 new shares to C and then caused the corporation to redeem 25 shares each from A and B. The Service announced that it was proper to rely on *Zenz* in determining whether the redemption distributions to A and B satisfied the §302(b)(2) "substantially disproportionate distribution" test. As long as the issuance of new shares and the redemption are "clearly part of an overall plan to reduce the shareholder's interest, effect will be given only to the overall result for purposes of section 302(b)(2) and the sequence in which the events occur will be disregarded."[103] A and B met the §302(b)(2) mathematical tests and were entitled to sale or exchange treatment, since each were viewed as having a 50% interest immediately before and a $33\frac{1}{3}$% interest immediately after the overall redemption transaction.

Not surprisingly, taxpayers are delighted with the *Zenz* bootstrap acquisition approach and it has become an important component of acquisition planning. Notice that a bootstrap acquisition may include a redemption as part of the plan when the selling shareholder is an *individual* taxpayer. The goal of the individual taxpayer is to get §302(b) sale or exchange gain rather than dividend income on amounts received for stock, while simultaneously lowering the purchase price to the buyer. A bootstrap acquisition generally will not include a redemption where the selling shareholder is a *corporate* taxpayer. The interest of the *corporate* seller is to classify any pre-sale distribution as a dividend in order to take advantage of the §243 dividends-received deduction or the consolidated return provisions.[104]

---

101. United States v. Carey, 289 F.2d 531 (8th Cir. 1961); Rev. Rul. 77-226, 1977-2 C.B. 90.

102. Rev. Rul. 75-447, 1975-2 C.B. 113.

103. *Id*. at 114.

104. Bootstrap acquisitions involving a corporate shareholder seeking to take advantage of the §243 dividends-received deduction were considered in Chapter 5.

Redemptions by Related Corporations: §304

Overview

The §302 redemption distribution rules covered in this chapter apply not only to *actual* redemptions, but also to certain sales of stock that are *deemed* to be redemptions for policy reasons. Section 304 provides a complex set of rules by which sales of stock involving related corporations will be treated as redemptions. Perhaps the best way to begin to approach §304 is through an example. Suppose that shareholder A owned 100% of the stock of both Corporations X and Y. In other words, X and Y Corporations are commonly controlled, sometimes referred to as brother-sister corporations. Assume that shareholder A sells some of his X shares to Corporation Y for cash. Absent §304, shareholder A would simply report gain or loss from the sale of stock under §§61(a)(3) and 1001, presumably as a capital gain. This transaction appears to be a straightforward sale of stock by shareholder A to Corporation Y. Why might it be necessary to complicate the universe by recharacterizing the transaction as something other than a simple stock sale? The concern here is that the shareholder controls the corporation from which he is receiving the sales proceeds (Y Corporation). In effect, he is taking property out of Corporation Y in exchange for stock in a related corporation over which he also has control (X Corporation). Viewed in this fashion, the transaction looks very much like a redemption and §304 requires that it be tested under the redemption rules.

Notice that §304 simply recharacterizes certain sales as redemptions. It says nothing directly about the tax consequences of such redemptions. Once a particular sale is recharacterized as a redemption for purposes of §304, tax consequences of the redemption to the shareholders will be governed by the §302 provisions considered at length earlier in this chapter. If the deemed redemption is treated as a sale or exchange under §302(b), any gain will be treated as capital gain. If the deemed redemption fails the §302(b) sale or exchange tests, the property received will be treated under the §301 distribution rules. The §304 rules are largely designed as anti-abuse provisions to prevent shareholders from bailing out corporate profits at capital gains rates rather than ordinary income rates, and from offsetting the amount of the distribution by their stock basis for distributions that resemble dividend distributions.[105]

Deemed redemptions covered by §304 fall into two categories. The first

---

105. This abuse concern applies primarily to *individual* shareholders, who prefer sale or exchange redemption treatment. *Corporate* shareholders, on the other hand, may *prefer* a §304 redemption that will be considered a §301 distribution. Under new provisions in §1059(e), a §304 redemption to which §301 applies may now be treated as an extraordinary dividend. Taxpayer Relief Act of 1997, Pub. L. No. 105-34, 111 Stat. 788, §1011(b) (codified at I.R.C. 1059(e)(1)).

involves acquisitions by related corporations other than subsidiaries, sometimes referred to as commonly controlled or brother-sister corporations.[106] The second involves acquisitions by subsidiaries.[107] Before getting into the details of each of these transactions, however, it will be useful to consider the special definition of control used for purposes of §304.

Measuring Control for Purposes of §304

Determining whether §304(a)(1) or (a)(2) applies to a particular sale or exchange of stock will first require an assessment of whether one or more persons is in *control* of each of two corporations (§304(a)(1)) or whether one corporation *controls* another (§304(a)(2)). The term "control" has a unique definition for purposes of §304, meaning "the ownership of stock possessing at least 50 percent of the total combined voting power of all classes of stock entitled to vote, *or* at least 50 percent of the total value of shares of all classes of stock."[108] In applying this 50% test, §304 explicitly provides that the constructive ownership rules of §318 shall apply, with some variations. These variations tend to broaden application of the constructive ownership rules and increase the likelihood that a particular transaction will be governed by §304.

First, if a person or persons controls one corporation, which in turn controls another corporation, the shareholders of the first corporation will also be in control of the second.[109] Second, 9 for purposes of §304, the §318(a)(2)(C) and (a)(3)(C) attribution rules shall be applied by substituting 5% for 50%.[110] Ordinarily, §318 constructive ownership to and from the corporation only kicks in where the shareholder is a majority shareholder; that is, where the shareholder owns 50% or more of the value in stock in a corporation. Under §318(a)(2)(C), a person who owns, directly or indirectly, more than 50% of the stock of a corporation shall be considered as owning stock owned by the corporation *in that proportion which the value of the stock owned bears to the value of all of the stock in the corporation.* So, a 50% shareholder of Corporation X will be deemed to own 50% of the stock that Corporation X owns.[111] For the purpose of measuring control under §304, a shareholder who has more than 5% of the stock of a corporation will be

---

106. I.R.C. §304(a)(1).

107. I.R.C. §304(a)(2).

108. I.R.C. §304(c)(1) (emphasis added). Notice that §304 uses a 50%, as opposed to 80%, control test. Compare I.R.C. §368(c).

109. Without this variation, the shareholders of the first would only receive *proportionate* attribution from the corporation under §318(a)(2)(C).

110. I.R.C. §304(c)(3).

111. Note that under the first variation described above, if Corporation X is in *control* of Corporation Y, the 50% shareholder here will be deemed to control both Corporations X and Y. I.R.C. §304(c)(1).

deemed to own the stock owned by the corporation. The attribution here will still be in proportion to the value of the stock owned by the shareholder. Thus, if shareholder A owns 5% of Corporation X, shareholder A will be deemed to own 5% of the stock that Corporation X owns.

Under §318(a)(3)(C), if a shareholder owns, directly or indirectly, more than 50% of the value of stock in a corporation, that corporation will be deemed to own the stock owned, directly or indirectly, by that shareholder. Thus, if shareholder A owns 50% of Corporation X and also owns 10% of Corporation Y, Corporation X will be deemed to own *all* of the shareholder's Corporation Y stock. Notice here that, unlike the §318(a)(2) rules, attribution under (a)(3) is not proportionate. Once the shareholder has 50% control, *all* stock owned by the shareholder is attributed to the controlled corporation. The §304 variation to the constructive ownership rules reduces the 50% threshold to 5%, but also provides that in any case where §318 would not apply but for this variation, the attribution rules shall be applied proportionately.[112] Assume, for example, that shareholder A owns 5% of the stock in Corporation X and also owns 50% in Corporation Z. Ordinarily, under the constructive ownership rules of §318, no shares would be attributed from shareholder A to Corporation X. Under the §304 variation, however, Corporation X will be deemed to own 5% of the Z shares that shareholder A owns.

Commonly Controlled or Brother-Sister Corporations: §304(a)(1)

Imagine that unrelated shareholders A and B each own 50% of the stock (50 out of 100 outstanding shares) of both Corporations X and Y and that Shareholder A sells 10 of her X shares to Corporation Y for cash.

---

112. I.R.C. §304(c)(3)(B)(ii)(II).

Brother-Sister Corporations: §304

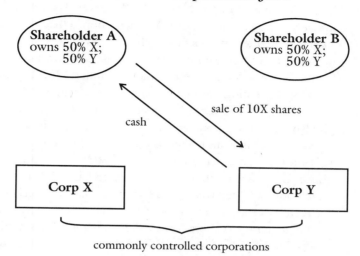

commonly controlled corporations

Under §304(a)(1), if "one or more persons are in control of each of two corporations, and in return for property, one of the corporations acquires stock in the other corporation from the person (or persons) so in control, then . . . such property shall be treated as a distribution in redemption of the stock of the corporation acquiring such stock." Slow and careful parsing of the words will help. First of all, A in our example is in control of each of the two corporations, X and Y, since she owns 50% of each corporation. Next, one of the corporations (Y Corporation) has acquired stock in the other corporation (X Corporation) from a person or persons in control of each of the corporations (shareholder A) in return for property (cash).

According to §304(a)(1), the property transferred by Y Corporation to shareholder A shall be treated as a distribution in redemption of the acquiring corporation (Y Corporation).[113] Thus, the next step is to test the deemed redemption to determine whether it will get sale or exchange as opposed to dividend treatment. For the most part, this will involve application of the same §302 rules considered earlier in this chapter. A few special considerations should be noted in the §304 context, however. For example, notice that the deemed redemption under §304(a)(1) is of the *acquiring* corporation's stock, in this case, Y Corporation. Since the funds are transferred from

---

113. For purposes of the §302 before and after analysis in testing the redemption, the §318(a)(2)(C) and §318(a)(3)(C) attribution rules are applied "without regard to the 50 percent limitation contained therein." I.R.C. §304(b)(1). Recall that for purposes of *measuring control,* the 50% threshold was reduced to 5%. Keep in mind that the provisions in §304(c) go only to the definition of control. These rules determine whether or not §304 will govern a particular transaction in the first instance. In contrast, the §304 elimination of the 50% threshold altogether is only for the purposes of testing the redemption under §302.

Y Corporation to shareholder A, this treatment initially makes some sense. There is a major logistics problem, however. We are told to test this case under §302 as a Corporation Y redemption. Ordinarily, this would require a before and after analysis of shareholder A's interest in Y Corporation. Here, however, there has been no change at all in the ownership of Y stock. Thus, for purposes of *testing* the redemption under §302(b), the statute looks to stock of the issuing corporation, here Corporation X.[114]

If the shareholder is entitled to sale or exchange treatment under §302(b), she will simply report the distribution as her amount realized from the sale, offsetting this by her basis in the X shares transferred to Corporation Y. If the deemed redemption fails the §302(b) tests and is treated as a §301 distribution, the statute expressly provides that the stock transferred by the shareholder and received by the acquiring corporation (10X shares) should be treated as transferred in a §351(a) transaction followed by a redemption by the acquiring corporation of the shares it was treated as issuing in the hypothetical §351 exchange.[115] In the above example, shareholder A owned 50% (50 out of 100 shares) of Corporation X immediately before the deemed redemption. Immediately after the deemed redemption, she owns 44% (40 out of 90 remaining shares). Shareholder A does not qualify for complete termination of interest treatment under §302(b)(3), nor will she qualify for the §302(b)(2) safe harbor.[116] Unless she can qualify the distribution for sale or exchange treatment under §302(b)(1) "not essentially equivalent to a dividend" test, shareholder A must report the amount received from Corporation Y as a §301 distribution, taxable as a dividend to the extent of earnings and profits.[117] In the end, §304(a)(1) creates a number of fictional events to work its magic. In effect, the transaction is treated as if shareholder A first transferred 10X shares in exchange for fictional shares of the acquiring corporation (Corporation Y). These fictional Y shares are immediately redeemed, but the redemption is tested with reference to shareholder A's ownership of stock in the issuing corporation (Corporation X). If the deemed

---

114. I.R.C. §304(b)(1).

115. I.R.C. §304(a)(1)(B) (last sentence) (as amended by the Taxpayer Relief Act of 1997, Pub. L. No. 105-34, 111 Stat. 788, §1013(a)).

116. Although she meets the less than 50% test, she fails the 80% test, since her interest immediately after the redemption (44%) is more than 80% of her interest immediately before the redemption (50% x .8 = 40%).

117. The §301 distribution rules were considered fully in Chapter 4. To calculate the amount which is a dividend, §304 first looks to the acquiring corporation to the extent of its earnings and profits, and then to the issuing corporation to the extent of its earnings and profits. I.R.C. §304(b)(2). In other words, the earnings and profits of both corporations effectively are pooled when necessary. Given the relationship between the entities, it makes sense to look also to the other corporation's earnings and profits in the case where those of the acquiring corporation are insufficient to cover the dividend.

redemption is treated as a §301 distribution, shareholder A is viewed as making a §351 contribution to the acquiring corporation. Thus, the shareholder should increase her basis in shares of the acquiring corporation (Corporation Y) by her basis in the 10 shares she transferred in Corporation X.[118] If the shareholder owns no remaining shares in the acquiring corporation directly, she may increase her basis in remaining shares of the issuer.[119] Here again, we see a variation of the mystery of disappearing basis.[120]

The acquiring corporation in the above example now owns 10 shares of stock in Corporation X. Ordinarily, a stock purchaser would simply take a cost basis in the purchased shares under §1012. Again, to the extent that the deemed redemption distribution is treated as a §301 distribution to the "selling" shareholder, §304(a)(1) treats the acquired shares as a §351 contribution.[121] As such, the purchasing corporation will take the shareholder's basis—a substituted basis—in the acquired stock.[122] In the above example, Corporation Y would hold the 10X shares transferred by shareholder A with the same basis that shareholder A had.

Acquisitions by Subsidiaries: §304(a)(2)

A slightly different set of rules applies under §304 when the corporations involved are parent and subsidiary, as opposed to brother-sister corporations. For example, suppose now that shareholders A and B each own 50% of the stock of Corporation X. Corporation X, in turn, owns 100% of Corporation Y. In other words, Corporation X is a parent and Corporation Y is its wholly owned subsidiary.

---

118. Treas. Reg. §1.304-2(a).

119. *Id.*

120. If the shareholder holds no direct shares in either the acquiring or the issuing corporation, the Service's view is that the seller's basis in the shares sold really does disappear. Rev. Rul. 70-496, 1970-2 C.B. 74. This is unfair to the shareholder. Some way should surely be found at an appropriate time to permit the shareholder or related parties the recovery of basis to which they are entitled. See Coyle v. United States, 415 F.2d 488, 493 (4th Cir. 1968) (discussion to the effect that basis will not disappear).

121. I.R.C. §304(a)(1) (last sentence).

122. I.R.C. §362(a)(2).

Parent-subsidiary corporations: §304

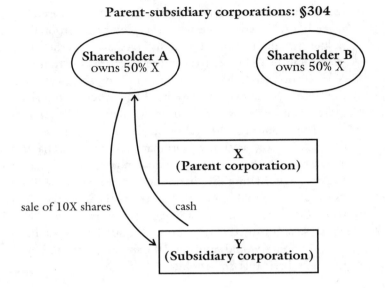

Assume again that shareholder A sells 10 of her X shares to Corporation Y for cash. Absent special statutory provisions, shareholder A would simply report gain or loss from the sale of stock. Again, however, §304 requires that the property she receives from Corporation Y be treated as a deemed redemption. The operation of the rules in this parent-subsidiary case is a bit different, however. Section 304(a)(2) provides redemption treatment "if in return for property, one corporation acquires from a shareholder of another corporation stock in such other corporation, and the issuing corporation controls the acquiring corporation." In our example, the issuing corporation (X Corporation) owns 100%, and thus controls, the acquiring corporation (Y Corporation). In return for property (cash), Y Corporation acquired stock in the issuing or parent corporation from shareholder A. Under §304(a)(2), the cash received by shareholder A "shall be treated as a distribution in redemption of the stock of the *issuing* corporation." One might envision this transaction as if X Corporation (the parent) first transferred cash to its subsidiary, Y Corporation, which in turn used the cash to acquire the X stock on behalf of its parent.

Notice some technical differences between the deemed redemption provided under (a)(2) as opposed to (a)(1). In the parent-subsidiary case covered by (a)(2), the deemed redemption is a redemption by X Corporation — the issuing corporation. Since shareholder A has parted with some of her X Corporation shares, the before and after analysis of her interest in X required by §302 can be performed without the logistics dilemma produced in the brother-sister case covered by (a)(1).[123] If the deemed redemption

---

123. I.R.C. §304(b)(1) states that in the case of any acquisition of stock to which subsection (a) of this section applies, determinations as to whether the acquisition is

meets one of the §302(b) sale or exchange tests, the shareholder simply will report the amount received from Corporation Y as an amount realized, offset by her basis in the X shares transferred. On the other hand, if the deemed redemption fails the §302(b) tests, the transaction will be governed by the §301 distribution rules. Unlike the brother-sister context, however, this transaction in the parent-subsidiary context is not envisioned as a contribution to capital. As a consequence, shareholder A will not increase her basis in Corporation Y stock by the basis in the X shares transferred. Instead, the regulations provide that basis in the remaining parent corporation stock is determined by including the basis in the shares sold to the subsidiary.[124] In other words, shareholder A will have the same basis in the 40X shares retained that she previously had in the full 50X shares. The acquiring subsidiary's basis in the parent corporation stock will be a §1012 cost basis.[125]

Overlaps Between §304(a)(1) and (a)(2)

Determining whether a particular transaction falls within §304(a)(1) or (a)(2) can become tricky. Bizarre results occur after application of the constructive ownership rules. For example, any parent-subsidiary relationship can be seen as a brother-sister relationship. Take, for example, our earlier parent-subsidiary case in which A and B each own 50% of the stock in Corporation X and Corporation X, in turn, owns 100% of Corporation Y. Under the constructive ownership rules as modified in §304(c), since A and B control Corporation X, they shall be treated as in control of the subsidiary, Corporation Y.[126] Thus, A and B are persons in control of each of two corporations and §304(a)(1) also would appear to apply. Section §304(a)(1) explicitly prevents this overlap, however, stating that it will apply "unless paragraph (2) applies." Thus, the §304(a)(2) parent-subsidiary rule trumps the commonly controlled corporation rule in §304(a)(1).

One can also argue that every brother-sister relationship also is a parent-subsidiary relationship after application of the constructive ownership rules. If A and B each own 50% of both Corporations X and Y, Corporation X is considered as owning all of the stock that A and B own in Corporation Y.[127] In other words, Corporation X is deemed to be the parent of Corporation Y.[128] If the statute is taken literally, §304(a)(1) is superfluous, since

---

by reason of §302(b), to be treated as a distribution in part or in full payment in exchange for stock shall be made by reference to stock of the issuing corporation.

124. Treas. Reg. §1.304-3(a).

125. Rev. Rul. 80-189, 1980-2 C.B. 106.

126. I.R.C. §304(c)(1) (last sentence).

127. I.R.C. §318(a)(3)(C).

128. One could also do this attribution in reverse. In reverse, Corporation Y is deemed to own all of A and B's stock in Corporation X. In other words, Corporation Y is the deemed parent of Corporation X.

every 50% control relationship could be recharacterized as a parent-subsidiary relationship. Here, however, the regulations suggest that the direct brother-sister relationship will prevail over the constructive parent-subsidiary relationship.[129]

Tax Consequences to the Corporation

From the corporation's perspective, the distribution of cash or property to the shareholder in a redemption distribution is a "distribution with respect to stock" for purposes of §311. Thus, the corporate tax consequences will be governed by the nonliquidating distribution rules considered in Chapter 5. When the corporation uses appreciated property in a redemption distribution, gain will be recognized.[130] Losses from the distribution of depreciated property will not be recognized.[131]

With regard to earnings and profits adjustments, redemptions that are treated as dividend distributions will be treated exactly as any other dividend distribution would be.[132] Different earnings and profits rules apply, however, with respect to redemptions treated as sales. Some reduction to earnings and profits is appropriate, since the corporation is, after all, distributing earnings to repurchase its shares. On the other hand, in order for the distribution to be classified as a sale or exchange for purposes of §302(a), the selling shareholder generally must have experienced a substantial reduction in proportionate interest. To some extent, then, the corporation is dipping into its capital to restore a portion of the selling shareholder's investment. A reduction in earnings and profits to the *full* extent of the redemption distribution would reduce the amount of dividend income on subsequent distributions to the remaining shareholders. Thus, the amount distributed in redemption would never be treated as dividend income with respect to the redeemed shares or the remaining shares. The statutory solution in §312(n)(7) is to limit the earnings and profits reduction to an amount "not in excess of the ratable share of earnings and profits . . . attributable to the stock so redeemed." This provision imposes a ceiling, or cap, on the e&p reduction following a redemption distribution that is treated as a sale or exchange to the redeemed shareholder. Thus, for example, if the corporation completely redeems a 50% shareholder, the redemption distribution could not generate an e&p reduction greater than the 50% of earnings and profits attributable to the shares redeemed.

---

129. See Treas. Reg. §1.304-2(c), ex. (1).

130. I.R.C. §311(b).

131. I.R.C. §311(a).

132. I.R.C. §312(a), (b). For a detailed discussion of these e&p adjustment rules, see Chapter 5.

As a final observation regarding tax consequences to the distributing corporation, note that §162(k) denies deductions for amounts paid or incurred in connection with the corporation's redemption of its own stock.[133]

EXAMPLES

1.   Complete Salvation, Inc. (CSI) was established for the sale of religious gifts and artifacts. It is not affiliated with any particular religion and is operated as a for-profit corporation. CSI has five shareholders: Mr. Roberts, Mr. Swaggert, Mr. Baker, Mrs. Baker, and Mr. Baker's girlfriend. Other than the Bakers (husband and wife), the other shareholders are unrelated. Each of the shareholders owns 20% of the 1000 shares of common voting stock outstanding. The overall net worth of the corporation is $5 million. The corporation decided to redeem Mr. Baker completely and distributed $1 million cash to him in return for all of his stock. The corporation's current earnings and profits for the year of the redemption is $2,500,000. It has no accumulated e&p. Mr. Baker's basis in his shares was $300,000. What tax consequence to Mr. Baker? To CSI? To the remaining shareholders?

Variations on Example 1

2a.   What if CSI distributed property worth $1 million (basis to CSI of $250,000) instead of cash to redeem Mr. Baker's stock?

2b.   What if CSI redeemed only 10 shares of Mr. Swaggert's stock and no stock from Mr. Baker? Mr. Swaggert's basis in the redeemed shares was $20,000.

2c.   Would the results in Example 1 change if all five shareholders had agreed to a "buy out" arrangement pursuant to which each agreed to first offer sale of the shares to the other shareholders before selling to a third party?

2d.   Would your answers to any of the above change if, in addition to their interests in CSI, Mr. Baker and Mr. Swaggert were partners in an unrelated partnership?

Meaningful Reductions?

3.   SlimFaster, Inc. is a corporation engaged in the business of selling weight loss products and consulting individuals seeking weight loss advice. Mr. Jim Slim, founder of the corporation, and his two daughters each own 250 of the 750 shares of common voting stock. In addition, the corporation recently issued 750 shares of nonvoting preferred stock. Mr. Slim holds all

---

133. I.R.C. §162(k)(1). The Code states an exception, however, for interest allowable as a deduction under §163. I.R.C. §162(k)(2).

of the preferred shares. What are the tax consequences to Slim and the corporation if the corporation redeems all of Slim's preferred stock for cash? What if the corporation redeems all of Slim's common *and* preferred stock?

4a. Assume the same facts as in Example 3, except that Slim owns only 250 shares of preferred stock with the remaining 500 held by the public. What are the tax consequences now if all of Slim's preferred shares are redeemed?

4b. One member of the public originally bought 100 shares of SlimFaster nonvoting preferred stock. The corporation redeems 10 shares from this shareholder. What result?

Fun and Games with Attribution

5.   Mr. Smith owns 50 of the 100 outstanding common shares of corporation X. X, a parent corporation, owns 100% of Corporation Y. Corporation Y owns 40 of the 100 outstanding shares in Corporation Z. Mr. Smith owns 60 shares of Corporation Z stock. What tax consequence if Z redeems the 60Z shares owned by Mr. Smith?

6a. Would your answer to Example 5 change if Mr. Smith did not own any X shares directly, but his wife owned 50X shares?

6b. Would your answer to Example 5 change if Mr. Smith did not own any X shares directly, but his mother-in-law owned 50X shares?

6c. What tax consequences in Example 5 if Z redeems the 40Z shares owned by Corporation Y?

Incestuous Corporations

7a. Three unrelated shareholders, Rex, Alexia, and Lee, each owned 300 of the 900 outstanding common shares of Oedipus Yarn and Needles, Inc. and 600 of the 1800 outstanding common shares of Queens Eyeglasses, Inc. Queens Eyeglasses had a substantial cash surplus, while Oedipus had no current earnings and a deficit in its accumulated e&p account. Oedipus did hold inventory and other assets of value, however. On the same day, Rex and Lee each sold 200 shares of their Oedipus stock to Queens in return for $10,000. How should Rex and Lee treat the sale for tax purposes?

7b. Would your answer in Example 7a differ if Oedipus held all of the shares in Queens Eyeglasses and the individual shareholders owned no direct shares in Queens?

7c. How would your answer to Example 7a differ if Rex and Alexia were husband and wife?

7d. How would your answer to Example 7b differ if Rex and Alexia were husband and wife?

EXPLANATIONS

1. Although at first blush, the redemption appears to qualify for sale treatment to Mr. Baker as a §302(b)(3) complete termination of interest, this will not be the case. Mr. Baker is deemed to own his wife's shares under §318(a)(1) and, thus, has not been completely terminated. Mr. Baker directly owned 200/1000 or 20% and indirectly owned an additional 200/1000 or 20% by attribution from his wife immediately before the redemption. Thus, immediately before the redemption, Mr. Baker held 400/1000 or 40%. Immediately after the redemption, Mr. Baker no longer held any shares directly, but continued to constructively own his wife's shares. Unless Mr. Baker files an appropriate waiver of family attribution under §302(c)(2), immediately after the redemption, he will be deemed to constructively own 200/800 or 25%. Even without a waiver, however, since the percentage owned immediately after the redemption is less than 50%, Mr. Baker satisfies the threshold test of §302(b)(2)(B). In addition, Mr. Baker meets the 80% test since his post-redemption ratio of 25% is less than 80% of his pre-redemption ratio of 40%.

Since Mr. Baker qualifies under the §302(b)(2) safe harbor, §302(a) provides that the redemption will be treated as a sale. The amount realized upon the sale is the $1 million received from the corporation. From this, he will subtract his $300,000 basis in the shares, resulting in a taxable gain of $700,000. This gain will be capital gain, assuming that the stock was a capital asset in Mr. Baker's hands.

Since the corporation distributed cash, there is no gain or loss to worry about from the corporation's perspective. The corporation will be required to reduce its earnings and profits to reflect the distribution. Pursuant to the §312(n)(7) limitations to §312(a), the corporation's e&p reduction shall not exceed the redeemed stock's ratable share of e&p. Thus, the reduction will be limited to 20% of $2.5 million, or $500,000. The remaining e&p after the redemption is $2 million.

Since the remaining shareholders had no primary and unconditional obligation to buy out his shares, there should be no tax consequence to the remaining shareholders from the redemption of Mr. Baker's shares.

2a. If the corporation used property instead of cash to redeem Mr. Baker's stock, the tax consequences to Mr. Baker would be the same. He has still received property worth $1 million in a "sale" redemption under §302(a). His gain will still be $700,000. Mr. Baker's basis in the property will be equal to its fair market value at the time of the redemption distribution, in this case, $1 million. Since the transaction was taxable to Mr. Baker, he should be entitled to a fair market value ("tax cost basis") in the property received.

If the corporation uses property with a fair market value of $1 million and a basis of $250,000 to redeem Mr. Baker's shares, the corporation will have a $750,000 taxable gain under §311(b). This reflects appreciation in the value of the property that was not previously taxed at the corporate level. The character of the gain will depend upon the asset distributed. The corporation's e&p would first be increased by the $750,000 gain to $3.25 million. I.R.C. §312(b). E&p would then be reduced by $650,000. Note that while §312(a), (b) would otherwise permit an e&p reduction in the amount of the $1 million value of the property, the reduction here is limited by §312(n)(7) to the redeemed stock's ratable shares of e&p (20% of $3.25 million). There would still be no tax consequence to the remaining shareholders.

2b. If the corporation redeemed 10 shares from Mr. Swaggert, he would clearly not qualify for sale treatment as a complete termination of interest. It appears that he also would not qualify under the §302(b)(2) substantially disproportionate distribution test. Immediately before the redemption, Mr. Swaggert owned 200/1000 or 20%. Immediately after the redemption, he owns 190/990 or 19%. In order to qualify under the 80% test, Mr. Swaggert's post-redemption ratio must be less than 16% (80% of his pre-redemption ratio of 20%). Although he meets the 50% threshold test because he owns less than 50% immediately after the redemption, he fails the 80% test.

To determine whether Mr. Swaggert might receive sale treatment under the §302(b)(1) "not essentially equivalent to a dividend" test, a facts and circumstances analysis will be necessary. The Senate legislative history indicated that §302(b)(1) was intended primarily for the protection of preferred minority shareholders who had no control over redemptions. Mr. Swaggert, however, is a minority voting common shareholder. He might argue that prior to the redemption, he shared voting control equally with four others and that immediately after the redemption, his interest is slightly lower than the remaining shareholders, thus eliminating his shared control. If successful with this argument, Mr. Swaggert will be eligible for sale treatment. He would subtract his basis of $20,000 from the amount received from the corporation to figure his gain or loss.

If Mr. Swaggert is unsuccessful in his argument that §302(b)(1) applies, the corporate distribution will be treated as a dividend since the corporation has sufficient e&p. He will not get any basis offset. His $20,000 basis in the redeemed shares should not be lost. He should be entitled to add the $20,000 back into the basis of the CSI shares he continues to hold. The corporation simply will reduce its e&p by the cash distribution. Notice that the §312(n)(7) limitation only applies to sale or exchange redemptions.

2c. From Mr. Baker's perspective, there would be no change. He would still have a $700,000 taxable gain. Moreover, there should be no effect on the remaining shareholders. The agreement here was only that the shareholders would first *offer* to the other shareholders. There was no binding obligation to purchase. If the remaining shareholders had previously entered into a *binding contract* to "buy out" Mr. Baker's shares and if, instead, the corporation redeemed the shares in satisfaction of that obligation, the remaining shareholders would be viewed as receiving a constructive dividend.

2d. No, the answers would not change if Mr. Swaggert and Mr. Baker were partners in an unrelated partnership. In such a case, each of the partners' 200 shares would be attributed to the partnership under §318(a)(3)(A). Absent a special rule, the shares might then be reattributed to the partners under §318(a)(2)(A). The attribution cut-off rule in §318(a)(5)(C) prevents this result. One partner shall not be deemed to own the shares of an unrelated partner.

3. This question is close to the facts in the *Davis* case. Mr. Slim owns one-third of the common voting stock directly and owns the remaining two-thirds indirectly through attribution from his daughters. After application of the constructive ownership rules, he is the sole shareholder. He surely does not qualify for the complete termination of interest safe harbor since only his preferred shares were redeemed. Moreover, he will not qualify for §302(b)(2) since there has been no reduction in his interest. He also fails the "not essentially equivalent to a dividend" test since there has been no reduction in his interest, meaningful or otherwise. As the *Davis* case indicated, a sole shareholder can never qualify for the §302(b)(1) "not essentially equivalent to a dividend" safe harbor. Since Slim will fail all of the §302(b) tests, the redemption will be treated as a dividend to the extent of the corporation's e&p. Since he continues to own common stock, his basis for the preferred shares redeemed will be added to the basis of his common stock. The corporation simply will reduce its e&p by the cash distributed pursuant to §312(a).

If the corporation redeemed both Slim's common and preferred stock, Slim would own no shares directly immediately after the redemption. Nevertheless, Slim would still own 100% of the remaining stock by attribution from his daughters and would therefore not qualify under any of the §302(b)(2) sale or exchange tests. The redemption distribution would be taxed as a dividend to the extent of e&p. Slim can avoid this dividend result by filing a waiver of family attribution and by agreeing to have no further interest in the corporation other than an interest as a creditor under §302(c)(2). Now Slim would qualify for sale or exchange treatment as a complete termination of interest under §302(b)(3). He would simply subtract his basis in the shares redeemed from the distribution received from the corporation to measure his gain or loss.

If Slim does not file a waiver and the distribution is treated as a dividend, Slim must address a potential mystery of disappearing basis problem. Unlike the situation above, Slim no longer holds any shares of his own to which he can add the basis of the redeemed stock. The mystery should be resolved here by giving Slim's basis to his two daughters in proportion to their relative stock holdings. Again, the corporation simply will reduce e&p by the cash distributed.

4a. If Slim held only 250 of the preferred shares all of which were redeemed, he still would not qualify for §302(b)(3) complete termination of interest treatment since he still would own one-third of the common stock directly and two-thirds indirectly, unless he files a family attribution waiver. In addition, he cannot qualify for the §302(b)(2) safe harbor because he does not meet the 50% threshold test. Directly and through attribution, he owns 100% of the common voting stock. The only possibility here is §302(b)(1). There was no reduction in Slim's voting stock interest. Since two-thirds of the preferred stock was owned by the public, there was some reduction in his preferred stock interest. Was this reduction meaningful under the *Davis* test? Probably not. Since Slim continues to have dominant voting control, he would most likely fail the *Davis* meaningful reduction test.

4b. If one member of the public purchased 100 shares of SlimFaster stock and 10 shares are redeemed, there is no complete termination of interest, since the shareholder still holds 90 shares. The §302(b)(2) substantially disproportionate interest test is not applicable here since the minority shareholder owned no voting stock in the first place. This case represents precisely the situation that the Senate Finance Committee was concerned with in keeping the "essentially equivalent to a dividend" language in the statute. A minority shareholder of nonvoting preferred stock has little or no control over corporate redemptions. Consequently, the §302(b)(1) safe harbor is liberally applied in such cases. Even minor reductions in the shareholder's interest have been considered meaningful. See, e.g., Rev. Rul. 76-385, 1976-2 C.B. 92. The minority shareholder should be entitled to sale treatment of the redemption distribution under §302(b)(1) and §302(a). The corporation will reduce its e&p, subject to the limitations in §312(n)(7).

5. If Z Corporation redeems the 60Z shares owned by Mr. Smith, at first blush it would appear that he qualifies for sale or exchange treatment under the complete termination of interest safe harbor. This will not be the case, however. Mr. Smith will be deemed to own 20Z shares by attribution in two steps. First, since X Corporation owns 100% of Y Corporation, X will be deemed to own 100% of the shares that Y owns under §318(a)(2)(C). Thus, X constructively owns Y's 40Z shares. And, since Mr. Smith owns 50% of X Corporation, he will be deemed to own 50% of the 40Z shares that X owns through attribution from Y. This multiple application of the attribution rules involves a (2)/(2) combination, which is not cut off by any of the operating rules in §318(a)(5).

After determining the proper attribution, Mr. Smith must compare the pre-redemption ratio to the post-redemption ratio. Immediately before the redemption, Mr. Smith owned 60% of the Z shares directly and 20% indirectly for a total of 80%. Immediately after the redemption, he owns no shares directly, but 50% of the remaining 40 shares through attribution. The reduction from 80% to 50% will not qualify for the §302(b)(2) substantially disproportionate distribution safe harbor. Note that the 50% threshold test requires that the shareholder hold *less than* 50% of the voting stock immediately after the redemption. Since Mr. Smith holds exactly 50%, this test is not met. The next question, then, is whether a reduction from 80% to 50% is a meaningful reduction under §302(b)(1). Since Mr. Smith shares control with a "friendly" party, the Service in this case will likely conclude that the reduction is not meaningful. If so, the redemption distribution will be treated as a dividend to the extent of earnings and profits. What about Smith's basis in his 60Z shares? The mystery of disappearing basis appears again. Mr. Smith's basis in the redeemed shares might be added to Y Corporation's basis in the remaining 40Z shares. On the other hand, Smith can argue that the change from a position of absolute power to one of equally shared power should be considered meaningful. If he wins, the redemption distribution will be entitled to sale treatment and Smith will get his basis offset through the §1001 computation on the exchange.

6a. No. The answer would be the same. Mr. Smith would still be deemed to constructively own one-half of Y's 40Z shares, now through a *three*-step application of the attribution rules. As above, the 40Z shares would be constructively owned by X under §318(a)(2)(C). Mr. Smith's wife would be considered to own one-half of these shares (20Z) through a second application of this attribution rule. Finally, Mr. Smith will be deemed to own the 20Z shares just attributed to his wife through the family attribution provisions of §318(a)(1). This (2)/(2)/(1) punch is also not prohibited by any of the cut-off rules in §318(a)(5).

6b. Yes. The first two attribution steps in this variation of the facts would not change, however. X Corporation would be deemed to own the 40Z shares under §318(a)(2) and X's mother-in-law would be deemed to own one-half of the 40Z shares through a second application of §318(a)(2). There is no direct attribution between in-laws, however. The mother-in-law's stock could only be attributed to Mr. Smith by going through his wife. This double application of the family attribution rules of §318(a)(1) is cut off by the operating rule in §318(a)(5)(B). Thus, the redemption of Mr. Smith's stock will completely terminate his interest under §302(b)(3) and he will be entitled to report the redemption distribution as a sale.

6c. If Z Corporation redeemed the 40Z shares owned by Y Corporation, again it would first appear to be a complete termination of interest. However, Y Corporation will be deemed to own Mr. Smith's Z stock. Since Mr. Smith owns 50% of X, X corporation will be deemed to own Mr. Smith's 60Z shares under §318(a)(3)(C). Since X owns 100% of Y, Y will be deemed to own X's shares under a second application of §318(a)(3)(C). Note that the attribution rules here are not proportionate. Thus, *all* of Mr. Smith's shares will be attributed to Y Corporation. As a result, Y will be considered a 100% owner of the Z shares both immediately before and immediately after the redemption and will fail all of the §302(b) tests. Y Corporation will report the redemption distribution as a dividend to the extent of Z's e&p. Y Corporation will take a §243 dividends-received deduction. Since this is a non pro rata redemption, it will be treated as an "extraordinary dividend" to Y Corporation subject to the special rules of §1059(a)(1) and (2). Y Corporation's basis in the Z stock will first be reduced by the nontaxed portion of the dividend under §1059(a)(1). To the extent that the nontaxed portion of the dividend exceeds Y Corporation's basis in the Z shares, gain will be recognized under §1059(a)(2).

7a. Since the shareholders are unrelated and each owns only *one-third* of the corporation's stock, no single shareholder controls either corporation, as control is defined in §304(c). One's initial instinct might be to say that §304 does not cover this case at all. If so, the sales would simply be treated as sales under §§61(a)(3) and 1001. Nevertheless, §304(a)(1) refers to "one or more persons . . . in control of each of two corporations." The issue here is whether to aggregate at least the shares owned by the two transferring shareholders for purposes of §304. The regulations provide that §304 will apply in such a case "provided the sales by each of such persons are related to each other." Treas. Reg. §1.304-2(b). Whether the sales are related will depend upon the facts and circumstances. In our case, the sales took place on the same day. In addition, the corporation is closely held. One suspects that the two shareholders consulted with each other, and probably with the third shareholder, regarding these sales. Assuming that the sales are related, both sales will be governed by §304(a)(1). In return for property (cash) one corporation (Queens) acquired stock of the other corporation (Oedipus) from the persons in control. The sales are deemed under §304(a)(1) to be a distribution in redemption of Queens stock. This redemption must now be tested under the §302 redemption rules. Even though §304(a)(1) tells us that this is a redemption of Queens stock, the statute tells us to test the redemption by reference to stock of the issuing corporation, in this case, Oedipus. I.R.C. §304(b)(1). Since the three parties are unrelated, attribution will not be a factor. Immediately before the redemption, each of the transferring shareholders had 300/900 or one-third of the stock outstanding. Immediately after the redemption, each of the transferring shareholders had 100/500 or one-fifth of the shares "outstanding." Remember here that this is a *deemed* redemption. The shares were not really redeemed, but are now owned by Queens. Nevertheless, for purposes of §304, we treat these shares as if they were, in fact, redeemed. The shareholders here have gone from a $33\frac{1}{3}\%$ ownership to a 20% ownership. Nothing in the facts suggests a corporate contraction. Thus, the (b)(4) partial liquidation exception will not apply. Since the shareholders still own stock, this is not a (b)(3) complete termination of interest redemption. They will qualify, however, for the (b)(2) safe-harbor since they each have less than 50% of the stock immediately after the exchange and the 20% interest immediately after the exchange is less than 80% of the $33\frac{1}{3}$% interest immediately before the exchange. In other words, this is a sufficient reduction in their interest in the corporation to qualify as a sale redemption. The shareholders, then, will recover their basis in the 200 Oedipus shares sold through the basis offset in the §1001 formula. Queens now holds the shares with a cost basis.

7b. No. If Oedipus was the parent and Queens was a subsidiary, the transaction technically would be covered by §304(a)(2) instead of (a)(1). The only difference here is that (a)(2) itself tells us that this is a deemed redemption of the issuing corporation's stock (Oedipus). The §302 analysis would be the same. Thus, the shareholders would be entitled to sale or exchange treatment under §302(b)(2). The corporation again would receive a cost basis in the shares.

7c. The analysis changes for Rex if he is married to Alexia. Under the attribution rules, Rex is deemed to own the shares that Alexia owns. Thus, before the deemed redemption, he held a 2/3 interest in Queens. After the redemption, he has a 4/5 interest in the corporation, since he holds 100 shares directly and 300 shares by attribution from his wife. This actually reflects an *increase* in his interest in the corporation. He will not be eligible for any of the §302(b) safe harbors. Consequently, he must treat the distribution as a dividend to the extent of Queen's e&p. Under §304(a)(1), a deemed redemption that is treated as a §301 distribution is treated as a §351 contribution. As such, Rex's basis in the shares transferred will be added to the basis in his remaining Queens shares. Queens will take the shares with a substituted basis — whatever basis Rex previously had in the shares transferred. There should be no difference in the tax consequences to Lee.

7d. This deemed redemption would now be governed by §304(a)(2). The tax differences would be minor. Rex would still fail the safe-harbor tests and, thus, would be required to treat the distribution as a dividend to the extent of Queen's e&p. The differences would arise regarding basis issues. Rex would add the basis in the transferred shares to the remaining shares in *Oedipus,* rather than Queens. In addition, Queens would get a cost basis in the shares received.

7

Stock Dividends

Introduction

From time to time during a corporate lifetime, the corporation will make distributions of its own stock to its shareholders. The reasons for such stock distributions are varied. Often, the distribution reflects a corporate surplus that was retained as working capital rather than distributed to the shareholders. The stock dividend is tangible evidence to the shareholders of that surplus, even though the shareholders have withdrawn no assets from the corporation.

This was precisely the type of distribution involved in the landmark decision of the Supreme Court in Eisner v. Macomber.[1] In that case, Standard Oil of California issued a 50% stock dividend on its outstanding capital stock. The taxpayer, as owner of 2200 shares, received a certificate for an additional 1100 shares. At the time, Congress had provided for taxation of stock dividends.[2] The Supreme Court declared the taxation of stock dividends unconstitutional on the grounds that a stock dividend was not income under the Sixteenth Amendment.

The *Macomber* opinion provides a useful discussion of the "essential nature of a stock dividend" and, more broadly, the concepts of income and realization. First, the Court described the "essential nature of a stock dividend" as a distribution that "takes nothing from the property of the corporation, and adds nothing to the interests of the shareholders. Its property is not diminished, and their interests are not increased. . . . The proportional interest of each shareholder remains the same. The only change is in the evidence which represents that interest, the new shares and the original shares

---

1. 252 U.S. 189 (1920).
2. Revenue Act of 1916, §2(a), c. 463, 39 Stat. 756.

195

together representing the same proportional interest that the original shares represented before the issue of the new ones."[3] The Court went on to describe a stock dividend as showing "that the company's accumulated profits have been capitalized, instead of distributed to the stockholders or retained as surplus available for the distribution. . . . Far from being a realization of profits of the stockholder, it tends rather to postpone such realization, in that the fund represented by the new stock has been transferred from surplus to capital, and no longer is available for actual distribution."[4]

The Supreme Court in *Macomber* correctly concluded that there is no realization of gain from the distribution of a pro rata stock dividend that does not alter the shareholder's proportionate interests in the corporation. The shareholder simply has additional pieces of paper reflecting the same interest that he had before. The key here is realization. As the corporation's surplus was building, the value of each shareholder's interest in the corporation was increasing. Economists would surely view this increase in value as income. Nevertheless, there is no *realization* of that income until the shareholder sells or disposes of the stock. Modern scholars take the view that the *Macomber* case developed an overly narrow definition of income and was wrongly decided as a constitutional matter. Most scholars today would agree, however, that Congress *could* constitutionally tax stock dividends if it chose to do so. Yet, as a matter of tax policy, the principle of realization is well-entrenched.

The Court's description of the "essential nature of a stock dividend" does not apply to all stock dividends. Unless all shareholders participate in proportion to their interests in the corporation, a stock dividend *will* alter the proportionate interests of shareholders. Some shareholders may increase their interest in the corporate enterprise at the expense of other shareholders. Thus, the holding in Eisner v. Macomber was later limited to "true stock dividends" that did not alter the shareholders' proportionate interests in the corporation. If the interest received by the shareholder was sufficiently different from the underlying stock upon which the stock dividend was issued, the stock dividend was taxable.[5] The lower courts had difficulty distinguishing stock dividends that were tax-free under the *Macomber* analysis from those that were taxable. Congress attempted to provide greater certainty by codifying rules on stock dividends in §§305 and 306. The remainder of this chapter will be devoted to these statutory rules and their current interpretation.

---

3. 252 U.S. 189, 202-203 (citing Gibbons v. Mahon, 136 U.S. 549, 559-560 (1890)).

4. 252 U.S. 189, 211 (1920).

5. See, e.g., Koshland v. Helvering, 298 U.S. 441 (1936) (common stock dividend on preferred stock).

Tax Consequences to the Shareholders

The Basic §305(a) Nonrecognition Rule

When a corporation distributes its own stock or rights to acquire such stock, the corporation is not making a distribution of "property" that would be covered by the §301 distribution rules.[6] Instead, stock dividends are governed by special provisions found in §305.

Under the §305(a) general rule applicable to stock dividends, distributions of the corporation's own stock or options to acquire such stock are not taxable to the shareholders.[7] Five exceptions to the general rule are enumerated in §305(b). In addition, Congress provided reasonably broad authority to the Treasury Department in §305(c) to promulgate regulations under which certain stock and option distributions and other transactions not covered by the five enumerated exceptions nevertheless may be treated as taxable distributions. These exceptions will be considered in later sections of this chapter.

The nonrecognition rule reflected in §305(a) simply codifies the general nonrecognition principle established by the Supreme Court in Eisner v. Macomber. Recall that the thrust of the Court's ruling in that case was to protect stock dividends that did not alter the shareholders' proportionate interest in the corporation. In keeping with that spirit, §305 ordinarily protects from taxation pro rata distributions issued with respect to common stock. Non pro rata distributions are likely to be covered by one of the exceptions to the general rule provided in §305(b).

Notice also that nonrecognition is limited under §305(a) to distributions of the corporation's stock made "with respect to its stock." Thus, only distributions to shareholders *qua* shareholders will be covered by §305. The stock dividend provisions of §305 will not apply to stock distributions when the facts and circumstances suggest that the distribution was intended as compensation for services or as satisfaction of corporate debt, for example.[8]

---

6. For purposes of the §301 rules, property includes "money, securities, and any other property; *except that such term does not include stock in the corporation making the distribution (or rights to acquire such stock)*." I.R.C. §317(a) (emphasis added). For a discussion of the rules applicable to nonliquidating distributions, see Chapter 5.

7. For purposes of §305, the term "stock" includes "rights to acquire such stock." I.R.C. §305(d)(1).

8. Section 301 contains a similar limitation. See discussion in Chapter 5.

Basis Rules: §307

There are no immediate tax consequences to the shareholder upon the receipt of a tax-free stock dividend under §305(a). However, the shareholder must compute basis for the dividend shares received. When new shares are received in a distribution to which the general rule of §305(a) applies, §307 requires an allocation of the old basis. More specifically, it provides that the "basis of such new stock and of the stock with respect to which it is distributed (referred to in this section as 'old stock'), respectively, shall . . . be determined by allocating between the old stock and the new stock the adjusted basis of the old stock." In other words, the shareholder will take the basis in the old stock with respect to which the new stock was issued and spread that basis over all of the shares, old and new, owned immediately after the stock distribution. The regulations specify that the allocation will be "in proportion to the fair market values of each on the date of distribution."[9] To determine the basis in dividend shares under this allocation rule, the shareholder will multiply the basis in the old stock by a fraction, the numerator of which is the fair market value of the new shares on the date of distribution and the denominator of which is the fair market value of *all* of the shares owned (old and new) on the date of the distribution.[10] Suppose, for example, that shareholder S owns 100 shares of stock in Corporation X ("old shares") with a basis of $1500. Corporation X declares a 50% stock dividend pursuant to which S receives 50 new shares. Immediately after the distribution, the fair market value of the old shares is $10,000 and the fair market value of the new shares is $5000. To determine her basis in the new shares, S will multiply her basis in the old shares of $1500 X 5000/15,000 or 1/3. One-third of her old basis is allocable to the new shares. Thus, the shareholder's basis in her 50 new shares will be $500. Her basis remaining in the old shares will be $1000. Notice that the shareholder's overall basis in her stock ownership remains at $1500 — the amount she originally invested. The original basis simply is spread over more shares of stock. Although the basis in each individual share is reduced, the overall basis remains the same.

The Shareholder's Holding Period

Since stock generally is considered a capital asset, it will be important for shareholders to know the proper holding period for shares received by way of a stock dividend. A special holding period rule for stock with a basis

---

9. Treas. Reg. §1.307-1(a).

10. The calculation of fair market value should be immediately after the stock distribution. Treas. Reg. §1.307-1(b) (example).

determined under §307 permits tacking of the period during which the underlying shares were held.[11] Returning to the example above, if shareholder S had owned her shares for three years, she would be entitled to add or "tack" that three year period to the holding period for the new shares. Remember that this stock dividend was tax-free under §305(a) and was subject to the §307 basis allocation rules. Like the stock dividend in Eisner v. Macomber, such stock dividends represent little other than a balance sheet adjustment whereby the shareholders receive additional shares of stock, but experience no change in their relative proportionate interest. In substance, shareholder S owns nothing different from what she had before. Under these circumstances, tacking of the holding period makes sense.

The §305(b) Exceptions

a) In General

Congress enumerates five specific types of stock dividends in §305(b) for which the general nonrecognition rule of §305(a) will not apply. The five §305(b) exceptions appear to be connected by a theme — the exceptions generally cover distributions that alter or may alter the proportionate interests of shareholders. The exceptions reflect a congressional effort to codify the "shift in proportional interest" test developed in Eisner v. Macomber and its progeny. When the stock dividend changes proportionate interests of the shareholders, the distribution is more than a mere paper transaction.

If one of the five §305(b) exceptions applies, the stock dividend will be treated as a §301 distribution. Remember that under the §301 rules, distributions will be taxable as dividends to the extent of earnings and profits. Thus, to the extent that there are sufficient earnings and profits to cover the distribution, a §305(b) stock dividend will be taxable. The shareholder will report the fair market value of the stock distributed as ordinary income and the shares will receive a fair market value basis under §301(d), rather than the §307 allocated basis that applies to stock received tax-free under §305(a).[12]

---

11. More specifically, the Code provides that "[i]n determining the period for which the taxpayer has held stock or rights to acquire stock received on a distribution, if the basis of such stock or rights is determined under section 307 . . . there shall (under regulations prescribed by the Secretary) be included the period for which he held the stock in the distributing corporation before the receipt of such stock or rights upon such distribution." I.R.C. §1223(5). The regulations clarify that the holding period for the dividend shares is the period for which the taxpayer held "the stock in respect of which the dividend was issued." Treas. Reg. §1.1223-1(e).

12. The §301 distribution rules were considered fully in Chapter 5.

b) Election to Take Other Property: §305(b)(1)

If any of the shareholders can elect to have a distribution payable in stock or property other than stock, the stock dividend will be taxable to all shareholders receiving stock pursuant to §305(b)(1). Surely, any shareholder who receives property *other than stock* should be taxable according to the §301 distribution rules. More important, §305(b)(1) also requires those who receive stock to report the distribution under the §301 rules. If some shareholders receive stock and other shareholders receive cash or other property, the stock dividend recipients increase their proportionate interest in the corporation at the expense of the other shareholders. Even if only one shareholder had an election to take cash or other property, all shareholders will be tainted by this election and the entire stock distribution will be taxable.

Notice that the §305(b)(1) exception sweeps rather broadly to deal not only with distributions that are actually disproportionate, but even those that are *potentially* disproportionate. The §305(b)(1) exception will apply even if all shareholders with an election to take property other than stock choose to take stock after all.[13] It is conceivable that a perfectly pro rata stock distribution will fail to get §305(a) nonrecognition simply because some shareholder had an unexercised election to take other property. The logic behind the §305(b)(1) exception is that where one or more shareholders choose to take property, usually cash, and other shareholders take stock, a shift in proportionate interest occurs. Those who receive stock have received something different from what they had before. Theoretically, even the mere option to take something other than stock suggests that what has happened, in substance, is that those shareholders with elective rights first received cash and then simply chose to reinvest that cash in the corporation.

An election to take stock or property may not be obvious from the stock dividend declaration itself, but may be found in the corporate charter or, more generally, in the circumstances surrounding the distribution.[14] For example, if the corporation has two classes of stock, one of which pays cash dividends and the other stock dividends, the arrangement is treated as one where the shareholders may elect to receive property or stock. The shareholders who receive stock dividends will be covered by the §305(b)(1) exception and, thus, will be taxable under §301 along with the other shareholders who received cash.

Shareholders who participate in an automatic dividend reinvestment plan

---

13. The regulations state that the exception will apply regardless of "[w]hether the distribution is actually made in whole or in part in stock or in stock rights." Treas. Reg. §1.305-2(a)(1).

14. Treas. Reg. §1.305-2(a)(4).

generally will be taxable on the shares received through the plan under §305(b)(1).[15] Such plans permit shareholders to elect to have their cash dividends automatically reinvested in shares of the corporation, often at a slight discount below the fair market value of the shares and for a service charge paid for administration of the plan. In effect, participating shareholders under such a plan have an election to take dividends in the form of cash or stock. From an economic perspective, those who receive stock may be viewed as if they had first received cash and then chosen to reinvest that cash in the corporate enterprise.

c) Disproportionate Distributions: §305(b)(2)

Under the disproportionate distribution exception, a stock distribution will be taxable if it results in the receipt of property by some shareholders and an increase in the proportionate interest of others in assets or earnings and profits. Under this provision the property often received is cash, but may be any other type of property. This requirement that some shareholders receive property often is referred to as the "companion distribution" requirement. As a first illustration of a taxable stock dividend under §305(b)(2), suppose that a corporation has two classes of stock, one of which pays cash distributions and the other simultaneously pays stock distributions. Those receiving the stock distribution will increase their proportionate interests in the corporation at the expense of those receiving cash. The stock dividend will be taxable under §305(b)(2).[16] The distributions need not be simultaneous, however. The §305(b)(2) exception applies to a distribution "or a series of distributions" that results in the receipt of property by some and an increase in proportionate interests of others.

Notice the breadth of §305(b)(2). First, if a stock distribution is part of a series of distributions that result in an increase in the proportionate interest of some shareholders and the receipt of cash or property by others, the stock dividend is taxable even though there was no plan to achieve this result.[17] If a series of distributions have the effect described in §305(b)(2), the stock distribution will be taxable "whether or not the stock distributions and the cash distributions are steps in an overall plan or are independent and unrelated."[18] Since no plan is required and since the Code and regulations provide no other definition of a "series of distributions," it is difficult to know when such a series exists. The regulations simply indicate that "[w]here

---

15. Rev. Rul. 76-53, 1976-1 C.B. 87; Rev. Rul. 78-375, 1978-2 C.B. 130.
16. Notice that there may be some overlap between §305(b)(1) and (b)(2).
17. Treas. Reg. §1.305-3(b)(2).
18. *Id.*

the receipt of cash or property occurs more than 36 months following a distribution or series of distributions of stock, or where a distribution or series of distributions of stock is made more than 36 months following the receipt of cash or property, such distribution or distributions will be presumed not to result in the receipt of cash or property by some shareholders and an increase in the proportionate interest of other shareholders, unless the receipt of cash or property and the distribution or series of distributions of stock are made pursuant to a plan."[19] Given the lax interpretation of the "companion distribution" requirement, it seems silly to bother with it at all.[20] The requirement adds needless complexity. In addition, in the case of an insolvent corporation, the lack of a companion distribution of cash or other property may even result in a disproportionate stock dividend *not* being subject to the §301 distribution rules.

Second, the companion distribution need not come from the corporation itself. The regulations continue that "there is no requirement that the shareholders receiving cash or property acquire the cash or property by way of a corporate distribution with respect to their shares, so long as they receive such cash or property in their capacity as shareholders."[21] Although the cash or other property need not come from the corporation itself, it must be paid to the shareholders in their capacity as shareholders and must be a distribution governed by §301 or other similar dividend-like provision mentioned in the regulations.[22] By way of illustration, the regulation describes a transaction in which some shareholders receive a stock distribution and other shareholders sell their shares in a prearranged plan to a related corporation for cash. In such a case, the stock dividend will be taxable under §305(b)(2).

d) Distributions of Common and Preferred: §305(b)(3)

If a distribution or series of distributions results in some common shareholders receiving common stock and others receiving preferred stock, the entire stock distribution will be taxable under §305(b)(3). The logic here presumably is that common shareholders' rights with respect to voting, earnings, and assets upon liquidation are significantly different from the rights of other shareholders. If a stock distribution results in some common shareholders receiving additional common shares and others receiving only preferred

---

19. Treas. Reg. §1.305-3(b)(4).

20. For an excellent critique, see James Holden, Unraveling the Mysteries of Section 305, 36 N.Y.U. Inst. Fed. Tax'n 781 (1978).

21. Treas. Reg. §1.305-3(b)(3).

22. The distribution must be one to which §§301, 356(a)(2), 871(a)(1)(A), 881(a)(1), 852(b), or 857(b) applies. Treas. Reg. §1.305-3(b)(3).

stock, a shift in proportionate interest has occurred. Notice, however, that the exception in §305(b)(3) applies only to distributions with respect to common stock. Distributions on preferred stock generally will be taxable under the exception provided in §305(b)(4).

e) Distributions on Preferred Stock: §305(b)(4)

A stock distribution issued with respect to preferred stock will be taxable under §304(b)(4), with one statutory exception for distributions to certain convertible preferred shareholders.[23] Unlike the other §305(b) exceptions, §305(b)(4) will apply even to a pro rata distribution. For example, if the corporation issues a pro rata stock distribution of additional preferred shares to all holders of preferred stock, this will be a taxable stock distribution unless it fits within the convertible preferred exception.

The logic behind the §305(b)(4) exception has a slightly different quality from that behind all of the other §305(b) exceptions, which are based on variations to the "shift in proportionate interest" theme. In each of the other cases, Congress identified situations that either shifted, or potentially shifted, the shareholders' proportionate interests and, thus, should not be covered by the Eisner v. Macomber reasoning. In contrast, the §305 legislative history notes that preferred stock generally pays specified cash dividends. Congress viewed stock dividends paid with respect to preferred stock as substitutes for cash dividends, concluding that such stock dividends should be taxed.[24]

f) Distributions of Convertible Preferred: §305(b)(5)

When shareholders receive a stock dividend in the form of preferred shares that are convertible into common stock, some shareholders may convert and others may not. If so, those shareholders who choose to convert increase their proportionate interest in the common stock relative to other shareholders. The final exception in §305(b)(5) provides that a distribution of convertible preferred will be taxable "unless it is established to the satisfaction of the Secretary that such distribution will not have the result described in paragraph (2)." In other words, a distribution of convertible preferred will be taxable unless the shareholders can show that the distribution will not result in an increase in proportionate interest for some shareholders and the

---

23. The exception covers only distributions to convertible preferred shareholders in order to increase the conversion ratio solely to take into account a stock dividend or stock split with respect to the stock into which the stock may be converted. I.R.C. §305(b)(4).

24. See S. Rep. No. 522, 91st Cong., 1st Sess. 55 (1969).

receipt of property by others. If *all* of the shareholders convert the shares or *all* of the shareholders choose not to convert, then the effect of the distribution is pro rata and the distribution is much like those covered by the general nonrecognition rule in §305(a). On the other hand, if some shareholders are likely to convert and others likely not to convert, the effect of the distribution is much like the taxable stock dividends provided for in §305(b)(2). The §305 regulations conclude that the distribution is likely to result in a disproportionate distribution when conversion rights must be exercised within a relatively short period of time and when factors such as dividend rates, redemption provisions, marketability and conversion price suggest that some shareholders will convert and some will not.[25] On the other hand, if conversion rights are available over a period of years and the dividend rates is consistent with market conditions, the regulations conclude that "there is no basis for predicting at what time and the extent to which the stock will be converted and it is unlikely that a disproportionate distribution will result."[26]

Deemed Stock Distributions: §305(c)

Recognizing that certain transactions may have the effect of a stock dividend even though no shares are actually distributed, Congress directed the Secretary to promulgate regulations under which certain transactions will be treated as distributions of stock for purposes of §305. Section 305(c) lists five categories of transactions that will be deemed constructive stock dividends to "any shareholder whose proportionate interest in the earnings and profits or assets of the corporation is increased" as a result of the particular transaction. The deemed stock distribution will be taxable under §301 if it has the result described in one of the five exceptions provided in §305(b).[27] In any constructive stock dividend case, one must first determine whether the transaction is a deemed distribution transaction that increases the proportionate interest of some shareholders and second, whether it would be taxable under one of the §305(b) exceptions.

The five categories of deemed transactions specified in §305(c) include:

(1) a change in conversion ratio,
(2) a change in redemption price,
(3) a difference between redemption price and issue price,
(4) a redemption treated as a distribution to which §301 applies, or

---

25. Treas. Reg. §1.305-6(a)(2).
26. *Id.*
27. Treas. Reg. §1.305-7(a)(2).

(5) any transaction (including a recapitalization) having a similar effect on the interest of any shareholder.[28]

Looking first at conversion ratios, if the corporation has one class of stock that is convertible into another, a change in the conversion ratio can result in an increase in the proportionate interest of some shareholders. Even though no stock is actually issued, the effect of such a change is similar to a non pro rata stock dividend. For example, imagine a corporation that has two classes of stock outstanding. Class B shares initially are convertible into Class A at a ratio of one to one; that is, each Class B share can be converted into one Class A share. Imagine further that the corporation pays cash dividends to the Class A shareholders and increases the conversion ratio of the Class B shareholders so that each Class B share now can be converted into 1.5 Class A shares. Even though no stock was actually issued, this increase in the conversion ratio reflects an increase in the Class B shareholders' proportionate interest at the expense of the Class A shareholders.[29] The constructive stock dividend will be treated as a disproportionate stock distribution under §305(b)(2).[30] The Class B shareholders are deemed under §305(c) to have received a stock dividend in the amount of the fair market value of the additional one-half share per Class B share previously owned.[31]

On the other hand, a change in conversion ratio sometimes may be necessary in order to prevent the dilution of the convertible shareholders' interest. Suppose in the above example, that the Class A shareholders received a dividend of additional Class A shares. An adjustment to the Class B shareholders' conversion rights will be necessary to prevent dilution of the Class B holders' interests. The regulations provide that a change in conversion ratio "made pursuant to a bona fide, reasonable adjustment formula" to prevent dilution of the convertible shareholders' interest will not be considered a deemed distribution of stock.[32]

The second category of transactions that may result in a deemed distribution is a change in the redemption price. Suppose, for example, that the corporation increases the price at which it will redeem preferred shares. Such a change increases the preferred shareholders' claim on corporate assets and will be viewed as a deemed stock distribution to the preferred shareholders.

Under the third category, a difference between the issue and redemption price may result in a deemed distribution. If the corporation provides for a

---

28. I.R.C. §305(c).

29. Technically speaking, the increase in proportionate interest does not occur until the Class B shareholders actually convert their shares.

30. The companion distribution requirement of §305(b)(2) is met, since the Class A shareholders received cash dividends.

31. For a similar example, see Treas. Reg. §1.305-3(e), ex. (6).

32. Treas. Reg. §1.305-7(b)(1).

redemption premium above the issue price, the premium may be treated as a distribution of additional stock. On the other hand, the regulations recognize that corporations will sometimes provide for a reasonable call premium designed as a penalty for premature redemption by the corporation. Thus, the regulations provide that the premium will only be a deemed distribution to the extent that it exceeds a "reasonable redemption premium." For purposes of this rule, "a redemption premium not in excess of 10 percent of the issue price on stock which is not redeemable for five years from the date of issue shall be considered reasonable."[33] Assume that the issue price for Class B preferred shares is $100 per share. The corporation provides that the shares are redeemable at any time after five years for $110. The $10 premium per share will not be a deemed distribution since this is considered a reasonable premium.[34] On the other hand, if the stock is redeemable after five years for $200, there will be a deemed distribution in the amount of $90 — the excess above the reasonable $10 premium.

Another potential deemed stock dividend may result from a non pro rata stock redemption. Recall that a redemption of stock from one shareholder causes an increase in the other shareholders' interests.[35] Under §305(c), Congress directed the Treasury Department to promulgate regulations addressing when a redemption treated as a §301 distribution to the redeemed shareholder should be treated as a deemed or constructive stock dividend to the remaining shareholders. The regulations include examples indicating that an isolated redemption from one shareholder resulting in an increase to other shareholders' proportionate interests will not be a constructive stock dividend to the shareholders whose interests are increased.[36] On the other hand, a periodic redemption plan under which a portion of some shareholders' stock is periodically redeemed while the proportionate interests of other shareholders' increases will be a constructive dividend to the shareholders whose interests are increased.[37]

Tax Consequences to the Corporation

Generally speaking, the issuance of a pro rata stock dividend has little or no tax consequence to the issuing corporation. For accounting purposes, the stock dividend merely is reflected on the corporation's balance sheet by appropriate changes to the equity and surplus accounts. On the other hand,

---

33. Treas. Reg. §1.305-5(b)(2).
34. See Treas. Reg. §1.305-5(d), ex. (4).
35. For a complete discussion of redemption distributions, see Chapter 6.
36. Treas. Reg. §1.305-3(e), ex. 10.
37. *Id.*, ex. 8 (describing method for computing the amount of distribution).

a distribution that is not pro rata should raise red flags. The additional shares resulting in an increase in proportionate interest may have been intended as compensation to a shareholder who performed services for the corporation. If so, the corporation should be entitled to an ordinary and necessary business expense deduction under §162. More generally, where there is a non pro rata distribution, the corporation should identify the economic substance of the transaction and treat it accordingly. If assets have left the corporation, an adjustment to earnings and profits will be necessary.

The Preferred Stock Bailout: §306 Stock

Background and History

Despite the many different varieties of preferred stock, certain shared characteristics tend to predominate. For example, preferred stock generally is senior stock in that it has a right to its share (usually specified as a percentage much like an interest rate) of dividends before dividends are paid to common shareholders. On the other hand, preferred shareholders often have no voting rights at all, or perhaps junior voting rights, in relation to the common shareholders. In addition, since dividends available to preferred shareholders are usually fixed, preferred shareholders generally have a lesser right to share in the unlimited growth of the corporation. Shareholders who own both common and nonvoting preferred stock can sell off preferred shares without compromising their voting rights and their share in unlimited growth. Combined with the tax-free nature of stock dividends under §305 discussed above, this opportunity gave rise to the "preferred stock bailout."

The first step in such a bailout was for the corporation to issue a pro rata stock dividend of preferred shares with respect to the common stock outstanding. Since none of the §305(b) exceptions applies to a pro rata distribution of preferred with respect to common, the distribution was a nontaxable stock dividend under §305(a). The second step was either for the corporation to redeem the preferred shares or for the shareholders to sell the preferred shares, usually in a prearranged plan. Upon sale or redemption of the stock, the shareholders would report any gain as capital gain. The preferred stock bailout was then complete. Instead of distributing its profits as a dividend taxable to the shareholders as an ordinary income dividend, the corporation reflected its profits in a tax-free distribution of its own stock. The shareholders realize gain upon later sale of the stock, but at capital gains rates. The technique permitted shareholders to bail out corporate earnings at capital gains rates.

The corporate bailout is easier to see in the case of a preferred stock dividend followed by a redemption of the dividend stock. The corporation is using its own funds to repurchase stock previously issued as a tax-free stock dividend. Funds for the bailout have been paid by the corporation directly to its shareholders. If the redemption is treated as a sale or exchange redemption under §302, the shareholder will report capital gain from a sale or exchange of stock as opposed to ordinary income from a dividend.[38] Where the shareholder sells the preferred stock received from the stock dividend to an outside third party, the corporate bailout may be more difficult to see. The funds for purchase of the shares come not from the corporation, but from some outside source. The case of Chamberlin v. Commissioner provides a good example of a successful preferred stock bailout through shareholder disposition of dividend shares to a third party.[39] The corporation in *Chamberlin* found itself with a substantial earned surplus. The primary shareholders, owning approximately an 85% interest, objected to the distribution of such a surplus as a dividend taxable at ordinary income rates. Instead, the corporation and its primary shareholders contacted two insurance companies regarding investing in the corporation's preferred stock. The insurance companies carefully investigated the corporation and agreed to purchase the preferred shares. The corporation arranged a pro rata preferred stock dividend to the common shareholders. Shortly thereafter, and in accordance with a plan worked out in advance, the shareholders then sold their preferred shares to the insurance companies. One important feature of the preferred shares was a mandatory redemption feature under which the shares would be redeemed by the corporation over a seven-year period. As the court put it, the "dominant and decisive issue" was whether the stock dividend, which "by reason of its redemption feature, enabled the corporation to ultimately distribute its earnings to its stockholders on a taxable basis materially lower than would have been the case by declaring and paying the usual cash dividend, was a bona fide one, one in substance as well as in form."[40] Although the shareholders received cash from the insurance companies as part of a sale of stock, the corporation's cash was ultimately used to satisfy the corporation's mandatory redemption obligation to the insurance companies. The Commissioner argued that this transaction was a taxable dividend to the shareholders. Rejecting this claim, the court concluded that both the stock dividend and the sale to the insurance companies were bona fide. In a useful and candid passage in its opinion, the court noted that:

> [i]n deciding this case it must be kept in mind that it does not involve a ruling that the profit derived from the sale of the stock dividend is or is not taxable income. Such profit is conceded to be taxable. The issue is whether it is taxable as income from a cash dividend or as income resulting from a long-term capital gain. Accord-

---

38. For a more detailed discussion of the redemption provisions of §302, see Chapter 6.

39. 207 F.2d 462 (6th Cir. 1953), *cert. denied*, 347 U.S. 918 (1954).

40. *Id*. at 470.

ingly, it is not the usual case of total tax avoidance. Congress has adopted the policy of taxing long-term capital gains differently from ordinary income . . . [I]t has specifically excluded certain transactions with respect to stock dividends from the classification of a capital gain. The present transaction is not within the exclusion. If the profit from a transaction like the one here involved is to be taxed at the same rate as ordinary income, it should be done by appropriate legislation, not court decision.[41]

Congress responded rather quickly to the court's invitation to adopt appropriate legislation to combat the preferred stock bailout. The result was the complex set of provisions found in §306.

Tainted §306 Stock

Preferred stock dividend distributions do not always result in a bailout of corporate earnings at capital gains rather than ordinary income rates. Since the preferred stock bailout resulted not from the initial tax-free receipt of the stock dividend, but from the later disposition of the dividend shares, Congress responded by creating a special provision in §306, entitled "Dispositions of Certain Stock." Preferred stock dividends remain eligible for nonrecognition under §305(a). Once received, however, the stock may be designated as §306 stock, sometimes known as "tainted stock." When the shareholder disposes of this "tainted stock," either through sale or redemption, the normal sale or redemption rules will not apply. Instead, the gain may be treated as ordinary income under rules provided in §306. To unravel the mysteries of §306, one must start by identifying the stock that will be covered by its web.

The Definition of §306 Stock

By its terms, §306 stock is "[s]tock (other than common stock issued with respect to common stock) which was distributed to the shareholder selling or otherwise disposing of such stock if, by reason of section 305(a), any part of such distribution was not includible in the gross income of the shareholder."[42] Notice first that §306 only applies to stock initially received tax-free under §305(a). The bailout concern was that shareholders could receive a *nontaxable* stock dividend that they could later convert to capital gain income through disposition of the shares. If the initial stock dividend is taxable, Congress is not concerned about subsequent disposition of the shares.

---

41. *Id.* at 472.

42. I.R.C. §306(c)(1)(A). Options to acquire stock and certain stock acquired through the exercise of options will also be considered §306 stock. I.R.C. §306(d).

Second, notice that §306 will not apply to common stock issued to common shareholders. Preferred shares were thought to be the perfect vehicles for corporate bailouts since shareholders can dispose of these shares without losing any of their proprietary interest reflected in the underlying common stock. If a corporation issues a common stock dividend to shareholders who later dispose of the dividend shares, the disposition causes a reduction in the shareholders' voting rights and rights to unlimited growth in the corporation. Thus, it makes some sense that Congress carved out common stock distributions from §306 coverage. Since the adoption of §306, several rulings and cases have focused on the question of what constitutes "common stock" for purposes of §306. A corporation might create a class of stock that smells a lot like preferred, but label it common stock. Labels will not be determinative for purposes of §306.[43]

In several rulings, the Service has indicated that in deciding whether or not particular stock is common stock for purposes of the §306(c)(1) definition, one must look to the underlying purpose of Congress to eliminate the preferred stock bailout. For example, Rev. Rul. 81-91 involved Class A and Class B shares with equal par values and equal voting rights. The Class B shares, however, had a 6% preference with respect to dividends before any dividend was payable on Class A shares. In addition, the Class B shares had a prior right to repayment up to par value in the event of liquidation. Although one might be tempted to label the Class B share as "voting preferred," the Service ruled that, for purposes of §306, the Class B stock was common stock, the distribution of which was not covered by §306. In reaching this conclusion, the Service said that "[i]n determining whether newly issued stock is 'common stock' for purposes of §306, the 'preferred stock bailout' abuse Congress sought to prevent by enactment of that section provides guidance. . . . The potential for a preferred stock bailout exists if . . . the stock . . . can be disposed of without a surrender by the shareholders of significant interests in corporate growth. Thus, stock is other than 'common stock' for purposes of section 306 not because of its preferred position as such, but because the preferred position is limited and the stock does not participate in corporate growth to any significant extent."[44]

In addition to the definition provided in §306(c)(1), Congress defined §306 stock to include two other categories. The second category classifies as §306 stock any stock other than common stock received tax-free in a reorganization, "but only to the extent that either the effect of the transaction was substantially the same as the receipt of a stock dividend, or the stock was received in exchange for §306 stock."[45] Under this definition, if the share-

---

43. See, e.g., Rev. Rul. 79-163, 1979-1 C.B. 131, where stock classified as common by the corporation was not considered common for §306 purposes because it did not have an unrestricted right in the equity growth of the corporation.

44. Rev. Rul. 81-91, 1981-1 C.B. 123.

45. I.R.C. §306(c)(1)(B)(ii).

holder receives new preferred shares in a tax-free reorganization to replace previously owned preferred shares, the new ("replacement") preferred shares should not be classified as §306 stock. On the other hand, if the shareholder receives preferred shares designed to provide him with an additional preferred interest, these additional shares will be classified as §306 stock. In addition, if the shareholder previously had §306 stock and, as part of a tax-free reorganization, receives preferred shares to replace the §306 stock, the replacement shares will be considered §306 stock as well. In the reorganization context, Congress assures that the taint remains even if the shareholder exchanges §306 stock for new preferred stock in a reorganization.

The third category of preferred stock is stock that has a substituted basis. Congress defines §306 stock to include "stock the basis of which (in the hands of the shareholder selling or otherwise disposing of such stock) is determined by reference to the basis (in the hands of such shareholder or any other person) of section 306 stock."[46] Here again, Congress was concerned with preserving the taint upon certain exchanges or transfers of §306 stock. For example, assume that a parent received tainted stock, as defined in the first definition above, from a stock dividend. Thereafter, the parent transfers the tainted stock to a child by way of a gift. Since property received by gift generally takes a substituted basis, the child will have tainted stock under this third category. Congress often uses substituted basis rules when property is exchanged without immediate recognition of gain or loss. The substituted basis assures that the previously unrecognized gain or loss is preserved in some fashion. When a parent makes a gift of stock to a child, for example, the parent's gain or loss effectively is preserved in the child's hands through use of a substituted basis under §1015. The third category included in the §306 stock definitions assures that not only the gain or loss, but also the §306 taint, will remain with the shares when they are transferred.

As an exception to the three categories of §306 stock described above, §306 stock "does not include any stock no part of the distribution of which would have been a dividend at the time of the distribution if money had been distributed in lieu of the stock."[47] This exception really gets to the heart of §306. It focuses on bailout *potential* by identifying the extent to which the stock distribution *would have been* taxable as a dividend if cash had been used instead of stock. Although the *bite* of §306 is usually not felt until ultimate disposition of the shares, the *taint* is identified upon the initial stock distribution. Bailout potential exists if the corporation had sufficient earnings and profits to cover the distribution if it had been a cash distribution instead of a stock distribution. If a corporation issued preferred stock to common shareholders in a year for which there were no current or accumulated

---

46. I.R.C. §306(c)(1)(C).
47. I.R.C. §306(c)(2).

earnings and profits, no part of the distribution would have been a dividend if cash had been distributed under the §301 distribution rules. Under the §306(c)(2) exception, the stock distributed will not be §306 stock. This exception is consistent with the purpose of §306 to prevent bailouts of corporate profits at capital gains as opposed to ordinary income rates. If no part of the distribution would have been a dividend, there would have been no ordinary income from the distribution in any event. Be aware, however, that the exception in §306(c)(2) explicitly requires that *no part* of the distribution would have been a dividend. If the corporation distributes preferred stock to common shareholders in a year for which there were some, but not sufficient, earnings and profits to cover the distribution, the §306(c)(2) exception will not apply. The preferred stock distributed will be tainted §306 stock.

Disposition of §306 Stock

Shareholders may dispose of tainted stock either through a redemption or a sale or exchange other than a redemption. The §306 operating rules cover each of these types of dispositions separately.

a) Dispositions by Redemption

A redemption distribution ordinarily is treated as a sale or exchange to the redeemed shareholder if it meets one of the §302(b) tests.[48] On the other hand, the amount realized to the shareholder upon redemption of tainted §306 stock automatically is "treated as a distribution of property to which section 301 applies."[49] The effect of this provision is to bypass the redemption provisions of §302. In other words, there is no opportunity for capital gain treatment under the §302 redemption provisions. The shareholder will not be entitled to a basis offset and the redemption proceeds will be treated as ordinary income to the extent that the corporation has sufficient earnings and profits to cover the distribution under the §301 rules.[50]

One odd feature of the §306(a)(2) disposition by redemption provision is that the corporation's earnings and profits at the time of the initial tainted stock distribution appear to be irrelevant. The §306(a)(2) rules simply direct the shareholder to §301. Thus, the relevant earnings and profits to determine tax consequences to the shareholder will be those in the year of the disposition or redemption, *not* the year when the tainted stock was distributed. This

---

48. The redemption provisions of §302 were considered in detail in Chapter 6.

49. I.R.C. §306(a)(2).

50. The §301 distribution rules were covered in detail in Chapter 5. Consistent with the ordinary distribution rules, any basis that the shareholders had in the §306 stock will be added back to the basis in their other shares in the corporation.

seems inconsistent with §306's focus upon bailout potential and the extent to which the initial stock dividend would have been taxable as a dividend if it had been paid in cash. Perhaps testing the redemption disposition of §306 stock by e&p at the time of redemption can be explained by the fact that the bailout is achieved through a distribution of funds directly from the corporation. In a sense, we see the actual bailout of corporate funds, as opposed merely to bailout potential. Another unique feature of the §306(a)(2) redemption bailout is that since the redemption is simply treated as a §301 distribution, a corporate shareholder will be entitled to a §243 dividends-received deduction.

b) Dispositions Other than by Redemption

Sales or other dispositions of §306 tainted stock *other than by redemption* are governed by §306(a)(1). The provision itself is rather awkwardly worded. Before diving into the mechanics, it might be useful to provide an overview of what §306(a)(1) achieves in the end. First, a portion of the amount realized from disposition of the tainted stock will be ordinary income. This portion essentially reflects the amount that would have been a dividend if the corporation had distributed cash instead of stock. Second, to the extent possible, the shareholder will be entitled to recover basis in the shares tax-free. Finally, any excess gain will be treated as gain from the sale of stock.[51] Notice that these three steps parallel the distribution rules in §301(c)(1), (2), and (3). This is precisely the idea—Congress is attempting here to provide for dividend-like treatment.

The mechanics of §306(a)(1) can be confusing. The only solution is slow and patient analysis of the statute. To illustrate the mechanics of §306(a)(1), suppose that Corporation X has two shareholders (A and B) who equally own all of the common stock. In a year when the corporation has only $100,000 in earnings and profits, it distributes a §305(a) nontaxable stock dividend of $500,000 worth of preferred stock ($250,000 to each shareholder). Shareholder A later sells the tainted preferred shares for $300,000 to an unrelated third party. Assume that shareholder A's basis in the stock, determined after a §307 allocation, is $225,000. If shareholder A's stock was not tainted and she simply sold it to a third party for cash, her taxable gain under §1001 simply would be her amount realized of $300,000 less her basis of $225,000 for a capital gain of $75,000. Shareholder A's preferred stock is §306 stock, however.[52] Since her shares are tainted, she will be required to report the gain in accordance with §306(a)(1).

---

51. I.R.C. §§306(a)(1)(A) and (B).

52. The exception to the §306 stock definition in §306(c)(2) will not apply here, since *some part* of the distribution would have been taxable as a dividend if cash had been distributed.

The §306(a)(1) rules begin by treating the amount realized from a disposition of §306 stock (other than by redemption) as ordinary income.[53] The statute continues, however, that there shall *not* be ordinary income to the extent that amount realized exceeds the §306 stock's "ratable share of the amount which would have been a dividend at the time of the distribution if (in lieu of section 306 stock) the corporation had distributed money in an amount equal to the fair market value of the stock at the time of distribution."[54] This language requires an answer to a hypothetical question—if the corporation had distributed cash instead of stock, what would be the shareholder's ratable share of the amount that would have been a dividend? Unlike the disposition by redemption provision in §306(a)(2), this exercise requires the shareholder to look back to the year in which the tainted stock was initially distributed. The earnings and profits in the year of disposition are irrelevant. Since the corporation had only $100,000 of earnings and profits in the year the tainted stock was distributed, and since shareholder A was a 50% shareholder, her ratable share of the amount that would have been a dividend if she had received cash is $50,000. Although §306(a)(1) starts by suggesting that the entire $300,000 received for the preferred shares will be treated as ordinary income, it provides an exception to the extent that the amount realized ($300,000) exceeds the $50,000 ratable share. In other words, $250,000 will *not* be treated as ordinary income and only $50,000 is treated as ordinary income.[55] This, after all, is the shareholder's portion of the bailout potential that existed at the time of the initial tainted stock distribution and the amount that Congress wanted to tax at ordinary income rather than capital gains rates.

The next step is to determine how the remaining $250,000 of her amount realized should be treated. Under §306(a)(1)(B), the excess of amount realized ($300,000) over the amount treated as ordinary income ($50,000) plus the adjusted basis of the stock ($225,000) will be treated as gain from the sale of the stock. Thus, under §306(a)(1)(B), shareholder A will report the excess $25,000 as capital gain from the sale of stock. Notice that the *amount* of shareholder A's gain under §306(a)(1) remains the same $75,000 she would have reported under §1001 if the stock had not been tainted §306 stock. The critical difference has to do with the *character* of gain. A sale of untainted stock would have resulted in a $75,000 capital gain, whereas the sale of §306 stock results in $50,000 of ordinary income and $25,000 of capital gain. Put differently, §306 breaks shareholder A's $300,000 amount realized into three pieces: $50,000 ordinary income,

53. I.R.C. §306(a)(1)(A).

54. I.R.C. §306(a)(1)(A)(ii).

55. When the dust settles, the "ratable share" figure determined under §306(a)(1)(A)(ii) is usually the amount that is taxable as ordinary income upon the disposition of the tainted stock.

$225,000 tax-free recovery of capital, and $25,000 capital gain from the sale of stock. For the most part, the §306(a) operating rules parallel the provisions in §301(c). When a corporation makes a distribution to a shareholder, only that portion that is a dividend is treated as ordinary income under §301(c)(1). Thereafter the shareholder is entitled to a tax-free recovery of basis under §301(c)(2). Finally, any excess is treated as gain from the sale of stock under §301(c)(3).

Despite the parallels to §301(c), there are some differences. For example, §306 refers to the shareholder's "ratable share" of earnings and profits whereas §301 does not. If the corporation had distributed $300,000 to shareholder A when its earnings and profits were $100,000, shareholder A would have had ordinary dividend income of $100,000 (assuming no other distributions). Under §306, however, she has only $50,000 of ordinary income. After all, the corporation did issue the preferred stock dividend on a pro rata basis. Shareholder B's ratable share of the hypothetical dividend may be taxed later when he disposes of his tainted stock.

In the above hypothetical, shareholder A was able to recover her entire basis tax-free. This will not always be possible upon a disposition of §306 stock. Suppose, for example, that shareholder A's basis in her tainted shares had been $275,000 instead of $225,000. If the stock had been untainted, she would simply have realized and reported a capital gain of $25,000 under §1001.[56] Under §306(a)(1), however, she must still report $50,000 of ordinary income under §306(a)(1)(A). Notice that this amount is already *more* than her realized gain. Under §306(a)(1)(B), gain is recognized to the extent of the excess of the amount realized ($300,000) over the amount treated as ordinary income ($50,000) plus the adjusted basis of the stock ($275,000). There is no excess here and, therefore, no gain. Notice that shareholder A was taxed on $50,000 when her realized gain was only $25,000. Put differently, §306(a)(1)(B) deprives her of a full basis offset or tax-free recovery of basis. The absence of a tax-free recovery of basis is common in the context of §301 dividend distributions. If a corporation has sufficient earnings and profits, the shareholder must report the entire distribution as a taxable dividend without any basis offset.[57] In the dividend scenario, however, the shareholder continues to own the shares, whereas the shareholder in the §306 stock sale has sold her shares to an unrelated third party. Absent §306, the shareholder would be entitled to a full basis recovery. Shareholder A might argue that since she has a $25,000 investment in the stock that she was not entitled to recover tax-free, she should be entitled to a loss. She will be denied the loss because §306(a)(1)(C) explicitly provides that "no loss shall be recognized." She will not lose her basis, however.

---

56. Amount realized of $300,000 less adjusted basis of $275,000.
57. See Chapter 5 for discussion of nonliquidating distributions.

Although §306 disallows losses, shareholders are permitted to add any un-
recovered basis from the tainted shares to the basis of the common shares
with respect to which the tainted shares were issued.[58]

Exceptions to the §306 Rules: §306(b)

The §306(b) exceptions to the §306(a) tainted stock rules are connected by
a common theme. Remember that Congress designed §306 to combat the
preferred stock bailout. If the shareholders retain their interest in the underlying common stock with respect to which the preferred stock dividend was
issued, they retain voting rights and rights to share in unlimited growth of
the corporation. By disposing of the tainted shares and retaining the underlying common shares, the shareholders essentially have taken earnings from
the corporation without sacrificing any of the proprietary interest reflected
in the underlying common shares. The first two exceptions in §306(b) cover
circumstances where the shareholder's interest in the corporation is completely terminated. In such cases, the shareholder has parted with not only
the tainted stock, but also the underlying common with respect to which the
tainted stock was issued. This is not the bailout scenario that Congress was
concerned with. In the most extreme case, if the corporation redeems tainted
stock as part of a complete liquidation of the corporation, *all* of the shareholders' interests are terminated. Thus, §306(a) will not apply to complete
liquidations.[59] Short of complete liquidation, §306(a) also will not apply to
complete termination of interest redemptions under §302(b)(3) or partial
liquidation redemptions under §302(b)(4).[60] In addition, §306(a) will not
apply if the disposition other than by redemption completely terminates the
shareholder's interest and is not a disposition to a related party under the
§318 attribution rules.[61]

As a third exception, §306(a) will not apply to the disposition of tainted
stock to the extent that gain or loss is not recognized under any other income
tax provisions in the Internal Revenue Code.[62] In other words, §306 will
not trump other nonrecognition provisions. This exception is not as generous
at it might seem at first glance. Keep in mind that most nonrecognition
provisions in the Code come paired with substituted basis rules designed to
preserve gain or loss left unrecognized. Since the §306 stock definition
includes stock the basis of which is determined in reference to the basis of

---

58. Treas. Reg. §1.306-1(b)(2), ex. (2), (3).

59. I.R.C. §306(b)(2). For a full discussion of complete liquidations, see Chapters
8 and 9.

60. I.R.C. §306(b)(1)(B).

61. For a more detailed discussion of the §318 attribution rules, see Chapter 6.

62. I.R.C. §306(b)(3).

§306 stock (substituted basis), the stock will retain its taint even after a nonrecognition exchange. Although §306(a) does not apply on the disposition of the tainted shares in the nonrecognition exchange, the §306(a) rules will apply upon ultimate disposition of the shares in a taxable exchange. For example, the owner of §306 stock who transfers the shares by gift will not recognize any gain upon the disposition. The recipient of the gift, however, takes the shares with a substituted basis under §1015 and the stock retains its taint in the new owner's hands. In addition, a shareholder may exchange tainted §306 shares for new shares as part of a tax-free reorganization. Although the disposition of the tainted shares was tax-free, the shares received in exchange for the tainted shares are considered §306 stock under §306(c)(1)(B). Thus, §306(a) will apply to a later disposition of the shares received tax-free as part of the reorganization.[63]

The final exception to the §306(a) rules is for "transactions not in avoidance." Since the §306 rules were designed to combat certain deliberate and tax motivated bailouts, Congress left the taxpayer with an opportunity under §306(b)(4) to argue that the transaction was not motivated by tax avoidance. The §306(b)(4) exception contains two categories of transactions. First, the taxpayer can avoid §306(a) by establishing to the satisfaction of the Secretary that the distribution *and* the disposition or redemption were "not in pursuance of a plan having as one of its principal purposes the avoidance of federal income tax."[64] Second, where there is a prior or simultaneous disposition of the underlying stock with respect to which the tainted stock was issued, the taxpayer can avoid §306(a) by establishing to the satisfaction of the Secretary that the disposition of the tainted stock "was not in pursuance of a plan having as one of its principal purposes the avoidance of federal income tax."[65]

The standard in each case is the same: pursuance of a plan having tax avoidance as *one* of its principal purposes. This may prove a very difficult standard for the taxpayer to address. Most taxpayers choosing one route or another for a particular transaction consider tax consequences to some extent. Although there have not been many litigated cases to date, cases that have been decided suggest that the taxpayer will have an uphill battle in making a case for this exception. Even if there is an otherwise legitimate business reason for the transaction, at least one court has held that the

---

63. Tax-free reorganizations are discussed in Chapters 11-14.

64. I.R.C. §306(b)(4)(A).

65. I.R.C. §306(b)(4)(B). With regard to the first nonavoidance exception category, the taxpayer must establish that *both* the initial stock distribution *and* the later disposition of the tainted stock meet the nonavoidance standard. With regard to the second category, involving prior or simultaneous sale of the underlying stock, the taxpayer must meet the standard only once with respect to the disposition.

transaction fails §306(b)(4) if *one* of the principal reasons for structuring the particular transaction was tax avoidance, apparently read "tax reduction."[66]

The rationale for the second category of nonavoidance exceptions is similar to the rationale for the complete liquidation and complete termination of interest exceptions discussed above. If the shareholder either already has disposed of the underlying stock or is disposing of the underlying stock along with the tainted shares, the bailout abuse arguably is no longer present. Congress was concerned that shareholders could get profits out of the corporation at capital gains rates without sacrificing much proprietary interest in the corporation. In the case of Fireoved v. United States,[67] the shareholder had previously sold some, but not all, of the underlying common stock with respect to which the §306 stock had been issued. Rejecting his claim for a §306(b)(4) exception, the court argued that:

> [I]t is reasonable to assume that Congress realized the general lack of a tax avoidance purpose when a person sells *all* of his control in a corporation and then either simultaneously or subsequently disposes of his section 306 stock. However, when *only a portion* of the underlying common stock is sold, and the taxpayer retains essentially all the control he had previously, it would be unrealistic to conclude that Congress meant to give that taxpayer the advantage of section 306(b)(4)(B) when he ultimately sells his section 306 stock.[68]

Under the particular circumstances in the *Fireoved* case, although the shareholder had sold some of his shares to another shareholder, he retained effective veto power, and hence, control over the corporation. A taxpayer with anything less than a prior or simultaneous sale of *all* of the underlying common will have a difficult time making a case under §306(b)(4). The case may be strengthened, however, if the prior or simultaneous sale of the underlying common results in a loss of effective control.

Charitable Bailout

In an early ruling, the Treasury Department ruled that although §306(a)(1) generally applies to dispositions other than redemptions, a disposition by gift is not a taxable event to the donor.[69] Thus, §306(a)(1) will not apply to dispositions by gift. Instead, the donee will receive a substituted basis under §1015 and, under the definition of §306 stock in §306(c)(1)(C), the donee will own tainted stock. In other words, the recipient of the gift takes the stock not only with the donor's basis, but also with the donor's §306 taint. If the taxpayer donates tainted stock to a tax-exempt charitable organization, the taxpayer has no taxable gain from making the gift. The charity presumably

---

66. Fireoved v. United States, 462 F.2d 1281 (3d Cir. 1972).

67. *Id.*

68. *Id.* at 1289 (emphasis added).

69. Rev. Rul. 57-328, 1957-2 C.B. 229.

has the stock with a substituted basis and with the §306 taint. The donor will never pay tax on the appreciation reflected in the shares received in the form of a stock dividend and later transferred to charity. Although the charity holds tainted stock, as a tax-exempt organization, it is unlikely to report any income from disposition of the shares. And, to add icing to the cake, the taxpayer donating the stock is entitled to a charitable contributions deduction under §170.

In a modest effort to combat this particular bailout transaction, Congress limits the amount of the taxpayer's charitable deduction. Ordinarily, a taxpayer can deduct the full fair market value of property contributed to charity.[70] Under a limitation in §170(e), however, the amount shall be reduced by "the amount of gain which would not have been long-term capital gain if the property contributed had been sold by the taxpayer at its fair market value." In the §306 context, the taxpayer must reduce his charitable deduction amount to the extent that the disposition would have resulted in ordinary income under §306(a)(1).

EXAMPLES

Basic §305 Problems

1. Tara Corporation was an industrial farm owned and operated by the O'Hara family. Mr. and Mrs. O'Hara owned 75% of the common stock with a basis of $600,000 and their daughter, Scarlet, owned the remaining 25%, with a basis of $200,000. Tara declares and distributes a stock dividend of newly authorized nonvoting preferred shares valued immediately after the distribution at $1 million. Mr. and Mrs. O'Hara receive $750,000 worth and Scarlet receives $250,000 worth of the preferred shares. Immediately after the preferred stock distribution, the total value of the common shares outstanding is also $1 million. Assume that the corporation has sufficient e&p to cover any distribution falling under the §301 rules. What are the tax consequences of the stock distribution to the O'Hara family?

Variations on a Theme from Example 1

2a. If Scarlet was able to convince the corporation to make her share of the stock dividend payable in cash in lieu of stock, what tax consequences to Scarlet? To her parents?

2b. What if the corporation issues a stock dividend of convertible preferred shares? Assume that each preferred share can be converted into one common share.

2c. If the corporation had two classes of voting common stock, one owned entirely by Mr. and Mrs. O'Hara (Class A) and the other owned by Scarlet

---

70. Treas. Reg. §1.170A-1(c).

(Class B) and the corporation declares a preferred stock dividend on the Class A shares and a cash dividend on the Class B shares, what result?

2d. What if the corporation issues a stock dividend to the Class B shareholders and nothing to the Class A shareholders? Is it relevant that one year later the Class A shareholders have deeded to them a portion of the farm property with a small cabin in which they plan to retire?

2e. What result if several years after the preferred stock dividend described in Example 1, the corporation decides to distribute additional common shares with respect to the preferred shares?

Deemed Distributions

3a. Miss Pitty Pat's Dress Shop started out as a small family business, but is now a large corporate chain with retail stores throughout the country. It has two classes of shares outstanding. Class A is regular voting common stock, while Class B is subject to mandatory, regular redemptions over a 10-year period. After the 10-year period, all of the Class B shareholders will have been completely redeemed. What tax consequences result from the regular, planned redemptions of the Class B shareholders?

3b. Now imagine that Miss Pitty Pat's simply had two classes of stock, one owned by the founding family and the other owned by the public, and as part of a plan to take the corporation private again and vest control in the family, the corporation was able to redeem all of the shares owned by the public through a one time tender offer. What tax consequences result?

4.   What if, in Example 2b above, Tara Corporation changed the conversion privileges of the preferred stock so that each share of preferred could now be converted into two shares of common stock?

Tainted Stock Problems

5a. Returning to Tara from Example 1, remember that Mr. and Mrs. O'Hara owned 75% of the common stock with a basis of $600,000 and their daughter, Scarlet, owned the remaining 25%, with a basis of $200,000. Tara declared and distributed in year one a stock dividend of newly authorized nonvoting preferred shares valued at $1 million. Mr. and Mrs. O'Hara receive $750,000 worth and Scarlet receives $250,000 worth of the preferred shares. Immediately after the preferred stock distribution, the total value of the common shares outstanding is also $1 million. Assume now that the current earnings and profits for year one were $1 million and that there were no accumulated earnings and profits. In year two, Tara redeems the preferred shares held by Scarlet for $1.2 million in cash. Assume further that this is the only distribution for year two and that the corporation's current earnings and profits for year two are $500,000 and that there are no accumulated earnings and profits for year two. What tax consequences to Scarlet when her preferred shares are redeemed?

5b. If instead of having her preferred shares redeemed for $1.2 million, Scarlet sells her shares to Rhett Butler for $1.2 million, what tax consequences to Scarlet?

5c. Would your answers to Examples 5a or 5b change if Tara had no earnings and profits for year one?

5d. Would your answers to Examples 5a or 5b change if the total earnings and profits for year one had been only $400,000?

5e. Would your answer to Example 5a change if the corporation simultaneously redeemed *all* of Scarlet's stock (the preferred and the common) in year two? What if the corporation simultaneously redeemed one-half of Scarlet's common stock along with the preferred?

6a. Pitty Pat's Dress Shops, Inc. and Ashley Enterprises entered into merger negotiations and arranged for a tax-free reorganization. Melonie had 200 common and 100 preferred shares in Ashley Enterprises. As part of the reorganization, she traded her Ashley shares for 200 Pitty Pat's shares (of equal value to her original common shares) and 200 preferred shares (double the value of her original Ashley preferred shares). What are the tax consequences to Melonie upon receipt of these shares?

6b. If Melonie gives her new preferred shares in Pitty Pat's to her daughter April on her birthday, any tax consequences to Melonie or April upon the initial transfer? What if April later sells the shares to an unrelated third party?

EXPLANATIONS

1. The distribution of preferred shares to the Tara shareholders is a pro rata distribution of preferred stock with respect to common stock. As such, it will be a tax-free stock dividend under §305(a). Note, however, that the shares will be considered tainted §306 stock. This will be considered further in Example 5. The basis of the preferred shares received as part of the stock distribution is determined under §307 by allocating the basis in the common shares according to a ratio based upon the fair market value of the classes of stock immediately after the distribution. Since the preferred shares had a value of $1 million immediately after the distribution and the total fair market value of all of the shares immediately after the distribution was $2 million, the ratio will be 50%. Thus, Mr. and Mrs. O'Hara will now have a basis of $300,000 in their new preferred shares (50% of $600,000) and $300,000 in the common shares, and Scarlet will have a basis of $100,000 in her new preferred shares (50% of $200,000) and $100,000 in the common shares.

2a. If Scarlet convinces the corporation to pay her distribution in cash, she will of course be taxable on a cash distribution in accordance with the §301 rules. In addition, the fact that she receives cash will make the stock distribution to her parents taxable under the §301 distribution rules as well under either §305(b)(1) or (2). Her parents' basis in the new shares will be fair market value under §301(d).

2b. If the corporation issues a dividend of convertible preferred shares, this distribution will be taxable under §305(b)(5) unless the shareholders can establish to the satisfaction of the Secretary that the distribution will not result in the increase in the proportionate interests of some shareholders and the receipt of property by others. In other words, if the shareholders can establish either that all of the shareholders will convert or that all of the shareholders will not convert, either event would leave the shareholders in the same relative positions vis-à-vis the corporation that they had held before. In either of these two cases, the distribution would not be taxable. If the shareholders cannot establish either of these two cases, they will be taxable on the stock distribution in accordance with §301 distribution rules. They will take a fair market value basis in the shares under §301(d).

2c. When there are two classes of stock, one of which receives cash and the other of which receives stock, the shareholders effectively have been able to elect (in deciding which class of stock to acquire) to receive either cash or stock. As such, the stock distribution would be taxable under §305(b)(1). In addition, under §305(b)(2), the distribution has the effect of the receipt of property by some shareholders (cash) and an increase in the proportionate interest of others. Whether you view it as under §305(b)(1) or (b)(2), the result is the same — a taxable dividend to all and a fair market value basis in the stock for those who receive stock.

2d. If the corporation issues a stock dividend to one class of shareholders and nothing to the other class, the shareholders receiving stock have increased their proportionate interest in the corporation at the expense of the other shareholders. As a policy matter, one would think that this increase in proportionate interest alone would be enough to justify taxation of the stock dividend. Under §305(b)(2), however, a companion distribution is required. In other words, one group of shareholders must receive stock and another group of shareholders must receive other property. The fact that the class A shareholders received some property from the corporation a year later is relevant. The regulations provide a 36-month window of time during which the companion distribution requirement can be met. Treas. Reg. §1.305-3(b)(4). Thus, one group of shareholders in this problem has received stock and another group has received property. The stock distribution will fall under §305(b)(2) and is taxable under the §301 distribution rules.

2e. If the corporation issues common shares with respect to its preferred shares, this will be a taxable stock dividend under §305(b)(4). All stock distributions on preferred stock are taxable.

3a. The regular and ongoing redemption of one group of shareholders causes the remaining shareholder's proportionate interests in the corporation to increase. Even though the remaining shareholders have received no formal stock distribution, this will be regarded as a deemed stock dividend under §305(c). The shareholders whose interests are increased will be taxable pursuant to the §301 distribution rules. See Treas. Reg. §1.305-7 and Treas. Reg. §1.305-3(e), ex. 8.

3b. Where an isolated redemption causes the interests of another group of shareholders to increase their proportionate interest, this isolated redemption does not give rise to a deemed distribution under §305(c). There will be no tax consequences to the family. Treas. Reg. §1.305-3(e), ex. 10.

4.   If Tara alters the conversion ratio so that every share of preferred stock can now be converted into two shares of common, this dilutes the interest of the common shareholders and increases the interests of the preferred shareholders. Although there has been no formal stock distribution, the preferred shareholders will be taxed upon a deemed stock distribution under §305(c). Treas. Reg. §1.305-7(a)(2).

5a.   Since the preferred shares issued by Tara were other than common shares received tax-free under §305(a), they are considered tainted §306 stock. There was no tax consequence upon the initial receipt of the preferred stock dividend (review answer to Example 1). When Scarlet has her shares redeemed for $1.2 million in cash, she has a distribution governed by §306(a)(2). Under §306(a)(2), her $1.2 million amount realized is treated as a §301 distribution. Since the redemption took place in year two, the §301 analysis be will applied for year two. Since the corporation had only $500,000 in earnings and profits for year two, Scarlet will have ordinary dividend income of $500,000. An additional $100,000 will be a tax-free recovery of her basis in the shares under §301(c)(2). (See answer to Example 1 for an analysis of the §307 basis allocation, arriving at a $100,000 basis for her preferred shares.) The remaining $600,000 will be capital gain under §301(c)(3).

5b.   If Scarlet sold her preferred shares to Rhett Butler for $1.2 million, the tax consequences would be slightly different. This is a disposition other than by redemption covered by §306(a)(1). We start with §306(a)(1)(A), which provides that the amount realized ($1,200,000) shall be treated as ordinary income. However, the provision continues that it shall *not* apply to the extent that the amount realized ($1,200,000) exceeds the stock's ratable shares of the amount which would have been a dividend at the time of the stock distribution if money had been distributed in lieu of stock. In this problem, the corporation had sufficient earnings and profits to cover the full stock distribution in year one. Thus, Scarlet's ratable share of the amount that would have been a dividend is $250,000, the full fair market value of the preferred shares that she received. So, of the $1,200,000 total amount realized, the ordinary income result shall *not* apply to the extent of $950,000. This leaves Scarlet with $250,000 ordinary income under §306(a)(1)(A). In the end, notice that she has ordinary income to the extent of her tainted stock's ratable share of the amount that would have been a dividend.

Next, we turn to §306(a)(1)(B). Any excess of amount realized ($1,200,000) over the *sum* of (i) the amount treated under (A) as ordinary income ($250,000) and (ii) the adjusted basis of the stock ($100,000) is treated as gain from the sale of stock. So, we subtract $350,000 from the $1,200,000 to arrive at $850,000, which will be treated as capital gain. Notice what we've done here. The $250,000 was already accounted for as ordinary income. This was her ratable shares of e&p for the year of the tainted stock distribution and thus the stock's bailout potential. Section 306(a)(1)(B) then takes her $100,000 basis into account, giving her a tax-free recovery of basis. Scarlet's total taxable income from the sale to Rhett is $1,100,000 ($250,000 ordinary income and $850,000 capital gain). Compare this result with the tax consequences if §306 were not in the Code. Under §1001, she would simply report her amount realized ($1,200,000) less basis ($100,000) for a gain of $1,100,000. The total taxable income from the transaction is the same. The only difference is the character of the income.

5c. The answers to 5a and 5b would be quite different if Tara had no earnings and profits in year one. Under such circumstances, the preferred stock distributed would not have been tainted stock at all under §306(c)(1)(C) since no part of the distribution would have been a dividend if the corporation had distributed money instead of stock. Thus, if there had been no earnings and profits in year one, a redemption of Scarlet's shares simply would be dealt with under the §302 redemption provisions. A sale to Rhett Butler would be governed by the sale or exchange rules in §1001.

5d. The answer to 5a would not change. Under §306(a)(2), Scarlet treats the redemption in year two as a §301 distribution. The relevant e&p is the e&p for year two. The answer to 5b would change, however. We would still start under §306(a)(1)(A) with ordinary income of $1.2 million *but not* to the extent that amount realized exceeds the stock's ratable shares of the amount that would have been a dividend. This amount would only have been $100,000. So, we subtract $1,100,000 from $1,200,000, leaving us with only $100,000 ordinary income under §306(a)(1)(A). Since e&p was limited in year one, the idea here is that the bailout potential was limited. Turning to §306(a)(1)(B), any excess of amount realized ($1,200,000) over the sum of (i) the amount treated as ordinary income ($100,000) plus basis in the stock (also $100,000) shall be treated as capital gain. So here, $1 million is treated as capital gain. Notice again that the total amount taxed is $1.1 million ($100,000 ordinary income and $1 million capital gain). The §306 anti-bailout provisions simply recharacterize a portion of the gain as ordinary income.

5e. Unlike the answer in 5a, Scarlet *may* be able to get sale or exchange treatment. Under §306(b)(1)(B), the §306(a) rules do not apply where the redemption of tainted §306 stock is part of a §302(b)(3) complete termination of the shareholder's interest. Although her interest appears to be completely terminated, she is still deemed to own her parents' stock under the §318 attribution rules. However, Scarlet would qualify for §302(b)(3) treatment and the redemption of the tainted shares would not be governed by §306(a) if she files the appropriate waiver of attribution under §302(c)(2).

If the corporation simultaneously redeems only one-half of Scarlet's common stock, her only hope of avoiding §306(a) ordinary income treatment would be to argue under §306(b)(4) that the redemption "was not in pursuance of a plan" having tax avoidance as one of its principal purposes. The Service will not automatically consider Scarlet eligible for the §306(b)(4) exception unless she has parted with *all* of her underlying common stock in the corporation. To make a claim under §306(b)(4), Scarlet would have to show that she parted with a *substantial* interest in the corporation and must also negate the inference of a tax avoidance plan. The §306(b)(4) exceptions do not explicitly cross-reference the §318 attribution rules. The extent to which the Service will consider attribution from Scarlet's parents as a factor in assessing her claim for §306(b) relief is unclear.

6a. When a shareholder receives shares in a tax-free reorganization, they will be considered tainted shares "to the extent that . . . the effect of the transaction was substantially the same as the receipt of a stock dividend." I.R.C. §306(c)(1)(B). Here, since Melonie received twice the value in preferred shares that she held previously, the excess preferred shares that she received will be regarded as tainted stock. There will be no immediate tax consequence other than designating the shares as tainted.

6b. When Melonie transfers the tainted shares by gift to her daughter, April, there is no immediate tax consequence to either Melonie or April. However, April will have tainted stock since the stock in her hands has a basis that is determined by reference to the basis of §306 stock under §306(c)(1)(C). Assuming that the stock appreciated in value during Melonie's term of ownership, April takes the stock under §1015 with her mother's basis in the preferred tainted shares. Thus, the basis of these shares in April's hands is determined by reference to the basis of tainted stock. If April later sells the shares, her sale will be governed not by §1001, but rather by §306(a)(1).

PART FOUR

Corporate Liquidation and Related Issues

8

General Liquidation Rules

Introduction

The closing events of a corporate lifetime involve liquidation of the corporate enterprise. The Code and regulations fail to provide a precise definition of the term liquidation, however. Some guidance is provided by regulations providing that "[a] status of liquidation exists when the corporation ceases to be a going concern and its activities are merely for the purposes of winding up its affairs, paying its debts, and distributing any remaining balance to its shareholders."[1] Thus, it is useful to think of liquidation as a *process* through which the corporation winds up its affairs and distributes remaining assets to its shareholders rather than a single event.

A corporation may liquidate in one of two ways. After paying off creditors, it may distribute the assets remaining directly to the shareholders in-kind. Alternatively, the corporation may sell off its assets for cash, first paying off creditors and then distributing the remaining cash to its shareholders. In either case, since the liquidation distribution effectively terminates the shareholder's interest in the corporation, distributions in liquidation, whether in-kind or cash, are treated as taxable events as if the shareholders sold their stock back to the corporation in return for corporate assets in-kind or for cash.[2]

From the corporation's perspective, an in-kind liquidating distribution also will be a taxable event.[3] If the government is to collect a corporate level

---

1. Treas. Reg. §1.332-2(c). The regulation also specifies that "legal dissolution of the corporation is not required." *Id.*

2. I.R.C. §331.

3. I.R.C. §336.

tax on appreciated assets or permit a loss on depreciated assets, this generally is the last opportunity to do so. If the corporation chooses instead to sell its assets and distribute cash in liquidation, it will report taxable gain or loss on the sale of assets.[4] Thus, the tax consequences of the two liquidating techniques are parallel for both shareholders and the liquidating corporation — liquidation generally is a taxable event to both the shareholders and the liquidating corporation.[5]

You might have noticed that the birth and death of the corporation do not receive parallel treatment. Under §§351 and 1032, formation of the corporation generally is a nonrecognition event to both the shareholders and the corporation. The stated rationale for such nonrecognition treatment is that formation of the corporate enterprise represents merely a change in form.[6] Dissolution of the corporation arguably represents a mere change in form as well. Yet under §§331 and 336, dissolution *is* a taxable event to both the shareholders and the corporation. The justification for this difference in treatment is that assets distributed to shareholders on liquidation represent value that has not yet been subject to shareholder level taxation. Nonrecognition treatment to shareholders would permit a "bailing out" of this value without the double tax envisioned by Subchapter C. In addition, liquidation distributions often are cash distributions. Since cash is not an asset to which a substituted basis can attach, there is no opportunity to preserve gain for later taxation. If the shareholders are to be taxed on the previously untaxed amounts, the liquidation distribution is the last moment to do so. Similarly, previously unrealized gain or loss on the corporation's assets would never be subject to the corporate level tax unless liquidation was treated as a taxable event to the dissolving corporation.

In summary, one important reason for treating complete liquidation as a taxable event is commitment to the scheme of double taxation developed in Subchapter C. If liquidation of the corporate enterprise is not treated as a taxable event, the opportunity for imposing this double tax on previously untaxed items is lost. Ordinarily, however, the regime imposed by Subchapter C is a double tax at ordinary income rates. Corporate profits are taxed as ordinary income and are included in the current or accumulated earnings and profits accounts available for taxable dividend distributions to shareholders. These dividend distributions also are taxed as ordinary income to the shareholders. Upon a §331 complete liquidation, however, the earnings and profits accounts go to earnings and profits heaven without ever being taxed at the shareholder level. To the extent that there is a double tax here, it occurs at different rates — the corporation paid tax on its profits as ordinary income,

---

4. I.R.C. §§1001, 61(a)(3).

5. Different rules will apply to the liquidation of a subsidiary. The parent-subsidiary context will be considered in Chapter 9.

6. For a discussion of §351 and its policy underpinnings, see Chapter 4.

while the shareholders presumably will report §331 liquidation gain as capital gain. If Congress is truly committed to double taxation of corporate profits, why are earnings and profits irrelevant for purposes of §331? Why not impose upon liquidation an ordinary income dividend tax on undistributed earnings and profits?

One explanation is that the shareholders can sell stock to a third party and, in that case, would have capital gain or loss treatment determined without regard to earnings and profits. Similar treatment arguably should be available upon a "sale" of the same shares back to the corporation upon liquidation. Moreover, Congress provided sale or exchange treatment for certain other purchases of stock by the corporation itself in the redemption provisions of §302.[7]

Another explanation is that under §351 and the corresponding substituted basis rule in §358, Congress provided the shareholders with a deferral of recognition on appreciation or depreciation in contributed assets. These contributed assets may have been capital assets. Thus, the previously unrecognized gain or loss should be capital gain or loss. This explanation fails to fully account for the current treatment of liquidation distributions — after all, the §331 provisions apply regardless of whether the underlying assets contributed by the shareholders were capital assets or not.

For the time being, Congress remains committed to the corporate double taxation regime, but not to double taxation at ordinary income rates. Shareholder income realized in the form of dividends will be taxed as ordinary income, while shareholder income realized in the form of gain from the sale or exchange of stock generally will be taxed as capital gain.[8] The policy generating this difference in treatment is the rate structure policy in general and not any specific policy regarding liquidations in particular.

Tax Consequences to Individual Shareholders: §331

Overview

Amounts received by the shareholders in complete liquidation are treated under §331 as "full payment in exchange for the stock."[9] The gain or loss

---

7. For a complete discussion of redemptions, see Chapter 6.

8. One exception is gain from the sale of stock in, or gain from a distribution in liquidation of, a "collapsible corporation," which is treated as ordinary income under special rules in I.R.C. §341.

9. A parent corporation that receives a liquidating distribution from a subsidiary will not be governed by §331. Instead, treatment of receipts by parent corporations in complete liquidation of a subsidiary are governed by §332. See Chapter 9.

on this exchange is computed in the same manner that the taxpayer would compute gain from any other sale or exchange.[10] Thus, the amount realized by the shareholder will be the fair market value of property plus the cash received from the corporation upon liquidation. From this, the shareholder will subtract his basis in the shares.

Since stock for most shareholders is a capital asset, the resulting gain or loss generally will be capital gain or loss.[11] The amount realized on liquidation will be allocated to blocks of shares purchased at different times. So, for example, if the shareholder purchased two-thirds of his shares several years ago and one-third of his shares within the last two months, he will allocate two-thirds of the amount realized to the first block and the remaining one-third to the more recently purchased block of shares. Long-term capital gain treatment will only be available for the first block of shares.[12] Moreover, the shareholder may have a gain on one block of shares and a loss on another.

If the shareholder receives an in-kind distribution and reports gain or loss under §331, the basis of the property received will be the fair market value of the property at the time of distribution under §334(a). Since the receipt of the property was a taxable event, the shareholder essentially is credited with a cost basis.

Dividends Distinguished

In contrast to liquidating distributions, shareholders must treat nonliquidating distributions under §301 as dividends to the extent that they are paid out of earnings and profits.[13] Three significant differences should be noticed here. First, earnings and profits are not relevant in determining the shareholder's taxable gain or loss on liquidation. Second, upon liquidation, the shareholder is entitled to a basis offset that is not available in the §301 dividend setting unless the corporation has insufficient earnings and profits to cover the distribution.[14] Finally, dividend income is treated as ordinary income, whereas liquidation gain generally will be capital gain. Given the lower tax rates on capital gains and the opportunity for a basis offset, shareholders generally prefer sale or exchange treatment to dividend treatment.[15] Complete liquidation offers shareholders the opportunity to take

---

10. Treas. Reg. §1.331-1(b). The regulation explicitly refers to §§1001 and 1002 governing sales or exchanges generally.

11.   Shares in the hands of a dealer in stock will not be capital assets with the exception of shares held for the dealer's own investment. I.R.C. §1236.

12. Treas. Reg. §1.331-1(e).

13. See Chapter 5. Section §331(b) states explicitly that the §301 distribution rules do not apply to complete liquidations.

14. The §301(c) dividend rules were considered in great detail in Chapter 5.

15. One exception will be the corporate shareholder, which will generally prefer dividend treatment to take advantage of the §243 dividends-received deduction.

earnings out of corporate solution at capital gains rather than ordinary income rates.

One transaction used by shareholders to take advantage of the capital gains rates on liquidation distributions was for the shareholders to receive appreciated corporate assets in complete liquidation and to reincorporate shortly thereafter simply by contributing the same assets to a newly formed corporation. If effective, gain on the liquidation distribution would be treated to the shareholders under §331 as capital gain, rather than dividend income. The assets received by the shareholders in the liquidation would take a fair market value basis under §334(a). The subsequent contribution to a new corporation would result in no further gain to the shareholders under §351.[16] Moreover, the new corporation would take the shareholder's basis in the asset under §362(a), effectively providing the corporation with a stepped-up basis. The shareholders' basis in the new stock under §358 would also be the same as their basis in the assets transferred, also the fair market value of the assets received in liquidation. Thus, the shareholders also effectively received a stepped-up basis in their stock holdings.

Prior to 1986, this liquidation/reincorporation technique was especially attractive since the liquidating distribution was not taxable to the distributing corporation. The corporation was able to get the stepped-up basis without having to pay any tax on the appreciation. Since 1986, however, a liquidating distribution of appreciated property is treated as a taxable event to the distributing corporation, thus somewhat diminishing the attractiveness of the liquidation/reincorporation technique.[17]

The government response to the liquidation/reincorporation technique is to argue, usually successfully, that the liquidation and subsequent reincorporation should be treated as part of an overall or integrated plan. In many cases, the transaction so integrated is recast as a tax-free reorganization, resulting in no tax upon the liquidating distribution or the incorporation and a retention of the asset's old basis to the corporation and a retention of the shareholder's old basis in stock in the corporate enterprise.[18]

Liquidation in Installments

a) Series of Liquidation Payments

Since liquidation is a process of winding up the affairs of a corporation that may take place over a period of months or even years, §346(a) provides that

---

16. Even if the contribution failed to qualify for §351 treatment, there would be no taxable gain to the shareholder, since the basis and the fair market value of the asset would now presumably be the same.

17. I.R.C. §336. This provision is discussed in greater detail in the sections that follow in this chapter.

18. The tax-free reorganization provisions are examined in detail in Chapters 11-14.

a distribution "shall be treated as in complete liquidation of a corporation if the distribution is one of a series of distributions in redemption of all of the stock of the corporation pursuant to a plan." In other words, each distribution is considered part of a complete liquidation as long as the series of distributions is part of an integrated, overall plan of complete liquidation. A few special §331 issues arise, however, in determining the proper shareholder tax treatment of a series of distributions in complete liquidation.

First, as a factual matter, it may be difficult to determine when a series of payments amounts to a series of distributions in complete liquidation. More specifically, the difficulty is in distinguishing a series of distributions in complete liquidation from a series of ordinary dividend payments. Given the advantages to the shareholders of §331 complete liquidation treatment, corporations and their individual shareholders have incentives to disguise what would have been dividend payments as part of a series of distributions in complete liquidation.[19] Whether or not the series of distributions in fact is one in complete liquidation will be decided by a facts and circumstances test. If the corporation wishes §331 complete liquidation treatment for its shareholders, the careful tax advisor, at a minimum, will insist that the corporation adopt a formal plan of complete liquidation and make liquidating distributions in accordance with that plan.

A second issue stems from the resemblance between a series of payments in complete liquidation and an installment sale of the shares. Under §453, an installment sale is defined as a "disposition of property where at least 1 payment is to be received after the close of the taxable year in which the disposition occurs."[20] Particularly since §331 and its regulations explicitly treat the complete liquidation exchange as a sale or exchange under §1001, a series of complete liquidation payments where at least one payment is received in the year after the disposition of the stock would appear to be an installment sale. It seems that the shareholders should use the installment method, reporting gain under §453(c) as each payment is received. On the other hand, if the stock was traded on an established securities market, the installment provisions would not apply at all pursuant to §453(k)(2), which requires all payments received upon the disposition of publicly traded stock to be treated as received in the year of disposition of the stock. In other words, §453(k)(2) denies the preferential installment sale reporting privilege on the sale of publicly traded stock.

Despite an apparent inconsistency with installment method reporting, the Service in Rev. Rul. 85-48 adopted the old basis recovery first approach in the complete liquidation setting.[21] Under this method, each payment that

---

19. Corporate shareholders, on the other hand, often will prefer dividend payments eligible for a dividends-received deduction.

20. I.R.C. §453(b)(1).

21. 1985-1 C.B. 126. Oddly enough, this is essentially the "open transaction" approach adopted by the Court in Burnet v. Logan, 288 U.S. 404 (1931), and since

the shareholder receives in liquidation is tax-free until basis has been recovered. This ruling is not only inconsistent with §453, but also is contrary to the modern trend toward denial of deferral advantages in the case of certainly publicly traded stock,[22] and toward generally substituting regular reporting requirements in lieu of deferral provisions.[23]

Recently finalized regulations now disallow installment reporting for shareholders who receive installment obligations in liquidation of a corporation whose stock is traded on an established securities market.[24] In addition, although the Service has not technically revoked Rev. Rul. 85-48, its preamble to the proposed version of Treas. Reg. §1.453-11, acknowledged the inconsistencies of a "basis first" recovery method with installment reporting.[25] Notice that §453(h)(1), which authorizes installment method reporting for shareholders who receive a distribution of a promissory note "acquired in respect of a sale or exchange by the corporation," does not technically apply to a mere series of distributions in liquidation. Nevertheless, the language of recently finalized Treas. Reg. §1.453-11(d) appears to extend more generally to a series of distributions in liquidation. If a series of liquidation payments from the corporation *is* to be governed by this regulation, the shareholder would be required to allocate basis for purposes of calculating gain.[26] The authority for this regulation apparently comes from I.R.C. §453(h)(2), which applies when the shareholder's liquidating distribution includes an *installment obligation acquired by the corporation in connection with a liquidating sale of assets*, as described in §453(h)(1). It is unclear whether the Treasury Department expects its new regulations to apply to situations in which the corporation did not distribute a formal installment obligation, but simply made a series of distributions in liquidation spanning more than one taxable year. Certainly the logic should extend to a series of liquidation distributions as well. On the other hand, the technical

---

rejected by the Treasury Department under most circumstances. See, e.g., Treas. Reg. §15A.453-1(c).

22. See, e.g., I.R.C. §453(k)(2).

23. See, e.g., rules requiring current inclusion in income of original issue discount on debt instruments. I.R.C. §1272.

24. Treas. Reg. §1.453-11(a)(2) (added by T.D. 8762, 63 Fed. Reg. 4168 (Jan. 28, 1998)).

25. 62 Fed. Reg. 3244, 3245 (Jan. 22, 1997) ("Generally, a shareholder that receives liquidating distributions in more than one taxable year may recover the basis in the shareholder's stock completely before recognizing any gain. This general rule is inconsistent with installment method reporting, which requires that basis be ratably recovered as payments are received.").

26. These regulations provide that "if a qualifying shareholder receives liquidating distributions to which this section applies in more than one taxable year, the shareholder must reasonably estimate the gain attributable to distributions received in each taxable year. In allocating basis to calculate the gain for a taxable year, the shareholder must reasonably estimate the anticipated aggregate distributions." Treas. Reg. §1.453-11(d).

statutory language of §453(h) does not appear to support such extension. In the meantime, the Treasury Department should rethink and clarify the status of Rev. Rul. 85-48.

b) Contingent Payments over Time

Ordinarily, the fair market value of property distributed upon complete liquidation will not be difficult to determine. In some cases, however, the shareholders receive contingent payment assets that cannot be valued. For example, rights to royalties or mineral rights provide for a series of payments over time, the overall value of which may be difficult to discern. In such cases, the liquidation will be treated as an "open transaction." Open transaction treatment permits the shareholder to treat payments first as tax-free recovery of basis and thereafter as capital gain from the sale of stock.[27] It should be noted that this will be a "rare and unusual" circumstance. Although appraisals may be difficult and complex, the Service ordinarily will require valuation and a closing of the liquidation transaction. Moreover, most of the case law on the "open transaction" doctrine was decided before the Installment Sales Revision Act of 1980. Section 453(j)(2) directed the Treasury Secretary to promulgate regulations "providing for ratable basis recovery in transactions where the gross profit or total contract price (or both) cannot be readily ascertained." In contingent payment cases where there is no maximum selling price and no fixed period over which payments will be made, the Treasury now requires that basis be recovered in equal increments over 15 years.[28] Again, however, it is not clear that the Service will apply the installment sale provisions to contingent payments received on complete liquidation. As a policy matter, these installment reporting provisions should apply.

c) Corporate Sale of Assets Followed by Distribution of Notes to Shareholders

Instead of distributing assets in-kind to the shareholders, the corporation may sell its assets in return for third party promissory notes and thereafter distribute these notes to the shareholders.[29] Ordinarily, the shareholders

---

27. The landmark case on the "open transaction" doctrine is Burnet v. Logan, 283 U.S. 404 (1931). The doctrine was explicitly applied to the corporate liquidation context in Comm'r v. Carter, 170 F.2d 911 (2d Cir. 1948).

28. Treas. Reg. §15A.453-1(c)(4).

29. The distribution of an installment note by the corporation will be considered a disposition of the note, triggering recognition of gain to the corporation on the difference between the fair market value of the obligation and the basis of the obligation. I.R.C. §453B(a)(2). In any event, under recent statutory amendments, an accrual basis corporation is no longer entitled to report income from an install-

under §331 are required to include the fair market value of any property received, including promissory notes. Section 453(h), however, provides special rules permitting the shareholders to report gain under the installment method when they receive such third party notes upon liquidation.[30] Under §453(h), shareholders may treat the receipt of *payments* under the obligation, rather than the obligation itself, as the consideration received in exchange for stock under §331. This provision effectively extends to the shareholders the same installment reporting privilege that would have been available to the corporation if it had retained the notes.[31] To qualify for this treatment under §453(h), the installment obligation must have been acquired by the corporation from a sale during the 12-month period beginning upon adoption of a plan of complete liquidation and the liquidation, in fact, must be completed during the same 12-month period. In order to prevent abuse of this transfer of the installment reporting privilege, Congress includes some restrictions on the use of §453(h). For example, the shareholders are not entitled to treat payments under the installment method where the note was received from a sale of stock in trade or other inventory of the corporation,[32] or in the case of certain sales where the obligor on the note and the shareholder are related.[33]

Distributions Involving Liabilities

If the shareholders assume a corporate liability or take property in liquidation subject to a liability, the liability will reduce the amount realized under §331. When the shareholders later make payments on debt, no further deduction will be permitted to the shareholders—the liability has already been taken into account, reducing the amount realized in the initial liquidation exchange.

In the case of a contingent or uncertain liability that was not taken into account in the initial liquidation exchange, a shareholder who later pays the

---

ment sale on the installment method. I.R.C. §453(a)(2) (added by the Ticket to Work and Work Incentives Improvement Act of 1999, Pub. L. No. 106–170, 113 Stat. 1860, §536 (1999) (repeal of installment method for accrual basis taxpayers)). Thus, most corporations will already have recognized gain on the initial installment sale itself and should not be taxed again upon distribution of the note in liquidation.

30. Upon distribution of these notes to the shareholders in liquidation, the liquidating corporation will report any previously unreported installment gain. I.R.C. §453B(a). This rule will not apply to distributions in liquidation of a subsidiary. I.R.C. §453B(d). For further discussion, see Chapter 9.

31. Recently finalized regulations under §453(h) disallow the installment reporting privilege in the case of installment obligation distributions in liquidation of a corporation whose stock is traded on an established securities market. Treas. Reg. §1.453-11(a)(2).

32. I.R.C. §453(h)(1)(B).

33. I.R.C. §453(h)(1)(C).

debt will be entitled to a deduction. Based upon the Supreme Court's decision in Arrowsmith v. Commissioner,[34] this deduction generally will be treated as a capital loss. In *Arrowsmith,* the corporation was completely liquidated and the shareholders reported capital gain on the liquidation exchange. In a subsequent year, the shareholders were held to have transferee liability for certain of the defunct corporation's debts. The shareholders reported payments on the debts as ordinary business losses. The Supreme Court, however, required the shareholders to take the losses as capital losses, noting that the shareholders "were required to pay the judgment because of liability imposed on them as transferees of liquidation distribution assets. And it is plain that their liability as transferees was not based on any ordinary business transaction of theirs apart from the liquidation proceedings."[35] The Court examined all of the liquidation transaction events occurring over several years to determine the proper character of the loss.[36]

Tax Consequences to the Liquidating Corporation: §336

Overview of the New World (1986 and Beyond)

Although there are some differences, the tax treatment to the corporation of liquidating distributions parallels the treatment of nonliquidating distributions under §311 considered earlier in Chapter 5. The general rule of §336 is that "gain or loss shall be recognized to a liquidating corporation on the distribution of property in complete liquidation as if such property were sold to the distributee at its fair market value." Just as the shareholders are viewed in §331 as selling their stock back to the corporation in return for corporate assets, the liquidating corporation is viewed as selling its assets to the shareholders. Thus, gain or loss *will* be recognized to the distributing corporation on in-kind distributions. In other words, a liquidating distribution generally is both a realization and recognition event to the distributing corporation.[37]

---

34. 344 U.S. 6 (1952).

35. *Id.* at 8.

36. The *Arrowsmith* decision is quite brief and subject to varying interpretations. Its implications extend far beyond the complete liquidation context, raising issues about the nature of our annual accounting system and the character of gains and losses from related events occurring in different tax years. These broader implications are beyond the scope of this book. For a useful discussion of the issues, see Deborah H. Schenk, Arrowsmith and Its Progeny: Tax Characterization by Reference to Past Events, 33 Rutgers L. Rev. 317 (1981).

37. Section 337 provides an exception to these rules in the case of distributions to a parent corporation in complete liquidation of a subsidiary. See Chapter 9.

Distributions Involving Liabilities

For purposes of computing gain or loss, the corporation is viewed as having sold the distributed property to the shareholders at fair market value. When the shareholders assume a liability or property is distributed subject to a liability, however, §336(b) provides that the amount realized on the sale "shall be treated as not less than the amount of such liability." This provision simply codifies in the liquidation context the notion that amount realized on the sale or exchange of property subject to liabilities must include the full liability, even if the liability exceeds fair market value.[38]

Treatment of Losses

a) General Loss Recognition

Despite parallels between the §311 nonliquidating distribution and §336 liquidating distribution rules, one key difference between the two sets of rules involves the treatment of losses. Remember that §311 does not permit recognition of losses to the distributing corporation upon nonliquidating distributions. In contrast, if the same property is distributed in a liquidating distribution, the liquidating corporation *will* be permitted to recognize loss. The policy explanation for this difference is a bit of a mystery. One possible explanation is that an operating corporation is more likely to deliberately undervalue property for purposes of recognizing loss than a liquidating corporation. Another explanation is that operating distributions offer greater opportunities for manipulation or "cherry picking." A corporation may distribute loss property so as to recognize losses while retaining gain property and not recognizing gain on unrealized appreciation. On the other hand, when the corporation is liquidating, it is selling or distributing *all* of its assets and the cherry picking problem presumably is not present. This explanation is not entirely satisfactory.

b) Loss Limitations

Although Congress established a general loss recognition rule in §336, its concern with potential abuses led to some restrictions. Section §336(d) provides two basic sets of loss limitations.[39]

---

38. Comm'r v. Tufts, 461 U.S. 300 (1983). These issues were discussed earlier in the chapter on nonliquidating distributions. Remember that §311(b)(2) provides that "[r]ules similar to the rules of section 336(b) shall apply" for purposes of §311. See discussion in Chapter 5.

39. A third loss limitation in §336(d)(3) involves liquidation of a subsidiary and will be considered later in Chapter 9.

i)   Related Person Rule: §336(d)(1)

First, the "related party" rules in §336(d)(1) disallow certain losses on distributions to related persons. Before going any further with §336(d)(1), you should first determine whether any of the shareholders receiving the in-kind loss property distribution is a "related person." For a definition of "related person," §336 cross-references to §267. An individual shareholder is related under that provision if she directly or indirectly owns more than 50% in value of the outstanding stock of the corporation — a controlling shareholder.[40] A corporate shareholder is related if it is a member of the same controlled group.[41]

Next, you must look carefully at the distribution in question. If the distribution to the related person is either non pro rata or is a distribution of "disqualified property," §336(d)(1) will disallow the recognition of *any* loss.[42] Disqualified property, for purposes of §336(d)(1), is any property received in a §351 contribution or contribution to capital during the five years prior to the liquidating distribution.[43] In other words, §336(d)(1) disallows the loss where the corporation distributes back out to related shareholders property that was recently contributed in a nontaxable §351 transaction.

The §336(d)(1) "related person" provisions respond to two perceived abuses. First, the corporation may be distributing recently contributed property with loss already built-in. Since the corporation took a substituted basis under §362 and the shareholder also received a substituted basis under §358 upon contribution of the property, there is potential in this situation for double recognition of loss. Notice that this potential results from the double tax structure of Subchapter C. Congress is prepared to permit double recognition of loss in some cases as a consequence of the double tax regime imposed upon corporations and their shareholders generally. On the other hand, Congress feared that double loss recognition would lead to abusive transactions designed simply to double up the losses in situations where the corporation and its shareholders are "related parties" willing to cooperate in such a double loss scheme with little economic substance.

---

40. I.R.C. §267(b)(2). Constructive ownership rules found in §267(c) will be used to determine stock indirectly owned.

41. I.R.C. §267(b)(3), (f). Section 267(f) adopts the controlled group definition from §1563(a) with the exception that a 50% control test is substituted for the 80% control test wherever it appears in §1563(a). Controlled groups include parent-subsidiary chains, brother-sister corporations commonly owned by five or fewer persons, and combinations of the two, as provided in §1563.

42. For purposes of this rule, "non pro rata" refers to a non pro rata distribution of the loss asset itself, as opposed to a distribution that is non pro rata in the aggregate. See Boris I. Bittker and James S. Eustice, Federal Income Taxation of Corporations and Shareholders ¶10.05[3][a] (7th ed. 2000).

43. I.R.C. §336(d)(1)(B).

The second perceived abuse was a transaction in which the liquidating corporation makes disproportionate distributions of loss property to related shareholders. The corporation might choose to make a disproportionate distribution of loss property to related shareholders to generate a double loss while leaving the unrelated shareholders without a comparable distribution. This abuse would not only hurt the federal fisc, but also deprive the unrelated shareholders of a fair share of the distribution.

ii)   Anti-Stuffing Rules: §336(d)(2)

The second basic loss limitation rule also responds to the potential for double losses on contributed property. It is sometimes referred to as the "anti-stuffing" rule because it responds to congressional concern that the shareholders deliberately would "stuff" the corporation initially with loss property in a §351 transaction. Absent the §336(d) loss limitations, "unstuffing," or liquidating, the corporation would result in both a loss to the corporation and a loss to the shareholder. This concern over double loss recognition drives both the related party rules in §336(d)(1) *and* the anti-stuffing rules in §336(d)(2). Congress was more troubled with the related party case, however, since related parties may more easily join together to cooperate for tax advantage. As you will see in the discussion below, the §336(d)(1) related party rules impose a more severe penalty than the §336(d)(2) anti-stuffing rules.

To illustrate the anti-stuffing rules, assume that several unrelated shareholders transferred property with a basis of $50,000 and a fair market value of $10,000 solely in exchange for stock in a §351 transaction. The shareholders' realized loss of $40,000 is not recognized under §351. The corporation's basis in the property under §362 will be the same as it was in the shareholders' hands — $50,000. The shareholders' collective basis in the stock under §358 will be the same as the property exchanged—also $50,000. Without the §336(d) limitations, if the corporation liquidates when the value of the property remains at $10,000, it will recognize a $40,000 loss under §336(a). The shareholders will also recognize a loss of $40,000 under §331. The §336(d)(2) rules are designed to prevent this double loss.

Two elements are necessary for the §336(d)(2) limitation to apply. First, the property in question must have been acquired by the liquidating corporation in a §351 transaction or as a contribution to capital.[44] Second, the acquisition must have been "part of a plan the principal purpose of which was to recognize loss by the liquidating corporation with respect to such

---

44. If the originally contributed property was transferred by the corporation in exchange for other property that takes a substituted basis from the contributed property — a §1031 like-kind exchange, for example — distribution of the property received in that exchange will be covered by the §336(d)(2) anti-stuffing rule. I.R.C. §336(d)(2)(B)(i).

property in connection with the liquidation."[45] Determining whether the §351 acquisition was part of a plan with such a purpose will not be easy. Here, however, Congress created a *presumption* that any §351 or capital contribution within two years before adoption of a plan of complete liquidation was part of a plan the principal purpose of which was to recognize loss. This presumption will be rebuttable under regulations to be drafted by the Secretary of the Treasury. In the meantime, the legislative history suggests some clues to transactions that may successfully rebut the presumption. The Conference Report issued in connection with the enactment of §336(d) stated that

> [t]he conferees intend that the Treasury Department will issue regulations generally providing that the presumed prohibited purpose for contributions of property two years in advance of the adoption of a plan of liquidation will be disregarded *unless* there is no clear and substantial relationship between the contributed property and the conduct of the corporation's current or future business enterprises.[46]

For the time being, then, it appears that if the contributed assets were an integral part of the trade or business of the corporation or substantially related to the business, rebuttal of the two-year presumption should be possible.

Unlike the "related person" limitation in §336(d)(1), the "anti-stuffing" rule will not necessarily disallow the *entire* loss upon a distribution of loss property. Rather than disallow loss outright, §336(d)(2) achieves its magic by adjusting the basis of the distributed property. The liquidating corporation must reduce the basis of the distributed property by the excess of the adjusted basis over the fair market value of the contributed property *immediately after its acquisition by the corporation.*[47] Returning to the example above involving contributed property with a basis of $50,000 and a fair market value of $10,000, the corporation would be required to reduce its §362 basis of $50,000 by the excess of basis over fair market value at the time of the §351 contribution—$40,000. Thus, the corporation's basis for purposes of determining gain or loss under §336(a) is now $10,000. Since the fair market value of the property is $10,000, there will be no loss to the corporation upon liquidation. Section 336(d)(2) thus operates rather elegantly to disallow *only* the loss built-in at the time of contribution. If the contributed property had declined further in value to $2000, the corporation's basis would still be $10,000. Of the overall decline in value of $48,000 the $40,000 built-in loss is disallowed and the remaining $8000 loss is permitted.

If the same distribution had been made to a related shareholder covered

---

45. I.R.C. §336(d)(2)(B)(i)(II).

46. H.R. Rep. 841, 99th Cong. 2d Sess. at II-201 (1986).

47. I.R.C. §336(d)(2)(A) (emphasis added).

by §336(d)(1), the entire $48,000 loss would have been disallowed. In other words, the (d)(1) related party rules disallow both built-in *and* subsequent losses. The rationale for the more draconian disallowance rule in §336(d)(1) probably is the control element. Congress tends to be more suspicious of abuse and manipulation in related party transactions where the parties can more easily cooperate to manipulate tax rules to their advantage.

The two loss limitation rules in §336(d)(1) and (d)(2) can overlap so that the same transaction appears to be covered by both sections. The General Explanation of the Tax Reform Act of 1986 explains that if a particular transaction could fit within either (d)(1) or (d)(2), the harsher provisions of (d)(1) will prevail.[48]

Although the related party rule is more severe than the anti-stuffing rule in most respects, one aspect of the §336(d)(2) provisions sweeps more broadly than its sister limitation in §336(d)(1). Notice that the "anti-stuffing" loss limitation in §336(d)(2) applies not only to distributions, but also to sales or exchanges of the previously contributed property covered by the rule.[49] Thus, if instead of distributing the loss property to its shareholders, the corporation *sold* the previously contributed property to a third party and distributed cash to the shareholders in liquidation, the built-in loss would still be disallowed under §336(d)(2).

The Old World of General Utilities

The rules presently found in §336 are of reasonably recent vintage. In 1986, Congress placed the final nail in the coffin of the old *General Utilities* rule. Under that old rule as applied in the liquidation context, corporations did not recognize gain or loss upon in-kind liquidating distributions.[50] Moreover, in order to achieve parity between in-kind liquidation distributions and sales of assets followed by cash distributions in liquidation, old rules permitted the corporation to avoid recognition of gain on the sale of assets in pursuance of a plan of complete liquidation. Prior to 1986, a corporate liquidation could be designed to avoid corporate level tax upon the distribution of appreciated property. The shareholders would report gain upon the receipt of corporate assets in liquidation under §331 and would receive

---

48. Staff of the Joint Comm. on Tax'n, Gen. Explanation of the Tax Reform Act of 1986, at 342 n.86 (1987).

49. Some commentators suggest that §336(d)(2) is less severe than §336(d)(1) in order to compensate for the broader scope of the former. See, e.g., Boris I. Bittker and James S. Eustice, Federal Income Taxation of Corporations and Shareholders ¶10.05[3][b] (7th ed. 2000).

50. The present §336 rules providing for general recognition of gain or loss to the corporation upon liquidation were added by the Tax Reform Act of 1986. For a discussion of the old *General Utilities* rule, see Chapter 5.

a fair market value (stepped-up) basis in the distributed property under §334(a). Subsequent sale of the assets by the shareholders to a third party resulted in no further gain to the shareholders on the appreciation that accrued up to the time of liquidation. The double corporate tax on asset appreciation was thus avoided. One danger in this technique was that the Service might successfully argue that the substance of the transaction was a taxable sale of assets by the corporation followed by a distribution of cash to the shareholders in liquidation. This danger was especially great in cases where the shareholders technically sold the property recently received in liquidation, while the corporation had done the groundwork of contracting with the buyer or negotiating the terms of the sale.[51] On the other hand, if the corporation was careful not to contract with a buyer or negotiate the details of a shareholder sale before the liquidation, the corporation might successfully avoid double taxation.[52]

Future generations of law students and tax lawyers may be able to forget the old *General Utilities* world. For the moment, however, the tax system is still suffering the growing pains resulting from the demise of the *General Utilities* rule. Many important cases, regulations, and rulings were written in the old world. To understand those precedents in proper context, one must be aware of that world. Moreover, as we will see in subsequent chapters, some small pieces of the old world remain in the Code. Taxpayers are creatively designing transactions to take advantage of the few remaining vestiges of the old world and the Treasury Department and Congress are trying to keep up with these transactions.

EXAMPLES

A Basic Liquidation

1a. ABC Corporation was initially formed with cash contributions totaling $50,000 from its five unrelated shareholders. The shareholders have made no further contributions. Assume that none of the shareholders are dealers in stock, so that their stock investment is a capital asset. After several years of operations, the corporation adopts a plan of complete liquidation and distributes assets with a basis to the corporation of $50,000 and a fair market value of $125,000. At the time of liquidation, the corporation had $125,000 in its current earnings and profits account and no accumulated earnings and

---

51. The Commissioner successfully raised this argument in the landmark case of Comm'r v. Court Holding Co., 324 U.S. 331 (1945).

52. Through careful planning, the taxpayers in United States v. Cumberland Public Service Co., 338 U.S. 451 (1950), achieved what the taxpayers in *Court Holding* had been unable to — liquidation without corporate level tax on corporate asset appreciation.

profits. What are the tax consequences to the corporation and its shareholders upon liquidation?

1b. How would your answer change if the fair market value of the assets distributed in liquidation was $30,000 instead of $125,000?

1c. What if the corporation sold these assets to a third party for $30,000 and distributed the cash to the shareholders upon liquidation?

1d. Assume that one 20% shareholder had purchased 50 of her 100 shares for $1000 in one year and the remaining 50 for $10,000 fifteen years later. What are the tax consequences to the shareholder upon receipt of assets worth $15,000 on liquidation?

Adding Liabilities

2. How would your answers to Examples 1a and 1b change if the shareholders took the property in liquidation subject to a $100,000 mortgage?

Series of Distribution Problems

3a. Confronted with competition from other children's book publishers and having lost its primary book author, Cat in the Hat Books, Inc. has decided to liquidate. It adopts a plan of liquidation pursuant to which it will make three distributions over a two-year period. Mr. Weiss, the primary shareholder, holds 100 shares. His basis in the shares is $20,000. In the year the liquidation plan is adopted, he receives distributions totalling $12,500. In the next year, he receives another $12,500. What are the tax consequences to shareholder Weiss upon receipt of these distributions in complete liquidation?

3b. How would your answer change if there was no formal plan of liquidation?

4. Lorax, Inc. is a mining company with coal operations in West Virginia. Upon liquidation, it distributes $20,000 cash and a 30-year right to receive royalties on the Berkley seam of coal to shareholder Tim. Tim's basis in his Lorax shares is $15,000. What are the tax consequences to the Lorax corporation and to Tim?

Sale of Asset/Distribution of Note Problems

5. Yak Enterprises is a corporation that runs travel tours to Nepal. On January 1 it adopted a plan of complete liquidation. Its assets had a basis of $250,000. In February of the same year it sold most of its assets to an interested buyer for $1 million, payable in 5 equal installments of $200,000 over 5 years plus 8% interest reflected in a promissory note received from the buyer. In March the corporation distributed the note to its shareholders in

complete liquidation before the corporation had received any payments on the note. What are the tax consequences to Yak and its shareholders?

Loss Limitation Problems

6a. Horton Enterprises is owned by two unrelated shareholders. Daisy holds 60% and Yertle holds 40% of the outstanding common stock. The company engages in the business of real estate development. The corporation purchased real estate in New York for a purchase price of $10 million. Given the decline in real estate values, the property was worth only $7 million when the corporation distributed the real estate to its shareholders as tenants in common in complete liquidation. What are the tax consequences to Horton?

6b. How would your answer to 6a change if the shareholders had purchased the same real estate in year one for $10 million, contributed it to the corporation in a §351 transaction in year five when the fair market value was $7 million, and got the real estate back upon complete liquidation in year twelve when the property was still worth $7 million?

6c. How would your answer to 6b change if the §351 contribution had taken place in year eleven? What if the real estate value had dropped to $6 million by the time of the liquidation? Would your answer differ if none of the shareholders were "related persons" for purposes of §336(d)(1)?

6d. How would your answer to 6c change if the corporation sold the property to a third party for $7 million and distributed cash in complete liquidation to the shareholders?

7.   Grinch Greeting Cards is a Missouri-based corporation owned by 10 unrelated shareholders, each of whom owns 10% of the outstanding common stock. One shareholder had previously operated a printing business and made her §351 contribution in year one in the form of a printing plant in St. Louis, Missouri. At the time of contribution, the plant had a basis of $800,000 and a fair market value of $500,000. The corporation used this plant to print Christmas cards. Another shareholder made his §351 contribution in the form of undeveloped real estate in New Mexico with a basis of $600,000 and a fair market value of $500,000. The corporation had no plans to use this real estate, but held it for investment purposes. A third shareholder made her §351 contribution in the form of real estate in Missouri that the corporation might use for expansion. At the time of contribution, this real estate had a basis of $500,000 and a fair market value of $150,000. The remaining shareholders contributed cash. Assume that these were the only contributions made by the shareholders. In year two, Grinch adopted a plan of complete liquidation and immediately thereafter distributed its assets to the shareholders pursuant to that plan. Each shareholder received the property that he or she originally contributed.

7a. What are the tax consequences to Grinch and its shareholders of the liquidating distributions assuming no change in the values of the various assets?

7b. What if the New Mexico real estate had dropped to $300,000 by the time of liquidation?

7c. What if the §351 contributions had been made three years earlier?

EXPLANATIONS

1a. ABC corporation will be treated under §336(a) as if it sold its assets to the shareholders for fair market value. Thus, the corporation will report a gain of $75,000 upon the liquidating distribution ($125,000 fair market value of the distributed assets less $50,000 basis). The character of the gain will be determined by the character of the assets distributed. The corporation's stock will now be canceled and the corporation is effectively dissolved. Its earnings and profits account, along with its other tax characteristics, disappear along with the corporation.

The shareholders collectively have received assets worth $125,000. Under §331, the liquidation distribution will be treated as full payment in exchange for stock. Each shareholder will report his or her share of this liquidation distribution and will subtract his or her basis in the stock. Depending on the particular shareholder's basis, this could be a gain or a loss. The gain or loss from this exchange will be considered capital gain or loss. The earnings and profits account of the corporation is irrelevant in determining shareholder gain or loss under §331. Under §334(a), the shareholders' basis in assets received in the taxable §331 exchange will be the fair market value of the assets upon liquidation.

1b. Again, under §336(a), ABC corporation will be treated as if it sold the assets to the shareholders for fair market value. In this case, since the fair market value of the assets is only $30,000 and the corporation's basis is still $50,000, the corporation will report a *loss* of $20,000. Unlike the §311 operating distribution rules, §336(a) *does* permit recognition of loss on liquidating distributions. The character of the loss will again depend upon the character of the asset distributed. Since none of the shareholders are related persons and none of the distributed property was acquired by the corporation from the shareholders in a §351 contribution, the §336(d) loss limitations are not applicable.

Although the amount of the overall liquidating distribution is much less than before, the technique for computing gain remains the same. As in the answer to 1a, the shareholders will treat their share of the $30,000 value distribution as an amount realized from the sale of stock. From this, they will subtract their basis in the stock. The resulting gain or loss will be capital gain or loss and the shareholders will take a fair market value basis in the assets received.

1c. If the corporation sold its assets to a third party for $30,000, it would also realize and recognize a $20,000 loss on the sale. The character of the gain or loss would depend upon the character of the assets sold. The subsequent distribution of the cash would be taxable to the shareholders under §331. Notice that the tax result is the same whether the corporation distributes the assets directly (as in 1b) or sells the assets and then distributes the cash.

1d. Since the shareholder has two blocks of shares, the amount realized on the liquidating distribution must be allocated to each block. She will allocate one-half of the distribution—$7500—to each block. She will report a $6500 long-term capital gain from the first block of shares and a $2500 long-term capital loss from the second block of shares. See Treas. Reg. §1.331-1(e). Note that if she had aggregated the shares, she would have had an overall gain of $4000. The allocation approach more accurately traces gain and losses for specific blocks of shares. The shareholder will have a fair market value basis in the assets received upon liquidation under §334(a).

2a. If the shareholders upon liquidation of the ABC Corporation took the $125,000 value property subject to a $100,000 mortgage, the transaction still will be treated under §336(a) to ABC as if the property had been sold at fair market value to the shareholders. Thus, the corporation will still have a $75,000 gain. The answer to question 1a does not change. In effect, the amount realized by ABC includes the $100,000 mortgage amount as well as the value in excess of the mortgage.

From the shareholders' perspective, however, addition of the liability does change the answer. The amount realized by the shareholders upon liquidation is net of the liability. Thus, the liability must be subtracted from the amount realized on the exchange. Collectively, the net amount received by the shareholders is only $25,000 ($125,000 value less the $100,000 mortgage). From his or her share of the $25,000 net distribution, each shareholder will subtract his or her stock basis to determine gain or loss as above. The shareholders' basis under §334(a) will be the fair market value of $125,000. You might think of this $125,000 as including the mortgage amount in the same way the taxpayers generally are entitled to include borrowing in basis.

2b. If the fair market value of the assets upon liquidation is only $30,000, but the property is still subject to a $100,000 mortgage, the tax consequences to ABC will change. Although ABC is still treated under §336(a) as if it sold the property to the shareholders, under §336(b), fair market value shall be treated as not less than the liability. Thus, the amount realized on the exchange is $100,000 — the amount of the liability. From this, the corporation will subtract its basis of $50,000, resulting in a $50,000 gain. Note that without the liability, this distribution resulted in a $20,000 loss to ABC. (See answer to 1b.) When shareholders take property subject to a corporate liability, the corporation benefits to the extent that it is relieved of the liability. Where the liability exceeds the fair market value, the amount realized must include the liability.

From the shareholders' perspective, the amount realized on liquidation should be net of liabilities. In this example, the fair market value of the liquidating distribution was $30,000 and the shareholders took the property subject to a $100,000 mortgage. There is actually a net negative value to this distribution from the shareholders' perspective. There is little or no case law or regulatory authority guiding our way here. Perhaps the reason for the sparsity of guidance is that corporations rarely make such distributions to their shareholders. One would expect shareholders to be unhappy to acquire liabilities that exceed the value of the assets. More often than not, the corporation probably avoids these problems by "dumping" the assets. Limited liability will protect the shareholders from the clutches of creditors. The presence of §336(b) suggests that Congress anticipated such transactions to occur from time to time. However, §336(b) only answers the corporate level questions. Section 331 itself says nothing about liabilities taken on by the shareholders at liquidation. One possible answer in our problem is to permit the shareholders to recognize an immediate capital loss in the amount of the mortgage plus their basis in the shares less the $30,000 fair market value of the property received. Their basis in the property would then be limited to the fair market value of $30,000 under §334(a).

If §301(b) is used by analogy, however, the amount of the distribution should not be reduced below zero. Thus, the shareholders would not report gain or loss on the exchange. As for the basis in the new property, §334(a) technically would not apply since no gain or loss was recognized on the exchange. What then should be the shareholders' basis in the property? One possibility is to give the shareholders a $100,000 basis on the assumption that they will pay the mortgage. This way, the shareholders at least will be entitled to a loss upon disposition of the property. A final alternative would be to permit the shareholder to take a capital loss when they pay the liability.

3a. The distribution will be treated as an exchange of shareholder Weiss's stock under §331. Although the shareholder is not receiving a formal promissory note, this series of distribution effectively is an installment sale. Under the §453 installment method, the shareholder would have a gross profit ratio of $5000/$25,000 or 20%. Thus, 20% of each $12,500 distribution ($2500) would have been taxable each year. Under the authority of Rev. Rul. 85-48, however, the shareholder may be permitted to recover his basis before reporting any gain. Since his receipts of $12,500 in the first year are less than his $20,000 basis, he would have no gain for year one. The $12,500 would be applied against his stock basis, however, leaving the shareholder with a $7500 basis in the shares. When he receives the $12,500 distribution in year two, he would report a $5000 capital gain. This deferral of gain is inconsistent with the installment method, which technically should apply here. Since this was not an installment note from a corporate sale of assets in liquidation, §453(h)(1) is not technically applicable. Nevertheless, the language of recently finalized Treas. Reg. §1.453-11(d) appears to extend more generally to a series of distributions in liquidation. If so, the shareholder would be required to allocate basis for purposes of calculating gain. The status of Rev. Rev. 85-48 is unclear.

3b. It is not necessary that there be a formal plan of liquidation in order for the provisions of §§331 and 336 to apply. Clear indication of an intent to liquidate should suffice. On the other hand, when liquidation involves a series of distributions, there is a risk that early distributions will be viewed as dividends. Whether a particular distribution is a dividend or part of a series of liquidating distributions is a question of fact to be determined under all of the facts and circumstances. To be safe, the corporation ordinarily will want to adopt a plan of liquidation. If the Service regarded the first payment in this series as a dividend and only the final payment as a liquidating distribution, the shareholder would report ordinary income on the first $12,500 distribution (assuming sufficient earnings and profits to cover the distribution). The second distribution would be treated as a §331 exchange, resulting in a $7500 capital loss ($20,000 basis less $12,500 distribution).

4.   Tim's receipt of the cash and royalty rights should be treated as an amount realized in a §331 liquidation exchange. The Service will expect Tim to make every effort to value the royalty rights, to include that amount in amount realized, and to "close" the transaction. Under a "closed transaction" approach, Tim would report capital gain on the difference between the assets received (cash plus royalty rights) less his basis in the shares. The royalty rights would receive a basis equal to the fair market value assigned to them for purposes of §331. As Tim received future royalty payments, he should be permitted to amortize this basis. Gain from the royalties will otherwise be treated as ordinary income.

   If the royalty rights truly cannot be valued, Tim may be entitled to treat this as an "open liquidation transaction." Since the cash of $20,000 exceeds his $15,000 basis by $5000, he should report $5000 in long-term capital gain upon liquidation. Thereafter, each royalty payment will be considered continuing payment in exchange for stock and, therefore, treated as capital gain. This open transaction treatment is inconsistent with installment sale provisions that now require ratable basis recovery over a 15-year period. The Service does not appear to be applying the installment sale provisions to distributions in complete liquidation, however.

5.   Until recently, corporations were entitled to installment reporting upon receipt of a promissory note in connection with a sale of assets to a third party. Subsequent distribution of the installment note in complete liquidation would be considered a disposition of the note for purposes of §453B, effectively triggering recognition of gain deferred through use of the install-

ment method. Under new §453(a)(2), most accrual basis taxpayers are no longer entitled to use the installment method. Since most corporations use the accrual method, an installment sale of assets now would trigger an immediate recognition of gain. Assuming that Yak uses the accrual method, it will report an immediate gain of $750,000 ($1 million amount realized less $250,000). Since the sale was taxed, Yak's basis in the note would then equal its $1 million face value. I.R.C. §453B(b). Thus, there should be no further taxable gain upon distribution of the note in complete liquidation. Even if Yak did not use the accrual method, the tax consequences would be the same, as a practical matter, since all of the events in Example 5 took place in the same taxable year. The only technical difference would be that the gain in the latter case would be triggered by the disposition of the note, as opposed to the underlying sale itself.

Ordinarily, the shareholders would be required to report the full fair market value of the note as part of the amount realized on the §331 exchange. Under §453(h), however, the shareholders will be entitled to treat each payment as payment in the §331 exchange. Thus, each $200,000 payment will be treated under the installment method. The shareholders will use their stock basis to determine a gross profit ratio and report a portion of each payment as gain accordingly. The shareholders will report this as capital gain or loss. Any interest received by the shareholders will be treated as ordinary income.

6a. Horton Enterprises should be permitted to recognize a $3 million loss upon distribution of the real estate in complete liquidation ($7 million value of real estate less $10 million basis). Daisy is a "related person" for purposes of §336(d)(1), since she owns 60% of the stock. I.R.C. §267(b)(2). However, the §336(d)(1) loss limitation rules apply only to non pro rata distributions or distributions of disqualified property. Since the real estate in this problem was not contributed, but rather purchased by the corporation, it is not disqualified property. Assuming that the distribution was a pro rata distribution, the (d)(1) loss limitation will not apply.

6b. The corporation should still be entitled to recognize a $3 million loss. Again, the loss limitations apply only to non pro rata or disqualified property distributions. Since this property was acquired by the corporation in a §351 contribution more than five years before the date of distribution, it is not disqualified property. Assuming that the distribution was pro rata, the corporation will be entitled to recognize the entire loss under §336(a).

6c. If the §351 contribution had taken place in year eleven and the liquidation took place in year twelve, the contribution was within five years of the liquidation and the property now is disqualified property. The corporation will not be entitled to recognize the $3 million loss. Note here that technically the provisions of §336(d)(2) also apply to this transaction. Where both provisions apply, the (d)(1) provisions will prevail. If the property had dropped in value to $6 million, the now $4 million loss would be disallowed as well. Section 336(d)(1) disallows *any* loss upon non pro rata or disqualified property distributions to related persons.

If none of the shareholders were "related persons," the §336(d)(1) loss limitations rules would not apply. Instead, the distribution would be governed by §336(d)(2). If the property was contributed in a §351 transaction in year 11 and distributed in year 12, it would be presumed to be property described in §336(d)(2)(B). The property would have a $10 million basis in the corporation's hands under §362. Unless the corporation could rebut the presumption that the acquisition of the property was part of a "plan a principal purpose of which was to recognize loss by the liquidating corporation," the $3 million loss would be disallowed. The loss limitation is achieved under §336(d)(2), however, by reducing the corporation's basis to the extent of the "built-in" loss at the time of contribution. Thus, for purposes of determining loss on the liquidating distribution, the corporation's basis is deemed to be $7 million. If the property had declined in value to $6 million, the corporation would be entitled to recognize a $1 million loss.

6d. If the corporation sold the property to a third party for $7 million, the loss would not be prevented by §336(d)(1). However, it may be covered by §336(d)(2). Note that unlike (d)(1), the §336(d)(2) loss limitation provision applies to any "sale, exchange or distribution" of property. Since the §351 contribution and the liquidation were within the two-year period specified in §336(d)(2)(B)(ii), the transaction will be presumed to be part of a plan the principal purpose of which was recognition of loss by the corporation. The corporation may be able to rebut this presumption by arguing that the assets were part of its business operations.

7a. Upon distribution of the printing plant, Grinch realizes a $300,000 loss (fair market value of $500,000 less $800,000 basis.)[53] However, the loss is technically subject to the §336(d)(2) limitations since the property was acquired in a §351 transaction and the acquisition is treated as part of "a plan a principal purpose of which was to recognize a loss by the liquidating corporation with respect to [the contributed] property." I.R.C. §336(d)(2)(B)(i)(I) and (II). By congressional fiat, distributions of the contributed property in complete liquidation are presumed to be part of such a plan. I.R.C. §336(d)(2)(B)(ii). Notice, however, that the statutory two-year presumed prohibited purpose clause contains the proviso that the two-year presumption shall apply "except as provided in regulations." While no regulations have been finalized, the legislative history contains unusually explicit descriptions of the types of exceptions Congress expects to see in the regulations. Where the property at issue is integrally related to the corporation's business operations, Congress suggested that the presumed prohibited pur-

---

53. Grinch received a substituted basis of $800,000 from the shareholder upon the §351 contribution pursuant to §362.

pose should be disregarded. If we disregard the clause here, we are left to examine the facts and circumstances to determine whether the acquisition of the plant was part of a plan a principal purpose of which was for Grinch to recognize a loss. Assuming that it was not part of such a plan, Grinch should be excepted from the loss limitation rule, thereby being able to recognize a $300,000 loss. Since the plant was presumably eligible for depreciation, it will not be considered a capital asset and the loss should be considered an ordinary loss. On the other hand, if the acquisition was part of a plan for Grinch to take a loss, then the §336(d)(2) limitation will apply. In that case, §336(d)(2)(A) would reduce the adjusted basis of the property ($800,000) by the excess of its adjusted basis immediately after acquisition by the corporation (also $800,000 pursuant to §362) over the fair market value at that time ($500,000). In other words, the property's basis would be reduced by $300,000. This $300,000 reflects the built-in loss at the time of contribution. Since the distributed property would now have a basis and a fair market value of $500,000, Grinch would not be entitled to recognize any loss upon the distribution in complete liquidation.

In either case, upon return of the plant in complete liquidation, the shareholder would report a loss of $300,000 under §331. Since she is exchanging stock, the character of the loss will be capital. The amount realized is the fair market value of the plant — $500,000. Her basis in her stock was the same as her basis in the contributed property under §358 — $800,000. Notice that the shareholder is permitted loss here even if the corporation's loss is limited. After all, the shareholder did experience loss in the value of the property. The idea behind §336(d)(2) is to prevent *double* recognition of the "built-in" loss.

The same statutory analysis applies to the New Mexico real estate distribution. This real estate had a built-in loss of $100,000 (shareholder's basis of $600,000 less fair market value of $500,000). The §336(d)(2) limitations will apply to Grinch's distribution of the property in complete liquidation. Since the real estate is unrelated to the business and at a great physical distance from business operations in Missouri, forthcoming regulations are unlikely to provide any exception to the presumed prohibited purpose. Legislative history accompanying the §336(d)(2) provisions indicates congressional belief that a contribution of *unrelated* loss property followed by a distribution in complete liquidation within two years is more likely to be part of an abusive plan to double loss recognition than a similar transaction with integrally related business property. Under §336(d)(2)(A), Grinch's basis in the property ($600,000) will be reduced by the $100,000 built-in loss. Since the basis of $500,000 now is the same as the fair market value of $500,000, Grinch will not be entitled to recognize any loss upon distribution of the New Mexico real estate in complete liquidation. The shareholder receiving the property previously contributed, however, still would be entitled to his loss under §331.

The Missouri real estate presents a closer case. Again, the literal terms of §336(d)(2) are applicable and the presumed prohibited purpose clause appears to apply. Unlike the New Mexico real estate, however, this property *is* related to the business, but not *as* related as the plant itself. Without regulations regarding exceptions to the two-year presumptive rule, this one is harder to call. If excepted under forthcoming regulations, Grinch would be entitled to recognize a $350,000 loss. If not excepted, Grinch would reduce its basis by the $350,000 built-in loss. This would leave Grinch with a basis and fair market value of $150,000 and no recognized loss.

7b. If the New Mexico real estate's value had dropped to $300,000 by the time of the liquidation, the §336(d)(2) limitation still would reduce Grinch's basis in the property ($600,000), but *only* by the excess of adjusted basis immediately after its acquisition ($600,000) over its fair market value *at that time* ($500,000); in other words, basis is reduced *only* by the $100,000 built-in loss. Since Grinch's basis is now $500,000, a distribution when the fair market value of the property is $300,000 results in a $200,000 capital loss. Notice that the overall loss in value of the real estate was $300,000 — a $100,000 built-in loss followed by a $200,000 decline in value while Grinch held the property. Despite the §336(d)(2) loss limitation rule, Grinch is entitled to recognize the latter part of this loss. If the shareholders had been "related parties" under §336(d)(1), the entire $300,000 loss would be disallowed.

7c. If the contributions had been made three years earlier, the two-year presumed prohibited purpose rule would not apply. This does not mean that the corporation is automatically free of §336(d)(2) restrictions. If the facts and circumstances indicate that acquisition of the property was "part of a plan a principal purpose of which was to recognize loss by the liquidating corporation," the loss restrictions still will apply.

9

Liquidation of Subsidiaries

Introduction

Unlike general liquidations, which typically are taxable events to both the liquidating corporation and to the shareholders who receive distributions in liquidation,[1] liquidations of subsidiary corporations generally are not taxable to either the liquidating subsidiary or to the shareholder parent corporation. One rationale for the different treatment of subsidiary liquidations is that Congress wished to encourage the simplification of complex corporate structures by permitting the elimination of subsidiary corporations without immediate tax consequence. A parent and its subsidiaries are part of the same "corporate family" and are eligible to file consolidated tax returns.[2] Since a distribution in liquidation does not cause assets to leave this larger corporate solution, Congress decided not to impose an immediate tax upon liquidation of a subsidiary, but instead to defer taxation of gain or loss. Put another way, the liquidation of a subsidiary effectively is a merger of the subsidiary into the parent corporation. The nonrecognition treatment provided these transactions is comparable to the nonrecognition otherwise provided to tax-free reorganizations.[3]

The different tax treatment afforded to subsidiary liquidations can also be understood by thinking back to the basic double tax imposed by Sub-

---

1. See Chapter 8.
2. I.R.C. §1501.
3. For a detailed discussion of tax-free reorganizations, see Chapters 11-14.

chapter C. The corporate tax regime is designed to impose a double tax on corporate earnings, but not multiple layers of taxation beyond the two tiers. Without special rules, the liquidation of a subsidiary would result in a triple, or even greater, multiple tax. The liquidating subsidiary would be taxed upon making the distribution under §336. The parent would be taxed upon receiving the distribution under §331. Finally, the parent corporation's shareholders would report gain or loss under §331 when the parent corporation eventually liquidates and distributes the assets received from the subsidiary or they will be taxed under §301 if the parent later distributes the assets in an operating distribution.[4]

The special subsidiary liquidation rules considered in this chapter avoid this potential triple or greater multiple tax result. The rules are designed to collect *one* shareholder level tax and *one* corporate level tax in connection with the subsidiary liquidation. Since a shareholder level tax will be reported eventually by the parent corporation's shareholders, Congress chose to eliminate the shareholder level tax that would otherwise be imposed on the parent corporation under §331 at the time of liquidation of a subsidiary. As described in more detail below, §332 operates as an exception to the general recognition rule in §331, providing nonrecognition of the shareholder level tax to the parent upon receipt of a liquidating distribution from a subsidiary. In addition, §337 operates as an exception to the general recognition rule in §336, providing nonrecognition of the corporate level tax to the liquidating subsidiary. This corporate level gain or loss in the subsidiary's assets will be preserved, however, through use of substituted basis rules. The distributed assets will retain in the parent corporation's hands the same basis they had while in the subsidiary's hands. Let's turn now to some of the details.

Tax Consequences to the Parent Corporation: §332

Overview

Section 332(a) provides that "[n]o gain or loss shall be recognized on the receipt by a corporation of property distributed in complete liquidation of another corporation." Despite the broad language used here, this nonrecognition rule will not apply to just *any* corporation, but is limited by §332(b)(1) to corporations owning stock that meets the requirements of §1504(a)(2)—a direct reference to the provision that defines affiliated corporations eligible to file consolidated returns. To meet the requirements of §1504(a)(2), a

---

4. If the parent shareholders sell their stock in the meantime, the sales price for the stock presumably will reflect the value of these assets as well.

corporation must own at least 80% of the total voting power *and* at least 80% of the total value of another corporation's stock.[5] Although the Code itself does not use the term "parent," a corporation meeting this two-part 80% ownership test is commonly referred to as a parent corporation. The corporation in which the parent holds this 80% interest is commonly referred to as a subsidiary.

In order to be eligible for §332(a) nonrecognition, the distribution must be in complete cancellation or redemption of all of the liquidating corporation's stock. In addition, the liquidating corporation must either transfer all of its property within the taxable year *or* make a series of distributions in accordance with a plan of liquidation under which all of the property is distributed within three years.[6] To be eligible for §332 nonrecognition, the parent corporation must meet the two-part 80% control test on the date of adoption of a plan of liquidation and at all times until receipt of the property in liquidation.[7]

If the subsidiary is indebted to the parent at the time of liquidation, payments in satisfaction of indebtedness will be taxable to the parent despite the nonrecognition rules of §332. Such payments are made to the parent in its capacity as a creditor rather than as a shareholder. As an example, the regulations provide that "if the parent corporation purchased its subsidiaries' bonds at a discount and upon liquidation of the subsidiary the parent corporation receives payment for the face amount of such bonds, gain shall be recognized to the parent corporation."[8]

Assuming that the corporate parent meets the control test and that the distributions in liquidation otherwise meet the requirements of §332, the parent corporation will recognize no gain or loss upon receipt of property in liquidation from the subsidiary. Property for purposes of §332 includes in-kind property as well as cash. Under §334(b) the basis of distributed property now in the parent corporation's hands "shall be the same as it would be in the hands of the transferor."[9] To use a simple example, assume that the subsidiary distributes property in liquidation with a basis of $25,000 and a fair market value of $100,000. The liquidating subsidiary is entitled to

---

5. Affiliated corporations may or may not elect to file consolidated returns. Regardless of whether or not consolidated returns are filed, the corporation is eligible for §332 nonrecognition as long as it meets the requirements of §1504(a)(2).

6. I.R.C. §332(b)(2), (3).

7. Although §332 is a mandatory provision, the 80% control test effectively makes it elective. If the parent corporation disposes of enough stock to cause its ownership to fall below the required 80%, it will fail the control test and the liquidation will not be covered by §332. See, e.g., Comm'r v. Day & Zimmerman, Inc., 151 F.2d 517 (3d Cir. 1945); Granite Trust Co. v. United States, 238 F.2d 670 (1st Cir. 1956).

8. Treas. Reg. §1.332-7.

9. This will be referred to as transferred basis. See I.R.C. §7701(a)(43).

nonrecognition of its $75,000 realized gain under §337.[10] In addition, the parent corporation will receive this $100,00 property without any immediate gain under §332(a). The parent corporation's basis in the property under §334(b) will be the same $25,000 basis that the subsidiary had. Thus, if the parent later were to sell the property for $100,000, it would report a $75,000 gain. The §334(b) basis rules effectively transfer responsibility for reporting the liquidating subsidiary's gain or loss on the liquidation distribution from the subsidiary to the parent.

There is one exception to the transferred basis rule of §334(b)(1). If gain or loss is recognized by the subsidiary on the distribution of property in liquidation, the basis of the distributed property in the parent's hands will be fair market value. There are a few situations in which the subsidiary may be required to recognize gain or loss despite the general nonrecognition rule for the subsidiary provided in §337.[11] The fair market value basis in such cases is sensible. Since the subsidiary has already reported gain or loss, there is no need to preserve gain or loss through a transferred basis.

Observations About "Outside" and "Inside" Basis

A parent corporation owns stock in its subsidiary for which it has a basis. This stock represents the parent's indirect ownership interest in the underlying subsidiary's assets. The subsidiary's assets themselves also have a basis. A parent corporation's basis in its subsidiary's *stock* sometimes is called its "outside" basis. The basis of the subsidiary's *assets* themselves sometimes is called the "inside" basis. When a parent corporation sells or disposes of its subsidiary's stock, gain or loss in its investment in the subsidiary stock is measured by subtracting the outside stock basis from the amount realized on the stock disposition. When the subsidiary sells or disposes of its assets, gain or loss is measured by subtracting the inside asset basis from the amount realized on asset disposition.

Notice the effect of the subsidiary liquidation rules. After liquidation, the subsidiary stock disappears and the parent is left owning the old subsidiary's assets directly. The parent corporation's "outside" basis in the subsidiary stock simply disappears and the unrealized gain or loss from the parent corporation's stock in the subsidiary will never be taxed. The parent takes a transferred basis in the old subsidiary's assets. By thus retaining the "inside" basis, Congress has chosen to preserve the unrealized gain or loss in the subsidiary's assets rather than the gain or loss in the stock. In many cases, the parent's "outside" basis in the stock and the subsidiary's "inside" basis

---

10. Detailed discussion of §337 appears later in this chapter.

11. For example, if the parent corporation is a tax-exempt organization, the subsidiary may not be eligible for §337 nonrecognition. The §337 provisions are considered in greater detail later in this chapter.

in its assets will be the same. In such cases, the preservation of the subsidiary's asset basis rather than the parent's stock basis makes little difference. In either event, the basis figure is the same. Since Congress was concerned with collecting only one corporate level tax, it will be sufficient to collect that tax upon sale or distribution of the assets received in liquidation. On occasion, however, the parent's "outside" basis in its subsidiary stock will not be equal to the subsidiary's basis in its assets.[12] This situation can create troubling distortions. For example, in the above hypothetical, assume that the parent corporation had a basis of $120,000 in the subsidiary stock. Since the fair market value of the assets received on liquidation is only $100,000, the parent corporation has suffered a $20,000 loss. However, the loss will not be recognized and the parent will take the assets with a $25,000 basis. In this case, the parent arguably is disallowed a loss that it should be entitled to recognize at some point. On the other hand, if the parent corporation's basis in its stock had been only $10,000, there is a potential $90,000 gain in the stock. By giving the parent a $25,000 basis in the assets, only a $75,000 gain is preserved. Here the government comes up short.

Tax Consequences to Minority Shareholders: §331

If the parent corporation owns 100% of the subsidiary's stock, there obviously will be no other shareholders to worry about. Since §332 equally applies to corporations with as little as 80% of the subsidiary's stock, however, one needs to consider minority shareholders holding the remainder of the subsidiary's stock. These minority shareholders may be individuals or corporations. Since §332 does not apply to minority shareholders, such shareholders are left to the recognition rules of §331 for general liquidations.[13] Minority shareholders generally will recognize gain or loss under §331 and take a fair market value basis in the assets received under §334(a).[14]

---

12. This situation can occur, for example, if the parent purchased the subsidiary's stock from a third party or acquired the subsidiary stock in a tax-free reorganization or other nonrecognition transaction.

13. See discussion in Chapter 8.

14. Minority shareholders may be entitled to nonrecognition if the overall transaction fits within one of the reorganization provisions of §368. Reorganizations are covered in Chapters 11-14.

Tax Consequences to the Liquidating Subsidiary: §337

Distributions to the Parent Corporation

The in-kind distribution of assets to the parent corporation in liquidation of a subsidiary generally is not a taxable event to the liquidating subsidiary. More specifically, §337(a) provides that "[n]o gain or loss shall be recognized to the liquidating corporation on the distribution to the 80-percent distributee of any property in a complete liquidation to which §332 applies." As noted earlier, the rationale behind this nonrecognition is that the *parent* corporation eventually will recognize gain or loss on its distribution or sale of the assets, since it takes a transferred basis from the subsidiary. Congress means to collect only one corporate level tax and, thus, provides nonrecognition to the liquidating subsidiary.[15] Responsibility for reporting gain or loss from appreciation or depreciation in the subsidiary's assets is transferred upon liquidation to the parent.

When a subsidiary is indebted to the parent corporation at the time of liquidation, it can be difficult to distinguish distributions in satisfaction of indebtedness from other distributions in payment for stock upon liquidation. As a consequence, §337(b)(1) provides that for §332 liquidations in which the subsidiary is indebted to the parent, any transfer of property to the parent in satisfaction of indebtedness shall be treated as a distribution in the §332 liquidation. In other words, the subsidiary will not recognize gain or loss. Pursuant to §334(b), the parent must take a transferred basis in these, as well as any other, assets.

It should be noted here that if the subsidiary sells off its assets for cash, it will be subject to taxation on the cash sale, even if the cash is shortly thereafter distributed to the parent corporation in complete liquidation.[16] This may initially appear inconsistent with the observation in the previous chapter on general liquidations that in-kind distributions and asset sales in liquidation followed by cash distributions should achieve similar tax results. The problem in the parent-subsidiary liquidation context is that §337 provides for nonrecognition, in part, because the subsidiary gain or loss is

---

15. As further confirmation of this rationale behind §337, notice the exception provided in §337(b)(2) for distributions to tax-exempt distributees. If the parent corporation is tax-exempt, the subsidiary will not receive nonrecognition treatment unless the property distributed will be used by the parent in an unrelated business and, thus, subject to tax to the parent.

16. This is in sharp contrast to the pre-1986 provisions. Old §337 (before repeal of *General Utilities*) permitted certain sales of assets in connection with liquidation of the corporation to be tax-free. This provision was repealed along with *General Utilities*.

preserved by giving the parent a transferred basis in the subsidiary assets. If the parent corporation gets only cash, there is no asset to which the Code can attach a transferred basis. If corporate level gain is to be taxed, the tax must be collected at the time of the cash sale by the subsidiary. One way around this problem is for the subsidiary to sell its assets for an installment note instead of cash. The installment note is an asset that can take a transferred basis. In addition, although §453B(a) generally requires recognition of gain or loss upon disposition of an installment note, the liquidating subsidiary here is protected from recognition by §453B(d), which provides an exception for distributions to which §337 applies.

Distributions to Minority Shareholders

Distributions to minority shareholders are not covered by §337, but instead are covered by the general liquidation rules in §336.[17] Recall that under §336, gain or loss shall be recognized *except to the extent provided in §337*. Since §337 limits its nonrecognition rule to distributions "to the 80% distributee," or parent, the liquidating subsidiary *will* recognize *gain* on any in-kind assets distributed to minority shareholders. However, no loss will be permitted to the liquidating subsidiary on such in-kind distributions. Losses are prohibited by §336(d)(3), which provides that "[i]n the case of any liquidation to which §332 applies, no loss shall be recognized to the liquidating corporation on *any* distribution in such liquidation." Notice the double standard. Gains on distributions to minority shareholders must be recognized, but losses cannot be recognized.

To understand the loss limitation on distributions to minority shareholders, it will be helpful to take a step back for a moment to look at the big picture. Remember the general rule now codified in §336 that in-kind distributions in complete liquidation are taxable to the liquidating corporation. As discussed in Chapter 8, this provision overruled or repealed the old *General Utilities* nonrecognition rule. Subsidiaries still can get nonrecognition treatment on distributions in complete liquidation under §337. Thus, §337 stands as one of the remaining exceptions to the repeal of *General Utilities*. Under the circumstances, Congress and the Treasury Department were, and continue to be, sensitive to potential abuses. The concern reflected in §336(d)(3) is that a liquidating subsidiary might deliberately arrange its affairs so as to distribute *gain* assets to the parent, thus taking advantage of the nonrecognition provided in §337, and at the same time distribute *loss* assets to the minority shareholder, thus taking advantage of the general recognition rules of §336.

---

17. Treas. Reg. §1.332-5.

Additional Anti-Abuse Provisions

Given that §337 remains as an exception to repeal of the old *General Utilities* nonrecognition rules, taxpayers have been rather creative in designing gain transactions to fit within §337, thereby avoiding taxation of gains and designing loss transactions to fall outside of §337, thereby recognizing loss. Many such transactions have taken advantage of special provisions in the consolidated return regulations. As taxpayers have come up with such transactions, Congress and the Treasury Department have promulgated statutory provisions and regulations to combat them.

For example, one consolidated return regulation allows several affiliated corporations to combine their shares for purposes of meeting the 80% control tests necessary to be eligible for §§332 and 337 nonrecognition.[18] This consolidated return provision led creative taxpayers to design a transaction known as the "mirror transaction." Assume that a purchasing corporation is interested in acquiring some, but not all, assets of a target corporation. Since the assets are highly appreciated, a direct sale of the wanted assets would result in a substantial taxable gain to the target. In a "mirror transaction," the wanted and unwanted assets would be isolated in different members of the target's consolidated group. For example, the target might hold the wanted assets in subsidiary T1 (asset basis $500, fair market value $2000) and the unwanted assets in subsidiary T2 (asset basis $500, fair market value $2000). The purchasing corporation would then create two subsidiaries, P1 and P2, to "mirror" the target's two subsidiaries. P would create these subsidiaries by contributing cash to P1 equal to the value of T1's assets ($2000) and cash to P2 equal to the value of T2's assets ($2000). P's basis in the stock of each of its new subsidiaries, P1 and P2, is $2000.[19] P now causes P1 to purchase one-half of T's stock for $2000 and P2 to purchase the other half of T's stock, also for $2000.

T now liquidates, distributing the T1 assets in complete liquidation to P1 and the T2 assets in complete liquidation to P2. By themselves, P1 and P2 only own 50% of T's stock. Thus, the liquidation would not be treated as a liquidation of a subsidiary under §§332 and 337. Under the consolidated return regulations, however, P1 and P2, as members of a consolidated group, will aggregate their shares in determining whether or not §332 applies.[20] Together, P1 and P2 own all of T's stock. As a result, the liquidation will be tax-free to P1 and P2 under §332 and tax-free to T under §337. No gain is recognized on the appreciation of T's assets. Since T1 has the wanted assets, P1 presumably will retain the T1 stock or cause T1 to liquidate so that P1

---

18. Treas. Reg. §1.1502-34.
19. I.R.C. §358(a).
20. Treas. Reg. §1.1502-34.

can hold the assets directly. In the meantime, P can sell off its P2 stock, thus getting rid of the unwanted assets. Since the fair market value of the P2 stock is equal to $2000 and P's basis in its P2 stock is also $2000, no gain will result from this sale of stock. When the dust settles, P and T have accomplished the transfer of appreciated assets without tax recognition of any gain.

To eliminate this particular end-run around repeal of the *General Utilities* rule, §337(c) now provides that the term "80% distributee" includes *only* the corporation meeting the stock ownership requirements of §332(b) and that the determination of an 80% distributee "shall be made without regard to any consolidated return regulation." As a result of §337(c), the liquidation of T in the above example would not receive nonrecognition treatment under §§332 and 337. Pursuant to §336, T now *will* report gain upon distribution of the T1 and T2 stock in complete liquidation.

In addition to this specific provision in §337(c), Congress in §337(d) gave the Treasury Secretary specific authority to prescribe regulations to ensure that the purposes of the Tax Reform Act of 1986 — most important, the repeal of the old *General Utilities* rule as applied to liquidations — not be circumvented. Shortly after Congress eliminated advantages of the "mirror transaction" with §337(c), creative taxpayers came up with yet a different transaction using another consolidated return regulation. The so-called "son of mirror" transaction took advantage of investment adjustment basis rules contained in the consolidated return regulations.[21] The Treasury Department has used its §337(d) authority to promulgate regulations disallowing losses in "son of mirror" as well as other potentially abusive transactions.[22]

As an illustration of the "son of mirror" transaction, assume the target corporation, S, owns only one asset (basis $500, fair market value $2000). Purchasing corporation, P, purchases all S's stock for $2000. S is now a subsidiary of P and the new P/T group elects to file consolidated returns. If S sells its asset to a third-party buyer for $2000, the sale will generate $1500 in earnings that must be reported as taxable gain to S. In the meantime, the investment adjustment rules included in the consolidated return regulations require P to increase its basis in the S stock by the $1500 gain that was taxed to S.[23] Consequently, P's basis in its S stock is now $3500. If P now sells the S stock, P will have a $1500 *loss*. The transaction has created an artificial loss. In the end, S's $1500 gain is offset by P's $1500 loss. No gain or loss was reported on the disposition of appreciated property.

Pursuant to its §337(d) authority to promulgate regulations, the Treasury Department responded to the "son of mirror" transaction with a rule generally disallowing loss recognition by a member of a consolidated group

---

21. Treas. Reg. §1.1502-32.
22. Treas. Reg. §1.337(d).
23. Treas. Reg. §1.1502-32.

upon disposition of a subsidiary's stock.[24] As a result, P's $1500 loss in the above illustration is not permitted under the new "loss disallowance" regulations. The §337(d) "loss disallowance" regulations have a long and tortured history. In its effort to prohibit artificial losses created through creative use of the consolidated return regulations, the Treasury Department swept rather broadly, sometimes disallowing even economic losses that arguably should have been permitted. Fine tuning of the "loss disallowance" regulations has resulted in the addition of exceptions designed to permit genuine economic losses to be recognized.[25]

Given their complexity, the consolidated return regulations in general and the loss disallowance regulations in particular are beyond the scope of most introductory corporate tax courses. On the other hand, dealing with the consolidated return regulations and their implications increasingly has become part of the corporate tax lawyer's work. The references to the consolidated return regulations and related issues in this chapter are not meant to be comprehensive, but rather simply to introduce the student of corporate taxation to some of the issues presented.

EXAMPLES

A Basic Subsidiary Liquidation

1a. Queen of the Night, Inc. (QNI), a mattress and bed discounter, has only one class of voting common stock outstanding. Papageno, Inc. (PI) owns 80% of the QNI stock with a basis of $200,000. The remaining 20% is owned by Papagena. Papagena has a basis of $5000 in her shares. The QNI shareholders adopt a plan of liquidation on January 1 and QNI distributes all of its assets in liquidation on December 31. The QNI assets distributed to PI on liquidation were as follows:

	basis	fair market value
real estate	$150,000	$750,000
building	$30,000	$25,000
mattresses	$20,000	$25,000

In addition, QNI distributes the following assets to Papagena:

	basis	fair market value
cash	—	$50,000
portfolio stock	$100,000	$150,000

---

24. Treas. Reg. §1.1502-20.

25. Despite this fine tuning, some problems remain. Even the Treasury Department concedes that it has been unable to find a perfect solution that would also be administratively feasible.

What are the tax consequences of the liquidation to PI? To Papagena? To QNI?

1b. If the basis in the portfolio stock that was distributed to Papagena had been $200,000 instead of $150,000, how would the tax consequences to QNI and Papagena be different?

1c. What if PI's basis in its QNI stock had been $150,000 instead of $200,000?

Effective Electivity of §332

2a. Figaro, Inc. is a wholly owned subsidiary of Bridal Shops, Inc. Figaro's primary asset is real estate with a basis of $800,000. The real estate has declined in value to $300,000. After Figaro adopts a plan of liquidation, but before distribution of the property in liquidation, Bridal Shops sells 21% of its Figaro stock to unrelated Buyer Bob. Figaro shortly thereafter liquidates, distributing the property to Bridal Shops and cash to Buyer Bob in complete liquidation. Assume that the liquidation distribution was pro rata, meaning that Bridal shops receives 79% of the value and Buyer Bob receives 21% of the value upon liquidation. What are the tax consequences to Figaro, Bridal Shops, and Buyer Bob?

2b. Assume that instead of Bridal Shops selling shares to Buyer Bob, Figaro decides to sell its real estate to Buyer Bob for $300,000 cash. Shortly thereafter, Figaro distributes the cash to Bridal Shops in complete liquidation. What tax consequences to Figaro? To Buyer Bob? To Bridal Shops?

Installment Notes

3. Tutti Corporation is a wholly owned subsidiary engaged in the business of selling and renting musical instruments. It owns a piece of real estate with a basis of $250,000 and a fair market value of $1 million. In addition, it maintains an inventory of musical instruments, also with a basis of $250,000 and valued at $1 million. Tutti sold the real estate to Buyer Bob for a five-year installment note calling for payments of $200,000 at the end of each year (plus interest). Before receiving any payments on the note, Tutti liquidates, distributing the note and the instruments to its parent in complete liquidation. What tax consequences to Tutti and its parent?

Debt to Parent Corporation

4. JFC is an American company that imports paper fans from Japan. JFC owns all of the outstanding stock of Butterfly Corporation. Several years ago, when Butterfly was short of cash, it borrowed $500,000 from JFC. Upon liquidation, Butterfly is distributing assets with an overall basis of $200,000 and a fair market value of $600,000. Of this amount, $500,000 is to cover the principal amount of the loan from JFC, $20,000 is to cover interest on

the loan, and the remainder is payment for the stock in liquidation. What are the tax consequences to JFC and Butterfly?

EXPLANATIONS

1a. The parent corporation, PI, received assets with an overall fair market value of $800,000 upon liquidation. Absent §332, PI would report a gain of $600,000 under §331 (amount realized of $800,000 less $200,000 stock basis). Section 332 operates as an exception to §331. Since PI owns stock meeting the two-part control test of §1504(a)(2) and since QNI is completely liquidating and transferring all of its property within the taxable year, PI will be eligible for nonrecognition under §332(a). Thus, PI will report no gain or loss upon receipt of the property from QNI.

The basis of the assets now in PI's hands will be the same as it was in QNI's hands under §334(b)(1). Thus, the real estate's basis will continue to be $150,000, the building's basis will be $30,000 and the basis in the mattresses will be $20,000. PI's $200,000 basis in the QNI stock will disappear.

QNI, the subsidiary, has distributed three assets to its parent, PI, in a complete liquidation to which §332 applies. There is a potential gain of $600,000 in the real estate, a potential loss of $5000 in the building, and a potential gain of $5000 in the mattresses. Under §337(a), none of this gain or loss will be recognized to QNI.

The minority shareholder, Papagena, has received cash and property, the total value of which is $200,000. From this, she will subtract her $5000 basis, resulting in a $195,000 taxable gain under §331. This will be capital gain from the sale of her stock. Her basis in the portfolio stock received will be its fair market value of $150,000 under §334(a). Since §332 only applies to distributions to the 80% distributee, QNI will be taxed on a gain of $50,000 upon distribution of its portfolio stock to Papagena under §336.

1b. Even if the basis of QNI's portfolio stock had been $200,000, Papagena's gain under §331 would still be $195,000. She still received cash and property valued at $200,000 and can subtract her $5000 basis. Her basis in the stock received will still be the fair market value of $150,000. The change in basis does affect the tax consequences to QNI, however. QNI now has a loss of $50,000 on the distribution of the portfolio stock. QNI will not be entitled to recognize this loss under §336(d)(3).

1c. This variation presents a discrepancy between the parent's (PI's) outside basis in its subsidiary's (QNI's) stock and the subsidiary's inside basis in the assets. In the first version of the hypothetical, PI's outside basis in the stock was $200,000 and QNI's overall inside basis in the assets attributable to PI was also $200,000. Thus, the potential gain of $600,000 with regard to PI's stock was the same as the overall gain reflected in QNI's assets. With a combination of §§332, 334(b), and 337, Congress has chosen to preserve only one level of corporate tax. When, as in the first variation of this hypothetical, the parent's gain in the stock and the subsidiary's gain in the assets is the same, it doesn't much matter which of the gains is preserved (except, perhaps, for character issues). In this variation, however, PI's unrealized gain in the stock was $650,000. The potential gain reflected in QNI's assets, however, still is only $600,000. Nevertheless, the tax consequences of this variation are exactly the same as in problem 1a. PI still will receive the assets on liquidation without recognizing any gain under §332. QNI still will get nonrecognition treatment on the distributions of assets under §337. Moreover, PI's basis in the assets will be the same as it was in QNI's hands. Thus, only $600,000 of potential future gain is preserved through use of a transferred basis. PI's basis in the QNI stock disappears and along with it the opportunity for the government to collect the extra $50,000 unrealized parent gain in the subsidiary stock.

2a. The issue here is whether the transfer of 21% of the stock successfully takes the transaction outside the scope of §332. Under §332, the distributee corporation must meet the 80% control tests at the time of adoption of a plan of liquidation and at all times until the property is distributed in complete liquidation. In effect, §332 is an elective provision. Put differently, the rigid rules of §332 also can operate as a trap for the unwary. Since the parent, Bridal Shops, in this case does not meet the 80% control test throughout the relevant period of time, the liquidation is not covered by §332. Upon receipt of the real estate, Bridal Shops will report gain or loss under §331 (amount realized of $300,000 less Bridal Shop's basis in its remaining 79% of the Figaro stock). The real estate now in Bridal Shop's hands will take a fair market value basis of $300,000.

Figaro has realized a $500,000 loss in real estate that it would like to recognize upon the liquidating distribution. Since §337 nonrecognition only applies to complete liquidations under §332 and Bridal Shops failed the §332 80% distributee test, Figaro should be entitled to recognize the loss.[26]

Buyer Bob recently purchased stock for cash and took a cost basis in his shares. He will subtract this cost basis from the cash amount received on liquidation and report the resulting gain or loss under §331.

2b. If Figaro sells the loss property to Buyer Bob, it will be entitled to recognize the $500,000 loss. By its terms, §337 nonrecognition applies only on distributions in liquidation. On the other hand, the Treasury Department has §337(d) authority to prescribe regulations as necessary or appropriate to carry out the purposes of the Tax Reform Act of 1986 — the critical purpose in this context is repeal of the *General Utilities* doctrine. Under this authority, the Treasury Department may extend the scope of regulations beyond simply dealing with actual liquidation distributions. The regulations to date do not

---

26. Assume for purposes of this question that the real estate was purchased by Figaro rather than contributed in a §351 transaction and, thus, does not raise loss limitation issues under §336(d)(1) or (d)(2). Notice also that the loss limitation rule of §336(d)(3) only applies to §332 liquidations and will not apply here.

prohibit the type of loss taken by Figaro in this problem. Although the sale of the loss property may well have been designed to avoid nonrecognition, the loss in this case is economic, as opposed to artificial. In addition, the culprit that leads to recognition of loss here is the Code's different treatment of sales as opposed to contributions and distributions. Similar problems arise in other areas as well. Shareholders with loss property will sell loss property and contribute cash to the corporation under §351 in order to be able to recognize the loss. Corporations will sell property rather than distribute it under §311 in order to recognize the loss. Congress and the Treasury Department have not yet decided to tackle these types of loss problems.

Bridal Shops will receive $300,000 cash without recognition of any gain under §332. Its basis in the Figaro stock disappears. Buyer Bob simply owns the real estate with a $300,000 cost basis under §1012.

3.   Assuming that Tutti is an accrual basis taxpayer, it will report immediate gain upon sale of the real estate for an installment note under new §453(a)(2), which disallows installment reporting for most accrual basis taxpayers. After reporting this gain, Tutti's basis in the installment obligation should equal its $1 million face value. Pursuant to §337, Tutti will not recognize any gain upon distributing the note and instruments in complete liquidation. The parent will take a transferred basis in the note and instruments from Tutti under §334. Since Tutti has already reported gain from the installment sale and the note has a $1 million basis, there should be no further taxable gain to the parent as payments are received. If Tutti were not an accrual basis taxpayer, it would be entitled to use the §453 installment method upon sale of the real estate, thus allowing it to report income as payments are received. Ordinarily, a corporation must recognize gain upon disposition of an installment note to the extent of the difference between the fair market value of the note and the basis of the obligation under §453B(a). In the case of liquidation distributions, however, §453B(d) provides an exception for distributions to which §337(a) applies. Since Tutti is distributing the notes in a §332/§337 liquidation, it will report no gain upon distribution of the installment note. Nor will it report any gain upon the distribution of the instruments under the terms of §337 itself. The parent will take a transferred basis in the note and the instruments from Tutti under §334(b). Any installment gain that would have been reported by Tutti effectively will now be reported by the parent as payments are received. The special relief provided in §453(h) for shareholders who receive installment notes in a liquidation distribution is unnecessary here since receipt of the note is eligible for nonrecognition in any event. Notice that the §453(h) relief is limited to liquidations to which §331 applies. (See Chapter 8 for further discussion of this provision.)

4.   The repayment of principal on the loan will not be taxable to JFC under the tax principles applicable to borrowing generally. The payment of interest

will be taxable. Repayments of the principal and interest are considered to be paid to the parent in its capacity as a creditor, not as a shareholder. Such payments are therefore outside the scope of §332. Any excess payments above the principal and interest on the loan will be tax-free under §332.

Butterfly has repaid the full amount of the loan and there is no cancellation of indebtedness income to worry about. In any event, §337(b)(1) provides that distributions in satisfaction of indebtedness will be considered part of the §337 distribution. Therefore, the subsidiary Butterfly will report no gain or loss.

PART FIVE

Corporate Acquisitions, Divisions, and Other Corporate Restructuring

SUBPART A

Taxable Acquisitions

10

Taxable Mergers and Acquisitions

Introduction

Corporate Acquisitions in General

Corporations sometimes purchase stock in other corporations to hold for investment or purchase assets from other corporations to hold for investment or to use for business operations. The tax lawyer or tax professional generally would not refer to these day-to-day corporate purchases of stock or assets as corporate acquisitions. In common tax parlance, "corporate acquisition" generally refers to an acquisition of *control* by one corporation over another.[1] One corporation may acquire control over another through two different transaction types. First, a simple *asset* acquisition from the target corporation itself offers the purchaser direct control over the selling corporation's assets. Second, a *stock* acquisition from the target corporation's shareholders provides the purchaser with indirect control over the selling corporation's assets through its ownership of the target corporation's stock.

In a stock purchase, the purchasing corporation (P) acquires a controlling interest in the target corporation's (T) stock from the target's shareholders, thus becoming a parent to its newly acquired subsidiary (T). The parent may continue to operate T as a separate entity or may cause T to distribute its assets in a complete liquidation. In the case of a stock purchase followed immediately by a liquidation of T, the purchasing corporation acquires

---

1. For purposes of this chapter, "control" refers to the 80% control requirement under I.R.C. §1504 ("Affiliated Group Defined").

control over T's assets upon the liquidation distribution. If the purchase of the target's stock and the subsequent liquidation of the target are viewed as an integrated transaction under the step transaction doctrine, the stock purchase transaction looks much like a direct asset acquisition. When the dust settles, T has disappeared, P has direct control over the T assets, and the T shareholders hold the consideration paid by P.

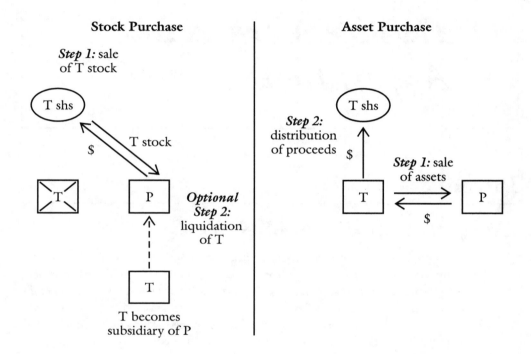

Over the years, the courts and Congress have developed rules to determine when certain stock acquisitions should be treated as asset acquisitions for tax purposes. The current provisions in §338 provide an election to qualified purchasing corporations to treat certain stock acquisitions as asset acquisitions. In the end, the acquiring corporation can choose among three basic techniques for a taxable acquisition of control: 1) an asset acquisition; 2) a stock acquisition without a §338 election; and 3) a stock acquisition treated as an asset acquisition pursuant to a §338 election.

For any corporate acquisition transaction to proceed substantially beyond the initial discussion stages, the parties to the transaction must make several basic decisions regarding the structure of the transaction. This chapter begins with a brief discussion on the choice of acquisition structure and corporate acquisitions tax planning. Following this introduction, the chapter considers the particular structure and tax consequences of taxable asset acquisitions, taxable stock acquisitions *with* a §338 election, and taxable stock acquisitions *without* a §338 election.

Choice of Acquisition Structure

a) Taxable Acquisition vs. Tax-Free Reorganization

The parties to a corporate acquisition must first decide whether the transaction is to proceed as a taxable acquisition or a tax-free reorganization.[2] The label "taxable acquisition" is used simply to indicate that the selling corporation is taxable upon the sale of its assets or that the selling shareholders are taxable upon the sale of their stock. Any particular transaction will be classified as a tax-free reorganization only if it fits within one of the precise meanings of the term "reorganization" as defined in §368(a).[3] By definition, a corporate acquisition transaction that fails to fit within such a statutory nonrecognition provision is a taxable acquisition.

Under the statutory nonrecognition provisions applicable to corporate organizations and reorganizations, classification of an acquisitive transaction as tax-free depends largely upon the consideration used by the purchasing corporation in the exchange. Generally speaking, where the consideration paid by the purchasing corporation provides the target corporation or its shareholders with a substantial continuing proprietary interest in the reorganized corporate entity, the transaction is likely to meet one of the "reorganization" definitions.

Two relatively easy cases appear at the extremes. Imagine first a purchasing corporation acquiring target assets or stock entirely for cash and/or notes. Surely, such consideration provides no continuing proprietary interest in the corporate enterprise to the target corporation or its shareholders. The simple corporate acquisition of assets or stock for cash and/or notes is the classic "taxable acquisition"—the target corporation is taxable upon the sale of its assets or the target shareholders are taxable upon the sale of their stock under §§61(a)(3) and 1001. At the other extreme, imagine that the purchasing corporation (P) acquires all of the target's assets in exchange for P *voting stock* or acquires all of the target's stock from the T shareholders in exchange

---

2. This chapter will focus upon *taxable* acquisitions of control. The brief material presented here on tax-free reorganizations is designed simply to illustrate the key distinctions between taxable and tax-free acquisitions. Most of the discussion of tax-free reorganizations appears in subsequent chapters. Chapter 11 provides an introduction to basic tax-free reorganization principles, and Chapter 12 includes a detailed analysis of acquisitive tax-free reorganizations in particular.

3. In addition, a transfer of property to a controlled corporation in return for stock will be a tax-free transaction under §351. See discussion in Chapter 4.

for P voting stock. In either case, the P voting stock provides the target corporation or its shareholders with a continuing proprietary interest in the reorganized corporation. Both transactions will fit one of the "reorganization" definitions of §368(a).[4]

The first, and most important, difference in tax consequence between taxable acquisitions and tax-free acquisitive reorganizations is that the seller typically recognizes gain or loss in a taxable acquisition, but is eligible for nonrecognition treatment in the case of a tax-free reorganization.[5] In a tax-free asset acquisition, the target corporation is entitled to nonrecognition upon the exchange of its assets for eligible consideration, usually purchasing corporation stock.[6] In a tax-free stock acquisition, the target shareholders will not recognize gain or loss upon the transfer of T shares for eligible consideration from the purchasing corporation, also usually P stock.[7]

The second key distinction in tax consequence between taxable acquisitions and tax-free reorganizations involves an important set of corollary basis rules. The purchasing corporation in a taxable asset acquisition is entitled to a §1012 cost basis in assets purchased from the target. Consequently, the term often used to describe a taxable asset acquisition is a "cost basis acquisition." In contrast, the purchasing corporation in a tax-free asset acquisition is not entitled to a "cost basis," but instead takes the target corporation's assets with the same basis that the target corporation had.[8] The effect of this basis rule is a deferral of gain or loss recognition with respect to the target's assets until the purchasing corporation later sells, exchanges or otherwise disposes of the target's assets in a taxable transaction. The term often used to describe this type of tax-free acquisitive reorganization is a "transferred" or carryover basis acquisition.[9]

---

4. The asset acquisition will fit within §368(a)(1)(C) (Type C reorganization). The stock acquisition will fit within §368(a)(1)(B) (Type B reorganization). For a full discussion of both types of tax-free acquisitions, see Chapter 12.

5. This is not to say that the target or its shareholders will *never* recognize gain or loss in a tax-free acquisitive reorganization. Shareholders will be taxable immediately, for example, on boot received as part of the transaction as well as payments received for accrued interest. These particular instances are considered in detail in Chapter 12.

6. I.R.C. §361. The tax-free asset acquisition may take the form of a direct transfer of assets by the target to the purchaser or, instead, a state-law merger of the target into the purchaser.

7. I.R.C. §354.

8. I.R.C. §362.

9. The Treasury Department itself, along with many practitioners, continues to use the term "carryover basis." The technically correct term provided in the Code is "transferred basis." Property with a transferred basis is defined as property the basis of which is "determined in whole or in part by reference to the basis in the hands of the donor, grantor, or other transferor." I.R.C. §7701(a)(43). For purposes of this chapter, the terms "transferred basis" and "carryover basis" are used interchangeably.

In a taxable stock acquisition, the purchasing corporation is entitled to a §1012 cost basis only in the T shares purchased.[10] In contrast, the purchaser in a tax-free stock reorganization is not entitled to a cost basis in the acquired stock, but instead takes the stock with the same basis that it had in the shareholder's hands. In addition, the target corporation's assets will retain the same basis that they had immediately before the acquisition, again deferring recognition of gain or loss with respect to target's assets.

Given the dramatic difference in tax consequence, proper classification of a corporate acquisition transaction as either a taxable acquisition or a tax-free acquisitive reorganization is critically important to the parties to the transaction and to the government. Unless otherwise indicated, however, the remainder of this chapter is devoted to taxable acquisitions. The definitional boundaries distinguishing taxable acquisitions from tax-free reorganizations are considered in subsequent chapters on tax-free reorganizations.

b) Stock vs. Assets

The second basic decision required of the parties to a corporate acquisition is whether the purchaser will acquire stock or assets. Both tax and nontax factors will influence this decision. With regard to nontax factors, the purchaser's choice between stock or assets may be limited because the corporation is unwilling to negotiate a transfer of assets, the shareholders are unwilling to negotiate a transfer of stock, or some other outside restrictions prevent the sale or transfer of the assets or the stock. In addition, the choice of a stock or asset acquisition may be heavily influenced by the purchasing corporation's desire to minimize its exposure to any outstanding target corporation liabilities to creditors. Finally, an asset acquisition makes it easier for the purchasing corporation to isolate and avoid acquiring any "unwanted assets."

Both buyer and seller also will have several tax factors to consider in deciding between a taxable stock or asset sale. The taxable sale of assets results in an immediate taxable gain to the selling corporation and a cost basis in the assets to the purchasing corporation. The purchasing corporation's desire to acquire assets will depend upon the extent to which the assets are depreciable or otherwise would benefit from a cost basis. The selling corporation's willingness to sell assets will depend on the extent of the gain or loss reflected in the assets and the possibility of using any offsetting losses to reduce gains. The selling corporation also must consider the tax consequences to its shareholders. After a simple sale of all of its assets for cash, the target company presumably will distribute the cash to its shareholders in a liquidation distribution taxable to the shareholders. Thus, an asset acquisition often involves

---

10. The purchasing corporation will not also get a "cost basis" in T's assets unless it makes a proper election pursuant to §338. These issues are considered in subsequent sections of this chapter.

a rather immediate double tax—the corporation recognizes gain or loss on the sale of its assets for cash and the shareholders recognize gain or loss on receipt of the cash proceeds upon the liquidation of their stock holdings. In contrast, a stock sale by the shareholders generally results in the immediate recognition of only the shareholder level tax — the shareholders recognize gain or loss upon the sale of their stock while the target corporation's assets remain with the target and retain their historic basis. These tax considerations will be considered further throughout this chapter.

c) To Elect or Not to Elect Under §338

Finally, in the case of a qualifying stock acquisition, the parties must decide whether or not the purchasing corporation will make a §338 election. Such an election essentially will provide the purchaser with a "cost basis" in the target's assets, but will also require the target to recognize gain or loss as if it had sold all of its assets. These significant tax consequences to both buyer and seller are considered in detail in subsequent sections of the chapter.

Taxable Asset Acquisitions

The Transaction

In a typical taxable asset acquisition, the selling or target corporation (T) transfers all or substantially all of its assets to the purchasing corporation (P) or a P subsidiary (S)[11] in exchange for cash and/or notes.[12] As part of the taxable acquisition, the purchasing corporation often will assume some or all of the selling corporation's liabilities. Generally, the target corporation will liquidate shortly after the exchange, distributing cash, notes and other consideration received to the T shareholders in exchange for their T shares. Sometimes, however, T may be kept alive for various reasons. For example, elderly shareholders may wish to keep the corporation alive in order to assure a stepped-up basis in the stock upon their death.[13]

---

11. A taxable asset acquisition need not necessarily involve a purchasing *corporation.* Instead, the purchaser might be a partnership, sole proprietor, or other entity. For purposes of this chapter, however, discussion of taxable asset transfers assumes a corporate purchaser.

12. P also may use other consideration, including P stock. Even where some P stock is used, the transaction will continue to be classified as a taxable acquisition unless the type and amount of P stock otherwise cause the transaction to fit within one of the tax-free reorganization definitions or the §351 contribution to a controlled corporation provision.

13. I.R.C. §1014. The shareholders also might wish to keep the corporation alive as a personal holding company, regulated investment company, or Subchapter S corporation.

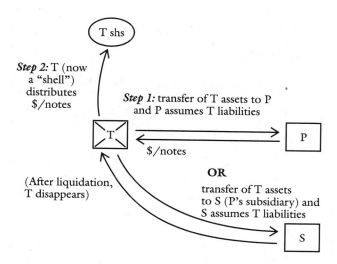

Another form of taxable asset acquisition is a state-law merger of the target into P or a P subsidiary[14] for cash, notes, or other consideration that would not qualify for tax-free reorganization treatment, sometimes referred to as a "cash merger." In this type of transaction, the consideration is transferred directly by P (or S) to the T shareholders and there is no need for T to formally liquidate. For tax purposes, however, the Service treats this transaction as a taxable asset transfer by T followed by T's complete liquidation.[15] For purposes of this chapter, reference to a "taxable asset acquisition" includes either the direct sale of assets or the taxable "cash merger."

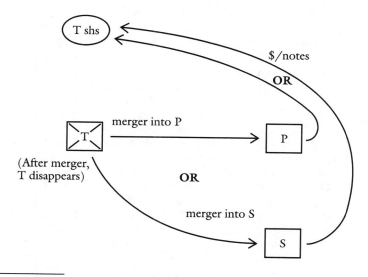

14. Merger of the target into a P subsidiary is called a "forward triangular merger." Discussion of such forward mergers in the tax-free reorganization context appears in Chapter 12.

15. See Rev. Rul. 69-6, 1969-1 C.B. 104; Treas. Reg. §1.368-1(b).

Tax Consequences to the Selling Corporation and Its Shareholders

a) Tax Consequences to the Target Corporation

In a taxable asset acquisition, the selling target corporation (T) will recognize a taxable gain or loss immediately upon the sale of assets under §§61(a)(3) and 1001.[16] The amount and character of gain or loss on the sale of assets must be determined on an individual, asset-by-asset basis.[17] In the event of a sale of a going business for a lump-sum price, it will be necessary to allocate a portion of the purchase price to each asset sold. Since some of the assets sold will result in capital gain or loss while others will result in ordinary income,[18] the particular method used for allocating the purchase price will be important to the seller. Congress now requires the "residual allocation method" for purposes of measuring the seller's gain or loss on the assets sold.[19]

Consistent with the rules for sales generally, T must include in its amount realized from the sale any liabilities assumed by the purchaser, and the amount of liability to which any property transferred was subject.[20] In

---

16. To the extent that T receives notes from the purchaser in exchange for its assets, T may be entitled to report gain under the installment method provided in §453. However, installment reporting is no longer available to most accrual basis taxpayers pursuant to new §453(a)(2). In addition, use of the installment method is not permitted with respect to the sale of certain assets such as inventory, I.R.C. §453(b)(2)(B). Moreover, if the aggregate face amount of receivables arising from asset sales for the year exceeds $5 million, Congress imposes an interest charge on the tax liability deferred through use of the installment method. See I.R.C. §453A.

17. The landmark case requiring this fragmented, individual asset approach to a sale of business assets is Williams v. McGowan, 152 F.2d 570 (2d Cir. 1945).

18. In addition to ordinary income reported on ordinary income assets sold, the selling corporation may be required to report ordinary income on recapture items such as certain previously deducted depreciation, I.R.C. §§1239, 1245, 1250, and previously deducted tax benefit items. See I.R.C. §111. In addition, T will be required to report ordinary income with respect to any imputed interest on P notes bearing less than a market rate of interest, §483, or original issue discount (OID) with regard to P notes received in the exchange, §§1271-1275. A detailed discussion of recapture items, imputed interest, and OID rules is beyond the scope of this book.

19. The same method also will be used by the purchaser for purposes of allocating basis to the assets purchased. See discussion in subsequent section of this chapter entitled "Tax Consequences to the Purchasing Corporation." New §1060 regulations explicitly cross-reference to and adopt the allocation rules in Treas. Reg. §1.338-6T and 7T. Treas. Reg. §1.1060-1T(c)(2). A discussion of the §§338 and 1060 residual allocation provisions follows in the section of this chapter entitled "Allocation of the Purchase Price."

20. The amount realized by T on any particular asset transferred subject to a mortgage will include the mortgage amount. Lest there be any doubt, the regulations

addition, if the purchasing corporation assumes liabilities for accrued, but as yet unpaid operating expenses of a cash basis target corporation, the liabilities assumed should be included in T's amount realized from the sale. Once T has included the assumption of operating expense liabilities as proceeds from the sale, T should be entitled to deduct these assumed operating expenses.[21]

After a sale of all or substantially all of the target's assets, the target corporation is simply a "shell" holding the consideration received from the purchasing corporation along with any unsold assets. In most cases, a liquidation of the target will quickly follow the sale. Unless the target is making a liquidating distribution to a corporate parent,[22] the subsequent liquidation distribution will be a taxable event to the distributing target. In a simple sale of substantially all of the target's assets for cash, T will already have paid gain or loss upon the initial sale of assets. As a practical matter, there should be little remaining gain or loss to be reported by target upon subsequent liquidation distributions. Keep in mind, however, that the target corporation still will be required to report gain or loss upon the liquidating distribution of any "unwanted assets" not sold to the purchaser as part of the asset acquisition.[23]

b) Tax Consequences to the Target Shareholders

When the target corporation distributes cash and other assets to its shareholders in liquidation following T's taxable asset sale, the shareholders generally will report gain or loss upon the liquidating distribution pursuant to §331.[24] Consequently, a taxable asset acquisition usually results in a rather

---

explicitly state that even though the fair market value used for purposes of allocation of the purchase price is *gross* fair market value for purposes of determining the amount of the seller's gain or loss, "the fair market value of any property subject to a nonrecourse indebtedness shall be treated as being not less than the amount of such indebtedness." Treas. Reg. §1.338-6T(a)(2).

21. See, e.g., Commercial Security Bank v. Comm'r, 77 T.C. 145 (1981); James M. Pierce Corp. v. Comm'r, 326 F.2d 67, 71-72 (8th Cir. 1964).

22. Subsidiary liquidations generally are not taxable to the distributing subsidiary pursuant to §337. See generally Chapter 9.

23. If, instead of a cash sale, T had sold substantially all of its assets for P notes eligible for installment treatment, T would have reported gain from the initial sale of assets only upon the receipt of installment payments pursuant to §453. A subsequent distribution of the P notes to T's shareholders upon liquidation would be considered a "disposition of an installment obligation," triggering recognition of any gain previously deferred through use of the installment method. I.R.C. §453B. Given that most accrual basis taxpayers can no longer use installment reporting pursuant to §453(a)(2), corporations now will be eligible only rarely to treat P notes under the installment method in any event.

24. See Chapter 8. Notice, however, that liquidation of a controlled subsidiary (an "upstream merger") generally is treated as a nonrecognition event under tax rules

immediate double tax—the selling target is taxed upon receipt of consideration for the assets sold and the target shareholders subsequently are taxed when the target distributes this consideration to its shareholders.[25] If T sells assets in exchange for P installment notes and subsequently distributes the P notes in complete liquidation, the note distribution will trigger T's recognition of any gain previously deferred through installment reporting.[26] Despite the general recognition provisions in §331, however, the *T shareholders* who receive P notes upon T's liquidation may be eligible to report payments on the notes under the installment method as if they had sold their T stock directly to P.[27]

Tax Consequences to the Purchasing Corporation

The purchasing corporation in a taxable asset acquisition is entitled to a §1012 cost basis in assets purchased from the target.[28] Since the target corporation is fully reporting gain or loss on the asset transfer and since the purchasing corporation is paying full consideration for each asset, there is no reason to deny the purchaser the same cost basis generally available under §1012 for any purchase of assets. The overall price paid by the purchaser must be allocated among all the assets purchased in order to determine the cost basis of each particular asset in the purchaser's hands. Some of the acquired assets may be depreciable or amortizable and others may not, and some of the assets may be intended for resale and others not. Thus, the particular method used for allocating the purchase price also will be important to the purchaser.[29] Pursuant to §1060, the purchaser must use the same residual allocation method to compute basis in the purchased assets that was used by the seller to allocate purchase price in computing gain or loss on the asset sale.

---

more akin to the tax-free reorganization rules. See Chapter 9. If the target corporation is not liquidating, the distribution to the shareholders will be taxable pursuant to the §301 dividend rules. See Chapter 5.

25. The shareholder level reporting may be deferred to some extent if the target remains alive. In most cases, the liquidation of the target follows rather quickly upon the sale, and any period of deferral is likely to be brief.

26. See note 23.

27. See I.R.C. §453(h), (k). For a more detailed discussion of shareholder installment reporting under §453(h), see Chapter 8.

28. Assuming an arm's-length purchase, this cost basis should be equal to the fair market value of the assets.

29. Transaction costs are not taken into account for purposes of this allocation. Treas. Reg. §1.338-6T(a)(2)(ii). Investigatory costs in determining *whether* to acquire a business and *which* business to acquire may be amortizable over a 60-month period under §195. See Rev. Rul. 99-23, 1999-20 I.R.B. 3.

Allocation of the Purchase Price

a) Tax Stakes for Buyer and Seller

Historically, buyer and seller in a taxable asset acquisition have had somewhat adverse interests regarding the allocation of purchase price to particular assets. Where appreciated capital assets are involved, the seller generally prefers as much as possible allocated to capital gain as opposed to ordinary income assets.[30] On the other hand, the buyer generally prefers as much as possible allocated to assets that are depreciable or amortizable or intended for resale, many of which are not considered capital assets. For example, sellers historically preferred allocation to goodwill or going concern value over covenants not to compete since sale of goodwill or going concern value generated capital gain while sale of covenants generated ordinary income. Buyers typically preferred allocation to covenants not to compete, since payments for such covenants were amortizable while payments for goodwill and going concern value were not. Because of these adverse interests, the Service generally respected an arm's-length agreement between buyer and seller containing a purchase price allocation.[31]

Although sellers generally still prefer allocations to capital assets and buyers generally still prefer allocations to depreciable or amortizable assets, recent tax changes have altered the tax landscape and the dynamics of the allocation of purchase price. First, the Code now includes a general provision in §197 for "amortization of goodwill and certain other intangibles." Under this provision, specified purchased intangibles that are held in connection with the conduct of a trade or business or investment activity are now amortizable over a fifteen-year period.[32] Most important from the buyer's point of view, the intangibles covered by §197 include goodwill, going concern value *and* covenants not to compete, along with several other intangibles. This change should eliminate the buyer's incentive to allocate as much of the purchase price as possible to covenants not to compete as opposed to goodwill.

---

30. In the case of loss assets, this preference would be reversed.

31. Comm'r v. Danielson, 378 F.2d 771 (3d Cir.), *cert. denied*, 389 U.S. 858 (1967).

32. See I.R.C. §197(a)-(d). Some limitations apply, however. For example, §197 amortization is not permitted "if the intangible is created in connection with a transaction (or series of related transactions) involving the acquisition of assets constituting a trade or business or substantial portion thereof." §197(c)(2). In addition, §197(f) disallows recognition of loss in the case of certain dispositions of §197 intangibles.

b) Special Allocation Rules: §1060[33]

i) Scope of the Special Allocation Rules

In addition to the §197 rules on amortization of purchased intangibles, Congress also recently added provisions in §1060 adopting "special allocation rules for certain asset acquisitions." The §1060 special allocation rules apply only to "applicable asset acquisitions," defined to include transfers "of assets which constitute a trade or business" and "with respect to which the transferee's [buyer's] basis in such assets is determined wholly by reference to the consideration paid for such assets."[34] In other words, the rules are limited to taxable asset acquisitions of a *group* of assets that together constitute a trade or business.[35] The classic example of a transaction covered by the §1060 allocation rules is a direct acquisition of all or substantially all of the target's assets for cash or notes.[36]

ii) The Residual Method

Under the residual allocation method prescribed by §1060, as revised by recent temporary regulations, the "consideration received for the assets" is allocated to seven different classes of assets.[37] The overall purchase price for the group of assets is allocated to each class in sequence, with the "residual," or leftover, amount allocated to Class VII assets. Class I assets generally include cash and general deposit accounts.[38] The total amount to be allocated

---

33. This section will provide only an overview of the §1060 allocation rules.

34. I.R.C. §1060(c). New regulations clarify that the acquisition will be governed by §1060 if the "assets transferred constitute a trade or business in the hands of either the seller or the purchaser." Treas. Reg. §1.1060-1T(b)(1) (added by T.D. 8858, 65 Fed. Reg. 1236 (Jan. 7, 2000)).

35. The regulations here first cross-reference to the "active trade or business" requirement of §355(b), but continue to provide that even if the group of assets does not constitute a "trade or business" under §355, it will constitute a trade or business for purposes of §1060 "if its character is such that goodwill or going concern value could under any circumstances attach to such group." Treas. Reg. §1.1060-1T(b)(2). For discussion of the §355 "trade or business" requirement, see Chapter 13.

36. The discussion of §1060 here is limited to corporate transfers. Notice, however, that the special allocation rules are not limited to corporate asset sales.

37. Section 1060 and its accompanying regulations adopt the same allocation method used to allocate basis to various assets under §338(b)(5). The rationale for borrowing from §338 for the taxable asset acquisitions allocation rules was to provide roughly parallel treatment for taxable asset acquisitions and taxable stock acquisitions *treated as* asset acquisitions upon a proper §338 election. A detailed discussion of §338 transactions follows later in this chapter.

38. Treas. Reg. §1.338-6T(b)(1). Class I assets are essentially cash and cash equivalents.

is first reduced by the amount of such Class I assets transferred, effectively allocating the purchase price to these assets on a dollar-for-dollar basis. Once the Class I assets are subtracted, the remainder is allocated first to Class II assets (actively traded personal property, including publicly traded stock, certificates of deposit, and foreign currency), then to Class III assets (accounts receivable, mortgages, and credit card receivables), then to Class IV assets (inventory or property held primarily for sale to customers), then to Class V assets (all assets other than those in Classes I-IV and VI-VII), then to Class VI assets (all §197 intangible assets except goodwill and going concern value), and finally to Class VII assets (intangibles in the nature of goodwill and going concern value) in proportion to the fair market value of the assets on the purchase date.[39] An allocation to any particular asset cannot exceed the asset's fair market value.[40] This important restriction effectively assures that any surplus value paid for the assets will be allocated to Class VII assets such as goodwill.

Early residual allocation method regulations were undoubtedly designed to assure that any premium paid for the target's assets would be attributed to goodwill or going concern value. Since goodwill and going concern value were not then amortizable, the practical effect was to limit the buyer's ability to amortize. Put slightly differently, the residual method was designed to prevent the undervaluation of goodwill in the allocation process. The buyer's disadvantage from the residual method was often the seller's advantage. By allocating the premium paid to goodwill or going concern value, the method increased the portion of any gain eligible for capital gains treatment. Now that §197 provides 15-year amortization to intangibles, including goodwill and going concern value, the Treasury Department has retained the "residual method," but includes all of the amortizable §197 intangibles (as opposed to just goodwill and going concern value) in the residual Classes VI and VII.[41]

---

39. Notice that the common thread for Class I assets is extreme liquidity. Continuing this thread, Class II assets are highly liquid, but not *as* liquid as Class I assets, which, in turn, are not quite *as* liquid as those in Class III, which include "fast pay" assets such as accounts receivable.

40. Treas. Reg. §1.338-6T(c)(1). See Treas. Reg. §1.338-6T(a)(2) for the definition of "fair market value" for purposes of §§338 and 1060 allocations.

41. The separation of §197 intangibles into two separate classes probably reflects the notion that §197 intangibles such as customer lists, workplace in force, and patents (now included in Class VI) are slightly more "tangible" than goodwill and going concern value (now included in Class VII).

Taxable Stock Acquisitions

The Transaction

In a typical stock sale, the selling shareholders transfer some or all of their target corporation (T) stock to the purchasing corporation (P) or a P subsidiary (S) in exchange for cash and/or notes.[42] Assuming the purchase of a controlling interest, the purchasing corporation now becomes a parent to its newly acquired subsidiary. P may simply retain T as a distinct subsidiary. Since T remains intact as a corporate entity and remains liable to its creditors, P need not formally assume T's liabilities. As an alternative, the purchasing corporation may completely liquidate T in an upstream merger. Upon such merger, P will become responsible for T's liabilities.

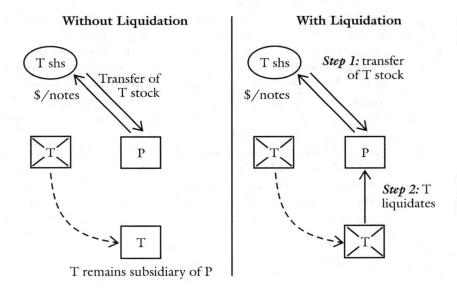

Tax Consequences to the Selling Corporation and Its Shareholders

The selling target shareholders will report gain or loss from sale of their T shares to P pursuant to $\S\S61(a)(3)$ and 1001. If the T shareholders receive

---

42. As in the case of taxable asset acquisitions, the consideration also may include other assets, and even P stock. The transaction will be classified as a taxable acquisition as long as it does not meet one of the reorganization definitions in I.R.C. §368(a). Although an individual may acquire a controlling interest in a target corporation, the focus of this chapter is upon corporate purchasers.

P notes in exchange for their T shares, they will be entitled to report gain under the installment method in §453.[43] The target corporation itself bears no immediate tax consequence. T simply remains intact, albeit now as a P subsidiary. Each T asset simply retains the same basis that it had prior to the stock acquisition. If T liquidates, it will recognize no gain or loss on the liquidating distribution pursuant to §337.[44]

A complex set of statutory and regulatory provisions addresses the extent to which the target corporation may continue to use any pre-existing net operating losses (NOLs) after the stock acquisition. In cases where the acquisition results in an "ownership change,"[45] the carryforward of unused NOLs is subject to limitations provided in §382.[46] If the target is liquidated or merged into P after the acquisition, P can continue to use T's unused NOLs, subject to restrictions provided in §381 and in the consolidated return regulations.[47] The details of these rules are beyond the scope of most basic courses in corporate taxation. In general, the rules allow P to use the NOLs to offset T's future income, but *not* to offset P's future income.

Tax Consequences to the Purchasing Corporation

In a taxable stock acquisition, the purchasing corporation is entitled to a §1012 cost basis in the T shares purchased. Since the shareholders fully reported gain or loss on the sale of stock and the purchasing corporation paid full consideration for the shares, there is no reason to deny such a cost basis in the stock. Absent an election under §338,[48] however, the target corporation (now a subsidiary of the purchasing corporation) retains its assets with no change in asset basis. If the purchasing corporation distributes T's assets in liquidation, P will not be required to recognize gain or loss pursuant to §332, and the parent will receive the assets with the same basis that the subsidiary had.[49] Thus, even after liquidation, the T assets will retain their historic basis. In the end, notice that the tax consequences to both T and P

---

43. I.R.C. §453(a), (b).

44. See Chapter 9.

45. There is an "ownership change," as defined in §382(g), if the percentage of target stock held by one or more 5% shareholders has increased by more than 50% over the lowest percentage of stock owned by such shareholders during the three-year testing period defined in §382(i).

46. In certain tax avoidance cases, the carryforward of NOLs may be denied entirely under special provisions in §269. The §382 rules are considered further in Chapter 12.

47. See Treas. Reg. §1.1502-21A(c).

48. Detailed discussion of the §338 election appears later in this chapter.

49. I.R.C. §334(b). See Chapter 9 for a detailed discussion of subsidiary liquidations.

are the same whether or not T liquidates. In either case, there is no immediate corporate level recognition of the gain or loss on T's assets, but instead a deferral of gain or loss until the purchasing corporation sells, distributes or otherwise disposes of the assets. In some cases, this deferral of the corporate level tax with respect to T's assets makes a stock acquisition more attractive than an asset acquisition.

Stock Acquisitions Treated as Asset Acquisitions: §338

Section 338: Roots and Background

When a purchasing corporation acquires a controlling stock interest in a target followed immediately by receipt of the target's assets in a liquidating distribution, the transaction begins to resemble an asset acquisition. The direct asset acquisition transfers assets from T to P in one step, whereas P's acquisition of T stock followed by T's liquidation transfers assets in two steps.

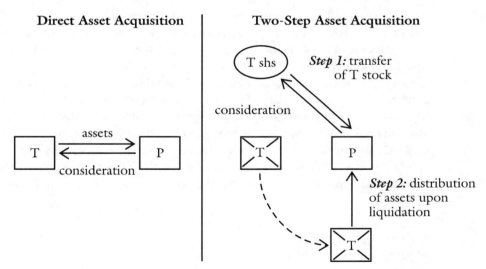

Consistent with the notion that economically equivalent transactions generally should receive equivalent tax treatment, Congress has attempted to achieve some parity between certain stock acquisitions and asset acquisitions. The remainder of this chapter addresses those efforts, culminating in the adoption of §338.

The starting point in any historical discussion of §338 is the case of Kimbell-Diamond Milling Co. v. Comm'r.[50] The corporate taxpayer in *Kim-*

---

50. 14 T.C. 74 (1950), *aff'd per curiam*, 187 F.2d 718 (5th Cir.), *cert. denied*, 342 U.S. 827 (1951).

bell-Diamond sustained a fire casualty that destroyed its mill. In its search to replace the mill property, Kimbell-Diamond found Whaley, a target corporation with a comparable mill. Kimbell-Diamond purchased 100% of Whaley's stock and shortly thereafter liquidated the target, thus acquiring direct ownership of the mill. The issue before the court in *Kimbell-Diamond* was the proper basis in the mill for purposes of depreciation. Kimbell-Diamond argued that it had legitimately liquidated the target, Whaley, and that the mill should have the same basis in its hands that it had in the target Whaley's hands under the predecessor to §334(b). The Commissioner argued that since Kimbell-Diamond *intended* an asset acquisition of the mill, the purchase of stock and the subsequent liquidation should be collapsed into one transaction and viewed as a purchase of assets under the step transaction doctrine. The Court agreed that the transaction should be viewed as an asset acquisition, leaving Kimbell-Diamond with a cost basis in the mill instead of a substituted basis from the target, Whaley.[51]

The government's success in *Kimbell-Diamond* was a Pyrrhic victory, however. Taxpayers quickly discovered that they could receive a cost basis in assets of an acquired subsidiary simply by establishing an *intent* to acquire assets. This intent-based standard led to great uncertainty. In 1954, Congress enacted old §334(b)(2), which codified the basic approach of *Kimbell-Diamond,* while attempting to eliminate the uncertainty of an intent-based test. Under old §334(b)(2), a purchaser of stock was entitled to a cost basis in the target company's assets if the purchaser acquired at least 80% of another corporation's stock during a 12-month period and the distribution of target assets was pursuant to a plan of liquidation adopted not more than two years after the stock purchase. Old §334(b)(2) was not elective and thus led to many traps for the unwary. In addition, the target corporation had to be liquidated in order to achieve a stepped-up basis for the purchasing corporation. In 1982, Congress replaced old §334(b)(2) with §338.[52] Since 1982, Congress has tinkered with details and ironed out kinks, but the *Kimbell-Diamond* case and the old §334(b)(2) roots of modern §338 are unmistakable.

Qualifying Stock Purchases (QSPs)

Unlike the early statutory response to *Kimbell-Diamond* in old §334(b)(2), modern §338 is explicitly elective. The election is available only to corpora-

---

51. The roles of the taxpayer and the Commissioner in *Kimbell-Diamond* are somewhat unusual. In acquisitions such as these, the purchaser's cost basis tends to be higher than a substituted basis in the target's assets. One would expect the purchaser to argue for cost basis. In *Kimbell-Diamond,* however, the purchaser's cost basis was lower than the target company's basis in the mill.
52. Tax Equity and Fiscal Responsibility Act of 1982, §224(a), Pub. L. No. 97-248.

tions that have made a "qualified stock purchase," (QSP) defined as a transaction (or series of transactions) in which the purchasing corporation acquires stock in another corporation that meets the two-part 80% control test of §1504(a)(2) during a 12-month acquisition period.[53] In other words, §338 only applies to stock purchases of *control* sufficient to meet the 80% ownership test required for consolidated return reporting. Although such control need not be acquired in one transaction alone, it must be acquired during one 12-month period. The purchasing corporation must make a timely §338 election and, once made, the election is irrevocable.[54]

Note that §338 only applies to qualified stock *purchases.* The definition of "purchase" provided in §338(h)(3) excludes certain stock acquisitions. For example, target stock in which the purchasing corporation takes a transferred or substituted basis from the transferor or a §1014 basis from a decedent is not acquired by purchase. In addition, any stock acquired by P in a §351 or other tax-free reorganization is not acquired by purchase.[55] Finally, any stock acquired from a person the ownership of whose stock would be attributed to P under the §318 attribution rules is not acquired by purchase. A moment's reflection on these exclusions from the §338 "purchase" definition reveals an important underlying theme. The idea is that §338 should apply only to *taxable* acquisitions. In the ordinary taxable stock acquisition, the selling shareholders report gain or loss on the sale of stock and the purchasing shareholder takes the stock with a cost basis. Congress was willing to permit an elective cost basis[56] in the target's assets upon a transfer of control that was taxable to the selling shareholders.[57] The elective step-up is *not* available for acquisitions of control through a tax-free reorganization.

In addition to the shareholder level tax reported on the stock sale, §338

---

53. I.R.C. §338(d)(3). The "acquisition period" is the "12-month period beginning with the date of the first acquisition by purchase of stock included in a qualified stock purchase." I.R.C. §338(h)(1).

54. To be timely, the election must be "not later than the 15th day of the 9th month beginning after the month in which the acquisition date occurs." I.R.C. §338(g)(1). The "acquisition date" is the "first day on which there is a qualified stock purchase," in general, the day on which the purchasing corporation's stock acquisitions during the 12-month period first meet the 80% tests. I.R.C. §338(h)(2).

55. To be acquired by "purchase" for purposes of §338, the stock must not have been acquired in an exchange to which §§351, 354, 355 or 356 applies. I.R.C. §338(h)(3)(A)(ii).

56. By its terms, §338 does *not* refer to the target's asset basis following a §338 election as either a "cost" or "stepped-up" basis, but instead as a "grossed-up" basis. This term and the mechanics of §338 are discussed later in this chapter.

57. Note the exception upon a §338(h)(10) election, discussed later in this chapter. Although the (h)(10) election permits the selling shareholder to avoid recognition of gain, the shareholder in that case is a corporation, whose shareholders, in turn, will presumably report taxable gain or loss in the future.

also assures corporate level recognition to the target on the appreciation or depreciation in the value of its assets, using a "deemed sale" of the target's assets as a trigger for recognizing gain or loss. In the end, the tax consequences of a stock acquisition under §338 essentially parallel the tax consequences of a direct asset acquisition. In each case, the target corporation recognizes a gain or loss on either the actual or the "deemed sale" of its assets and the target shareholders recognize capital gain or loss on either the sale of target stock to the purchasing corporation or the receipt of distributions in liquidation of the target. In addition, the purchasing corporation in either case effectively receives the target's assets with a cost basis.

Deemed Sale and Repurchase of Assets by Target

If the purchasing corporation makes a §338 election following a QSP, the target corporation will be deemed to have engaged in two significant transactions. First, under §338(a)(1), the target is treated as if it "sold all of its assets at the close of the acquisition date at fair market value in a single transaction."[58] This sale triggers recognition of gain or loss to the target and is often described as the deemed sale by "old target" (old T). Second, under §338(a)(2) the target is treated "as a new corporation which purchased all of the assets referred to in paragraph (1)" on the following day. This deemed repurchase of the target corporation's assets is the transaction that effectively provides the purchaser with a cost basis in the target's assets and is often described as the deemed repurchase by "new target" (new T).

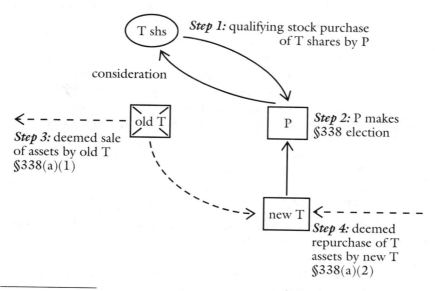

---

58. Recall that under §338(h)(2), the acquisition date is the first date on which the purchasing corporation has acquired enough target stock to meet the 80% control tests.

At first glance, the fictional two-step sale and repurchase provided by §338(a) seems unnecessarily complex. If Congress meant to permit a cost basis to the purchasing corporation in the target corporation's assets, why not just say so? First, step one of the two-step process extracts a heavy price for the cost basis ultimately permitted to the purchasing corporation in the target corporation's assets. Congress was unwilling to provide the cost (usually stepped-up) basis to the purchasing corporation unless the target corporation paid tax on the previously unrealized gain or loss in the target assets. The §338(a)(1) deemed sale of target assets requires recognition of that gain or loss to the old target.

Second, notice that the deemed repurchase in step two takes place on the day *after* the acquisition date and the target is treated as a new corporation. The new target created by the fiction in §338(a)(2) has lost most of its tax attributes. With few exceptions, "new target is treated as a new corporation that is unrelated to old target."[59] Thus, new target no longer has any earnings and profits, net operating losses or other relevant tax attributes.[60] By creating this new target for the deemed repurchase in step two, Congress meant to eliminate trafficking in tax attributes that might otherwise occur. For example, purchasing corporations might otherwise shop around for target corporations with net operating losses.

Another consequence of having the deemed sale by the old target on one day and the deemed repurchase on the following day, is isolation of the old target's gain or loss from the §338(a)(1) deemed sale. Special rules included in §338 provide that "the target corporation shall not be treated as a member of an affiliated group with respect to the sale described in subsection (a)(1)."[61] This provision is also designed to prohibit trafficking—in this case, trafficking in the tax characteristics of the old target's deemed sale itself. Notice that §338(h)(9) restricts the target's membership in both the selling *and* purchasing affiliated groups with respect to the deemed sale. Thus, the restriction generally prevents the target from using gains or losses of other members of the selling consolidated group to offset gains or losses resulting from the §338(a)(1) deemed asset sale.[62] In addition, the old target is not

---

59. Treas. Reg. §1.338-1T(b)(1).

60. The exceptions provided for in the regulations include various employee benefit, pension, annuity, profit sharing, stock bonus, or options plans. Treas. Reg. §1.338-1T(b)(2). Thus, new target will continue to be liable for such obligations to its employees. In addition, new target will continue to be liable for old target's federal income tax liabilities. Treas. Reg. §1.338-1T(b)(3)(i), (ii).

61. I.R.C. §338(h)(9).

62. Also in §338(h)(9), however, Congress authorized the Treasury Department to formulate exceptions. If old T is the common parent of an affiliated group, the deemed sale gain can be reported on a final consolidated return for old T. Treas. Reg. §1.338-10T(a)(1). On the other hand, if the target is otherwise a member of a selling group, the old target is treated as "disaffiliated" from the group immediately

considered a member of the purchasing corporation's affiliated group with respect to old T's deemed asset sale.[63] Consequently, the purchasing corporation will not be entitled to use the old target's gain or loss from the deemed sale to offset gain or loss on the purchasing group's consolidated return.

Mechanics of the §338(a)(1) Deemed Sale

The statutory language in §338(a)(1) merely provides that "the target shall be treated as having sold all of its assets at the close of the acquisition date at fair market value in a single transaction." The extensive §338 regulations had gone through so many ad hoc revisions since 1982 that they had become "difficult to follow" and needed a facelift.[64] A new and improved version of the §338 regulations was recently finalized.[65]

Instead of adopting a traditional "arms-length buyer and seller" definition of fair market value, the regulations use aggregate deemed sales price (ADSP) as the price at which target is deemed to have sold all of its assets for purposes of §338(a)(1).[66] Under prior regulations, the primary component of the ADSP was the purchasing corporation's price for the QSP. In other words, the old regulations used the buyer's cost for the T stock as a surrogate for the fair market value of T's assets, reasoning that in an arm's-length transaction between unrelated parties, the buyer's cost should reflect fair market value. The revisions reflected in the new §338 regulations were designed to provide for greater consistency in the treatment of *actual* asset sales and §338 *deemed* asset sales. Under the new regulations, ADSP is no longer linked to the purchasing corporation's cost for the QSP. In recommending this change, the Treasury Department observed that "[s]uch link does not exist . . . in the case of an actual asset between two parties. In actual asset sales the timing and amount of the seller's amount realized and the timing of the amount of the buyer's basis may differ."[67] ADSP is

---

before the deemed sale of its assets and will file a separate "deemed sale return," including *only* items resulting from the deemed sale and limited carryover items. Treas. Reg. §1.338-10T(a)(2)(i).

63. Treas. Reg. §1.338-10T(a)(5).

64. Preamble to proposed regulations, 64 Fed. Reg. 43,461, 43,465 (Aug. 10, 1999) ("The current regulations are difficult to follow. Thus, the I.R.S. and Treasury determined that a review of the regulations was appropriate."). In fact, the preamble lists "organization of the regulations" as the first of four major components of the new regulations.

65. T.D. 8858, 65 Fed. Reg. 1236 (Jan. 7, 2000) (codified, as amended, at Treas. Reg. §§1.338-1T-10T and (h)(10)-1T).

66. Treas. Reg. §1.338-4T(a).

67. 24 Fed. Reg. 43,461, 43,465 (Aug. 10, 1999). As an example, except under rare and unusual circumstances, amount realized to the seller includes the full value of future contingent payments. Treas. Reg. §1.1001-1(g). On the other hand, a cash

now based upon the amount realized on the sale to the purchasing corporation.[68]

In addition, ADSP includes any old target liability "that is properly taken into account in the amount realized under general principles of tax law that would apply if old target had sold its assets to an unrelated person for consideration that included that person's assumption of, or taking subject to, the liability."[69] This inclusion of liabilities in the §338(a)(1) deemed sales price is consistent with the general tax principle that the amount realized on any sale includes liabilities assumed by the buyer or liabilities to which the assets sold were subject. For purposes of computing ADSP, the target's liabilities also include any tax liability from the deemed asset sale itself, including recapture items arising from the deemed sale.[70] Since gain or loss from the deemed asset sale is determined on an asset-by-asset basis, old target must allocate the overall ADSP price among its assets.[71] The allocation method used for this purpose generally will be the same allocation method used for determining the basis of each asset in the purchaser's hands.[72] Character of the old target's gain or loss as capital or ordinary will depend upon the character of each asset sold. In addition, the target will be taxed at ordinary income rates on various recapture items.

---

method buyer would not be entitled to include the amount of such contingent payments in basis until the payments were made, and an accrual method buyer would not be entitled to include them before "economic performance" under §461(h). The new §338 regulations take these sorts of differences into account in computing the amount realized to old T on the deemed sale and in computing the basis in old T's assets on the deemed repurchase.

68. The regulations actually refer to the "grossed-up amount realized on the sale to the purchasing corporation of the purchasing corporation's recently purchased target stock." Treas. Reg. §1.338-4T(b)(i). This amount realized is "determined as if old target were the selling shareholder and the installment method were not available. . . ." *Id.* at (c)(i). The amount realized is then "grossed-up" by "divid[ing] by the percentage of target stock (by value, determined on the acquisition date) attributable to that recently purchased target stock. *Id.* at (c)(ii). Finally, old T is entitled to subtract from amount realized those selling costs that would ordinarily be permitted in a sale of stock to an unrelated third party. *Id.* at (c)(iii).

69. Treas. Reg. §1.338-4T(d)(1).

70. *Id.* The regulations acknowledge that the deemed sale itself can increase or decrease ADSP by creating or reducing a tax liability. Thus, the determination of ADSP "may require trial and error computations." Treas. Reg. §1.338-4T(d)(3).

71. See earlier discussion in this chapter on taxable asset sales.

72. This is the residual method proscribed by the Treasury Department pursuant to authority granted in §338(b)(5). Treas. Reg. §1.338-6T. See also discussion in this chapter on "Mechanics of the §338(a)(2) Deemed Repurchase." The residual method also is used for direct taxable asset acquisitions pursuant to §1060. See earlier discussion in this chapter on taxable asset acquisitions.

Mechanics of the §338(a)(2) Deemed Repurchase

Although the idea behind the deemed repurchase of assets by the new target is to provide a cost basis to the purchasing corporation in the target's assets, the mechanics of the repurchase can be a bit puzzling for the novice. Notice that §338 never uses the term "cost basis." Instead, §338(b)(1) provides that the purchase price for purposes of the deemed repurchase is the sum of "(A) the grossed-up basis of the purchasing corporation's recently purchased stock, and (B) the basis of the purchasing corporation's nonrecently purchased stock."[73] There are two reasons for the complexity here. First, the purchasing corporation need only purchase the required 80% interest during the 12-month acquisition period. The purchasing corporation itself already may own additional target stock that it acquired before this acquisition period. The Code refers to this stock as "nonrecently purchased" stock. More colloquially, it is sometimes referred to as "old and cold" stock. The purchasing corporation generally is not entitled to a cost basis with respect to old and cold stock that was not part of the QSP. Thus, absent an additional special election, the cost basis is permitted only for the qualifying shares.[74]

A second reason for the complexity is that the purchasing corporation will not necessarily own all of the target company's stock after the qualified acquisition. Up to 20% of the target stock still may be owned by minority shareholders. Nevertheless, since the old target recognized the full gain or loss on the deemed sale of its assets, Congress wanted to provide a full step-up in basis for the target assets. This is achieved through use of a "grossed-up" basis. To figure the "grossed-up" basis, §338(b)(4) instructs the purchasing corporation to multiply the cost basis for stock purchased during the 12-month acquisition period by a fraction the numerator of which is 100% minus the old and cold (nonrecently purchased) stock and the denominator of which is the percentage of qualifying or recently purchased stock.[75] If there are no minority shareholders, this fraction will always be

---

73. The new §338 regulations use the term "adjusted grossed-up basis" (AGUB) to refer to "the amount for which new target is deemed to have purchased all of its assets in the deemed purchase under section 338(a)(2)." Treas. Reg. §1.338–5T(a). Under the regulations, AGUB "is the sum of (i) The grossed-up basis in the purchasing corporation's recently purchased target stock; (ii) The purchasing corporation's basis in nonrecently purchased stock; and (iii) The liabilities of the new target." *Id.* at (b)(i)-(iii).

74. Ordinarily, the historical basis for the old and cold shares is simply added to the "grossed-up" basis of the recently purchased shares according to §338(b)(1)(B). If the purchasing corporation would like to receive a cost basis with respect to this old stock as well, it is possible to do so by making a second election under §338(b)(3). The price extracted for this secondary election is recognition of gain on a deemed sale of the old and cold, or nonrecently purchased, target corporation stock.

75. "Recently purchased stock" is the T stock acquired by P during the 12-month acquisition period and held by P on the acquisition date (i.e., the 80% or more QSP).

equal to one. Obviously, multiplying the cost basis of the stock by one will leave the cost basis unchanged. Thus, where there are no minority shareholders, the purchase price for the deemed repurchase by the new target simply will be the cost of the qualifying or recently purchased stock plus the basis of any old and cold or nonrecently purchased shares of target stock that the purchasing corporation may happen to own.

Assume, for example, that the purchasing corporation (P) acquired 10% of the target corporation (T) many years ago for $1000. This 10% of the T stock in P's hands is nonrecently purchased or old and cold stock. In a qualified stock purchase, P acquires the remaining 90% for $900,000. As of the acquisition date, T owns assets with a basis of $50,000 and a fair market value of $1 million. Whether or not P makes a §338 election, the T shareholders will report gain or loss on the sale of their T shares under §§61(a)(3) and 1001. If P does not make a §338 election, T will simply be a new subsidiary of P, retaining its historical basis of $50,000 in its assets. Even if P liquidates T, neither P nor T will recognize gain or loss under §§332 and 337 and the target assets still will have a $50,000 transferred basis in P's hands under §334(b).

On the other hand, if P makes a §338 election, old T will be deemed to sell all of its assets on the acquisition date. Old T will report a gain of $950,000 on this deemed sale. On the following day, new T will be deemed to repurchase the same assets. The purchase price will be the grossed-up basis in P's recently purchased stock plus the basis of the nonrecently purchased stock. To determine grossed-up basis here, P will multiply the basis of the 90% recently purchased ($900,000) by a fraction of 90%/90% or 1.[76] In other words, the grossed-up basis is simply the cost basis of the recently purchased shares of $900,000. This will always be the case where no minority shareholders are involved. To this grossed-up basis, P can add the $1000 basis from the old and cold shares.[77] Thus, new T's basis in the assets after the deemed repurchase will be $901,000. This overall basis then must be allocated among new T's assets.[78] Notice that the asset basis is not fully stepped-up to the $1 million fair market value. This is because P is not eligible for the step-up in basis with respect to the 10% nonrecently purchased stock.[79]

I.R.C. §338(b)(6)(A). "Nonrecently purchased stock" includes any T stock held by P on the acquisition date that is *not* recently purchased stock (i.e., P's "old and cold" T stock). I.R.C. §338(b)(6)(B).

76. Under §338(b)(4), the numerator of the fraction is 100% less the 10% old and cold stock, and the denominator is the 90% recently purchased stock.

77. I.R.C. §338(b)(1)(B).

78. I.R.C. §338(b)(5); Treas. Reg. §1.338-6T, 7T.

79. P may be able to get the additional step-up in basis with respect to these shares by making a secondary election under §338(b)(3) and recognizing gain on the appreciation in those old shares.

Changing the facts slightly, assume that P purchases 90% in a QSP, but that the remaining 10% is owned by minority shareholders. If P makes a §338 election, old T still is deemed to sell all of its assets as of the acquisition date. Thus, old T will still report a $950,000 gain. Since P has no nonrecently purchased stock, the purchase price on the deemed repurchase by new T under §338(b)(1) is just the grossed-up basis of the 90% recently purchased stock. P now will multiply its $900,000 cost basis in the recently purchased shares by a fraction of 100%/90%.[80] Note that the grossed-up basis then is $1 million, the fair market value of T's assets as of the acquisition date. Since T reported full gain on the deemed sale of its assets, and since all of P's shares were recently acquired as part of a QSP, §338 here permits a full step-up in the basis of T's assets.

Qualified Stock Purchase Without *a §338 Election Followed by Liquidation or Reorganization of Target*

One lingering question after the adoption of old §334(b)(2) and its §338 successor was whether a purchaser that *failed* to meet the formal statutory requirements for a stepped-up basis in assets under old §334(b)(2) or failed to make a §338 election following a QSP still could receive a stepped-up basis in the target's assets by arguing an intent to acquire assets under the *Kimbell-Diamond* step-transaction doctrine. The legislative history behind §338 attempted to resolve the lingering question, declaring that §338 was "intended to replace any nonstatutory treatment of a stock purchase as an asset purchase under the Kimbell-Diamond doctrine."[81] Despite this declaration, the *Kimbell-Diamond* doctrine has refused to disappear quietly.

In the case of Yoc Heating Corp. v. Commissioner,[82] the purchasing corporation (P) was unable to negotiate a purchase of the target corporation's assets, but subsequently acquired 85% of the target corporation's stock for cash and notes.[83] P indicated that it was only interested in the target stock acquisition if it could subsequently transfer the target (old T) assets to

---

80. Under §338(b)(4), the numerator is 100% less the nonrecently purchased shares. In this case, there are no such shares. The denominator is the recently purchased stock, here 90%.

81. H.R. Conf. Rep. No. 760, 97th Cong., 2d Sess. 467, 536 (1982). See also Rev. Rul. 90-95, 1990-2 67, 68 ("Section 338 of the Code replaced the *Kimbell-Diamond* doctrine and governs whether a corporation's acquisition of stock is treated as an asset purchase.").

82. 61 T.C. 168, 178 (1973).

83. Under the current provisions in §338, this stock acquisition would be considered a QSP.

a new corporate subsidiary (new T) and receive a stepped-up basis in the assets equal to the cost of the target stock. Shortly after the stock acquisition, P formed new T and offered the old T shareholders, including P itself, one share of new T stock in exchange for every three shares of old T stock. Not surprisingly, P accepted this offer to exchange its recently acquired 85% interest in old T for new T shares. The old T minority shareholders were "bought out" for cash.

The government in *Yoc Heating* took the position that the stock exchange was covered by the tax-free reorganization rules under which new T retained the same asset basis that old T had under §362(b). The purchaser, on the other hand, argued under the step-transaction doctrine that its various steps were integral parts of a plan to acquire a controlling interest in the target's assets. Noting that it was relying on the step-transaction doctrine generally rather than the narrower *Kimbell-Diamond* doctrine, the Tax Court agreed to view the various steps involved in the acquisition as part of an integrated transaction. Before the overall integrated transaction, 85% of the target was owned by unrelated shareholders. After the overall transaction, the purchaser held an 85% controlling interest. Since the historic shareholders no longer held a substantial interest in the corporate enterprise, the Tax Court found that the transaction failed to meet the continuity of proprietary interest test necessary to classify the acquisition as a tax-free reorganization.[84] Since it was not a tax-free liquidation of a subsidiary or a tax-free reorganization, the Tax Court held that the transaction was "by way of purchase with an accompanying step up in basis."[85] In the end, the taxpayer in *Yoc Heating* received a stepped-up basis in the appreciated target assets following an acquisition of the target's stock *without* satisfying the statutory requirements of old §334(b)(2).

The *Yoc Heating* integrated transaction rule seemed to support a stepped-up basis in target assets after a qualified stock acquisition even in some cases where the purchaser does *not* make a §338 election. The Treasury Department reacted by adding a new provision to the §338 regulations, commonly known as the "anti-*Yoc Heating*" regulations.[86] The "anti-*Yoc Heating*" regulations apply only if target assets are transferred to the purchasing corporation (or an affiliate) following a qualified stock purchase for which a §338 election was *not* made.[87] In such cases, the regulations deem the purchasing corporation to be an historic shareholder for purposes of

84. The Treasury Department has substantially changed its position regarding "historic" continuity of interest. For further discussion, see Chapter 11.

85. 61 T.C. 168, 178.

86. Treas. Reg. §1.338-3T(c)(3).

87. Treas. Reg. §1.338-3T(c)(3)(i).

measuring continuity of interest under the tax-free reorganization principles.[88] Recall that the only element lacking for tax-free reorganization treatment in *Yoc Heating* was continuity of interest because the historic
shareholders of old T did not hold a substantial interest in new T after the
transaction. The §338 regulations solved the dilemma by deeming the recent
purchaser to be an historic shareholder. As a result, the acquisition can be
treated as a tax-free reorganization, resulting in a substituted basis for the
target assets pursuant to §362(b). In any event, recent changes to regulations
under §368 have virtually eliminated the historic shareholder continuity of
interest requirement for purposes of tax-free reorganizations. Moreover, the
new §338 regulations clarify that a QSP for which a §338 election is *not*
made can be immediately followed by a tax-free reorganization.[89]

Notice the unusual and creative regulatory response provided by the
Treasury Department in the "anti-*Yoc Heating*" regulations. The regulation
effectively "bifurcates" the transaction, treating the acquisition as a tax-free
reorganization as to the purchaser and target, but a taxable acquisition as to
minority shareholders. The regulation provides that tax-free reorganization
treatment will not be available to minority shareholders unless the transaction
would otherwise qualify as a reorganization.[90] Thus, the minority shareholders "bought out" for cash in the *Yoc Heating* transaction would not be
eligible to treat the exchange of their old T shares as received in tax-free
reorganization pursuant to §354. The Treasury Department defends this
treatment as "the simplest and most effective means" of achieving the intent
of §338.[91] The Treasury Department believed that extension of this regulatory reorganization treatment to minority shareholders would "inappropri-
ately alter general reorganization principles, and would not be grounded in
the policies of section 338."[92]

Deciding Whether or Not to Make the §338 Election

Prior to the 1986 repeal of the *General Utilities* rule, §338 elections were
rather attractive because the §338 deemed sale by old T did not result in

---

88. Treas. Reg. §1.338-3T(c)(3)(ii).

89. See Chapter 11 for a full discussion of the new continuity of interest regulations
and the potential overlaps between §338 and the tax-free reorganization provisions.

90. Treas. Reg. §1.338-3T(c)(3)(i). For a detailed discussion of acquisitive reorganization rules, see Chapter 12.

91. T.D. 8626 (preamble to final "anti-*Yoc Heating*" regulations).

92. *Id.*

taxable gain or loss.[93] As a result, the purchasing corporation could acquire the target's assets with a stepped-up basis without the target ever having recognized gain on the unrealized appreciation in its assets. Since 1986, however, the deemed sale by old T *will* trigger recognition of the target's gain or loss. Thus, the step-up in basis provided by a §338 election often comes at a heavy price. In our example above, old T was required to report a taxable gain of $950,000. Even though responsibility for this gain technically belongs to T, as a practical matter, the price to P of the overall acquisition often will increase substantially if the purchaser plans to make a §338 election. Given the large "toll charge" in the form of a taxable gain to T, a §338 election will be unwise for many taxpayers. On the other hand, if T's assets are depreciable or include unimproved property that P plans to sell reasonably quickly, a step-up in the basis of T's appreciated assets may be attractive to P. To decide whether such an election is sensible, the taxable gain from the deemed sale by the target must be weighed against the value to the purchasing corporation of the basis step-up. For example, it may be that the discounted present value of additional depreciation allowances provided by the higher basis will exceed the taxable gain to the target under §338(a)(1).[94]

Special Problems Under §338: Affiliated Corporations and Consistency Rules

Target as Part of a Selling Affiliated Group

Special tax concerns emerge when the target corporation is part of an affiliated group of corporations, and the target recognizes gain as a result of a §338 election. Imagine, for example, that T's sole asset is all of the stock of corporation T-1. In other words, T is a parent holding company of a wholly owned subsidiary. If P acquires all of T's stock and makes a §338 election with respect to its qualified stock purchase, T will be deemed to have sold its T-1 stock under §338(a)(1) and to repurchase the same T-1 stock under §338(a)(2). The deemed repurchase under §338(a)(2) is also a QSP. Absent special rules, if T makes a §338 election with respect to its deemed acquisition of T-1 stock, T-1 now will be deemed to have sold all of its assets

---

93. Prior to 1986, the deemed sale of assets by the target was considered to be a tax-free sale in connection with liquidation under *old* §337. For discussion of these rules prior to repeal of *General Utilities,* see Chapter 8.

94. For an effort to describe mathematically the assessments involved, see Mark Kotlarsky, Stepping-Up Basis: Purchase of Stock or Purchase of Assets, 39 Tax Notes 1011 (1988).

under §338(a)(1). Thus, T would be taxed on the sale of its T stock and T-1 would be taxed on the deemed sale of its assets.

The potential for cascading taxes multiplies as the corporate chain of tiered subsidiaries lengthens. For example, assume that T-1's only asset, in turn, is all of the stock of second-tier subsidiary, T-2. T is taxed on its sale of T-1 stock to P. Again, assuming a §338 election by P and an actual or deemed §338 election by T and T-1, T-1 is taxed on its deemed sale of T-2 stock and T-2 is taxed on the deemed sale of its assets. Under certain conditions, the §338 regulations provide relief from this multiple tax potential.[95] If eligible for this regulatory relief, the target (T) will not recognize gain or loss from the deemed sale of the target affiliate's (T-1) stock, but T-1 still will be required to recognize gain or loss on the deemed sale of its assets. This regulatory provision is known as the "anticascading rule."

The Special §338(h)(10) Election

A related concern for a target and its affiliates arises when the target is a wholly owned subsidiary of a corporate seller, CS. Assume, for example, that purchaser P makes a cash purchase of all of T's stock from CS. CS will be

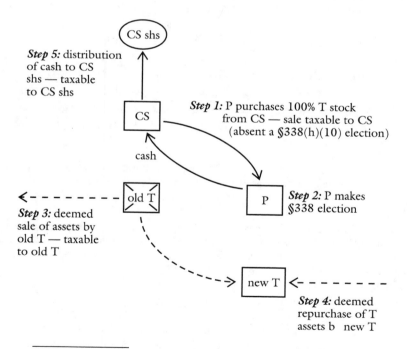

95. Treas. Reg. §1.338-4T(h)(1), (2). The regulation only applies to the deemed sale of a target affiliate where a §338 election was made for the target and the target affiliate. Treas. Reg. §1.338-4T(c)(2), (8), exs. 1, 2. The relief provided for in this regulation is not available when a §338(h)(10) election has been made for the target affiliate. A discussion of §338(h)(10) appears in the next section.

taxed upon the sale of the T stock. CS's shareholders also will report gain or loss when the cash received from P is distributed to them in the form of a dividend or liquidating distribution. In addition, if P makes a §338 election, T will report gain or loss from the deemed sale of its assets under §338(a)(1).

The target group's concern is the multiple taxes imposed upon old T, CS and the CS shareholders. If T simply had distributed its assets to CS in complete liquidation, CS and T would have been entitled to nonrecognition under §§332 and 337. CS then could have sold the T assets directly to P in a taxable asset sale. As an alternative, T could have sold its assets directly to P in a taxable asset sale followed by a liquidating distribution to its parent, CS. Again, CS would have been entitled to nonrecognition under §332. In either case, these alternative transactions would provide a cost basis in assets to the purchaser while imposing only one layer of corporate tax on the selling target and its parent.

In some circumstances, however, P may demand, or require, a stock rather than an asset acquisition. To give P a cost basis in the T assets only when both the selling target and its parent recognize gain would be inconsistent with the general notion that economically equivalent transactions should result in reasonably equivalent tax consequences.[96] In response to these concerns, §338(h)(10) permits a special election,[97] under which CS will recognize no gain or loss on the sale of its T stock.[98] Under the §338(h)(10) regulations, old T is treated as if it sold all of its assets to an unrelated person in a single transaction at the close of the acquisition date and subsequently transferred all of its assets to members of the selling consolidated group or selling affiliate.[99] This special (h)(10) election is available only if the purchasing corporation makes a QSP of target stock from a member of a selling consolidated group.[100] In addition, the election is

---

96. In addition, while Subchapter C imposes a double tax on corporate earnings, Congress has generally provided relief designed to prevent more than two layers of tax in the case of tiered corporations. See, e.g., the dividends-received deduction in §243.

97. Unlike the initial §338 election made by the purchasing corporation alone, the §338(h)(10) election is made jointly by P and the selling consolidated group or the selling affiliate. Treas. Reg. §1.338(h)(10)-1T(c)(2). The timing of the (h)(10) election coincides with the timing required for the §338 election itself under §338(g).

98. I.R.C. §338(h)(10)(A).

99. Treas. Reg. §1.338(h)(10)-1T(d)(3), (4). "In most cases, the [latter] transfer will be treated as a distribution in complete liquidation. . . ." *Id.* at (4)(i).

100. The statute itself provides for an (h)(10) election only when the target corporation was a member of a consolidated group filing a consolidated return. Pursuant to regulatory authority granted in §338(h)(10)(B), however, the Treasury Department recently extended eligibility for the (h)(10) election to cases in which the target merely is a member of an affiliated group of corporations, whether or not they file a consolidated return. Treas. Reg. §1.338(h)(10)-1T(c)(1).

available only if the target recognizes gain or loss from a §338(a)(1) deemed sale of assets resulting from a §338 election.[101]

While the attractiveness of §338 elections generally has diminished since the 1986 repeal of the *General Utilities* rule, a general §338(a) election combined with a secondary §338(h)(10) election can provide numerous advantages, making it one remaining stock acquisition transaction for which a §338 election often is sensible. In addition to providing for nonrecognition of shareholder gain upon the sale of target's stock, a §338(h)(10) election allows the target corporation to be treated as a member of the selling consolidated group for purposes of the deemed sale.[102] Recall that the target generally is not considered to be a member of a consolidated group with respect to the §338(a)(1) deemed asset sale.[103] Absent a special §338(h)(10) election, the deemed sale would be reported on a single day special "deemed sale return." Thus, gain or loss from the target's deemed asset sale ordinarily cannot be consolidated or offset against other gains or losses within the target's affiliated group. The §338(h)(10) election will be especially attractive where the target has losses elsewhere in the selling group that can be used to offset gain from the deemed §338(a)(1) sale of assets.

Consistency Rules

a) Background

When §338 was first enacted in 1982, the old target's deemed sale of assets was eligible for nonrecognition pursuant to the old *General Utilities* doctrine.[104] By making a §338 election, the purchaser could get a stepped-up basis in T's appreciated assets without T recognizing gain on the transfer. Consequently, the §338 election was extremely attractive to the purchaser and imposed little tax cost on the target. In designing §338, Congress wanted to prevent corporate purchasers from acquiring a stepped-up basis for some target assets by making a §338 election while acquiring a transferred or carryover basis for other assets. In addition, Congress sought to prevent

---

101. I.R.C. §338(h)(10)(A)(ii).

102. If P has purchased the T stock for installment notes, new §338 regulations permit old T to report gain from the deemed sale on the installment method. Treas. Reg. §1.338(h)(10)-1T(d)(8)(i) ("Old T is treated as receiving in the deemed asset sale new T installment obligations, the terms of which are identical (except as to the obligor) to P installment obligations issued in exchange for recently purchased stock of T."). In addition, on the subsequent "deemed liquidation, "[o]ld T is treated as distributing . . . the new T installment obligations that it is treated as receiving in the deemed asset sale." *Id.* at (d)(8)(ii).

103. I.R.C. §338(h)(9). See earlier discussion in this chapter.

104. The doctrine was codified in old §337 and in the original language of §338. See earlier discussion in this chapter and in Chapter 8.

purchasers from preserving certain target tax attributes by making separate stock acquisitions from the target or a target affiliate without making a §338 election. Congress included consistency rules in §§338(e) and (f) to prevent this type of selectivity. The "asset consistency" rules in §338(e) created a "deemed §338 election" if the purchasing corporation acquired any assets from the target or a target affiliate[105] within a defined "consistency period."[106] The "stock consistency" rules in §338(f) effectively made the purchaser's decision to elect or not to elect under §338 with respect to a first QSP binding as to subsequent QSPs from one or more target affiliates during the "consistency period."

Since repeal of the *General Utilities* rule in 1986, the §338 election has been less advantageous for most taxpayers and the concern for abuse through selective use of §338 has greatly diminished. New consistency rule regulations under §§338(e) and (f) reflect this diminished concern. Nevertheless, the consistency rules remain in the Code and must be considered by the purchasing corporation, particularly in transactions with a target corporation that is part of a selling group including one or more affiliated corporations. The following sections of this chapter take a closer look at these rules.

b) Asset Consistency Rules: §338(e)

According to the terms of §338(e), the purchasing corporation is deemed to make a §338 election if it acquires any asset of the target or a target affiliate at any time during the consistency period. Imagine, for example, that P made a QSP of T-1 stock from T, the parent and sole shareholder of T-1, and that P decided *not* to make a §338 election. Imagine further that at some time during the consistency period, P also bought a small piece of property directly from T-1.[107] Under the actual language of §338(e), P is *deemed* to have made a §338 election with respect to the T-1 stock purchase because P bought an asset from T-1 during the consistency period. Pursuant to the statute, it appears that the purchase of one small asset from T-1 in this example triggers a "deemed §338 election," requiring T-1 to recognize gain or loss as if it

---

105. I.R.C. §338(e)(1). See §338(e)(2) for some exceptions to the §338(e)(1) rule.

106. The consistency period includes the 12-month acquisition period up to and including the acquisition date. In addition, the consistency period extends back in time to include the 1-year period before the beginning of the 12-month acquisition period and forward to include the 1-year period beginning on the day after the acquisition date. I.R.C. §338(h)(4). Thus, the consistency period may be as long as 3 years.

107. I.R.C. §338(e)(1). The deemed election rule of (e)(1) does not apply, however, to the acquisition of target (or affiliate) assets in the ordinary course of the target (or affiliate) trade or business, §338(e)(2)(A), or to the acquisition of a target (or affiliate) asset taking a transferred basis from the selling target or affiliate, §338(e)(2)(B). The statute granted the Treasury Department regulatory authority to promulgate additional exceptions. I.R.C. §338(e)(2)(D).

had sold all of its assets pursuant to §338(a)(1). The purchased asset triggering the deemed election often was referred to as a "tainted asset."

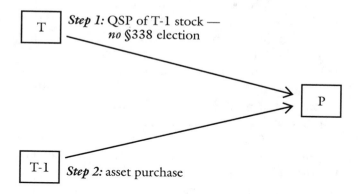

Step 1: QSP of T-1 stock — *no* §338 election

Step 2: asset purchase

Congress was concerned that without this special asset consistency rule, P could pick the T-1 assets for which it wished to receive a cost basis and simply buy those assets directly. At the same time, P could acquire control over the remaining assets through a QSP of T-1 shares *without* making a §338 election. The remaining assets indirectly acquired through this purchase of the T-1 stock would retain the same basis that they had before the transaction. Moreover, since no §338 election was made, T-1 would not lose its identity as "old T-1" and find itself reincarnated as "new T-1," thus enabling P to acquire T-1 with many of its tax attributes still intact.

Strictly applied, §338(e) asset consistency rules created traps for the unwary, and sometimes draconian results. Target selling groups often include several corporations and many assets. Purchasing corporations were at risk that their officers and managers might unwittingly make an asset purchase from some member of the T group, not knowing that even a small asset acquisition could trigger a deemed §338 election with respect to a QSP from T or a T affiliate. Since the deemed election triggered recognition of gain or loss on *all* of the target's assets, this could prove to be a costly mistake. The Treasury Department's initial response to this trap for the unwary was a set of extremely complex temporary regulations.[108] Pursuant to the temporary regulations, unless the government affirmatively imposed the "deemed §338 election," the purchasing corporation was viewed simply as acquiring the "tainted asset" with a carryover basis.[109] In other words, rather than impose

---

108. Temp. Treas. Reg. §1.338(b)-4T, removed and replaced with Treas. Reg. §1.338-8(b)-(d).

109. The technical device used to achieve this result was to deem P to have made an "affirmative action carryover election" under which "the P group's basis in the tainted asset equals the S group's basis in the asset (a carryover basis)." CO-111-90, 1992-1 C.B. 1000, 1001 (description of temporary regulations in preamble to proposed final §338 regulations).

the draconian rule under which the target recognized gain or loss as if it had sold all of its assets, the Treasury Department simply denied P a stepped-up basis with respect to the tainted asset. Also under the temporary regulations, P was able to avoid the possibility of a deemed election altogether by making a "protective carryover basis election."[110] Here again, the purchaser simply took a carryover basis with respect to the tainted asset and the target was not viewed as having sold all of its assets.

The final consistency regulations under §338(e) offer an important lesson on the need to examine regulations and not to rely on statutory language alone. In language directly contradicting the terms of §338(e) and (f), the final regulations state that "no election under section 338 is deemed made or required with respect to target or any target affiliate. Instead, the person acquiring an asset may have a carryover basis in the asset."[111] Under the "carryover basis rule" now provided in Treas. Reg. §1.338-8(d), when a purchasing corporation makes a QSP without a §338 election and also acquires a "tainted asset" during the consistency period, it simply takes the tainted asset with "its adjusted basis immediately before its disposition." In addition to eliminating the §338(e) deemed election, the final §338 regulations further limit the scope of the consistency rules. Although the language of §338(e) itself applies the asset consistency rules to tainted asset acquisitions from any target or target affiliate, the regulations generally apply the consistency rules only when the target is a subsidiary in a consolidated group.[112]

The dramatic relaxation of rules reflected in the final §338 regulations reflects a diminished concern for taxpayer abuse through selective asset acquisition given repeal of the *General Utilities* rule. The remaining concern is more narrowly focused on the combined use of consolidated return reporting provisions with a selective acquisition of assets. This concern is best illustrated in an example offered by the Treasury Department in its preamble to the proposed final §338 regulations. In this example, S and T file consolidated returns. In S's hands, the T stock has a basis of $100 and a fair market value of $200. Assume that T recognizes a $100 taxable gain upon sale of an asset to P and that P shortly thereafter makes a QSP of the T stock from

---

110. Temp. Treas. Reg. §1.338-4T(f), removed and replaced with Treas. Reg. §1.338-8(b)-(d).

111. Treas. Reg. §1.338-8(a)(1). Indeed, the final regulations no longer permit the government even to impose a deemed §338 election. CO-111-90, 1992-1 C.B. 1000, 1001 (preamble to proposed consistency regulations). The final regulation is so inconsistent with the statutory language of §338(e) that it arguably goes beyond the scope of the Treasury Department's authority. *But see* I.R.C. §338(e)(2)(D). In any event, since this is a "taxpayer friendly" regulation, a taxpayer challenge to its constitutionality is unlikely.

112. Treas. Reg. §1.338-8(a)(2). In addition, the regulations will apply when the target is not a member of a consolidated group, but uses a 100% dividends-received deduction "to achieve an effect similar to that available under the investment adjustment provisions of the consolidated return regulations." Treas. Reg. §1.338-8(a)(4).

S for $200. Under the consolidated return regulation "investment adjustment rules," S was entitled to increase the basis in its T stock by the $100 gain recognized by T upon the sale of its asset.[113] As a result, the subsequent sale of the T stock to P resulted in no taxable gain to S. The Treasury Department noted that "[i]f the consistency rules did not apply in such a case, P could acquire assets from T with a stepped-up basis in the assets, and then acquire T stock at no additional tax cost to the S group."[114]

c) Stock Consistency Rules: §338(f)

Under the terms of §338(f), the choice P makes on the first QSP of a selling group of corporations is binding as to subsequent QSPs from the group during the consistency period. Imagine, for example, that T-1 and T-2 are wholly owned T subsidiaries. Assume that P first made a §338 election with respect to the QSP of T-1 stock and later makes a QSP of T-2 stock without a §338 election. Under the actual language of §338(f), P is deemed to have made a §338 election with respect to a QSP of T-2 stock during the consistency period.[115] Similarly, if P had not made a §338 election with respect to the T-1 stock purchase, it would not be permitted to make a §338 election on the subsequent T-2 purchase.[116]

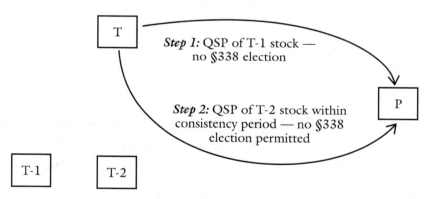

Little is left of the §338(f) stock consistency rules as interpreted by the final §338 regulations, however. First, the final regulations eliminate deemed elections altogether for purposes of both the §338(e) asset consistency rules and the §338(f) stock consistency rules.[117] Thus, if P makes a §338 election with respect to one stock purchase, it can no longer be deemed to make a

---

113. Treas. Reg. §1.1502-32.

114. CO-111-90, 1992-1 C.B. 1000, 1001. Similar concerns arise when S and T do not file a consolidated return, but T pays a $100 dividend eligible for a 100% dividends-received deduction immediately after T's sale of the asset to P. *Id.* at 1002.

115. I.R.C. §338(f)(1).

116. I.R.C. §338(f)(2).

117. Treas. Reg. §1.338-8(a)(2).

§338 election with respect to a subsequent stock purchase within the consistency period. Second, the scope of both sets of consistency rules is limited by the regulations to targets that are subsidiaries in a consolidated selling group and certain other transactions involving an affiliated selling group using the 100% dividends-received deduction.[118] Third, the final regulations specifically limit the stock consistency rules to "cases in which the rules are necessary to prevent avoidance of the asset consistency rules."[119] The only such case described in the final regulations is the sale of stock following a QSP for which a §338(h)(10) election was made.[120]

An example from the final regulations illustrates the remaining selectivity concern in certain cases involving §338(h)(10) elections. Imagine a selling group including S and its wholly owned subsidiary, T. S has a basis of $100 in its T stock. T, in turn, owns all of the stock of second-tier subsidiary T-1, and T-1 owns all of the stock of third-tier subsidiary T-2. T-2's assets have a basis of $100 and a fair market value of $200. Assume that P first purchases all of T-2's stock from T-1 for $200 and makes both a §338 and a §338(h)(10) election with respect to the T-2 stock purchase.

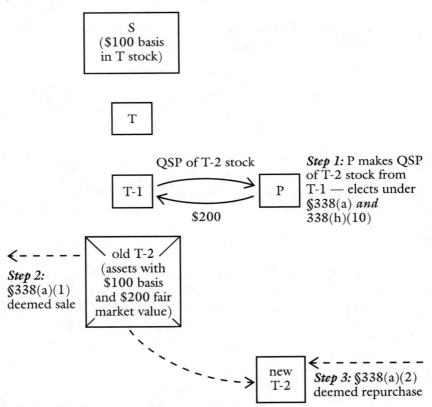

---

118. See discussion in preceding section of this chapter concerning the scope of the asset consistency rules.

119. Treas. Reg. §1.338-8(a)(6).

120. *Id*. See also Treas. Reg. §1.338-8(b)(2).

As a result of the basic §338 election, T-2 is deemed to have sold and repurchased all of its assets, thus recognizing a $100 gain, and P effectively receives a $200 cost basis in the T-2 assets. In addition, pursuant to the §338(h)(10) election, T-1 will report no gain or loss on the sale of the T-2 stock and the selling group will be entitled to include any gain or loss from T-2's deemed sale of assets on its consolidated return. Under the investment adjustment provisions in the consolidated return regulations,[121] the $100 gain recognized upon the deemed sale of T-2 assets will increase S's basis in its T stock to $200. Absent special consistency rules, P might now purchase T stock from S without making a §338 election. If successful, the end result of this selective stock acquisition is a stepped-up basis to P in the T-2 assets and a carryover basis to P in the T-1 assets. Moreover, this result would have been achieved without any taxable gain to either T-1 on the sale of its T-2 stock or to S upon the sale of its T stock.[122] In this limited type of selective §338(h)(10) case, the final regulations treat the (h)(10) acquisition as an asset acquisition subject to the carryover basis rule incorporated into the asset consistency provisions of the regulations. Thus, P is denied a stepped-up basis in the T-2 assets and these assets will retain the same basis that T-2 had immediately before P's QSP of T-2.[123]

Creative Acquisition Strategies

Eliminating One Layer of the Corporate Tax

At least historically, one important component of taxable acquisitions tax planning was to devise a way to transfer control of corporate assets without imposing a *double* tax on the target corporation and its shareholders. Before congressional repeal of the *General Utilities* doctrine, corporations could distribute assets to their shareholders without recognizing corporate level gain or loss with respect to the distributed assets.[124] Thus, a corporation could arrange first to distribute assets to the shareholders and then to have the shareholders sell the recently distributed assets to the purchaser. If successful, this technique permitted an asset acquisition with a cost basis in the assets to the buyer without a corporate level tax to the selling corporation; in other words, an asset acquisition without the full weight of the corporate "double tax." Congress even extended this opportunity for a "single tax"

---

121. Treas. Reg. §1.1502-32.

122. As an additional bonus, under §338(h)(10), T-2's gain from the deemed asset sale would be included on the S group consolidated return.

123. See Treas. Reg. §1.338-8(e)(2), ex. 2.

124. Discussions of the old *General Utilities* nonrecognition rules appear in Chapter 5 (in the context of nonliquidating distributions) and Chapter 8 (in the context of liquidating distributions).

acquisition of assets by permitting corporations themselves to sell their assets to a purchaser without recognizing corporate level tax under *old* §337 as long as the sale was pursuant to a "plan of liquidation" and certain other conditions were met.[125] For a time, the "single tax" asset acquisition technique was successful in some cases and unsuccessful in others. Cases that were unsuccessful usually involved a court finding under the step-transaction doctrine that the distribution and the subsequent asset sale by the shareholders should be viewed as a single, integrated transaction in which the corporation really sold assets directly to the purchaser, using the shareholders as a "conduit" for the sale.

Since repeal of the *General Utilities* rule, corporate distributions of assets to shareholders generally trigger recognition of gain or loss to the distributing corporation. Consequently, it has become quite difficult to structure a taxable asset acquisition without a "double tax."[126] On the other hand, creative tax planners continue to seek out new routes to the "single-tax promised land." The playing field in this regard seems to be taking advantage of the one distribution transaction for which the *General Utilities* rule was *not* repealed—distributions in liquidation of a subsidiary under §337. Using the subsidiary liquidation rules along with provisions found in the complex consolidated return regulations, creative tax acquisitions planners have been able to structure unusual acquisition transactions in which the corporate level tax is avoided. As each of these transactions has come to the government's attention, the Treasury Department or Congress have responded with changes to the Code or its regulations. Several of these "mirror" and related transactions were described earlier and will not be revisited here.[127]

Another technique for eliminating or substantially reducing the corporate level tax to the purchasing corporation in corporate acquisitions is the heavy use of debt or leveraging by the purchasing corporation. In a leveraged buy-out (LBO), the purchasing corporation incurs substantial corporate interest expense for the acquisition and hopes to use interest deductions to shelter income. Here again, Congress has responded with statutory provisions that reduce opportunities for using interest deductions to eliminate or substantially reduce the corporate level tax.[128]

The brief description just provided should be sufficient to illustrate the limits on opportunities to eliminate the *corporate* level tax in connection with

---

125. See Chapter 8 for discussion of *old* §337 and its extension of *General Utilities* nonrecognition to corporate sales of assets in complete liquidation.

126. Corporate level gain on target assets can be deferred, but not eliminated entirely, through a stock acquisition. See earlier discussion in this chapter on the choice between stock and asset purchases.

127. See discussion of "mirror" and "son of mirror" transactions in Chapter 9 on Liquidation of Subsidiaries.

128. See, e.g., I.R.C. §279.

corporate acquisitions of control. Creative techniques for eliminating the *shareholder* level tax in connection with corporate acquisitions of control also are available, but subject to legal and practical limitations as well. One technique has been for the selling corporation to transfer assets to the purchasing corporation in an asset sale taxable to the corporation. Instead of liquidating, the selling corporation may remain alive as a "shell" and its shareholders will receive a stepped-up basis upon death under §1014. If successful, this transaction results in a transfer of assets to the purchasing corporation without the imposition of a shareholder level tax. This technique is limited under the Internal Revenue Code by the personal holding company and accumulated earnings tax rules. Moreover, as a practical matter, it is limited to circumstances involving individual shareholders, who are both eligible for the §1014 step-up in basis and old enough to make this technique viable.

EXAMPLES

Each of the following questions will use the same terminology. The purchasing corporation will be P. The target corporation will be T. If a §338 election is made, the target will be old T for purposes of the deemed sale of assets and new T for purposes of the deemed repurchase of assets under §338(a). Affiliated corporations of P or T will be referred to as P-1 or T-1 and so on.

Basic Asset Acquisition

1a. Lorax, Inc. (T) is a publisher of children's books and is solely owned by Dr. Weiss. Dr. Weiss's basis in the Lorax shares is $2500. Immediately before the asset acquisition described below, T had the following assets:

	basis	fair market value
portfolio of securities	100	500
inventory (books)	400	500
printing equipment	0	1000
building	4000	3000
land	2000	5000
goodwill	0	?

For the purposes of this problem, assume that the securities were readily marketable. Arthur Books, Inc. (P) acquired all of T's assets, except the old and obsolete printing equipment, for a total cash purchase price of $9500. Shortly thereafter, T liquidates, distributing the cash and the unwanted equipment to Dr. Weiss in complete liquidation. What are the tax consequences of this acquisition to Lorax, Dr. Weiss, and Arthur Books?

Adding a Liability Twist

1b. How would your answer to 1a change if the building had been subject to a $500 mortgage, assumed by P as part of the acquisition transaction?

Bargain Sale

1c. How would your answer to 1a change if the total purchase price for the desired assets was only $8000?

Basic §338 Stock Acquisition

2a. P is a small-town newspaper publisher looking for a new printing plant. P discovers that T has just the plant it's looking for. T recently closed its newspaper operation and the business no longer has any goodwill or going concern value. T's basis in the plant is $20,000. On January 1, P acquired 50% of the T stock for $300,000 in cash. The fair market value of the plant on January 1 was $400,000. T's other assets at that time had a basis of $50,000 and a fair market value of $200,000. On July 1, P acquired the remaining 50% of the T stock for $300,000 in cash. The value of T's assets had not changed between January 1 and July 1. What are the tax consequences to P, T and the T shareholders if P makes no §338 election? How would these tax consequences be different if P makes a §338 election?

2b. How would your answer to 2a change if P acquired the remaining 50% in February of the following year?

Adding Minority Shareholders

2c. How would your answer to 2a change if P had acquired the first 50% of T stock on January 1 for $300,000, but only 30% of the T stock on July 1 for $180,000 cash? Assume that P is unable to acquire any more T shares.

Old and Cold Complications

2d. How would your answer to 2a change if P purchased 20% of T on January 1 for $100,000 cash and the remaining 80% on February 1 of the following year for $480,000 cash?

Affiliated Corporations: §338(h)(10) Elections

3a. Bigco owns all of the stock in subsidiary, T. Its basis in the T shares is $400,000 (outside basis). Bigco and T file consolidated returns. T's assets have a basis of $400,000 (inside basis) and a fair market value of $1 million. Bigco has an unused $700,000 net operating loss from last year. P acquires all of the T stock from Bigco for $1 million cash in a QSP and makes a general §338 election. What are the tax consequences to Bigco, T, and P?

3b. What would the tax consequences be if P and the selling group also made a joint §338(h)(10) election?

Trouble With Consistency

4a. T is a parent corporation with subsidiaries, T-1, T-2, and T-3. T-1 owns depreciable equipment with a basis of $10,000 and a fair market value of $60,000. T-2 owns only one piece of highly appreciated property with a basis of $50,000 and a fair market value of $450,000. T-3 owns a large inventory of paper supplies that it sells to newspaper publishers, with a basis of $15,000. P acquires the depreciable equipment for $60,000 cash directly from T-1 on January 1. On July 1, P acquires 100% of the T-2 stock from T for $450,000 and chooses *not* to make a §338 election. What are the tax consequences to P and the T group?

4b. Assume instead that P acquires 100% of the stock of both T-1 and T-2 on July 1. P chooses *not* to make a §338 election. On January 1 of the following year, P acquires paper supplies from T-3. What are the tax consequences to P and the T group?

4c. Assume instead that P acquired 100% of the stock of T-1 on January 1 and filed a timely and proper §338 election. On July 1, P acquired 100% of the T-2 stock and does not wish to make a §338 election. What are the tax consequences to P and the T group?

EXPLANATIONS

1a. The seller, Lorax (T) will be required to report gain or loss on each asset sold pursuant to §§61(a)(3) and 1001. To determine the amount of gain or loss on each asset, the $9500 purchase price must be allocated in accordance with regulations under §1060. The first step in this residual method allocation process is to identify the assets in each Class. No Class I assets such as cash or general deposit bank accounts were included in the sale. The only Class II asset is the portfolio of securities, with a fair market value of $500. No Class III assets were included in the sale. The inventory, with a fair market value of $500, is considered a Class IV asset under the new §§338 and 1060 regulations. The building and land are Class V assets, with an overall fair market value of $8000. T will begin with the $9500 purchase price, allocating fair market value (but no more) to the Class II asset. Thus, the allocation to the stock portfolio is $500, resulting in a $400 taxable gain to T (amount realized of $500 less $100 basis). Since this is an investment portfolio, the gain presumably will be capital gain. Next, T will allocate the fair market value of $500 to inventory, resulting in a $100 gain (amount realized of $500 less $400 basis), presumably ordinary income.

Notice that the remaining $8500 of the purchase price exceeds the total fair market value of the Class V assets. Since no asset can be allocated more than its fair market value, each of the Class III assets simply receives an allocation equal to its fair market value, resulting in the following gains to T:

building: $3000 amount realized less $4000 basis = ($1000) loss (ordinary loss)

land: $5000 amount realized less $2000 basis = $3000 gain (probably capital gain)

After allocating a total of $8000 to Class V assets, a surplus of $500 remains. This surplus is allocated to goodwill. Assuming a zero basis in the goodwill, T will report a $500 capital gain.

Upon liquidation, Lorax distributed $9500 cash plus the unwanted printing equipment worth $1000. Lorax will report a gain of $1000 upon this liquidating distribution pursuant to §336.[129] Dr. Weiss received $9500 in cash, plus printing equipment valued at $1000, for a total liquidating distribution of $10,500. Since his basis in the Lorax shares is $2500, he will report an $8000 capital gain ($10,500 less $2,500) from the sale of his shares pursuant to $331.

Arthur Books (P) is entitled to a cost basis in the assets purchased. The same allocations just determined with respect to T also will apply for P. Thus, P's acquired assets have the following §1012 cost basis:

stock portfolio:	$500	
inventory:	$500	
building:	$3000	
land:	$5000	
goodwill:	$500	
TOTAL	$9500	purchase price

P will use its basis of $3000 for purposes of computing depreciation allowances on the building and will be entitled to amortize the $500 expense for goodwill over 15 years under §197.

1b. Under the §1060 regulations, the purchaser's "consideration" to be allocated among the purchased assets is the "cost of purchasing the assets . . . that is properly taken into account in basis," and the seller's "consideration" to be allocated among the assets sold is the seller's "amount realized" under §1001(b).[130] Under general tax principles, the purchaser's "cost" includes liabilities or mortgages assumed and the seller's amount realized also

---

129. This gain will probably be included as ordinary income under the §1245 recapture provisions.

130. Treas. Reg. §1.1060-1T(c)(1).

includes liabilities or mortgages from which the seller is relieved. Thus, P's assumption of T's $500 mortgage on the building is considered additional consideration received for the assets, increasing the total purchase price to be allocated to $10,000. Notice that by agreeing to assume the $500 mortgage on the building, P is paying $500 *more* than it paid in Example 1a for the same assets. Since the mortgage relates to the building, P arguably has paid $500 more than the building's $3000 alleged fair market value. Why would the buyer do this? Assessing fair market value is not an exact science. Perhaps the buyer is willing to speculate on property it expects to rapidly increase in value, or perhaps the buyer believes that the current fair market value actually *is* $3500. On the other hand, the buyer may believe that the overall assets as a package are worth $500 more.

As before, since there are no Class I assets, the purchase price first will be allocated to the Class II stock portfolio in the amount of $500, again resulting in a $400 taxable capital gain to T from the sale of investment stock. Next, $500 will be allocated to the Class IV inventory, again resulting in $100 of ordinary income. The remaining $9000 will be allocated to Class V assets, but no allocation shall exceed the asset's fair market value. Thus, the land again will receive a fair market value allocation of $5000, resulting in a $3000 capital gain from the sale of land.

What about the building? Ordinarily, the amount realized from the sale of an asset subject to a mortgage includes the mortgage amount in the amount realized. Thus, one would expect an allocation of $3500 to the building, resulting in a loss of $500. Notice, however, that fair market value is defined as "*gross* fair market value (i.e., fair market value determined without regard to mortgages, liens, pledges, or other liabilities)."[131] Also, §1060 permits an allocation of *no more than* the fair market value of $3000. Consequently, despite P's assumption of a $500 mortgage on the building, T's loss from the sale of the building is $1000.[132]

After the above allocation of $500 to Class II assets, $500 to Class IV assets, and $8000 to Class V assets, the $1000 surplus remaining is allocated to goodwill, resulting in a taxable capital gain to T from the sale of goodwill. In the end, the answers to 1b are the same as 1a, with the exception of the additional $500 allocation to goodwill.

---

131. Treas. Reg. §1.338-6T(a)(2). Notice that the §1060 regulations now direct that the allocation of consideration and basis be made under the §338 allocation regulations, substituting the term "consideration" for ADSP and AGUB. Treas. Reg. §1.1060-1T(c)(2). The only exception to this use of *gross* fair market value under the regulations is when a *nonrecourse* debt exceeds the fair market value of the property. In such cases "the fair market value of any property . . . shall be treated as not less than the amount of such indebtedness." Treas. Reg. §1.338-6T(a)(2).

132. Since T has a *loss* on the building, the gross fair market value rule works to its advantage by increasing the permissible loss. Conversely, the gross fair market value rule would have worked to T's disadvantage if there had been a gain on the property.

Notice that the additional "consideration" provided to T through P's assumption of T's mortgage apparently is allocated to the sale of goodwill rather than the building. This may seem an odd result, allocating too much to goodwill and too little to the building. Given that goodwill now is amortizable under §197 over a shorter period than the ACRS recovery period for the building under §167, P may prefer this outcome. If P paid the additional $500 because it believed the overall package of assets was worth $500 more, an allocation of the excess purchase price to goodwill makes sense. On the other hand, the excess $500 should be allocated to the building if the building is undervalued and its *true* fair market value is $3500. Absent some evidence that the building, in fact, was undervalued, the better default rule would seem to be to allocate any excess purchase price to goodwill.

The tax consequencies to Lorax and shareholder Weiss upon liquidation will be the same as it was in Example 1a.

1c. Since the overall value of the desired assets is $9000, P's acquisition for $8000 is a below-market or "bargain purchase." Under the §1060 regulations, $500 still will be allocated to the Class II stock portfolio and $500 to the Class IV inventory. The remaining $7000 of the purchase price will be allocated to Class V assets in proportion to their fair market value. Since only $7000 in purchase price remains to be allocated, and the overall fair market value of the Class V assets transferred is $8000, the allocation to each Class V asset will be less than its full fair market value. To allocate the remainder, T must determine the proportionate fair market value of each Class V asset:

		allocated basis
building:	$3000/$8000 = .38 × $7000 =	$2660
land:	$5000/$8000 = .62 × $7000 =	$4340
TOTAL ALLOCATED TO CLASS V		$7000

Nothing remains to be allocated to goodwill. This allocation may not reflect the economics of the transaction. Perhaps T was anxious to sell quickly and agreed to sell the entire package, including goodwill, at a discounted price rather than wait for a better offer. If so, it would seem that some portion of the purchase price should be allocable to goodwill.

2a. Whether or not P makes a §338 election, P will have an overall cost basis in the T shares of $600,000. Also, whether or not P makes an election, the T shareholders will report gain or loss on the sale of their T shares.

If P chooses not to make the §338 election, T simply will be a wholly owned subsidiary of P and will retain its historical basis of $20,000 in the plant and $50,000 in the other assets. P may continue T as a subsidiary or it may choose to liquidate T and take direct control over the assets. If T is liquidated, T will report no gain from the distribution pursuant to §337 and P will similarly report no gain under §332. P will take T's assets with the same basis they had in T's hands. In other words, P will not be entitled to a step-up in basis to fair market value.

On the other hand, if P makes a §338 election, this will trigger a deemed sale by T of all of its assets at the close of the acquisition date. The acquisition date in this case is July 1, the first day on which P had acquired the 80% interest necessary to make this a QSP. Under the §338 regulations, the price at which T is deemed to sell its assets is the aggregate deemed sales price (ADSP) of the acquisition. This is the grossed-up amount realized on the sale to P of P's recently purchased T stock. The overall ADSP must be allocated to the assets deemed to be sold according to allocation regulations in Treas. Reg. §1.338-6T. Assuming that all of T's assets are Class V assets and included no goodwill or going concern value, the purchase price of $600,000 simply is allocated to each asset in proportion to its fair market value as of the acquisition date. Since the fair market value of the plant on July 1 still was $400,000 and T's basis was $20,000, T will report a gain of $380,000 from the deemed sale of the plant. Since the fair market value of the other assets on July 1 was $200,000 and the basis $50,000, T will report a $150,000 gain from the sale of its other assets. T will report this deemed sale gain on "the final return of old target filed for old target's taxable year that ends at the close of the acquisition date." Treas. Reg. §1.338-10T(a)(1).

On July 2, the day after the acquisition date, new T will be deemed to repurchase all of the assets that it sold in the deemed sale on July 1. The purchase price for these assets will be the grossed-up basis of P's recently purchased stock. Since recently purchased stock under §338(b)(6)(A) includes any T stock held by P on the acquisition date that was acquired within the 12-month acquisition period, *all* of P's stock is recently purchased. The grossed-up basis in this case simply is the cost basis of P's stock in T, $600,000, multiplied by 100/100 or $600,000. Thus, as a result of the deemed repurchase, new T will have a basis of $600,000 in its assets. According to the §338 regulations, this overall basis will be allocated among T's assets under the same residual method used for purposes of measuring T's gain on the deemed asset sale. Thus, the plant will receive a $400,000 basis and the other assets will receive a $200,000 basis. The effect of the deemed sale and repurchase is to give P a step-up in the basis of T's assets. To get this step-up, however, T is required to report gain on the deemed sale. P may or may not choose to liquidate T at this point.

2b. If P acquired the first 50% of its T stock on January 1 and the remaining 50% in February of the following year, P would not be eligible to make a §338 election since P has not made a QSP. A QSP is limited under §338(d)(3) to a transaction or series of transactions in which stock meeting the 80% ownership tests is acquired during a 12-month acquisition period. The second purchase was more than 12 months after the first purchase and, therefore, fails this definition. As a result, T simply will be a subsidiary of P and retain the T assets with their historical bases. T will not be required to report any gain or loss. As before, the selling T shareholders will report gain or loss on the sale of stock.

2c. Even though P was unable to acquire 100% of T, P has still made a QSP since it has acquired the necessary 80% during a 12-month acquisition period. The remaining 20% of the shares are held by minority shareholders. If P makes a §338 election, T still will be deemed to have sold all of its assets on the close of the acquisition date, which is still July 1. Thus, T will still report a gain of $380,000 on the plant and a gain of $150,000 on its other assets. On July 2, new T will be deemed to repurchase all of its assets. The computation of the purchase price will change a bit here, however. The purchase price again will start with P's basis for the recently purchased stock. Since all of P's stock in T was recently purchased, all of it will be considered here. P's overall basis in its T stock is now $480,000. This cost basis will be multiplied by 100/80 (1.25) as provided in §338(b)(4). Recall that the numerator is 100% minus the nonrecently purchased stock, in this case zero. The denominator is the percentage of recently purchased stock, in this case the full 80% purchased. The result is an overall basis of $600,000 for all of T's assets. Again, this basis must be allocated among T's assets. Notice that P gets the same basis in the assets whether it acquires 100% of the stock, as in example 1a, or only 80% of the stock, as in this variation. In other words, the effect of the "grossed-up basis" computation is to provide a full step-up in basis with regard to *all* of T's assets. Why? Even though P acquired only an 80% interest in T, T still was treated as if it sold *all* of its assets in the §338(a)(1) deemed sale. Since T was taxed as if it had sold all of its assets, P should get a cost basis as if it had acquired all of T's assets. The §338(b) basis formula effectively achieves this result by "grossing-up" the basis to take the additional 20% into account. As before, the selling T shareholders will report gain or loss on the sale of stock.

2d. Although the second purchase was more than 12 months after the first, it was a purchase of 80%. This second purchase alone is a QSP. The first 20% will be considered nonrecently purchased or old and cold stock. If P makes a §338 election, T again will be deemed to sell all of its assets as of the acquisition date, which is now February 1 of year two. The gain reported by old T will be the ADSP as of that date less T's basis in the assets. On the day following the acquisition date, new T will be deemed to repurchase the assets. The purchase price now will include the grossed-up basis of the 80% recently purchased stock plus the basis of the 20% nonrecently purchased stock. For the first computation, P will start with its cost basis of $480,000 and multiply it by 80/80 leaving a grossed-up basis of $480,000. To this amount, P will add the basis for the nonrecently purchased shares of $100,000. Thus, the overall basis in new T's assets will be $580,000. Again, this amount will need to be allocated among T's assets in accordance with Treas. Reg. §1.338-6T.

     Notice here that each asset is *not* entitled to a full step-up in basis. Consequently, the "cost" basis for each asset will be less than the fair market value of each asset. This is because the "old and cold" stock that P holds was not acquired as part of the QSP and no gain was taxed with respect to the portion of appreciation reflected in these "old and cold" shares. If P wishes to get a full stepped-up basis, P must make a secondary election under §338(b)(3) and recognize gain as if it had sold the "old and cold" stock.

As before, the selling T shareholders will report gain or loss on the sale of stock.

3a. Bigco will report a taxable gain of $600,000 on its sale of T stock under §§61(a)(3) and 1001. Bigco can use $600,000 of its NOL to offset its taxable gain on the stock sale. P's §338 election will trigger a deemed sale by old T of all of old T's assets, resulting in another $600,000 taxable gain to T under §338(a)(1). Bigco's remaining $100,000 NOL *cannot* be used to offset T's gain on the deemed sale, since §338(h)(9) provides that T is not considered a member of the selling affiliated group for purposes of the deemed sale. The deemed repurchase of assets by new T under §338(a)(2) will result in a $1 million basis in new T's assets. As the new parent of T, P effectively receives a step-up in the basis in T's assets.

3b. If P and the selling group also make a joint (h)(10) election, Bigco will *not* report any taxable gain on the sale of T stock. P's §338 election still will trigger a deemed sale by old T, resulting in a $600,000 gain. However, T will be able to use affiliate Bigco's NOL to fully offset this gain, since §338(h)(10) provides that T *shall* be considered a member of the selling consolidated group with respect to the deemed sale. Old T is deemed to be liquidated under §338 while it was a member of the selling affiliated group. Treas. Reg. §1.338(h)(10)-1T(d)(4). As a result, Bigco may be entitled to retain certain T tax attributes that otherwise would have been lost. P still will get the new T assets with a $1 million basis under §338(a)(2). Comparing the two answers to this question should make it clear that the §338(h)(10) election will be rather attractive in many cases involving sales of stock in an affiliated group.

4a. The purchase of T-2 stock by P is a QSP. Under the *statutory* asset consistency rules in §338(e), P was deemed to have made a §338 election on the T-2 stock purchase since P purchased assets from a target affiliate during the 12-month acquisition period. As a result, T-2 was deemed to have sold its one asset under §338(a)(1), resulting in a $400,000 taxable gain ($450,000 amount realized less $50,000 basis).[133] The price for the §338(a)(2) deemed repurchase will be P's grossed-up basis in its T-2 stock ($450,000), leaving P with a stepped-up (cost) basis of $450,000 in the acquired asset.[134] P may have deliberately designed these two purchases in

---

133. The ADSP for the T-2 stock is $450,000. Since T-2 had only one asset, however, no allocation will be necessary. The entire amount is attributed to the sale of T-2's sole asset.

134. All of P's stock in T-2 is recently purchased. Thus, under §338(b)(4), the grossed-up basis is P's $450,000 cost multiplied by 100/100, or $450,000. Again, since T-2 has only one asset, the entire price is allocated to the one asset.

order to acquire depreciable assets from the target group with a cost basis of $60,000 for depreciation purposes while acquiring T-2's asset from the target group without T-2 having to recognize gain on appreciation. The §338(e) statutory consistency rules prevented this result by permitting P to have the $60,000 cost basis in the depreciable assets, but deeming a §338 purchase of T-2 stock, resulting in a substantial taxable gain to T-2. Given the complexity of the §338 rules, P may not have deliberately designed this transaction, but instead may have unwittingly fallen into a trap with rather harsh results.

Under the new consistency rules provided in Treas. Reg. §1.338-8(d), no deemed §338 election with respect to T-2 will occur. In fact, the consistency rules will not apply at all unless T-2 is part of a consolidated group filing a consolidated return and T-1's gain from the sale of the depreciable assets is reflected in T's basis in its T-2 stock under the investment adjustment provisions of the consolidated return rules. Moreover, even if the consistency rules *do* apply, P simply will be denied the cost basis in the depreciable asset acquired from T-1, instead acquiring a carryover basis of $10,000. T-2 would not be required to report any taxable gain.

4b. Here P has made QSPs of both T-1 and T-2 stock. The issue is whether the asset purchase from T-3, an affiliated corporation, triggers a deemed §338 election. If the sale of paper supplies by T-3 was a sale in the ordinary course of its trade or business, this particular purchase should not trigger a deemed §338 election. I.R.C. §338(e)(2)(A). In any event, under the new regulatory consistency rules, there would be no deemed election and the "tainted" assets (paper supplies) will retain their historic basis of $15,000.

4c. P is now potentially in trouble with the stock consistency rules. Since P made an election with respect to one affiliated corporation during the consistency period, the statute deems P to have made a similar election with respect to the second qualified purchase during the consistency period under the express statutory provisions in §338 (f). Under the new consistency regulations, however, there is *no* deemed election. The statute and regulations here are in direct conflict.

SUBPART B

Tax-Free Reorganizations

11

Introduction to Basic Corporate Reorganization Principles

Introduction

One who has not studied corporate taxation may be surprised to discover that the term "reorganization" for purposes of Subchapter C does not have the same meaning that it might have in the ordinary business setting. A corporation might restructure departments, reassign or redefine personnel responsibilities, or modify or change business operations. Tax consequences do not ordinarily flow from this kind of business change. Corporations also "reorganize" in bankruptcy to restructure debt and to satisfy creditors. Although there are certainly tax consequences to this restructuring in bankruptcy, a "reorganization in bankruptcy" is different from a corporate "reorganization" for purposes of Subchapter C of the Internal Revenue Code.

In the corporate tax context of Subchapter C, the term "reorganization" is a statutory term of art. Rather than provide a general definition, Congress attempted to provide precise definitions for the term "reorganization" in §368(a)(1) with an exclusive list of seven specific types of transactions that will be considered "reorganizations." Subparagraphs (A) through (G) of §368(a)(1) each provide a description of a particular reorganization transaction. Unless a transaction fits within one of the seven categories listed in subparagraphs (A) through (G), it simply is not a corporate reorganization.

As a shorthand, most tax lawyers, corporate taxpayers, and academics study-ing Subchapter C identify reorganizations by referring to the appropriate subparagraph. Thus, a Type A reorganization simply is a reorganization that fits within the §368(a)(1)(A) definition, a Type B reorganization is a reor-ganization that fits within the §368(a)(1)(B) definition, and so on.

At the outset, it is important to notice that §368(a) merely provides a definition of "reorganization." The definitional section says nothing of the tax consequences that flow from classification of a transaction as a corporate reorganization. In general, reorganization exchanges are eligible for nonrec-ognition treatment and the basis of assets or stock received in the nonrecog-nition exchange will be a substituted, rather than a cost, basis.[1] The reorganization definition covers several very different types of transactions, the details of which will be considered in the chapters that follow. After a brief description of the different types of transactions that fall within the "reorganization" umbrella, this introduction to general reorganization prin-ciples offers an overview and history of tax-free reorganizations and a discus-sion of the rules and policy considerations that the different types of reorganizations share in common.

Categories of Reorganization

Acquisitive Reorganizations

Although the §368(a)(1) reorganization definition contains seven distinct transactions, these distinct transactions fit loosely into three general catego-ries. The first general category is the acquisitive reorganization. In an acquisi-tive reorganization, the purchasing or acquiring corporation acquires control over or combines with another corporation, usually referred to as the target corporation.[2] This is not to suggest that every corporate acquisition of control over another corporation will be a tax-free reorganization. The critical distinction between a tax-free acquisition of control and a taxable acquisition of control is the consideration used by the purchasing corporation. In a tax-free acquisition, the seller typically receives compensation in the form of stock of the acquiring corporation or an affiliated corporation, thus retaining

---

1. The specific tax consequences of reorganization exchanges are outlined at the end of this introductory chapter and are considered in more detail in subsequent chapters.

2. For purposes of §368(a), control generally is defined to mean "the ownership of stock possessing at least 80 percent of the total combined voting power of all classes of stock entitled to vote and at least 80 percent of the total number of shares of all classes of stock of the corporation." I.R.C. §368(c). For further discussion of this control test, see Chapter 4.

a proprietary interest in the reorganized or restructured corporate enterprise.[3] In contrast, sellers in a taxable acquisition typically receive cash or other fairly liquid assets in exchange for stock, thus ending their investment relationship with the corporation.[4] Subparagraphs (A) through (C) of §368(a)(1) generally cover this type of acquisitive reorganization.[5] A Type A reorganization is a "statutory merger or consolidation."[6] In a Type B reorganization, the acquiring or purchasing corporation uses voting stock to acquire a controlling interest in the *stock* of another corporation.[7] This is referred to as a "stock for stock" acquisition. In contrast, a Type C reorganization is a "stock for assets" acquisition in which one corporation uses voting stock to acquire substantially all of the *assets* of another corporation.[8]

Divisive Reorganizations

In contrast to the acquisitive reorganization in which two or more corporations are combined, the second major category of reorganizations defined by §368(a)(1) is the divisive reorganization in which one corporation is divided into two or more corporate enterprises in a spin-off, split-off or some other form of division. Most of these transactions are accomplished using §368(a)(1)(D). In a Type D reorganization, one corporation transfers all or part of its assets to another corporation. Immediately after the asset transfer, the new corporation must be controlled by the transferring corporation itself, shareholders of the transferring corporation, or some combination of the two.[9] Notice that the new corporation essentially must be controlled by the shareholders of the transferring corporation. Where there once was only one corporation, now there will be two or more corporations controlled by shareholders of the original corporation.

---

3. A more detailed discussion of the continuity of proprietary interest requirement follows in this introductory chapter and in subsequent chapters regarding specific types of reorganization transactions.

4. Taxable acquisitions were covered in Chapter 10.

5. Although §368(a)(1)(D) reorganizations generally are thought of as "divisive," some acquisitive reorganization transactions use the Type D reorganization definition.

6. I.R.C. §368(a)(1)(A).

7. I.R.C. §368(a)(1)(B).

8. I.R.C. §368(a)(1)(C).

9. I.R.C. §368(a)(1)(D). An additional requirement for a Type D reorganization is that stock or securities of the new corporation must be distributed pursuant to §§354, 355, or 356. Further discussion of the details of divisive reorganizations appears in Chapter 13. A divisive reorganization also can be accomplished through a simple distribution of stock in a subsidiary without using the Type D reorganization definition.

Internal Restructuring

The third general category of reorganizations is internal restructuring. This last category of reorganizations generally is the simplest in the sense that it involves only one corporation that is engaged in restructuring itself. Included here are Type E and F reorganizations.[10] A Type E reorganization is a "recapitalization" in which the bondholders or shareholders of one corporation exchange their bond or stock interests for a different kind of equity interest in the same corporate enterprise.[11] A Type F reorganization involves a "mere change in identity, form, or place of organization of one corporation, however effected."[12]

Overview and History: Doctrine Underlying Tax-Free Reorganizations

The most frequently cited policy reason for the tax-free reorganization rules is that the exchange represents a "mere change in form" of the shareholders' interest in the business enterprise. The participants to a reorganization arguably have not "cashed out" on their investment; rather they have substituted one investment in the business enterprise for a similar investment in the same or related business enterprise. Since the immediate transaction effects only the "readjustment of continuing interest in property under modified corporate forms," recognition of gain or loss is deferred.[13] When shareholders sell their stock in a target corporation for cash or notes from the purchasing corporation, immediate recognition of the shareholders' gain or loss is appropriate. On the other hand, when shareholders exchange their stock in a target corporation entirely for stock of the purchasing corporation, the transaction can be viewed as a mere change in form.

Another explanation for tax-free treatment is the potential hardship imposed upon those required to pay tax when they receive property in a reorganization, usually stock, and may not have the cash with which to pay a heavy tax. This reasoning should sound familiar — it is quite similar to the policy behind the tax-free incorporation rules of §351.[14] The hardship argu-

---

10. A Type G reorganization, the last of the §368(a)(1) reorganization definitions, covers certain internal reorganization of one corporation in the bankruptcy setting. I.R.C. §368(a)(1)(G).

11. I.R.C. §368(a)(1)(E); Treas. Reg. §1.368-2(e).

12. I.R.C. §368(a)(1)(F).

13. Southwest Natural Gas Co. v. Comm'r, 189 F.2d 332, 334 (5th Cir. 1951). This language is now incorporated into the Treasury Department regulations. See Treas. Reg. §1.368-1(b).

14. For a detailed discussion of incorporation transactions, see Chapter 4.

ment is even stronger in the context of a reorganization involving minority shareholders who are effectively forced to involuntarily exchange their shares in the target corporation. In fact, both the §351 incorporation rules and the reorganization rules appear in Part III of Subchapter C, entitled "Corporate Organizations and Reorganizations." The substituted basis rules in §§358 and 362 that apply to corporate reorganizations are the same basis rules that apply to §351 transactions.

As discussed in Chapter 4 on §351 transactions, the "mere change in form" or "continuity of investment" rationale appears sensible in theory. In practice, however, the nonrecognition rules in some cases sweep so broadly as to include transactions that most would not regard as "mere changes in form" and in other cases to exclude transactions that most would regard as "mere changes in form."

Judicial Glosses on the Statute

In General

Simply fitting within one of the apparently precise definitions in §368(a)(1) will not be enough to classify a transaction as a tax-free reorganization. Perhaps more than in any other area of Subchapter C, the courts have added, and Treasury Department regulations confirm, additional requirements necessary to achieve "reorganization" status. The regulations now summarize law created over the years by court decisions that focused on the purpose and scope of the reorganization provisions:

> The purpose of the reorganization provisions of the Code is to except from the general rule certain specifically described exchanges incident to such readjustments of corporate structures made in one of the particular ways specified in the Code, *as are required by business exigencies and which effect only a readjustment of continuing interest in property under modified corporate forms.* Requisite to a reorganization under the Code are a continuity of the business enterprise under the modified corporate form as described in paragraph (d) of this section, and . . . a continuity of interest as described in paragraph (e) of this section.[15]

This regulatory provision incorporates three requirements governing all of the §368(a)(1) corporate reorganization definitions that are not otherwise explicitly included in the statutory language: 1) continuity of proprietary or

---

15. Treas. Reg. §1.368-1(b) (emphasis added). Recently finalized amendments to the regulation added paragraph (e), which provides details regarding the continuity of shareholder interest requirement and substantially modifies the Treasury Department's position on continuity of interest. The new regulatory provisions are discussed later in this chapter.

investment interest; 2) continuity of the business enterprise; and 3) business purpose.

Continuity of Proprietary Interest

a) Background and History

Continuity of proprietary interest is central to the tax-free reorganization provisions. Taxpayers are entitled to nonrecognition treatment on a reorganization exchange since they are viewed as continuing their investment in the old, albeit now modified, corporate enterprise. If investors remain invested in the modified corporate enterprise, the logic is that the transaction should not trigger immediate recognition of gain or loss. The continuity of proprietary interest test evolved from court opinions interpreting an early version of the statutory reorganization provisions. Several of the modern reorganization definitions in §368(a)(1) now include a statutorily built-in continuity of investment requirement, making the application of a the judicially developed "continuity of proprietary interest" test unnecessary. In these cases, the type and amount of proprietary interest that the transferor must receive to be eligible for tax-free nonrecognition treatment is defined by the statute itself. Under §368(a)(1)(B), for example, the exchange must be *solely* for all or part of the purchasing corporation's voting stock or solely for all or part of the voting stock of the purchasing company's parent corporation. In other words *all* of the consideration paid to the sellers must be in the form of voting stock; no cash consideration is permitted. The language of §368(a)(1)(C) is similar, but subsequent paragraphs provide more flexibility with regard to the required proprietary interest in the case of Type C reorganizations.[16]

Recently finalized Treasury Department regulations summarize and clarify the continuity requirement, stating:

> The purpose of the continuity of interest requirement is to prevent transactions that resemble sales from qualifying for nonrecognition of gain or loss available to corporate reorganizations. Continuity of interest requires that in substance a substantial part of the value of the proprietary interests in the target corporation be preserved in the reorganization. A proprietary interest in the target corporation is preserved if, in a potential reorganization, it is exchanged for a proprietary interest in the issuing corporation[17] . . . , it is exchanged by the acquiring corporation for a direct interest in the target corpora-

---

16. These issues will be considered more fully in Chapter 12.

17. The issuing corporation means "the acquiring corporation (as that term is used in section 368(a)), except that, in determining whether a reorganization qualifies as a triangular reorganization (as defined in §1.358-6(b)(2)), the issuing corporation means the corporation in control of the acquiring corporation." Treas. Reg. §1.368-1(b).

tion enterprise, or it otherwise continues as a proprietary interest in the target corporation.[18]

The judicially developed continuity of interest test provides historical background with respect to reorganizations generally and continues to be directly applicable in the case of statutory mergers or consolidations pursuant to §368(a)(1)(A).[19] Under the Revenue Act of 1921, the term "reorganization" included a "merger or consolidation (including the acquisition by one corporation of at least a majority of the voting stock and at least a majority of the total number of shares of all other classes of stock of another corporation, *or substantially all the properties of another corporation*)."[20] A corporate sale of assets for cash and promissory notes technically fit within the early reorganization definition since it was, after all, an "acquisition by one corporation of substantially all of the properties of another." Nevertheless, the courts were reluctant to grant nonrecognition treatment in the case of essentially cash asset sales. The Second Circuit in Cortland Specialty Co. v. Commissioner[21] rejected tax-free reorganization treatment in the case of a transfer of substantially all of the target corporation's assets in exchange for cash and promissory notes. Even though the transaction technically fit the then applicable reorganization definition, the court found lacking the "requisite that there must be some continuity of interest on the part of the transferor corporation or its stockholders in order to secure exemption. Reorganization presupposes continuance of business under modified corporate forms."[22] The transaction did not satisfy the continuity of proprietary interest test since the target corporation received only cash and notes, rather than an interest in the purchasing corporation.

The Supreme Court considered a similar cash transaction in *Pinellas Ice & Cold Storage* and also refused to interpret the reorganization definition literally. The *Pinellas* Court found that:

> the mere purchase for money of the assets of one company by another is beyond the evident purpose of the [reorganization] provision, and has no real semblance to a merger or consolidation. Certainly, we think that to be within the exemption the seller must *acquire an interest in the affairs of the purchasing company more definite than that incident to ownership of its short-term purchase-money notes.*[23]

---

18. Treas. Reg. §1.368-1(e) (added by T.D. 8760, 63 Fed. Reg. 4174 (Jan. 28, 1998)).

19. These issues regarding continuity of interest will be addressed in more detail in Chapter 12.

20. Revenue Act of 1921, ch. 135, §202(c)(2), 42 Stat. 227, 230 (1921) (emphasis added). This language was reenacted in Revenue Acts through 1932.

21. 60 F.2d 937 (2d Cir. 1932), *cert. denied,* 288 U.S. 599 (1933).

22. *Id.* at 940.

23. Pinellas Ice & Cold Storage Co. v. Comm'r, 287 U.S. 462, 470 (1933).

In other words, the Supreme Court required some continuity of proprietary interest — receipt by the sellers of only cash and short-term notes was not sufficient.

Two years later, in the case of Helvering v. Minnesota Tea Co.,[24] the Court interpreted the same language[25] in the case of an asset acquisition for cash and voting trust certificates. To the earlier *Pinellas* requirement that the seller receive "an interest in the affairs of the purchasing company more definite than that incident to ownership of its short-term purchase-money notes," the Supreme Court added that "this interest must be definite and material; it must represent a substantial part of the value of the thing transferred."[26]

An unpacking of the *Minnesota Tea* test reveals two components. First, the sellers must receive a "definite and material" interest in the purchasing corporation. The focus here is on the *quality* or type of consideration sufficient to represent a "definite and material" interest in the acquiring corporation. Voting stock of the acquiring corporation, whether common or preferred, represents a definite and material interest in the acquiring corporation. The Court in *Minnesota Tea* found that voting trust certificates representing the purchasing corporation's voting stock also were sufficient. In John A. Nelson Corp. v. Commissioner,[27] a companion case decided on the same day as *Minnesota Tea*, the Supreme Court held that a transfer of assets in exchange for cash and the entire issue of the purchasing corporation's nonvoting preferred stock provided the selling corporation with a "definite and substantial interest in the affairs of the purchasing corporation"[28] sufficient to qualify the transaction as a tax-free reorganization. The *Nelson* case established that the continuity of proprietary interest test did not necessarily require retention of a voting or management interest in the modified corporate enterprise; nonvoting preferred stock was sufficient. The Supreme Court later held in LeTulle v. Scofield[29] that the continuity of interest test is not met when the transferor receives only cash and long-term bonds of the purchasing corporation. In such a case, the Court remarked, "we think it cannot be said that the transferor retains any proprietary interest in the enterprise. On the contrary, he becomes a creditor."[30]

The second component of the *Minnesota Tea* test focuses on the *pro-*

---

24. 296 U.S. 378 (1935).

25. The language from §203 of the Revenue Act of 1926 had been carried over to §112(a)(1)(A) of the Revenue Act of 1928.

26. 296 U.S. 378, 385 (1935).

27. John A. Nelson Corp. v. Helvering, 296 U.S. 374 (1935).

28. *Id.* at 377.

29. 308 U.S. 415 (1940).

30. *Id.* at 421.

portion of the total consideration that must come from these "definite and material" types of consideration. Some portion of the consideration may be paid in the form of cash, notes, securities, or other property without disqualifying the reorganization. As to this second component, the *Minnesota Tea* Court was not bothered by the fact that a large part of the consideration paid to the sellers was cash.[31] "This, we think, is permissible so long as the taxpayer received an interest in the affairs of the transferee which represented a material part of the value of the transferred assets."[32] The Internal Revenue Service takes the position that the continuity of interest test is satisfied if the former shareholders of the target corporation receive a stock interest "equal in value, as of the effective date of the reorganization, to at least 50 percent of the value of all of the formerly outstanding stock of the acquired or transferor corporation as of the same date."[33]

The courts apply the continuity of interest test in the aggregate. Even if some shareholders receive only cash and other shareholders receive only stock, a transaction will generally qualify for tax-free treatment as long as the overall consideration package paid to all of the participating target shareholders meets the continuity of interest requirements and otherwise fits one of the reorganization definitions in §368(a)(1).[34]

b) The New Continuity of Interest (COI) Regulations

In its recently finalized continuity of interest (COI) regulations, the Treasury Department added a new subparagraph interpreting the COI requirement. The new regulations begin with the general observation that COI:

> requires that in substance a substantial part of the value of the proprietary interests in the target corporation be preserved in the reorganization. A proprietary interest in the target corporation is preserved if, in a potential reorganization, it is exchanged for a proprietary interest in the issuing corporation . . . , it is exchanged by

---

31. Approximately 37% of the purchase price was paid in cash, with the remaining 63% paid in the form of voting trust certificates.

32. 296 U.S. at 386.

33. Rev. Proc. 77-37, 1977-2 C.B. 568. Until recently, this was the Service's position for purposes of issuing advance letter rulings. The Service has announced that it will no longer issue advance rulings on routine Type A reorganizations. Rev. Proc. 2000-3, 2000-1 I.R.B. 103, sec. 3. Nevertheless, an example included in recently finalized regulations confirms that the Service will be satisfied in a Type A reorganization with consideration from the acquiring corporation that is 50 percent stock and 50 percent cash. Treas. Reg. §1.368-1(e)(6), ex. 1. The case law is even more forgiving. For example, in John A. Nelson Corp. v. Helvering, a transaction with only 38% equity qualified as a tax-free reorganization.

34. See Rev. Rul. 66-224, 1966-2 C.B. 114.

the acquiring corporation for a direct interest in the target corporation enterprise, or it otherwise continues a proprietary interest in the target corporation. However, a proprietary interest in the target corporation is not preserved if, in connection with the potential reorganization, it is acquired by the issuing corporation for consideration other than stock of the issuing corporation, or stock of the issuing corporation furnished in exchange for a proprietary interest in the target corporation in the potential reorganization is redeemed. All facts and circumstances must be considered in determining whether, in substance, a proprietary interest in the target corporation is preserved.[35]

Notice that the new regulations do not reflect *fundamental* changes in concept. The basic quality and quantity components of the continuity of interest requirement, discussed earlier in this chapter, remain in place. Nevertheless, the new regulations *do* change the concept underlying continuity of interest requirements in subtle ways. The new regulations are designed to refocus the continuity requirement "on its initial purpose of ensuring that the acquiring corporation furnishes the proper type of consideration."[36] Put differently, the emphasis of the Treasury Department's earlier continuity analysis was on what the target shareholders *retained* after the reorganization. The emphasis now will be on what the acquiring corporation *furnished* as part of the reorganization transaction.[37] The most dramatic changes resulting from this shift in focus involve the effect of pre- and post-reorganization transfers of stock by target shareholders. These issues are discussed in the sections that follow.

In addition to the detailed interpretation of requirements necessary to satisfy the COI test, the new regulations specifically suggest two situations in which the COI requirement is *not* met. First, a transaction fails the COI test if the target corporation is acquired with consideration other than the issuing corporation's stock.[38] This is essentially a restatement of the quality component of traditional continuity analysis. Second, a transaction fails the COI requirement if stock furnished by the acquiring corporation in the reorganization is redeemed. This seems a sensible result. If the purchasing

---

35. Treas. Reg. §1.368-1(e)(1). The proposed COI regulations, 61 Fed. Reg. 67,512 (Dec. 23, 1996), were revised in response to comments and issued as final regulations generally applicable to transactions occurring after January 28, 1998. T.D. 8760, 63 Fed. Reg. 4174 (Jan. 28, 1998).

36. Fed. Reg. 67,512, 67,513 (Dec. 23, 1996) (preamble to proposed COI regulations).

37. For an interesting discussion, see David F. Shores, Reexamining Continuity of Shareholder Interest in Corporate Reorganizations, 17 Va. Tax Rev. 419 (1998).

38. The issuing corporation will generally be the acquiring corporation, except in certain triangular mergers in which the issuing corporation, will be the corporation in control of the acquiring corporation. A definition of "issuing corporation" is provided in Treas. Reg. §1.368-1(b).

corporation immediately redeems for cash the stock that it recently issued in connection with a reorganization, it has effectively made a cash purchase.[39]

One concern under the new COI regulations was the effect of a sale of purchasing corporation (P) stock recently received by the former target shareholders back to P under a corporate stock repurchase program. In a recent ruling on stock repurchase programs, the Service sanctioned reorganization treatment even where the purchasing corporation modified its stock repurchase program in order to prevent dilution that might result from the issuance of its stock in a merger transaction.[40] The ruling disregards any former target corporation (T) shareholders' sales of stock to P under the repurchase program as "mere dispositions" to unrelated persons.[41] The ruling was careful, however, to stress that the repurchase program was not a matter negotiated by the T shareholders as part of the reorganization and that the "mechanics of an open market repurchase" did not favor participation by the former T shareholders. Even if it could be established that some of the former T shareholders participated in the repurchase, the ruling concludes that such purchases would be coincidental.[42]

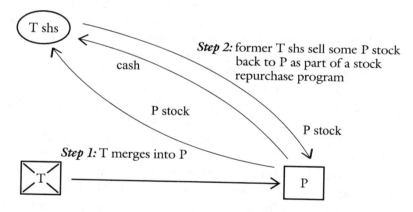

c) Post-Reorganization Continuity

(i) Background

One concern regarding the continuity of interest requirement is the length of time that investors of the old corporate enterprise must *retain* a continuing proprietary interest in the modified corporate form *after* the reorganization

---

39. See Treas. Reg. §1.368-1(e)(6), ex. 5.

40. Rev. Rul. 99-58, 1999-52 I.R.B. 701.

41. A more detailed discussion of the new regulations' treatment of post-reorganization sales follows in section (c)(ii) of this chapter.

42. The ruling does not mention the "small percentage" caveat from the regulatory example.

exchange. Imagine, for example, a transaction in which shareholders exchange their stock in the target corporation entirely for stock of a purchasing corporation. Shortly thereafter, a substantial proportion of the old target shareholders sell their recently acquired stock in the purchasing corporation for cash. In the end, these target shareholders will have cashed out on their investment. Surely, the old target shareholders who sell their new stock for cash will be taxed upon this stock sale. The more difficult question is whether or not the post-reorganization sale by a substantial percentage of the old target shareholders will jeopardize the tax-free nature of the reorganization to the other shareholders or to the corporations involved. Subchapter C itself contains no specific requirements on the length of time that participating investors must *retain* their continuity of proprietary interest, suggesting that simply satisfying the continuity requirements immediately after the exchange should be sufficient. Until recently, however, the Internal Revenue Service took the position that "[s]ales, redemptions, and other dispositions of stock occuring . . . subsequent to the exchange which are part of the plan of reorganization will be considered in determining whether there is a 50 percent continuing interest through stock ownership."[43]

This position came back to haunt the Treasury Department in the case of McDonald's Restaurants of Illinois, Inc. v. Commissioner,[44] a case in which a group of McDonald's franchisees were interested in being bought out for cash. For various reasons, McDonald's preferred to acquire the franchisees' interests as part of a stock merger. To satisfy the franchisees' demands for cash, the merger agreement provided that the McDonald's stock transferred to the old franchisees would later be included in a registered public sale of stock for cash arranged by the purchasing corporation. Consistent with this plan, the franchisees' corporations were first merged into numerous McDonald's subsidiaries in exchange for McDonald's stock. Several months later, the franchisees sold the McDonald's stock they had received in the earlier merger for cash as part of a McDonald's registered public stock sale.

Taking the position that the transaction was a cash purchase rather than a tax-free reorganization, McDonald's used a cost (or stepped-up) basis in the assets acquired. Viewing the transaction under step-transaction analysis, the Seventh Circuit agreed with McDonald's, concluding that the transaction failed to satisfy the continuity of interest requirement. Integrating the various parts of the transaction together, the court concluded that the transaction

---

43. Rev. Proc. 77-37, 1977-2 C.B. 568, 569, sec. 3.02. Recently finalized new regulations, however, reflect a dramatically different view. Under the new regulations, the post-reorganization continuity requirement is all but eliminated. These new regulations are discussed in detail later in this section.

44. 688 F.2d 520 (7th Cir. 1982).

was not a tax-free reorganization, but instead was a cash sale. Although the franchisees had no formally binding commitment to sell the shares for cash, the court found that the merger would not have taken place without guarantees of saleability to the franchisees who insisted on cash.

The Seventh Circuit's opinion in *McDonald's* took the position that post-reorganization sales of the acquiring corporation's stock by the target shareholders should be taken into account in testing for continuity of shareholder interest. Commentators were quick to criticize the Seventh Circuit opinion, commenting that post-reorganization target shareholder sales should be troublesome only when the target shareholders sold the stock back to the acquiring corporation or a party related to the acquiring corporation. If, shortly after the exchange, the target shareholders' recently acquired stock in the purchasing corporation is redeemed or otherwise repurchased by the purchasing corporation, it would appear that such target shareholders have "sold" their interest rather than participate in a reorganization exchange. The post-reorganization sale by the target shareholders in *McDonald's* was to third parties unrelated to the purchasing corporation and was merely *arranged* by the purchasing corporation. This type of post-reorganization sale to an unrelated third party arguably should not defeat continuity of shareholder proprietary interest. The Treasury Department has finally adopted this approach in its new regulations.

(ii) Impact of the New COI Regulations

Reversing its earlier position, the Treasury Department now effectively eliminates any post-reorganization continuity requirement as long as target shareholders' sales of stock after the reorganization are made to unrelated parties:

> For purposes of the continuity of interest requirement, . . . a mere disposition of stock of the issuing corporation received in a potential reorganization to persons not related . . . to the issuing corporation is disregarded.[45]

Lest there be any doubt that the Treasury Department has changed its position in the *McDonald's*-type case, the regulations include an example that is eerily reminiscent of the *McDonald's* facts. In this example, the T shareholders receive only P stock in a merger transaction. At the same time, P agrees to register the stock issued to the T shareholders in the merger, thus enabling them to quickly sell their P shares for cash. The example confirms that the T shareholders' sales of P stock immediately after the merger will be disregarded, since the sales were to unrelated parties.[46] Even a *binding*

---

45. Treas. Reg. §1.368-1(e)(1)(i).
46. Treas. Reg. §1.368-1(e)(6), ex. 3.

contract on the part of target shareholders to sell acquiring corporation stock received in a reorganization will not defeat continuity of interest as long as the target shareholders are selling to unrelated parties.[47] Thus, with the exception of sales to related parties, the new regulations now disregard post-reorganization sales altogether, even if they were part of an integrated transaction.

(iii)   Sales to Related Parties

Post-reorganization transfers to related parties that are part of an integrated transaction, however, will cause the reorganization to fail the COI test. The regulations provide:

> A proprietary interest in the target corporation is not preserved if, in connection with a potential reorganization, a person related (as defined in paragraph (e)(3) of this section) to the issuing corporation acquires, with consideration other than a proprietary interest in the issuing corporation, stock of the target corporation . . . in the potential reorganization, except to the extent those persons who were direct or indirect owners of the target operation prior to the potential reorganization maintain a direct or indirect proprietary interest in the issuing corporation.[48]

Two corporations[49] are considered "related" for purposes of the regulations if they are members of the same affiliated group, as defined in §1504, or if purchase by one corporation of stock of the other would be considered a redemption under §304(a)(2).[50] As a basic illustration of such a post-reorganization sale to a related party, imagine that T merges into a subsidiary (S) of the parent corporation (P), with the T shareholders receiving only P stock in the exchange.[51] Immediately after the merger, S purchases the P stock received by the T shareholders for cash. Such a transaction would violate the COI test, since the former T shareholders made an immediate post-reorganization sale of P stock received in the exchange to a party related to P.[52]

---

47. *Id.* at ex. 1.

48. Treas. Reg. §1.368-1(e)(2).

49. Individuals or other noncorporate shareholders are not included in the definition of "related persons" for purposes of these regulations. Statements accompanying the announcement of the final regulations explained: "[B]ecause the final regulations focus generally on the consideration P exchanges, related persons do not include individuals or other noncorporate shareholders." T.D. 8760, 63 Fed. Reg. 4174 (Jan. 28, 1998).

50. Treas. Reg. §1.368-1(e)(3)(i). Section 304's treatment of certain stock sales between related corporations as redemptions is discussed in Chapter 6.

51. Such Type A triangular mergers are considered in detail in Chapter 12.

52. Treas. Reg. §1.368-1(e)(6), ex. 4(iii).

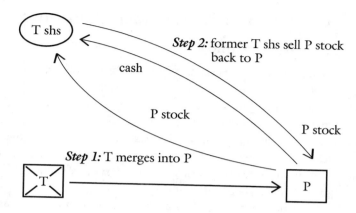

Special rules clarify that corporations are considered related if they meet either of these definitions immediately before or immediately after the stock sale involved.[53] So, for example, imagine that T shareholders receive stock representing 35 percent of the outstanding stock of P in connection with a merger of T into P. Immediately after the merger, X Corporation, which already owns 50 percent of P, purchases all of the P stock received by the T shareholders in the merger. Since X owns 85 percent of the P stock immediately after the purchase, X is considered a related person. The transaction will fail the COI test, since a related person acquired T stock with consideration other than a proprietary interest in the issuing corporation.

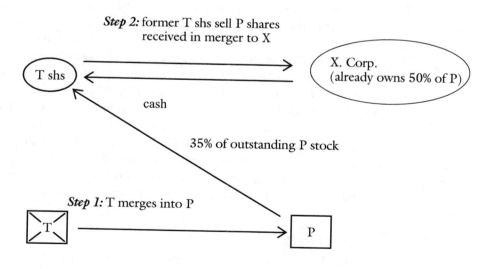

_____

53. Treas. Reg. §1.368-1(e)(3)(ii)(A).

d) Historic Shareholder Continuity

(i) Background

The issue of *pre*-reorganization sales arises in cases where the historic share-holders of a target corporation transfer their interest in the target shortly before a reorganization transaction. The new owners of the target stock then participate in a reorganization in which they receive a proprietary interest in the acquiring corporation. The transaction may meet the continuity of inter-est test with respect to the *recent* target shareholders. Should it matter that continuity does not exist as to the *historic* shareholders of the target, who have been cashed-out?

Rules regarding historic shareholder continuity of interest continue to evolve. One major early case is Yoc Heating Corp. v. Commissioner,[54] in which the purchasing corporation acquired approximately 85% of the target corporation's stock from the target shareholders for cash and notes. As new owner of an 85% interest in the target, the purchasing corporation then arranged for transfer of all of the target's assets to a newly formed subsidiary in exchange for the new subsidiary's stock, which was distributed to partici-pating target shareholders. Not surprisingly, the only target shareholder to participate was the purchasing corporation itself, which received the subsidi-ary stock in exchange for its 85% interest in the target. The minority share-holders who disapproved of the asset transfer were paid cash.

The government in *Yoc Heating* took the position that the transaction was a reorganization under §368(a)(1)(D),[55] which requires that the trans-feror, or one or more of its shareholders, have control of the new corporation immediately after the exchange. Since the purchasing corporation was the primary shareholder of the target transferor immediately before the exchange, and since the purchasing corporation controlled the new corporation im-mediately after the exchange, the government argued that the control requirements of §368(a)(1)(D) were met. Under §362, the purchasing cor-poration's basis in the target assets in a reorganization transaction should be the same as the basis of the assets in the target corporation's hands.

The purchasing corporation in *Yoc Heating* used an integrated transac-tion argument to claim that the target transferors did not have sufficient "control" immediately after the exchange to be considered a reorganization. The purchasing corporation argued that the transaction should be viewed as

---

54. 61 T.C. 168 (1973).

55. A §368(a)(1)(D) reorganization is "a transfer by a corporation of all or part of its assets to another corporation if immediately after the transfer the transferor, or one or more of its shareholders . . . or any combination thereof, is in control of the corporation to which the assets are transferred; but only if, in pursuance of the plan, stock or securities of the corporation to which the assets are transferred are distributed in a transaction which qualifies under section 354, 355, or 356."

a cash purchase, resulting in a stepped-up basis in the target's assets.[56] The Tax Court agreed with the purchasing corporation that the transaction should be viewed as an integrated transaction, beginning with the cash sales by the original target shareholders and ending with the later exchange for the new subsidiary's stock. Since approximately 85% of the original target shareholder had been bought out for cash, the target or its shareholders were not in "control" immediately after the exchange as required by §368(a)(1)(D). The court also found that there was no reorganization "[b]y a parity of reasoning rooted in the judicial 'continuity of interest' principle applicable to reorganizations."[57] In other words, it is not enough to meet the literal requirements of the §368 reorganization definitions; the Tax Court in *Yoc Heating* held that the *historic* shareholders must retain a continuity of proprietary interest in the newly reorganized enterprise. Since the original or *historic* shareholders in *Yoc Heating* had sold their stock for cash and were no longer invested in the reorganized corporation, the Tax Court held that the transaction was not a reorganization and that the purchasing corporation was entitled to a stepped-up basis in the acquired target assets.

A more recent development in the historic shareholder continuity of interest doctrine is the Tax Court's decision in J.E. Seagram Corp. v. Commissioner,[58] which involved a take-over battle for corporate control. DuPont and Seagrams, along with several other corporations, were competing for control over the target corporation, Conoco. Each of the competitors successfully acquired substantial amounts of Conoco stock for cash. DuPont, however, was the ultimate winner, having acquired approximately 46% of Conoco's stock. DuPont then arranged for a merger of Conoco into one of its subsidiaries. Conoco shareholders received DuPont stock in connection with the merger. The Conoco shareholders included in this exchange included DuPont itself (approximately 46%), Seagrams (approximately 32%) and the public (approximately 22%).

Seagrams hoped to recognize its realized loss on the exchange of its Conoco stock for DuPont stock. Loss recognition was unavailable to Seagrams, however, if the transaction was classified as a tax-free reorganization and if Seagrams had received its DuPont stock as part of a "plan of reorganization." Although the merger appeared to be a legitimate §368(a)(1)(A) reorganization, Seagrams argued that the transaction failed to meet the shareholder continuity of interest requirements, since only 22% of the participating shareholders to the merger were the original or *historic* sharehold-

---

56. The *Yoc Heating* case was decided before Congress added §338, which provides an election for such a stepped-up basis following a "qualified stock purchase." This provision, and its relationship to *Yoc Heating,* is discussed in detail in Chapter 10.

57. 61 T.C. 168, 177.

58. 104 T.C. 75 (1995).

ers who owned Conoco stock before the integrated series of events relating to the take-over battle. Seagrams argued that:

> because it acquired approximately 32 percent of [the] shares for cash pursuant to its own tender offer, and DuPont acquired approximately 46 percent of [the] shares for cash pursuant to its tender offer, the combined 78 percent of Conoco shares acquired for cash after the date of the agreement destroyed the continuity of interest requisite for a valid reorganization.[59]

The Tax Court in *Seagrams* took a limited view of the historic shareholder test, distinguishing *Yoc Heating* by observing that in *Yoc Heating* it was the *acquiring* corporation *itself* whose recently acquired shares were not counted towards meeting the continuity of interest requirements. Under this view of the historic shareholder continuity of interest doctrine, the shares recently acquired by the *purchasing* corporation should not count toward continuity of interest. Thus, DuPont's recently acquired 46% of the target Conoco's stock would not count toward continuity. On the other hand, the Tax Court in *Seagrams* held that the 32% of Conoco shares held by Seagrams immediately before the merger *should* be counted towards meeting the continuity of interest requirement even though Seagrams had recently acquired these shares. Thus, the Tax Court in *Seagrams* has limited the historic shareholder continuity requirement, concluding that:

> we must look not to the identity of the target's shareholders, but rather to what the shares represented when the reorganization was completed. In this case, a majority of the old shares of Conoco were converted to shares of DuPont in the reorganization, so that in the sense, at least, that a majority of the consideration was the acquiring corporation's stock, the test of continuity was met.[60]

The court continued to observe that:

> sales of target stock for cash after the date of the announcement of an acquisition can be neither predicted not controlled by publicly held parties to a reorganization. A requirement that the identity of the acquired corporation's shareholders be tracked to assume a sufficient number of 'historic' shareholders to satisfy some arbitrary minimal percentage receiving the acquiring corporation's stock would be completely unrealistic.[61]

In the end, the Tax Court in *Seagrams* held that the transaction was a reorganization despite the fact that 78% of the transferring shareholders in

---

59. *Id.* at 99.
60. *Id* at 103.
61. *Id.*

the merger had recently acquired their stock in the target and, therefore, arguably were not the historic shareholders.

(ii)   Impact of the New COI Regulations

The originally proposed changes to the COI regulations focused only on the effect of *post*-reorganization sales on continuity of shareholder interest. The preamble to the final regulations, however, states that "the IRS and Treasury Department believe that issues concerning the COI requirement raised by dispositions of T stock *before* a potential reorganization correspond to those raised by subsequent dispositions of P stock furnished in exchange for T stock in the potential reorganization."[62] Thus, "the final regulations apply the rationale of the proposed COI regulations to transactions occurring both prior to and after a potential reorganization."[63] These final regulations virtually eliminate the historic shareholder or remote continuity of interest requirement providing that:

> For purposes of the continuity of interest requirements, a mere disposition of stock of the target corporation prior to a potential reorganization to persons not related . . . to the target corporation or to persons not related to the issuing corporation is disregarded. . . .[64]

This regulatory language in §1.368-1(e)(1) gives its blessing to the result in the *Seagrams* case. Under the new regulations, Seagrams' cash purchases of Conoco stock immediately prior to the reorganization would be disregarded as "mere dispositions," since Seagrams in that case was unrelated to the purchaser, DuPont, or to the target, Conoco. In other words, shares held by Seagrams immediately before the reorganization *would* be counted toward the COI test, even though Seagrams was not a historic shareholder. On the other hand, target corporation stock recently acquired for cash by DuPont would not count toward the COI test, since DuPont would be considered a related person under the new regulations.

---

62. T.D. 8760, 63 Fed. Reg. 4174 (Jan. 28, 1998) (emphasis added).

63. *Id.*

64. Treas. Reg. §1.368-1(e)(1). In this regard, it is important to note that the potential reorganization transaction *itself* can create a relationship meeting the definition of "related persons" under the regulations. For example, the regulations describe a transaction in which X Corporation already held a 60% interest in the purchasing corporation (P) and a 30% interest in the target (T). X bought the remaining 70% of T for cash immediately before a merger of T into P. When the new P shares that X received in connection with the merger are combined with the 60% in P that X already owned, X has an 80% interest. The example concludes that X is a related person whose purchases cannot be disregarded. Since X, now considered a related person, acquired a proprietary interest in T for something other than P stock, the transaction fails the COI test. Treas. Reg. §1.368-1(e)(6), ex. 2.

The *Yoc Heating* fact pattern presents interesting questions of overlap between the reorganization provisions and the taxable acquisition provisions in §338. In that fact pattern, P first purchases 85% of the T stock for cash.[65] Shortly thereafter, T is merged into S, a subsidiary of P. Since P is a related party that acquired a proprietary interest for cash, the regulations conclude that the COI requirements are not met.[66] This conclusion actually has the most serious implications for the minority shareholders who exchange their 15% interest in T for P stock in connection with the merger. They will be ineligible for tax-free reorganization treatment.

Regulations under §338 address the overlap issues surrounding a transfer of the target corporation's assets to the purchasing corporation in a reorganization following a QSP for which the purchaser does *not* make a §338 election. The regulations conclude that "the purchasing corporation's target stock acquired in the qualified stock purchase represents an interest on the part of a person who was an owner of the target's business enterprise prior to the transfer that can be continued in a reorganization."[67] In other words, it is possible for the purchasing corporation, or one of its affiliates, to participate in a tax-free reorganization immediately following a QSP. At the same time, however, the §338 regulation cautions that tax-free reorganization treatment "cannot apply to any person other than the purchasing corporation or another member of the same affiliated group as the purchasing corporation unless the transfer of target corporation assets is pursuant to a reorganization as determined without regard to this paragraph. . . . "[68] The regulatory example provided involves a QSP by P Corporation of 85% of T Corporation from shareholder A. Shortly after the QSP, and as part of an integrated plan, T merges into X Corporation, a subsidiary of P. Both P Corporation and T Corporation's 15% minority shareholder, K, receives P stock in connection with the merger.

---

65. Although the provision was not applicable at the time, this purchase today would be considered a QSP under §338. For a discussion of §338 and taxable acquisitions, see Chapter 10.

66. Treas. Reg. §1.368-1(e)(6), ex. 4(ii). The regulations go on to say, "However, see [the §338 regulation] (which may change the result in this case by providing that, by virtue of section 338, continuity of interest is satisfied for certain parties after a qualified stock purchase)." *Id.*

67. Treas. Reg. §1.338-3T(c)(3)(ii).

68. Treas. Reg. §1.338-3T(c)(3)(i).

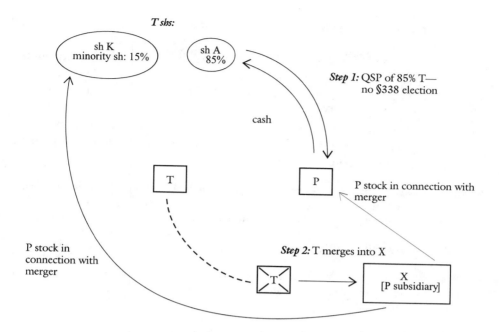

The regulations conclude that "*[b]y virtue of section 338*, the transfer of T assets to X is a reorganization" with respect to P.[69] On the other hand, the regulations conclude that the transfer will *not* be treated as a tax-free reorganization with respect to the minority shareholder "because P's stock purchase and the merger of T into X are pursuant to an integrated transaction in which A, the owner of 85 percent of the stock of T, received solely cash in exchange for A's stock."[70] The bottom line here is that a purchasing corporation that does *not* make a §338 election following a QSP will be held to a substituted basis under §362. Without this special §338 regulation, P might claim a cost basis in the assets its subsidiary receives in the merger, arguing that the merger is not a tax-free reorganization. If so, it would be too easy for P get a cost basis in the T assets acquired by its subsidiary without meeting the requirements of §338. The regulations effectively preserve the §338 election as the sole route to a stepped-up basis after a QSP, but do not otherwise convert the transaction into a tax-free reorganization for minority shareholders.

At the same time that it finalized the new COI regulations, the Treasury Department issued temporary regulations more specifically addressing the issue of pre-reorganization redemptions and dividends.[71] The temporary regulations swept quite broadly, finding that a proprietary interest in T is not

---

69. Treas. Reg. §1.338-3T(c)(3)(iv), ex. (iv) (emphasis added).
70. *Id.* at ex. (v).
71. T.D. 8761, 63 Fed. Reg. 4183 (Jan. 28, 1998).

preserved if *any* pre-reorganization redemptions or extraordinary dividends are made with respect to T in connection with a potential reorganization. Commentators pointed out that this approach was inconsistent with authorities holding that a pre-reorganization redemption would not violate the "solely for voting stock" requirement for Type B and C reorganizations as long as funds for the redemption did not come directly, or indirectly, from P.[72] Responding to this concern, the Treasury Department removed the temporary regulations and amended its final regulations, substituting a narrower rule. The new rule provides that:

> A proprietary interest in the target corporation . . . is not preserved to the extent that consideration received prior to a potential reorganization, either in a redemption of the target corporation stock or in a distribution with respect to the target corporation stock, is treated as other property or money received in the exchange for purposes of section 356, or would be so treated if the target shareholder also had received stock of the issuing corporation in exchange for stock owned by the shareholder in the target corporation.[73]

In effect, the redemption or distribution will cause the transaction to fail COI requirements if it was directly or indirectly funded by P. A pre-reorganization redemption or distribution funded entirely by T should not affect continuity of interest.[74]

Continuity of the Business Enterprise (COBE)

In theory, even if the original shareholders retain a substantial proprietary interest in the reorganized corporate enterprise, a reorganization represents more than a "mere change in form" if the type of business conducted or the use of business assets is dramatically transformed. In early cases, the government took the position that to qualify for tax-free reorganization treatment, the new corporation had to engage in a business identical to or similar to the transferor corporation's business.[75] After losing several cases in the courts,[76] the Service revoked its earlier position, concluding that "the surviving corporation need not continue the activities conducted by its prede-

---

72. See discussion of Type B and C reorganizations in Chapter 12.

73. Treas. Reg. §1.368-1(e)(1)(ii), as amended, T.D. 8898, 65 Fed. Reg. 52,909 (Aug. 31, 2000).

74. Treas. Reg. §1.368-1(e)(6), ex. 9. This revised rule is more consistent with the treatment of pre-reorganization redemptions in Type B and C reorganizations.

75. See, e.g., Rev. Rul. 56-330, 1956-2 C.B. 204, *revoked,* Rev. Rul. 63-29, 1963-1 C.B. 77, *superseded,* Rev. Rul. 81-25, 1981-1 C.B. 132.

76. See, e.g., Bentsen v. Phinney, 199 F. Supp. 363 (S.D. Tex 1961).

cessors."[77] Regulations now provide that the continuity of the business enterprise requirement is satisfied if the issuing corporation *either* 1) continues the target corporation's historic business *or* 2) "use[s] a significant portion of [the target's] historic business assets in a business."[78]

As it has evolved, the continuity of the business enterprise requirement is rather loose and reasonably easy to satisfy. If the target corporation has more than one line of business, all that is required to continue the target's historic business is for the purchasing corporation to continue *one* significant line of business. In the alternative, the continuity of the business enterprise requirement is satisfied if the purchasing corporation simply uses a significant portion of the target's historic business assets in *any* business. For the purposes of this provision, "significance" is a facts and circumstances analysis based upon the relative importance of the assets to the operation of the business.[79] As one example of a transaction that fails the continuity of the business enterprise requirement, the regulations describe a merger of a farm machinery corporation into a lumber mill corporation. Immediately after the transaction, the purchasing lumber corporation disposes of all of the target's farm machinery manufacturing business and continues to engage in milling operations. The purchasing corporation does not continue the farm machinery manufacturing business nor does it continue to use the historic farm machinery business assets. Thus, continuity of the business enterprise is lacking.[80]

Recently finalized amendments to the COBE regulations continue the Treasury Department's loose approach. They clarify that the acquiring corporation need not *directly* continue the target's business or use the target's assets. These new regulations add flexibility by permitting the acquired assets to be transferred after a reorganization to any member of a "qualified group," defined as "one or more chains of corporations connected through stock ownership with the issuing corporation, but only if the issuing corporation owns stock meeting the requirements of section 368(c) in at least one other corporation, and stock meeting the requirements of section 368(c) in each of the corporations . . . is owned directly by one of the other corporations."[81]

---

77. Rev. Rul. 63-29, 1963-1 C.B. 77, *suspended,* Rev. Rul. 79-433, 1979-2 C.B.155 *superseded,* Rev. Rul. 81-25, 1981-1 C.B. 132.

78. Treas. Reg. §1.368-1(d)(1). Note that the continuity of the business enterprise requirement applies only to the business assets of the *target* corporation, and not to the business assets of the purchasing corporation. See Rev. Rul. 81-25, 1981-1 C.B. 132.

79. Treas. Reg. §1.368-1(d)(2).

80. Treas. Reg. §1.368-1(d)(5), ex. (5).

81. Treas. Reg. §1.368-1(d)(4)(ii). These new COBE regulations were issued along with the new COI regulations discussed above. T.D. 8760, 63 Fed. Reg. 4174 (Jan. 28, 1998).

For purposes of the COBE requirement, the issuing corporation "is treated as holding all of the businesses and assets of all of the members of the qualified group."[82] In addition, the regulations specify circumstances in which the issuing corporation will also be treated as conducting a business of a partnership for purposes of the COBE requirement.[83]

To the extent that the continuity of the business enterprise requirement has any remaining bite, its purpose is to prevent a tax-free reorganization where the target corporation sells all or most of its assets and shortly thereafter, transfers its new assets in exchange for stock in a mutual fund or regulated investment company. For example, assume that a clothing manufacturer sells all of its assets for cash and a highly diversified portfolio of stocks and bonds. Although this is a taxable asset sale, assume that the asset basis is high so that the asset sale does not generate significant taxable income for the selling corporation. Shortly thereafter the corporation transfers the recently acquired stocks and bonds to a mutual fund or regulated investment company in return for mutual fund or regulated investment company stock, which it then distributes to its shareholders. This transaction meets the technical statutory requirements for a Type C reorganization. It fails the continuity of business enterprise requirement, however, because investment activity is not the target's historic business and stocks and bonds are not the target company's historic assets.[84] The target shareholders are thus prevented from converting their equity interest in a clothing manufacturer tax-free into an equity interest in a mutual fund or regulated investment company.

The Business Purpose Test

A nonrecognition rule permitting taxpayers to defer taxation upon the exchange of appreciated property is obviously appealing to taxpayers. In an early landmark case, the taxpayer structured a transaction so as to fit literally within the definition of a reorganization, but nevertheless failed to convince the Court that she was entitled to reorganization treatment since the reorganization plan had no "business purpose."[85] Mrs. Gregory's solely owned corporation held appreciated stock in another corporation. If her corporation had distributed this appreciated property directly to Mrs. Gregory, she would have received a dividend, taxable as ordinary income. Instead, Mrs. Gregory arranged for transfer of the appreciated stock to a newly formed corporation

---

82. Treas. Reg. §1.368-1(d)(4)(i).

83. Treas. Reg. §1.368-1(d)(4)(iii).

84. See Treas. Reg. §1.368-1(d)(5), ex. (3); see also Rev. Rul. 87-76, 1987-2 C.B. 84.

85. Gregory v. Helvering, 293 U.S. 465 (1935). The statute involved was the Revenue Act of 1928.

in which she would hold all of the stock.[86] Shortly thereafter, the new corporation distributed the appreciated stock to Mrs. Gregory in a complete liquidation of the recently formed corporation. The corporation was in existence for only three days and never conducted any business. Mrs. Gregory hoped to treat the liquidating distribution as sale or exchange gain pursuant to §331, taxable at the lower capital gains rates, thus attempting to convert what otherwise would have been ordinary income into capital gains.[87]

In a famous opinion for the Second Circuit, Judge Learned Hand said first that:

> a transaction, otherwise within an exception of the tax law, does not lose its immunity because it is actuated by a desire to avoid, or, if one choose, to evade, taxation. Any one may so arrange his affairs that his taxes shall be as low as possible; he is not bound to choose that pattern which will best pay the Treasury; there is not even a patriotic duty to increase one's taxes.[88]

Reading this far, Mrs. Gregory surely would have thought that she had won the case. However, Judge Hand went on to say that:

> the meaning of a sentence may be more than that of the separate words, as a melody is more than the notes. . . . The purpose of the [nonrecognition] section is plain enough; . . . the underlying presupposition is plain that the readjustment shall be undertaken for reasons germane to the conduct of the venture in hand, not as an ephemeral incident, egregious to its prosecution. To dodge the shareholder's taxes is not one of the transactions contemplated as corporate "reorganizations."[89]

In less colorful language, the Supreme Court affirmed the Second Circuit's opinion, firmly establishing the "business purpose" test. In Mrs. Gregory's case, the Court concluded that the operation had no "business or corporate purpose," but was rather "a mere device which put on the form of a corporate reorganization as a disguise for concealing its real character, and the sole object and accomplishment of which was the consummation of a preconceived plan, not to reorganize a business or any part of a business, but to transfer a parcel of corporate shares to the petitioner."[90]

---

86. Under the modern definitions of reorganization, this transaction would be regarded as a "divisive reorganization" under §368(a)(1)(D).

87. For a complete discussion of §331 sale or exchange treatment to the shareholder upon a liquidating distribution, see Chapter 8.

88. Helvering v. Gregory, 69 F.2d 809, 810 (2d Cir. 1934), aff'd, 293 U.S. 465 (1935).

89. Id. at 810-811. Ironically, Judge Hand's opinion is most often cited for the first quotation without mentioning the second.

90. 293 U.S. at 469.

Although the "business purpose" test has never been formally incorporated into the statutory language of the reorganization provisions, it is built into the regulations in several places. First, the general regulation regarding the purpose and scope of the tax-free reorganization provisions states that the nonrecognition rules apply to "such readjustments of corporate structures . . . *as are required by business exigencies*."[91] In addition, in order for the shareholders or the corporation to qualify for tax-free treatment under §§354 or 361, the transfers must be "in pursuance of a plan of reorganization." The regulations defining "plan of reorganization" require that:

> the readjustments involved in the exchanges or distributions . . . must be undertaken for reasons germane to the continuance of the business of a corporation a party to the reorganization. Section 368(a) contemplates genuine corporate reorganizations which are designed to effect a readjustment of continuing interests under modified corporate forms.[92]

Finally, the Treasury Department states that "[i]n order to exclude transactions not intended to be included, the specifications of the reorganization provisions of the law are precise. Both the terms of the specifications *and their underlying assumptions and purposes* must be satisfied in order to entitle the taxpayer to the benefit of the [nonrecognition] exception from the general rule."[93]

Step-Transaction Doctrine

Although the new COI regulations have limited its application in the context of pre- and post-reorganization stock transfers, the "step-transaction" doctrine continues to play an important role with regard to tax-free reorganizations.[94] Step-transaction principles will apply in determining the applicable subparagraph of §368(a)(1). For example, if the end result of a series of corporate transactions is the acquisition of assets by the purchasing corporation, an intermediate acquisition of stock might be ignored under the step-transaction doctrine.[95] As a result, the transaction may be recast as a Type C asset acquisition rather than a Type B stock acquisition. This introductory chapter on basic reorganization principles cannot illustrate fully the ways in which step-transaction principles apply regarding reorganizations under Sub-

---

91. Treas. Reg. §1.368-1(b) (emphasis added).
92. Treas. Reg. §1.368-2(g).
93. Treas. Reg. §1.368-1(b) (emphasis added).
94. See discussion of the impact of new COI regulations on pre- and post-reorganization transfers earlier in this chapter.
95. See, e.g., Rev. Rul. 76-123, 1976-1 C.B. 94. But see Rev. Rul. 88-44, 1984-1 C.B. 105.

chapter C. Subsequent chapters detailing the reorganization provisions will address circumstances in which the step-transaction doctrine might be applied.

Overview of Corporate Reorganization Tax Consequences

Tax Consequences to Shareholders

a) General Nonrecognition Rule: §354

A shareholder who transfers stock in connection with a reorganization and receives stock or other assets in return has realized a gain to the extent that the value of the stock or other assets received exceeds the shareholder's basis in the stock transferred. Similarly, the shareholder has realized a loss to the extent that the shareholder's basis in the stock transferred exceeds the value of the stock or assets received in the exchange. Absent a special nonrecognition rule, gains and losses realized from these exchanges generally would be recognized for tax purposes pursuant to §§61(a)(3) and 1001. Losses also generally would be recognized pursuant to §1001, and subject to the loss rules provided in §165. In §354, Congress provides just such a nonrecognition rule for shareholders who, "in pursuance of a plan of reorganization" exchange stock or securities in a corporation that is a "party to a reorganization" for stock or securities in the same corporation or another corporation that is a "party to the reorganization."[96] Thus, a properly structured reorganization will be tax-free to the participating shareholders.

The §354 nonrecognition rule contains several parallels to the §351 nonrecognition rule applicable to incorporation transactions.[97] The initial motivating policy behind each of the provisions is similar; that is, providing nonrecognition to exchanges (whether as part of the organization or reorganization) that reflect "merely a change in form." In addition, a shareholder who receives nonrecognition treatment under either §351 or §354 takes a substituted basis in the stock or securities received pursuant to §358. One significant distinction between §§351 and 354, however, is that §354 pro-

---

96. I.R.C. §354(a). Some limitations to this nonrecognition rule apply in the case of transfers of securities. I.R.C. §354(b). In addition, certain "nonqualified preferred stock" will not be considered "stock or securities" for purposes of §354 under a new provision added by the Taxpayer Relief Act of 1997, Pub. L. No. 105-34, 111 Stat. 788, §1014(b) (codified at I.R.C. §354(a)(2)(C)). For a more detailed discussion of the tax consequences to shareholders and the definitions of "plan of reorganization" and "party to a reorganization," see Chapters 12 and 13.

97. For an in-depth discussion of §351 and its underlying policy, see Chapter 4.

vides nonrecognition upon receipt of "stock or securities" while §351 only permits nonrecognition upon receipt of stock.[98] Moreover, a second significant distinction between §§351 and 354 is that the shareholders in the §351 context must receive a quantum of stock representing "control" whereas the shareholders of a target may receive only a minuscule ownership in the acquiring corporation and yet be entitled to nonrecognition treatment.

While §354(a)(1) establishes a general nonrecognition rule, limitations are set forth in §354(a)(2). Nonrecognition is not available to the extent that the principal amount of any securities received exceeds the principal amount of securities surrendered.[99] In other words, an exchange of securities for the same principal amount of securities in a reorganization will be a tax-free exchange. Any *excess* securities that the shareholder receives will be considered boot and will be taxable.[100] Similarly, if any securities are received and no securities are surrendered, the securities received also will be considered boot.[101] In addition, a new provision, added by the Taxpayer Relief Act of 1997, now provides that certain "nonqualified preferred stock" will *not* be treated as stock or securities for purposes of §354.[102] As a result, "nonqualified preferred stock" also will be considered boot, subjecting those who receive such preferred stock in an otherwise tax-free exchange to potentially taxable "boot gain."[103] For purposes of the new §354(a)(2)(C) boot rule,

---

98. In addition, recent regulatory amendments generally provide that, for purposes of §354, "the term *securities* includes rights issued to a party to a reorganization to acquire its stock." Treas. Reg. §1.354-1(e) (as amended by T.D. 8752, 63 Fed. Reg. 409 (Jan. 6, 1998)). These new regulations are discussed further in Chapter 12. For many years, §351 did provide nonrecognition upon receipt of "stock or securities." The words "or securities" were deleted from §351 as part of the Omnibus Budget Reconciliation Act of 1989. See Chapter 4.

99. I.R.C. §354(a)(2)(A)(i).

100. *Id.* See also I.R.C. §356(d)(2)(B). Stock rights are now considered to be "securities" for purposes of §354. See note 98. However, "a right to acquire stock has no principal amount." Thus, receipt of a stock option or warrant should not generate any additional principal amount in securities received for purposes of §§354 and 356. Treas. Reg. §1.356-3(b).

101. I.R.C. §354(a)(2)(A)(ii). In addition, under limitations provided in §354(a)(2), shareholders will not be eligible for nonrecognition to the extent that receipt of stock, securities, or other property is attributable to accrued interest on securities. I.R.C. §354(a)(2)(B).

102. I.R.C. §354(a)(2)(C), added by the Taxpayer Relief Act of 1997, Pub. L. No. 105-34, 111 Stat. 788, §1014(b).

103. One exception to the new boot rule is the receipt of "nonqualified preferred stock" in the case of a §368(a)(1)(E) recapitalization of a family-owned corporation. I.R.C. §354(a)(2)(C)(ii). Recently finalized regulations add that the term "stock or securities" does not include nonqualified preferred stock (NQPS) received in exchange for stock or rights to acquire stock other than NQPS. Treas. Reg. §1.356-6(a)(2). In other words, receipt of NQPS generally will be considered taxable boot. However, an exchange of NQPS for other NQPS or for rights to acquire such stock should be tax-free.

"nonqualified preferred stock" carries the same definition that it has under the parallel new boot rule applicable to §351 exchanges.[104]

b) Shareholder Receipt of "Boot": §356

The nonrecognition language in §354 itself appears quite rigid. It requires that the exchange of stock or securities in one corporation a party to a reorganization be *solely* for stock or securities in the same corporation or another corporation a party to a reorganization. This apparently strict requirement is loosened by §356, which provides that if §354 would apply, but for the fact that something other than stock or securities is received, "then gain, if any, to the recipient shall be recognized, but in an amount not in excess of the sum of . . . money and the fair market value of . . . other property."[105] Thus, to the extent that shareholders receive any "boot" or property other than property permitted to be received tax-free under §354, the "boot" will be taxable under §356 to the extent of realized gain.[106] Any excess securities or "nonqualified preferred stock" received as described in §354(a)(2) will be considered "boot" for purposes of §356.[107]

The §356 "boot" rules are rather unusual. The shareholder who receives §356 boot will either have boot in the form of capital gain under §356(a)(1) or "boot" in the form of a dividend under §356(a)(2). The latter provision simply states that if the boot distribution "has the effect of the distribution of a dividend . . . then there shall be treated as a dividend to each distributee such an amount of the gain . . . as is not in excess of [the shareholder's] ratable share of the undistributed earnings and profits of the corporation . . ."[108] Although the statute uses the term "dividend," the term as used here is quite different from an ordinary dividend under §§301 and 316. Two aspects of the §356(a)(2) dividend provision are rather unique. First, under §356, the *amount* of the dividend is limited to the amount of *gain* recognized on the exchange. In contrast, assuming that a distribution meets the §316 dividend definition, the §301 dividend rules impose a tax on the entire amount received without any basis offset. As a result of this difference in

---

104. I.R.C. §351(g) now treats "nonqualified preferred stock" received in a §351 exchange as boot. For a detailed discussion of this new provision and the definition of "nonqualified preferred stock," see the section entitled "Nonqualified Preferred Stock Treated as Boot" in Chapter 4.

105. I.R.C. §356(a)(1)(B). For purposes of §356, the term "other property" includes "nonqualified preferred stock" unless the preferred stock was permitted to be received tax-free in a §368(a)(1)(E) recapitalization of a family-owned corporation. Taxpayer Relief Act of 1997, Pub. L. No. 105-34, 111 Stat. 788, §1014(d) (codified at I.R.C. §356(e)).

106. The "boot" rules in §356 are similar, but not identical, to the "boot" rules provided in the incorporation context in §351(b).

107. I.R.C. §356(d).

108. I.R.C. §356(a)(2).

treatment, §356(a)(2) sometimes is described as a special "dividend within a gain" rule. The second distinction between the §356(a)(2) dividend and an ordinary dividend is that, unlike §316, the §356(a)(2) dividend is limited to the shareholder's "ratable share of earnings and profits." Moreover, §356(a)(2) looks only to accumulated earnings and profits, unlike §316, under which dividends can arise from either current or accumulated earnings and profits.

A brief look at the history behind §356(a)(2) is useful to get a feel for the underlying purpose or policy behind the "dividend boot" provisions in §356(a)(2). Prior to the addition of the special "dividend boot" provision, boot received in a tax-free reorganization was taxed simply as capital gain. The example used in the legislative history provides a good illustration of congressional concerns leading to adoption of the "dividend boot" provision now found in §356(a)(2). In the example, Corporation A had accumulated earnings of $50,000. A direct distribution of these earnings would result in ordinary dividend income to the shareholders. On the other hand, Corporation A could create, and then merge with, a new Corporation (B), transferring all of its assets and liabilities to the new corporation. As part of the merger transaction, the old Corporation A shareholders would receive B stock and $50,000 cash in exchange for their old A shares. Since this exchange qualified as a tax-free reorganization, the shareholders were entitled to nonrecognition on the receipt of Corporation B stock. And, under the old boot rules, the cash was taxed at capital gains rates. As the example illustrates, §356(a)(2) was designed to prevent an "evasive" bailout of corporate earnings at capital gains rather than ordinary income rates.[109]

From the time of its enactment, the most difficult and controversial §356 issue has been determining when the shareholder has received a distribution that "has the effect of the distribution of a dividend," thus bringing it within the §356(a)(2) dividend rule as opposed to the §356(a)(1) capital gain rule.[110] After a period during which boot received in tax-free reorganizations was virtually always treated as an "automatic dividend" to the extent of earnings and profits,[111] the Treasury Department and the courts finally agreed that they should look to the §302 redemption rules in designing a "dividend equivalence" test for purposes of §356(a)(2). After all, the point of the §302 redemption rules is to distinguish sale or exchange type redemp-

---

109. H.R. Rep. No. 179, 68th Cong. 1st Sess. 15 (1923).

110. Individual taxpayers would generally prefer to have the boot classified under §356(a)(1) to take advantage of the preferential capital gains rates. Corporate shareholders, on the other hand, would generally prefer to have boot classified under §356(a)(2) to take advantage of the §243 dividends-received deduction.

111. Comm'r v. Estate of Bedford, 325 U.S. 283 (1945). The Service at first adopted this "automatic dividend" approach, Rev. Rul. 56-220, 1956-1 C.B. 191, but later abandoned it. Rev. Rul. 74-515, 1974-2 C.B. 118.

tion distributions eligible for capital gains treatment from dividend-like redemption distributions to be treated as ordinary income dividends. The idea behind §302 is that shareholders receiving distributions in redemption without significantly reducing their proportionate interest in the corporation should not be entitled to capital gain treatment.[112] Similarly, it was thought that shareholders receiving boot in a reorganization transaction should experience a significant reduction in their proportionate interest before being entitled to capital gain treatment under §356(a)(1). Despite agreement that §302 was the appropriate analogy, disagreement quickly emerged regarding how the redemption rules should be applied in the reorganization context. In an acquisitive reorganization, should the redemption tests be applied to stock of the target corporation or to stock of the purchasing corporation? Should the redemption tests be applied just before or just after the reorganization exchange? And finally, whose earnings and profits should count?

The major disagreement between the pre-reorganization and post-reorganization views was finally resolved by the Supreme Court's decision in Commissioner v. Clark.[113] The taxpayer, Clark, was the sole shareholder of a small corporation. He agreed to a transaction in which his wholly owned corporation was merged into a subsidiary of a large publicly held corporation. Clark turned down an offer of 425,000 purchasing corporation common shares in exchange for his stock in the target corporation. Instead, Clark ultimately received only 300,000 shares of the purchasing corporation's stock and over $3 million in cash "to boot." Clark's ownership interest in the publicly held corporation after the reorganization was 0.92%.

Under the pre-reorganization view advocated by the government,[114] the cash boot payment should be regarded as a hypothetical redemption by the target corporation immediately *before* the reorganization. Since Clark was the *sole* shareholder of the target, treating the boot as a hypothetical redemption of target stock would have resulted in dividend treatment under the United States v. Davis principle that a redemption from a *sole* shareholder does not result in a meaningful reduction in the shareholder's interest.[115]

The Supreme Court rejected this approach, instead adopting a post-reorganization view. To reach this result, the Court held that the transaction should be viewed "as a whole" in determining whether it has the effect of

---

112. For a full discussion of the §302 redemption provisions and the logic behind them, see Chapter 6.

113. 489 U.S. 726 (1989).

114. This was the approach adopted in Shimberg v. United States, 577 F.2d 283 (5th Cir. 1978). The Fifth Circuit in *Shimberg* applied a pre-reorganization test under §356, asking "whether the distribution would have been taxed as a dividend if made *prior to* the reorganization or if no reorganization had occurred." *Id*. at 288 (emphasis added).

115. The *Davis* "meaningful reduction" test under §302 was discussed in Chapter 6.

the distribution of a dividend.[116] Under the post-reorganization approach, the Court treated the distribution of boot to Mr. Clark as a redemption by the *purchasing* corporation immediately after the acquisitive reorganization transaction. The Court viewed the transaction as if Mr. Clark had received the full 425,000 purchasing corporation shares originally offered and then had 125,000 shares redeemed for cash, thus leaving him with the 300,000 shares he actually received in the transaction. So viewed, his interest in the purchasing corporation was hypothetically reduced from 1.3% to 0.92%. Since this reduction would have been sufficient to qualify as a §302(b)(2) redemption, the Court found that Mr. Clark was entitled to capital gain, as opposed to dividend, treatment under §356(a).

In its reasoning, the Court adopted the rule of statutory construction that exceptions to the general rule are to be narrowly construed. Since §356(a)(2) is an exception to the general capital gain rule in §356(a)(1), its scope should be limited. Moreover, it was important to the Court that this was an arm's-length transaction with a purchasing corporation in which Mr. Clark had no prior interest. The Court concluded that "unlike traditional single corporation redemptions and unlike reorganizations involving commonly owned corporations, there is little risk that the reorganization at issue was used as a ruse to distribute a dividend."[117]

Since the Court in *Clark* applied §356(a)(1), it did not reach the issue of which corporation's earnings and profits are relevant in the case of boot which "has the effect of the distribution of a dividend" under §356(a)(2). The traditional view is that one must look to the earnings and profits of the acquired or target corporation for purposes of §356(a)(2). On the other hand, the Supreme Court's view of the *Clark* transaction "as a whole" may suggest that one should look to the earnings and profits of the purchasing corporation, or perhaps, both corporations.[118]

Tax Consequences to the Corporation in a Reorganization

Absent special rules, a corporation that transfers property in return for stock or securities of another corporation *realizes* gain or loss from the exchange

---

116. 489 U.S. at 737. In adopting this post-reorganization view, the Supreme Court sided with the Eighth Circuit, which applied a post-reorganization test in Wright v. United States, 482 F.2d 600 (8th Cir. 1973). The Eighth Circuit there compared the boot received from the purchasing corporation with what the shareholder hypothetically *would* have received if he had taken stock only from the purchasing corporation without any boot.

117. 489 U.S. at 744.

118. In at least one early case, the Fifth Circuit looked at the earnings and profits of both corporations for §356(a)(2) purposes. Davant v. Comm'r, 366 F.2d 874 (5th Cir. 1966), *cert. denied,* 386 U.S. 1022 (1967).

under §§61(a)(3) and 1001. In addition, corporations that distribute property to shareholders realize, and ordinarily must recognize, gains and losses.[119] A special nonrecognition rule is provided in §361 for a corporate "party to a reorganization" that "in pursuance of a plan of reorganization" exchanges property in return for stock or securities of another corporate "party to the reorganization."[120] Even if the corporation receives property other than stock or securities in the exchange, the receiving corporation will not be required to recognize gain if the other property is distributed pursuant to the plan of reorganization.[121] Finally, the corporation is entitled to nonrecognition treatment on distributions to shareholders of certain qualified property in connection with the reorganization.[122] Thus, a properly structured corporate reorganization will be tax-free to the participating corporations.

In addition, under §1032, no gain or loss is recognized when a corporation receives money or property in exchange for its own stock.[123] Thus, a corporation that acquires stock or assets in a tax-free reorganization generally will not recognize gain or loss. Finally, in addition to concerns about gain or loss recognition, the acquiring corporation will be concerned about the survival of net operating losses and other tax characteristics of the acquired corporation. These issues will be discussed in the next chapter on acquisitive reorganizations.[124]

Meaning of "Party to a Reorganization" and "Plan of Reorganization"

The various shareholder and corporate nonrecognition rules incorporated into the tax-free reorganization provisions require transaction participants to be a "party to a reorganization" and further require that the exchange take place pursuant to a "plan of reorganization." For example, the shareholder

---

119. Gains and losses generally are recognized upon liquidating distributions under §336. In the case of nonliquidating distributions, §311 requires recognition of gain, but does not permit losses. For a detailed discussion of §§311 and 336, see Chapters 5 and 8, respectively.

120. I.R.C. §361(a).

121. I.R.C. §361(b).

122. I.R.C. §361(c).

123. This provision also was discussed earlier in connection with incorporation transactions. See Chapter 4. Notice that the scope of §1032 is not limited to organizations or reorganizations. A corporation that receives money or other property in return for its own stock recognizes no gain or loss, even if the transaction does not qualify as a tax-free §351 exchange or as a reorganization under §368(a).

124. See Chapter 12 for discussion of the survival of net operating loss and other tax characteristics following a reorganization.

nonrecognition rule in §354 requires the exchange of stock or securities in a corporation that is a "party to a reorganization" in return for stock or securities of the same corporation or another corporation that also is a "party to a reorganization." Similar language shows up in the §361 nonrecognition rule applicable to the distributing corporation. Under §361, a corporation that is a "party to the reorganization" is eligible for nonrecognition only upon the exchange of its property in return for stock or securities in another corporation that is a "party to a reorganization."

This frequently used term is defined in §368(b) to include a corporation resulting from a reorganization and both corporations, in the case of an acquisitive reorganization. As the opportunities for triangular reorganizations have expanded over the years, Congress has expanded the §368(b) "party to a reorganization" definition to include the multiple corporate participants in the transaction. For example, when a purchasing corporation uses a subsidiary to acquire stock or property of a target, the target corporation, the purchasing corporation and its subsidiary all will be considered parties to the reorganization.[125]

For the participants to be eligible for nonrecognition treatment, the tax-free reorganization provisions of Subchapter C also generally require that the transaction be pursuant to a "plan of reorganization."[126] The Code itself provides no definition, but the regulations refer to:

> a *consummated transaction* specifically defined as a reorganization under section 368(a). The term is not to be construed as broadening the definition of "reorganization" . . . but is to be taken as limiting the nonrecognition of gain or loss to such exchanges or distributions *as are directly a part of the transaction specifically described as a reorganization in section 368(a).*[127]

The regulatory definition of "plan of reorganization" reflects the government's concern that the boundaries of the transaction for which nonrecognition is available not be loosely defined. Nonrecognition should be limited to a discrete reorganization transaction with a beginning and an end and should not extend to peripheral or related transactions.

Reorganization Basis Rules

Given the nonrecognition provisions of §§354, 361, and 1032, most accountants, lawyers, and academics working with Subchapter C refer to cor-

---

125. See Chapter 12 for a more detailed discussion of this expansion of the "party to a reorganization" definition in the case of triangular acquisitions.

126. See, e.g., §§354(a), 361(a).

127. Treas. Reg. §1.368-2(g) (emphasis added).

porate reorganizations as "tax-free reorganizations." As is the case with most nonrecognition provisions in the Internal Revenue Code, however, the nonrecognition comes at a price. Specifically, the property permitted to be received tax-free generally receives a substituted, as opposed to a cost, basis. An understanding of substituted basis will be quite central to understanding tax-free reorganizations.

The shareholders who receive stock or securities tax-free under §354 will take the same basis that they previously had in the shares transferred as their basis in the shares received.[128] Similarly, a corporation receiving property tax-free under §1032 will take the same basis that the transferor had.[129] The substituted basis rules preserve the realized gain or loss for potential later recognition upon subsequent transfer of the property. Thus, the tax-free reorganization provisions will not necessarily permanently exclude, but simply defer, realized gains and losses.[130] These basis rules will be taken up in the context of particular reorganization transactions in the chapters that follow.

---

128. I.R.C. §358.

129. I.R.C. §362(b).

130. It should be noted, however, that a shareholder who receives stock in a tax-free reorganization effectively can transfer the stock with a fair market value basis upon death under §1014. Thus, in some cases, the realized gain or loss may never be recognized.

12

Acquisitive Reorganizations

Introduction

Just as taxable acquisitions can be arranged as either transfers of stock or of assets,[1] tax-free acquisitive reorganizations also can be arranged as either stock or asset deals. A tax-free acquisitive stock acquisition can be structured under §368(a)(1)(B), while a tax-free acquisitive asset acquisition is possible under either §368(a)(1)(A) or (C). Before moving on to the detailed requirements for each of these transactions, stop for a moment to reconsider the policy for affording nonrecognition treatment to acquisitive reorganizations — the now familiar notion of "mere change in form." In a taxable transaction, the target corporation and its shareholders are ending their corporate investment — "cashing out." In the tax-free acquisition, the target corporation and its shareholders have not "cashed out" their investment, but instead have traded an investment in target assets or stock for an investment in the newly reorganized corporate entity. Under these circumstances, Congress felt that recognition of gain or loss could wait until a subsequent sale or disposition by the target shareholders of the purchasing corporation stock received in the acquisition or a sale by the purchasing corporation of the target assets received in the acquisition. The parties to the reorganization transaction remain substantially invested in the restructured corporate enterprise, and gain or loss left unrecognized can be deferred through the use of substituted basis rules.[2] Since the transaction represents a "mere change in form," it is not an appropriate moment to impose tax recognition.

---

1. Taxable acquisitions were covered in detail in Chapter 10.

2. For a complete discussion of this underlying policy and other basic principles applicable to reorganizations generally, you may wish to review Chapter 11.

Unfortunately, the policy works better in theory than in practice. The Supreme Court itself noted in an acquisitive reorganization case that "[b]ecause of the arbitrary and technical character, and the somewhat 'hodgepodge' form, of the statutes involved, the interpretation problem presented is highly complicated."[3] My best advice in mastering the mechanics is to take a deep breath and to proceed slowly and carefully. More importantly, try to keep your eye on the big picture. Keep the underlying nonrecognition policy in mind as you work through the following materials on tax-free reorganizations. Finally, read critically. You will find that many specific aspects of the tax-free reorganization provisions are difficult to justify based upon coherent tax policy objectives. An understanding of these difficulties will serve you well in understanding discussions of corporate tax reform.

Recall that there are two key differences between taxable acquisitions and tax-free acquisitive reorganizations. First, and most importantly, the seller will recognize gain or loss in a taxable acquisition, but is eligible for nonrecognition treatment in the case of a tax-free reorganization.[4] In a taxable asset acquisition, the target corporation will report gain or loss on the sale of the assets under §§61(a)(3) and 1001. The target shareholders will also report gain or loss when the target distributes the consideration it received for the asset sale. In a taxable stock acquisition, the selling shareholders report gain or loss upon sale of the target stock under §§61(a)(3) and 1001. In contrast, the target corporation and its shareholders in a tax-free asset acquisition are eligible for nonrecognition treatment under §§361 and 354. Similarly, the selling shareholders in a tax-free stock acquisition are eligible for nonrecognition under §354.

The second key distinction in tax consequence between taxable acquisitions and tax-free reorganizations involves basis rules. Taxable acquisitions often are referred to as "cost basis" transactions. In a taxable asset acquisition, the purchasing corporation simply acquires a cost basis in the target corporation's assets under §1012.[5] In a taxable stock acquisition, the purchasing corporation acquires a cost basis in the target corporation's stock and may effectively receive a cost basis in the target assets with an appropriate election to step-up the basis under §338.[6] Tax-free reorganizations, on the other hand, often are referred to as "substituted basis" transactions. In a tax-free asset acquisition, the acquiring corporation takes the target corporation's assets

---

3. Turnbow v. Comm'r, 368 U.S. 337, 339 (1961).

4. This is not to say that target shareholders will *never* recognize gain or loss in a tax-free reorganization. Shareholders *will* be taxable immediately on boot received as part of the transaction as well as payments received for accrued interest. The tax treatment of §356 boot was discussed in Chapter 11. These matters will be considered in further detail later in this chapter.

5. Assuming an arm's-length purchase, this cost basis should be equal to the fair market value of the assets.

6. The stepped-up basis election under §338 was covered in detail in Chapter 10.

with the same basis that the target corporation had under §362. In a tax-free stock acquisition, the target corporation's assets simply retain their historic bases.[7]

The combined effect of the nonrecognition and basis rules for reorganizations is effective *deferral* of gain or loss. Although the target and its shareholders in a tax-free reorganization do not recognize *immediate* gain or loss, they will not necessarily escape taxation in the long run. The gain or loss not recognized at the time of the reorganization is preserved through special substituted basis rules. Thus, for example, if the old target shareholders later dispose of the purchasing corporation shares acquired as part of the reorganization, they will measure their gain or loss using the basis from their old target shares. Gain or loss in the old target shares is thus preserved.[8] If the purchasing corporation later disposes of the old target's assets, it will measure its gain or loss using the target's old basis, thus preserving the gain or loss in the assets.

Acquisitive Stock Reorganizations: The Basic Type B Reorganization

Description of the Basic Type B Transaction

In a simple Type B reorganization, the purchasing corporation (P) acquires a controlling interest in the target corporation (T) stock from the T shareholders solely in exchange for all or part of P's voting stock.[9] Two significant elements of the Type B reorganization should be noted at the outset. First, and most importantly, the purchasing corporation must have *control* over the target corporation immediately after the stock acquisition from the target shareholders. "Control," for purposes of §368, generally requires ownership by the acquiring corporation of "at least 80 percent of the total combined voting power of all classes of stock entitled to vote" *and* "at least 80 percent of the total number of shares of all other classes of stock."[10]

---

7. A subsequent upstream merger of the subsidiary into the parent also will preserve the target corporation's historic basis in the assets. I.R.C. §334(b). See Chapter 9 for a full discussion of subsidiary liquidations.

8. One way for the shareholders to escape this preserved gain or loss is to leave the purchasing corporation shares to beneficiaries upon death. The beneficiaries will received a stepped-up (or possibly stepped-down) basis under §1014, and the otherwise preserved gain or loss from the target shares will be lost.

9. I.R.C. §368(a)(1)(B).

10. I.R.C. §368(c). Notice that the "control" test used for purposes of the tax-free reorganization provisions is the same control test used for purposes of §351 incorporation transactions. For a discussion of the control requirement in connection with incorporation transactions, see Chapter 4.

Second, the Type B reorganization provides explicit rules regarding the type of consideration that may be used to compensate target shareholders for their stock. The target shareholders must exchange T stock *solely* for all or part of the acquiring corporation's voting stock or *solely* for all or part of the voting stock of the acquiring corporation's parent. Thus, the *only* consideration that may be used in a Type B reorganization is *voting* stock of the acquiring corporation or its parent.[11] One minor exception to this rule is that the "'solely for voting stock' requirement . . . will not be violated where the cash paid by the acquiring corporation is in lieu of fractional share interests to which the shareholders are entitled, representing merely a mechanical rounding-off of the fractions in the exchange, and is not separately bargained for consideration."[12]

As a result of the rigid rules in §368(a)(1)(B), no "boot" is permitted in a B reorganization. By specifying that *only* voting stock may be used in a Type B reorganization, Congress has built the continuity of proprietary interest requirement directly into the statute itself, assuring a continued connection between the target shareholders and the assets of the old target corporation. Such continuity of proprietary interest surely exists when the target shareholders receive consideration entirely in the form of the purchasing corporation's voting stock, as required by §368(a)(1)(B). Remember, however, that the transaction must also meet the continuity of business enterprise and business purpose tests discussed in Chapter 11 to qualify for nonrecognition.

Tax Consequences of the Basic Type B Reorganization

The simplest Type B reorganization is one where the purchasing corporation (P) acquires 100% of the stock of the target corporation (T) from T's shareholders entirely in exchange for P voting stock in a single transaction.

---

11. The stock used in the Type B reorganization may be either common or preferred, as long as the stock is voting stock.

12. Rev. Rul. 66-365, 1966-2 C.B. 116, 117.

Type B Reorganization

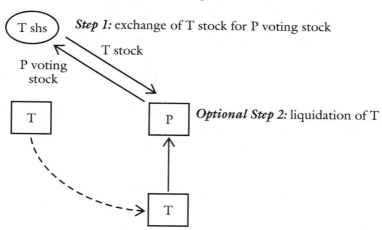

Step 1: exchange of T stock for P voting stock

T stock

T shs

P voting stock

Optional Step 2: liquidation of T

Since the T shareholders exchanged stock in one corporation a party to a reorganization (T) solely for stock in another corporation a party to a reorganization (P), they will not report gain or loss on the exchange.[13] Under §358(a)(1), the T shareholders' basis in P stock received in the exchange will be the same basis that they previously had in their T shares — a substituted basis.[14] As a result of its acquisition of all of the T stock, P is the new owner of T, now a wholly owned P subsidiary. Under §1032, P has no gain or loss upon the receipt of T stock in exchange for its own stock.[15] P's basis in its new T shares will be the same basis the old T shareholders previously had in their T shares pursuant to §362(b).[16] T will retain its historic basis in its assets. Put another way, T's assets will not receive a stepped-up basis as a result of the acquisition.

P may choose to continue to operate T as a subsidiary, or instead may choose to liquidate or merge T into P in an upstream merger. If the initial Type B reorganization and the subsequent liquidation are respected as separate transactions, T's liquidation will be governed by the subsidiary liquidation rules provided in §332.[17] On the other hand, if the merger of T into P

---

13. I.R.C. §354(a)(1). The term "party to a reorganization" includes "both corporations, in the case of a reorganization resulting from the acquisition by one corporation of stock or properties of another." I.R.C. §368(b)(2).

14. The holding period for the P stock received will include the period during which the shareholder held the T stock under "tacking" rules provided in §1223(1).

15. I.R.C. §1032(a).

16. Where the target is a publicly held corporation, it may be difficult for P to know each T shareholder's basis in the T shares. P is entitled to use a statistical sampling. See Rev. Proc. 81-70, 1981-2 C.B. 729.

17. For a detailed discussion of the tax consequences upon liquidation of a subsidiary, see Chapter 9.

was part of an overall integrated plan, the initial transaction may not be regarded as a Type B reorganization at all, but instead, recast for tax purposes under the step-transaction doctrine as a Type C asset acquisition.[18]

P may acquire less than 100% of the T stock solely in exchange for P voting stock and the transaction still will qualify as a Type B reorganization as long as P has control immediately after the exchange, as defined in §368(c).[19] If P acquires only 80% of the T stock in the reorganization, the tax consequences to T, to P, and to the participating T shareholders essentially are the same as above.

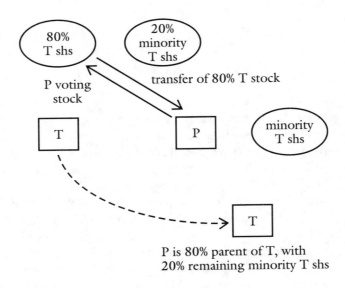

P is 80% parent of T, with
20% remaining minority T shs

The participating T shareholders will not recognize gain or loss and the T assets will retain their historic basis. P also will recognize no gain or loss and its basis in its T stock will be the same as the participating old T shareholders' basis in their old shares. Here, however, P is not the *sole* owner of T, but instead a part owner of its new subsidiary, T. The nonparticipating T shareholders are left as co-owners or minority shareholders of the new subsidiary.[20] Their basis in the T shares they continue to hold will remain the same.

18. See, e.g., Rev. Rul. 67-274, 1967-2 C.B. 141. Discussion of the Type C asset acquisition appears later in this chapter.

19. A Type B reorganization also can occur over time in what is referred to as a "creeping acquisition." Such acquisitions are discussed later in this section.

20. The minority shareholders may wish to be "bought out" at some point rather than remain as minority shareholders. Efforts to "buy out" minority shareholders in a Type B reorganization may result in tax difficulties that will be discussed later in this chapter.

Rigidity of the "Solely for Voting Stock" Requirement

The statutory language of §368(a)(1)(B) explicitly requires that the exchange in a Type B reorganization be solely for all or part of the acquiring corporation's voting stock or solely for all or part of the voting stock of a corporation in control of the acquiror (a parent). This requirement is quite strictly enforced. In the early landmark case of Helvering v. Southwest Consolidated Corporation,[21] the parties adopted a plan of reorganization under which the acquiring corporation purchased assets for voting stock and stock purchase warrants. In addition, some security holders of the old corporation who wished not to participate in the reorganization were bought out for cash. This transaction was held to be an invalid reorganization for several reasons, among them that part of the acquisition was for stock purchase warrants and part for cash. The transaction thus failed the "solely for voting stock" requirement. The Supreme Court noted that:

> Congress has provided that the assets of the transferor corporation must be acquired in exchange "solely" for "voting stock" of the transferee. *"Solely" leaves no leeway. Voting stock plus some other consideration does not meet the statutory requirement.*[22]

Strict application of the "solely for voting stock" requirement leaves little room for flexibility in structuring a Type B reorganization.[23] As some put it, there can be "no boot in a B." Since the acquiring corporation cannot use any consideration other than its own voting stock or voting stock of a parent corporation, it will be difficult to compensate target shareholders who wish not to participate in the reorganization. There is no direct way to "buy out" dissenting shareholders. As a policy matter, it makes little sense for Congress to be so rigid with regard to Type B reorganizations when similar economic results can be achieved through a Type A or Type C acquisitive reorganization with much greater flexibility. Nevertheless, the distinctions between the different types of acquisitive reorganizations remain.[24]

Given the strict "solely for voting stock" restriction applied in the Type B reorganization context, acquiring corporations must be creative in dealing with minority or nonparticipating target corporation shareholders. Any cash

---

21. 315 U.S. 194 (1942).

22. *Id.* at 198 (emphasis added).

23. Congress has relaxed the "solely for voting stock" requirement for asset acquisitions under §368(a)(1)(C), however. These more relaxed rules will be considered in subsequent sections of this chapter.

24. Further discussion of proposals to eliminate traps for the unwary created by the technical and rigid distinctions between the different types of tax-free acquisitions appears at the end of this chapter.

or notes paid to any shareholders may cause the transaction to violate the requirements of §368(a)(1)(B).

One technique sometimes used to buy out target shareholders who do not wish to participate in the acquisition transaction is a redemption of the nonparticipating shareholder's interests by the target corporation. Until recently, the Treasury Department agreed that if the target corporation redeemed stock from some of its shareholders prior to the reorganization using its own funds or funds borrowed on its own credit, the subsequent Type B stock-for-stock exchange would still qualify.[25]

Target Corporation Liabilities in a Type B Transaction

Ordinarily, if a taxpayer's liability is assumed by another, or if the taxpayer's property is transferred subject to a liability, the taxpayer will have cancellation of indebtedness income or the amount of the liability will be included in the amount realized on the sale. Technically, a Type B reorganization is not a transfer of assets, but a transfer of stock ownership. After the exchange, the target corporation has a new owner, but remains liable to creditors for its debts. Since T simply remains liable for its debts, there technically is no assumption of liability by P and thus no violation of the "solely for voting stock" requirement.

On the other hand, the target's security holders sometimes do exchange T debt for cash or P debt in connection with a Type B reorganization. Historically, the government took the position that such ancillary exchanges were separate transactions not governed by the tax-free reorganization rules. Surely, debt holders should be taxed to the extent that they receive cash in exchange for debt. Under the government's old position, ancillary debt-for-debt exchanges were considered taxable as well. In a significant change of position, the Service recently ruled that a debt-for-debt exchange that accompanies a Type B reorganization "is not part of the stock-for-stock exchange which qualifies as a reorganization. *It is, however, an exchange of securities in parties to a reorganization which occurs in pursuance of the plan of reorganization and, therefore, meets all the conditions of §354(a)(1)*."[26] In other words, the debt-for-debt exchange should now be eligible for tax-free reorganization treatment except to the extent of boot received under §356.

---

25. See, e.g., Rev. Rul. 68-285, 1968-1 C.B. 147. In using this technique, however, the parties had to be careful to assure that no funds used in the target shareholder redemption came from the acquiring corporation or an affiliate of the acquiring corporation. See, e.g., Rev. Rul. 75-360, 1975-2 C.B. 110 ("solely for voting stock" requirement not met where cash from acquiring corporation was used to pay off target company bank loan). See also Rev. Rul. 74-565, 1974-2 C.B. 125.

26. Rev. Rul. 98-10, 1998-1 C.B. 643 (emphasis added).

Revenue Rule 98–10 is most notable for extending tax-free treatment to these debt-for-debt exchanges. It is also notable, however, because some of the target debentures exchanged for acquiring company debentures were held by target shareholders. Nevertheless, the ruling concludes that the "solely for voting stock" requirement is met because the target shareholders received only voting stock "in their capacity as shareholders."[27]

A more difficult question arises if the target corporation's shareholders guaranteed the target debts and the debts are later paid off by the acquiring corporation. In such a case, the relief from a guarantor obligation paid by the acquiring corporation may be considered additional consideration other than voting stock. As long as the acquiring corporation's payment of the debt was not a condition for the exchange of stock, the Internal Revenue Service regards the payment of debt as a separate transaction from the reorganization and the stock-for-stock exchange should still qualify as a Type B reorganization.[28]

Type B Acquisitions over Time

a) Old and Cold Target Stock Acquired for Consideration Other than Stock

An acquiring corporation does not necessarily purchase all of its stock in the target corporation at one time. The acquiring corporation might own a small amount of the target corporation's stock that it acquired years before, perhaps with no intention of making any additional purchases. Subsequently, the acquiring corporation might acquire additional interests in the target corporation sufficient to acquire control over the target. An issue that arises here is whether the "old and cold stock" held by the purchasing corporation acquired with consideration other than voting stock will prevent the subsequent acquisition from qualifying as a Type B reorganization. The regulations provide an example of a corporation that purchased 30% of the target corporation's stock for cash in 1939. Sixteen years later, in 1955, the purchasing corporation acquired an additional 60% of the target corporation's stock in exchange solely for its own voting stock. Immediately after the acquisition, the purchasing corporation owned 90% of the target. The regu-

---

27. *Id.* One should be cautious in relying upon this ruling for transactions in which there is a substantial overlap of ownership between the target shareholders and security holders. The Service was careful to note that "[t]he fact that a substantial proportion of the Y debentures is held by bondholders who own no stock in Y has the effect of ensuring that the value of the debentures of Y realistically reflects the value of the Y debentures alone and does not constitute indirect nonqualifying consideration for the Y stock." *Id.*

28. Rev. Rul. 79-4, 1979-1 C.B. 150; Rev. Rul. 79-89, 1979-1 C.B. 152.

lation concludes that this transaction was a Type B reorganization.[29] This regulatory example clarifies that it is not necessary that the acquiring corporation actually acquire an 80% controlling interest in the reorganization exchange itself and that ownership of some "old and cold stock" in the target corporation will not prevent the acquiring corporation from arranging a subsequent Type B acquisitive reorganization. The statute simply requires that the acquiring corporation have control immediately after the exchange.

Dangers may be lurking, however, for the acquiring corporation with "old and cold" stock. If the earlier cash purchase and the subsequent stock-for-stock acquisition are regarded as part of an integrated transaction under the step-transaction doctrine, the transaction will violate the solely for voting stock requirement of §368(a)(1)(B). In Chapman v. Commissioner, the taxpayer argued that it satisfied §368(a)(1)(B) when it acquired 80% control over the target corporation solely in exchange for its own stock even though it had acquired target shares for cash in an earlier acquisition that was conceded to be part of an integrated plan. The First Circuit disagreed, stating:

> We believe that the presence of nonstock consideration in [a Type B reorganization], regardless of whether such consideration is necessary to the gaining of control, is inconsistent with treatment of the acquisition as a nontaxable reorganization.[30]

One way to avoid these dangers is for the acquiring corporation to unconditionally sell all of the earlier acquired shares to a third party prior to any offer to acquire the target shareholders' stock in a subsequent Type B reorganization.[31]

b)   Creeping Acquisitions

Despite the rigidity regarding the *type* of consideration used in a Type B reorganization, there is some flexibility regarding *timing*. An acquiring corporation need not necessarily take control of the target corporation in one fell swoop. The acquiring corporation may make a "creeping acquisition" in which a controlling interest in the target corporation's stock is acquired over a period of time. The fact that the acquisition takes place over a period of time will not necessarily disqualify it from Type B reorganization treatment as long as each acquisition was part of an integrated plan and as long as the

---

29. Treas. Reg. §1.368-2(c).

30. 618 F.2d 856, 862 (1st Cir. 1980).

31. See, e.g., Rev. Rul. 72-354, 1972-2 C.B. 216, in which the Treasury Department permitted Type B reorganization treatment in a case in which the acquiring corporation sold stock previously acquired for cash in an unconditional sale with no agreement or arrangement to reacquire the stock and subsequently entered into a Type B stock-for-stock exchange.

transaction meets the "solely for voting stock" requirement. If the acquiring corporation uses any consideration other than its own voting stock for any piece of a transaction viewed as an overall integrated plan, then the acquisition will not be a proper Type B reorganization. After the lessons learned from the *Chapman* case, the acquiring corporation must be careful to assure that *each purchase* that is part of the overall acquisition plan meets the "solely for voting stock" requirement, even though 80% or more of the T stock was acquired for P stock.

Acquisitive Asset Reorganizations: Basic Statutory Mergers and Consolidations

Description of the Basic Type A Reorganization

Section 368(a)(1)(A) simply provides that a "statutory merger or consolidation" is a reorganization. To qualify as a Type A reorganization, the transaction must satisfy all of the applicable merger or consolidation requirements under the corporation laws of the federal or state government.[32] In the typical merger transaction, one corporation is absorbed into another corporation, with only one of the two corporations surviving. In a typical consolidation, two corporations are combined into a new entity, and both of the old corporate entities disappear.

Type A Merger	**Type A Consolidation**
merger under state law	consolidation under state law

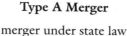

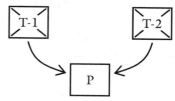

T is absorbed by P and ceases to exist	T-1 and T-2 are absorbed by P and cease to exist
T shs must retain a substantial proprietary interest in P	T-1 and T-2 shareholders must retain a substantial proprietary interest in P

Historically, state corporation laws that permitted mergers or consolidations incorporated strict standards. These included requirements that the

---

32. Treas. Reg. §1.368-2(b)(1).

target and purchasing corporation engage in similar businesses, that the target shareholders receive a substantial equity interest in the purchasing corporation, and that the target corporation cease to exist. Thus, when Congress first restricted tax-free reorganization treatment to mergers or consolidations meeting state statutory requirements, the idea was to *limit* tax-free treatment to reorganization transactions that met such stringent continuity of interest requirements.[33] Over time, however, it became clear that state corporation laws were hardly uniform. A transaction might technically meet the state-law definition of a merger and yet look very much like a sale. Thus, the courts soon began to require that, in addition to qualifying as a state law merger or consolidation, the transaction must meet the continuity of proprietary interest, continuity of business enterprise, and business purpose tests.[34] Some modern state statutes now even include within the definition of a merger transactions in which both the target and the purchasing corporations survive.[35] Such transactions more closely resemble divisive reorganizations than acquisitive reorganizations. The Service recently ruled not only that a Type A reorganization must meet business purpose, continuity of business enterprise, and continuity of interest tests, but also that "a transaction effectuated under a corporate law merger statute must have the result that one corporation acquires the assets of the target corporation by operation of the corporate law merger statute and that the target corporation ceases to exist."[36]

Unlike the Type B and C reorganizations, Congress failed to specify precise statutory requirements for the continuity of proprietary interest requirement in the case of Type A reorganizations. Consequently, the early case law on continuity of proprietary interest continues to apply. Recall that under the test from *Minnesota Tea*, continuity requires that the target shareholders receive a "definite and substantial interest" in the acquiring corporation and that this interest must represent a "material part of the value of the transferred assets."[37] As discussed in Chapter 11, this test addresses both the *type* of consideration necessary for a proprietary interest and the *propor-*

---

33. For an interesting and useful discussion of this history, see Steven A. Bank, Federalizing the Tax-Free Merger: Toward an End to the Anachronistic Reliance on State Corporation Laws, 77 N.C. L. Rev. 1307 (1999).

34. These rules have since been incorporated into the §368 regulations. Treas. Reg. §1.368-1(b). For a detailed discussion of the judicial development of these requirements, see Chapter 11.

35. See, e.g., Tex. Bus. Corp. Act Ann. arts. 1.02A(18), 5.01 (West Supp. 1999).

36. Rev. Rul. 2000-5, 2000-5 I.R.B. 436.

37. 296 U.S. 378, 386 (1935). For a more detailed discussion of the *Minnesota Tea* case and the early development of the continuity of proprietary interest test, see Chapter 11.

tion of total consideration in the reorganization exchange that must consist of such a proprietary interest. Under the Internal Revenue Service interpretation, fully *one-half* of the consideration paid in a Type A reorganization may be something other than stock.[38] The opportunity to use a substantial proportion of assets other than stock as consideration in a Type A reorganization makes this type of acquisitive transaction far more flexible than the Type B reorganization. Thus, one advantage to the Type A reorganization is its greater flexibility regarding the buy out of dissenting or otherwise nonparticipating shareholders.[39] On the other hand, the absence of precise statutory rules regarding the continuity of proprietary interest test in the Type A reorganization context creates uncertainty for taxpayers.

Tax Consequences of the Basic Type A Reorganization

Assume that the target corporation (T) is merged into the purchasing corporation (P) in a state law merger that qualifies as a Type A reorganization. T shareholders who receive only P stock will have no gain or loss pursuant to §354 and their basis in the P shares will be the same basis they previously had in their T shares under §358.[40] Shareholders who receive P stock *and* boot will get tax-free treatment with respect to the stock, but will be taxable on the boot to the extent of realized gain under §356. The boot will either be taxed as capital gain under §356(a)(1) or as a dividend under §356(a)(2).[41]

P will not report any gain or loss upon the receipt of assets from T as part of the merger transaction pursuant to §1032. P's basis in the assets acquired from T will be the same basis as in T's hands under §362(b).[42] In

---

38. Treas. Reg. §1.368-1(e)(6), ex. 1. The case law is even more forgiving. For example, in John A. Nelson Corp. v. Helvering, 296 U.S. 374 (1935), a transaction with only 38% equity qualified as a tax-free reorganization. For a more detailed discussion, see Chapter 11.

39. Similarly, a Type C reorganization provides somewhat greater flexibility in this regard than a Type B reorganization, but still less flexibility than the Type A reorganization. Details regarding the Type C reorganizations are considered later in this chapter.

40. Again, the holding period for the P stock received will include the period during which the shareholder held the T stock under "tacking" rules in §1223(1).

41. For a more complete discussion of the §356 boot rules, see Chapter 11.

42. Notice that §362(b) provides for an increase in the amount of gain recognized to the transferor. Since T is regarded as the transferor and T has no gain or loss in a Type A reorganization, there will be no step-up in the basis of T's assets now held by P. There is no step-up permitted to P for the *shareholders'* gain on any boot because they are not the transferors of the assets within the meaning of §362(b).

effect, the transaction is viewed as if T first transferred its assets and liabilities to P in exchange for P stock and then immediately distributed the P stock to its shareholders. T has no gain or loss upon the receipt of P stock or securities under §361(a). Further, T is entitled to nonrecognition even for any boot under §361(b), since the boot is viewed as immediately distributed to the shareholders as well. As a matter of course, T's liabilities to its creditors continue and will be the liabilities of the merged entity. On the other hand, if P had any liabilities to T that were discharged as a result of the transaction, P may have cancellation of indebtedness income.

Assumption of Liabilities in Type A Transactions

In a basic two-party merger of a target into a purchasing corporation the target's liabilities simply become the liabilities of the purchaser, by operation of law, with no immediate tax consequence. T remains eligible for nonrecognition under §361(a). And, under §357(a), if another party assumes a liability as part of the consideration in a §361 exchange, the assumption of liability will not prevent the exchange from qualifying for nonrecognition. In other words, the liability assumption will not be considered boot.

A related issue in the Type A reorganization is the treatment of creditors who exchange target securities or debentures for parent securities or debentures. Such creditors are entitled to nonrecognition under §354, subject to taxation on the excess principal amount of securities received over the securities surrendered under §§354(b) and 356.

Type A Acquisitions over Time

In a statutory merger, one corporation merges into another at a particular moment in time. At first blush, the concept of a "creeping acquisition" would not appear to be applicable. However, an acquiring corporation may make stock purchases over time with a plan to eventually merge the target. Moreover, unlike the Type B reorganization, under the Service's interpretation, up to 50% of the consideration in a Type A reorganization may take the form of nonequity consideration. Consequently, it may be possible for P to acquire up to 50% of T's stock for cash and 50% of T's stock for P stock over a period of time culminating in the ultimate merger of T into P. The issue here is whether the ultimate merger of T into P should be treated as a Type A reorganization or instead treated simply as a liquidation of a subsidiary.[43] If all of the purchases of stock are considered part of an integrated acquisition the upstream merger of the subsidiary into the parent will be governed by §332.

---

43. The upstream merger of a subsidiary into a parent is governed by §332 and was considered in further detail in Chapter 9.

Acquisitive Asset Reorganizations: The Basic Type C Reorganization

Description of the Basic Type C Reorganization

a) The "Substantially All of the Properties" Requirement

In a basic Type C reorganization, the purchasing corporation acquires "substantially all of the properties" of another corporation.[44] Consequently, the Type C transaction is referred to as an "asset acquisition."

Type C Reorganization

Step 2: liquidation of T

Step 1: transfer of "substantially all" of T's assets

P voting stock (some "boot" permissible)

If the target transfers *less* than substantially all of its assets, the transaction is not "acquisitive" in nature. A transfer of only *part* of a corporation's assets may still qualify for tax-free reorganization treatment, but authority for such nonrecognition will be found in §368(a)(1)(D), which generally applies to *divisive* reorganizations.[45]

Given the tremendous importance of the "substantially all of the properties" requirement in distinguishing acquisitive from divisive reorganizations, it is surprising to discover that neither the statute itself nor the regulations specify what constitutes "substantially all" of a corporation's properties for purposes of §368(a)(1)(C). There is no precise percentage of assets rule. One should take care to look not only to the percentage of assets transferred, but to compare the nature of the property transferred with the nature of the property retained. If the assets transferred are the major

---

44. I.R.C. §368(a)(1)(C).

45. For a full treatment of §368(a)(1)(D) and divisive reorganizations, see Chapter 13. It also is possible to use §368(a)(1)(D) in connection with an acquisitive reorganization where *all* of the target's assets are transferred. See the subsequent section in this chapter entitled "Nondivisive Type D Reorganizations."

operating assets of the business and the assets retained are largely liquid assets retained to pay off debts, the "substantially all" requirement should be satisfied even though the percentage of liquid assets retained is rather high.[46] For purposes of issuing advanced rulings, the Internal Revenue Service takes the position that "substantially all" means 90% of the fair market value of T's net assets and 70% of the fair market value of T's gross assets.[47]

b) Disregarding the Assumption of Liabilities

With regard to permissible consideration paid to target shareholders, the language in §368(a)(1)(C) is virtually identical to the language in §368(a)(1)(B). In each case, the statutory definition requires that the acquisition be in exchange "solely for all or part of its [the acquiring corporation's] voting stock (or in exchange solely for all or a part of the voting stock of a corporation which is in control of the acquiring corporation)."[48] Despite the virtually identical language, Type C reorganizations are different in several respects. One unique issue in the Type C reorganization context is treatment of the assumption of target liabilities. In a Type B stock acquisition, the purchasing corporation simply becomes the new owner of the target. There is no formal assumption of the target's liabilities; the liabilities simply remain with the target. On the other hand, in a Type C reorganization, the purchasing corporation becomes the new owner of substantially all of the target's assets. The target corporation's liabilities do not transfer to the purchasing corporation along with these assets unless an express agreement to assume liabilities is made part of the transaction. As a practical matter, however, it is common for asset acquisitions to include an assumption of liabilities. Consequently, Congress added a clause to the Type C reorganization definition to assure that the mere assumption of liabilities would not threaten eligibility for tax-free treatment of an asset acquisition. This clause provides that "in determining whether the exchange is solely for stock the assumption by the acquiring corporation of a liability of the other, or the fact that property acquired is subject to a liability shall be disregarded."[49] Thus, the "solely for voting stock" requirement is met if the only other consideration is an as-

---

46. See, e.g., Rev. Rul. 57-518, 1957-2 C.B. 253 (emphasizing the nature of properties retained). See also Robert A. Rizzi, Corporate Organizations and Reorganizations: Quantity and Quality in the Substantially All Requirement, 20 J. Corp. Taxation 171 (1993).

47. Rev. Proc. 77-37, §3.01, 1977-2 C.B. 568. The fair market value of "net assets" is the value of those assets *net* of liabilities.

48. Compare I.R.C. §368(a)(1)(B) with (a)(1)(C).

49. Note, however, that liabilities that were *created* as part of the reorganization transaction itself are not protected by this clause. So, for example, P's assumption of T's liability to pay cash to its dissenting shareholders is not considered a liability for purposes of this clause. See Rev. Rul. 73-102, 1973-1 C.B. 186.

sumption of liabilities.[50] Notice that the assumption of liabilities is disregarded *only* in determining whether the transaction meets the "solely for voting stock" requirement. The regulations are careful to stress that disregarding the assumption of liabilities for this limited purpose "does not prevent consideration of the effect of an assumption of liabilities on the general character of the transaction."[51] In some cases, the assumption of liabilities may "so alter the character of the transaction as to place the transaction outside the purposes and assumptions of the reorganization provisions."[52] So, for example, if the bulk of the transaction consists of an assumption of liabilities with only a small asset component, the transaction may not be eligible for reorganization treatment.

c) The Relaxed Solely for Voting Stock Requirement

Perhaps the most significant statutory distinction between Type B and C reorganizations is the boot relaxation rules for Type C asset acquisitions found in special rules in §368(a)(2)(B). Under this provision, a transaction that would otherwise qualify as a Type C reorganization will not be disqualified by the addition of money or other property (boot) so long as the purchasing corporation does acquire, solely for voting stock, target property with a fair market value of at least 80% of the fair market value of all of the target corporation's property.[53] In other words, despite the "solely for voting stock" requirement explicitly stated in §368(a)(1)(C), the use of consideration other than voting stock for up to 20% of the acquisition will *not* disqualify the Type C reorganization. Thus, in a case where P is acquiring 100% of T's assets, as long as 80% of the acquisition was "solely for voting stock," the remaining 20% of the assets may be acquired for other consideration or "boot." Notice that the boot relaxation rule in §368(a)(2)(B) requires that at least 80% of *all* of the property of the target corporation be acquired in exchange solely for voting stock. Thus, where the purchasing corporation acquires less than *all* of the assets, the amount of boot that will be permitted is reduced accordingly. For example, if P is acquiring only 90% of T's assets, only 10% of the T assets may be acquired for boot.

One caution should be noted, however. In computing the allowable 20% "boot" in a Type C reorganization, the statute requires that liabilities assumed or liabilities to which any property acquired is subject shall be con-

---

50. If the consideration includes both assumption of liabilities and other boot, additional issues arise. These will be considered shortly.

51. Treas. Reg. §1.368-2(d)(1).

52. *Id.*

53. I.R.C. §368(a)(2)(B)(iii).

sidered as money (boot) paid for the property.[54] Remember that this provision considers the assumption of liability as boot *solely* for purposes of the §368(a)(2)(B) boot relaxation rule. Consequently, if the assumption of liabilities is the *only* consideration other than voting stock, the limitation generally should not present problems. On the other hand, if P is to assume liabilities *and* also pay cash or other boot, the 20% permissible boot must be reduced by the liabilities assumed. In many cases, the practical effect will be that no other boot will be permitted.

Imagine, for example, that P is acquiring 100% of T's assets, valued at $1 million, solely in exchange for P voting stock, plus the assumption of T's liabilities in the amount of $300,000. Even though the liabilities represent 30% of the total fair market value of T's assets, the transaction still qualifies as a Type C reorganization, since the terms of §368(a)(1)(C) itself disregard liabilities in determining whether the exchange is "solely for voting stock." Changing the transaction slightly, imagine that, in addition to the P voting stock and the assumption of T's liabilities, P includes $5 of cash boot in exchange for the T assets. The transaction no longer qualifies as a Type C reorganization since the liabilities *are* considered boot *solely* for purposes of the §368(a)(2)(B) boot relaxation rule. In this transaction, the 20% boot that would otherwise be permissible cannot be used since the liabilities already represent more than 20% of the fair market value.

It is worth taking a moment here to compare the different rules regarding permissible consideration in acquisitive reorganizations. The rules for Type B reorganizations are the most strict, permitting only cash to pay target shareholders for fractional shares. The Type C rules permitting up to 20% boot are more relaxed, but still rather restrictive as a practical matter. Finally, the Type A rules are the loosest, permitting as much as 50%, or perhaps more, boot in a statutory merger or consolidation.[55] Given that the different reorganization definitions in §§368(a)(1)(A), (B), and (C) simply represent different routes to achieve similar acquisition results, the differences in these rules are difficult to justify. They create traps for the unwary in some cases, and needlessly increase the cost of transactions in many cases, as taxpayers look for ways around the various restrictions and decide which of the alternative types of acquisition transactions is best for them.

d) The Liquidation Requirement

Immediately after the target's sale of substantially all of its property to the purchasing corporation, the target holds its remaining assets along with the

---

54. This is an exception to the provision in §368(a)(1)(C) discussed above that such liabilities should be disregarded.

55. The Treasury Department's position for purposes of issuing advanced letter rulings limits boot to 50%. See note 38, *supra.*

voting stock and other boot consideration received from the purchasing corporation. The target is no longer a going concern. Until 1984, however, the target could continue as a holding company. By failing to distribute money or other boot received from P to its shareholders, the T shareholders thus avoided reporting §356 gain on the boot. Responding to this and other related types of perceived manipulation, Congress added the special requirement in §368(a)(2)(G) that, unless the target receives a waiver from the Treasury Secretary, the target corporation in a Type C reorganization *must* distribute stock, securities, and other properties received in pursuance of the plan of reorganization. Distributions to creditors in connection with the plan of liquidation will be treated as pursuant to the reorganization for purposes of this rule.

Tax Consequences of the Basic Type C Reorganization

Let's begin by looking at a simple Type C reorganization in which the target corporation (T) transfers all of its assets to purchasing corporation (P) solely in exchange for P voting stock.

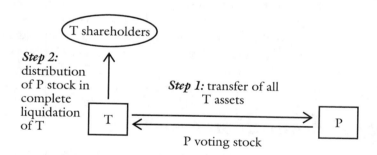

Notice, first of all, that the T shareholders are not exchanging anything directly with the purchasing corporation. T itself is transferring its assets to P in return for P voting stock. This exchange will not be taxable to T pursuant to §361(a). T's basis in the P voting stock will be the same basis it had in the transferred assets. Remember, though, that unless the requirement is waived by the Treasury Secretary, the target corporation in a Type C reorganization will be required to distribute the stock received from P pursuant to a plan of reorganization.[56] T will not be taxed on this distribution pursuant to §361(c). Since the T shareholders are exchanging their T stock for P stock upon this liquidation, they also will be entitled to nonrecognition treatment

---

56. I.R.C. §368(a)(2)(G).

under §354.[57] The T shareholder's basis in the stock received will be the same as the T shares surrendered in the liquidation under §358.

If the purchasing corporation takes advantage of the opportunity to pay up to 20% of the consideration in the form of boot, T will not be required to report any gain pursuant to §361(b) so long as the boot is distributed to the T shareholders in pursuance of the plan of reorganization[58] or to creditors in connection with the reorganization.[59] Since such distribution is *required* as part of a Type C reorganization, there will be no taxable gain to T upon the receipt of boot. Nor will T be entitled to deduct any losses.[60] P's assumption of T's liabilities will not be considered boot under §357(a), except in cases involving tax-avoidance motives.[61] The rationale for permitting nonrecognition to T even upon receipt of boot is that T is simply acting as an agent or conduit selling assets on behalf of the shareholders. The T shareholders will be taxable on the boot received pursuant to §§354(a)(2) and 356. P will report no gain upon receipt of T's assets under §1032 and the assets acquired from T will retain the historic basis in P's hands.[62]

Notice that the example described above envisions a transaction in which T transferred *all* of its assets to P. In such cases, there should be no taxable gain to T either upon the transfer of assets to P, pursuant to §361(a), or upon the subsequent distribution of assets to the T shareholders, pursuant to §361(c). Recall, however, that the Type C reorganization requires only the transfer of *substantially all* of T's assets. When T has transferred substantially all, but retained some, of its assets, T's subsequent liquidation will involve a distribution of both "qualified property" eligible for §361(c) nonrecognition[63] and also the retained assets. T will recognize gain, but is not permitted to recognize loss, upon the distribution of the retained assets.

Type C Acquisitions over Time

Until recently, a purchasing corporation that already held some target stock and later wished to acquire control through a Type C acquisition of substantially all of T's assets had to be careful to avoid the pitfalls encountered by

---

57. The §354 nonrecognition rule here operates as an exception to §331, under which the shareholders would ordinarily report gain or loss upon the complete liquidation of a corporation.

58. I.R.C. §361(b)(1)(A).

59. I.R.C. §361(b)(3).

60. I.R.C. §361(b)(2).

61. I.R.C. §357(b).

62. I.R.C. §362(b).

63. "Qualified property" for purposes of §361(c) generally includes stock or obligations of the distributing corporation (T) itself or stock or obligations of the purchasing corporation (P) acquired by T in the reorganization exchange.

the taxpayer in Bausch & Lomb Optical Co. v. Commissioner.[64] In that case, Bausch & Lomb already owned 79% of the stock in Riggs corporation and wished to acquire complete control over Riggs' assets.[65] Bausch & Lomb (B&L) acquired control in a two-step transaction, the first part of which was an acquisition of all of Riggs' assets in return for B&L voting stock, followed by a liquidation whereby Riggs distributed its recently acquired B&L voting stock. This surely looks like a Type C acquisition of substantially all of the target's assets followed by the required liquidation of the target under §368(a)(2)(G). The rub is that as a Riggs shareholder itself, B&L surrendered its previously owned Riggs shares as part of the liquidation transaction. The Commissioner took the position that the two steps were part of an integrated plan and that the Riggs stock surrendered by B&L was additional consideration paid by B&L in the acquisition in violation of the "solely for voting stock" requirement. The Tax Court and the Second Circuit agreed. Thus, the liquidation was not considered part of a Type C reorganization, but instead a liquidation taxable to B&L as a shareholder under §331.

In another change of position, the Treasury Department recently amended its §368 regulations, effectively overturning the longstanding *Bausch & Lomb* doctrine. For purposes of Type C reorganizations, the regulations now provide that "prior ownership of stock of the target corporation by an acquiring corporation will not by itself prevent the solely for voting stock requirement . . . from being satisfied."[66] Example 1 of the new regulatory provision involves P, which acquired 60% of T for cash years ago in an unrelated transaction and now wishes to acquire the remaining 40% of T from X, an unrelated corporation. T transfers all of its assets, with a fair market value of $110, to P in exchange for P stock, $10 in cash, and P's assumption of T's $10 in liabilities. T then liquidates, distributing the P stock and cash to X. The example concludes that the Type C "solely for voting stock" requirement is met, since the $10 in cash and the $10 assumption of liabilities do not exceed 20% of the value of T's assets.[67]

---

64. 267 F.2d 75 (2d Cir.), *cert. denied*, 361 U.S. 835 (1959).

65. Notice that this was just short of the 80% necessary to make Riggs a subsidiary for purposes of §332.

66. Treas. Reg. §1.368-2(d)(4)(i) (added by T.D. 8885, 65 Fed. Reg. 31,805 (May 19, 2000)). The preamble to these new provisions explicitly addresses Rev. Rul. 69-294, in which the *Bausch & Lomb* doctrine was applied to a Type B reorganization. Although application to Type B reorganizations was outside the scope of the new regulation, the Treasury announced that it may reconsider this old ruling and the application of *Bausch & Lomb* principles as applied to Type B reorganizations. *Id.* at 31,806.

67. Treas. Reg. §1.368-2(d)(4)(ii), ex. 1. The results would be different, however, if the prior cash purchase of 60% had been part of an integrated plan. In such a case, the amount of cash involved in the transaction would far exceed even the relaxed boot rules applicable to Type C reorganizations. *Id.* at ex. 2.

Triangular Reorganizations

Introduction

Each of the basic acquisitive reorganization transactions discussed earlier in this chapter included only two corporate parties — a target corporation (T) and a purchasing corporation (P). Such basic reorganization exchanges sometimes prove inadequate to meet the needs of the parties to certain acquisition transactions. For various nontax reasons, the purchasing corporation might not wish to own T assets or stock directly, but might prefer to have the T stock or assets owned by a subsidiary. Similarly, T or its shareholders might not wish to sell P directly. A triangular reorganization typically involves *three* corporations — a target (T) on one side of the transaction and a parent (P) and subsidiary (S) on the purchaser side of the transaction. Extension of tax-free reorganization treatment to triangular reorganizations has evolved in piecemeal fashion — one now can structure a triangular reorganization as a Type A, B, or C reorganization.

The "Drop-Down" Transaction

Under case law interpreting early versions of the statutory reorganization provisions, P's acquisition of T stock or assets followed by an immediate contribution of the T stock or assets to a P subsidiary was not eligible for tax-free treatment.[68] Under the step-transaction doctrine, the *true* stock purchaser was the subsidiary. Consequently, P was not a "party to the reorganization" and the T shareholders receiving P stock did not receive stock of another party to the reorganization as required by §354. Moreover, under a doctrine sometimes known as the "remote continuity of interest" doctrine, this transaction failed the continuity of proprietary interest test because the target's stock or assets were not held by the corporation that issued the stock in the reorganization. In 1954, however, Congress added a special rule in §368(a)(2)(C) providing that a transaction otherwise qualifying as a Type A, B, or C reorganization will not be disqualified if the stock acquired is transferred or "dropped-down" to a subsidiary.[69]

Thus, for example, in a Type B stock-for-stock reorganization, P can now acquire T shares in exchange for P shares and subsequently drop the T shares down into a subsidiary (S).

---

68. See, e.g., Helvering v. Bashford, 302 U.S. 454 (1938).

69. In addition, the definition of "party to a reorganization" was amended to ensure that P would be considered a "party" in this drop-down transaction. The stock may be dropped down to second-tier as well as first-tier subsidiaries of the parent acquiring corporation. See, e.g., Rev. Rul. 64-73, 1964-1 C.B. 142.

Drop-Down Following a Type B Reorganization

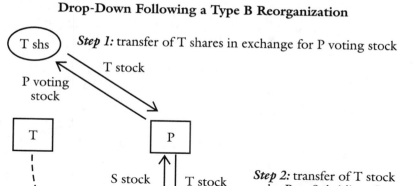

Step 1: transfer of T shares in exchange for P voting stock

Step 2: transfer of T stock by P to Subsidiary S

T becomes a subsidiary of S

The initial tax consequences will be the same as described above for the "basic Type B" transaction — the T shareholders are entitled to nonrecognition under §354. The T shareholders' basis in the P shares is determined under §358. P has no gain or loss upon exchange of its P stock for T stock under §1032 and P briefly takes a substituted basis in the T shares from the T shareholders under §362(b).

In transactions involving a "drop-down" of stock after a Type B reorganization, the statute explicitly provides only that "the term 'party to the reorganization,' includes the corporation controlling the corporation to which the acquired . . . stock [is] transferred."[70] Thus, P is considered a party, but S is not considered a party to the reorganization. The result here is that P's receipt of S stock in the drop-down portion of the transaction is ineligible for §354 nonrecognition. This should not be a matter of great concern since P should be eligible for nonrecognition under §351.[71] Under the §358 basis rules, which apply to §351 as well as to §354, S's basis in the T shares will be the same basis that P had immediately before the transfer— the T shareholders' basis in the shares before the exchange.

A similar drop-down technique can be used following a transfer of T's assets as part of a Type A merger or a Type C asset acquisition. Under this drop-down technique, T is merged into P in a Type A reorganization or

---

70. I.R.C. §368(b)(2).
71. For a full discussion of §351, see Chapter 4.

transfers assets in a Type C reorganization, and P shortly thereafter transfers the T assets to an existing or a newly created P subsidiary.[72]

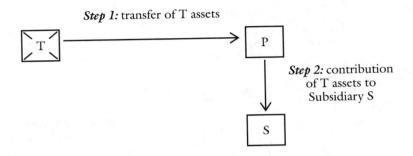

Step 1: transfer of T assets

Step 2: contribution of T assets to Subsidiary S

In a drop-down of the T assets received by P following a basic Type A merger or Type C asset acquisition, the tax treatment of the initial Type A or Type C transaction is the same as that described above — no gain or loss to the T shareholders, except to the extent of boot received, and no gain or loss to P or to T. T's asset basis carries over to the assets now in P's hands. Again notice that while T and P are both considered "parties to the reorganization," the subsidiary (S), to which the assets are dropped, is not a "party to the reorganization" under §368(b). The subsequent drop-down of assets will be treated as an incorporation transaction under §351. There will be no gain or loss to P upon the exchange. The one exception would be a case in which the target's liabilities assumed exceed the basis of the target's assets. In such a case, the drop-down could trigger a §357(c) gain to P to the extent of the excess of liabilities over basis. Under §362, S's basis in the assets will be the same basis that P had in the assets — T's historic basis in the assets.

Direct Triangular Reorganizations

In a more direct triangular reorganization, the purchasing corporation may compensate the target corporation or its shareholders with a *parent* corporation's voting stock instead of using its *own* voting stock to make an acquisition. In this triangular acquisition, the subsidiary corporation (S) technically is the acquiror, but the target corporation or its shareholders receive stock of the acquiring subsidiary's parent corporation (P) in the exchange. Since the rules for direct triangular Type A, B, and C reorganizations vary slightly, each of them is considered separately in the following materials.

---

72. I.R.C. §368(a)(2)(C).

a) The Type B Triangular Reorganization

In the Type B triangular reorganization, T shareholders transfer T stock to P's subsidiary (S) solely in exchange for P voting stock.

Type B Triangular Merger

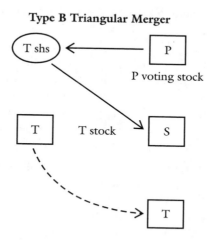

This transaction, too, was not always effective as a tax-free reorganization. Under early case law, the parent was not a "party to the reorganization" and the transaction violated the continuity of proprietary interest requirement under the "remote continuity of interest" doctrine — the T stock was not ultimately held by the corporation issuing the stock (P). Consequently, T shareholders who received the parent corporation's stock were ineligible for §354 nonrecognition.[73] Under statutory language revised in 1964, the acquiring subsidiary (S) may use solely voting stock of the parent in a direct triangular Type B reorganization. The rationale for permitting this direct triangular merger was that if the same results could be achieved through a simple two-party reorganization followed by a drop-down, it made little sense to prohibit corporations from achieving those results more directly through a triangular reorganization.

Notice, though, that the consideration must be *entirely* voting stock of the acquiring corporation (S) itself or *entirely* voting stock of a parent of the acquiring corporation (P). It is not possible to mix parent and subsidiary stock in a compensation package to the target shareholders.[74] The reason for this restriction is not entirely clear. Perhaps Congress was concerned that

---

73. Groman v. Comm'r, 302 U.S. 82 (1937).

74. The regulations provide that the transaction will not be a Type B reorganization "if stock is acquired in exchange for voting stock *both* of the acquiring corporation and of a corporation which is in control of the acquiring corporation." Treas. Reg. §1.368-2(c) (emphasis added).

with a mix of consideration, target shareholders could sell the more readily marketable parent shares without giving up the equity interest reflected in the subsidiary shares.

In the direct triangular Type B reorganization in which the T shareholders transfer their stock to S in exchange for P stock, all three of the corporations now are considered "parties to the reorganization."[75] T shareholders who receive P stock clearly are entitled to §354 nonrecognition.

Resolving the proper treatment for P and S in the Type B triangular reorganization is a bit more difficult. S should be entitled to nonrecognition upon its exchange of P shares for T shares. Although this is uniformly accepted as the right answer, the precise statutory authority is less clear. Technically, §1032 nonrecognition applies upon the corporation's exchange of its *own* stock. In the triangular Type B reorganization, S is exchanging its *parent's* stock rather than its own. Under recently finalized regulations under §1032, S will not recognize gain as long as the P stock was provided by P to S or directly to the T shareholders on behalf of S pursuant to the plan of reorganization. On the other hand, S *will* recognize gain or loss to the extent that it uses P stock that it did not receive from P pursuant to the reorganization plan.[76] With regard to basis, since S is entitled to nonrecognition treatment upon receipt of the T shares, it follows that S's basis in the T stock should be a substituted basis from the T shareholders. This result is provided under §362(b).

What about the tax consequences to P? P was not directly involved in the exchange, which technically took place between T and S. Nevertheless, P's stock was used in the exchange and it is the parent corporation now indirectly in control of T through its subsidiary. New regulations under §1032 treat the transfer of P shares by S "as a disposition by P of shares of its own stock for T's . . . stock."[77] Thus, P is entitled to §1032 nonrecognition upon the exchange.

A more difficult issue is determining P's basis in its S stock after the triangular reorganization. Under the new regulations, the Treasury Depart-

---

75. In this example, S is acquiring T stock. T and S, then, are considered parties by virtue of the general language of I.R.C. §368(b)(2) including "both corporations, in the case of a reorganization resulting from the acquisition by one corporation of stock . . . of another." S's parent, P, also is a party by virtue of language providing that "[in] the case of a reorganization qualifying [as a Type B reorganization] . . . if the stock exchanged for the stock . . . is stock of a corporation which is in control of the acquiring corporation, the term 'party to a reorganization' includes the corporation so controlling the acquiring corporation." I.R.C. §368(b)(2) (flush language).

76. Treas. Reg. §1.1032-2. For example, if S used P stock that it previously acquired in a transaction unrelated to the reorganization, S would be required to report gain or loss upon disposition of those previously acquired shares.

77. Treas. Reg. §1.1032-2(b).

ment provides that P's basis in its subsidiary stock should be adjusted after the triangular reorganization as if P had first acquired the T stock *directly* from the T shareholders and then transferred the T stock to S in a transaction in which P's basis in its S stock was determined under §358.[78] In other words, imagine first that P had done a simple two-party Type B reorganization rather than a triangular type. As such, P would take the T shares with a substituted basis from the T shareholders under §362(b). Second, imagine that in a subsequent transfer under §351, P contributed the T shares to its subsidiary. The effect of this new regulation is to permit P to increase its prior basis in its S stock by the T shareholders' bases.[79] The end result of this "over-the-top" method of adjusting P's basis in its S stock is the same as if the transaction had been structured as a simple two-party Type B reorganization followed by a drop-down of the T stock to S.

b) The Type A Triangular Reorganization

(i) Type A Forward Triangular Merger

Special rules in §368(a)(2)(D) provide authority for a forward Type A triangular merger. In this transaction, the target corporation (T) merges directly into a P subsidiary (S). The parent corporation (P) may establish a new subsidiary for this purpose or may use an already existing subsidiary.

Type A Forward Triangular Merger

---

78. Treas. Reg. §1.358-6(c)(3). This method is known as the "over-the-top" method for adjusting basis.

79. This adjustment will not apply, however, to the extent that the P shares used by S in the exchange were not provided by P pursuant to the plan of reorganization.

Several conditions apply to the forward triangular merger under §368(a)(2)(D), however. First, the acquiring subsidiary corporation must receive "substantially all" of the target's properties.[80] In the context of a Type A merger, the requirement that S acquire "substantially all" of T's assets appears a bit odd. After all, by its very nature, a merger involves the acquisition of all of T's assets. The concern that led Congress to include this requirement is the same concern that drove it to include a "substantially all" requirement in the Type C asset acquisition. Specifically, Congress wanted to prevent corporations from using the acquisitive reorganization provisions in a transaction that was truly divisive in nature. Imagine, for example, that the purchasing corporation is interested in only one part of the target's business. The parties might arrange for the target to first spin-off or otherwise rid itself of the unwanted assets followed by an acquisition of T, now holding only the desired assets. In determining whether the "substantially all" requirement is met, one should look at the entire integrated transaction. Under the step-transaction doctrine, a spin-off of a substantial portion of T's assets that were unwanted followed by an acquisition that was part of an integrated plan would violate the "substantially all" of the assets requirement.

The second requirement for a Type A forward subsidiary merger is that no stock of the acquiring corporation (S) be used in the transaction.[81] Thus, the stock consideration used is limited to P stock; it will not be possible to use a mixture of P and S stock as consideration in a forward subsidiary merger. One finds very little in searching for a sensible policy explanation for this restriction. Perhaps Congress was thinking about its 1964 changes to the definition of the Type B reorganization. With those changes, Congress permitted a direct triangular Type B reorganization using solely the voting stock of the acquiror's parent (P), but not a combination of both P and S. Yet, the Type A reorganization much more closely resembles a Type C asset acquisition, which includes boot relaxation provisions. Why not permit the use of 20% S stock, but treat the receipt of S stock as taxable boot? Looking at the problem differently, if T had merged into S in a simple two-party merger, it could presumably have paid half of the consideration in the form of P stock and half in the form of S stock without running into continuity of proprietary interest problems. Why not permit some similar mix of consideration for forward triangular Type A reorganizations? Whatever the reason, the limit on the use of S stock in a Type A forward triangular merger remains. If the purchasing group wishes to use some S stock in the transac-

---

80. I.R.C. §368(a)(2)(D). The regulations specify that "the term 'substantially all' has the same meaning as it has in section 368(a)(1)(C)." Treas. Reg. §1.368-2(b)(2). The Type C triangular asset acquisition is considered in detail in the following section of this chapter.

81. I.R.C. §368(a)(2)(D)(i).

tion, alternatives to the Type A forward triangular transaction must be explored.

Notice that the restriction added by §368(a)(2)(D)(i) only prohibits the use of S stock. Since the Type A reorganization is rather generous with regard to permissible boot, a Type A forward triangular merger may include as consideration cash, debentures, and other types of boot, including S debt. Thus, although it is impermissible to use S *stock* in the transaction, it is permissible to use S *debt*.[82]

The final requirement for a Type A forward triangular merger is that the transaction *would have* qualified as a Type A reorganization if it had been a merger of T directly into P.[83] A merger of T into a P subsidiary will be permissible under §368(a)(2)(D) as long as it meets the business purpose, continuity of proprietary interest, and other tests that would apply in the context of a simple two-party Type A merger. The regulations further clarify that "it is not relevant whether the merger into the controlling corporation could have been effected pursuant to State or Federal corporation law."[84] In fact, one common nontax reason for a triangular, as opposed to a simple two-party, merger is that state or federal law restricts T and P from merging.[85]

In a forward triangular merger in which T merges directly into S, the T shareholders upon receipt of P stock will receive the same nonrecognition treatment under §354 and boot treatment under §356 as described for the basic Type A merger. What about the tax consequences to P and S? Here again, the "right answer" appears to be nonrecognition for both corporations on the acquiring side of the corporation, yet the Code is not clear with respect to the proper tax treatment for P and S. Nonrecognition under §1032 technically applies only upon the corporation's use of its *own* stock. Again, new regulations under §1032 provide that no gain or loss is recognized to P or S in a forward triangular merger, except to the extent that S uses P stock in the transaction that it did not receive from P under the reorganization plan.[86] T's assets will retain their historic basis as in the basic Type A merger.

One further issue in the forward triangular Type A merger is P's basis in its S stock after the merger. Under the new §1.358-6 regulations, P's basis in its S stock is adjusted as if P first received the T assets and liabilities through a direct merger of T into P and subsequently P transferred the T assets and liabilities to S in a §351 transaction.[87] In other words, imagine that P had

---

82. Treas. Reg. §1.368-2(b)(2).

83. I.R.C. §368(a)(2)(D)(ii).

84. Treas. Reg. §1.368-2(b)(2).

85. Various federal and state banking and insurance laws and regulations, for example, prevent the merging of certain entities.

86. Treas. Reg. §1.1032-2. For an earlier discussion of this regulation applied in the Type B reorganization context, see text accompanying notes 76-79, *supra*.

87. Treas. Reg. §1.358-6(c)(1).

done first a simple two-party Type A merger in which P would take T's assets and liabilities with a substituted basis under §362(b). Next imagine that P contributed those assets and liabilities in a subsequent §351 nonrecognition transaction in which P's basis in the S stock is equal to the basis of the assets transferred under §358. Thus, P's basis in its S stock will include the basis of T's assets plus any basis that P previously had in the S stock. This is the same "over-the-top" method used in connection with triangular Type B transactions. As was the case in the triangular Type B reorganization, the end result is the same as if the parties arranged a simple two-party reorganization followed by a drop-down of the assets into a subsidiary.

(ii)   Type A Reverse Triangular Merger

Special rules in §368(a)(2)(E) also permit a "reverse triangular merger" to qualify as a Type A reorganization. Congress saw no reason "why a merger in one direction should be taxable when the merger in the other direction [under §368(a)(2)(D)], in identical circumstances is tax-free."[88] In the reverse subsidiary merger, the purchasing corporation's (P's) subsidiary (S) is merged directly into the target corporation (T) so that the *target* survives the merger and the acquiring subsidiary (S) disappears. The target shareholders exchange their T stock for P stock.[89]

Type A Reverse Triangular Merger

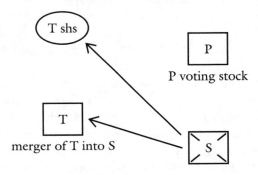

_____

88. H.R. Rep. No. 91-1778, 91st Cong., 2d Sess. (1970).

89. This "reverse triangular merger" is explicitly authorized assuming that the merger of the acquiring subsidiary into the target would otherwise qualify as a Type A reorganization. I.R.C. §368(a)(2)(E).

Here again, Congress imposes conditions, some of which parallel the conditions for the forward subsidiary merger. As in the forward triangular merger, the basic merger of S into T must otherwise qualify as a Type A merger. The reverse subsidiary merger provision also contains a "substantially all" of the assets requirement, which now appears in two parts. First, the corporation surviving the merger (T) must hold substantially all of *its own* properties after the merger.[90] It seems sensible to require that substantially all of the target assets remain in corporate solution. Otherwise, the transaction appears divisive in nature. The second part of the "substantially all" test requires that after the transaction T also hold substantially all of the *merged* corporation's (S's) properties (other than P stock distributed in the transaction).[91] Thus, cash or other property contributed by P to S for use as boot consideration to T shareholders or to pay off dissenting T shareholders does not count toward the "substantially all" test and it should not be a problem that T no longer holds these assets. The regulations clarify that "[i]n applying the 'substantially all' test to the merged corporation, assets transferred from the controlling corporation to the merged corporation in pursuance of the plan of reorganization are not taken into account."[92]

One unique quality of the reverse subsidiary merger is the possibility that some of the old T shareholders will dissent and continue to hold T shares as minority shareholders. In the forward subsidiary merger, in contrast, T disappears. The old T shareholders either receive P stock and boot or, as dissenters, are "bought out," usually with cash. This unique characteristic of the reverse subsidiary merger necessitated a final condition for a successful tax-free reverse triangular merger — former shareholders of the surviving corporation (T) must have transferred a controlling interest in T in exchange for P *voting* stock.[93] Given that the reverse subsidiary merger is an acquisitive reorganization, the requirement that the T shareholders transfer control makes sense.

Although forward and reverse triangular Type A reorganizations share several characteristics in common, there are several differences. One inexplicable difference is that the use of S stock as consideration to the T shareholders is expressly prohibited in the former, while it is permitted in the latter. If Congress wished to create reasonable parity between the two types of triangular transactions, these differences are hard to justify. Another sig-

---

90. I.R.C. §368(a)(2)(E)(i).

91. *Id.*

92. Treas. Reg. §1.368-2(j)(3)(iii).

93. I.R.C. §368(a)(2)(E)(ii). The regulations specifically provide that "*in the transaction*, shareholders of the surviving corporation must surrender stock in exchange for voting stock of the controlling corporation." Treas. Reg. §1.368-2(j)(3)(i) (emphasis added). Since the control must be acquired "in the transaction," a creeping acquisition will not be possible.

nificant difference between the forward and reverse subsidiary merger is the requirement in the case of reverse subsidiary mergers, that the P stock used to acquire the 80% control over the target be *voting* stock. This may initially appear a bit odd, given that in the simple Type A merger or the forward subsidiary merger, P nonvoting stock is permissible. The differences between these transactions reflect deeper and more fundamental problems permeating the whole subject of tax-free reorganizations. It simply makes no sense to have the tax consequences to functionally and economically equivalent transactions turn on the kinds of details now built into the acquisitive reorganization rules. A final section of this chapter briefly considers proposals to provide more simplicity and coherence to the area of acquisitive reorganizations.

As for tax consequences, the T shareholders exchanging T stock for P stock in the reverse subsidiary merger are entitled to nonrecognition pursuant to §354, subject to the §356 boot rules. Treatment of the other parties to the transaction is a bit more complex. By analogy to the simple Type B reorganization, nothing of much tax consequence has happened to T; it has simply been acquired. Its assets and liabilities remain with historic basis intact. On the other hand, T, as the surviving corporation, is receiving S assets upon the merger of S into T. There should be no gain or loss on the receipt of these assets, although the statutory authority is not entirely clear. One might argue that nonrecognition should be provided by analogy to §1032. Interestingly, the new §1032 regulations directly address the forward triangular merger, but not the reverse subsidiary merger. The regulations simply refer to §361 for "rules governing the use of P stock in a reverse triangular merger."[94] Even though the T stock technically is coming from the T shareholders, T arguably is receiving the S assets in return for T stock. In any event, as a practical matter, T is unlikely to be receiving significant assets from S. S often is merely a transitory shell corporation set up solely for the purpose of the merger. Perhaps the best authority for nonrecognition to T, however, is the §118 contribution to capital provision, which covers contributions to capital both from shareholders and nonshareholders.

When P contributes its stock and other assets to S to be used as consideration to the T shareholders, there will be no gain or loss to P pursuant to §351 and no gain or loss to S under either §§1032 or 118. When S is merged into T, again there are no tax consequences to S. Its assets simply transfer to T along with their historic bases. P should receive nonrecognition treatment upon the receipt of T stock pursuant to §1032. In general, the new regulations treat P's basis in the T stock in the same manner as a forward triangular merger under the "over-the-top" method — P is viewed first as

---

94. Treas. Reg. §1.1032-2(b).

acquiring the assets directly by a merger of T into P and then P is viewed as transferring the assets to T in a §351 transaction.[95]

c) The Type C Triangular Reorganization

The statutory language of §368(a)(1)(C) itself permits the acquiring corporation to use stock of a parent corporation as consideration in the acquisitive Type C reorganization. In this transaction, the target corporation (T) transfers its assets directly to a P subsidiary (S) in exchange for P stock.

Type C Triangular Reorganization

T shs

Step 2: liquidation of T

Transfer of P voting stock (some "boot" permissible)

T ← P

Step 1: Transfer of substantially all of T's

S

As with the Type B reorganization, however, the acquiring corporation (S) must use entirely its own stock or entirely its parent's stock, but not a mixture of the two.[96]

In the Type C triangular asset acquisition, the target corporation will have no taxable gain from the receipt of P stock or S stock pursuant to §361. The target shareholders who receive P stock upon liquidation of T will be eligible for §354 treatment and will take as their basis the same basis they previously had in the T shares under §358. Any boot received by T will not be taxable to T under §361(b). Distributions of the boot also will not be taxable to T under §361(c), but *will* be taxable to the T shareholders pursuant to §356. S now is considered a "party to the reorganization" and

---

95. Treas. Reg. §1.358-6(c). In the forward triangular merger, the latter §351 transfer would be to the surviving corporation, S. Here, since T is the survivor, the transfer is regarded as made to T.

96. See Treas. Reg. §1.368-2(d)(1).

S will not report any gain upon receipt of the assets under §1032.[97] New regulations using an "over-the-top" method would adjust P's basis in its S stock as if it first received the assets in a direct Type C asset acquisition and then transferred the assets to its subsidiary in a §351 transaction.[98] In other words, P would increase its previous basis in its S shares by the basis in the T assets acquired in the transaction.[99]

Nondivisive Type D Reorganizations

Although *most* reorganizations that rely upon §368(a)(1)(D) to qualify as nonrecognition transactions are divisive reorganizations, the section itself can encompass both acquisitive and divisive transactions. In a Type D reorganization one corporation transfers "all *or part* of its assets to another corporation" and the transferring corporation or one or more of its shareholders (or a combination of the two) must be in control of the corporation to which the assets are transferred immediately after the transfer.[100] Notice that the Type D reorganization definition does not require the purchasing corporation to use its own stock or securities or stock or securities of a subsidiary. Instead, continuity of proprietary interest is assured by requiring that the target (T), or one or more of T's shareholders, be in control of the *purchasing* corporation (P) immediately after the transfer of assets.[101]

Notice that the transferor corporation and/or its shareholders in a Type D reorganization must retain control over the purchasing corporation. This is quite *unlike* the typical acquisitve reorganization, in which the target shareholders typically *lose* control over the target and its assets.

Since the Type D reorganization involves transfer of "all or part" of the target's assets, there can be overlaps with the Type A and Type C acquisitive asset reorganization definitions. Imagine, for example, that shareholder A controls two corporations, T and P. T transfers all of its assets to P in exchange for P voting stock. This transaction surely fits within the Type C

---

97. Under Treas. Reg. §1.1032-2(b), S is entitled to nonrecognition except to the extent that the P stock it used as consideration in the exchange was stock that it did not receive from P pursuant to the plan of reorganization.

98. Treas. Reg. §1.358-6(c)(1).

99. This basis in the T assets would, of course, be a substituted basis under §362(b).

100. I.R.C. §368(a)(1)(D).

101. In the case of *nondivisive* Type D reorganizations, the applicable "control" test is the 50% test provided in §304(c), rather than the 80% control test in §368(c) that would otherwise apply. See I.R.C. §368(a)(2)(H). This reduced 50% threshold for control in nondivisive Type D transactions more readily enables the government to recast certain liquidation-reincorporation transactions, in which the liquidating corporation attempts to recognize loss upon a liquidating distribution, as Type D reorganizations in which recognition of loss is not permissible.

acquisitive reorganization definition. At the same time, it fits within the Type D reorganization definition — T has transferred all of its assets to another corporation (P) and T's shareholder (A) is in control of the acquiring corporation (P) immediately after the exchange. One might initially wonder whether this overlap is any more than a technicality, since both transactions are within the tax-free reorganization definition in §368(a). As long as P acquires *substantially all* of T's assets in the Type D reorganization, the target shareholder should still be eligible for §354 nonrecognition.[102] Whether the transaction is classified under the Type C or Type D definition can make a significant difference, however. First, if the target corporation's liabilities exceed its basis in the assets transferred, there is the potential for §357(c) gain in a Type D reorganization.[103] In addition, the Type D reorganization provisions explicitly require that stock or securities of the purchasing corporation be distributed in a transaction meeting the requirements of §§354, 355, or 356. To resolve the potential overlap issue, §368(a)(2)(A) explicitly provides that a transaction meeting the Type C and Type D definitions will be treated as a Type D reorganization. The Treasury Department takes the same position with respect to transactions meeting both the Type A and Type D definitions.[104] Since the Type D transaction involves many more restrictions than the Type C asset acquisition, most tax-free asset acquisitions will be structured so as to qualify as Type A or Type C transactions and to avoid meeting Type D definition.[105]

Acquisitive Reorganizations in Insolvency: The Type G Reorganization

Congress in 1980 added a special category to the §368 reorganization definition dealing with reorganizations of corporations in bankruptcy. The Type G reorganization involves a "transfer by a corporation of all or part of its assets to another corporation in title 11 or similar case; but only if, in pursuance of the plan, stock or securities of the corporation to which the assets are transferred are distributed in a transaction which qualifies under section 354, 355 or 356."[106] The Type G reorganization definition is similar to the Type D definition, permitting a transfer of all or a part of T's assets.

---

102. I.R.C. §354(a), (b)(1).

103. By its terms, §357(c) applies to an exchange "to which section 361 applies by reason of a plan of reorganization within the meaning of section 368(a)(1)(D)." I.R.C. §357(c)(1)(B). Issues related to §357(c) were addressed in Chapter 4. Details regarding Type D reorganizations are considered in Chapter 13.

104. Rev. Rul. 75-161, 1975-1 C.B. 114.

105. For detailed coverage of the Type D reorganization provisions, see Chapter 13.

106. I.R.C. §368(a)(1)(G).

Some Type G reorganizations will involve a transfer of substantially all of the bankrupt corporation's assets to another corporation and, thus, will resemble a Type C acquisitive reorganization. Thus, new corporation effectively may acquire control over the bankrupt corporation's assets as a result of a reorganization in bankruptcy. Even though a Type G transaction falls within the §368(a)(1) reorganization definition, the shareholders and security holders will not be eligible for §354 nonrecognition unless the transaction also meets special requirements in §354(b). First, the corporation to which the assets are transferred must acquire substantially all of the assets of the transferor.[107] Thus, §354 nonrecognition applies only in the case of acquisitive Type G transactions and not in the case of divisive Type G transactions. Second, the stock, securities and other properties received by the transferor, as well as all other properties of the transferor, must be distributed as part of the plan of reorganization.[108]

Overlaps in the Acquisitive Reorganization Definitions

One aspect of the tax-free acquisitive reorganization that generates tremendous confusion is the many overlaps between various reorganization definitions and other provisions in the Internal Revenue Code. Some reorganization transactions fit one or more of the specific reorganization definitions described above. Since the requirements for each are different one must be clear about which of the definitions applies. For example, if a transaction can be cast both as a Type B and as some other type of reorganization, will it be disqualified by virtue of some small amount of boot included in the transaction? Another overlap problem arises because many complex corporate transactions involve many steps. Viewed separately, the steps may appear to be one specific type of reorganization. If the step-transaction doctrine is applied, the transaction may take on the characteristics of another specific type of reorganization. This section will address some of the more common overlap problems in the acquisitive reorganization context.

An upstream merger of a subsidiary corporation into its parent technically may be both a Type A statutory merger or consolidation and, at the same time, a liquidation of a subsidiary under §332. In such circumstances, regulations provide that the §332 liquidation rules generally prevail over the reorganization provisions.[109]

---

107. I.R.C. §354(b)(1)(A).

108. I.R.C. §354(b)(1)(B).

109. Treas. Reg. §1.332-2(d). This is certainly the case when the parent has held stock in the subsidiary for a substantial period of time. If the parent's stock in the subsidiary was recently acquired, however, the upstream merger of the subsidiary into the parent might be recast as an asset acquisition.

Another overlap issue arises when a Type B reorganization is followed shortly thereafter by a liquidation of the newly acquired subsidiary. After application of the step-transaction doctrine, the acquisition may be recast as a Type C asset acquisition or perhaps a Type A merger.[110] A Type B reorganization where the target corporation is a holding company whose only asset is stock in a subsidiary corporation may also be recast as a Type C reorganization.[111]

In addition to these overlap areas, there are also substantial overlaps between the incorporation provisions in §351 and the reorganization provisions. This should not be surprising in that all of these provisions can be found in Part III of Subchapter C, entitled "Corporate Organizations and Reorganizations." Remember that §351 provides for nonrecognition to persons who transfer property solely in exchange for stock if those persons are in control of the corporation immediately after the exchange. The nonrecognition rule provided for §351 incorporation transactions parallels, in many respects, the nonrecognition provided in §354 for tax-free reorganizations.[112] Since both of these provisions permit nonrecognition, one might wonder if it makes much difference whether the taxpayer is entitled to §351 or §354 nonrecognition. The key difference is that the assumption of liabilities is treated differently in §351 transactions. In the case of incorporation transactions, §357(c) requires the recognition of gain to the extent that liabilities assumed or property taken subject to liability exceeds the basis of property transferred in the nonrecognition exchange. In contrast, in the reorganization context, it is often possible to disregard liabilities and to avoid taxable gain from the assumption of liabilities under §357.[113] In addition, securities received by the transferors in a §351 exchange are *always* considered boot, whereas securities received are not necessarily boot under §354.

Proposals to Eliminate the Reorganization Definitions

Given the complexities of the acquisitive reorganization definitions and the overlaps between the various definitions, many commentators have suggested eliminating the tax-free reorganization framework altogether and substitut-

---

110. Rev. Rul. 67-274, 1967-2 C.B. 141.

111. Rev. Rul. 70-65, 1970-1 C.B. 77.

112. Control, for purposes of §351, is the same 80% test in §368(c) that is used for reorganizations. Also, the basis rules in §§358 and 362 are applicable both to §351 incorporation transactions and reorganizations. For a detailed discussion of §351, see Chapter 4.

113. One exception is in the case of Type D reorganizations. See I.R.C. §357(c)(1)(B).

ing a more workable and less complex set of rules. Under such proposals, the parties to a corporate acquisition could simply elect to treat the transaction as a taxable acquisition in which the shareholders who sell their stock report gain, the corporation acquiring the stock receives a stepped-up basis in the assets acquired, and the target corporation reports any gain or loss on its transfer of assets.[114] On the other hand, the parties could elect to treat the acquisition as a tax-free acquisition in which the shareholders who transfer stock are not be required to report gain and the acquiring corporation receives a carryover basis in the target corporation's assets. Under these proposals, whether the transaction was taxable or tax-free would be explicitly elective rather than being left to the technical details of the §368(a)(1) reorganization definitions.

Carryover of Tax Attributes Following Tax-Free Acquisitive Reorganizations

Every corporation has its own distinct tax characteristics, including its methods of accounting, its earnings and profits accounts, its various available tax credits, its capital loss carryovers, and its net operating losses. After a *stock* acquisition, the target corporation remains a distinct legal entity and one would suspect that its tax attributes remain intact. This generally will be the case. After an *asset* acquisition, one would suspect the distinct tax attributes of the target to remain with the target and *not* to transfer to the purchasing corporation. This is certainly true for taxable acquisitions. In the case of tax-free asset acquisitions, however, tax attributes of the target *should* generally survive in the hands of the acquiring corporation. After all, tax-free status was afforded these transactions on the theory that the transaction represented a "mere change in form," and that the original business enterprise continued, albeit in modified form.

As a *general* rule, tax attributes of the target corporation will continue after the target's stock or assets have been acquired in a tax-free acquisitive reorganization. This general rule is subject to numerous judicial and statutory restrictions and limitations, however, designed to prevent "trafficking" in tax characteristics. As one corporate tax treatise has observed, "[i]t seems safe to say . . . that the judicial climate is hostile to taxpayer efforts to secure corporate tax benefits by merger or other forms of acquisitions; some judges and commentators apparently feel that traffic in corporate tax benefits (most notably, net operating loss carryovers) is akin to original sin."[115] As suggested

---

114. This transaction would be quite similar to the current taxable acquisition with a §338 election. See Chapter 10.

115. Boris I. Bittker and James S. Eustice, Federal Income Taxation of Corporations and Shareholders ¶14.01[2] (7th ed. 2000). One might safely add that the statutory climate is similarly hostile.

by this quote, the tax attribute most frequently subject to perceived "trafficking" abuse is the net operating loss. Consequently, many of the judicial and statutory restrictions and limitations address this attribute in particular. The material that follows presents a brief overview of the rules regarding the carryover of tax attributes following a tax-free acquisition.

To begin, notice that no special rule is required to provide that the tax attributes of the target corporation generally remain intact following a stock acquisition. Such attributes survive simply because the target survives as a distinct entity. On the other hand, absent a special rule, the tax characteristics of the target might well disappear if the purchasing corporation were to liquidate the target immediately after a stock acquisition, or if the purchasing corporation acquired assets directly in the case of a Type A merger or a Type C asset acquisition. Congress provided in §381 for the general carryover of tax attributes for §332 liquidations (upstream mergers) and other tax-free acquisitive reorganizations.[116] Although §381 generally permits the target's tax attributes to survive, this general rule is subject to numerous restrictions and limitations included in §381 itself, as well as further restrictions in §§382 and 384 and elsewhere. These restrictions and limitations generally apply mechanically, and do not require a finding of tax avoidance motivation or deliberate tax attribute "trafficking." At the same time, the Treasury Secretary is authorized to completely disallow any deduction, credit, or other allowance following an acquisition of control if "the principal purpose for which such acquisition was made is evasion or avoidance of federal income tax by securing the benefit of a deduction, credit, or other allowance which [the acquiror] would not otherwise enjoy."[117]

Section 382, substantially revised by the Tax Reform Act of 1986, imposes limitations on net operating loss carryforwards (NOLs) following certain ownership changes resulting from either taxable or tax-free acquisitions.[118] In general, §382 addresses the extent to which the acquiring corporation (P) may continue to use the target corporation's pre-acquisition NOLs. The §382 limitations will not apply to all acquisition transactions, but must be triggered by an "ownership change."[119] Generally, a tax-free acquisitive reorganization will constitute such an ownership change if the target shareholders own less than 50% of the acquiring corporation's stock immediately after an acquisitive reorganization. Under §382, T's NOLs are eliminated entirely unless the target meets the continuity of business enter-

---

116. I.R.C. §381(a). The particular tax items that carry over include net operating loss carryovers, earnings and profits accounts, capital loss carryovers, and other items listed in §381(c).

117. I.R.C. §269(a).

118. The §382 limitations, as applied to taxable acquisitions, were considered briefly in Chapter 10.

119. Details regarding the definition of "ownership change" are extremely complex and beyond the scope of most introductory courses in corporate taxation. The statutory definition appears in §382(g).

prise test during the two-year period following the ownership change.[120] Even if the target meets the continuity of business enterprise test, the use of T's pre-acquisition NOLs is subject to an annual limitation. This limitation is computed by multiplying T's fair market value immediately before the reorganization by a rate equal to the long-term tax-exempt rate.[121] The idea here is to imagine that the target's value will continue to grow after the acquisition. Rather than look at the *actual* rate of growth, §382(b) presumes a rate of growth equal to the long-term tax-exempt rate. The logic behind the §382(b) annual limitation is to try to allow P to use T's pre-acquisition NOLs to the same extent that T alone would have been entitled to use them if T had continued on its own and had experienced a reasonable rate of growth.

In addition to providing limitations on P's ability to use T's pre-acquisition NOLs, the Code imposes limitations on either party's ability to use its pre-acquisition NOLs to offset the other party's built-in gains — unrealized gains with respect to assets for which the pre-acquisition fair market value was higher than the asset's basis. Special rules in §§382(h) and 384 prevent the fusing of such NOLs with such built-in gains for a period of five years following the acquisition.

EXAMPLES

The Basic A,B,Cs

1. Brady Construction, Inc. (BC) is a design/construction corporation, incorporated in the State of Delaware, that is considering an expansion of its operations into a service industry. BC has its eyes on Alice's Housekeeping Services, Inc. (AHS), also incorporated in Delaware. AHS provides housekeeping services on a contract basis to commercial buildings. With this expansion, BC hopes to provide housekeeping services under separate contract in commercial buildings that it constructs, as well as continuing to offer such services to others. At the time of the acquisition discussions, AHS had the following assets:

	basis	fair market value
cash	$200,000	$200,000
equipment/trucks	250,000	350,000
cleaning supplies	0	50,000
investments	250,000	800,000
customer lists	0	600,000
Total	$700,000	$2,000,000

---

120. I.R.C. §382(c).
121. I.R.C. §382(b).

Alice was the founder and primary shareholder of AHS. At the time of the proposed acquisition, she held 75% and her original business partner, Sam, held 15% of the authorized and outstanding common stock. Alice's basis in her AHS shares was $825,000. Sam's basis in his shares was $165,000. The remaining 10% was owned by numerous minority shareholders, no one of which held more than 1% of the stock. Alice and Sam are amenable to the acquisition, but the minority shareholders are not.

Assume that the parties agree to a stock-for-stock deal under which Alice and Sam will exchange all of their AHS shares in return for 5 shares of newly authorized BC voting stock for each AHS share exchanged. Assume further that the BC voting stock Alice received in the exchange is valued at $1.5 million and the BC voting stock received by Sam in the exchange is valued at $300,000. For the moment, BC plans to retain AHS as a subsidiary.

1a. What are the tax consequences of the stock-for-stock exchange to BC, AHS, Alice, Sam? What happens to the minority shareholders? What happens to AHS's liabilities to its creditors?

1b. What if the parties agreed to a stock-for-stock deal in which Alice and Sam exchanged all of their AHS shares in return for 4 shares of newly authorized BC voting stock and 1 share of newly authorized BC nonvoting stock for each AHS share surrendered? For 4 shares of newly authorized voting stock and 10-year 8% BC debentures for each share surrendered? Assume that the compensation package to Alice still is valued at $1.5 million and the compensation package to Sam still is valued at $300,000.

1c. How would your answer to Example 1a change if BC paid $200,000 in cash to buy out the dissenting minority shareholders? How would your answer to Example 1a change if, instead, AHS redeemed its minority shareholders with the $200,000 cash on hand immediately before the acquisition?

1d. Based upon the facts in Example 1a, what would be the tax consequence of a subsequent liquidation of AHS in which the $200,000 cash is distributed to the minority shareholders and the remaining assets are distributed to BC?

2.   How would your answers to Examples 1a through 1c change, if at all, if the transaction was structured to meet all of the requirements for a statutory merger of AHS into BC under the laws of the State of Delaware?

3.   Suppose now that BC arranged to acquire directly all of the AHS assets (described in Example 1), except for the cash. According to the agreement, AHS transfers these assets in exchange for BC voting stock valued at $1.7 million. Assume for the moment that AHS has no outstanding mortgages or liabilities. The BC voting stock received by AHS is subsequently distributed in liquidation to Alice, who receives $1.5 million worth of BC stock, and Sam, who receives $300,000 worth of BC stock. The $200,000 cash is distributed to the minority shareholders in complete liquidation of AHS.

3a. What are the tax consequences, if any, of the transaction to BC, AHS, Alice, and Sam? What happens to the minority shareholders?

3b. How would your answer to Example 3a change, if at all, if AHS decided to retain the BC stock and cash as a holding company?

3c. How would your answer to Example 3a change, if at all, if BC explicitly assumed all of AHS's liabilities to creditors, amounting to $300,000?

3d. How would your answer to Examples 3a and 3c change, if at all, if the exchange of AHS assets was for BC voting stock (valued at $1.7 million) and BC nonvoting stock (valued at $100,000)?

3e. How would your answers to Example 3a change, if at all, if the exchange of AHS assets was for BC voting stock (valued at $1.7 million) and 10-year 8% BC debentures (valued at $100,000)?

3f. How would your answer to Example 3a change, if at all, if the asset acquisition called for transfer of all AHS assets *other than* cash and investments?

Acquisition Geometry

4. Greg, Bobby, and Peter were the founders and shareholders of Interior Decorators, Inc, (IDI) incorporated in the State of Delaware. Greg held 50%, Bobby held 25% and Peter held 25% of the common voting stock. Father Michael lent $50,000 to the corporation in return for a 5-year installment note at 8% interest.

Carol, Jan, Marsha, and Cindy were the founders and shareholders of a competing firm, Design Studios, Inc. (DSI), also incorporated in Delaware. Each of them holds 25% of DSI's common voting stock. After negotiations, the corporate boards of the two corporations agreed that DSI would acquire IDI. Compare the tax results and the advantages and disadvantages of structuring the transaction in the following different ways:

4a. DSI creates a new subsidiary, S. DSI then acquires all of the IDI stock from Greg, Bobby, and Peter in return for DSI voting stock. Immediately thereafter, DSI contributes the recently acquired IDI stock to S.

4b. DSI creates a new subsidiary, S, by transferring DSI stock in return for S stock. S acquires all of the IDI stock from Greg, Bobby, and Peter in return for DSI voting stock. What difference if S acquired all of the IDI stock in return for DSI voting stock and S voting stock? For DSI voting stock and S debentures?

4c. DSI acquires all of IDI's assets in return for DSI voting stock. Immediately thereafter, DSI contributes the assets to S, a newly created subsidiary.

4d. DSI creates a new subsidiary, S, by transferring DSI voting stock in return for S stock. S acquires all of the assets of IDI in return for the DSI voting stock. IDI then liquidates distributing the DSI stock to its shareholders. What difference if S acquired all of the IDI assets in return for DSI voting stock and S voting stock? For DSI voting stock and debentures?

4e. DSI creates a new subsidiary, S, by transferring DSI stock in return for

S stock. IDI then merges into S in a statutory merger under the laws of the State of Delaware. What difference if S merged into IDI?

4f. For each of the above transactions, would it make any difference if, as part of the transaction, DSI pays off the debt to Michael in cash? If DSI contributes cash to S, which S then uses to pay off Michael's debt?

4g. For each of the above transactions, would it make any difference if DSI used an already existing as opposed to an newly created subsidiary?

EXPLANATIONS

The Basic A,B,Cs

1a. Since the AHS shareholders are exchanging their AHS stock solely for BC voting stock, the transaction qualifies as a Type B stock-for-stock reorganization. I.R.C. §368(a)(1)(B). Purchaser BC now owns 90% of the target AHS stock, more than sufficient to meet the 80% control tests of §368(c). BC will not recognize any gain upon receipt of the AHS stock in exchange for its own voting stock. I.R.C. §1032. BC's basis in the AHS shares acquired from Alice and Sam will be the same as it was in Alice and Sam's hands (totalling $990,000) pursuant to §362(b).

Alice and Sam each have a *realized* gain from the exchange of AHS stock for BC stock. Alice's realized gain amounts to $675,000 (amount realized of $1.5 million less adjusted stock basis of $825,000) and Sam's realized gain amounts to $135,000 (amount realized of $300,000 less adjusted stock basis of $165,000). Neither Alice nor Sam will *recognize* this gain from the exchange, however, since both AHS and BC are parties to the reorganization and the shareholders are each exchanging stock of one corporation that is a party to the reorganization for stock of another corporation that is a party to the reorganization pursuant to §354(a). Alice's basis in her BC shares will be the same basis she had in the AHS shares transferred ($825,000). Sam will similarly receive a substituted basis ($165,000) pursuant to §358(a).

AHS is now a controlled subsidiary, owned 90% by its new parent (BC) and 10% by the dissenting minority shareholders. If the dissenting shareholders have dissenters' rights under state law requiring that they be bought out, they may jeopardize the Type B status of the reorganization if they insist on being bought out with BC assets and if the buy-out is considered an integrated part of the acquisition transaction. The payment of any BC assets (other than BC voting stock) to minority shareholders will cause the entire transaction to violate the "solely for voting stock" requirement. AHS's assets will retain the same basis that they had prior to the acquisition and AHS will remain liable to its creditors.

1b. If Alice and Sam receive any BC nonvoting stock or any BC debentures in the exchange, the transaction no longer qualifies as a Type B reorganization since it violates the "solely for voting stock" requirement. Even if it could be shown that BC acquired 80% control over AHS for BC voting stock and the remaining 10% of AHS for BC nonvoting stock or debentures, the transaction would still be disqualified if the two purchases are part of an integrated transaction.[122] Assuming the transaction does not qualify under any of the other reorganization definitions, this failed reorganization would be taxable to Alice and Sam. Alice would realize and recognize a $675,000 capital gain and Sam would realize and recognize a $135,000 capital gain. (See figures in explanation 1a above.) Since the transaction is taxable to them, Alice and Sam would now take a cost basis in the BC stock and debentures received in the exchange rather than a §358 substituted basis. This cost basis would be the fair market value of the AHS stock transferred, which in an arm's-length transaction is presumed to be the same value as the consideration received.[123] Thus, Alice will take a $1.5 million cost basis and Sam will take a $300,000 cost basis and each of them will apportion the basis between the voting stock and nonvoting stock or between the voting stock and the debentures in accordance with the relative fair market values.

BC would hold its 90% of the AHS stock with a cost basis of $1.8 million (the value of the BC stock transferred to Alice and Sam.) Since the transaction is already disqualified from tax-free treatment under the reorganization rules, BC would be free to pay off the minority shareholders without risk. Unless BC made a §338 election in connection with the acquisition, AHS assets would retain the same basis that they had before the transaction. AHS remains liable to its creditors as before the transaction.

1c. As noted in the answer to Example 1a, any cash paid by BC to buy out minority shareholders would cause the entire transaction to fail as a Type B reorganization since it would now violate the "solely for voting stock" requirement. A failed Type B reorganization would be treated as described above. On the other hand, if AHS redeemed the minority shareholders with *its* cash on hand before the acquisition, the transaction could be saved as a tax-free reorganization.[124]

1d. As long as the subsequent liquidation is not viewed as integrated with the initial acquisition, a subsequent liquidation of AHS will be treated by the parent, BC, as a liquidation of a subsidiary under rules in §332.[125] BC will report no gain or loss upon the receipt of AHS's assets in liquidation under §332(a), and BC's basis in the assets will be the same basis that the assets

---

122. See Chapman v. Comm'r, 618 F.2d 856 (1st Cir. 1980); Rev. Rul. 75-123, 1975-1 C.B. 115.

123. Philadelphia Park Amusement Co. v. United States, 126 F. Supp 184 (Ct. Cl. 1954).

124. Scofield v. San Antonio Transit Co., 219 F.2d 149 (5th Cir. 1955), *cert. denied,* 350 U.S. 823 (1955); Rev. Rul. 68-285, 1968-1 C.B. 147.

125. If the subsequent liquidation is integrated with the initial stock purchase, the entire reorganization might be recast as a Type C reorganization.

had in AHS's hands before the liquidation pursuant §334(b)(1). The minority shareholders will treat the cash as amounts received in exchange for stock pursuant to §331. Gain or loss to the minority shareholders will be computed by subtracting the basis in their AHS shares from the amount of the cash received. The cash distribution to the minority shareholders results in no taxable gain to AHS since cash is presumed to have a basis equal to its value. AHS also will not report any gain or loss upon its distribution of assets to its parent, BC, pursuant to §337(a).

2. If the transactions described in Example 1a were structured to meet all of the requirements for a statutory merger of AHS into BC, they would now fit the reorganization definition in §368(a)(1)(A) — statutory merger or consolidation. Once the transaction fits any of the reorganization definitions, the same operating Code sections providing nonrecognition and substituted basis will apply as in the explanation of 1a above. The tax consequences in Example 1a would remain the same.

Restructuring the transaction in Example 1b as a Type A reorganization makes a significant difference. When the transaction was structured as a Type B reorganization, the presence of any nonvoting BC stock or any BC debentures tainted the entire transaction, causing it to fail to meet the reorganization definition. While the Type A reorganization definition requires a continuity of proprietary interest, it does not require that this proprietary interest take the form of solely voting stock. Nonvoting stock is considered a sufficient proprietary interest for purposes of §368(a)(1)(A). Thus, if Alice and Sam received 4 shares of BC voting stock and 1 share of BC nonvoting stock for each share of AHS stock, the transaction still would qualify as a Type A reorganization. BC still will not recognize any gain upon receipt of the AHS stock in exchange for its own voting and nonvoting stock. I.R.C. §1032. As before, BC would hold the AHS shares with the same basis that Alice and Sam had in the shares immediately before the exchange (totalling $990,000.) I.R.C. §362(b). As before, Alice and Sam would be entitled to full nonrecognition under §354(a). Their basis in the BC voting and nonvoting stock would be the same basis that they previously had in the AHS stock. They would allocate this basis over the voting and nonvoting shares in accordance with §358(b). BC would now also have more freedom with respect to the dissenting minority shareholders, who could be bought out for cash without jeopardizing tax-free reorganization status for the others. As before, AHS's assets will retain the same basis that they had before the acquisition and, under most states' merger statutes, BC would become liable after the merger for AHS liabilities.[126]

---

126. P's continued responsibility for T's liabilities following a Type A merger is a serious concern for many purchasers. Despite the more rigorous requirements of the Type B reorganization, some purchasers may attempt a Type B stock-for-stock reorganization to avoid problems with such liabilities.

If Alice and Sam received 4 shares of BC voting stock and 1 BC debenture for each AHS share transferred, the tax consequences would differ slightly. The debentures would not be considered a proprietary interest for purposes of the continuity of proprietary interest test. Nevertheless, if the BC voting stock reflects at least 50% of the value of the consideration paid for the AHS shares, the transaction should still safely qualify as a Type A reorganization.[127] BC will not report any gain upon receipt of the AHS shares in exchange for BC stock pursuant to §1032. In addition, BC should not have any gain upon the receipt of AHS shares in exchange for BC debentures. The issuance of a security in exchange for property is effectively a purchase of the property by BC, resulting in no gain or loss to the buyer, BC.

Alice and Sam still will be entitled to nonrecognition on the exchange of AHS stock for BC stock. However, §354 nonrecognition will *not* apply to the extent that the principal amount of the securities received exceeds the principal amount of the securities surrendered. Since Alice and Sam surrendered no securities, the securities received will be treated as taxable boot under §356. Whether the boot gain is treated as capital gain or dividend income will depend upon the outcome of the §356 boot analysis described in Chapter 11.

Since the Type A reorganization does not contain the "solely for voting stock" limitations of the Type B reorganization, BC should be able to buy out the minority shareholders for cash without jeopardizing the tax-free reorganization status of the transaction. Thus, the acquisition described in Example 1a (as modified) would result in nonrecognition of gain to Alice and Sam under §354. The minority shareholders receiving cash will be taxable on their stock sales. BC will not report any gain upon the receipt of the AHS stock. Similarly, there should be no problem with tax-free reorganization treatment if, instead, AHS were to redeem the minority shareholders immediately before the acquisition.

3a. This acquisition will qualify as a tax-free asset-for-stock reorganization under §368(a)(1)(C). AHS is transferring all of its assets, except for cash. Since the cash represents only 10% of the $2 million value of AHS's assets, AHS has transferred "substantially all of its assets," as required in a Type C reorganization. Since only BC voting stock is used as consideration in exchange for the AHS shares, the transaction meets the Type C "solely for voting stock" requirement. The cash distributed to the minority shareholders in the subsequent liquidation of AHS will not cause the transaction to fail the reorganization definition even though the liquidation is part of an integrated transaction. Notice that the cash in this case comes directly from the target, AHS, and not from BC. Even if the cash had come from BC, under

---

127. The *Service's* position is that continuity of proprietary interest in a Type A reorganization requires that 50% of the consideration take the form of stock. A Type A transaction could conceivably qualify with a smaller percentage.

the boot relaxation rules in §368(a)(2)(B), as long as the acquiring corporation acquires 80% of the fair market value of the target's property for voting stock, the transaction would still have qualified.[128] BC will have no gain upon receipt of the AHS assets in return for voting stock under §1032. BC's basis in the assets will be the same basis that the assets had in AHS's hands under §362(b).

The subsequent liquidation of AHS is required by §368(a)(2)(G) and is considered part of the reorganization transaction. AHS will report no gain or loss upon receipt of the BC voting shares under §361(a), nor will it report any gain or loss upon the distribution of the BC voting stock in liquidation pursuant to §361(c). Alice and Sam will be entitled to nonrecognition under §354 upon receipt of the BC voting shares in liquidation of AHS. Their basis in the BC voting shares will be the same basis they previously had in the AHS shares pursuant to §358(a). The minority shareholders will report the cash received as an amount realized in exchange for their stock under §331.

3b. Unless granted a waiver by the Secretary pursuant to §368(a)(2)(G)(ii), AHS *must* liquidate in order for this transaction to qualify as a Type C reorganization. Absent such a waiver, if AHS survives as a holding company, the transaction no longer qualifies for nonrecognition. Alice and Sam would report gain upon receipt of the BC stock. BC would acquire the AHS assets with a cost basis.

3c. As long as BC otherwise uses solely its own voting stock as consideration for the AHS assets, its explicit assumption of AHS's liabilities to creditors should cause no problem. The §368(a)(1)(C) reorganization definition itself instructs that assumptions of liabilities should be disregarded. In other words, the assumption of liabilities is not considered boot paid in this transaction. The tax consequences would remain as described in the answer to example 3a.

3d. Under the "boot relaxation" rule, the transaction in example 3a would still qualify as a Type C reorganization as long as BC acquires 80% of the fair market value of AHS's property for BC voting stock. Here, BC is acquiring 90% of AHS's assets. Since 80% must be acquired for BC voting stock, this leaves room for 10% of AHS's assets to be acquired for something other than voting stock. BC is acquiring 85% of AHS's assets for BC voting stock ($1.7 million) and only 5% for nonvoting stock ($100,000). Thus, the transaction still qualifies as a Type C reorganization. Since BC is acquiring assets in exchange for its own voting and nonvoting stock, it will have no gain under §1032. The tax consequences will be the same as described in

---

128. See, e.g., Rev. Rul. 73-102, 1973-1 C.B. 186 (cash paid by acquiring corporation to dissenting shareholders did not violate Type C "solely for voting stock" requirement, since acquiror acquired 80% of the value of the target's assets for voting stock).

the answer to Example 3a. Alice and Sam will apportion their substituted basis between the voting and nonvoting stock in accordance with §358(b).

The answer to Example 3c changes dramatically by the change in facts described here. Although §368(a)(1)(C) instructs us to disregard liabilities, the "boot relaxation" rule *does* consider liabilities as money paid for property solely for purposes of deciding whether the acquired corporation is acquiring 80% of the fair market value of the property solely for voting stock. Thus, the acquiror has paid $400,000 in "boot" for purposes of the boot relaxation rule ($300,000 liabilities assumed plus $100,000 in BC nonvoting stock). Since BC is acquiring only 90% of AHS's assets, it has room to pay for 10% with something other than voting stock.[129] Including liabilities here causes BC to violate the "solely for voting stock" requirement even as relaxed by §368(a)(2)(B). The transaction no longer qualifies as a Type C reorganization. The sale of assets by AHS now becomes a taxable sale requiring it to report gain or loss on the sale of each of its assets. Its basis in the BC stock received will be a cost basis. AHS would no longer be required to liquidate. If it did liquidate, however, the distribution in liquidation would be taxable to Alice and Sam under §331. BC would now acquire the assets with a cost basis.

3e.   The issue again is whether the transaction fails the Type C reorganization definition for violating the "solely for voting stock" requirement. The exchange would still qualify as a Type C reorganization since the debentures (liabilities) are within the 10% permissible "boot" for this transaction. In other words, as long as BC acquires 80% of the fair market value of AHS's property for BC voting stock, the use of debentures will not disqualify the transaction. Note, however, that Alice and Sam will report gain pursuant to §356 to the extent that the principal amount of securities received exceeds the principal amount of securities surrendered. BC's basis in the assets under §362(b) will be increased by the amount of Alice and Sam's gain.

3f.   The issue now raised is whether BC is acquiring "substantially all of the properties" from AHS. The $800,000 fair market value of the investments and the $200,000 cash retained represents fully one-half of the value of AHS's properties. At first glance, one might conclude that the transfer of the other half does not meet the "substantially all" test. On the other hand, the assets that *are* transferred are AHS's operating assets: equipment and trucks, cleaning supplies, and customer lists, while the assets retained are liquid assets that are not integral to the business. Moreover, it does not appear that the investments and cash are being retained to achieve a disguised divisive reorganization. Under these circumstances, the parties have a strong argument

---

129. Note that if BC had acquired *all* of AHS's assets, the $400,000 boot would constitute 20% of the $2 million of assets, leaving the transaction within the permitted boot relaxation range.

that, for purposes of the Type C reorganization definition, BC has acquired "substantially all" of AHS's properties.

Acquisition Geometry

4a. This transaction is a Type B reorganization followed by a drop-down of IDI stock into a subsidiary, thus creating a three-tier corporate chain with DSI as parent, S as a first-tier subsidiary and IDI as the new third-tier subsidiary. The initial Type B reorganization will not be disqualified by virtue of the drop-down. I.R.C. §368(a)(2)(C). Even though Michael will continue to be paid on his installment note, this should not be a problem if the payments to creditors are considered a transaction separate from the acquisition transaction.

The initial incorporation of S is governed by §§351 and 1032 and will not be taxable to either DSI or S. The subsequent stock-for-stock exchange between DSI and the IDI shareholders is treated as a simple Type B reorganization. The IDI shareholders' receipt of DSI stock is entitled to nonrecognition under §354(a). The shareholders' basis in the DSI stock is the same basis they previously had in the IDI shares transferred. DSI has no gain upon receipt of the IDI shares from the IDI shareholders under §1032. DSI's basis in the IDI shares is the same basis that the IDI shareholders had pursuant to §362(b). The subsequent drop-down of the IDI stock to S is not part of the Type B exchange, but instead will be governed again by §§351 and 1032. Under these sections, neither DSI nor S will report any gain or loss from the drop-down transaction.[130] S's basis in the IDI shares will be the same basis that DSI had, which in turn was the same basis that the IDI shareholders had. Put more simply, the IDI stock retains its substituted basis. The basis in the IDI assets will remain as it was.

4b. This transaction is a direct triangular Type B reorganization. The definition of the Type B reorganization itself permits the use of solely voting stock of a corporation which is in control of the acquiring corporation. Since the acquiring corporation, S, is using solely the stock of its parent, DSI, this transaction will qualify. Notice that the transaction would *not* qualify as a Type B reorganization if S used a combination of DSI and S voting stock to acquire the AHS shares. For purposes of the Type B reorganization, the acquiror must use solely its own voting stock *or* solely the voting stock of a corporation that controls the acquiror, but not a combination. This rigid rule is a disadvantage to the triangular Type B reorganization. Similarly, a combination of DSI voting stock and S debentures will cause the transaction to violate the Type B definition.

Again, the initial formation of the new subsidiary is governed by §§351 and 1032. Unlike the drop-down transaction, however, the remainder of the

---

130. For a more detailed analysis of §351 incorporation, see Chapter 4.

transaction is covered by the reorganization rules. S is now treated as the acquiring corporation and S, DSI, and IDI are considered parties to the reorganization. S is entitled to nonrecognition upon the exchange of DSI stock for IDI stock. Under Treas. Reg. §1.1032-2, S would report gain only to the extent that it used DSI stock that it did *not* receive as part of the reorganization. Since S was newly incorporated for purposes of this transaction, it should be fair to assume that all of the DSI stock used by S was received by S as part of the reorganization plan. S's basis in the IDI shares received will be the same basis that the IDI shareholders had. I.R.C. §362(b). The IDI shareholders receive nonrecognition under §354 and take as their basis in the DSI shares the same basis that they previously had in their IDI shares under §358.

4c. This is now a simple Type C asset acquisition followed by a drop-down of the assets to a subsidiary. This type of drop-down will not disqualify an otherwise qualifying Type C acquisition. I.R.C. §368(a)(2)(C). Since DSI has acquired *all* of IDI's assets solely in exchange for DSI voting stock, this transaction will qualify as a Type C reorganization. DSI will report no gain or loss upon the receipt of IDI assets in exchange for voting stock. I.R.C. §1032. DSI will hold the assets with the same basis that IDI had. I.R.C. §362(b). IDI will report no gain or loss upon receipt of the DSI voting stock in exchange for all of its assets. I.R.C. §361. The subsequent drop-down of assets is governed by §§351 and 1032 with no gain or loss to DSI or S. S will now hold the assets with the same basis that DSI had under §358, which, in turn, is the same basis that IDI had in the assets. In other words, the assets retain the substituted basis from IDI. IDI will be required to distribute the DSI voting stock received to its shareholders in liquidation. The shareholders will report no gain or loss upon receipt of the DSI shares under §354 and will use the same basis that they previously had in the IDI shares as the basis in their new DSI shares.

4d. This is now a direct forward triangular Type C reorganization permitted by the Type C definition itself. The Type C definition, like the Type B definition, permits the use of solely voting stock of the acquiring corporation *or* solely the voting stock of a corporation in control of the acquiring corporation. As a result, S may use DSI stock to acquire IDI's assets. The liquidation of IDI is a required component of the transaction. I.R.C. §368(a)(2)(G). The initial incorporation of S is again governed by §§351 and 1032. In the subsequent Type C reorganization, S is treated as the acquiror, but S, DSI, and IDI are all considered parties to the reorganization. S's receipt of IDI assets in exchange for DSI voting stock is treated as a nonrecognition event under Treas. Reg. §1.1032-2. Its basis in the assets will be the same basis IDI had. I.R.C. §362(b). IDI's receipt of DSI voting stock in return for its assets will not be taxable under §361(a) and its subsequent distribution of the stock to its shareholders will also not be taxable. I.R.C. §361(b). The IDI shareholders who receive the DSI voting stock in liquidation will not report any gain or loss under §354 and will receive a substituted basis under §358.

As in the answer to 4c, the use of a combination of DSI voting stock and S voting generally is not permitted under the regulations. Using both DSI and S stock may threaten Type C reorganization status. On the other hand, if the S stock used as a consideration constitutes 20% or less of the total consideration, the S stock may be considered legitimate boot under the Type C reorganization "boot relaxation" rules. If the transaction is disqualified as a Type C reorganization, the sale of assets for DSI voting stock and S voting stock would be taxable to IDI. S would be viewed as purchasing the assets in a taxable acquisition and would be entitled to a §1012 cost basis in the assets. Since the transaction did not qualify, the liquidation would be treated as a taxable exchange to the IDI shareholders under §331.

The use of DSI voting stock and debentures will work as a triangular Type C acquisition so long as the debentures fall within the 20% boot relaxation provision. In other words, as long as S acquires 80% of IDI's assets for DSI voting stock, the transaction will still qualify as a Type C reorganization. The tax consequences will be the same as those just described with the exception that the IDI shareholders will report boot gain or loss to the extent that the principal amount of the debentures (securities) received exceeds the principal amount of the securities surrendered pursuant to §356.

4e. A merger of IDI into S would be a forward triangular Type A acquisition. Under §368(a)(2)(D), use of the parent DSI's stock will not disqualify an otherwise qualified Type A reorganization if no S stock is used in the transaction and if the transaction would have qualified if the merger had been a merger of IDI directly into DSI. Since both of these requirements are met, the transaction remains a tax-free reorganization. Under recently finalized regulations, S's exchange of its parent DSI stock for IDI assets "is treated as a disposition by P [here DSI] of shares of its own stock for T's [here IDI's] assets." Treas. Reg. §1.1032-2(b). In other words, DSI will report no gain or loss under §1032. Similarly, S will report no gain or loss unless S uses P stock that it did *not* receive pursuant to the plan of reorganization. Treas. Reg. §1.1032-2(c). The IDI assets will retain the same basis in S's hands that they previously had in IDI's hands under §362(b). Under the so-called "over-the-top" method, DSI's basis in its subsidiary stock will be adjusted as if DSI first acquired the assets directly from IDI, thus determining its basis in the assets under §362(b), and subsequently transferred the assets to S in a §351 exchange. In other words, DSI's previous basis in its S stock will be increased by the amount of §362(b) substituted basis in the IDI assets. Treas. Reg. §1.358-6(c)(1). The IDI shareholders are entitled to nonrecognition under §354 upon the exchange with S of their IDI shares for DSI voting shares. Their basis in the DSI shares will be the same basis that they had in the IDI shares pursuant to §358(a).

In the alternative, a merger of S into IDI would be a reverse triangular Type A acquisition. Pursuant to §368(a)(2)(E) an otherwise qualified Type A reorganization is not disqualified by the use of stock of a controlling corporation if the surviving corporation, here IDI, holds substantially all of its properties and the merged corporation's properties [here S's properties] after the exchange. In addition, former shareholders of IDI must have exchanged a sufficient amount of IDI stock for DSI voting stock to constitute control. The first requirement is easily met since S had no assets other than the DSI voting stock used as part of the reorganization. This stock used in the reorganization is not counted for purposes of determining whether the surviving corporation holds substantially all of its own properties after the reorganization. The second requirement is also met since all of IDI's assets were transferred for DSI voting stock.[131]

In the reverse triangular merger, the parent corporation, DSI is entitled to nonrecognition pursuant to §361. See also Treas. Reg. §1.1032-2(b) (last sentence). To the extent that the surviving corporation receives any properties from S, it too receives nonrecognition treatment under §361. Since the IDI assets simply are remaining with IDI, the assets will retain the same basis that they had before the reorganization transaction. IDI now is a controlled subsidiary of DSI. Under recently finalized regulations, DSI's basis in the IDI stock acquired in the reverse triangular merger "equals its basis in its S stock immediately before the transaction adjusted as if T [here IDI] had merged into S in a forward triangular merger to which paragraph (c)(1) of this section applies." Treas. Reg. §1.358-6(c)(2). In other words, DSI's basis will be computed as described in the paragraph above describing the forward triangular merger. The IDI shareholders remain entitled to nonrecognition under §354 upon the receipt of DSI voting stock and will use their IDI stock basis as the basis in their new DSI shares under §358.

4f.   The key factual question here is whether the payment to Michael is part of, or integrated with, the reorganization plan. To the extent that the payment to Michael is separated from the reorganization plan, it should not affect the answers above. On the other hand, if the payment to Michael is an integral part of the plan, some significant issues arise. In the Type B reorganization followed by a drop-down and the direct Type B triangular reorganization described in examples 4a and 4b, the use of DSI cash to pay off the debt to Michael (whether directly by DSI, or through a contribution

---

131. Notice that the second requirement in the reverse subsidiary merger provides more flexibility than that provided by the forward triangular merger. As long as the IDI shareholders transferred 80% control in return for DSI voting stock, the remaining 20% of the consideration could take the form of S stock. This combination of parent and subsidiary stock consideration is not permissible in the forward merger.

of cash to S, which in turn is used to pay Michael) will disqualify the entire transaction from tax-free reorganization since the transaction no longer meets the "solely for voting stock requirements." In the Type C reorganization followed by a drop-down and the direct triangular C reorganization, the payment of the liability to Michael can be disregarded. Thus, the payment should not disqualify the transaction. If any consideration other than DSI voting stock was used in the transaction, however, the debt to Michael, other liabilities, *and* other consideration together could not exceed the 20% "boot relaxation" provision. The forward triangular reorganization provides the greatest flexibility here. Under the Service's interpretation, as long as no more than 50% of the consideration takes a nonequity form, the Type A transaction still will qualify. In the reverse triangular merger, however, §368(a)(2)(E) requires that IDI shareholders transfer 80% control in return for DSI voting stock.

4g. In each case, it is permissible for the parent to use an already existing subsidiary, as opposed to a newly created subsidiary, for purposes of a triangular reorganization. One concern under the recently finalized §§358 and 1032 regulations is that the subsidiary will report gain or loss to the extent that it uses parent stock that it did not receive as part of the reorganization transaction. Thus, the reorganization may trigger taxable gain with respect to previously owned parent stock. In addition, in the case of an existing subsidiary, the parent's old basis will be adjusted in accordance with the new regulations. In a reverse triangular merger, the parent must also consider the tax consequences of any old stock in the target corporation that it held before the reorganization transaction.

13

Corporate Divisions

Introduction

Corporate Divisions in General

The corporate acquisition transactions considered in earlier chapters involved amalgamating or joining the shareholder investments reflected in two or more corporations.[1] Corporate *divisions* involve the reverse — breaking the investment reflected in one corporation into investments in multiple corporations. The reasons for a corporate division or separation can be quite varied. A corporate division might be mandated by an antitrust decree or might otherwise be necessary to comply with statutory or regulatory restrictions imposed by federal, state, or local governments. For example, banking regulations might require a bank holding company to separate its banking operations from other business operations. Corporate divisions can also be used to resolve conflicts between opposing groups of shareholders. Separating the business into two corporations may be more sensible than forcing warring shareholder factions to coexist under one corporate roof. Corporate division also can be useful when two or more separate corporations will have better access to credit or other sources of funding than the single corporate enterprise. Finally, corporate division sometimes is used in connection with merger and acquisition transactions. Such a division might be used defensively to make an unfriendly or unwanted takeover less attractive to the acquiror or offensively to facilitate a desired merger or acquisition.

Like the acquisitive transaction, the divisive transaction can be either taxable or tax-free. To illustrate a "taxable division," imagine a corporation

---

1. See Chapters 10 (Taxable Acquisitions) and 12 (Acquisitive Reorganizations).

with two individual shareholders that has been operating a hotel business and a restaurant business as separate divisions. The corporation might arrange a corporate division simply by distributing the hotel business assets to one shareholder and the restaurant business assets to the other in a complete liquidation.[2] Or, the corporation might distribute the hotel assets to its shareholders in a nonliquidating distribution, remaining alive as a corporation operating only a restaurant business.[3] Finally, the corporation might arrange to distribute all of the hotel business assets in redemption of all of one shareholder's stock, leaving the other shareholder as sole owner of a corporation with only restaurant assets.[4] Although the proper character of gain or loss as ordinary or capital may be at issue for some of these transactions, each of the above variations reflects a taxable division of the shareholders' investment in one corporation.

In contrast to a "taxable division," the corporation in the above illustration could arrange a tax-free division by using special rules in the "Corporate Organizations and Reorganizations" provisions appearing in Part III of Subchapter C.[5] A tax-free division usually refers to the separation of one corporation into two or more corporations, along with an accompanying distribution of stock or securities to the shareholders or security holders of the original corporation in a distribution that qualifies for nonrecognition under §355.[6] This division or separation may or may not be a "reorganization." Recall that "reorganization" is a term of art, referring only to those transactions defined in §368(a). The term "divisive reorganization" generally refers to a transaction meeting *both* the requirements of §355 *and* the reorganization definition in §368(a).[7] The remainder of this chapter discusses tax-free divisions, including the subclass of tax-free divisions generally referred to as "divisive reorganizations."

---

2. Such a liquidating distribution would be taxable to the shareholders under §331 and to the distributing corporation under §336. See Chapter 8.

3. Such a nonliquidating distribution would be taxable to the shareholders under §301 and to the corporation under §311. See Chapter 5.

4. Such a redemption distribution would be taxable to the shareholders under §302 and taxable to the corporation under §311. See Chapter 6.

5. I.R.C. §§351-368.

6. If a corporation simply transfers some of its assets to a new subsidiary without distributing the subsidiary's stock to its shareholders, the transaction is covered by §351. While this type of transaction technically constitutes a tax-free corporate division, the focus of this chapter is on divisive transactions that include a distribution of stock or securities to shareholders (other than a distribution pursuant to §351). For detailed discussion of §351 and incorporating a subsidiary, see Chapter 4.

7. The "reorganization" definition typically invoked in divisive reorganization cases is §368(a)(1)(D).

Rationale for Nonrecognition Treatment Balanced Against Potential for Taxpayer Abuse

As discussed in earlier chapters, corporate formation and certain acquisitive reorganizations are entitled to nonrecognition treatment on the theory that these transactions represent "mere changes in form."[8] A corporate division also can be viewed as a mere change in form. Imagine, for example, that the corporation operating a hotel and restaurant business as two divisions of a single entity decides to transfer all the hotel division assets to a newly formed subsidiary. Shortly thereafter, the corporation distributes the new subsidiary stock pro rata to its two equal individual shareholders. Immediately after the transaction, the same two shareholders own the same two business operations in the same proportions as before, but now the businesses are contained in two separate corporate entities rather than as divisions of one corporate entity. This breaking of corporate divisions into separate corporate entities owned in the same proportions by the same shareholders arguably represents a mere change in form. Consistent with the "mere change in form" rationale, §355 provides nonrecognition treatment for both the distributing corporation and the shareholder or security holder distributees upon certain corporate distributions of stock and securities in a controlled corporation. Unlike many other provisions of Subchapter C that deal with tax consequences to the corporation and its shareholders in separate sections, §355 addresses both the tax consequences to shareholder distributees *and* to the distributing corporation.

Even though many corporate divisions can be appropriately described as "mere changes in form," Congress feared that an overly broad nonrecognition provision would lead to abuses. The drafting challenge presented in connection with §355 was to distinguish genuine "mere change in form" divisive stock or security distributions from other corporate distributions, which generally are taxable events. When §355 was first enacted, the primary concern was potential bailout of corporate earnings at capital gains rates that would otherwise be taxable as ordinary income dividends. To illustrate, imagine a corporation holding a highly appreciated asset not needed in current business operations. The corporation might transfer such an asset to a new subsidiary and distribute the subsidiary stock to its shareholders. A subsequent sale of stock at a gain by the shareholders would result in gains taxable at preferential capital gains rather than ordinary income rates. Assuming that the distribution of stock to the shareholders was pro rata and that all shareholders subsequently sell the subsidiary stock, the shareholders have effectively bailed out corporate earnings and profits at capital gains rates

---

8. See Chapters 4 (Incorporation and Other Contributions to Capital) and 12 (Acquisitive Reorganizations).

without otherwise altering their proportionate interest in the corporate enterprise.[9] If the distribution successfully qualified for §355 nonrecognition, there would be no tax upon distribution of the asset either to the distributing corporation or to the shareholders receiving the distribution.

In the end, this corporate separation transaction resembles a direct distribution of the appreciated asset to the shareholders, followed by a shareholder sale of the asset. In either case, the value of the assets has been transferred out of corporate solution to the shareholders. In contrast to a tax-free divisive distribution, direct distribution of the asset surely would result in ordinary dividend income to the shareholders[10] and taxable gain to the distributing corporation.[11] Absent special restrictions to §355, corporations could isolate selected assets in a controlled subsidiary and then distribute stock in the subsidiary to its shareholders, thus allowing shareholders to avoid shareholder recognition of ordinary dividend income on the distribution, reporting only capital gain from the later sale of the shares. Congress responded to this bailout potential by including in §355 a requirement that both the distributing corporation and the controlled subsidiary be engaged in the active conduct of a trade or business immediately after the distribution[12] and a separate requirement that the distribution not be used principally as a device for the distribution of the distributing corporation's earnings and profits.[13]

Since §355 was enacted, Congress has made several significant tax changes. First, it has tinkered with the differential between ordinary income and capital gains rates, initially eliminating the difference in rates in 1986, only to reintroduce a difference in rates in 1989. Recent reductions in capital gains rates restore a significant difference between ordinary income and capital gain rates. As the rate differential increases, incentives to bail out corporate earnings at lower capital gains rates also increase, placing renewed emphasis on the §355 "anti-bailout" provisions.[14]

---

9. Notice that the concern here is quite similar to that underlying §306. Rather than disqualify the transaction altogether, another alternative would be to "taint" shares received in a §355 distribution in similar fashion to the taint imposed on §306 stock. For a detailed discussion of the §306 provisions designed to combat bailouts of earnings and profits, see Chapter 7.

10. The dividend result to the shareholders assumes that the distributing corporation has sufficient earnings and profits to cover the distribution. I.R.C. §§301, 316. See Chapter 5. Since the shareholders' basis in the asset received upon distribution would be the asset's fair market value at the time of distribution under §301(d), there should be little or no further taxable gain upon the shareholders' immediate resale of the asset.

11. I.R.C. §311. See Chapter 5.

12. I.R.C. §355(a)(1)(C). A more detailed discussion follows later in this chapter.

13. I.R.C. §355(a)(1)(B). A more detailed discussion follows later in this chapter.

14. For a discussion of preferential capital gains rates under §1(h), as amended, see Chapter 1.

The second major change since §355's enactment is repeal of the *General Utilities* nonrecognition rule — corporations now generally are taxable on distributions of appreciated property.[15] Yet the distributing corporation recognizes no gain or loss upon a distribution of appreciated property in a §355 transaction.[16] The corporate nonrecognition provision in §355 is among the primary remaining statutory exceptions to *General Utilities* repeal, thus inviting another potential taxpayer abuse — using §355 as a loophole to avoid corporate level tax on distributions of appreciated property. While the primary concern originally driving §355 was preventing bailout of corporate earnings to the shareholders at capital gain rates, the primary concern now has shifted to preventing tax avoidance at the corporate level. Unfortunately, several of the specific requirements found in §355 are ill-suited to the new concerns raised by the repeal of *General Utilities*. Other requirements are arguably redundant and unnecessary. As long as the Code includes a differential between ordinary income and capital gain rates, the §355 requirements must continue to respond to the corporate earnings bailout concern. At the same time, however, §355 should not provide an easy loophole permitting corporate taxpayers to avoid corporate level recognition of gain upon distributions of appreciated property. These dual concerns make an otherwise difficult statute even more challenging. The statutory and regulatory response to these underlying concerns are addressed throughout this chapter.

Some Introductory Terminology: Spin-Offs, Split-Offs, and Split-Ups

Corporate divisions tend to come in three basic flavors: spin-off, split-off, or split-up. Each variation involves a slightly different type of distribution of stock or securities. In general, if the transaction successfully runs the gauntlet of §355, the tax treatment to the shareholders and the corporation will be the same regardless of whether the transaction is a spin-off, split-off, or split-up.

In a *spin-off*, the distributing corporation distributes stock of a controlled corporation (a subsidiary) to its shareholders. This subsidiary may be either a recently created subsidiary "spun off" through the parent corporation's transfer of assets in return for stock or an existing subsidiary. The shareholders in a spin-off generally receive a pro rata share of the controlled corporation's stock and do not transfer anything in return for this stock. If the transaction fails to qualify for nonrecognition under §355, the distribu-

---

15. I.R.C. §§311, 336. For detailed discussion of these provisions and repeal of the *General Utilities* principle, see Chapters 5 and 8.

16. I.R.C. §355(c). A similar nonrecognition rule applies to distributions in connection with a "divisive reorganization." I.R.C. §361(c). These rules are discussed later in this chapter.

tion is treated as a dividend to the shareholder distributees to the extent of the corporation's earnings and profits[17] and any gain on the distribution of the appreciated assets is taxable to the distributing corporation.[18]

Spin-Off

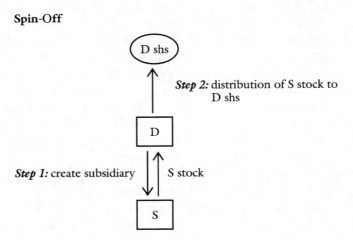

A *split-off* is very much like a spin-off except that the parent's shareholders receive stock in the subsidiary *in return for* some of their stock in the parent corporation. In other words, the transaction is structured more like a redemption than a dividend. If the transaction fails to qualify for §355 nonrecognition treatment, the distribution will be subject to the redemption provisions of §302. Consequently, the redemption distribution might be treated by the shareholders either as a dividend under §302(d) or as a sale or exchange redemption under §302(a).[19]

Split-Off

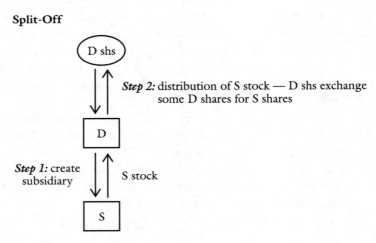

17. I.R.C. §301. For detailed discussion of the §301 distribution rules, see Chapter 5.

18. I.R.C. §311.

19. The corporation would be taxable on any gain pursuant to §311. For a detailed discussion of redemptions, see Chapter 6.

In a *split-up,* the corporation transfers all of its assets to two or more new corporations (controlled corporations) in return for stock, which is then distributed to the shareholders of the parent corporation in return for all of the parent stock. The split-up effectively liquidates the original parent corporation. If the transaction fails to qualify for §355 nonrecognition, the distribution will be treated as a complete liquidation to the shareholders, who will report gain or loss based upon the difference between the fair market value of the stock received and their basis in the original corporation's stock.[20] In addition, the corporation would be taxable on any gain upon a distribution of assets in complete liquidation.[21]

Split-Up

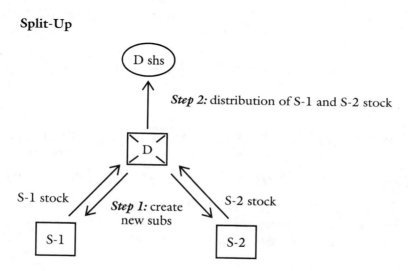

Overview of §355 Requirements

A distribution of stock or securities in a controlled corporation will be eligible for §355 nonrecognition treatment only if it meets numerous statutory and nonstatutory requirements. The statute itself requires:

1. *Control immediately before the distribution*—the distributing corporation must distribute solely stock or securities of a corporation which it controls immediately before the distribution;[22]

2. *Distribution requirement*—the distributing corporation must distribute

---

20. I.R.C. §331. For a detailed discussion of §331, see Chapter 8. But see §332 (liquidation of subsidiary), discussed in Chapter 9.

21. I.R.C. §336. But see §337 (liquidation of subsidiary).

22. I.R.C. §355(a)(1)(A).

all of the stock and securities in the controlled corporation held immediately before the distribution;[23]

3.   *Trade or business requirement* — both the distributing corporation and
    the controlled corporation must be engaged immediately after the dis-
    tribution in the active conduct of a trade or business;[24]

4.   *Non-device requirement* — the transaction was not used principally as a
    device to distribute earnings and profits of the distributing corporation,
    the controlled corporation, or both.[25]

In addition to these statutory requirements, §355 incorporates several
judicially developed requirements paralleling those required for the reorganization provisions genrally.[26] These include business purpose,[27] continuity of
the business enterprise,[28] and continuity of proprietary interest requirements.[29]

The following sections of this chapter will consider each of these statutory and nonstatutory requirements.

A Closer Look at the §355 Requirements

Control "Immediately Before the Distribution"

Nonrecognition under §355 is limited to corporate distributions of stock or
securities of a *controlled* corporation.[30] Such distribution of stock or securities
in a controlled subsidiary to shareholders of the parent arguably reflects a

---

23. I.R.C. §355(a)(1)(D)(i). As an alternative, the distributing corporation may
distribute an amount sufficient to constitute control. In such a case, however, the
distributing corporation must also establish to the satisfaction of the Secretary that
any retention of stock was not in pursuance of a tax avoidance plan. I.R.C.
§355(a)(1)(D)(ii).

24. I.R.C. §355(a)(1)(C), (b). The "trade or business" requirement actually incorporates *both* a *post-distribution* and a *pre-distribution* rule, since the statutory definition of an "active trade or business" requires that the corporation's trade or business
have been "actively conducted throughout the 5-year period ending on the date of
the distribution." I.R.C. §355(b)(2)(B).

25. I.R.C. §355(a)(1)(B).

26. For a discussion of the judicially developed requirements in the reorganization
context, see Chapter 11.

27. Treas. Reg. §1.355-2(b).

28. Treas. Reg. §1.355-1(b).

29. Treas. Reg. §1.355-2(c).

30. I.R.C. §355(a)(1). Section 355 uses the same 80% control tests from §368(c)
that are used for purposes of §351 transactions, discussed earlier in Chapter 4, and
for certain acquisitive reorganizations, discussed in Chapters 11-12. In the context
of a *nondivisive* Type D reorganization, however, the control test is reduced to a 50%
threshold. See I.R.C. §368(a)(2)(H).

"mere change in form." One might visualize the §355 tax-free stock distribution as a rough complement to the §351 tax-free transfer to a corporation which the transferring shareholders control immediately after the exchange.[31] Reversing directions, a parent corporation under §355 distributes stock or securities in a corporation which *it* controls "immediately *before* the distribution."[32] The distributing parent may distribute stock or securities in either a preexisting or a newly created subsidiary.[33] As a practical matter, corporations planning for a division frequently create new subsidiaries for the purpose of effecting a spin-off or split-off. So, for example, the distributing corporation may create a new subsidiary under §351 or as part of a Type D reorganization or other tax-free reorganization provision. On the other hand, if the distributing corporation recently acquired control through a *taxable* purchase, §355 will not apply to the subsequent distribution of the stock.[34] The idea here is to restrict nonrecognition to divisions of corporations with a reasonable history of operating a business or at least a business recently created or acquired in a "mere change in form" nonrecognition type transaction.[35]

Distribution of Control

A further requirement for §355 nonrecognition involves the amount of stock or securities distributed.[36] The distributing corporation must either distribute *all* of the stock or securities of the controlled corporation held immediately

---

31. See Chapter 4.

32. I.R.C. §355(a)(1)(A) (emphasis added).

33. Treas. Reg. §1.355-1(b).

34. One example in the regulations describes a transaction in which the distributing corporation owned 75% of the outstanding stock of another corporation. The corporation acquires the remaining 25% of the stock in a taxable purchase transaction and distributes stock of the controlled corporation six months thereafter. The regulations conclude that §355 will not apply to this distribution. Treas. Reg. §1.355-2(g)(2), example (last sentence).

35. The restriction with regard to recent taxable acquisitions is built into §355 via the "active conduct of a trade or business requirement." The "active trade or business requirement" is not met when the distributing corporation acquired control of the controlled corporation within the past five years in a taxable transaction. I.R.C. §355(b)(2)(D). These restrictions will be discussed in greater detail later in this chapter.

36. Also note that the distribution must be to a shareholder "with respect to its stock." I.R.C. §355(a)(1)(A). This language parallels language in the §301 distribution rules. As in the case of §301 distributions, this language is designed to limit application of the rules to distributions to the shareholders qua shareholders. For example, a corporation may make a distribution to a shareholder as compensation for services, or payment for goods, or repayment of debt. Such distributions will not be covered by §355. For more detailed discussion of the "with respect to stock" restriction in the context of §301 distributions, see Chapter 5.

before the distribution or enough stock to constitute control.[37] If the distributing corporation exercises the latter option, it must also establish to the satisfaction of the Secretary that retention of stock (or stock and securities) was not principally for tax avoidance purposes.[38]

The distribution requirements of §355(a)(1)(D) probably stem from concerns that the corporation might otherwise take advantage of the tax-free distribution rules of §355 as a substitute for taxable dividends. If the corporation could periodically distribute small amounts of the controlled corporation's stock, the distribution begins to look more like a distribution of earnings and profits.[39]

Although §355 requires distribution of all, or a controlling amount, of the controlled subsidiary stock, the distributing corporation has substantial flexibility regarding the structure of the distribution. For purposes of §355, the stock need not be distributed pro rata among the shareholders.[40] This flexibility can be especially useful in structuring corporate separations to resolve conflicts among shareholders. In addition, it does not matter whether the shareholders surrender any distributing corporation stock.[41] Finally, the distribution often is, but need not be, part of a Type D reorganization.[42]

Active Trade or Business Requirement

a) Post-Distribution Active Trade or Business Requirement

Much of §355's complexity enters through the "active trade or business" requirements detailed in §355(b). In addition to the requirements already

---

37. I.R.C. §355(a)(1)(D). Section 355(a)(1)(D)(ii) itself requires only a distribution of an amount of *stock* constituting control and says nothing about securities. The regulations clarify that all, or part, of the securities of the controlled corporation may be distributed. Treas. Reg. §1.355-2(e)(1).

38. *Id.*

39. This concern is already addressed by the requirement in §355(a)(1)(B) that the transaction not be used "principally as a device for the distribution of the earnings and profits of the distributing corporation or the controlled corporation or both," leading some commentators to question whether the additional restrictions in §355(a)(1)(D) are really necessary. See, e.g., Boris I. Bittker and James S. Eustice, Federal Income Taxation of Corporations and Shareholders ¶11.07 (7th ed. 2000). This "device" restriction is addressed in further detail later in this chapter.

40. I.R.C. §355(a)(2)(A).

41. I.R.C. §355(a)(2)(B). This is the provision that permits the flexibility to structure the corporate division as a spin-off (involving no surrender of stock), a split-off (involving a surrender of *some* of the distributing corporation's stock), or a split-up (involving a surrender of *all* of the distributing corporation's stock).

42. I.R.C. §355(a)(2)(C).

mentioned, §355 requires that both the distributing corporation and the controlled corporation or corporations be "engaged immediately after the distribution in the active conduct of a trade or business."[43] In the case of a split-up, the distribution effectively is a liquidating distribution of stock in multiple controlled corporations after which the distributing corporation will cease to exist. In such cases, each of the controlled corporations must be "engaged immediately after the distribution in the active conduct of a trade or business."[44] The post-distribution active trade or business requirement is designed to assure that the distributing corporation is actually breaking off a part, or parts, of the business that will continue to operate after the distribution rather than simply distributing assets to shareholders.

The "definition" section in §355(b)(2) offers virtually no guidance on the meaning of the words "active conduct of a trade or business." Moreover, Treasury Department regulations make only a modest contribution. According to the regulations, a corporation is engaged in a "trade or business" if:

> a specific group of activities are being carried on by the corporation for the purpose of earning income or profit, and the activities included in such group include every operation that forms a part of, or step in, the process of earning income or profit. Such group of activities ordinarily must include the collection of income and the payment of expenses.[45]

Whether or not the corporation is *actively*, as opposed to passively, engaged in a trade or business will depend upon the facts and circumstances. To be considered an active trade or business, however, the corporation generally is "required itself to perform active and substantial management and operational functions."[46] If the corporation can establish that it provides significant operation and management services, the business will be considered an active trade or business. The regulations specifically eliminate from the active conduct of a trade or business definition the holding of stock, securities, land or other property, for investment purposes as well as certain ownership and operation of real or personal property.[47] Ownership and operation of real estate tends to be largely an investment activity and typically

---

43. I.R.C. §355(b)(1)(A). The provisions of §355(a) explicitly cross-reference to the active business rule, indicating that the requirements of subparagraph (b) must be met if the shareholder distributees are to be entitled to nonrecognition treatment. I.R.C. §355(a)(1)(C).

44. I.R.C. §355(b)(1)(B).

45. Treas. Reg. §1.355-3(b)(2)(ii).

46. Treas. Reg. §1.355-3(b)(2)(iii). Activities performed by persons outside the corporation, such as independent contractors, do not count as activities performed by the corporation. Nevertheless, the corporation can meet the active trade or business requirement even though "some of its activities are performed by others." *Id.*

47. Treas. Reg. §1.355-3(b)(2)(iv).

is not a business involving significant management and operational activity. Thus, the regulations eliminate such activity from the definition of an active trade or business unless the owner performs significant services with respect to the operation and management of the property.[48] These investment-type activity exclusions from the active trade or business definition reflect the concerns underlying §355. The idea is to limit nonrecognition to genuine corporate separations and, thus, to disallow tax-free distributions of investment assets.

b) Pre-Distribution Active Trade or Business Requirement

The pre-distribution active trade or business requirement appears rather inelegantly in the statutory language. The language in §355(b)(1) begins by including only a post-distribution trade or business requirement. The definition section that follows in §355(b)(2) treats a corporation as engaged in the active conduct of a trade or business for purposes of paragraph (b)(1) only if the trade or business "has been actively conducted throughout the five-year period *ending* on the date of the distribution."[49] Thus, the particular trade or business relied upon to meet this requirement cannot be a new trade or business, but must have a five-year history. Finally, the distributing corporation must not have acquired the trade or business, or control over the corporation conducting the trade or business, in a taxable transaction within five years prior to the distribution.[50]

Here again, Congress was trying to limit nonrecognition to "mere change in form" divisions and to prevent corporations from simply siphoning off assets to shareholders that otherwise would have been distributed to them in the form of taxable dividends. The suspicion raised when a corporation spins off a recently developed business is that the particular business was developed as part of a plan for sale of the business by the shareholders. Similar suspicions arise when the corporation spins off a business recently acquired in a taxable transaction.[51]

---

48. The issues regarding real estate as a passive activity are similar to issues in connection with the passive activity loss rules of §469.

49. I.R.C. §355(b)(2)(B) (emphasis added).

50. I.R.C. §355(b)(2)(C), (D).

51. Under §355(b)(2)(D), the distributing corporation will not meet the pre-distribution trade or business requirement if it acquired *control* within the five-year period ending on the date of the distribution. If the distributing corporation acquired not 80% control, but only a *50%* interest within this five-year period, restrictions in §355(d) and (e) may apply. These special provisions are considered later in this chapter.

c) Particular Applications of the "Active Trade or Business" Requirements

(i) Vertical Divisions of a Single Business

Although unresolved for a time, it is now well settled that §355 treatment is possible upon the corporate division of a single trade or business, sometimes referred to as a vertical division. In its early regulations, the Treasury Department had taken the position that the division of a single business was not eligible for §355 nonrecognition, arguing that the active trade or business requirement was met only if there were two or more separate and distinct businesses operating immediately after the distribution. In two landmark §355 cases, however, the Fifth and Sixth Circuits both declared these regulations invalid. In the Sixth Circuit case of Coady v. Commissioner,[52] a single corporation engaged in the business of constructing sewage disposal plants transferred half of its assets to a new subsidiary and then distributed the stock in the subsidiary to one of its shareholders in exchange for all of his stock. The corporate division effectively transferred one major construction contract to the new corporation and left the remaining major construction contract with the original corporation. The Fifth Circuit case of United States v. Marett[53] involved a single business manufacturing edible pork skins. The corporation had a contract with one major customer and others with several smaller customers. The corporation built a new factory to handle orders from its smaller customers and transferred the factory and related assets to a new subsidiary. The stock in this new subsidiary was then distributed to the parent corporation's shareholders. In each case, the courts found that the distributions were valid §355 distributions. Since losing these cases, the government has conceded that the division of a single business into two separate businesses can qualify under §355. In fact, the particular facts of the Coady and Marett cases are explicitly given the Treasury Department's blessing in two examples incorporated into regulations promulgated in 1989.[54]

Remember that to meet the "active trade or business" requirement, the distributing and controlled corporations must not only be engaged in an active trade or business immediately after the distribution, but such trade or business must have been actively conducted during the five-year period

---

52. 289 F.2d 490 (6th Cir. 1961), *affirming* 33 T.C. 771 (1960).

53. 325 F.2d 28 (5th Cir. 1963).

54. Treas. Reg. §1.355-3(c), exs. (4) (*Coady* case), (5) (*Marett* case). Beware, however, that there must also be a business purpose for the division and distribution. For example, the separation of the corporation into two corporations in Example 5 was designed to eliminate errors in packaging. See also Examples (6) and (7) involving separation of downtown and suburban retail or department stores into separate corporations.

preceding the distribution as well. Some difficult issues arise in determining whether a particular trade or business satisfies this five-year history requirement. The regulations specify that "[t]he fact that a trade or business underwent change during the five-year period preceding the distribution (for example, by the addition of new or the dropping of old products, changes in production capacity, and the like) shall be disregarded, provided that the changes are not of such a character as to constitute the acquisition of a new or different business."[55] In addition, the expansion of a business into new geographical areas should not be regarded necessarily as the creation of a new trade or business. If a corporation has been actively engaged in a trade or business in one state and recently expanded into a new state, it should be possible to arrange a corporate division into separate corporations, each conducting business in the separate state. The Treasury Department did not always agree. In one early case, for example, a corporation whose primary operations had been in Nebraska had recently opened a branch in Maine. The corporation transferred assets connected with the Maine office to a new subsidiary and then distributed the subsidiary's stock to its shareholders. The government took the position that this was not a valid §355 distribution since the Maine "trade or business" had not been conducted for the necessary five years prior to the distribution. The Eighth Circuit disagreed, holding that the active trade or business requirement was met. The court said that "[n]othing in the language of §355 suggests that prior business activity is only to be measured by looking at the business performed in a geographical area where the controlled corporation is eventually formed."[56] Again, the Treasury Department conceded the point in regulations promulgated in 1989.[57]

(ii) Horizontal or Functional Divisions of a Single Business

Corporations may wish to separate particular functions, such as research or sales, into separate corporate entities. The potential problem here is that a corporate entity created to engage in a single function of a larger business enterprise may not independently produce income. The new §355 regulations envision a corporation as engaged in a "trade or business" "if a specific group of activities are being carried on by the corporation for the purpose of earning income or profit, and the activities included in such group include every operation that forms a part, or a step, in the process of earning income or profit."[58] In order to satisfy the "active trade or business" requirement,

---

55. Treas. Reg. §1.355-3(b)(3)(ii).

56. Estate of Lockwood v. Comm'r, 350 F.2d 712, 715 (8th Cir. 1965).

57. Treas. Reg. §1.355-3, ex. (8).

58. Treas. Reg. §1.355-3(b)(2)(ii).

the activities separated in the new corporation must represent a separate and independent trade or business. Nevertheless, the Treasury Department regulations provide several examples of functional divisions that it says will satisfy the active trade or business requirement. One involves the spin-off of a research division, another a sales function, and another a supply function for a manufacturing business.[59] In each case, however, the regulation cautions that the division must also satisfy the separate requirement that the transaction not be used principally as a device for the distribution of earnings and profits.

Device for the Distribution of Earnings and Profits

In addition to all of the restrictions and requirements discussed above, §355 explicitly demands that "the transaction was not used principally as a device for the distribution of the earnings and profits of the distributing corporation or the controlled corporation or both."[60] Frequently described as the "device requirement," this condition is a nutshell statement of the general concern underlying §355. In fact, it is in the regulations pursuant to the "device" requirement that one finds perhaps the best statement of the underlying concern. The regulation states that "section 355 recognizes that a tax-free distribution of the stock of a controlled corporation presents a potential for tax avoidance by facilitating the avoidance of the dividend provisions of the Code *through the subsequent sale or exchange of stock of one corporation and the retention of the stock of another corporation.*"[61] In some measure, all of the restrictions and requirements found in §355 are directed at this goal of preventing bailout of corporate earnings and profits without paying the "dividend" toll. In fact, some §355 requirements arguably are redundant. The independent "device requirement" may serve as a general safeguard to catch bailouts that the more specific and technical §355 restrictions or requirements fail to cover.

Regulations on the "device" requirement list a number of "device factors" to be considered in making the facts and circumstances analysis required to determine whether the transaction was used to bail out earnings and profits. Not surprisingly, the regulations indicate that "the fact that a distribution is pro rata or substantially pro rata is evidence of device."[62] Moreover, a subsequent sale of the distributed stock can be evidence of a

---

59. Treas. Reg. §1.355-3, exs. (9)-(11).

60. I.R.C. §355(a)(1)(B).

61. Treas. Reg. §1.355-2(d)(1) (emphasis added).

62. Treas. Reg. §1.355-2(d)(2)(ii).

device.[63] The greater the percentage of the stock sold and the shorter the period of time between the distribution and the subsequent sale, the stronger the evidence of device becomes.[64] A prearranged or negotiated sale is considered "*substantial* evidence of device," whereas a subsequent sale that was not arranged or negotiated prior to the distribution merely is "evidence of device."[65] Any device factors present should be balanced against, and may be outweighed by, "nondevice factors." Regulations permit the taxpayer to use corporate business purpose as evidence that the transaction was not used as a device for the distribution of earnings and profits.[66] However, the same regulations caution that "[t]he stronger the evidence of device . . . , the stronger the corporate business purpose required to prevent the determination that the transaction was used principally as a device."[67]

Nonstatutory Requirements

Even if a §355 tax-free separation is not a §368(a) reorganization, the transaction nevertheless must meet business purpose and continuity of interest requirements reminiscent of the rules applied to reorganizations generally under §368. This should not be surprising given the substantial overlap and similarity of underlying concerns behind tax-free reorganizations and tax-free divisions. The same business purpose and continuity doctrines developed in early reorganization cases will apply to §355 distributions as well.[68]

---

63. However, the mere fact of a subsequent sale will not be construed as a "device" unless it was pursuant to an arrangement negotiated or agreed upon prior to the distribution. I.R.C. §355(a)(1)(B).

64. Treas. Reg. §1.355-2(d)(2)(iii).

65. Treas. Reg. §1.355-2(d)(2)(iii)(B), (C) (emphasis added). On the other hand, the I.R.S. has announced that the distributing corporation or a controlled corporation may repurchase the shares subsequent to the distribution in some cases for valid business reasons and will issue a "safe harbor" ruling in such cases in accordance with Rev. Proc. 91-63, 1991-2 C.B. 865.

66. Treas. Reg. §1.355-2(d)(3).

67. *Id.* Also under these regulations, the fact that the distributing corporation is publicly traded is evidence of nondevice. *Id.*

68. See Chapter 11. The "business purpose" test that now applies to both the §368 reorganization provisions and the §355 distribution provisions actually grew out of an early landmark case involving a divisive reorganization. Gregory v. Helvering, 293 U.S. 465 (1935). The shareholder in *Gregory* caused her solely owned corporation to transfer highly appreciated stock to a newly formed subsidiary that never conducted any business and was in existence for only three days. Although the transaction met the literal terms of the reorganization statute, the court denied tax-free reorganization treatment, since the transaction lacked a business purpose. For a detailed discussion of the *Gregory* case, see Chapter 11.

a) Business Purpose

Regulations under §355 explicitly incorporate an "independent business purpose" test under which the overall transaction must be motivated, "in whole or substantial part, by one or more corporate business purposes."[69] In recent years, the Treasury Department has been increasing its emphasis on the business purpose test while decreasing emphasis on the "active trade or business" and "device" requirements of §355. This changing emphasis reflects the changing tax landscape considered in the introduction to this chapter. The business purpose test better serves the government's interest in combating corporate level tax avoidance on distributions of appreciated property than the trade or business and device requirements, which were designed to combat bailouts of corporate earnings at capital gains rates.

Consistent with the increased focus on the business purpose test since the repeal of the *General Utilities* rule in 1986, the §355 regulations now insist that both the overall transaction *and* the §355 distribution itself be carried out for one or more business purposes.[70] Making matters even more difficult, a separation will not meet the corporate business purpose requirement if the business purpose can be achieved *without* the distribution of stock of a controlled corporation in a nontaxable transaction which is "neither impractical nor unduly expensive."[71] In other words, the §355 distribution must be the transaction structure of last resort to achieve the business purposes. To illustrate the point, the regulations include an example of a corporation engaged in the manufacture of candy and toys. In order to protect the candy business from the "risks and vicissitudes" of the toy business, the corporation transferred its toy manufacturing operations to a new controlled subsidiary and then distributed the stock in the new subsidiary to its shareholders. The example concludes that the legitimate business purpose of protecting the candy business is achieved simply by creating the new corporate entity. Since the subsequent distribution to the shareholders is unnecessary to achieve the business purpose, the shareholders are not eligible for §355 nonrecognition.[72]

As for the definition of "corporate business purpose," the regulations simply provide that it is "a real and substantial non-Federal tax purpose

---

69. Treas. Reg. §1.355-2(b)(1). In fact, much of the language in this regulation parallels the precise language of Treas. Reg. §1.368-1(b). The regulations declare that the potential for tax avoidance "is relevant in determining the extent to which an existing corporate business purpose motivated the distribution." *Id.*

70. Treas. Reg. §1.355-2(b)(3).

71. *Id.*

72. Treas. Reg. §1.355-2(b)(5), ex. (3).

germane to the business."[73] Given an increasing volume of corporate break-ups, the vague regulatory definition has left many corporate taxpayers searching for further indication as to what business purposes will be acceptable. In the meantime, some examples of acceptable business purpose already provided in the regulations include corporate separations designed to comply with federal antitrust or other regulatory restrictions, to settle shareholder conflicts, or to permit employees to share in corporate profits.[74]

b) Continuity of Proprietary Interest

The judicially developed "continuity of proprietary interest" doctrine goes to the heart of the "mere change in form" rationale behind the nonrecognition rules. The idea is to provide nonrecognition treatment in transactions where the investors holding an interest before the transaction remain substantially invested in the restructured corporate enterprise after the transaction. Continuity of interest is built in to the §368(a)(1)(D) divisive reorganization definition since the transferor corporation, or one or more of its shareholders, must be in control of the corporation acquiring the transferor's assets immediately after the transfer. Moreover, continuity of interest principles apply even to §355 tax-free distributions that do not meet the §368(a) reorganization definition. Mirroring language in the §368 regulations, the §355 regulations require that the separation effect "only a readjustment of continuing interests in the property of the distributing and controlled corporations."[75] As applied in the tax-free separation context, continuity requires that one or more prior owners own, in the aggregate, "an amount of stock establishing a continuity of interest in *each of the modified corporate forms in which the enterprise is conducted after the separation*."[76] In other words, if one corporate enterprise is separated into three distinct corporations, the continuity of interest requirement must be met with regard to each of the three corporate entities resulting from the separation.

c) Step-Transaction Doctrine

The judicially developed step-transaction doctrine potentially applies in the context of divisive reorganizations and §355 distributions just as it does

---

73. Treas. Reg. §1.355-2(b)(2).

74. See examples in Treas. Reg. §1.355-2(b)(5).

75. Treas. Reg. §1.355-2(c) ("section 355 requires that one or more persons who, directly or indirectly, were the owners of the enterprise prior to the distribution or exchange own, in the aggregate, an amount of stock establishing a continuity of interest in each of the modified corporate forms in which the enterprise is conducted after the separation").

76. Treas. Reg. §1.355-2(c)(1) (emphasis added).

elsewhere throughout the tax-free reorganization provisions and Subchapter C more generally.[77] Under this doctrine, a distribution otherwise qualifying for nonrecognition treatment under §355 could be disqualified if the distribution was considered part of a larger, integrated transaction that fails to meet §355 requirements. Until recently, the Service had made it clear that it would apply step-transaction analysis to such §355 cases.[78] In Rev. Rul. 98-27, however, the Service announced that it "will not apply Court Holding (or any formulation of the step transaction doctrine) to determine whether the distributed corporation was a controlled corporation immediately before the distribution under section 355(a) solely because of any postdistribution acquisition or restructuring of the distributed corporation."[79] This announcement seems consistent with the government's recently changed position with regard to post-reorganization continuity of interest principles more generally.[80]

Overlap of §368(a)(1)(D) and §355: Divisive Reorganizations

Many, but not all, distributions of stock in a controlled corporation will simultaneously be "reorganizations" under §368(a)(1)(D) and also distributions under §355. A Type D reorganization involves transfer of "all *or a part* of [a corporation's] assets to another corporation if immediately after the transfer, the transferor, or one or more of its shareholders . . . , or any combination thereof, is in control of the corporation to which the assets are transferred."[81] In addition, stock or securities of the corporation to which the assets were transferred must be distributed pursuant to the requirements of §§354, 355, or 356.[82] Remember that the Type D reorganization includes both acquisitive and divisive reorganizations. In general, acquisitive Type D reorganizations involve a transfer of *all* of the assets and a subsequent distribution of stock or securities pursuant to the requirements for nonrecognition under §354. On the other hand, a divisive reorganization involves

---

77. See earlier discussion of the step-transaction doctrine as generally applicable in connection with tax-free reorganizations in Chapter 11.

78. Rev. Rul. 96-30, 1996-1 C.B. 36., *declared obsolete by* Rev. Rul. 98-27, 1988-1 C.B 1159.

79. 1998-1 C.B. 1159, 1160. See also I.R.C. §§351(c), 368(a)(2)(H).

80. See discussion of the new continuity of interest regulations in Chapter 11.

81. I.R.C. §368(a)(1)(D) (emphasis added). Contrast the "acquisitive reorganization " provisions of §368(a)(1)(C), which require transfer of "substantially all" of the transferring corporation's assets. Discussion of the acquisitive Type D reorganization appeared in Chapter 12.

82. *Id.*

a transfer of *part* of the assets and a subsequent distribution of stock or securities pursuant to the requirements for nonrecognition under §355. Since Congress was more concerned with abuse possibilities in connection with divisive reorganizations, §355 imposes more rigorous requirements for nonrecognition than many of the other tax-free reorganization provisions.

Tax Consequences to Shareholders and Other Distributees

Basic Nonrecognition Rule: §355(a)

If all of the requirements for a tax-free division or tax-free reorganization are met, the shareholders and security holders will not report gain or loss or otherwise include any income upon receipt of stock or securities in the controlled subsidiary from the distributing parent corporation.[83]

Receipt of Boot

A transaction that otherwise satisfies the requirements of §355 will not be disqualified simply because the shareholders or security holders receive property other than stock or securities permitted to be received tax-free under §355.[84] Consistent with the other reorganization provisions in Subchapter C, however, any such additional property received will be treated as boot and taxable according to the reorganization boot rules in §356.[85] Under new provisions added by the Taxpayer Relief Act of 1997, "'nonqualified preferred stock' is *not* considered stock or securities" for purposes of §355.[86] Thus, any such "nonqualified preferred stock" will be treated as boot. Unlike the §351 nonrecognition rules, securities received will not automatically be treated as boot. However, the excess principal of securities in the controlled

---

83. I.R.C. §355(a)(1).

84. Recently finalized regulations now indicate that, with certain exceptions provided in Treas. Reg. §1.356-6, the term "securities" for purposes of §355 "includes rights issued by the distributing corporation or the controlled corporation to acquire stock of that corporation." Treas. Reg. §1.355-1(c). Thus, the Treasury Department now permits the tax-free receipt of these stock rights in a §355 transaction. This new position will allow more freedom for taxpayers to receive options or warrants in connection with a §355 distribution without having to recognize boot gain.

85. See I.R.C. §355(a)(4)(A), which explicitly cross-references to the §356 boot rules.

86. Taxpayer Relief Act of 1997, Pub. L. No. 105-34, §1014(c) (adding I.R.C. §355(a)(3)(D)). "Nonqualified preferred stock" is defined in new §351(g) and was discussed in detail in Chapter 4. See also Treas. Reg. §1.356-6 (rights to acquire nonqualified preferred stock).

corporation received over the principal amount of securities surrendered will be considered boot.[87] If securities are received and no securities were surrendered, then all of the securities received will be considered boot.[88]

In addition to the above boot rules, §355 includes a unique boot rule that applies to recently acquired stock in the controlled corporation. If the distributing corporation acquired stock of the controlled corporation within five years prior to the distribution in a taxable transaction, the distribution of such stock will be treated as the distribution of boot.[89] Presumably, the amount of recently acquired stock that would be considered boot under this provision would not exceed 20%, since the transaction would be disqualified from §355 altogether if the distributing corporation acquired *control* in a taxable transaction within the five years prior to the distribution.[90]

In the case of a straight §355 spin-off distribution in which the shareholders do not exchange or surrender any shares, §356 provides that the boot distribution shall be treated as a distribution of property to which §301 applies.[91] Thus, if the distributing corporation has sufficient earnings and profits to cover the boot distribution, the shareholders will report the boot as dividend income. In the case of a split-off or split-up in which the shareholders exchange some or all of their shares in return for the stock or securities received, the boot received in the exchange will be governed by §356(a). Unless the exchange is determined to have the effect of the distribution of a dividend, the boot under §356(a) will be treated as capital gain.[92]

Basis in the Stock or Securities Received

In the case of split-offs and split-ups, each of which involves an *exchange* of stock or securities by the shareholder or security holder, §358(a) provides that the basis of the stock or securities received shall be the same as the stock or securities surrendered, decreased in the amount of any boot received and

---

87. I.R.C. §§355(a)(3)(A), 356(d)(2)(B). This security boot rule parallels the §354(a)(2) boot rule that applies to reorganizations generally. For a detailed discussion of these boot rules as applied to other reorganizations, see Chapter 11. A right to acquire stock, which is now considered a "security" for purposes of §355, is considered to have no principal amount. Treas. Reg. §1.355-1(c). See also Treas. Reg. §1.356-3(b).

88. I.R.C. §355(a)(3)(A). Even though a stock option or warrant is considered a security for purposes of §355, it is *not* considered "other property" for purposes of the §356 boot rules, since it has no principal amount. Treas. Reg. §1.356-3(b). See also *id.* at exs. (7)-(9).

89. I.R.C. §355(a)(3)(B).

90. I.R.C. §355(b)(2)(D).

91. I.R.C. §356(b).

92. For a more detailed discussion of the §356 boot rules and the distinction between dividend boot and capital gain boot under these rules, see Chapter 11.

increased by the amount of gain or amount treated as a dividend. With regard to spin-offs, §358(c) deems the transaction to be an exchange in which the stock or securities of the distributing corporation retained is viewed first as surrendered and then received back in the exchange. The effect of both of the §358 basis rules is to allocate the old basis over all of the stock or securities owned after the distribution in accordance with fair market values on the date of distribution.

Tax Consequences to the Corporation

A corporation distributing stock or securities of a controlled subsidiary in a transaction meeting the requirements of §355 generally will recognize no gain or loss upon the distribution. Section 355(c) provides such nonrecognition for §355 distributions that are "not in pursuance of a plan of reorganization."[93] Lest there be any doubt, §355(c)(3) explicitly states that the general recognition rules in §§311 and 336 that would otherwise apply to corporate distributions will not apply to §355 distributions. Notice that §355(c) nonrecognition technically applies only to tax-free divisions that are not also "divisive reorganizations" under §368(a)(1)(D). Similar nonrecognition is provided to the distributing corporation in a Type D divisive reorganization via §361(c), and §361(c)(4) explicitly states that §311 shall not apply. If any appreciated property, other than stock or securities in the controlled corporation, is distributed as boot in connection with the §355 separation distribution, the corporation will be required to recognize gain upon the distribution of the boot.[94] Similar treatment is provided in §361 for boot distributed in a divisive Type D reorganization.[95]

Generally speaking, the tax consequences to the distributing corporation will be the same regardless of whether the transaction is a Type D divisive reorganization or a tax-free division not classified as a reorganization. One notable exception, however, is the treatment of certain liabilities. In a Type D divisive reorganization, the distributing corporation may be required to report capital gain to the extent that the liabilities transferred exceed the adjusted basis of the property pursuant to §357(c).[96]

Corporations planning a divisive transaction often will contribute assets to a new subsidiary immediately before distributing the subsidiary's stock to its shareholders. If the transaction qualifies as a Type D reorganization, the

---

93. I.R.C. §355(c)(1).

94. I.R.C. §355(c)(2).

95. I.R.C. §361(c)(2).

96. These are the same §357 rules that apply in the case of §351 exchanges. A detailed discussion of §357 appears in Chapter 4.

corporation is entitled to nonrecognition on its transfer of assets in exchange for subsidiary stock under §361. Even if the transaction technically is not a Type D reorganization, the corporation transferring assets to a new subsidiary in exchange for stock should be eligible for nonrecognition treatment under §351. Recall, however, that the transferors must have control immediately after the exchange in order to qualify for §351 nonrecognition.[97] Special provisions in §351(c) assure the corporate transferor that the control test is not violated if the stock received in the initial §351 exchange is distributed to its shareholders. Moreover, in the case of such a §355 distribution following a §351 exchange, recent amendments reduce the control required by the shareholders to 50% control, rather than the 80% control that would otherwise be required under §368(c).[98] The reduced control requirement should offer greater flexibility to corporations planning spin-off transactions.

Special Corporate Gain Recognition Rules: Preventing Corporate Escape from General Utilities Repeal

The corporate level nonrecognition provided for the distributing corporation in §355(c) is the primary remaining exception to the general rule requiring corporate recognition of gain or loss upon the distribution of appreciated property. Since the repeal of *General Utilities,* corporations have focused upon using §355 as the remaining opportunity to escape corporate level tax on appreciation. In recent responses to this potential loophole, Congress added two new provisions requiring the recognition of gain upon certain distributions of stock or securities in a controlled corporation.

a) Disguised Sales: §355(d)

Absent special restrictions to §355 nonrecognition, a corporation might convert an otherwise taxable sale of a controlling interest in a corporation into a tax-free sale through use of §355 nonrecognition distributions. Imagine, for example, a holding company (T) with two subsidiaries, T-1 and T-2. Unrelated corporations X and Y each acquire 50% of T's stock from the T shareholders for cash. Immediately thereafter, T liquidates, distributing the T-1 stock to X and the T-2 stock to Y.

---

97. For discussion of the §351 control test, see Chapter 4.

98. Taxpayer Relief Act of 1997, Pub. L. No. 105-34, §1012(c)(1) (codified at I.R.C. §351(c)(2)).

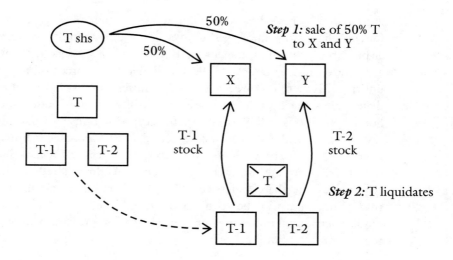

In this transaction, the holding company (T) effectively is selling its subsidiaries, T-1 and T-2, in a transaction that would otherwise trigger a corporate level gain to T.[99] T's liquidation ordinarily would trigger a corporate level gain under §336.[100] Notice, however, that the transaction is designed to meet the requirements of §355. The distributing corporation (T) is distributing solely stock of two controlled corporations (T-1 and T-2) to its shareholders, X and Y. Prior to the enactment of §355(d), the hypothetical transaction described above was eligible for §355 nonrecognition to both the shareholders receiving the distribution, X and Y, and the distributing corporation (T).

Congress responded to this type of "disguised sale" transaction, adding §355(d) in 1990.[101] Legislative history accompanying §355(d) notes a congressional intent "to prevent taxpayers from using section 355 to dispose of subsidiaries in sale-like transactions, or to obtain a fair market value stepped-up basis for future dispositions without incurring a corporate-level tax."[102]

Under §355(d), distributions of certain "disqualified stock" *will* trigger recognition of gain to the distributing corporation, contrary to the general corporate level nonrecognition rule in §355(c)(1). Briefly summarized, stock in the distributing corporation itself, or stock in a corporation controlled by the distributing corporation (its subsidiaries), is considered "disqualified

---

99. Since X and Y corporations are unrelated, their purchases will not be combined, and the transaction cannot be a §338 QSP eligible for a §338(h)(10) election that would eliminate the corporate level taxable gain. For a discussion of §338, see Chapter 10.

100. For a discussion of liquidations, see Chapter 8.

101. This new provision was added by the Revenue Reconciliation Act of 1990, Pub. L. No. 101-508, §1132(a) (codified at I.R.C. §355(d)).

102. H.R. Rep. No. 101-881, 341 (1990).

stock" under §355(d) if it was acquired by purchase within the five-year period ending on the date of the distribution.[103] Distribution of such disqualified stock is not a qualified distribution for purposes of §355(c)(2). As such, the distribution will trigger gain to the distributing corporation as if the stock were sold to the distributee shareholders at fair market value.[104] The §355(d) rules do not alter the nonrecognition available to the shareholder distributees, but T now *will* be taxable upon the distribution of its T-1 and T-2 stock to X and Y.

Despite the recent judicial trend in statutory interpretation cases to emphasize literal text, the conference report accompanying §355(d) explicitly invited the Treasury Department to promulgate regulations "to exclude from the provision transactions that do not violate the purposes of the provision."[105] The report further announced that "[t]he purposes of [§355(d)] are not violated if . . . the effect of the distribution is neither (1) to increase ownership in the distributing corporation or any controlled corporation by persons who have directly or indirectly acquired stock within the prior five years, nor (2) to provide a basis step-up with respect to the stock of any controlled corporation."[106] Pursuant to this authority, recently proposed regulations offer examples of transactions that will not be considered "disqualified distributions" for purposes of §355(d), even though the transactions otherwise fit the literal language of the statute.[107]

b) The New Anti-*"Morris Trust"* Rules: §355(e)

In another recent reaction to transactions designed to prevent recognition of corporate level gain, Congress added §355(e) as part of the Taxpayer Relief Act of 1997.[108] The new §355(e) provisions have come to be known as the *"Morris Trust"* rules, in reference to the early case which stimulated this statutory response. Commissioner v. W. Morris Trust[109] involved the merger of a state bank into a national bank. One barrier to the proposed merger was an insurance division operated for many years by the state bank to be merged—federal banking law prohibited national banks from engaging in insurance operations. To facilitate the merger, the state bank spun off its insurance operations by transferring them to a new subsidiary and immedi-

---

103. I.R.C. §355(d)(3).

104. I.R.C. §355(d)(1), (c)(2).

105. H.R. Conf. Rep. No. 101-964, 1092 (1990).

106. *Id*. at 1093.

107. Prop. Treas. Reg. §1.355-(b)(3)(v).

108. Taxpayer Relief Act of 1997, Pub. L. No. 105-24, §1012(a) (codified at I.R.C. §355(e)).

109. 367 F.2d 794 (4th Cir. 1966).

ately distributing stock in this new subsidiary to its shareholders in a transaction otherwise qualifying as a Type D divisive reorganization. The stock distribution included as part of the Type D reorganization also otherwise qualified for nonrecognition under §355. As planned, the state bank was then merged into the national bank in a Type A reorganization. The Fourth Circuit in *Morris Trust* gave its blessing to the tax-free divisive reorganization preceding the merger. The *Morris Trust* transaction offered a blueprint for transaction planners who wish to spin off unwanted assets in a Type D reorganization just prior to a tax-free acquisitive reorganization. If effective, target corporations could transfer *less than* substantially all of their assets and still be eligible for tax-free nonrecognition in the acquisition of the desired assets that follows.

The structure of §355(e) is similar to that of §355(d). If the §355(e) rules are triggered, the distribution of stock or securities will not be a distribution of qualified property eligible for §355(c)(1) nonrecognition to the distributing corporation. Briefly summarized, the corporate level gain recognition rules are triggered by a distribution that is "part of a plan (or series of transactions) pursuant to which 1 or more persons acquire" a 50% or greater interest in the distributing corporation or any controlled corporation.[110] Acquisition of a 50% or greater interest during the four-year period beginning two years before the date of the distribution is *presumed* to be part of such a plan unless the contrary can be established.[111] The Treasury Department recently proposed extensive regulations on the meaning of the "plan (or series of related transactions)" language in §355(e), focusing on conditions necessary to rebut the statutory presumption of a plan.[112]

A related provision included as part of the Taxpayer Relief Act of 1997 is §355(f), which provides that §355 will not apply to a distribution from one member to another member of an affiliated group if the distribution was part of a plan for one or more persons *outside* the group to acquire a 50% or greater interest as described in §355(e).

Subparts (d), (e), and (f) of §355 are controversial and complex. For many years prior to the enactment of §355(e), *Morris Trust*-type transactions had been blessed by the Service, and used regularly by taxpayers, as a technique to spin off a target corporation's unwanted assets prior to a tax-free reorganization. Practitioners argue that the new provision sweeps too broadly, extending far beyond the "abusive" transactions that provided the

---

110. I.R.C. §355(e)(2)(A).

111. I.R.C. §355(e)(2)(B).

112. Prop. Treas. Reg. §1.355-7. These proposed regulations have generated voluminous comments, most critical, from the practicing bar. See, e.g., ABA Comments on Proposed Regulations Under Section 355(e), letter to I.R.S. Commissioner Rossotti, reprinted in Tax Analysts, Highlights and Documents 89 (Jan. 4, 2000).

impetus for enacting §355(e).[113] These "abusive" transactions involved highly leveraged transactions, in which the purchasing corporation became responsible for substantial target corporation debts.[114] Nevertheless, §355(e) extends more generally to 50% or greater changes in interest in the distributing or the controlled corporation.

The text above has only touched upon the statutory details. We have surely not heard the last of the controversy, and much more remains to be spelled out in forthcoming regulations. For the moment, it is worth noting that §355's complexities stem from its multiple purposes. The §355 rules simultaneously attempt to prevent the shareholders from bailing out corporate earnings at preferential capital gains rates *and* to prevent the distributing corporation from escaping corporate level recognition, thus effectively escaping the repeal of *General Utilities*. Congress is packing a lot into one statutory provision.

EXAMPLES

Basic Separations

1a.   Shareholders A and B each own 50% of the outstanding common stock of Corporation C, which has been operating a flower delivery and a singing telegram business for ten years. The flower delivery business assets have an aggregate basis of $100,000 and a fair market value of $500,000 and the singing telegram business assets have an aggregate basis of $75,000 and a fair market value of $300,000. Shareholders A and B each have a basis in the C shares of $25,000. Because each of its operations requires different types of management skills and has different inventory requirements, Corporation C's Board of Directors has decided to separate the two businesses. To achieve this result, C first transfers its flower delivery business assets to Newco, a newly formed subsidiary, in exchange for all of Newco's stock. Newco will continue operating the flower delivery business. Immediately thereafter, C

---

113. *See, e.g.,* Mark J. Silverman and Lisa M. Zarlenga, Proposed Section 355(e) Regulations: Broadening the Definition of a Plan, 87 Tax Notes 117, 118 n.10 (2000) ("Section 355(e) is a poorly drafted statute based on flawed principles. . . . Section 355(e) was aimed at certain abusive transactions . . . one feature [of which is] that the corporation to be acquired borrows money (or assumes a large amount of debt) and distributes . . . the proceeds of such debt to its parent before a spin-off."). See also Scott Polsky, The Cause and True Effects of Code Section 355(e), 76 Taxes 29, 33 (1998).

114. The most frequently mentioned among these "abusive" transactions was the Viacom/TCI merger. Viacom contributed its "unwanted" assets along with $1.7 billion in borrowed funds to a spun-off subsidiary. The subsidiary stock was distributed to shareholders pursuant to §355. In the subsequent merger, TCI was left with the wanted assets and liability for the $1.7 billion debt.

makes a pro rata distribution of the Newco stock to shareholders A and B. What are the tax consequences of this transaction to shareholders A and B and to Corporation C?

1b. Assume instead that Corporation C itself had been operating only the singing telegram business, but had long been operating its flower delivery business through Oldco, a wholly owned subsidiary. C now makes a pro rata distribution of its stock in Oldco to shareholders A and B. What are the tax consequences to Corporation C and shareholders A and B?

1c. What if shareholders A and B were each required to surrender one-half of their C shares in exchange for the Newco shares in Example 1a?

1d. Would your answer to Example 1a differ if Corporation C instead transferred its flower delivery business assets to Newco 1 and its singing telegram business to Newco 2 in exchange for all of the stock of Newco 1 and 2, respectively, and thereafter distributed all of the Newco 1 and Newco 2 stock to shareholders A and B in exchange for all of their Corporation C shares?

1e. Would your answer to Example 1a differ if Corporation C had transferred only the real estate associated with the flower delivery operation to Newco in exchange for all of the Newco stock and subsequently distributed the Newco stock pro rata to shareholders A and B?

Shareholder Conflicts, Boot and Other Matters

2a. Corporation N is a magazine publisher, publishing largely sports magazines. It recently acquired a highly controversial, politically incorrect magazine in a tax-free reorganization. Shareholder group A, which holds 20% of N's stock, is quite upset and threatening to sell its N shares. Shareholder group B, which holds the remaining 80%, does not object to the recent acquisition. In response to this conflict, Corporation N transfers the new magazine business assets to Newco in exchange for all of the Newco stock and subsequently distributes the Newco stock to shareholder group B and cash to shareholder group A. What are the tax consequences to Corporation N and the two shareholder groups?

2b. Corporation D is a toy manufacturing company, with two distinct business operations. One division manufactures children's toys and the other manufactures games and puzzles designed for adults. D has owned and operated each of these businesses for at least ten years. D transfers its adult division to Newco, a newly formed subsidiary, and immediately thereafter transfers the Newco stock to its shareholders. Within two weeks of the distribution, 90% of the Newco shareholders sell their Newco stock to a purchasing corporation interested in getting into the adult game and puzzle business. The sale transaction was not prearranged at the time of the initial spin-off. What are the tax consequences of the spin-off transaction and the subsequent sale to D and its shareholders?

3. Shareholder A is the sole owner of Corporation X, which operates funeral homes in small communities a, b, and c. X's key, and only full-time, employee at the community c location threatened to quit and start a competing business. Loss of this key employee and subsequent competition from another funeral home in this small community would have a significant adverse impact on Corporation X's profits. Corporation X contributes all assets related to the community c location to Newco, a newly formed subsidiary, in exchange for Newco stock. Immediately thereafter, Corporation X distributes all of the Newco stock to shareholder A, who immediately sells 49% of the Newco stock to the key employee, pursuant to a prearranged plan, for cash and notes. What are the tax consequences of these transactions to Corporation X and shareholder A?

EXPLANATIONS

1a. The transaction described in this example is a basic spin-off. The initial exchange creating Newco will be tax-free to Corporation C under §351. Thus, the Newco stock in Corporation C's hands will have the same aggregate basis that the flower delivery business assets had before the exchange — $100,000.[115] The value of the Newco shares presumably is the same as the $500,000 value of the assets contributed by Corporation C. Thus, shareholders A and B have each received a distribution worth $250,000. Ordinarily, a distribution of stock other than the corporation's own stock would be taxable to the recipient shareholders under the rules of §301.[116] If this distribution qualifies under §355, however, shareholders A and B will report no gain or loss upon receipt of the Newco shares pursuant to §355(a). Their basis in the Newco shares received would be a substituted basis determined under §358. Under §358(a), the basis in property received in a tax-free exchange shall be the same as the property exchanged. In this spin-off, however, shareholders A and B have not "exchanged" anything in return for their Newco shares. Nevertheless, under §358(c), shareholders A and B will be regarded as if their shares in the distributing corporation were surrendered and then received back. In other words, they are viewed as having exchanged their C shares with a basis of $25,000 for a return of the same C shares along with the Newco shares. Thus, shareholder A and B's aggregate basis in the Corporation C and Newco shares is the same $25,000 basis they had before. This $25,000 now will have to be allocated between the C shares and the Newco shares. This allocation will be based upon the relative fair market

---

115. See Chapter 4 for a discussion of §351.
116. See Chapter 5 for a discussion of the §301 nonliquidating distribution rules.

values immediately after the distribution. Thus, five-eighths ($500,000 fair market value of Newco shares/$800,000 total value of Newco and C Corporation shares) will be allocated to the Newco stock and three-eighths ($300,000 value of the C Corporation remaining after distribution/$800,000 total value of Newco and C Corporation shares) will be allocated to the Corporation C stock.

Ordinarily, the distribution of appreciated property is taxable to the distributing corporation under §311.[117] If the distribution qualifies, §355(c) provides that Corporation C will not be taxed upon the $400,000 gain otherwise realized upon the distribution of Newco stock with a basis of $100,000 and a fair market value of $500,000.

This transaction appears to meet the statutory requirements of §355. Corporation C was in control of Newco immediately before the exchange, both corporations are engaged in the active conduct of a trade or business immediately after the exchange, both the flower delivery and singing telegram business have at least a five-year history, Corporation C has distributed all of its Newco stock, and the transaction does not appear to be principally a device for the distribution of C's earnings and profits.

There may be a problem, however, in meeting the nonstatutory business purpose test, however. The need to separate the two businesses due to different management requirements may be a perfectly appropriate business purpose. The regulations require, however, that the distribution of stock also have a business purpose. Since the initial creation of Newco *without* the subsequent distribution arguably fulfills the stated business purpose, this distribution may not be eligible for §355 treatment unless the corporation provides an additional business purpose for distributing the Newco shares to A and B.

1b. Although §355 transactions frequently include a new subsidiary, a newly created subsidiary is not necessary. Thus, assuming the business purpose issue is resolved in the taxpayers' favor, the distribution of Oldco stock in Example 1b also would be eligible for §355 treatment as provided in the answer to Example 1a.

1c. This variation is an illustration of a basic split-off, with similar tax consequences. The key difference in the transactions is that shareholders A and B now have each received $250,000 worth of Newco shares in exchange for one-half of their C shares. Ordinarily, such a distribution would be treated as a redemption and would be taxable to the shareholders pursuant to the rules in §302 and to the corporation under §311.[118] Assuming the transaction meets the business purpose hurdle discussed in the answer to Example 1a, however, A and B should be entitled to nonrecognition upon receipt of

---

117. See Chapter 5 for a discussion of the nonliquidating distribution rules.
118. See Chapter 6 for a discussion of redemptions.

the Newco shares under §355(a) and the corporation should be entitled to nonrecognition under §355(c). The shareholders' basis in the Newco shares will again be determined under §358. Unlike the spin-off in Example 1a, however, the shareholders now have actually exchanged shares. At first blush, it might appear that the substituted basis would be only $12,500 (one-half of the $25,000 basis of each shareholder in the C shares exchanged). However, §358(b)(2) provides a special rule for §355 cases under which the allocation of basis shall take into account not only the property permitted to be received without gain recognition, but also stock of the distributing corporation which is retained. In other words, the substituted basis for allocation purposes will include the full $25,000 basis that shareholders A and B had in the Corporation C shares and the basis will be allocated between the Newco and C shares as described in the answer to Example 1a.

1d. This variation now illustrates a basic split-up. Since shareholders A and B are exchanging *all* of their C shares in exchange for the Newco stock, this transaction is effectively a liquidation distribution, which would ordinarily be taxed to the shareholders under §331 and to the corporation under §336.[119] If the transaction overcomes the business purpose hurdle described in the answer to Example 1a, however, the shareholders again should be entitled to nonrecognition under §355(a) and the corporation should be entitled to nonrecognition under §355(c). The shareholders' basis in the Newco shares again would be determined under §358. The substituted basis rule works more simply in this case to reach the same $25,000 substituted basis result. Since all of the shares were exchanged in this variation, one need not resort to the metaphysical "deeming" rules of §358(b)(2) or §358(c).

1e. A transaction in which Corporation C transfers only the real estate associated with the flower business should appear quite suspicious. This transaction is unlikely to qualify for §355 nonrecognition for several reasons. First of all, the real estate held by Newco immediately after the distribution probably is not sufficient to constitute the active conduct of a trade or business. Second, the transaction does now appear to be a device for the distribution of earnings and profits.

2a. This transaction represents a spin-off of the new magazine business. Surely the cash received by shareholder group A will be taxable pursuant to the §301 distribution rules. The distribution of Newco shares to the shareholder group B raises several issues under §355. Corporation N had control of Newco immediately before the distribution, as required by §355(a)(1)(A). Moreover, it appears that both Corporations N and Newco will be engaged in the active conduct of a trade or business immediately after the distribution. Recall, however, that §355(b)(2)(B) also requires a trade or business "ac-

---

119. See Chapter 8 for a discussion of liquidations.

tively conducted throughout the five-year period ending on the date of the distribution." The statute goes on to require in §355(b)(2)(C) that this trade or business not have been acquired *in a taxable transaction* within the same five-year period. The facts in this question indicate that the new magazine business was acquired by Corporation N in a tax-free reorganization. Thus, even though Corporation N itself has not been operating the new business for five years, the business should be considered a business with the necessary five-year history. The fact that some shareholders are receiving cash and others are receiving Newco stock makes this a non pro rata distribution. This too should not prevent the transaction from qualifying for §355 nonrecognition since the statute explicitly states in §355(a)(2)(A) that the distribution need not be pro rata. Resolving conflicts among shareholders is among the acceptable business purposes for a §355 distribution. Thus, the distribution of Newco stock to the group B shareholders should be eligible for nonrecognition to the shareholders under §355(a) and to the distributing corporation under §355(c).

2b. This transaction appears to be a rather straightforward spin-off, which should be eligible for §355 nonrecognition treatment. However, the sale of 90% of the Newco stock within such a short time after the distribution raises questions as to whether or not the transaction was a "device for the distribution of earnings and profits." The statute itself provides, in §355(a)(1)(B), that the mere fact of a subsequent sale "shall not be construed to mean that the transaction was used principally as such a device." On the other hand, the regulations do consider such a sale to be "evidence of a device." The regulations further suggest that the greater the percentage of stock sold and the shorter the time period between the distribution and the subsequent sale, the stronger the evidence of a device for the distribution of earnings and profits.[120] These factors point toward a finding that the transaction was used as a device. At the same time, the corporation and its shareholders will point out that the transaction was not prearranged. Such a prearranged sale would have been considered *substantial* evidence of a device under the same regulation. In the end, whether the transaction was used as a device will be determined based upon *all* the facts and circumstances.

Corporation D should be eligible for nonrecognition on the contribution of assets in exchange for Newco stock under either §§361 or 351. Its basis in the Newco stock will be the same basis that it previously had in the assets contributed under §358. If the transaction qualifies under §355, both D and its shareholders will be eligible for nonrecognition upon the distribution of Newco stock. Pursuant to §358, the D shareholders will allocate a portion of the basis in their D shares to the Newco stock received. Those shareholders participating in the subsequent taxable sale of Newco stock will

---

120. Treas. Reg. §1.355-2(d)(2)(iii).

use the portion of basis allocable to the Newco shares as an offset to their amount realized.

If the transaction does *not* qualify under §355, D will be required to report gain on the distribution of the Newco stock under §311. The shareholders will report taxable income on the receipt of the Newco stock under the §301 distribution rules, under which the fair market value of the Newco shares will be taxable as an ordinary income dividend, assuming that D has sufficient earnings and profits to cover the distribution. Under §301(d), the shareholders would take the Newco shares with a fair market value basis. Assuming that the value of the shares did not increase or decrease within the two weeks before the subsequent sale, there should be no further taxable gain to the selling shareholders.

3.   If this transaction qualifies as a tax-free spin-off, shareholder A will not recognize any gain on the receipt of Newco stock from Corporation X pursuant to §355(a), nor will Corporation X recognize any gain on the distribution of the Newco stock pursuant to §355(c). Basis in the Newco shares will be determined under §358, and shareholder A will report capital gain or loss from the sale of Newco shares to the employee. If the transaction does not qualify under §355, and presuming sufficient earnings and profits to cover the distribution, shareholder A will report the fair market value of the Newco stock received as an ordinary income dividend under §301(c) and take a fair market value basis in the Newco shares under §301(d). Although the subsequent sale technically is a taxable event, there should be no further taxable gain if shareholder A receives a fair market value price for the Newco shares sold. Corporation X's distribution of the Newco stock would be governed by §311.

This transaction should raise serious questions about whether the transaction was "used principally as a device for the distribution" of earnings and profits under §355(a)(1)(B). Shareholder A's proceeds from the sale of Newco stock are treated as capital gain. If the distribution is tax-free under §355, shareholder A will have been able to bail out corporate earnings from a solely owned corporation at capital gain rather than ordinary income rates. Although the mere fact of a subsequent sale to the employee should not be construed to mean that the transaction was used principally as a device for distributing earnings and profits, numerous other "device factors" exist. First, the distribution is pro rata to a sole shareholder. According to the regulations, such a distribution "presents the *greatest potential for the avoidance of the dividend provisions*" and should be regarded as evidence of a device. Treas. Reg. §1.355-2(d)(2)(ii). Second, the immediate sale of a substantial amount of stock is evidence of a device. The regulations further provide that the "greater the percentage sold" and the "shorter the period of time between the distribution and the sale or exchange, the stronger the evidence of device." Treas. Reg. §1.355-2(d)(2)(iii). Moreover, since it was pursuant to a prearranged plan, the subsequent sale is *substantial* evidence of a device. *Id.*

These device factors must be balanced against nondevice factors under a facts and circumstances balancing test. On the "nondevice factor" side, shareholder A will point to the corporate business purposes of the transaction: avoiding loss of a key employee and the threat of competition. Treas. Reg. §1.355-2(d)(3)(ii). Note, however, the regulatory caution that "the stronger the evidence of device . . . , the stronger the corporate business purpose required to prevent the determination that the transaction was used principally as a device." *Id.* In addition, the alleged business purposes may not be sufficient for purposes of §355 if the "corporate business purpose can be achieved through a nontaxable transaction that does not involve the distribution of stock of a controlled corporation and which is neither impractical nor unduly expensive." Treas. Reg. §1.355-2(b)(3).

In an example similar to the transaction here, the regulations found that the transaction should be considered to have been used as a device, noting that the corporation *could* have achieved its business purpose by directly issuing shares to the employee. Treas. Reg. §1.355-2(b)(4), ex. 1. Surprisingly, in a case presenting facts remarkably similar to those here and in Example 1, the Tax Court ruled that the transactions *did* qualify for §355 tax-free treatment. Pulliam v. Comm'r, TCM 1997-274, RIA TC Memo, ¶97,274 (1997), *nonacq.* 1999-1 I.R.B. 5. In a rather weak effort to distinguish its case from the regulatory example, the Tax Court noted that the taxpayers before the court *thought* that they were required by state law to have the stock distributed to the sole shareholder, since only individual licensed funeral directors and embalmers could hold stock in an incorporated funeral business.

14

Recapitalization and Other Corporate Restructuring

Introduction

The reorganization definition in §368(a)(1) includes two types of transactions involving the restructuring of only *one* corporation, as opposed to an acquisition joining two or more corporations or a division resulting in two or more corporations. In each of these restructuring transactions, the shareholders exchange stock or securities for stock or securities in the same corporation.[1] As with any corporate reorganization, the participating shareholders will not report gain or loss upon the receipt of stock and certain securities in the reorganization transaction pursuant to §354, except to the extent that they receive taxable boot under §356. The shareholders' basis in the shares received will be governed by the substituted basis rules of §358. Similarly, there will be no gain or loss to the corporation.[2]

Various factors might encourage a corporation to adopt and implement a recapitalization plan. The corporation might recapitalize in order to simplify its capital structure.[3] Or the corporation might recapitalize to create stock

---

1. In the case of a Type F reorganization, the old corporate enterprise (the predecessor) technically may be transformed into a new corporate entity (the successor).

2. The corporation simply receives its own stock or securities. This receipt should be nontaxable under either §§361 or 1032.

3. See, e.g., Rev. Rul. 77-238, 1977-2 C.B. 115 (recapitalization to encourage the conversion of preferred stock into common stock to simplify capital structure); Rev. Rul. 72-57, 1972-1 C.B. 103 (subsidiary corporation simplifies capital structure by eliminating minority shareholders).

that will be more attractive in a public offering[4] or to improve its financial condition by restructuring its debt obligations.[5] In some cases, the corporation recapitalizes in order to increase the equity interest of management employees who have made a significant contribution to the corporate enterprise.[6]

In other cases, the corporation might recapitalize to reflect management changes upon the retirement of one of its key shareholders. For example, upon retirement of the corporation's founder, the corporation might adopt a plan of recapitalization in which the founder exchanges her voting common stock interest in return for newly issued nonvoting preferred stock. As a result of the recapitalization, the shareholder retains a financial interest in the corporation through her preferred stock, but eliminates her management interest previously reflected in her voting common stock.[7] One might initially think that the §302 redemption rules should apply to this retirement of the shareholder's voting common stock. Despite appearances, however, this is not a redemption. In a redemption, the corporation must acquire its stock from the shareholder in return for *property*,[8] which is defined to exclude the corporation's own stock.[9] When a corporation acquires old stock and issues new stock in return, the exchange will be treated as a recapitalization under §368(a)(1)(E), and not as a redemption under §302.

The simplest of the two internal restructuring reorganizations is a Type F reorganization involving a "mere change in identity, form, or place of organization of one corporation, however effected."[10] For example, the corporation might choose to change its incorporation from New Jersey to Delaware.[11] The Type E reorganization is slightly more complex. A Type E reorganization is defined, without further elaboration, as a "recapitalization." Each of these reorganizations will be considered in this chapter.

A third related type of corporate reorganization, a Type G reorganization, involves the restructuring of a corporation in bankruptcy. The Type G

---

4. See, e.g., Rev. Rul. 77-479, 1977-2 C.B. 311.

5. See, e.g., Rev. Rul. 77-415, 1977-2 C.B. 311.

6. See, e.g., Rev. Rul. 54-13, 1954-1 C.B. 109.

7. See, e.g., Rev. Rul. 74-269, 1974-1 C.B. 87.

8. I.R.C. §317(b).

9. I.R.C. §317(a). For a more detailed discussion of corporate redemptions, see Chapter 5. Notice, however, that the definition of "property" in §317(a) applies only for purposes of Part I of Subchapter C (§§301 through 318). Thus, the definition of property applies for redemption and distribution purposes, but not for reorganization purposes.

10. I.R.C. §368(a)(1)(F).

11. This was the situation in the early case of Marr v. United States, 268 U.S. 536 (1925), in which the Supreme Court held that the transaction was not a tax-free reorganization. The transaction surely would qualify today as a Type F reorganization.

reorganization permits more flexibility than the E and F types and, unlike the E and F internal restructuring reorganizations, may involve more than one corporation. The insolvent corporation may be acquired by another corporation as part of the bankruptcy reorganization, or the insolvent corporation may be divided into several separate corporate entities in the bankruptcy reorganization. Thus, Type G reorganizations may take an acquisitive or a divisive form.

Recapitalizations: The Type E Reorganization

A Stab at a Definition

Neither the Code nor the regulations provide a definition of the term "recapitalization" as used in §368(a)(1)(E). In an early reorganization case, the Supreme Court, in dicta, described recapitalization as a "reshuffling of a capital structure, within the framework of an existing corporation."[12] Although the regulations do not provide a definition, they do provide five examples of transactions that will be considered recapitalizations.[13] Deciding whether a particular transaction constitutes a recapitalization often simply involves a comparison with the illustrations provided in the regulations. The closer a transaction is to fitting the five described transactions, the more likely it is to be treated as a recapitalization.[14] Most of the examples in the Treasury regulation involve stock-for-stock transfers. Thus, shareholder exchanges of preferred stock for common stock or exchanges of common stock for preferred stock generally will be considered recapitalizations.[15] A transaction in which the corporation pays off bonds with preferred stock, as opposed to cash, is also considered a recapitalization.[16] Under appropriate circumstances, the conversion of common stock into preferred stock or preferred stock into common may constitute a recapitalization.[17]

One might imagine that a recapitalization requires an actual exchange or transfer of stock, securities, or other financial instruments. However, a

---

12. Helvering v. Southwest Consolidated Corp., 315 U.S. 194, 202 (1942). This particular case involved what would now be considered a Type G reorganization. Although the Court's definition of "recapitalization" was dicta, the case continues to be frequently cited as a starting point for the definition of recapitalization.

13. Treas. Reg. §1.368-2(e).

14. Certainly, one making a case to the I.R.S. also should be prepared to argue that the exchange results only in a change in form.

15. Treas. Reg. §1.368-2(e)(2)-(5).

16. Treas. Reg. §1.368-2(e)(1).

17. See, e.g., Rev. Rul. 77-238, 1977-2 C.B. 115.

simple amendment to the articles of incorporation may be a "deemed recapitalization" even if no shares actually are exchanged if "the change in the outstanding stock is so substantial as to constitute, in substance, an exchange . . . in a recapitalization of the corporation."[18]

The following sections of this chapter consider numerous different exchanges that fall within the "recapitalization" definition. Some of these exchanges are non pro rata, some change proportionate shareholder interests and otherwise may appear on the surface to be more than a "mere change in form." Again, the "change in form" rationale sounds nice in theory, but fails to account, in practice, for several nonrecognition transactions.[19] Keep in mind that none of the exchanges described here will be eligible for tax-free reorganization treatment unless it also meets the general business purpose requirement applicable to all reorganizations.[20]

Equity Exchanges

a) Common for Common or Preferred for Preferred

One of the simplest recapitalizations is an exchange by the shareholders of old common for new common shares or of old preferred for new preferred shares. Several changes may occur as the result of an exchange of old common shares for new common shares or old preferred shares for new preferred shares. The new shares may have different voting rights and thus alter the proportionate voting interest of the shareholders.[21] Or, the new shares may have different preemptive rights. The corporation may have had only one class of stock before the recapitalization and have several different classes of stock after the recapitalization. In the alternative, the number of classes of common shares might be reduced as a result of recapitalization. Despite these relative changes in shareholder rights, the transaction still is considered a "mere change in form" and still qualifies for nonrecognition treatment as a reorganization.

In fact, a simple exchange of common stock for common stock in the

---

18. Rev. Rul. 56-654, 1956-2 C.B. 216 (amendment to articles increasing the per share redemption price and liquidation value of preferred stock deemed to be a recapitalization).

19. In some cases, though, a recapitalization resulting in changes in proportionate interest will result in a deemed stock dividend taxable under §305(c). See Chapter 6 for a discussion of §305(c) deemed stock dividends.

20. See Chapter 11 for a full discussion of the business purpose requirement. The continuity of interest tests will not be applicable in the case of recapitalizations. See section later in this chapter entitled "Application of General Reorganization Principles."

21. See, e.g., Rev. Rul. 69-407, 1969-2 C.B. 50.

same corporation or of preferred stock for preferred stock in the same corporation is entitled to nonrecognition treatment under §1036. This provision simply states that "no gain or loss shall be recognized if common stock in a corporation is exchanged solely for common stock in the same corporation, or if preferred stock in a corporation is exchanged solely for preferred stock in the same corporation."[22] Notice that §§1036 and 368(a)(1)(E) overlap in their coverage of recapitalizations involving an exchange of common for common stock or of preferred for preferred stock.[23] A simple recapitalization involving an exchange of common for common stock or preferred for preferred stock generally can be handled under §1036. If "boot" is transferred as part of a such a recapitalization, however, the reorganization provisions will "trump" §1036.[24]

At this point, one may wonder why Congress has overlapping provisions providing nonrecognition treatment to the same transaction. Notice that the overlap is not perfect. Section 1036 nonrecognition is not limited to exchanges between the corporation and its shareholders, but also applies to an exchange between two shareholders.[25] Moreover, as noted, the more complex reorganization provisions will be necessary for transactions involving boot.

b) Common Stock for Preferred Stock

When shareholders exchange old common shares for new preferred shares, they are exchanging what often is referred to as a "junior" equity interest for a "senior" equity interest in the corporation. The preferred shares are "senior" in that they typically receive priority in dividend and liquidation rights.[26] A transfer of old common shares for new preferred is an "upstream equity exchange." Although the shareholders have received a more secure equity interest in the corporation, this transfer still is considered a recapitalization representing a "mere change in form." The exchange fits within the §368(a)(1)(E) reorganization definition.[27]

A shareholder who receives preferred stock in a recapitalization must

---

22. I.R.C. §1036(a).

23. The regulations are explicit that "a transaction between a stockholder and the corporation may qualify not only under section 1036(a), but also under section 368(a)(1)(E) (recapitalization)." Treas. Reg. §1.1036-1(a).

24. See, e.g., Rev. Rul. 72-57, 1972-1 C.B. 103, *modified by* Rev. Rul. 78-351, 1978-2 C.B. 148.

25. See Treas. Reg. §1.1036-1(a); Rev. Rul. 72-199, 1972-1 C.B. 228.

26. Although it is common for preferred shares to be senior to common shares in dividend rights or rights to assets upon liquidation, this will not always be the case. There may be common and preferred shares with equal dividend and liquidation rights.

27. See Treas. Reg. §1.368-2(e)(3).

also be concerned about the possibility that certain preferred shares received will be classified as "§306 stock," which could result in ordinary, as opposed to capital gain, income upon later sale or redemption of the shares.[28] The preferred shares will be "§306 stock" if they were received by the shareholder in a plan of reorganization and if gain or loss was not recognized, "but only to the extent that either the effect of the transaction was substantially the same as the receipt of a stock dividend, or the stock was received in exchange for §306 stock."[29] Under this definition, the shareholder should be concerned about tainted §306 shares where the shareholder in a recapitalization receives preferred shares in excess of the preferred shares surrendered. In the common for preferred exchange, the receipt of preferred shares in the exchange is much like the receipt of a preferred stock dividend. Unless the receipt falls within one of the §306(b) exceptions, the stock will be tainted stock.

c) Old Preferred for New Common

When shareholders exchange old preferred stock for new common, they generally are exchanging a "senior" interest for a more "junior" interest.[30] Even though the shareholders have received an interest somewhat different from the interest they previously held, this "downstream equity exchange" still is considered a "mere change in form."[31]

d) Convertible Shares

When the articles of incorporation provide stock conversion rights, shareholders who convert their common shares into preferred shares or those who convert preferred shares into common should be eligible for tax-free reorganization treatment under §354 if the transaction qualifies as a recapitalization. The transaction will qualify as long as the exchanges are pursuant to a plan of reorganization and there is a business purpose for the conversion privilege.[32]

---

28. For a complete discussion of tainted "§306 stock," see Chapter 6.

29. I.R.C. §306(c)(1)(B).

30. Here, there will be no issue with respect to §306, since the definition of "§306 stock" includes only "[s]tock which is not common stock." I.R.C. §306(c)(1)(B).

31. Treas. Reg. §1.368-2(e)(2), (4). In the latter paragraph, the regulations make it clear that the transaction will be treated as a recapitalization if the preferred stock carried certain priorities regarding dividends and assets upon liquidation which the common shares do not carry.

32. For further discussion of the "plan of reorganization" and "business purpose" requirements, see Chapter 11.

e) Dividend Arrearages and Other Potential §305 Issues[33]

Although a recapitalization technically is not a stock dividend, §305(c) authorizes the Treasury Secretary to prescribe regulations under which any transactions, including recapitalizations, resulting in a change in the proportionate interests of shareholders will be treated as deemed stock dividends taxable under §301. Since stock distributions with respect to preferred stock generally are thought to increase the preferred stockholders' proportionate interest, §305(b)(4) provides that such stock distributions are taxable. Recapitalizations may achieve comparable results. For example, if a corporation finds itself in arrears on dividend obligations to preferred shareholders, it may arrange a recapitalization in which the shareholders transfer their preferred stock, including the right to dividend arrearages, to the corporation in return for other stock of the corporation. Such a transfer is considered a recapitalization under §368(a)(1)(E).[34] However, if the stock received in the exchange increases the preferred shareholders' proportionate interest in the assets or earnings and profits of the corporation, the shareholders may have taxable income from a deemed stock dividend under §305(c). The regulations provide that an exchange of preferred stock with dividends in arrears for other stock increases the shareholders' proportionate interest whenever the fair market value or the liquidation preference of the new stock exceeds the issue price of the preferred stock surrendered in the exchange.[35] The amount of the deemed §305(c) distribution generally will be the lesser of (1) the amount in arrearage or (2) the excess of the fair market value of the new stock or the liquidation preference (whichever is greater) over the issue price of the stock surrendered.[36]

Assume, for example, that the corporation has preferred shares outstanding that are four years in arrears on dividends. The arrearages exceeded $20 per share and the issue price of the preferred shares was $100 per share. In a recapitalization, the shareholders exchange each old preferred share, including the right to dividend arrearages, in return for 1.2 newly authorized preferred shares. Immediately after the exchange, the new preferred shares are valued at $100 per share. Notice that the shareholders have increased their proportionate interest in the corporation since they have received $120 worth of new shares in return for the $100 issue price on each of the old

---

33. This section will consider limited applications of §305 in the context of recapitalizations. For a more detailed discussion of §305 stock dividends, see Chapter 7.
34. Treas. Reg. §§1.368-2(e)(5), 1.305-7(c)(1)(ii).
35. Treas. Reg. §1.305-7(c)(2)(ii).
36. See Treas. Reg. §§1.368-2(e)(5), 1.305-7(c)(2).

shares. Each shareholder will have a $20 taxable stock dividend on each share of old preferred exchanged for new preferred.[37]

In addition to the preferred stock with dividend arrearages transaction described above, other recapitalizations may have deemed stock dividend consequences under §305(c) where the recapitalization results in a change in proportionate interests among the shareholders. Under the regulations, a recapitalization will be deemed a taxable stock distribution if "[it] is pursuant to a plan to periodically increase a shareholder's proportionate interest in the assets or earnings and profits of the corporation."[38] Notice that an *isolated* recapitalization that is not part of a periodic plan to alter the shareholders' proportionate interests should not result in any deemed stock dividend consequences for the shareholders.[39] Corporations frequently take advantage of this exception in the regulations for recapitalizations in which a retiring shareholder exchanges old stock for new.

Debt and Equity Exchanges

a) Debt for Equity Exchanges

(i) Tax Consequences to the Debt Holders

A debt holder may receive stock in exchange for outstanding debt in a tax-free recapitalization. This type of transaction may be arranged as part of a "workout" to improve the financial condition of a troubled corporation by substituting equity interests for debt interests on the balance sheet. In fact, the first example in the regulations illustrating the definition of "recapitalization" describes a corporation with bonds outstanding that discharges the bond obligations by issuing preferred shares to the bondholders rather than paying the bonds off with cash.[40] As a result of this "downstream" exchange, the bondholders have exchanged a "senior" debt interest for a more "junior" equity interest in the form of preferred stock. The bondholders will be entitled to nonrecognition upon the exchange of their securities in return for stock under §354. Notice that §354 allows nonrecognition only where "stock or *securities*" are exchanged solely for stock or securities.[41] Thus, in order for the debt holder to qualify for nonrecognition under §354, the debt interest surrendered must be considered a "security." Short-term notes and

---

37. This $20 amount is the difference between the fair market value of the stock received over the issue price of the stock surrendered pursuant to Treas. Reg. §1.305-7(c)(2).

38. Treas. Reg. §1.305-7(c)(1)(i).

39. See, e.g., Treas. Reg. §1.305-5(d), ex. (2).

40. Treas. Reg. §1.368-2(e)(1). See also Lorch v. Comm'r, 605 F.2d 657 (2d Cir. 1979), *cert. denied*, 444 U.S. 1076 (1980).

41. Note the contrast to §351, which provides nonrecognition only for exchanges of property in return for *stock*. For a complete discussion, see Chapter 4.

other forms of indebtedness surrendered in the exchange that do not constitute "securities" will not be eligible for nonrecognition treatment. Although the debt holder generally is entitled to nonrecognition upon the exchange of debt for equity, §354 provides an exception to account for accrued interest on the surrendered debt. Neither §§354 nor 356 will apply to the extent that "any stock, securities, or other property received is attributable to interest which has accrued on securities on or after the beginning of the holder's holding period."[42] Note that §354(a)(2)(B) simply provides that the general nonrecognition rules of §354(a)(1) and the related §356 boot rules do *not* apply to that portion of the stock received in return for *interest accrued* on the debt surrendered in the exchange. This makes sense. Interest income is treated as ordinary income and typically is recognized for tax purposes as it is received or as it accrues under special provisions of the Code.[43] The shareholder involved in a debt-for-stock exchange should not be entitled to avoid tax on the interest income. All we know so far, then, is how *not* to treat the portion attributable to interest. Section 354 simply sends the taxpayer to the general definition of income in §61. The portion of the stock value that is received in return for accrued interest simply should be treated as ordinary income upon receipt of the stock.[44]

(ii) Tax Consequences to the Corporation

Under basic cancellation of indebtedness principles, when a corporation discharges its debt obligations with stock or other assets worth less than the principal amount of the debt, the corporation will be required to report cancellation of indebtedness income.[45] Under new rules adopted by Congress, a solvent debtor corporation that "transfers stock to a creditor in satisfaction of its indebtedness . . . shall be treated as having satisfied the indebtedness with an amount of money equal to the fair market value of the stock."[46] In other words, if the fair market value of the stock transferred is less than the principal amount of the debt, the corporation must report cancellation of indebtedness income. If the corporate discharge of indebtedness occurs in a Title 11 bankruptcy proceeding or occurs when the corporation is insolvent, however, the corporation may exclude the cancellation of indebtedness income.[47] This exclusion will provide the corporation with only

---

42. I.R.C. §354(a)(2)(B).

43. See, e.g., the original issue discount rules in §§1271-1275.

44. Amounts reflecting market discount are not immediately recognized. I.R.C. §1276(c)(2).

45. I.R.C. §61(a)(12); United States v. Kirby Lumber, 284 U.S. 1 (1931).

46. I.R.C. §108(e)(8).

47. I.R.C. §108(a)(1)(A), (B). Section 108(a) also provides more narrow exceptions for "qualified farm indebtedness," I.R.C. §108(a)(1)(C), and "qualified real property business indebtedness," I.R.C. §108(a)(1)(D).

a temporary break since the corporation will be required to reduce its tax attributes, potentially resulting in increased income in later years.[48]

b) Equity for Debt Exchanges

In contrast to the "downstream" exchange described above, a shareholder might transfer his stock to the corporation in return for a debt interest in an "upstream" exchange. By exchanging stock for debt, the shareholder has converted a "junior" stock interest for a more "senior" debt interest. He now typically has a priority interest assuring his payment of interest before dividends are paid to shareholders. Moreover, he now typically stands in line ahead of the shareholders when creditors are paid off upon liquidation. Although the exchange might technically qualify as a "recapitalization" under §368(a)(1)(E), limitations to the general shareholder nonrecognition provisions in §354 provide that the nonrecognition rules shall not apply if the principal amount of securities received exceeds the principal amount of securities surrendered, or if any securities are received and no securities are surrendered.[49] Any excess securities will be treated as taxable "boot" under §356.[50]

There is also the possibility in an "upstream" exchange of stock for debt, that the transaction may not qualify as a "recapitalization" at all. In the case of Bazley v. Commissioner,[51] a closely held family corporation arranged a plan of reorganization under which each shareholder would exchange one share of $100 par value stock in return for five shares of no par stock and new debenture bonds callable at any time. The corporation had substantial earnings and profits. The Supreme Court appears to conclude in this case that the transaction was not a tax-free reorganization *at all* since "nothing can be a recapitalization . . . unless it partakes of those characteristics of a reorganization which underlie the purpose of Congress in postponing the tax liability."[52] The Court apparently found that the distribution of debentures was a "disguised dividend," concluding that:

> if the Bazley corporation had issued the debentures to Bazley and his wife without any recapitalization, it would have made a taxable distribution. Instead, these debentures were issued as part of a family arrangement, the only additional ingredient being an unrelated modification of the capital account. The debentures were found to be worth at least their principal amount, and they were virtually cash because they were callable at the will of the corporation which in this case was the will of the taxpayer.

---

48. See I.R.C. §108(b).

49. I.R.C. §354(a)(2)(A).

50. For a further discussion of the §356 boot rules, see Chapter 11.

51. 331 U.S. 737, *reh'g denied*, 332 U.S. 752 (1947).

52. *Id.* at 741.

A "reorganization" which is merely a vehicle, however elaborate or elegant, for conveying earnings from accumulations to the stockholders is not a reorganization . . .[53]

At the end of its opinion the Court further concludes that *"even if this transaction were deemed a reorganization,* the facts would equally sustain the imposition of the tax on the debentures under [§356]."[54] Whether the transaction was classified as a recapitalization or not, the debentures would still be considered taxable boot under the reorganization boot provisions. The Supreme Court's opinion in *Bazley* leaves the legal uncertainty that, in some cases, an exchange of stock for debt might fail to qualify as a reorganization at all. As a result, the exchange of stock for stock may be a taxable event and the receipt of debt will be fully taxable as a dividend governed by §301 as opposed to §356. As such, the dividend would be taxable regardless of whether or not there was any realized gain on the exchange.

c) Debt for Debt Exchanges

(i) Tax Consequences to Debt Holders

Corporations sometimes restructure debt through an exchange of old debt for new debt. The new debt may provide for a reduced interest rate, a reduction in the principal amount, a delayed payment date, or other modification of terms. These debt exchanges have been especially useful to financially stressed corporations seeking a "workout" of their difficulties short of a formal declaration of bankruptcy.

In a debt-for-debt exchange, the debt holder realizes gain or loss from "the exchange of property for other property differing materially either in kind or in extent."[55] The difficulty here is determining when one debt differs "materially either in kind or extent" from another, resulting in realization under the §1001 regulations. In Cottage Savings Association v. Commissioner,[56] the Supreme Court reviewed mortgage swap transactions among various financial institutions. Cottage Savings Association exchanged mortgage participation interests for substantially identical mortgage participation interests from another lending institution. The loan interests exchanged were all similar-type, single-family residence loans with the same term to maturity, identical interest rates, and virtually identical terms and conditions. Cottage Savings deducted a loss on these exchanges. The Internal Revenue Service argued that there was no realization event since the mortgages exchanged were economic equivalents. According to the Service, the properties ex-

---

53. *Id.* at 742-743.

54. *Id.* (emphasis added). This result is now formally incorporated into Treas. Reg. §1.301-1(l).

55. Treas. Reg. §1.1001-1(a).

56. 499 U.S. 554 (1991).

changed were not "materially different." Rejecting the government's argument, the Supreme Court adopted "a much less demanding and less complex test,"[57] concluding that the exchanged mortgage interests were materially different since they embodied "legally distinct entitlements." Since the mortgage participation interests were made to different obligors and secured by different homes, the Supreme Court concluded that the taxpayer "received entitlements different from those it gave up,"[58] treating the exchange as a realization event. The Court thus upheld Cottage Savings' recognition of losses on the mortgage swaps.

The significance of *Cottage Savings* in the recapitalization context is that under the Supreme Court's "less demanding and less complex" test, most actual exchanges of one debt obligation for another will be considered realization events under the §1001 regulations. Even without a formal exchange of debt instruments, a "significant modification of the debt instrument" may be considered a realization event.[59] Assuming that there is an exchange of materially different properties or a significant modification of the debt instrument, the debt holders will recognize gain or loss *unless* the exchange or modification is a §368(a)(1)(E) recapitalization.[60]

For many years, the Internal Revenue Service regarded the exchange by debt holders of old debt for new debt in the same corporation, or the modification of debt terms without a formal modification of the corporation's capital structure, as a "mere refinancing" rather than a "recapitalization." In an early case, however, the Second Circuit noted that:

> in common financial parlance the long term funded debt of a corporation is usually regarded as forming part of its capital structure. . . . By changing the interest rate and date of maturity of its old bonds and adding a conversion option to the holders of the new, the corporation could strengthen its financial condition, while the bondholders would not substantially change their original investments by making the exchange. "Recapitalization" seems a most appropriate word to describe that type of reorganization.[61]

---

57. *Id.* at 562.

58. *Id.* at 567.

59. In regulations written and finalized after the *Cottage Savings* decision, the Treasury Department provides that a "significant modification of a debt instrument . . . results in an exchange of the original instrument for a modified instrument that differs materially either in kind or in extent." Treas. Reg. §1.1001-3(b). The regulations provide a detailed description of what constitutes a "significant modification," Treas. Reg. §1.1001-3(e), and a number of detailed examples, Treas. Reg. §1.1001-3(g).

60. Of course, if the exchange is of properties that are *not* materially different, or if the modification is *not* a "significant" modification, there is no realization event in the first instance. Consequently, there will be no gain or loss and there should be no need to consider the tax-free reorganization provisions.

61. Comm'r v. Neustadt's Trust, 131 F.2d 528, 529-530 (2d Cir. 1942), *acq.* 1951-1 C.B. 2.

As long as the exchange or significant modification of debt is part of a plan of reorganization with a business purpose, it should be treated as a recapitalization under §368(a)(1)(E).

Assuming that a debt-for-debt exchange is a recapitalization, the debt holders who exchange old securities for new securities should be eligible for nonrecognition under §354. Since §354 nonrecognition is limited to exchanges of "stock or securities," exchanges of short-term and other debt instruments that are not "securities" will not be eligible for §354 nonrecognition. Moreover, to the extent that the principal amount of securities received exceeds the principal amount of securities surrendered, the exchanging debt holders will recognize gain under §356.

(ii) Tax Consequences to the Corporation

A corporation issuing new debt in exchange for old debt has potential discharge of indebtedness income. Unless the discharge fits within one of the exclusions provided in §108(a),[62] gain from the cancellation of indebtedness must be recognized. In computing this gain, the "debtor shall be treated as having satisfied the indebtedness with an amount of money equal to the issue price of such debt instrument."[63]

Application of General Reorganization Principles

a) Business Purpose Test

As with any other reorganization, a recapitalization will not qualify as a tax-free reorganization unless it has a business purpose.[64] For example, the Treasury Department ruled that the conversion of stock pursuant to a conversion privilege may constitute a recapitalization if there is a sufficient business purpose for the conversion privilege. Rev. Rul. 77-238 involved a manufacturing business whose corporate employees owned substantial amounts of common stock. Upon retirement, employees were entitled either to have their stock bought out for cash or to convert the common stock into preferred shares according to the terms of the articles of incorporation. The Treasury Department concluded that the retiring shareholder employees' conversion of common stock into preferred was a recapitalization, emphasizing that the purpose of the conversion privilege was to "eliminate common

---

62. Section 108(a) excludes cancellation of indebtedness income if the discharge occurs in title 11 bankruptcy, when the taxpayer is insolvent and has qualified farm indebtedness or qualified real property business indebtedness. I.R.C. §108(a)(1).

63. I.R.C. §108(e)(10)(A).

64. The regulations provide that the tax-free reorganization provisions are available to "such readjustments of corporate structures . . . as are required by business exigencies." Treas. Reg. §1.368-1(b). For more detailed discussion of the general business purpose rule as applied to reorganizations, see Chapter 11.

stock ownership by retiring employees and to reduce the cash expenditures . . . that would otherwise result if the common stock of retiring employees were redeemed for cash."[65] The articles of incorporation of a second manufacturing corporation in the same revenue ruling provided preferred shareholders the privilege of converting their shares into common stock. Shareholder conversions in accordance with this privilege were also considered recapitalizations since the business purpose of the privilege was to "encourage the conversion of preferred stock into common stock in order to simplify the capital structure of the corporation by eliminating the preferred stock."[66]

b) Continuity of Interest Tests

In general, the continuity of proprietary interest and the continuity of the business enterprise test must be met before a transaction will be eligible for tax-free reorganization treatment.[67] The continuity of proprietary interest test first emerged in early acquisitive reorganization cases. In these cases, a purchasing corporation acquired stock from target corporation shareholders in exchange for cash or notes or debentures of various types. Because the transferors in these early cases had not retained a significant proprietary interest in the corporate enterprise, the court denied tax-free reorganization treatment. In numerous cases involving an exchange of common or preferred stock by the shareholders of one corporation in return for debentures in the same corporation, the Commissioner initially argued that the exchanges were not entitled to reorganization treatment because ownership of debentures did not represent a sufficient continuity of proprietary interest.[68] The courts rejected these arguments, holding that the "continuity of proprietary interest" test simply did not apply in the recapitalization setting. Since, by definition, a recapitalization involves only an internal reshuffling of the capital structure of a *single* corporation, continuity of proprietary interest is not at issue. The following passage from the *Hickok* case is representative:

> [T]he "continuity of interest" doctrine, which was developed by the courts to serve a necessary purpose in the merger and consolidation

---

65. Rev. Rul. 77-238, 1977-2 C.B. 115.

66. *Id.* One should not assume that all stock conversions pursuant to a conversion privilege in the articles of incorporation will necessarily be viewed as recapitalizations. The facts and circumstances in these cases are sufficiently complex that even the Service is unwilling to rule in advance regarding whether or not there is a sufficient business purpose for the conversion such that the conversion should be regarded as a recapitalization. See Rev. Proc. 2000-3, sec. 3.01(26), 2000-1 I.R.B 103.

67. For a detailed discussion of these requirements, see Chapter 11.

68. See, e.g., Penfield v. Davis, 105 F. Supp. 292 (N.D. Ala. 1952), *aff'd*, 205 F.2d 798 (5th Cir. 1953); Berner v. United States, 282 F.2d 720 (Ct. Cl. 1960).

types of reorganizations, need not be a necessary ingredient in the cases where a recapitalization occurs. It is quite apparent that the considerations which make such a doctrine necessary in the merger and consolidation cases are simply not present in a recapitalization. . . . We think that the "continuity of interest" doctrine has no application to a recapitalization such as took place in the instant case.[69]

The Treasury Department has now conceded and agrees that the continuity of proprietary interest test does not apply to recapitalizations.[70]

Under the continuity of the business enterprise requirement, reorganized corporations must either continue the target corporation's historic business or use a significant portion of the target corporation's historic business assets in a business.[71] Just as the courts and the Treasury Department have rejected application of the continuity of proprietary interest test to recapitalizations, they have similarly rejected application of the continuity of the business enterprise requirement.[72] Since only one corporation is involved in a recapitalization, the corporation in its newly reorganized form presumably will continue either to use its historic assets or continue its historic business. In any event, a single corporation could change its business or fail to use its historic assets without tax penalty. An internal restructuring of one corporation should have no different result.

Mere Change in Identity, Form, or Place: Type F Reorganization

A Type F reorganization involves "a mere change in identity, form, or place of organization *of one corporation,* however effected."[73] The highlighted language, added in 1982, was intended to simplify the Type F reorganization provision. The new language makes it clear that the Type F reorganization applies to the change in identity, form, or place of a single corporation, rather than an acquisitive or divisive reorganization. In its Conference Report

---

69. Hickok v. Comm'r, 32 T.C. 80, 89-90 (1959). See also Erwin Griswold, Securities — Continuity of Interest, 58 Harv. L. Rev. 705, 716-717 (1945).

70. See Rev. Rul. 77-415, 1977-2 C.B. 311. Moreover, since the the continuity of proprietary interest test does not apply to recapitalizations, the Treasury Department has ruled that a prearranged plan to sell stock received in a recapitalization will not disqualify the transaction from tax-free reorganization treatment. Rev. Rul. 77-479, 1977-2 C.B. 119.

71. Treas. Reg. §1.368-1(d)(2). For a more detailed discussion of the continuity of the business enterprise requirement, see Chapter 11.

72. Rev. Rul. 82-34, 1982-1 C.B. 59.

73. I.R.C. §368(a)(1)(F) (emphasis added).

accompanying the 1982 changes, however, the Committee clarified that "[this] limitation does not preclude the use of more than one entity to consummate the transaction provided only one operating company is involved. The reincorporation of an operating company in a different State, for example, is an F Reorganization that requires that more than one corporation be involved."[74]

The major tax advantage to classification as a Type F reorganization is the preferential set of rules that will apply after the transaction regarding the carryover of tax attributes. For example, following any other reorganization, the new corporation's opportunity to use net operating losses against the income of the old corporation will be restricted.[75] Since Type F reorganizations presumably involve continuation of the same corporation with the same shareholders, the rules regarding carryover of tax attributes are far less restrictive.[76] Thus, net operating losses can be more freely used to offset income from the old corporation prior to the reorganization.[77]

Prior to the 1982 changes, the scope of §368(a)(1)(F) had expanded to cover and overlap with many of the other reorganization definitions, creating much confusion for taxpayers. Since 1982, the Type F reorganization largely has returned to the more simple role that it once had.[78] The classic Type F reorganization is a reincorporation in another state. A California corporation may decide that it is more advantageous to incorporate in Delaware. Upon reincorporation in Delaware, the shareholders of the old California corporation will be issued shares in the new Delaware corporation.[79] Or the corporation might simply change its name. Another simple Type F reorganization is a change in the corporation's charter or articles of incorporation.[80] These "mere changes in form" will be treated as tax-free reorganizations to the shareholders.

Although the 1982 changes simplified the Type F reorganization pro-

---

74. H.R. Rep. No. 760, 97th Cong., 2d Sess. (1982).

75. I.R.C. §§381, 382. For a more detailed discussion of the carryover of tax attributes following corporate acquisitions, see Chapter 12.

76. See, e.g., I.R.C. §§381(b), 382.

77. A similar provision for recapitalizations (Type E reorganizations) is unnecessary, since the same corporation remains after the internal restructuring.

78. The Type F reorganization was so little used that the House of Representatives proposed its repeal in 1954. The provision was retained, however, and rulings and cases in the 1950s through the 1970s expanded the scope of §368(a)(1)(F) until Congress amended the language in 1982.

79. If the shareholders receive virtually identical interests in the new corporation that they previously held in the old corporation, the transaction will be a Type F reorganization. On the other hand, if the corporation also uses the transaction as an opportunity to do some capital restructuring, the transaction will be regarded as a recapitalization under §368(a)(1)(E).

80. Ahles Realty Corp. v. Comm'r, 71 F.2d 150 (2d Cir.), cert. denied, 293 U.S. 611 (1934).

visions, a Type F reorganization still may be used in connection with a more complex transaction. For example, one corporation may change its state of incorporation in a Type F reorganization in anticipation of an impending acquisitive reorganization transaction. Whether the transaction should be respected as a Type F reorganization followed by another type of reorganization in an independent transaction or should be integrated into one transaction may be determined under the step-transaction doctrine.

EXAMPLES

A Simple Starter

1a. Several years ago, Jerry received a large inheritance and decided to incorporate a lingerie business to be named Steinfeld's Lingerie, Inc. He persuaded several friends to provide capital. Jerry himself put in $170,000 for 85% of the common stock (850 shares). Elaine, George, and Kramer contributed $10,000 each in return for 5% of the common stock (50 shares each). Although the first few years were rough, the corporation began to see substantial profits after five years. The Board of Directors decided to issue five new shares of common stock in exchange for each old share. As a result of this stock exchange, Jerry received 4250 shares valued at $425,000 and Elaine, George, and Kramer each received 250 shares valued at $25,000. What are the tax consequences to each shareholder upon this exchange of stock? Are there any tax consequences to the corporation?

1b. Assume that Jerry and George were much more actively involved with the company than Elaine and Kramer. As a result, the Board decided to create two different classes of stock: voting common and nonvoting 10% preferred. Jerry exchanged his 4250 old shares for 4250 shares of voting common (valued at $450,000) and George exchanged his 250 old shares for 250 shares of voting common (valued at $26,470). Elaine and Kramer each exchanged their 250 old shares for 250 shares of nonvoting 10% preferred (valued at $26,500). What are the tax consequences to each shareholder upon the stock-for-stock exchange? Are there any tax consequences to the corporation?

1c. Now assume that George is annoyed with the whole enterprise. He can't agree with Jerry on anything and no longer wants to actively participate in the business. The Board of Directors agrees to accept his 250 voting common shares in return for 500 nonvoting 10% preferred (valued at $50,000). What are the tax consequences to George and the other shareholders? Any tax consequences to the corporation?

Financial Difficulties

2a. Kramer's Hair Studio, Inc. is owned 50% by Kramer (200 common shares with a basis of $5000) and 50% by his sister (200 common shares also with a basis of $5000). Kramer's father loaned the corporation $10,000 in return for a 10-year bond at 8% interest. The corporation encounters financial difficulties and is unable to make timely payments of principal and interest on the bond. The corporation is two years in arrears on interest payments. The corporation reaches an agreement with father under which he exchanges his bond for 400 shares of newly authorized preferred stock. What are the tax consequences to father and the other shareholders upon this exchange? What are the tax consequences to the corporation?

2b. Would your answer to Example 2a change if, instead of exchanging the bond for stock, father exchanged the bond for an identical bond except that the new bond's interest rate was reduced to 7.5% interest?

Throwing in a Little Boot

3a. Elaine owned 75 shares (basis $75,000) and her sister, Judy, owned 25 shares (basis $25,000) of the stock in Elaine's Advertising, Inc. They wanted to bring down the per share price to facilitate a possible future sale of shares to other stockholders. They agreed on a plan under which Elaine exchanged her 75 common shares for 225 new common shares (fair market value $80,000) plus a 10-year bond at 8% interest (fair market value $30,000). Judy exchanged her 25 common shares for 75 new common shares (fair market value $23,000) plus a 10-year bond at 8% interest (fair market value $14,000). To keep things simple, assume that the principal amount of the bonds in this question is equal to the fair market value of the bonds. What are the tax consequences to Elaine, Judy, and the corporation from the exchanges?

3b. How would your answer change if the value of the stock Elaine and Judy received had been $50,000 and $17,000 respectively, and the value of the bonds they received had been $25,000 and $8000 respectively?

EXPLANATIONS

1a. Each of the shareholders in this example has *realized* a gain. For Jerry, this realized gain is $255,000 ($425,000 fair market value of the shares received less $170,000 basis in the shares exchanged). For Elaine, George, and Kramer, this realized gain is $15,000 ($25,000 fair market value of the shares received less $10,000 basis in the shares exchanged).[81] Absent a special

---

81. In several respects, the transaction is similar to the type of stock dividend involved in Eisner v. Macomber. The only difference is that the shareholders here actually exchanged shares for the shares received. Recall that in the *Macomber* case, the Supreme Court found that no income had been realized from a similar common stock dividend issued with respect to common stock. The modern and widely accepted view, however, is that *Macomber* was wrong with regard to its definition of income. Most would view the stock dividend there, and the stock exchange here, as a realization event.

nonrecognition provision, these gains would be taxable as capital gains. Taxpayers may find it somewhat unusual to have two overlapping provisions permitting nonrecognition treatment for the same transaction. Yet, one can arrive at the answer to Example 1a under *either* §1036 or the tax-free reorganization provisions.

The more simple provision is §1036(a), providing nonrecognition where common stock is exchanged solely for common stock in the same corporation. Jerry now owns 4,250 shares in lieu of his old 850 shares and Elaine, George, and Kramer each own 250 shares in lieu of their old 50 shares. With regard to the basis of these new shares, §1036(b)(2) simply cross-references to §1031(d) — the basis rules attached to the like-kind exchange provisions. This cross-reference suggests that, although the like-kind exchange rules in §1031 generally do not apply to stock, one can conceptually think of the common stock received for common stock in the *same* corporation as a like-kind exchange. Under §1031(d), the basis in the new shares will be the same as the old shares exchanged. Thus, Jerry will have a basis of $170,000 in his new shares and Elaine, George, and Kramer will each have a basis of $10,000 in their new shares. Prior to the exchange, Jerry's basis *per share* was $200 ($170,000 basis/850 shares). After the exchange, the basis is allocated among the new shares under §1031(d). Thus, his basis *per share* will now be $40 ($170,000 basis/4,250 shares). Similarly, Elaine, George, and Kramer's *per share* basis was $200 ($10,000 basis/50 shares) and now will be $40 ($10,000 basis/250 shares).

One reaches the same tax results under the tax-free reorganization provisions. The exchange of common for common stock in the same corporation is a "recapitalization" under §368(a)(1)(E), and thus a "reorganization." Under §354(a), the shareholders shall not recognize the gain realized from the exchange. Under §358(a), the basis of the new shares will be the same as the basis in the old shares. The basis will be allocated among the new shares pursuant to §358(b)(1).

Notice that whether the shareholders use §1031(d) or §358(b) to determine basis, the basis in each case is a substituted basis. Gain not recognized at the time of the exchange is preserved through this substituted basis for potential taxation later on.

The corporation does not recognize any gain upon the receipt of property in exchange for stock pursuant to §1032. See Treas. Reg. §1.1032-1(b), (c). Notice that the corporation's own stock *can* constitute property for purposes of §1032. The §317(a) definition of property, which excludes the corporation's own stock, is limited to Part I of Subchapter C.

1b. Again, each of the shareholders has realized a gain from the exchange. Jerry's realized gain is $280,000 ($450,000 fair market value of shares received less $170,000 basis of the shares exchanged). George's realized gain is $16,470 ($26,470 fair market value of the shares received less $10,000 basis of the shares exchanged). Elaine and Kramer have a realized gain of $16,500 ($26,500 fair market value of the shares received less $10,000 basis in the shares exchanged).[82] Jerry and George again have the choice of relying upon either §1036 or the reorganization provisions, since they have exchanged common stock for common stock in the same corporation. Under either provision, it initially appears that they will not required to recognize any gain and their basis in the new shares will be the same basis as the basis in the shares exchanged. Since they received the same number of shares that they previously held, no allocation of basis will be necessary. Jerry and George may have problems, however, under §305(c). Stay tuned for more on this issue in a moment.

Since the §1036 provision is only available upon exchanges of common for common in the same corporation or preferred for preferred in the same corporation, Elaine and Kramer must treat this exchange under the reorganization provisions. An exchange of common for preferred in the same corporation will be considered a "recapitalization" covered under the tax-free reorganization rules. In other words, Elaine and Kramer will not report any gain pursuant to §354, and will have a substituted basis in the new shares under §358.

Notice that after this exchange, Jerry retains 85% of the overall stock and the others each retain 5% of the overall stock. Although the overall exchange does not change the proportionate stock holdings, it does change the proportionate *voting* rights. Elaine and Kramer's voting interest has been reduced from 5% to zero. Jerry's voting interest has increased from 85% to 94%.[83] George's voting interest has increased from 5% to 6%.[84] In addition, the exchange changes the shareholders' status vis-à-vis one another. Elaine and Kramer now have a "senior" interest relative to Jerry and George. One must consider here whether either Jerry and George's increase in proportionate voting rights or the change in shareholder status triggers a §305(c) deemed taxable stock dividend.

Recapitalizations in which shareholders receive new shares resemble stock dividends. The simple difference between a stock dividend and a recapitalization is that in the latter case, the shareholder actually exchanges old shares for new. Had this transaction been a simple stock dividend, it would have been taxable under §305(b)(3) as a distribution resulting in the receipt of preferred stock by some common shareholders and the receipt of common stock by other common shareholders. In other words, such a transaction is considered disproportionate.[85] This should give all of the shareholders in this problem cause for concern. On the other hand, several

---

82. Notice that at the time of the exchange, each nonvoting preferred share is valued just slightly higher than the voting common shares.

83. Of the total 4500 voting shares, he owns 4,250.

84. Of the total 4500 voting shares, George owns 250.

85. See Chapter 7 for a discussion of stock dividends.

examples in the §305 regulations indicate that an *isolated* transaction that is not part of a periodic plan will not trigger deemed §305(c) stock dividend treatment. Treas. Reg. §1.305-3(e), exs (10)-(13). If the shareholders here can satisfy the Secretary that this is an isolated transaction and not part of a periodic plan to alter proportionate interests, they can avoid the §305 pitfall, and the transaction will retain its nonrecognition treatment.

One additional issue for Elaine and Kramer is whether or not the nonvoting preferred shares received will be classified as tainted §306 stock. Recall that the §306 stock definition includes stock, other than common, received in a tax-free reorganization to the extent that "the effect of the transaction was substantially the same as the receipt of a stock dividend." I.R.C. §306(c)(1)(B). Since Elaine and Kramer exchanged *all* of the old common shares (none of which were §306 stock), this exchange does not appear substantially the same as a stock dividend of preferred stock to common shareholders. Moreover, since the underlying common shares have been relinquished, the anti-bailout purpose of §306 would not be served by classifying these shares as tainted. See I.R.C. §306(b)(4).

1c. Again, George has *realized* a $40,000 gain (the $50,000 fair market value of the shares received less his $10,000 substituted basis in the shares surrendered). He will not be required to *recognize* this gain, however. His basis in the new shares will remain $10,000 under §358. The potential §§305 and 306 issues should be analyzed as above in the answer to 1b. One might be tempted to treat this transaction as a redemption subject to §302. Note that this is not a redemption as defined in §317(b) since George is receiving the corporation's *own* stock. This will be treated as a recapitalization, the business purpose of which is to "retire" a major shareholder from active participation.

2a. One often sees application of the tax-free reorganization provisions as part of a workout for a financially troubled corporation such as this. The exchange of Dad's outstanding bonds for preferred stock is a recapitalization. See Treas. Reg. §1.368-2(e)(1). Assuming that the 10-year bond is considered a "security," Dad will not report any gain or loss pursuant to §354, providing nonrecognition upon exchange of "stock or securities" for "stock or securities" in a reorganization. Note, however, that §354 nonrecognition will not extend to the portion of the stock received that is attributable to the two years' accrued interest. I.R.C. §354(a)(2)(B). The amount realized (fair market value of the stock received) must be apportioned between accrued interest and the bond. The portion of amount realized attributable to interest will be taxable as ordinary income. The corporation has effectively cancelled a debt and will have cancellation of indebtedness income.

2b. Dad will *realize* a gain or loss upon this debt-for-debt exchange. Under Treasury regulations, "an exchange of property for other property differing materially either in kind or extent" is a realization event. Treas. Reg.

§1.1001-1(a). Given the change in interest rates, the properties should be considered materially different. See Prop. Treas. Reg. §1.1001-3(e).[86] Assuming a sufficient business purpose, however, this transaction should be treated as a recapitalization, with no gain or loss recognized to Dad under §354, except to the extent of amounts attributable to accrued interest as described above in the answer to 2a. As for the corporation, notice that the principal amount of its obligation remains the same. Since the only change is a prospective alteration of the rate of interest, there should be no cancellation of indebtedness to the corporation.

3a. Elaine has realized a $35,000 gain from the exchange of her old stock for new stock and a bond (fair market value received of $110,000 less basis in old shares of $75,000). Judy has realized a $12,000 gain from the exchange (fair market value received of $37,000 less basis in old shares of $25,000). The first issue here is whether the transaction should be classified as a tax-free Type E recapitalization. As in the *Bazley* case, the concern here might be that the distribution of bonds simply is a disguised dividend. A few distinguishing factors might make ours a stronger case than *Bazley*. First, the restructuring here arguably had a business purpose — reducing the price of shares for a potential future sale of stock. On the other hand, this alleged business purpose does not explain the need for including bonds in the exchange. Second, the bonds in the *Bazley* case were callable at will, and thus virtually the equivalent of cash. The bonds in our case are not callable and thus not cash equivalents.

Assume, then, that Elaine and Judy are successful in their claim that the exchange is a recapitalization. If so, they are eligible for §354 nonrecognition. In any event, §354 nonrecognition does *not* apply to the extent that the principal amount of any securities received exceeds the principal amount of any securities surrendered. I.R.C. §354(a)(2)(A). Moreover, Treasury Department regulations take the position that the bond distribution should be considered as a separate transaction from the stock exchange. Consequently, the regulations would treat the bond distribution as taxable under §301 to the extent of earnings and profits. Treas. Reg. §1.301-1(l).

3b. The analysis of the example is the same except that neither Elaine nor Judy has *realized* a gain from the exchange since each has received a value equal to her basis. Note that the §356 boot rules provide for taxation of boot income to the extent of gain. Since there was no gain here, neither shareholder will report taxable income even though boot has been paid to each of them.

---

86. Under this proposed regulation, a change in interest rate is considered a significant modification if the modified rate varies from the original rate by more than 1/4 of 1%.

Table of Cases

Table of Internal Revenue Code Sections

Table of Treasury Regulations and Revenue Rulings

Proposed Treasury Regulations

Temporary Treasury Regulations

Revenue Rulings

Index